Brian Head

Choosing Your Degree Course & University

D1428206

Brian Heap

12th edition

Choosing Your Degree Course & University

Mander Portman Woodward

Choosing Your Degree Course and University
This twelfth edition published in 2010 by
Trotman Publishing a division of Crimson Publishing Ltd
Westminster House, Kew Road, Richmond, Surrey TW9 2ND
© Brian Heap 2010

First–tenth editions published by Trotman and Company Ltd

Eleventh edition published by Trotman Publishing

Author Brian Heap

British Library Cataloguing in Publication Data
A catalogue record for this book is available from the British Library

ISBN 978 1 84455 248 1

All rights reserved. No part of this publication may be reproduced, stored in a retrieval system or transmitted in any form or by any means, electronic and mechanical, photocopying, recording or otherwise without prior permission of Trotman Publishing.

Typeset by RefineCatch Ltd, Bungay, Suffolk

Printed and bound in the UK by Ashford Colour Press, Gosport, Hants

LEEDS METROPOLITAN
UNIVERSITY
LIBRARY

1705482794
Ca.B
CC-116178/2010
2-11-10
378.41 HEA.

Founded in 1973, **Mander Portman Woodward (MPW)** is one of the UK's best known groups of independent sixth-form colleges with centres in London, Birmingham and Cambridge. It offers over 40 subjects at AS and A2 with no restrictions on subject combinations and a maximum class size of eight.

MPW has one of the highest numbers of university placements each year of any independent school in the country. It has developed considerable expertise over the years in the field of applications strategy and is frequently consulted by students facing some of the more daunting challenges that may arise in areas such as getting into Oxbridge, Medicine or Law. This expertise is available to a wider audience in the form of **Getting Into** guides on higher education and the seminars that are run for sixth-formers at its London centre. We are grateful to Trotman for publishing the Guides and hope that this latest edition of **Choosing Your Degree Course & University** will prove as popular and useful as ever.

If you would like to know more about MPW or Getting Into guides, please telephone us on 020 7835 1355 or visit our website, www.mpw.co.uk.

CONTENTS

Choosing Your University And Degree Course...And Completing Your UCAS Form?

Why not contact Brian Heap, the author of *Degree Course Offers*, *Choosing Your Degree Course and University* and *University Scholarships and Awards*, for a personal interview or a telephone consultation for advice on such issues as:

Choosing A-level subjects (which are the best subjects and for which courses!)
Degrees and Diploma courses (making the right choice from a list of thousands!)
Completing your UCAS form (will the admissions tutor remember your personal statement?)
Choosing the right university or college (the best ones for you and your courses)

For details of services and consultation fees contact:
The Higher Education Advice and Planning Service

tel: 01386 859355 email: heaps@dsl.pipex.com

ABOUT THIS BOOK

Students – read this book if you're just beginning to think about applying for university ... it's essential reading.

Parents – read this book if you want to know about higher education and you want to help your sons or daughters.

Careers staff and Sixth Form Tutors – read this book if you want to impress your sixth form with your extensive knowledge of universities and their courses! (A must if you have to take group career sessions.) (You could use Chapters 1 and 2 as your syllabus!)

THE DECISION

* A university course can last three, four or more years and includes tuition fees of at least £3110 each year, plus living costs and personal spending money.
* There are over 350 degree subjects on offer which include over 70,000 course options (single, joint, and combined honours), offered by over 300 universities and colleges.

If you are in Year 13 your application will probably have to be submitted in January. (Too many schools **demand** early applications in September each year, even when students haven't had enough time to decide. No wonder 30,000 university students drop out of courses each year!)

Choosing Your Degree Course is in two parts. Part One explains:

* how to make your first decision, listing ideas from examination subjects or career interests to vocational, partly vocational and academic interests
* how to make a first choice of degree subjects from the eight main subject areas – Business courses, Social Studies and Law, Medicine and Health, the Sciences, Engineering, Mathematics and Computing, Learning a Language, Creative subjects and the Arts and Humanities. Each 'option' lists all the alternative subjects available
* how to choose your university, which is the **best** university, reasons why you think a university is good – or not so good – some university characteristics, **and questions to ask when you go to an Open Day or an interview**.

Part Two provides:

* a list of over 80 main degree subject tables in detail. Each university is included which offers that course providing a short profile of the topics you will cover
* the final career destinations – types of jobs you could enter from your degree.

Good Luck!

Brian Heap

AUTHOR'S ACKNOWLEDGEMENTS

Initially, I wish to record my appreciation to my daughter, Jane Heap (Staff) Putney High School, for the research on university courses which she has undertaken in the preparation of this edition. In addition I also wish to acknowledge the support of many universities and colleges who have supplied data for this book and in particular the Surrey University Careers Service for providing details of graduate destinations.

Brian Heap BA, DA (Manc), ATD

Part 1

1 | THE CHOICE

For many students the idea of going to university has become a way of life – the obvious next step from school and college. Some do consider going into full-time employment but many probably feel that a simple office or lab job with fairly repetitive work lacks the excitement of university life or a gap year abroad (although a gap year in full-time employment could be even more challenging and 'educational' than tramping around Peru!). On the other hand, many hope that going to university will lead to 'management' careers and certainly many university courses seem to wish to convey this impression. But in the end even new graduates will still probably find themselves doing similar office jobs as the school leavers, the difference being that employers hopefully will consider that after three years at university they should have management potential and some will and some won't!

Many parents however will certainly see the benefits of and regard a university education as essential, although this is where their advice and influence might fall down because many only seem to consider a small number of degree subjects (and certain universities) as the best preparation for the best jobs which is quite misleading. So, for the applicants, the problem is to choose the right course – but be prepared for some difficult questions at home!

For example, you might have decided to apply for an English degree, but be ready for the obvious question – 'What can you do with English?' Well you could say that you had thought about becoming the Director of MI5 which is what Stella Rimington (one-time director) did after her English degree at Edinburgh! What about a degree in Classics and French? One graduate went into teaching and then became a millionaire ... when she wrote about Harry Potter! But then of course Sir Richard Branson didn't go to university at all! So take your pick, but remember whatever you choose to study at university very often bears little relation to your future career.

For a few surprises, a survey of graduate employment destinations at York University revealed that apart from those graduates who went into subject related careers, others went into a wide range of other occupations, eg:

* from Archaeology to – Care Assistant, Advertising, Youth Work (USA) and Retail Management
* from Biological Science to – Pensions Administrator, Insurance, Share Dealing and Catering Management
* from Chemistry to – Electricity Board Administration, Market Research, Music Promotion and Accountancy
* from Electronics to – Banking, Railtrack, News Assistant (TV) and Soccer Coach (USA)
* from English to – Publishing, Law, Ministry of Defence and Hospital Administration
* from Philosophy to – Building, Society Work, Local Government, Voluntary Youth Work and Data Processing
* from Politics to – Accountancy, an Army Commission, Journalism and the NHS

... and for more information turn to chapter 6.

Many parents – and students – still believe that a degree is meant to be a type of training for a future job, which in fact only applies in a very few cases, eg Medicine, Dentistry, Architecture and Physiotherapy etc. **A degree is meant to teach you how to learn.** On a university course you will be given a wide range of topics to study. In each case you will have to research the problem yourself, test your conclusions and present your decisions. Which is what every manager has to do every day, no matter what the job. So, as the saying goes **'learn how to learn and you can learn to do anything'**.

But no matter which subject you choose you will find that at university you will have to work on your own for most of the time, just as you will once you're in a job – the moral being – don't go to university if you are not prepared to be a self-starter. Also in today's society, people don't necessarily have the same job for life, many change their career direction at least once or even twice before they retire, so it's important to be able to know how to adapt to new careers and how to adjust to new systems.

But at the present time you still have four or five years to go before you start your first job and with plenty of time to think about what you really want to do, so choosing a career at this stage isn't absolutely necessary. However choosing a course and a university is, so browse through the next few chapters and the important decisions you need to make might become clearer.

MAKING THE FIRST DECISION

There are over 1800 degree subjects from which to choose and making the right choice has its problems! Much depends on the type of person you are which means that you need to do a bit of self-analysis.

To begin with, all university and college courses fall into one of three categories. Which one fits you?

Vocational courses

Vocational courses are really 'training courses' for entry to specific careers eg Medicine, Dentistry, Pharmacy, Architecture, Occupational Therapy, Radiography, Optometry, Podiatry and several others. These are professional courses, monitored by professional bodies and on graduation you will be qualified to practise from day one. In addition, some of these courses are planned so that you spend some time working with an employer (sandwich courses), in some cases for up to a year – on full pay. In many cases students are offered jobs with these firms on graduation. Some of these courses are very competitive, for example at one university there are 16 applicants for each place for Dentistry, at another there are 11 Pharmacy applicants per place and at yet another, 22 applicants for every Physiotherapy place. Thus admission tutors will expect you not only to have a good knowledge of the career, but also to have engaged in some work experience before applying and above all to know the disadvantages of the work as well as the attractions.

Partly vocational

These courses aim to provide you with a clear picture of the type of work done in certain careers. Courses include such subjects as Business Studies, Environmental Science, Biological Sciences, Chemistry, Physics and Media Studies. (Many of these also arrange work placements with firms.) Within each of these careers are many specialist fields so the degree itself isn't a specialist qualification in its own right, but only an introduction to the types of work you might be asked to do once you are employed. Once in your first job you will go on to specialise in a particular field, probably taking additional professional qualifications. So, for example, depending on their choice of career and firm, Business Studies graduates may go on to complete the examinations of the Institutes of Marketing and Public Relations or the Chartered Insurance Institute or the Institutes of Purchasing and Supply or Logistics and Transport.

Exam subjects or interests

The third way is to consider the academic or non-vocational subjects you are taking at school or college, with the possibility of continuing the same subject at university. If so which are your best subjects? Which are your favourite subjects? Would you like to study one or even two of them on a joint or combined course for the next three years? Alternatively you could take a subject which is new to you but which you find interesting such as American Studies, Philosophy, Anthropology, International Relations or a new foreign language such as Chinese, Japanese or Scandinavian Studies ... but more about these options later.

If you do choose an examination subject it's really quite important to choose the one which you also enjoy the most ... after all you've got to study it for the next three or four years! Every year about 20,000 students drop out of their courses, not because the work is too difficult, simply because they found the course too boring and not what they expected.

CHOOSING DEGREE SUBJECTS

Students are different in many ways not least in their attitudes to life and their interests, eg sport, music and the arts, the environment, politics, law, etc, and as a result you might feel that your personality and study interests are suited to certain types of jobs more than others.

Have a look at these main career groups and try some self-analysis.

1. **Science careers** Are you taking chemistry, biology or other science subjects, if so do you enjoy them? If not move on...
2. **Technical careers** These occupations often focus on maths and physics and are very appropriate for those with a practical outlook and aptitude. Interested? If not move on...
3. **Artistic careers** Do you enjoy art, music, dance, drama, creative writing, or designing things? In short are you a creative person? If not move on...
4. **Outdoor/active careers** Are you energetic? Do you enjoy the open-air life? If not move on...
5. **Communication careers** Do you enjoy meeting people, are you a leader, do you enjoy debating the problems and issues of the day? Or are you one of those quiet retiring types who likes to keep out of the limelight? if so move on...
6. **Social careers** Do you enjoy helping people? Do your friends always come to you first when they have problems? If you'd prefer they didn't ... then move on!
7. **Business careers** Are you an 'organiser'; if so these courses are well worth considering. Business Studies graduates join a range of industrial and commercial organisations and whether you are working in an office, a laboratory, or on a building site, business skills apply. Over 200,000 students applied for Business programmes last year, but not to worry, there are plenty from which to choose. So begin your degree subject journey in Option 1 ... the answer to your problems could be there or farther on!

2 | THE OPTIONS

OPTION 1: BUSINESS COURSES

There was a time not so long ago when some students – and quite a lot of parents – seemed to think that employers took a poor view of students with a Business Studies degree and certainly many years ago, when the new universities introduced these new degree courses, many people were still sceptical about their value. But now these courses are very well established and widely accepted. One university careers adviser said that many employers always gave first priority to good Business Studies Graduates since they are well-prepared in all those essential transferable skills. These skills cannot be overlooked, no matter what your course at university. The world of employment is looking for graduates with verbal, written and time management skills, information technology know-how and the ability to work in a team.

Unfortunately many sixth formers interested in business simply look for degrees called **Business Studies** or **Business Administration** and seem to forget that there are many other courses covering aspects of the business field such as **Hospitality Management**, **Environmental Management**, **Marketing** and **Property Development** and over a hundred more at the end of this section!

Business courses tend to fall into two main categories, the traditional three-year full-time course and the four-year sandwich programme which would mean that you will usually spend one year or two six month periods working full time in industry or commerce, often with full pay. One advantage of the sandwich option is that if you impress your employer then you could be offered a sponsorship or even a permanent job with the firm when you graduate. This often happens and sandwich course students usually come out top in the graduate employment stakes. And just another small point – it isn't unusual for sandwich students on placement in industry or commerce to earn £11,000 to £12,000 during their year which helps a lot when you are faced with a student loan, top-up fee or an overdraft!

Sandwich courses were introduced many years ago and now many institutions can offer a wide range of such courses. Among several good, well-established universities offering sandwich courses are Aston, Bath, Bradford, Brunel, City, Kent, Kingston, Loughborough, Oxford Brookes, Portsmouth, Salford and Surrey. In fact most universities have now introduced various types of work placement schemes.

In addition to choosing between full-time and sandwich courses, applicants should also check the range of topics offered in the many Business courses. Some programmes will offer an academic bias with a focus on the economic, mathematical and statistical elements of the subject, whilst other courses are more practical and 'hands-on'. Business courses provide a general grounding in all the main aspects of management, such as marketing, sales operations, human resources management (personnel management), industrial relations and finance. All courses will naturally involve IT and most universities will expect at least a GCSE grade C in maths, with the more academic courses a grade B or even an A and some may even require A-level maths.

If you are considering the possibility of working abroad, there are also **International Business** courses, some with a year in the USA as at Lancaster or Salford. In the case of **European Business Studies** degrees, students can use their language skills with placements in one of many European countries. Bradford is one of many universities offering these courses; one of their students went into the Diplomatic Corps when she graduated, which simply proves that you don't have to go into business when you've done a business course although part of her work was dealing with exports from Canada to the UK. But it doesn't end there. What about a course in one of the business specialisms such as **Marketing**, which is not just public relations and advertising but also product development, distribution of products, pricing and promotion. **Human Resources Management** is another popular option which covers such topics as industrial relations, employee development and the economic, financial, legal and human issues when dealing with people at work.

Alternatively other business options include **Hospitality Management** (a new title for hotel management) offered at a number of universities, or you could consider **Public Relations** or **Advertising** at Bournemouth, **Tourism** at Bangor or Aberystwyth in addition to many other universities and colleges. Other options open include **Sport Management** offered at London Metropolitan, and **Fashion Buying** at Westminster and the University of the Arts. There are also business courses dealing with property, such as **Planning and Property Development** at Sheffield Hallam and Kingston and **Estate Management** (not a course in agriculture) at Bristol UWE. Most of these courses lead to qualification as a surveyor. In the field of transport it's possible to study **Logistics** at Aston and **Transport Management** at Loughborough where there is also a degree specialising in **Air Transport Management**.

Then there is the huge area covered by courses in **Finance.** These involve degrees in **Accountancy**, **Banking, International Finance, Investment Banking, Risk Management, International Securities**, and **Actuarial Studies** and the broader field of **Financial Services**.

Finally, it's worth remembering that a very large proportion of graduates from other subjects – history, geography, geology, languages and law, etc – still go into business, being trained by firms to fit their own style of management operations. Employers are, after all, entitled to assume that if you are bright enough to get a degree then you should be able to adapt to their system!

One other point to remember is that you don't need to have done Business Studies at A-level or Vocational A-level to do a degree in the subject, but you do need to be able to show an understanding of the subject on the dreaded UCAS application! But how? Not simply by saying that 'I'm interested in it' but by getting some first-hand work experience and describing the work you have done and explaining what you have gained by it. Talk to people in business. Even if you are only stacking shelves in a super-market you should find out about the problems of running the store. Talk to the manager. What is the turnover of the store? What are the best-selling lines? Does he have any staffing problems and how does he overcome them? What problems are caused by customers? By discussing these topics on your personal statement you are demonstrating some awareness of the problems of business which is what admission tutors will expect.

Manchester Metropolitan University state that they insist on such experience before recommending students to employers, whilst the University of Wales Institute at Cardiff looks for sociable, ambitious, team players. Another university reported that students who are not interested in widening their horizons or who do not demonstrate leadership skills are likely to be rejected.

Putting information about your experiences on the UCAS application will demonstrate that you have given some serious thought to making your decision and the admissions tutor will take your application more seriously. (More about the dreaded UCAS application later!)

Course options
General courses
Administration, Business Administration, Business Decision Analysis, Business Finance, Business Information Management, Business Information Systems, Business Studies, combined degrees with Business, Commerce, Decision Studies, Management, Management Science, Operational Research, Operations Management, Organisation Studies and Quality Management.

Specialised courses
Accountancy, Accountancy and Finance, Actuarial Studies, Agricultural Management, American Business Studies, Animal Management, Antiques and Collections Management, Arts Management, Attraction Park Management, Banking, Beauty Therapy Management, Building Management, Business Computer Systems, Business Economics, Business Finance, Careers Management, Catering Management, Civil Engineering Management, Community Management, Conservation Management, Construction Management, Countryside Management, Countryside Recreation Management, Design Management, Distribution Management, Earth Resources Management, Engineering Management, Entertainment Management, Environmental Management, Equine Management, Estate Management, European Business Administration, Events Management, Exercise and Health Management, Facilities Management, Farm Management, Financial Services Management, Fisheries Management, Food Manufacturing Management, Food Marketing, Forestry Management, Garden Design Management,

Golf Course Management, Golf Management, Health and Safety Management, Health Care Management, Heritage Management, Horticultural Management, Hospital Management, Hospitality Management, Hotel Management, Housing Management, Human Resources Management, Information Management, Institutional Management, Insurance, International Hotel Management, International Marketing Management, International Tourism Management, International Transport Management, Investment Management, Land Management, Land Use Management, Landscape Management, Legal Practice Management, Leisure Management, Libraries Management, Licensed Retail Management, Livestock Management, Marketing Management, Music Industry Management, Optical Management, Pharmaceutical Management, Poultry Management, Print Management, Property Management, Public Administration, Quality Management, Real Estate Management, Recreation Management, Retail Management, Rural Resources Management, Social Administration, Sports Management, Stage Management, Supply Chain Management, Technical Management, Textile Management, Tour Management, Travel and Tourism Management, Urban Estate Management, Veterinary Management, Waste Management, Water Management, Wildlife Management.

OPTION 2: SOCIAL STUDIES AND LAW

Many applicants imagine that the **Social Sciences** are only appropriate if you are aiming to be a social worker which is certainly not the case. These degree courses cover a wide range of subjects. Take for example the combined honours degree programme at Durham in which students are able to design their own degree course and make a choice of subjects from **Anthropology, Archaeology, Economics, Education, Geography, History, Management Studies, Politics, Psychology, Sociology, Social Policy** and **Sport**. At Bristol a degree in **Accountancy and Finance** is included in the subjects offered in the Faculty of Social Sciences and at King's College, London, degree programmes include **War Studies** (a study of the impact of war on society, from ancient to modern times and the moral and ethical dilemmas it raises). Also there is **Environment and Society** which combines a study of the environment and at the same time allows students to choose subjects from the Departments of Geography and Education. **Town and Country Planning** courses are closely related to human geography since they explore the man-made environment and all the aspects in which towns and cities affect our lives including urban design, transport issues, industrial and tourist sites and conservation areas. Finally there is also Politics, Psychology and Sociology at Cambridge (PPS) replacing the title Social and Political Sciences (SPS).

However there are some people who would like to work with people and more importantly not only work with them but to provide care and other forms of support. Medical and health occupations cover many of the caring careers and some of these jobs come quite close to, or even overlap into social work. Although it is possible to go into social work from any degree or diploma course, students specially interested in this type of work could focus their attention on degrees in **Social Work, Social Policy, Social Sciences** or **Social Administration**. These subjects cover topics relating to sociology, politics, social history and economics and will include such issues as the family, unemployment, poverty, health, equal opportunities, housing and education.

Social work is a challenging and demanding career and degree courses will cover a range of problems which could involve race and ethnic identity, family problems, old age, drug addiction, health and illness, mental health, deviance, disability, housing and the penal system. Despite the challenging nature of the work however, statistics show a 90% increase in applications in recent years. It's obviously a career for which motivation is very important and many mature students are accepted on courses without the benefit of higher education or even A-levels, simply because they have the right qualities and usually some experience. An interest in social work will also extend to working in the community and several universities offer degrees in **Community Development, Youth and Community Studies, Community Arts** and **Education**.

One of the most popular courses in this huge field is that of **Psychology** with 20 applications for each place at Bath and similar ratios at many other universities. In many courses it's possible to specialise in certain aspects; for those interested in a medical emphasis there are studies in the field of clinical, abnormal and health psychology whilst other courses will cover occupational, consumer and educational psychology and child development. Those wishing to qualify as psychologists (about 20% of all applicants eventually do so) need to be sure that their chosen degree is validated by the British Psychological Society. Not all degree courses provide such validation and in particular, students should check the status of joint courses before applying. Some other courses worth considering in this sector include **Neuroscience** (a study of the nervous system), **Cognitive Science** (investigating human mental processes and the relationship between natural and artificial intelligence), **Developmental Psychology** (which focuses on how we become the people we are) and **Counselling** in which interpersonal skills are developed and which at Salford can be combined with Complementary Medicine, Health Sciences or Social Policy.

Degrees in **Education** are immediately associated with teacher training courses which is not necessarily the case since the subject can be studied on a much wider base than that which is normally undertaken by trainee teachers. Courses in Education focus not only on schools and children but on the history, sociology and philosophy of education. By comparison **Teacher Training** courses cater for a variety of student needs whether they wish to work with the very young or pupils in the secondary age range. Some courses offer specialisms in such subjects such as English, Design Technology, Mathematics, Physical Education, Religious Studies and Science.

Those students interested in the idea of a career in the teaching profession but who have not followed a teacher training course can choose to follow a degree course for example in English, Geography, History or languages and then take an extra year leading to a postgraduate certificate in education.

The **Social Sciences** also include **Sociology,** another popular course, which presents a broad view of social problems, exploring the structure of the society in which we live: the nature of crime and punishment, poverty, social protest and exclusion, social movements and social divisions of class, gender and ethnicity. Some courses go into much greater depth, covering human rights, criminology and criminal justice, women's studies, gender studies, race and ethnic studies and psychosocial studies. Courses in **Criminology** have become extremely popular in recent years and it should be noted that these degrees are not law courses as such, being more concerned with understanding major social problems and the means of dealing with them. **Criminal Justice** courses examine the causes of crime and the operation of the criminal justice system and will prepare graduates to work in the Probation and Prison Services as well as Social Services. However for those aiming for careers in Law, some Criminal Justice courses can lead on to the Common Professional Examination or the Postgraduate Diploma in Law. Alternatively, direct entry might be possible to the graduate training programme for those interested in the Police. Check with your university of choice.

Anthropology is a study of the human species from a totally different perspective, from a biological or a social emphasis. Scientific aspects could cover human evolution, genetics, nutrition and human disease whilst social studies could include political systems, religion and kinship studies focusing on countries throughout the world.

Other social issues are taken up in degree programmes in **Politics and Government** which has attracted increasing numbers of students in the past two years. Politics courses explore the main philosophies through history and will also cover parliamentary and presidential systems, party politics, conflict and social attitudes. Political systems abroad will also be included, with specialisms arising from the research fields of university staff. When choosing universities it is also worthwhile considering some four-year courses in which placements abroad are included. Another related course worth considering is a degree in **International Relations** which will include the diplomatic, economic and military relations between states, international agencies and multinational companies and the factors which lead to and determine the course of war and peace. A more detailed study of some of these factors is also developed in courses in **Peace Studies**, **War Studies**, **Conflict Resolution** and **War and Security Studies**.

In all societies however, legal issues arise and these are covered in the most comprehensive way in all **Law** degrees. It is however not necessary to have a degree in Law in order to become a solicitor or barrister, entry being open to graduates in many subjects providing they have a good class of degree. Law is one of the most popular degree course and involves a wide spectrum of subjects and students are well advised to read *Learning the Law* by Glanville Williams before embarking on a course. Only about half of those who follow law degrees will enter the career. In 1972 there were approximately 26,000 practising solicitors in the UK and by 2002 the total had risen to 89,000 with 80% of these working in private practice. Women account for 55% of newly qualified solicitors, and 7% are from ethnic minority groups. Be warned however because there is a high failure rate in law examinations at this level.

Economics is a subject which is primarily concerned with monetary issues such as exchange and interest rates, price increases, and movements in the stock market, there are also specialist areas covering business, labour, environmental and public-sector economics. Some universities will require mathematics at A-level which will be dictated by the content of the course, however it isn't widely known that an A-level in Economics is not a necessary requirement for many courses, although a background knowledge and an interest in the subject obviously helps students to make a decision to choose such courses.

Course options

Anthropology, Applied Social Studies, Behavioural Science, British Sign Language, Business Law, Business Studies, Childhood Studies, Citizenship, Cognitive Science, Communication, Community Studies, Conductive Education, Conflict Resolution, Consumer Studies, Counselling, Criminal Justice, Criminal Law, Criminal Psychology, Criminology, Deaf Studies, Development Studies, Early Childhood Studies, Economics, Environmental Studies, Ethics, Philosophy and Religion, Gender Studies, Housing Management, Human Communication, Human Resources Management, Human Rights, Industrial Relations, International Development Studies, International Relations, Marketing, Peace and Security, Peace Studies, Philosophy, Philosophy, Logic and Scientific Method, Police and Criminal Investigation, Policing, Politics, Politics, Philosophy and Economics, Population Science, Psychology, Psychosocial Studies, Public Administration, Race and Culture, Religious Studies, Security Studies, Social Administration, Social Research, Social Work, Society and Cities, Society, Culture and the Media, Sociology, Teaching, Town and Country Planning, Trade Union Studies, War Studies, Women's Studies, Youth Studies.

OPTION 3: MEDICINE AND HEALTH

Forty-five GCSEs at the same time – that's how one medical school admissions officer described a course in **Medicine**! This might appear to be a slight exaggeration but the fact remains that the workload should never be underestimated which is why medical schools are looking for a good spread of grade A's at GCSE, AS and A-levels. Consequently expect the normal offers to be high – often in the AAA–ABB range (NB the A* grade will be introduced from 2010), although some medical schools might be prepared to make slightly lower offers depending on their policies, the school or college references, the results of BMAT or UKCAT tests and the personal statement.

Bearing in mind then that all applicants are equally strong academically and will receive good references from their tutors, the only opportunity to make a personal bid for an offer comes in the personal statement. However before putting 'pen to paper' it's important to answer a few questions and not least: Why do you want to be a doctor? The hours are long, the work is arduous and the responsibilities are enormous and mistakes could be dire!

It's not enough just to want to be a doctor simply because you want to **'help people'**. The real question is **'are you a scientist?'** Because from the moment you become a medical student and throughout your career, you will be making scientific decisions every day of your working life. You will need to update your knowledge continuously, since new scientific developments in medicine, surgery and pharmacology are taking place on a very regular basis.

So how interested are you in science – not just your A-level subjects but the scientific world around you? You should be interested enough to follow articles in the news on topics such as pollution, public health and the spread of diseases. Do you read scientific journals, medical journals, magazine articles on health and developments in medicine? You might not understand all the medical terms but you should have a good general knowledge of current medical issues and personal opinions to support them.

At interview you could be asked such questions as: Do you agree with the principle of private medicine? Would you refuse to treat a patient with lung cancer who refused to give up smoking? What has been the most important advance in medicine in the past 50 years? Should we pay for blood donations or for donor organs?

Work experience, too, is essential. It might be in a hospital, but it could be in an old people's home, learning about geriatric conditions, homes for the mentally handicapped or the blind or even in a hospice for the terminally ill. Talk to doctors, matrons and nurses in these places, as well as health workers in the community. What problems do they face and how do they overcome them?

When you realise that all the other medical applicants have the same academic levels of achievement then these extra experiences are important. Special interests you might have in science and medicine, and other activities which you can discuss on the UCAS statement, could get you to the interview and finally a place in medical school. The advice from Imperial, London is standard for most medical schools:

We look for resourceful men and women with wide interests and accomplishments and a practical concern for others. Academic ability, motivation, character and depth of interests are all assessed.

For most applicants the next problem is where to study? London medical schools traditionally have had a good reputation and they attract a lot of applicants. But your first aim is to get a good basic medical education and all medical schools will provide an excellent start for any doctor. After completing the course you can then go on to specialise if that's your aim.

The popularity of any degree course or career however will always raise the stakes. Applications for entry to Medicine quite recently were up by 22% and for **Dentistry** by 14%. Expect high offers too for **Veterinary Medicine** for which girls represent the majority of applicants. **Optometry** is also popular, with about nine applicants per place at some universities, mainly because of the small number of institutions offering the course. In recent years **Pharmacy** has also become very popular, but be aware that there's a difference between **Pharmacy** and **Pharmaceutical Sciences**, the latter being a study of chemistry and biochemistry and medical issues pertaining to drugs whilst **Pharmacology** focuses on the study of and uses of drugs and **Toxicology** is the science of poisons.

Other courses allied to medicine include: **Nursing and Midwifery** (applications up by 18% and 27% respectively), **Physiotherapy**, another scientific career which also attracts a lot of applicants with 20 to 30 applicants per place being not uncommon, **Speech Therapy** involves assessing and treating speech and language disorders, **Audiology** is the treatment of hearing disorders, **Nutrition and Dietetics** a study of food intake, health and individual needs, **Radiography (Diagnostic** and **Therapeutic)** involves using healthcare technology to diagnose conditions and administer treatments eg radiotherapy for cancer patients, **Occupational Therapy** covers the treatment and management of physical and psychological conditions by the use of various activities, **Orthoptics** is the speciality for those interested in the investigation, diagnosis and management of visual defects and abnormalities of eye movement, **Podiatry** is management of disease and disability in the lower limbs and treatments involving feet, **Prosthetics and Orthotics** is the provision of artificial body limbs – prostheses – and the provision of supports for conditions of the limbs and spine. There are also other more specialist courses such as **Chiropractic** for the diagnosis and treatment of the disorders of the neuro-musculoskeletal system, whilst **Osteopaths** use manual and manipulative methods of treatment for conditions affecting the musculoskeletal system. Finally, Paramedic Practice is available at degree level at Plymouth and Hertfordshire universities with Higher National Diploma and Foundation courses available elsewhere.

Finally in addition to the vocational courses above in recent years there has been an increase in the number of Health Studies/Sciences degrees on offer. These include courses in **Health Psychology, Health Promotion, Health and Safety, Herbal Medicine** and **Homeopathic Medicine**.

For those students seeking a more scientific base for their studies and in some cases those hoping to proceed to a degree in Medicine after graduation there are also courses in **Biological Sciences** covering **Anatomy and Physiology, Microbiology** and **Genetics**.

Course options
Aromatherapy, Arts Therapy, Audiology, Beauty Therapy, Care Practice, Caring Services, Childhood Studies, Chiropractic, Clinical Science, Community Health, Complementary Medicine, Deaf Studies, Dental Technician, Dentistry, Dietetics, Dispensing Optician, Environmental Health, Health and Fitness Studies, Health Education, Health Psychology, Health Science, Herbal Medicine, Medicine, Midwifery, Naturopathic Medicine, Neuroscience, Nursing, Nutrition, Occupational Health and Safety, Occupational Therapy, Optometry, Orthoptics, Orthotics, Osteopathic Medicine, Paramedical Practice, Podiatry, Pharmaceutical

Science, Pharmacology, Pharmacy, Physiotherapy, Psychology, Public Health, Radiography (Diagnostic or Therapeutic), Rehabilitation, Sign Language, Speech Therapy, Sport and Health, Toxicology, Veterinary Medicine, Veterinary Nursing.

OPTION 4: THE SCIENCES

This group of courses covers a huge field and if you are studying the sciences then you will be familiar with many of them. Even so, check through all the options at the end of this section and see the range of possibilities ... which is after all what research scientists are doing all the time!

Biochemistry, **Biological Sciences**, **Biology**, **Chemistry** and **Physics** are the obvious starting points when choosing science courses. In fact, these are the safe, broad science courses which can lead to many of the specialised studies which follow because they form the foundation of science careers and in the universities these are the subject areas with a shortage of students.

Students taking courses in **Biological Science** can usually specialise in their chosen field in the second or third year of the course in such areas as **biomedical sciences**, **microbiology**, **physiology**, **immunology**, **genetics** or **botany**. At Lancaster for example 10 modules are taken in Year 1, five in biological subjects and a further five subjects related to biology or in 'stand alone' subjects reflecting the student's particular interests. Specialisation then begins in Year 2. Newcastle has a similar 'Deferred choice' arrangement and again at Warwick where further specialist subjects cover molecular genetics, cell biology, microbiology, virology or environmental resources.

Other more specialised courses include: **Medical Engineering** (the application of engineering principles to medicine including rehabilitation and orthopaedic engineering and medical physics), **Biotechnology** (the application of biology to industry eg agriculture, food or medicine), **Bioarchaeology** (links between archaeology and biology involving human skeletons, ecology and fossils) and **Biogeography** (ecology, the environment and earth sciences). However the more highly specialised your subject choice then the narrower will be the range of subject-related job opportunities available in that field. Biosciences however also include areas related to health and medicine such as pharmacy, and the paramedical professions which are covered in **Option 3**.

Agriculture and **Agricultural Sciences**, **Forestry**, **Animal and Equine Science** and **Aquaculture** (not just fish farming but the culture of aquatic species from prawns and shrimps to turtles and crocodiles) are other options with a biological emphasis. Many courses are multidisciplinary and have a strong scientific bias and can include biotechnology, fisheries management and food production, in addition to business aspects such as countryside management, marketing and rural tourism. It's also a short step from a course in agriculture to **Crop Science** and **Horticulture**, which are concerned with growth on a commercial scale, compared with the more scientific application of a degree in **Botany**, now more commonly referred to as **Plant Sciences.** It is not uncommon to study Plant Sciences after the first year of a course in Biological Science.

Chemistry, for which there is a great shortage of applicants, is the broadest of the traditional physical sciences and provides a considerable foundation for specialisation leading for example to **Forensic Science**. Unfortunately Forensic Science, like Media Studies, is currently attracting large numbers of applicants, due to certain TV programmes, and many students are going to be disappointed when they graduate and realise the limited job opportunities open to them. A **Chemistry** degree however is the passport to many careers including pharmaceuticals, the food science industry, environmental issues, the petroleum industry, cosmetics, plastics and ceramics to mention but a few. Applicants however should not overlook the fact that for a number of these courses an A-level, or at least an AS-level, in mathematics is important. Four year Master's degrees leading to an MChem are common and in many cases these courses include a year in industry.

Specialist areas in **Chemistry** which might be considered include Medicinal Chemistry, Pharmaceutical Chemistry, Environmental Chemistry, Colour and Polymer Chemistry, Cosmetic Science, Materials Chemistry, Forensic Chemistry, or Nanoscience or Nanotechnology (defined as the study of organic or inorganic materials with dimensions on the nanometre scale – a nanometre being one millionth of a millimetre) offered at Sussex and Leeds. **Chemical Engineering** and **Polymer Science** also come into the chemistry and technology field. Furthermore at some universities you can combine all science courses with almost any other science or non-science subject, such as education, computing, languages, business management, geography, history, music or politics.

The skills picked up in a **Physics** degree are not only mathematical and experimental but involve problem-solving, the analysis of information and team management, hence the reason why so many careers are open to the Physics graduate. As in the case of Chemistry, MPhys and MSc courses are also popular among about a third of Physics undergraduates. Those applying for **Physics** can also choose a range of specialisms which include for example Medical Physics at King's College and University College, London, Nuclear Physics at Surrey, Astrophysics at Kent, or Physics, Oceanography and Climate Studies at Liverpool. **Physics** is also involved in many other courses and is an essential A-level for most **Engineering** courses.

Some changes have taken place in recent years in the overall structure of degrees in **Geography** in which students now explore the natural environment in what is now a multidisciplinary subject. Courses will cover **Human Geography** and **Economic and Social Geography** whilst **Physical Geography** will include modules in climate change, river catchments, glacial processes and environmental management. In addition most courses will also focus on geographical issues worldwide and field courses and placements abroad are not uncommon. As such it is not a world away from **Environmental Science/Studies,** another broad subject which could include population biology, environmental chemistry and ecology as well as sociology, law and conservation. Along a similar theme, courses in **Geology** and **Earth and Marine Sciences** link closely with physical geography and a study of Planet Earth, its land forms, surface features, volcanoes, earthquakes, oceans and the changes in its structure over billions of years. **Marine Studies** can also include **Oceanography** (a study of wave formations, ocean currents, water density and tides), **Marine Chemistry** (seawater and pollutants), **Marine Biology** (marine plants and animals) and **Coastal Environmental Management.**

Environmental Science courses, some of which are interdisciplinary, meaning that they cover a range of subjects leading to one degree, could also suit students looking for breadth in a science degree. Some courses may have a bias however towards biology, as at Plymouth and Hull, or Coastal Conservation at Southampton Solent, Environmental Management with an agricultural bias at Harper Adams University College, or Environmental Hazards at Kingston. Alternatively courses may be tailored to the student's preference between chemistry, geology, ecology or management as at East Anglia. Then of course there is the geographical emphasis in courses in **Urban Studies** or **Town and Country Planning.** However, courses in **Environmental Science** or **Environmental Studies** shouldn't be confused with **Environmental Health** since this is a specialised career training leading to work as an environmental health officer.

As one would expect, at least one A-level or Vocational A-level in science is usually a requirement for all courses, except for Foundation courses which allow students to embark on the first year of a four-year course without the necessary science subjects. But don't confuse Foundation courses with Foundation degrees, which are quite different. Foundation degrees are offered to those who are in employment and who wish to add to their qualifications by aiming for a degree.

Whilst you can take a single honours degree in any science subject, there are several additional routes. Many universities will offer a whole batch of similar science degrees with all students taking the same course in the first year; these are called Modular courses. Thereafter in the second and third years students choose their specialist option. In most cases science subjects can be taken at some universities with industrial placement or with a year abroad, thus extending the course to four years, when you will usually be paid by the firm during your year away from university ... and often offered a job when you graduate.

As in the case of other degree courses, admissions tutors expect your interests to go beyond your studies at school. Information on the UCAS application should therefore include evidence of your interests culled from sources other than your A-level syllabus, such as scientific journals, the internet, newspapers and popular magazines. You're not expected to know everything about your chosen subject but you would be expected to have made an effort to focus on one or two areas of special interest if only to demonstrate a depth of interest.

Course options

Agricultural Biochemistry/Biology/Biotechnology/Zoology, Agriculture, Agroforestry, Anatomy, Animal Biology/Nutrition, Applied Biology, Applied Chemistry, Aquaculture, Aromatherapy, Astronomy, Astrophysics, Bacteriology, Biochemistry, Biological Sciences, Biology, Biomaterials Science, Biomedical Science, Biophysics, Bioscience, Biotechnology, Brewing and Distilling, Cell Biology, Ceramic Sciences, Colour Chemistry, Consumer Science, Crop Science, Cosmetic Science, Earth Science, Ecology, Environmental Biology/Chemistry/Science, Fisheries Science, Food Science, Forensic Science, Genetics, Geochemistry, Geology, Geophysics, Horticulture, Human Biology/Nutrition/Physiology, Immunology, Materials Science, Medical Microbiology, Molecular Biology, Ocean Science, Paper Science, Parasitology, Pharmaceutical Chemistry/Science, Physics, Physiology, Plant Sciences, Polymer Science, Soil Science, Toxicology, Underwater Science, Virology, Water Science, Zoology.

OPTION 5: ENGINEERING, MATHEMATICS AND COMPUTING

A few years ago, a sixth former applied for university sponsorship with a large engineering firm. He was called for an interview and on arrival he was sent to a waiting room. In the centre of the room there was a table and on it something rather bulky was covered with a cloth. The first question he was asked when he was interviewed was, 'What was underneath the cloth?' The model of a jet aircraft which was under the cloth however was not quite as important as the fact that the student was inquisitive enough to have a look. The interviewer's reasoning being that all good engineers are inquisitive!

Wanting to know how things work, wanting to make things work, or wanting to invent new ways to make things work therefore would seem to be a fairly good indication of a technically minded student. If you are one of these then you might have already thought about a career in engineering, although you might not be familiar with the very wide range of engineering specialisms available.

Most universities offer **Bachelor of Engineering (BEng)** and **Master of Engineering (MEng)** programmes, the latter with a higher entry requirement, although it is possible to move upwards from a BEng degree. Sandwich courses should also be considered since they include a year of paid work experience and often good contacts for future employment.

Some applicants might simply wish to do a broad course in Engineering which will involve different aspects of the work; if so, you could aim for a **General** or **Integrated Engineering** degree in which all first year students follow the same course, choosing their preferred specialism in Year 2. Several universities including Bath, Bradford, Cardiff, Durham, Leicester, Liverpool and Nottingham Trent offer these courses. The work of an engineer covers maintenance, research and development, irrespective of the branch of engineering you decide to follow – and there are up to 30 different specialisms from which to choose.

Electrical and Electronic Engineering is a major field in this industry concerned with electricity genera-tion, supply and distribution and includes **Software Engineering, Audio Engineering, Computer and Control Engineering** and **Communications Engineering. Aeronautical and Aerospace Engineering** covers both civil and military aircraft and at some universities a study of space exploration is included. In addition pilot training is offered by Brunel, Liverpool, Salford and Sheffield. It is also worth noting that many similarities exist between the design of aircraft and sea-going craft. Consequently the courses offered in **Naval Architecture** by four universities (Southampton, Newcastle, Plymouth and Strathclyde) could be worth more than a cursory glance, whilst **Boat and Yacht Design** can be studied at Southampton Solent, Cornwall College and Coventry University.

Mechanical Engineering is probably the most diverse field being specifically concerned with the design, development, installation, operation and maintenance of just about anything which has movable parts, and which also includes **Automobile, Acoustical, Marine** and **Agricultural Engineering.** Often linked to Mechanical Engineering is **Manufacturing Engineering** (at one time referred to as production engineering). These engineers cover the entire production process, designing manufacturing systems closely linked to the final product in the right quantities, at the right price for the right delivery date.

Engineering is not always concerned with 'engines' however, as in the case of **Civil Engineering** which focuses on the building structures and stresses and strains involved in high-rise buildings, railways, dams, airports, bridges, motorways, harbours and tunnels. Other specialisms in this category include **Structural, Highway, Transport, Mining, Environmental** and **Water Engineering,** as well as **Offshore Engineering** which includes the construction of drilling platforms used in North Sea oil exploration.

In considering the built environment, it's a short step from Civil Engineering to **Building and Construction Management.** Specialist areas in these careers cover **Building, Land, Hydrographic** and **Quantity Surveying** and also **Building Services Engineering** (heating and ventilation, refrigeration, lighting, air conditioning, water supply and elevators).

The field of **Chemical Engineering** involves several areas from the pharmaceutical, food, brewing and cosmetics industries, to the exploration of offshore gas and oil which in turn links with **Petroleum Engineering.** Courses in **Fire and Explosion** and **Nuclear Engineering** are other branches of this industrial field.

But probably the best kept secret in the careers library is **Materials Science and Engineering,** a great field for research and a mix of chemistry, physics and engineering. The simple fact is that sixth formers don't know what it is and never get round to reading about it, hence the shortfall of applicants! Materials science is the study of a range of materials; it originally developed from metallurgy, a study of metals and their properties, but now also involves product manufacturing in plastics, glass and ceramics.

The testing of materials is constantly taking place. Go into an aircraft establishment and you are likely to see a jet fighter on the rig being shaken continuously for days and weeks until something cracks! At one university they were testing an aero engine for bird-strike and had reached the limit of a 12lb bird hitting the engine at a speed of 700 mph, without too many ill effects for the plane!

Whilst mathematics and physics are the subjects most appropriate for engineering courses, graduates in both these subjects also enter careers in engineering, specialising in their own subject fields, in addition to a wide range of other occupations.

Mathematics is fundamental to every sphere of life, hence the vast range of careers open to graduates. Mathematics at university however is much broader than that experienced by the average student and prospectus information should be scanned carefully before choosing courses which can vary considerably with pathways leading into **Pure** and **Applied Mathematics, Statistics, Computing** and **Operational Research.** In addition joint courses with mathematics include related subjects such as physics, statistics, computer science, electronics, astronomy, accountancy and finance. Currently the largest percentage of graduates go into financial activities with many also going into other areas of business, education and manufacturing.

Finally in this group of subjects it is impossible to ignore the impact which **Computer Science** has had on the work of engineers, technologists and mathematicians. However, bearing in mind some of the misconceptions, students should recognise the range of openings in this area with opportunities existing for business analysts, systems analysts and designers, programmers and software development.

Most courses have a strong practical focus and many students are attracted to them because of their interests in information technology and various computer packages. Yet computer science degrees offer far more. Many embrace hardware and software network systems and database design, and some can involve electronic engineering and mathematics. When choosing courses therefore it is important to step carefully and to be aware of the range of optional subjects and degree courses in **Information Systems** and **Information Management, Artificial Intelligence, Cybernetics** and **Multimedia.**

Course options
Acoustics, Aerospace Engineering, Applied Mathematics, Applied Statistics, Architecture, Astronomy, Astrophysics, Automotive Engineering, Avionics, Civil Engineering, Communications Engineering, Computer Science, Computer Systems Engineering, Cybernetics, Electrical Engineering, Electronics Engineering, Ergonomics, Integrated Engineering, Marine Engineering, Mathematics, Mathematics Teaching, Mechanical Engineering, Meteorology, Mining Engineering, Naval Architecture, Offshore Engineering, Operational Research, Opto-electronics, Physics, Probability and Statistics, Quantity Surveying, Robotics, Statistics, Surveying, Systems Analysis, Systems Modelling, Teaching.

OPTION 6: LEARNING A LANGUAGE

There is a true story of a man who spent a week with a tribe of American Indians. He couldn't speak their language but he listened to the sounds they were making and at the end of the week he could put some of the sounds together and make himself understood. If you come to think about it, that's the way you learned your language – by listening. Learning a vocabulary and putting the words in the right order comes much later.

Unfortunately however one problem is that the British are too complacent when it comes to learning languages. We take it for granted that foreigners will be able to speak or at least understand English. Another problem seems to be that language students, who presumably enjoy studying and have a special ability for learning their chosen foreign language at school, seem to be unenthusiastic about extending this gift to learning new ones.

Many language students go on to study a foreign language at university, but all too often they choose the same language, **French**, **German** or **Spanish**, which they have studied at school for four or five years. That's fine but are they making such choices merely as a means to an end, just to spend three or four years at university to get a degree? One language applicant admitted at interview that she wasn't really interested in going abroad!

If you have this gift for languages why not set a target to see how many other languages you can learn in the next five or six years? Why not in fact take a two-language degree? Having a second language is an advantage when it comes to applying for a job – although if you are going to work abroad, having a knowledge of dialects is also important. One German from Munich spoke of the difficulties he sometimes faced with visitors from Hamburg and Frankfurt because of the differences in dialects.

In choosing a course it's important to establish the type of degree which you prefer and whether you want a literature option or a course which emphasises the written and the spoken word. Whilst A-levels in the target language are required for courses in **French**, **German**, **Spanish** and **Hispanic Studies,** other languages can be started from scratch (*ab initio*), although universities will expect applicants to have good grades in one or two modern languages, just to show that they have some flair for language study. So, why not choose **Chinese**, **Czech**, **Italian**, **Japanese**, **Modern Greek**, **Portuguese**, **Russian** or **Scandinavian Studies**? (For other languages see 'Course options' below.) In some respects there's probably a better chance of a subject-related job choosing an unusual language rather than French, German or Spanish from which several thousand students graduate each year and with competition coming from many Europeans able to speak perfect English. **Welsh**, **Irish** and **Gaelic** also offer a stimulating challenge for linguists although such interests are more likely to stem from an attraction to the historical, social and cultural aspects of these areas.

In addition and linked to European languages it is also possible to follow a broader course by way of a degree in **European Studies**, **European Business Studies**, **European Social and Political Studies**, **Contemporary Europe** or **European Union Studies**. For those particularly interested in Spanish studies, a degree in **Portuguese** or **Latin American Studies** might be considered. Latin America has 400 million inhabitants and in many ways represents a new world with considerable potential and opportunities with degree courses covering political, social and cultural aspects.

In addition, French, German and Spanish, which are offered by most universities, may be combined with a host of other subjects, for example French at Leeds can be taken with over 30 subjects. One very popular option at a number of universities is that of Business Studies in which it is often possible to spend a year with a firm abroad. Bath, Bradford, Aston and Loughborough are popular universities offering these combinations.

Finally, for something quite different, there are also courses in **Translating and Interpreting** at Aston, East Anglia and Heriot-Watt.

However when it comes to choosing one of the new languages below, don't do it just for the novelty; you should obviously have some interest in the country or region concerned!

Course options
Amharic, Anglo-Saxon Norse and Celtic, Applied Languages, Arabic, Asia-Pacific Studies, Bengali, Brazilian, Bulgarian, Burmese, Cambodian, Chinese, Czech/Slovak, Danish, Dutch, East European Studies, European Studies, European Union Studies, Finnish, French, Gaelic, Georgian, German, Greek, Hausa, Hebrew, Hindi, Hispanic Studies, Hungarian, Icelandic, Indonesian, International Business Studies, Iranian, Irish, Italian, Japanese, Korean, Latin, Latin American Studies, Linguistics, Malay, Modern Greek, Modern Languages, Nepali, Norwegian, Persian, Polish, Portuguese, Punjabi, Romanian, Russian, Sanskrit, Serbian/Croatian, Sinhalese, Somali, Spanish, Swahili, Swedish, Tamil, Thai, Tibetan, Translating and Interpreting, Turkish, Ukrainian, Urdu, Vietnamese, Welsh, Yoruba, Zulu.

OPTION 7: CREATIVE SUBJECTS
One could argue that creative people are the lucky ones, since artists, musicians, actors and actresses seem to have energy and enthusiasm to maintain their interests in their work throughout their lives without really thinking about retiring. They are often described as being 'gifted', almost as though painting pictures or playing musical instruments come without trying, which is far from the truth. Equally of course some people find mathematics, the sciences or languages easier than others, but as in the case of art and music, achievement doesn't come without a lot of effort.

Creative courses such as **Art and Design**, **Music** and **Drama** are specialist subjects which in turn can and often do lead to specific careers. One exception however is the field of **Fine Art**, with painting and sculpture being very difficult areas in which to get established. Many students will choose a degree subject with the intention of following it into a similar career, but in the case of creative subjects it's well worth realising that unlike business courses and computer studies, job opportunities can be limited. It's also important to realise that universities and colleges do not accept the responsibility of finding jobs for students when they graduate. So from the student's point of view, the best institutions will be those with good facilities for the chosen course and good contacts with the industry for job placements and if you are concerned about the latter check the destinations of graduates on Open Day visits or at interview.

Art and Design covers a vast area which probably accounts for the fact that it attracts more applicants than any other degree subject. **Fashion and Textile Design** is a particularly large and popular field which extends into contemporary fashion, knitwear design, clothing design, fashion marketing and promotion, textile surface decoration (carpets, tiles etc) and textile management.

Students choosing **Graphic Design** can follow specialisms in advertising, illustration and animation and job opportunities could be reasonably good. **Industrial Design** is more specialised still and covers furniture design, interior design, theatre and stage design and car and transport design, and finally there is **Three Dimensional Design** which can involve glassware, ceramics, silverware, metal and jewellery.

Architecture should also be regarded as a creative subject and whilst A-level art is not a requirement for most courses, evidence of the ability to express ideas visually is extremely important and is often seen as a requirement for entry to most schools of architecture. Most applicants will finally aim to work as architects and when applying for courses it's important to check that the degree offered by the university or college is validated by the Royal Institute of British Architects. One specialised field of architecture is that of **Landscape Architecture** which focuses on the design of the environment surrounding buildings. This is not to be confused with garden design, although landscaping building environs will include trees and other vegetation as well as the design of water features and pavings.

Finally in the art field and for those more interested in the theory than the practice there are courses in the **History of Art and Design**, currently attracting a high percentage of women. Courses can be chosen which offer specialised studies in various historical periods of art and architecture or aspects of applied art such as furniture and textiles or modern design.

Students applying for **Music** face similar problems and decisions with some aiming to be performers and others seeking other outlets at the end of their degree. **Music** courses can be quite broad in their approach. Some are exclusively performance courses, some are not, whilst others provide a range of topics such as that offered by Leeds University which covers analysis, aural training, counterpoint, harmony and historical studies, with second year students choosing to specialise in performance, notation, composition or history and criticism. Separate courses are offered in **Popular** and **World Music**, **Multimedia** and **Electronics** and **Music Theatre**. Southampton also offers a wide range of music subjects, covering everything from madrigals to jazz as well as joint courses with acoustics, languages and management. In addition several universities offer courses in **Music Technology** and **Music and Sound Recording**, notably Surrey.

Students interested in **Drama** or **Dance** can choose specialist courses in these areas or aim for **Performing Arts** which could include some acting, dancing and music, whilst other courses give a greater focus to drama and include stage management. Specialist fields on several drama courses include directing and the aspects of drama related to films, video, radio or live theatre. It's worthwhile remembering however that not all drama courses are acting courses although many have acting modules; some may also offer theoretical and practical studies in radio, TV, film and theatre techniques.

However, creativity is not restricted to art, music and drama. The ability to produce new ideas is basic in many jobs but none more so than careers in the media. This is a very wide field which can include courses in **Journalism**, **Radio and TV Production**, **Film and Video**, **Photography**, **Public Relations**, **Publishing**, **Creative Writing** and **Scriptwriting**. There are also broader courses, for example **Communication and Media Studies** at Loughborough University, which examines the social, political and economic impact of communication and the media. Needless to say you should also choose your media studies courses with care.

Course options

Art and Design
Animation, Art and Design, Art Education, Blacksmithing and Metalwork, Book Arts and Crafts, Calligraphy and Heraldry, Ceramics, Community Arts, Design Crafts, Embroidery, Fashion, Film and Television, Fine Art, Furniture Restoration, Furniture Studies, Graphic Design, Industrial Design, Interior Design, Jewellery, Leather Studies, Lettering, Metalwork, Modelmaking, Moving Image, Painting, Photography, Plastics, Printed Textiles, Product Design, Public Art, Sports Equipment Design, Surface Pattern, Textile Crafts, Textile Design, Three Dimensional Design, Virtual Reality Design, Wildlife Photography, Wood.

Dance
Art and Teaching of Ballet, Choreography, Community Dance, Costume for Stage and Screen, Dance and Movement Studies, Dance Education (Distance learning), Dance with Related Subjects, Performing Arts.

Drama
Acting Studies, Actor Musician, Alternative Theatre, Circus, Community Theatre, Contemporary Theatre, Directing, Drama, Drama Education, European Theatre Arts.

Music
Actor Musician, Applied Music, Audio and Music Technology, Commercial Music, Jazz, Music, Music Education, Music Industry Management, Music Production, Music Systems Engineering, Music Technology, Musical Theatre, New Music and Media, Performing Arts, Popular Music, Puppetry, Recording Arts, Technical Theatre, Theatre Sound.

Other creative courses
Architecture, Art Galleries and Heritage Management, Arts Management, Beauty Therapy, Communication Studies, Creative Studies, Creative Writing, Floristry, Hair and Beauty, History of Art and Design, Media and Special Effects, Media Studies, Screenwriting Studies, Television and Radio.

OPTION 8: OTHER ARTS AND HUMANITIES SUBJECTS

Arts degrees cover a wide field and apart from those subjects chosen as a preparation to enter the teaching profession they are non-vocational but (hopefully) studied for pleasure and scholarship and one of the most popular courses in terms of the numbers of applicants is **English**.

In the personal statement, on her UCAS form, one applicant wrote, 'I've just read *Birdsong* and *Charlotte Grey* by Faulks and couldn't put them down. I keep reading *The Famished Road,* which in the world of the bizarre is in a different realm to other works I have read. Locked away in book after book over the years, I enjoy literature because it opens windows into many worlds unreachable in any other way. That's ..... Why English?'

Such enthusiasm speaks for itself and such is the scope offered to applicants in a wide-ranging study of literature through poetry, fiction and drama that the extent of the subject seems limitless. In addition to Shakespeare, Chaucer, Donne, Milton, Swift, and others, students are able to engage with children's literature, science fiction and film literature and in recent years **Creative Writing** has appeared as a degree subject or as an option at a number of universities including East Anglia, Hull, Liverpool John Moores, London (Royal Holloway) and Warwick. *(If you are interested try this test, set by one university – Write a piece of creative writing between 400 and 500 words and include each of the following words twice. Each word must be used in a different context and/or with a different meaning on each occasion. All the words must be used – Shell; Flicker; Knit; Coin; Compose; Lark; Stream; Root.)*

However when choosing courses check the prospectuses carefully because a course listed as **English** might simply mean **English Literature** or **English Language** or both. There are also courses in **Literature and Modern Languages** which cross international boundaries, **American Studies** which covers the literature and history of North America and **Linguistics** focusing on a study of language itself, which may include topics such as children's language, dialect and slang, language handicap, and advertising language.

Degree courses in **History** vary enormously, exploring different ages in different countries and cultures and applicants should tread carefully to select those universities offering the course best suited to their interests. Another historical study is offered by way of courses in the **History of Art**, the principal areas of study being painting, sculpture and architecture, often referred to as 'high art'; however many courses have now expanded into other areas such as design, photographic and film history. **Economic and Social History** is another branch of the subject whilst **Ancient History** leads on to **Classical Studies**, **Classics** and on towards **Archaeology** which can be studied from a scientific as well as an historical base.

Courses in **Theology** and **Religious Studies** explore religious beliefs and how individuals practise their beliefs (a recent BBC poll stated that 70% of people in the UK believe in a 'higher being' or a spiritual force). These beliefs impact strongly on the world in which we live and whilst the subject is non-vocational in one sense, an awareness of these beliefs and an understanding of the major faiths and the standards and values of others in a multicultural society is now an essential part of our working lives. However, an examination of beliefs, the differences between knowledge and opinion, the nature of good and evil and ethical issues, can also take us into **Philosophy**, a subject which is close to the heart of anyone who enjoys an argument, balancing one issue against another, whether the topic might be one of free will or predestination or the existence of God. **Social and Cultural Anthropology** also explore religions, as well as kinship, ritual systems, art, politics within the organisation of society, whilst **Biological Anthropology** looks at the evolutionary processes, genetics and physical differences.

For something completely different, for those interested in **Physical Education** there are a number of degrees offered in sporting subjects such as **Sport Science** and **Sport Studies**. Courses are now offered in abundance, which can include **Leisure and Recreation Management**, **Coaching**, **Sport Therapy and Exercise Science**, **Fitness Management** and **Sport Psychology**.

Those students interested in the idea of a career in the teaching profession but who have not followed a teacher training course can follow a degree course, for example in English, Geography, History or languages, by taking an extra year leading to a postgraduate certificate in education.

Course options

Advertising, African Studies, American Studies, Ancient Civilisation, Ancient Greek, Ancient History, Ancient Mediterranean Studies, Anglo-Saxon, Anthropology, Archaeology, Arts Management, Asia-Pacific Studies, Australian Studies, Biblical Studies, Bioarchaeology, Broadcasting Studies, Byzantine Studies,

Canadian Studies, Caribbean Studies, Celtic Studies, Church History, Classical Archaeology, Classical Civilisation, Classical Studies, Communication Studies, Conservation, Countryside Management, Creative Writing, Cultural Studies, Development Studies, Divinity, Earth Sciences, East Mediterranean History, Ecology, Economic History, Economics, Egyptology, English, English Language, English Literature, European History, Film History, Film Studies, Fine Art Valuation, Furniture Restoration, Greek, Greek and Roman Studies, Heritage Management, History, History of Architecture, History of Art, Information Management, International Relations, Jewish History, Journalism, Land Management, Latin, Law, Linguistics, Literary Studies, Literature, Maritime History, Maritime Studies, Media Studies, Mediaeval Studies, Middle Eastern Studies, Peace Studies, Politics, Publishing, Religious Studies, Rural Resources Management, Scottish Studies, Scottish Literature, Sports Science, Sports Studies, Theatre Studies, Theology, TV Studies, Urban Land Economics, Urban Studies, Victorian Studies, War Studies, Welsh History.

CHOOSING A DEGREE BY WAY OF SCHOOL SUBJECTS

Below are lists of examination subjects, followed by a list of appropriate degree course subjects

Accounting/Applied Business
Accountancy
Actuarial Science/Studies
Agricultural Economics
Banking
Business Administration
Business Economics
Business Studies
Economics
Estate Management
Finance
Financial Services
Hospitality Management
Industrial Economics
Insurance
Land Economics
Management Sciences
Marketing
Quantity Surveying
Retail Management

Ancient History
Ancient Civilisation
Ancient Greek
Anglo-Saxon
Anthropology
Archaeology
Art and Archaeology of the Ancient World
Biblical Studies
Byzantine Studies
Celtic Studies
Classical Archaeology
Classical Civilisation
Classical Studies
East Mediterranean History
Egyptian Ecology
Greek (Ancient)
Greek and Roman Studies
Greek Archaeology
Heritage Management
History
History of Architecture
History of Art

Jewish History
Middle Eastern Civilisation/Cultures
Religious Studies

Archaeology
Anthropology
Archaeological Sciences
Art and Design
Bioarchaeology
Byzantine Studies
Celtic Studies
Classical Civilisation
Classical Studies
Combined Studies
Conservation (Restoration)
Conservation of Buildings
East Mediterranean History
Environmental Archaeology
Geoarchaeology
Geology
Greek and Roman Studies
Greek Archaeology
History of Architecture
History of Art
History of Design
Maritime History
Middle Eastern Studies

Art and Design/Applied Art and Design
Advertising
  Copywriting
  Design
  Management
  Photography
Animation
Applied Arts
Archaeology
Architecture
Art (Teaching)
Bookbinding
Ceramic Design
Combined Studies
Communication Studies

Conservation
  Archaeological
  Building
  Restoration
Costume Design
Creative Arts
Design Crafts
Designs for Media
Digital Modelling
Embroidery
Fashion Design
Fashion Promotions
Film Studies
Fine Arts
Fine Arts Restoration
Floral Design
Furniture Design
Garden Design
Glass Design
Graphic Arts
Heritage Management
History of Architecture
History of Art
History of Design
History of Film
Illustration
Industrial Design
Interior Design
Landscape Architecture
Media Studies
Model-making
Moving Image (Design)
Photography
Print Design
Product Design
Sculpture
Silversmithing, Goldsmithing and Jewellery
Textile Design
Theatre Design
TV Studies
Typography
Valuation (Fine Arts)
Virtual Reality Design
Visual Arts
Visual Communications
Visual Studies

Biology/Applied Science

Agricultural Biochemistry
Agricultural Biology
Agricultural Biotechnology
Agricultural Botany
Agricultural Zoology
Agriculture
Agroforestry
Agronomy

Anatomy
Animal Behaviour
Animal Biology
Animal Management
Animal Nutrition
Animal Science
Animal Welfare
Anthropology
Applied Biology
Aquaculture
Aquatic Bioscience
Arboriculture
Bacteriology
Behavioural Studies
Biochemical Engineering
Biochemistry
Biological Chemistry
Biological Sciences
Biology (Teaching)
Biomaterials Science
Biomedical Sciences
Biomolecular Chemistry
Biophysics
Bioprocess Engineering
Biosciences
Biosciences (Medical)
Biotechnology
Brewing and Distilling
Cell Biology
Childhood Studies
Conservation Biology
Consumer Sciences/Studies
Cosmetic Sciences
Countryside Management/Recreation
Crop Protection
Crop Science
Dental Technology
Dentistry
Developmental Psychology
Dietetics
Earth Resources
Earth Science Studies
Ecology
Environmental Biochemistry
Environmental Biology
Environmental Health
Environmental Management
Environmental Protection
Environmental Sciences/Studies
Environmental Toxicology
Equine Science/Studies
Exercise and Health
Farm Business Management
Floriculture
Food and Consumer Studies
Food Economics

Food Management
Food Manufacturing
Food Marketing
Food Production
Food Quality
Food Science
Food Technology
Forensic Science
Forest and Woodland Management
Forest Products (Wood) Technology
Forestry
Garden Design
General Science
Genetics
Golf Course Management
Health and Community Studies
Health and Exercise Psychology
Health and Fitness
Healthcare
Health Promotion
Health Sciences Studies
Herbal Medicine
Horticulture
Human Biology
Human Communication
Human Ecology
Human Geography
Human Life Sciences
Human Nutrition
Human Physiology
Human Psychology
Human Sciences
Immunology
Land Management
Land Use Studies
Landscape Architecture
Landscape Design
Learning Disabilities
Life Sciences
Marine Biology
Marine Biotechnology
Marine Environment
Marine/Maritime Studies
Marine Resources
Medical Biochemistry
Medical Biosciences
Medical Electronics
Medical Genetics
Medical Microbiology
Medical Physics
Medicinal Chemistry
Medicine
Microbiology
Midwifery
Molecular Biology
Molecular Sciences

Natural Resources
Natural Sciences
Neuroscience
Nursing
Nutrition
Nutritional Biochemistry
Occupational Health
Occupational Therapy
Ocean Science
Oceanography
Optometry
Orthoptics
Osteopathy
Palaeobiology and Evolution
Paramedical Science
Parasitology
Pathobiology
Pharmaceutical Chemistry
Pharmacology
Pharmacy
Physical Education (Teaching)
Physical Geography
Physiology
Physiotherapy
Plant Sciences
Podiatry
Polymer Science
Population Biology
Prosthetics and Orthotics
Psychology
Public Health
Radiography
Recreation Management
Rural Environment Management
Rural Resource Development
Social Anthropology
Social Care
Social Psychology
Social Work
Soil Science
Speech Sciences Therapy
Sports Science
Toxicology
Turf Science/Technology
Underwater Studies
Veterinary Nursing
Veterinary Science
Wildlife Management
Zoology

Business Studies/Applied Business

Accountancy
Administration
Advertising
American Business Studies
Arts Management

Banking
Building Management
Business
  Administration
  Analysis
  Computing
  Decision Analysis
  Economics
  Information Systems
  Information Technology
  Law
  Mathematics Studies
  Psychology
  Studies (Welsh)
Consumer Studies
Countryside Management
E-Business
E-Commerce
Economics
Estate Management
European Accountancy and Finance
European Business/Management
European Economics
European Logistics Management
European Management Science
European Tourism
Events Management
Farm Management
Financial Services
Food Marketing
Health Administration
Heritage Management
Hospitality Management
Hotel Management
Industrial Relations
Institutional Management
International Business Hospitality
International Management
International Marketing
International Tourism Management
Land Economy
Land Management
Leisure Management
Management Science/Studies
Marketing
Operational Research
Organisational Studies
Property Management
Public Administration
Publishing
Purchasing
Quality Management
Retail Management
Risk Management
Rural Business Management
Rural Economics

Social Administration
Stage Management
Surveying
Tourism Management
Transport Management

Chemistry/Applied Science

Agricultural Biochemistry
Agricultural Biology
Agricultural Chemistry
Agriculture
Analytical Chemistry
Animal Nutrition
Animal Sciences
Applied Chemistry
Bacteriology
Biochemical Engineering
Biochemistry
Biological Chemistry
Biological Sciences
Biomedical Sciences
Biotechnology
Brewing and Distilling
Cell Biology
Ceramic Science
Chemical Physics
Chemical Product Technology
Chemistry of Materials
Chemistry (Teaching)
Colour Chemistry
Cosmetic Science
Dental Materials
Dentistry
Engineering
  Chemical
  Fire
  Food
  Fuel and Energy
  Nuclear Process
  Petroleum
Environmental Biochemistry
Environmental Biology
Environmental Chemistry
Environmental Geoscience
Environmental Toxicology
Food Science
Forensic Science
Fuel Science
General Science
Genetics
Geochemistry
Health Sciences
Horticulture
Human Biology
Human Nutrition
Human Physiology

Human Sciences
Immunology
Life Sciences
Marine Chemistry
Materials Science
Medical Biosciences
Medical Microbiology
Medicinal Chemistry
Medicine
Minerals Engineering
Minerals Surveying
Molecular Biology
Molecular Genetics
Molecular Pathology
Molecular Sciences
Natural Sciences
Neurosciences
Nursing
Nutrition
Ocean Science
Parasitology
Petroleum Geology
Pharmaceutical Chemistry
Pharmacology
Pharmacy
Plant Science
Polymer Science
Soil Science
Sports Science
Toxicology
Zoology

Classics and Classical Civilisation

Ancient Civilisations
Ancient Greek
Ancient History
Ancient Mediterranean Studies
Archaeology
Biblical Studies
Classical Studies
Greek
History (Greek and Roman Studies)
History of Architecture
History of Art
Latin
Roman Civilisation

Computing/Applied ICT

Artificial Intelligence
Business Computing
Business Information Systems
Business Information Technology
Cognitive Science
Computational and Experimental Mathematics
Computational Chemistry
Computational Linguistics

Computational Physics
Computational Science
Computer-Aided Design
Computer-Aided Engineering
Computer Animation
Computer Studies
Decision Systems
Engineering
  Control and Systems
  Information Systems
  Software
Information Science
Information Systems
Intelligent Systems
Robotics

Dance
(See under **Theatre Studies**)

Design and Technology/ Applied Art and Design

Architecture
Art and Design
Building
Ceramic Design
Dental Technology
Design and Technology (teaching)
Design Crafts
Design History
Furniture Design
Industrial Design
Interior Design
Jewellery
Landscape Architecture
Product Design
Prosthetics and Orthotics
Silversmithing, Goldsmithing and Jewellery
Technical Illustration

Drama
(See under **Theatre Studies**)

Economics/Applied Business

Accountancy
Actuarial Science/Studies
Agricultural Economics
Applied Economics
Applied Mathematics
Applied Statistics
Banking
Business Administration
Business Analysis
Business Decision Management
Business Decision Mathematics
Business Economics
Business Information Systems

Business Studies
City and Regional Planning
Development Studies
Economic and Social History
Economics (Teaching)
Environment Economics and Ecology
European Business Administration
European Economics
European Logistics Management
European Marketing
European Politics
European Studies
Farm Management
Finance
Financial Economics
Financial Services
Food Marketing
Geography
Government
Human Resource Management
Industrial Economics
Information and Library Studies
International Business Economics
Land Economics
Management Science
Mathematical Economics
Mathematical Statistics
Mathematics
Money, Banking and Finance
Operational Research
Planning
Politics
Quantity Surveying
Social History
Social Sciences
Social Studies
Sociology
Statistics
Technological Economics
Tourism and Leisure Economics

Electronics/Engineering/Applied ICT

Astrophysics
Audio and Music Technology
Audiotechnology
Avionic Systems
Broadcasting
Communications Engineering
Computer Science/Systems
Control Systems
Digital Systems
Electroacoustics
Electronic Design
Electronic Media
Electronic Music
Electronic Systems

Engineering
  Aeronautical
  Aerospace Systems
  Computer Systems
  Electronic
  Information
  Mechatronic
  Physics
  Software
  Systems
  Telecommunications
Intelligent Systems
Internet Technology
Laser Systems
Media Systems
Medical Electronics
Microelectronics
Music Technology
Optoelectronic Engineering
Planetary Physics
Power Systems
Signal Processing
Telecommunications

English

Advertising (Copywriting)
American Studies
Anglo-Saxon
Arts
  Combined
  General
Broadcast Media
Broadcasting Studies
Communications Studies
Contemporary Writing
Creative Writing
Cultural Studies
Drama
English (Teaching)
English as a Foreign Language
English Literature
Information and Library Studies
Information Science
Journalism
Linguistics
Literary Studies
Literature
Media Studies
Publishing
Scottish Literature
Theatre Studies
TV Studies

Environmental Science/Applied Science

Agriculture
Agroforestry

Animal Science
Architecture
Biology
Botany
Chemistry
City and Regional Planning
Combined Studies
Conservation
Countryside Management
Crop Science
Development Studies
Earth Resources and Management
Ecology
Economics
Environmental Chemistry
Environmental Planning
Estate Surveying
Forestry
Garden Design
Geography
Geology
Heritage Management
Horticulture
Land Management
Landscape Architecture
Leisure Management
Marine Environment
Oceanography
Population Studies
Recreational Land Management
Rural Resources
Surveying
Topographic Science
Town and Country Planning
Underwater Studies
Urban Estate Management
Urban Studies

Film Studies
(See under **Media Studies**)

Geography/Applied Science
African Studies
Afro-Asian Studies
Agriculture
Agroforestry
Anthropology
Applied Ecology
Applied Geology
Archaeology
Canadian Studies
Caribbean Studies
City and Regional Planning
Countryside Management
Development Studies
Earth Sciences

East Asian Studies
Ecology
Economics
Environmental Planning
Environmental Studies
Estate Management
Estate Surveying
European Land Management
Food Marketing
Geochemistry
Geographical Information Systems
Geography (Teaching)
Geology
Geophysics
Geoscience
Government
Human Geography
Land Economy
Land Management
Land Surveying
Landscape Architecture
Marine Resources and Management
Maritime Studies
Meteorology
Mineral Surveying
Mining Geology
Nautical Studies
Oceanography
Planning
Politics
Population Studies
Recreational Land Management
Rural Resources Management
Strategic Studies
Surveying
  Estate
  Minerals
  Valuation
Surveying and Mapping
Topographic Science
Town and Country Planning
Transport
Travel and Tourism
Underwater Studies
Urban Estate Management
Urban Studies

Geology/Applied Science
Agriculture
Applied Ecology
Archaeology
Astronomy
Chemistry
Earth Science
Ecology
Environmental Science

Geochemistry
Geographical Information Systems
Geography
Geological Engineering
Geomorphology
Geophysical Science
Geotechnics
Human Geography
Hydrography
Meteorology
Mineral Surveying
Mining Engineering
Mining Geology
Natural Resources
Ocean Science
Offshore Engineering
Petroleum Geology
Physics
Rural Resources
Soil Science
Surveying
Topographic Science

Government and Politics
African Studies
Afro-Asian Studies
Agricultural Economics
American Studies
Anthropology
Applied Social Sciences/Studies
Asian Studies
Banking
Broadcasting Studies
Business Economics
Business Law
Business Studies
Canadian Studies
Caribbean Studies
Chinese Studies
City and Regional Planning
Commerce
Communication Studies
Community Sciences/Studies
Defence and Security Studies
Development Studies
Earth Resources and Management
Economics
Education (Not Teaching)
Environmental Policy
Environmental Protection
Environmental Studies
European Business Economics
European Community Studies
European Politics
European Social Policy
European Studies

Financial Economics
French Law
French Studies
German Law
German Studies
Government
Health Administration
History
Housing Management
Human Organisation
Industrial Relations
International Agriculture
International Business Economics
International Finance
International History
International Marketing
International Politics
International Relations
International Studies
Investment
Italian Studies
Japanese Studies
Law
Natural Resources
Peace and War Studies
Peace Studies
Political Economy
Politics
Philosophy
Public Policy and Administration
Public Sector Economics
Race Studies
Scandinavian Studies
Social Administration
Social Anthropology
Social Care
Social Ethics
Social History
Social Policy
Social Research
Social Work
Sociology
Strategic Planning
Town Planning
Urban Studies
Welfare and Social Policy
Youth and Community Work

History
African Studies
American Studies
Ancient Civilisations
Ancient History
Anglo-Saxon
Anthropology
Archaeology

Biblical Studies
Byzantine Studies
Canadian Studies
Chinese History
Church History
Classical Civilisation
Classical Studies
Classics
Conservation
  Building
  Restoration
Criminal Justice
Cultural Studies
Divinity
East Mediterranean History
Economic History
European History
Film History
History of Architecture
History of Art
History of Design
History of Ideas
History of Science
History (Teaching)
International History
International Relations
Irish Studies
Islamic Art and Archaeology
Italian Studies
Jewish History
Latin American Studies
Law
Medieval Studies
Near and Middle Eastern Studies
Peace Studies
Politics
Religious Studies
Scottish History
Social History
Social Sciences
Social Studies
Sociology
Strategic Studies
Victorian Studies
War Studies
Welsh History

History of Art/Applied Art and Design

Advertising
Anthropology
Archaeology
Architecture History
Art and Design
Art History
Arts Management
Church History

Conservation
  Archaeological
  Buildings
  Restoration
Costume Design
Crafts (Printmaking)
Film History
Fine Art Valuation
Furniture Restoration
Heritage Management
History
Victorian Studies

Home Economics/Applied Science/ Health and Social Care

This subject area also involves courses concerned with food and drink and the consumer.

Administration
Advertising
Animal Nutrition
Applied Consumer Studies
Behavioural Science
Biological Science
Biology
Brewing and Distilling
Business Studies
Chemistry
Chemistry of Food
Communications Studies
Community Studies
Consumer Product Design
Consumer Sciences
Consumer Studies
Culinary Arts
Dietetics
Environmental Studies
Fashion
Food
  Bioprocessing
  Economics
  Manufacturing
  Marketing and Management
  Production
  Quality
  Technology
Health and Community Studies
Health and Safety
Healthcare
Health Services
Home Economics (Teaching)
Hospitality (Hotel) Management
Housing Studies
Human Biology
Human Nutrition
Human Psychology
Human Sciences

Industrial Design
International Hospitality Management
Leisure Studies
Marketing
Media Studies
Nursing
Nutrition
Psychology
Retail Management
Social Administration
Social Policy
Social Studies
Sociology
Textile Arts
Women's Studies
Youth and Community Work

Languages

Students of modern (or ancient) languages frequently choose the same languages to study at degree level. It should be noted, however, that the ability to speak and write in a range of foreign languages can be an important asset when applying for jobs. It is therefore suggested that those students with an interest and ability in languages should look beyond their A-level skills into new languages.

African languages
Akkadian
Ancient Greek
Anglo-Saxon
Asian languages
Assyriology
Bantu
Bengali Studies
Breton
Bulgarian
Burmese Studies
Celtic
Chinese
Communication Studies
Czech and Slovak
Danish
Dutch
East European Studies
Egyptian
European Studies
  French
  German
  Italian
  Russian
  Spanish
European Tourism
Finnish
French
French (Teaching)
French Law

Gaelic
German
German (Teaching)
German Law
Greek (Modern)
Hausa
Hebrew
Hindi
Hispanic Studies
Hungarian
Indonesian
International Hospitality
  Management
International Studies
Interpreting and Translating
Iranian
Irish
Italian
Italian (Teaching)
Italian Law
Japanese
Korean
Languages for Business
Latin
Latin American Studies
Linguistics
Literature
Marathi
Modern Languages
Nepali Studies
Norse
Norwegian
Oriental Languages
Pakistan Studies
Persian
Polish
Portuguese
Romanian
Russian
Russian (Teaching)
Sanskrit
Scandinavian Studies
Serbo-Croat
Sinhalese
Slavonic Studies
South Asian Studies
Spanish
Spanish (Teaching)
Spanish Law
Swedish
Tamil
Tourism
Travel
Turkish
Urdu
Vietnamese Studies
Welsh

Law

American Legal Systems
Business Law
European Community Studies
European Law
Government
History
International History
International Relations
Legal Studies
Legislative Studies
Police Studies
Politics
Property Management
Public Administration
Social Administration
Social Policy
Strategic Studies
Urban Studies

Mathematics/Statistics

Accountancy
Acoustical Engineering
Actuarial Science
Applied Mathematics
Applied Statistics
Architecture
Astrophysics
Automotive Engineering
Banking
Building
Business Computing
Business Economics
Business Information Systems
Business Studies
Cognitive Science
Commerce
Computer Science
Decision Systems
Economics
Engineering
  Aeronautical
  Aerospace Systems
  Avionics
  Civil
  Communications
  Computer Systems
  Control Systems
  Electrical
  Electronic
  Marine
  Mathematical
  Mechanical
  Mining
  Physics
  Software
  Systems

Environmental Engineering
Ergonomics
European Business Economics
Financial Analysis
Financial Services
Industrial Mathematics
Information Science
Insurance
Integrated Engineering
Intelligent Systems
Investment
Management Science
Mathematics (Pure and Applied)
Mathematics (Teaching)
Mathematics and Statistics
Naval Architecture
Offshore Engineering
Operational Research
Opto-electronics
Probability and Statistics
Quantity Surveying
Risk Management (Financial)
Robotics and Cybernetics
Ship Science
Surveying
Systems Analysis
Systems Modelling

Media Studies

Advertising
Art
Art and Design
Arts Management
Audio-visual Production
Band Studies
Broadcasting
Communication Studies
Design (Advertising)
Drama
Electronic Music
Ethnic Studies
Film Studies
Human Organisation
Human Psychology
Jazz Studies
Journalism
Leisure Studies
Marketing
Media and Theatre Studies
Music
Music Technology
Photography
Politics
TV Studies
Visual Arts
Visual Performance

Music/Music Technology/Performing Arts
Acoustics
Band Musicianship
Book Publishing
Broadcasting
Creative Music Technology
Dance
Drama
Electronic Music
Ethnomusicology
Jazz Studies
Media Production
Media Studies
Music (Teaching)
Performance Arts
Stage Management
Theatre Studies

Performance Arts/Studies
(See under **Theatre Studies**)

Philosophy
Ancient Civilisation
Cognitive Science
Conflict Resolution
Divinity
Economics
Educational Studies (Not Teaching)
European Philosophy
Government
History
History and Philosophy of Science
History of Ideas
History of Religions
Law
Peace Studies
Philosophy of Science
Politics
Psychology
Religious Studies
Social Ethics
Theology
Women's Studies

Photography
(See under **Art and Design**)

Physical Education/Health and Social Care
Chiropractic
Coaching Science
Dance Studies
Exercise and Health
Exercise Science
Golf Studies
Health Education
Health Psychology

Health Science
Healthcare
Human Life Science
Nursing
Occupational Health and Safety
Occupational Therapy
Osteopathy
Outdoor Pursuits
Physical Education (Teaching)
Primary, Secondary (Teaching)
Physiotherapy
Sport and Exercise Science
Sport and Health
Sport Coaching
Sport Equipment Design
Sport Management

Physics/Engineering/Applied Science
Acoustics
Aerodynamics
Air Transport Engineering
Applied Physics
Architecture
Astronautics
Astronomy
Astrophysics
Automotive Engineering
Biophysics
Broadcasting
  Electronics
Building
Ceramic Science
Chemical Physics
Computer Science
Cybernetics
Digital Systems Engineering
Electro-acoustics
Engineering
  Aeronautical
  Aerospace Systems
  Agricultural
  Avionics
  Communications
  Computer Systems
  Electrical
  Electro-mechanical
  Electronic
  Mechanical
  Nuclear Physics
  Software
  Systems
  Telecommunications
Fire Engineering
Fuel and Energy Engineering
Geophysics
Glass Technology

Hydrography
Information Engineering
Laser Systems
Materials Science
Mechatronic Engineering
Metallurgy
Meteorology
Microelectronics
Mineralogy
Mining Engineering
Naval Architecture
Oceanography
Offshore Engineering
Optometry
Physics (Teaching)
Planetary Physics
Prosthetics and Orthotics
Radiography
Robotics
Ship Science
Signal Processing
Solid State Electronics
Technology

Psychology/Health and Social Care
Advertising
Animal Behaviour
Anthropology
Artificial Intelligence
Behavioural Science
Business Studies
Childhood Studies
Christian Ministry
Clinical Psychology
Cognitive Science
Community Studies
Counselling
Criminal Justice
Criminology
Drama
Education
Educational Psychology
European Social Psychology
Gender Studies
Health Administration
Health and Fitness
Health Psychology
Hospitality Management
Human Biology
Human–Computer Interaction
Human Evolution
Human Geography
Human Life Science
Human Organisations
Human Psychology
Human Resource Management

Industrial Relations
Journalism
Life Sciences
Management
Medicine
Neuroscience
Nursing
Occupational Psychology
Occupational Therapy
Organisational Behaviour
Psycholinguistics
Public Health
Public Policy
Public Relations
Robotics
Social Administration
Social Care
Social Ethics
Social Policy
Social Psychology
Social Work
Sociology
Speech Therapy
Tourism
Town Planning
Urban Studies
Women's Studies
Zoology

Religious Studies
Anthropology
Applied Theological Studies
Behavioural Studies
Biblical Studies
Christian Studies
Church History
Comparative Religion
Divinity
Education
Ethnic Studies
Health and Community Studies
Hebrew
History
History of Religion
Jewish Studies
Philosophy
Psychology
Psychosocial Sciences
Religious Studies (Teaching)
Social Administration
Social Anthropology
Social Ethics
Social Policy
Sociology
Theology

Science for Public Understanding
(See under **Science, Technology and Society**)

Science, Technology and Society/Applied Science/Engineering/Applied ICT
Agricultural Sciences
Agriculture
Animal Sciences
Astronomy
Biology
Biotechnology
Botany
Building
Chemistry
Computer Science
Conservation
Ecology
Engineering
Environmental Science
Food Studies
Forestry
General Engineering
General Science
Human Science
Marine Resources
Materials Science
Nutrition
Ocean Science
Sports Science
Technology
  Building
  Chemical
  Food
  Geological
  Leather
  Marine
  Polymers

Social Policy/Business/ Health and Social Care
Administration
Arts Management
Banking
Business Studies
City and Regional Planning
Community Studies
Education
Estate Surveying
European Planning
European Politics
European Social Policy
Government
Health and Community Studies
Housing
Human Organisations
Human Resource Management

Industrial Relations
International Relations
Land Management
Law
Leisure Management
Marketing
Organisation Studies
Police Studies
Politics
Public Administration
Public Health
Public Policy
Public Relations
Public Sector Economics
Public Services
Social Administration
Social Care
Social Work
Sport and Health
Tourism
Town and Country Planning
Transport
Urban Studies
Women's Health
Youth and Community Work

Sociology/Health and Social Care
Administration
Anthropology
Behavioural Studies
Broadcasting
Business Studies
City and Regional Planning
Communication Studies
Consumer Studies
Development Studies
Economic and Social History
Economics
Environmental History
Environmental Science
Geography
Government
History
Industrial Relations
Management Studies
Organisation Studies
Police Studies
Politics
Psychology
Public Administration
Social Administration
Social Policy
Social Work
Town and Country Planning
Urban Studies

Textiles/Applied Art and Design

Art and Design
Clothing Engineering
Consumer Studies
Costume Design
Fashion Design
Footwear Design
History of Art
History of Design
Home Economics
Industrial Design
Interior Design
Knitwear
Printed Textiles
Textile Design
Textile Economics
Textile Management
Textile Marketing
Textile Technology
Visual Arts

Theatre Studies/Leisure and Recreation/ Performing Arts

Acting
Arts Management
Broadcasting
Classical Civilisation
Communication Studies
Dance
Drama

Education
English Literature
Film Studies
Literature
Media Studies
Performance Arts
Stage Management
Theatre Design
Theatre Studies
TV Studies

Welsh

Celtic Civilisation
Celtic Studies
Communication Studies
Drama
Education
History
Irish Studies
Literature
Media Studies
Performance Arts
Welsh
  Drama
  History
  Literature
  Teaching

World Development

(See under **Government and Politics**)

4 | WHICH UNIVERSITY

Students – and parents – always ask the same question: **Which is the best university?!**

Let me answer by asking another question: Which is the best restaurant in town? To which you will reply: It depends on what you want – Chinese, Thai, French, Italian?

It's much the same with universities and colleges, since not all universities will necessarily offer the subject or subject combination or the type of course you want. Then again do you want to study in a town or city, in the country, on the coast or on a campus located out of town ... **and more importantly what grades are you going to get?**

In the minds of many students the reason for getting into a university with a 'good name' means only one thing – you will get a good job when you leave! Far from it, that depends on you, not just the name of the university. The universities won't find you a job – that's your problem although they all provide a careers advisory service and can suggest firms to which you could apply; after that it's up to you. Even a degree course at a top university won't prepare you to write an application or teach you how to cope with a job interview. Despite this however, many graduates get good jobs irrespective of where they studied. It's true that some employers might be more impressed if you have been a student at some of the very popular universities since they know that you will have had to achieve good grades to get a place, but they also look at many other factors when choosing employees and not just the university.

But, you may say aren't some universities better than others? This is a common enough question because students naturally become confused when yet another newspaper produces another set of league tables of 'best' universities. **Some students in fact don't seem to care where or even what they study so long as the university they choose is high up in the list, or is where their friends are headed!**

Many applicants and their parents rely too much on the information appearing in league tables, particularly those referring to 'teaching quality'. **Please note that these tables were first compiled in 1996 and ceased in 2002 and are now out-of-date since departments will probably have changed in the past ten years.** They are also misleading to students since individual members of staff were never 'inspected' as in school inspections. They are not about the ability of the staff to put over their subject; they are tables about the facilities in the department and the overall work of the subject department. As one university professor explained, the quality of the lectures, whether awful or brilliant, has no bearing on teaching quality league table scores ... points on these tables are only awarded for paperwork, systems and procedures, not for the effectiveness, stimulation, or the brilliance of the lectures!

It might be difficult therefore to decide which is the 'best' university but when it comes to getting a place we have a fairly good idea which ones are among the most popular at present and set high entry standards for many of their courses. These include **Bath, Bristol, Cambridge, Durham, Edinburgh, Exeter, Imperial** (no longer part of London University), **Leeds, London (King's College), (LSE), (University College), Newcastle, Nottingham, Oxford, Oxford Brookes, St Andrews, Southampton, Warwick** and **York.** All medical and veterinary schools, and law schools in the older universities are also high in the popularity stakes.

Some reasons why students and parents often consider a university to be good are:

* because it's an old established institution quite well-known eg Oxford, Cambridge, Edinburgh, Bristol, LSE.
* because it's located near an attractive town or city. (Not always a good reason although these universities do attract a lot of applicants so they can pick and choose their students and thus set high entry standards eg Bath, Warwick, York.)
* because your teacher went there and advises you to apply. (Not necessarily a good reason because it depends upon when he or she graduated and their advice might be a little out-of-date. (Universities and their courses have changed a lot in the past five years.)

* because some students say it's a good place. (These students can give you good advice about their own university and the course they are taking, but not about every course. Nor are they in a position to compare their university with any others.)
* because a lot of your friends are applying. (A bad reason because a lot of school leavers are afraid to leave their friends. Learn to make your own decisions.)

Some reasons why universities might be less popular are:

* because they are small. (There might be fewer facilities for students although smaller places are usually more friendly – eg Trinity St David (Lampeter) – but check out the university; you might be wrong and be missing a good course.)
* because it seems far away and difficult to reach by public transport. (Even so this doesn't seem to affect St Andrews, which is remote enough, but then a Prince went there, since when it's been overwhelmed with applications!) So check out Aberystwyth, Bangor, Stirling and Swansea – all first-rate universities with excellent track records.
* because it doesn't have a familiar name and it's difficult to identify where it's located eg Anglia Ruskin (Cambridge and Chelmsford) and Brunel (Middlesex), both universities offering a good range of courses. (The trouble with sixth formers these days is that they don't know their geographical locations – one student travelled from London to Bangor, thinking he was going to Bognor!)

Whilst everyone wants to go to a good university it's worthwhile reminding you that you are different from the next applicant. You must choose the course and the university which is right for you. Universities and colleges not only differ in their size and location, but also in the way in which they present their subjects and teach the courses.

Subjects are presented in a variety of ways:

* **Single honours** degree courses – you will graduate in one subject. Each university offering the same subject however will offer different options in years two and three – check the options.
* **Joint honours** courses – these involve the study of two different subjects. Your choice of subjects might be related, such as Mathematics and Physics, or quite different such as Computing and Creative Writing.
* **Combined honours** courses – similar to joint courses but some universities such as Durham and Newcastle offer up to three subject choices.
* **Major/minor** courses – students choose two subjects, one being studied over a longer period than the other eg 75% / 25%.
* **Sandwich** courses – alternating periods of study and work related experience (for up to a year) on full pay – in commerce and industry. Students are frequently offered full-time employment when they graduate.

SOME UNIVERSITY FEATURES

Whilst many universities offer the same subject, the way in which courses are organised can differ widely. Here are some examples. Check what your chosen universities can offer.

* **Modular courses.** Most universities now offer modular courses. This means that your degree course will consist of a study of compulsory and optional units. Compulsory units are essential to achieve a degree in your chosen subject. Optional units allow you to choose other specialised topics appropriate to your degree subject, which suit your special interests. On some courses it may be possible to study some subjects not related to your degree subject for part of the time. Modular courses are not offered in Medicine, Dentistry or Veterinary Science.
* **Change of degree course possible in some subject areas.**
  Aberdeen, Aberystwyth, Bangor, Cambridge, Cardiff, City, Dundee, Edinburgh, Essex, Glasgow, Loughborough, Reading, St Andrews, Stirling.
* **Universities offering sandwich ('professional placement') courses.**
  Aston, Bath, Bradford, Brunel, Loughborough, Salford, Surrey and most other universities now offer sandwich courses.

＊ **Some courses commence in February.**

Bolton, London Metropolitan, Stirling.

＊ **A private university. Full tuition fees apply. Some courses commence in January and July.**

Buckingham.

＊ **Combined studies/joint honours and other programmes offering flexibility and delayed choice of degree subject/s.**

Bradford, Central Lancashire, Derby, Durham, East London, Exeter, Glamorgan, Glasgow Caledonian, Gloucestershire, Greenwich, Heriot-Watt (BSc), Hull, Kent, Kingston, Trinity St David (Lampeter), Lancaster, Leeds, Leicester, Liverpool, London (RH), London Metropolitan, Manchester, Manchester Metropolitan, Newcastle, Northampton, Portsmouth, Roehampton, Staffordshire, Sunderland, Winchester.

＊ **A leading university for courses in Science and Engineering.**

Imperial, London.

＊ **Most students take dual honours courses.**

Keele.

＊ **A leading university for the study of the Social Sciences.**

London (LSE).

＊ **Focus on programmes concerned with Asia, Africa and the Middle East.**

London (SOAS).

＊ **Opportunity to continue a study of a foreign language or study a new language, for all students.**

Bangor, Bradford, East Anglia, Huddersfield, Hull, Keele, Loughborough, Salford, Westminster, Worcester, York, York St John.

＊ **One specialist course in the History of Art.**

London (Courtauld).

＊ **One specialist course in French Studies.**

University of London Institute in Paris.

＊ **One specialist course in Pharmacy.**

London (School of Pharmacy).

＊ **Specialist courses in Veterinary Studies.**

London (Royal Veterinary College).

＊ **Specialist courses in Theology, Philosophy and Psychology.**

London (Heythrop).

WORLD RANKING UNIVERSITIES (IN THE TOP 200)

Harvard (1), Cambridge (2), London (UCL) 4, Oxford (5=), Imperial London (5=), Edinburgh (20), London (King's) (23), Manchester (26), Bristol (34), Warwick (58), Birmingham (66), London (LSE) (67), York (70), Glasgow (79), Sheffield (82), St Andrews (87), Nottingham (91), Southampton (95), Leeds (99), Durham (103), Aberdeen (129), Cardiff (135), Liverpool (137), Bath (144), Newcastle (158), Lancaster (162).

QUESTIONS TO ASK STUDENTS AND STAFF
AT OPEN DAY OR INTERVIEW

About new students.

Are there induction courses for new students? Are students advised on study skills and time management? What student services are available? What advice and help can the Students' Union offer? Is it possible to purchase second-hand set books?

About the facilities in the department.

In science departments, is the equipment 'state of the art' or just adequate? Do students have to pay for materials? Are the libraries well-stocked? Are they open all hours? Are there plenty of places for private study or do rooms and work places become overcrowded?

About the teaching staff.

What is the quality of the teaching? Do the staff have flair and enthusiasm for their subject? What are their research interests? Are they approachable? Do they mark the work? How often? Is the feedback helpful?

About the teaching style.
How will you be taught, eg lectures, seminars, tutorials? What types of assessments are used? Are examinations seen or unseen? Are there good computer facilities? Are computer-assisted packages used in teaching? Are you taught how to use the computer facilities? How much will you be expected to work on your own? Will you be expected to attend field courses? If so, do you have to pay towards them?

About sandwich courses.
Will the department organise your work placement or are you expected to find your own firm? Are the placements good? Do they count towards your degree assessment? Can the staff advise on sponsorships? When you are on a sandwich placement will the staff keep in touch with you to advise you or will they visit you?

About transferable skills.
Does the department provide training and experience in communication skills, teamwork exercises, time management, information technology? (All these are regarded as important skills by employers irrespective of the subject you are studying.)

About accommodation.
Which types of accommodation does the university offer? Which types are the most popular? What are the costs? Which are the best halls of residence? Is transport provided from the halls of residence to the university?

About finance.
Does the university permit students to take part-time employment? What opportunities exist to earn money on a part-time basis (in the university/in the town)? Are students assisted in finding part-time employment? Are scholarships or other awards offered by the university or the department? What are the best ways of saving money? Do firms sponsor students on the course?

Part 2

5 | COURSE PROFILES

USING THE PROFILES

This chapter aims to give you a 'taster' of what is on offer in a whole range of major subject areas. Each subject table provides a profile of the course or courses available in that subject area at each university, thus enabling you to note the main differences between courses and the range available in that subject area. Information in each subject entry will give you an overview of the range of topics on offer.

You will also notice that in most subject areas many universities cover similar topics in the first year of a course. However, in Years 2 and 3 the range of different topics that you can choose might differ considerably, *so watch out for the options.*

When reading through the subject tables you should note that the information given under **Subject requirements/preferences** is provided as a *general guide only* to the GCE A-level and GCSE subjects that are normally required or preferred by the universities. However, each admissions tutor makes his or her own value judgement on each applicant and might be prepared to waive the need for preferred subjects or specific grades, depending on individual circumstances. Always check the prospectuses and websites before applying and if you are not sure that you will be able to meet course requirements or preferences, contact the university.

A-level applicants should also note that offers for university places may include a preference or require-ment for a GCE A-level subject, in some cases at a specific grade. Contact the university department and website and also refer to *Heap 2011: University Degree Course Offers* (also published by Trotman Publishing, see **Booklist**), the companion book to *Choosing Your Degree Course and University.*

Many of the vocational courses available (for example, Accountancy, Architecture, Engineering, Surveying) will give exemptions from professional body examinations. These exemptions will vary, depending on the course and modules taken. Contact the university department for details of the profes-sional body requirements and possible exemptions given for successful completion of the course. Also, you could write to the professional bodies themselves (again, see *Degree Course Offers* for contact details).

Many hundreds of subjects are offered by universities and, as described in this chapter, these are organ-ised in such a way as to produce many thousands of course combinations. Because of this, it is not possible to include all degree courses in this book, but the course profiles in this chapter give an insight into the range of subject combinations that institutions provide for students.

It is important also to recognise that universities frequently make changes to their courses and course titles each year and some courses are abandoned and new ones introduced. **It is therefore essential that you consult up-to-date prospectuses and websites before making your final decisions of course and university.** Remember, about 20% of students drop out of degree courses in their first year, many in their first term, simply because the course is not what they expected. Therefore you need to find out as much as possible from as many sources of information as you can find, so that you know **exactly** what your chosen courses involve – including any professional body accreditation – and the careers to which they might lead.

ABBREVIATIONS USED IN THE COURSE PROFILES

AI	Arts Institute
AMD	Academy of Music and Drama
BPS	British Psychological Society
BusSch	Business School
CA	College of Art(s)
CAD	College of Art and Design
CAFRE	College of Agriculture, Food and Rural Enterprise (Northern Ireland)
CAg	College of Agriculture
CAgH	College of Agriculture and Horticulture
CAST	College of Arts, Science and Technology
CAT	College of Advanced Technology or Arts and Technology
CBP	College of Building and Printing
CDC	College of Design and Communication
CFash	College of Fashion
CFE	College of Further Education
CFHE	College of Further and Higher Education
CHE	College of Higher Education
CHort	College of Horticulture
CmC	Community College
CMus	College of Music
CMusDr	College of Music and Drama
Coll	College
CSAD	College and School of Art and Design
CSM	Camborne School of Mines (Exeter University)
CT	College of Technology
HMS	Hospital Medical School
IAD	Institute of Art and Design
IEd	Institute of Education
IFHE	Institute of Further and Higher Education
IHE	Institute of Higher Education
Inst	Institute
IT	Institute of Technology
King's	King's College (London University)
LIPA	Liverpool Institute of Performing Arts
LSE	London School of Economics and Political Science
Marjon (UCP)	St Mark and St John University of Plymouth College
MS	Medical School
NESCOT	North East Surrey College of Technology
QM	Queen Mary (London University)
QTS	Qualified Teacher Status
RAcMus	Royal Academy of Music
RCMus	Royal College of Music
RegColl	Regional College
RegFed	Regional Federation
RH	Royal Holloway (London University)
RNCM	Royal Northern College of Music
RVC	Royal Veterinary College (London University)
SA	School of Art
SAC	Scottish Agricultural College
SAD	School of Art and Design
SCE	Scottish Certificate of Education
Sch	School
SchBus	School of Business
SchSciTech	School of Science and Technology
SchSpDr	School of Speech and Drama

SHCS	School of Health Care Studies
SOAS	School of Oriental and African Studies (London University)
SP	School of Physiotherapy
TAS	Trinity and All Saints (Leeds)
TC	Technical College
TrCMus	Trinity College of Music
UA	University of the Arts
UC	University College
UCL	University College London
Univ	University
UWIC	University of Wales Institute, Cardiff

ACCOUNTANCY/ACCOUNTING

(see also **Finance**)
(*indicates universities with the highest entry requirements)

SUBJECT REQUIREMENTS/PREFERENCES

GCE A-level: Mathematics preferred at some universities. **GCSE:** Mathematics essential for all courses.

SUBJECT INFORMATION

All courses offer financial management and accountancy training. Accountancy courses are not necessarily intended for those wishing to become accountants since they provide an excellent training for any career in business. Students should note that a degree in Accountancy or Accounting is not the only method of qualifying as an accountant. Applicants should note that in addition to degree courses many institutions offer foundation courses that provide opportunities to move directly into degree courses.

Most Accountancy courses will give graduates exemptions from the examinations of the various professional accounting bodies. Applicants should check with universities before applying since these examinations are essential for those wishing to qualify as accountants in various specialist fields.

Aberdeen* Accountancy at Levels 1 to 4 focuses on financial and management accounting and covers the practice of accountancy in modern society, financial reporting, management accountancy and taxation.

Abertay Dundee* This is a broad vocational degree in Accounting. The course includes information technology, industrial studies and the opportunity to continue (or begin) a language (French, German or Spanish), specialisms follow in Year 3. The course is subject to approval.

Aberystwyth The scheme in Accounting and Finance covers finance, financial accounting, management accounting and information systems. Special interests in such subjects as auditing, financial strategy and taxation are offered in Years 2 and 3. There is also a degree in Business Finance. Several joint Accounting schemes are available with subjects such as Law, Economics, a European language, Computer Science and Mathematics and with major/minor options. A voluntary year in employment is offered between Years 2 and 3.

Anglia Ruskin A degree course in Accounting and Finance is offered with key topics in management accounting and corporate finance. There is also a degree course in International Finance Markets. It is possible to commence this course in February.

Aston* The Accounting for Management course (with exemptions from some examinations of professional bodies) focuses on the crucial role that financial information plays in management decision making and in the monitoring and planning of a business organisation's activities. An optional sandwich year is available.

Bangor The Accounting and Finance course offers training in accounting skills. In addition, students are encouraged to develop an understanding of relevant theories and the role of accounting in organisations and society. An emphasis is placed on financial theory and decision-making techniques, providing integration with marketing, economics and banking disciplines. There are also courses in Banking and Finance which include management and marketing topics and Management with Accountancy.

Bath* The Accounting and Finance course is a specialist programme for those aiming for a career in the field of Accounting and Finance. Economics, Law, IT and People and Organisations are some of the topics included. A one-year industrial placement is an option including an opportunity to study abroad.

Bedfordshire The Accounting course is a vocational programme specially designed for the training of accountants. It is also offered as part of the modular credit scheme on a major, joint or minor programme. Accounting is also offered with Law.

Birmingham* The Accounting and Finance degree emphasises the study of accounting and finance throughout the three years of the course. The course includes business skills, development, computing, economics, industrial relations, law, information technology and marketing. Also check out Money, Banking and Finance.

Birmingham City Students on the Accountancy course take core subjects in each year in addition to project work with an option to take a 12 month placement after Year 2. Core subjects in the Accountancy course include law, computer studies, financial management and taxation, with options in the second and third years in organisational behaviour, international and management accounting and languages. See also **Finance**.

Bolton The course in Accountancy has a strong vocational emphasis and may be taken by way of full- or part-time studies.

Bournemouth* Financial and management accounting are covered in each year of the Accounting and Finance course, with options commencing in Year 2 that include taxation, money markets and vocational language studies. Accounting is also offered with Law and with Taxation. Accounting can also be taken with Business, Law or Taxation. There is also a Financial and Business degree with a compulsory 40 week placement.

Bradford Accounting and Finance can include a one-year work placement. Students follow the same pro-gramme as that of the Business and Management Studies degree in Year 1. Specialisms begin in Year 2.

Brighton Accounting and Finance is a three-year full-time or four-year sandwich course. The first-year course includes financial and management accountancy, law and economics. Years 2 and 3 are divided into two semesters and develop the accountancy and management themes with specialist options such as human resources management, marketing and small business development. There is also a course in Finance and Investment. (See **Finance**.)

Bristol* Accounting is offered with Finance, and with opportunities to study in continental Europe.

Bristol UWE Accounting and Finance is a vocational course (three-year or four-year sandwich alternative) and provides a sound basis for careers in other fields of management. The first-year course includes elec-tives from a wide range of subjects, with a range of options available in the third year including business languages. Accounting is also offered with Business Studies.

Brunel* Accounting is offered as part of the Business and Management programme with modules in auditing and taxation. There is also a course in Finance and Accounting.

Buckingham Accounting and Financial Management is a two-year course (starting in January or July) with a common preliminary programme for the first two terms. It also provides options in accounting and financial management, economics and insurance. This leads to more advanced studies, granting exemptions from foundation examinations of all the leading accountancy bodies. Tutorial groups are small – not exceeding eight students. Accounting is also available with Economics, Information Systems, French and Spanish, and there is also a degree in Financial Services.

Bucks New This practical course in Accountancy and Finance provides significant exemptions from the examination requirements of professional accountancy bodies.

Canterbury Christ Church The Accounting and Finance degree provides a general knowledge of Management with a specialised knowledge of Accounting. Accounting can also be taken with either Business or Marketing.

Cardiff* The Accounting course covers all aspects of accountancy and also provides supporting courses in relevant areas of financial and management accountancy, economics, business studies and law. Courses with French, German, Italian and Spanish are also offered with Year 3 being spent abroad. Accounting is also available in the BSc Economics joint honours course. There is also a course in Banking and Finance.

Cardiff (UWIC) All aspects of Accounting are covered in the BA degree with options in European Law and Investment Management.

Central Lancashire The Accounting course focuses on a study of the current practice, problems and developments in accounting and the practical applications of computers. Distinguishing features of the course include an integrated approach to the teaching of computing, an information technology course in Year 2, a case study approach to the teaching of law, with simulated meetings, and a choice of options in Year 3. Accounting is also offered with Business, Economics, Financial Studies, International Business Management, Marketing and Law. See also **Combined Courses** and **Finance**.

Chester The Accountancy course attracts partial exemptions from the main professional bodies and is also offered as part of the combined honours degree.

Chichester There is a practical and vocational focus to the Accountancy degree preparing students for a career in financial management.

City Several courses are offered with a financial bias including Accountancy with Economics, Accountancy and Finance, Actuarial Science, Banking and International Finance, Real Estate Finance and Investment and Financial Risk Analysis and Insurance. Optional placement years are possible on most of courses.

Coventry Accounting covers several business subjects in Year 1 with specialist subjects following in Years 2 and 3 and an optional year's work experience. Joint courses are also offered including Business and Accounting, Accounting and Economics and Accounting and Marketing.

Cumbria The Accounting and Finance course has a strong vocational bias.

De Montfort Accounting and Finance is offered as a vocational or non-vocational subject which can be studied with Law, Business and Computing. Finance is also offered as a joint honours course.

Derby Accounting and Finance is offered as a single honours course or with a year in industry. There is also a degree in Management Accounting that is offered on a full-time or sandwich basis. A joint honours programme is also offered.

Dundee The Accountancy course emphasises analytical and conceptual issues and does not deal at length with procedural matters. Specialisms include business finance, management information systems, languages, management or accountancy. Applied Computing, Management, languages and Mathematics can also be offered with Accountancy. A course in Finance is also available. The BSc course includes two science courses in Years 1 and 2 and three courses in Year 3. Scholarships offered.

Durham (Stockton) The degrees in Accounting and Finance, Business and Finance and Business share a common first year with the option to transfer at the end of Year 1. The degree in Accountancy leads to exemptions from some professional bodies.

East Anglia* The Accounting and Finance degree combines the traditional approach to accountancy with a focus on computing and management control. Core subjects are taken in Years 2 and 3; in Year 3 students choose from a wide range of options. There are also courses combining Accounting with Law and Management, and there is an Economics with Accountancy course. There is also a course in Actuarial Science which can include a year in industry.

East London Accounting and Finance is a three-year course that provides a business education covering law, management accountancy, taxation, computing and insurance finance. Information Technology, Law, Politics and Business Studies are offered with Accounting on the combined honours programme. There is also a degree in Finance, Money and Banking.

Edge Hill Accountancy work experience takes place in Year 2 of this three-year degree course for students aiming to enter the profession.

Edinburgh* Three joint courses are offered covering Business Studies, Economics or Law with Accounting taken in parallel with the Accounting degree.

Essex The Accounting course focuses on financial or management accountancy. Optional courses are offered in Year 3.

Exeter* The Accounting and Finance single honours course has a vocational emphasis, with work placement opportunities. Business, Economics, Management and Mathematics are also offered with Accounting.

Glamorgan There are three-year full-time courses in Accounting and Finance that include a third year in a commercial or industrial placement in the UK or abroad. International Accounting has options in European languages, marketing, European business and international financial management. There are also courses in Forensic and Management Accounting. Combined, joint, major/minor degrees are available.

Glasgow* The BAcc degrees in Accountancy or Accountancy with Languages, Finance or International Accounting all lead to professional recognition.

Glasgow Caledonian Three-year or four-year Accountancy courses are offered with two options from public sector or management accounting, international finance and financial reporting. Joint courses are also offered with Economics, Law and Management. There is also a degree in Financial Services covering all aspects of finance operations in the business field.

Gloucestershire The degree in Accounting and Financial Management gives some exemptions from the Association of Chartered Certified Accountants (ACCA) and the Chartered Institute of Management Accountants (CIMA) professional examinations and offers students an optional one-year paid work placement.

Glyndŵr A Business Accounting course is offered with the option to choose an alternative degree at the end of Year 1.

Heriot-Watt A four-year course is offered in Accountancy and Finance. Accountancy is also offered as a joint course with Business Law. There are opportunities to study abroad on both courses. Scholarships available.

Hertfordshire The degree in Accounting and Finance can include study abroad or in work placement. There is also a separate degree in Finance. Scholarships offered.

Huddersfield The first-year course in Accountancy and Finance consists of basic accounting, business law, financial and management accountancy. In the second and third years there is an emphasis on the use of financial information in business planning, control and decision making, insolvency and employee relations. Courses in Accountancy and/with Financial Services Information Systems/Law/Small Business are also available.

Hull Six Accounting courses are offered, one with an international bias with core subjects giving some exemption from the examinations of professional bodies. In the first year, students take compulsory courses in academic and professional skills, business economics, managing people, accounting and finance, and marketing, plus a sixth choice selected from a range of options. Financial accounting, management accounting and the principles of economics are taken in the second year. The course emphasis is on finance, accounting and computing. The course in International Accounting involves Year 3 being spent abroad. Other courses involve those with professional experience, Business Economics, Financial Management and Marketing.

Keele 30 dual honours degree courses in Accountancy are offered and similarly dual honours degrees in Finance a degree in Accounting and Finance with Computing is also offered. A single honours degree in Accounting and Finance with options in Banking and Economic Forecasting is available.

Kent* In addition to the single honours degree in Accounting and Finance (with the option of a year in industry) a degree in Accounting and Finance with Computing is also offered. An important feature of the School of Business is its links with France and Germany, which lead to joint Accounting and Finance courses in their languages and a Year 3 placement in Europe.

Kingston The Accounting and Finance course provides an in-depth study of accounting and financial management including company law, accounting and revenue law and taxation. The core subject in Year 1 is legal and financial strategy. Option choices include marketing, languages, international accountancy and computer systems.

Lancaster* The BA/BSc course in Accounting and Finance is intended for accounting specialists. The BSc Business Studies (Accounting) is a broader study of accounting in the context of management studies. There is also a broad study of Finance.

Leeds* The Accounting and Finance course covers the main aspects of financial and management accounting, economics, taxation and business finance.

Leeds Metropolitan The degree in Accounting and Finance is a three-year full-time degree that provides an academic foundation for a career in accounting or finance in either public or private sector organisations.

Lincoln Accountancy is studied as a single subject or can also be studied as a joint degree in combination with Advertising, Management, Marketing, Business, Human Resources Management and Finance.

Liverpool* The Accounting degree is both a theoretical and practical course covering micro and macro economics, mathematics, statistics, financial reporting, management accounting and options from accounting, business and economics modules. There is a joint course in Accounting and Computer Science.

Liverpool John Moores The course in Accounting and Finance which can include a year's sandwich placement concentrates on financial and management accountancy. Students choose from a wide range of options in Years 2 and 3.

London (LSE)* The Accounting and Finance course covers both managerial and financial accountancy. Other subjects such as anthropology, geography, history, psychology can be taken in Years 1, 2 and 3 in place of an accounting option. There is also a course in Actuarial Science.

London (RH)* Accounting is offered with a course in Management.

London Metropolitan The Accounting and Finance course is biased towards the qualitative aspects of economic and business analysis and decision making. There are over 20 joint courses with Accounting. See also **Finance**.

London South Bank The Accounting and Finance course covers financial and management accounting, law, economics, auditing, taxation, financial institutions. The course is accredited by the Association of Chartered Certified Accountants (ACCA). Accounting is also offered with a range of other subjects including Psychology, Law, Marketing, Forensic Science, and International Accounting.

Loughborough* Accounting and Financial Management is a four-year sandwich course that provides a broad educational base for a career in management. Various aspects of management are studied in depth. Economics and Mathematics are also offered with Accounting and there is a well-established course in Banking and Financial Management.

Manchester* In the BA (Econ) degree it is possible to specialise in Accounting or in Finance or in both areas. There are also degrees in Accounting with Business Information Systems and Accounting and Economics. Scholarships offered.

Manchester Metropolitan Accounting and Finance is a three-year full-time or four-year sandwich course with an emphasis on management accountancy and options in banking and insurance. There is also a course in Accounting Information Systems.

Middlesex Full-time and sandwich courses in Accounting and Finance can be taken whilst Accounting can also be studied with Business Economics or Statistics. There is also a Business Accounting degree.

Napier The Accounting degree is focused on training students for the profession. Information technology, financial management, taxation and law are important components of the course. There are also joint courses in Economics, Finance, Law and Marketing.

Newcastle* Economics and law are included in the first-year Accounting and Finance course with additional options in the second and third years. Accounting can be studied with Computer Science, Mathematics or Statistics. There is also a degree course in Business Accounting and Finance with paid work placements.

Newport The Accounting programme is part of the Newport Business School enabling students to transfer to other business courses at the end of the first year. Accounting can also be taken with Economics or Law.

Northampton In addition to the degree in Accounting and Finance, several joint courses with Accounting are offered all on a three year full-time basis.

Northumbria This is a three-year full-time Accounting course with a comprehensive overview of business operations leading to professional accreditation opportunities. There is also a course in Finance and Investment Management.

Nottingham* A degree in Finance, Accounting and Management provides a broad introduction to the world of finance, while a more specialised focus on finance is offered in the Industrial Economics with Insurance degree.

Nottingham Trent Accounting and Finance is offered as a three-year full-time or four-year sandwich course with industrial placement in Year 3. There is also a course in Accounting and Information Systems.

Oxford Brookes Several subjects are offered with Accounting and Finance in the single honours modular programme. There is an optional placement in Year 3.

Plymouth The Accounting and Finance course provides a broad overview of business, a detailed study of the accounting function and an understanding of business information systems. There is an optional year of work experience (paid).

Portsmouth Accounting is a three-year full-time or a four-year sandwich course. Part I covers the first two years; Part II includes the sandwich year and two operational studies. Courses are also available in Accounting with Finance, Business, or International Finance.

Queen's Belfast* The degree in Accounting is intended to provide an academic education in accounting and an introduction to professional studies. The course includes specialisms in Financial Accounting, Management Accounting and Taxation and Finance. Accounting is also offered with French, German or Spanish and there is a degree in Finance, and Actuarial Studies.

Reading Accounting is offered with Economics or Management. There are also courses in International Securities, Investment and Banking and Investment and Finance in Property.

Robert Gordon The Accounting and Finance degree is a four-year course with a 12-month paid placement. The degree is accredited by professional accountancy bodies.

Salford The degree in Finance and Accounting has a bias towards management and financial accounting with the option of an industrial placement and sends a good proportion of its graduates into industry in addition to the more usual destination of the chartered profession. There are also degrees in Business Finance and in Property Management and Investment.

Sheffield* First-year students following the Accounting and Financial Management course take an introductory course with two other subjects and a course in statistical methods. In the second and third year students take a number of core courses, some of which are options. Managerial analysis is studied in the third year by students working in groups.

Sheffield Hallam Accounting and Financial Management is a vocational course which is offered as a three-year full-time or four-year sandwich course with an optional placement in Year 3. Courses in Banking and Financial Services are also available.

Southampton* Accounting is offered with Economics, Finance and Management Sciences. Scholarships offered for Actuarial studies.

Southampton Solent Accountancy graduates may claim exemptions from the later stages of professional examinations of management and corporate accountants. There are also degrees in Finance.

Staffordshire Accounting and Business can be chosen in Year 2 after a common first year with other Business courses. In addition, there are courses in Accounting with Information Systems, Business and Economics.

Stirling The BAcc Accountancy course includes units of economics and business law and covers all the relevant aspects giving exemptions from all the professional accountancy bodies. Ten Accountancy combined honours degrees are also available including Accountancy with Business Law, Management Science, languages and Mathematics.

Strathclyde* In the Business with Accounting degree, financial accounting and finance are taken in Years 1 and 2 followed by options in business law, economics, finance, human resource management, law, management science, marketing or tourism. Accounting is also offered jointly with over 10 other subjects including languages and international business.

Sunderland A three-year course in Public Relations and Accountancy is on offer.

Surrey The Accounting and Financial Management degree leads to qualification in Management Accountancy. The degree offers a sandwich placement in industry or commerce.

Swansea Accounting is offered with Business Studies or Management Science.

Swansea Metropolitan The Accountancy course gives a number of exemptions from the professional chartered accountancy bodies. There is also a course specialising in Business Finance.

Teesside Accounting and Finance is part of the modular Business scheme in which students take eight subjects (common to all Business degrees) and progress to their special degree subject in Years 2 and 3. A degree in Accounting can also be studied with Law, and there is also a unique course in Finance, Accounting and Cybercrime.

Ulster The Accounting course provides a firm foundation in accounting and other related subjects. It is recognised by the professional accountancy bodies and exemptions are gained from their examinations. Final-year options include auditing and financial management and two from business policy, information systems management, public sector accounting or economics or finance. Combined courses are also offered.

Warwick* The first year of the Accounting and Finance degree is largely common with the Management Sciences course and provides a broad base for the study of accountancy. A choice of four specialist subjects is made in Year 3 from a list of financial options and includes a choice of one non-finance subject. The University has one of the largest business schools in the UK.

West London A course in Accounting and Finance is offered with modules in management accounting and taxation. Courses commerce in both September and February.

West Scotland Accounting can be taken as a three-year or four-year course. There are also courses in Business Accounting and Business Information Technology with Accounting.

Westminster A course is offered in Accounting with Management with an optional sandwich placement or studies abroad.

Wolverhampton Accounting is offered as a specialist route in a combined studies degree and can also be studied as a single honours course. It is also offered with Law, Marketing and Computing. There is also a three-year full-time or a four-year sandwich degree in Accounting and Finance.

Worcester (See under **Business courses**).

York A course is offered in Accounting, Business Finance and Management with an optional year in industry.

OTHER INSTITUTIONS OFFERING ACCOUNTANCY COURSES

Blackpool and Fylde (Coll), Bradford (Coll), Croydon (Coll), Duchy (Coll), East Lancashire (Coll), Highbury (Coll), Holborn (Coll), Kensington (Coll/Bus), Northbrook (Coll), Norwich City (Coll), Somerset (CAT), West Cheshire (Coll), Westminster Kingsway (Coll), Wirral Metropolitan (Coll).

ALTERNATIVE COURSES

Actuarial Studies, Applied Mathematics, Banking, Business Studies, Economics, Finance, Mathematics, Statistics.

ACTUARIAL SCIENCE/STUDIES

(*indicates universities with the highest entry requirements)

SUBJECT REQUIREMENTS/PREFERENCES

GCE A-level: Mathematics and one other subject. **GCSE:** Most institutions will require grade A or B Mathematics.

SUBJECT INFORMATION

Actuaries are reputed to have one of the highest paid careers in finance, and so naturally Actuarial Science courses attract a large number of applicants! Training as an actuary, however, is extremely demanding and must not be underestimated. An alternative route for actuarial work would be a Mathematics degree course. See also **Accountancy/Accounting** and **Finance**.

Courses usually offer full exemptions from some of the examinations of the Institute and Faculty of Actuaries that lead to professional qualifications.

City* The Actuarial Science course involves actuarial science, mathematics, statistics, economics and accounting. There are study placements in Canada and with firms in the UK.

Heriot-Watt Actuarial Mathematics and Statistics covers life office procedures, pension funds and risk theory. The course provides a sound grounding in mathematics probability, statistics and actuarial mathematics. A small number of students study abroad or take an industrial placement for one year.

Kent* A strong mathematical background is required for the Actuarial Science course that covers economics, computing, probability and inference, mortality, operational research and life contingencies. There is an optional year in industry.

Kingston* The single honours course in Actuarial Mathematics and Statistics prepares students for the actuarial profession.

London (LSE)* The Actuarial Science course covers statistics, mathematical methods, investigations and life contingencies. Options are offered in statistics, mathematics, economics, sociology, social psychology and population studies.

Queen's Belfast The Actuarial Studies programme combines courses in actuarial modelling, financial reporting, insurance, pensions economics and financial mathematics.

Southampton* The Actuarial Studies course (with either Economics or Mathematics) provides the opportunity to study French, German or Spanish. Scholarships offered.

Swansea* Three-year and four-year Actuarial Studies courses are offered, including a year abroad in the latter. The first year is largely common with other degree schemes in the Business School. Part 2 is approximately 50% actuarial and 50% financial maths, life insurance and management, while in Part 3 a wide range of specialist modules is on offer.

ALTERNATIVE COURSES
Accountancy, Applied Mathematics, Banking, Business Studies, Economics, Financial Services, Insurance, Mathematics, Statistics.

AFRICAN STUDIES

(*indicates universities with the highest entry requirements)

SUBJECT REQUIREMENTS/PREFERENCES
GCE A-level: Languages at grade A or B might be required. **GCSE:** English, Mathematics (grades A–C).

SUBJECT INFORMATION
African Studies is often combined with Caribbean Studies and can involve geography, history, popular culture, political science and sociology.

Birmingham* African Studies can be taken as a joint honours degree or with Anthropology or Development. The course combines perspectives from the history, cultures, environments and societies relating to the African sub-continent. An optional field work trip to Ghana occupies one month during a summer vacation.

London (SOAS) There are different approaches offered in the African Studies course by way of geographical region or its language and culture – Amharic (Ethiopia), Hausa (Nigeria), Somali (Eastern Horn of African), Swahili (East Africa), Yoruba (Nigeria) and Zulu (South Africa). In each case the language is supported by studies covering social anthropology, history, law, linguistics, art and archaeology. There are also joint courses with management, geography, law and politics.

London (UCL)* An African language is offered with French.

London Metropolitan The Caribbean Studies course covers history, colonisation, independence, literature and film. Over 10 joint courses are also on offer.

ALTERNATIVE COURSES
Anthropology, International Relations, Politics.

AGRICULTURE AND RELATED COURSES

(including **Plant Sciences, Forestry** and **Landscape Design.**)
(*indicates universities with the highest entry requirements)

SUBJECT REQUIREMENTS/PREFERENCES

GCE A-level: Science subjects required. **GCSE:** English and Mathematics usually required. Practical experience may be required.

SUBJECT INFORMATION

Agriculture is a wide-ranging subject covering practical farming, animal and crop science, biochemistry, bacteriology, food production and aspects of biology; other aspects include business studies and countryside management. Degree courses offered at colleges of agriculture are also indicated below.

Aberdeen Agriculture and Business Management, Agriculture, Animal Science, Crop and Soil Science and Forest Management can be studied by way of three-year designated and four-year (honours) courses. The Agriculture course allows for specialisation in crop protection, animal physiology and nutrition, rural tourism and agricultural and food marketing. Other courses are offered in Countryside and Environmental Management and Wildlife Management, Plant Biology and Forest Science. Scholarships offered. (High research rating)

Aberystwyth A four-year course in Agriculture is offered with work experience in Year 2. From a base of crop science and production, animal science and production, this modular course introduces farm business, management, marketing and crop and animal production in Years 3 and 4. The Welsh Institute of Rural Studies also offers degrees in Countryside Management, Conservation and Recreation, Animal Science, Plant Biology and Agriculture with Marketing and with Business and Management. Scholarships offered.

Bangor The degree in Agriculture, Conservation and Environment is a broad programme covering ecological and social aspects of land use. The focus is mainly agricultural with modules in soil and plant environments, livestock, grassland and crop production supported by wildlife conservation and environmental planning. There is also a Forestry degree involving studies in silviculture, forest operations, practical forestry, forest products and estate planning.

Birmingham City A course is offered in Garden Design covering landscape history, graphics and communication skills. It is taught at both the University and at Pershore College, a centre of excellence in this field and in Horticulture. A degree course in Landscape Architecture is also offered.

Bournemouth A three-year degree is offered in Landscape, Garden Design and Management.

Bristol* A degree in Botany is offered as part of the Biological Sciences programme.

Bristol UWE Conservation and Countryside Management is a three-year full-time course with modules as diverse as farm, woodland, game and deer management, environmental studies and conservation. There are also courses in Dairy Herd Management and Conservation Biology. Scholarships offered.

Central Lancashire A wide range of Agriculture-related courses is offered. There is also a degree in Conservation and Countryside Management offering graduates a preparation for careers in nature conservancy, wildlife and countryside management. Forest and Woodland Management courses are available at Newton Rigg College in Cumbria.

Cumbria There are vocational courses in Forestry, Forestry Management and Forestry and Woodland Conservation.

Derby The Conservation and Countryside Management course covers rural studies, landscape conservation and countryside management.

Durham* Two courses are offered in Plant Sciences, one of four years including an industrial placement.

East Anglia Development Studies is a very broad subject touching on topics such as agricultural production systems, environmental management and planning, resource development and conservation, natural resources, economics, sociology and politics. The focus extends to world problems. Courses in Conservation and Biodiversity and Landscape Design, Conservation and Plant Biology are also available.

Edinburgh* A course in Plant Science is offered.

Glasgow Courses are offered in conjunction with the Scottish Agricultural College at Auchincruive, Ayrshire. These include a Bachelor of Technology course in Agriculture, Countryside Management, Rural Tourism and Horticulture. See also **Biology**.

Gloucestershire The Garden Design course covers plant sciences and horticulture, the design of formal and informal gardens, and the history of landscapes. There is also a course in Landscape Management and Landscape Architecture.

Greenwich Courses are offered in Garden Design, International Agriculture, Medicinal and Commercial Horticulture, and Landscape Management (Land Use). (High research rating)

Harper Adams (UC) Agriculture is offered with Animal Science, Crop Management, Land and Farm Management, Marketing and Mechanisation.

Kent A course is offered in Biodiversity and Countryside Management and also Wildlife Conservation.

Leeds Metropolitan Garden Design and Landscape Architecture can be studied.

Kingston A course is offered in Landscape Architecture.

Manchester* Three courses in Plant Science are offered, one with industrial experience.

Manchester Metropolitan Courses are offered in Sustainable Development and Landscape Architecture.

Newcastle* The wide range of Agriculture courses on offer includes Agriculture, Agronomy, Animal Production Science, Countryside Management, Rural Resource Management, Farm Business Management, Rural Studies and Organic Food Production. Many of these subjects are degree options at the end of the Deferred Choice degree (D400). (High research rating)

Northampton Land Management, Horticulture and Garden Design courses are available.

Nottingham Pre-university practical experience desirable. Students in the Faculty of Agricultural Science are taught at the Sutton Bonnington campus. Courses are offered in Agriculture and in Crop Science, which are either three-year degrees or four-year courses with European Studies involving a European year out between Years 2 and 3. These courses came top in a survey of student satisfaction. Animal Science and Crop Science can also be studied including a four-year course in European Studies. (High research rating)

Nottingham Trent A course is offered in Conservation and Countryside Management covering rural skills, ecology, planning, leisure and business management. A degree course in Horticulture is also offered.

Plymouth The Applied Bioscience Programme has Pathways in Agriculture and Environment, Agriculture, Food and Nutrition, and Plant Sciences.

Queen's Belfast The new School of Agriculture and Food offers three degree courses. Food Quality, Safety and Nutrition covers diet, health and management. Land Use and Environmental Management includes biology, geography, economics and law. Agricultural Technology focuses on animal husbandry and crop production. (High research rating)

Reading The Agriculture course is divided into three parts: Part I (two terms) includes agriculture, crop production, animal production, plant and soil science and agricultural economics. Part II (three terms) includes crop physiology, crop protection, plant breeding and animal breeding. Part III (four terms) offers a choice of one of 12 options. Other courses offered include Agricultural Business Management, Horticulture and Landscape Rural Resources Management and Botany. (High research rating)

Royal Agricultural College One of the leading institutions offering courses in Agriculture including Animal and Land Management, Organic Farming and Crop Management.

Sheffield Three-year and four-year degrees in Plant Science can be followed and also three- and four-year courses in Landscape Architecture.

Stirling Courses are available in Conservation Management and Land Resources.

Strathclyde Degree courses are offered in Landscape and Garden Design.

Worcester The degree in Horticulture leads to specialisation in either Amenity and Landscape Management or in Crop Production. There is also a course in Sustainable Woodland Management.

OTHER INSTITUTIONS OFFERING AGRICULTURE COURSES
Askham Bryan (Coll), CAFRE, Duchy (Coll), Huddersfield (TC), Myerscough (Coll), SAC, Sparsholt (Coll), UHI Millennium Inst, West Anglia (Coll), Writtle (Coll).

ALTERNATIVE COURSES
Animal Sciences, Biochemistry, Biological Science, Biology, Botany, Chemistry, Conservation Management, Crop Science, Ecology, Environmental Sciences, Estate Management, Food Science and Technology, Forestry, Geography, Horticulture, Land Surveying, Plant Science, Veterinary Science and Zoology.

AMERICAN STUDIES

(including **Latin American Studies**)
(*indicates universities with the highest entry requirements)

SUBJECT REQUIREMENTS/PREFERENCES
GCE A-level: English and/or History may be required. **GCSE:** Grades A–C English, a foreign language, Mathematics and science may be required.

SUBJECT INFORMATION
American literature and history represent the core of most courses, with a year spent in the USA. Not all courses require a year to be spent in North America.

Aberdeen Courses in Hispanic Studies are offered with a focus on Latin American Studies.

Aberystwyth Part I of the American Studies course includes the history of the USA and an introduction to American literature and culture. Part II includes five core courses covering history, literature and politics, the American Revolution and also two optional courses. Seventeen joint courses are also offered with American Studies. (A good A-level pass in English or History is required for entry to Part I.) Exchanges take place with American universities in Year 3. There is also a course in American Studies and International Politics.

Bangor A course is offered in English and American Literature.

Birmingham* The American and Canadian Studies course consists of specialist studies in American history, literature and politics including Canada. This is a four-year course, Year 3 being spent in the USA or Canada. The subject can also be taken as a joint honours or major/minor course.

Bristol UWE Four courses are offered in Latin American Studies.

Canterbury Christ Church American Studies is offered with a study of either Canada, USA or Latin America or all three. There are also courses focusing on American Studies in the context of History and Politics, Film and Art, and Geography and Anthropology.

Central Lancashire American Studies is a three-year course with the opportunity to study in the USA. Literature, history, film, music, architecture and popular culture are studied. See also **Combined Courses**.

Derby American Studies is offered as an honours degree or in the Credit Accumulation Modular Scheme covering film, literature, music and history, with a semester in the USA.

Dundee* Students take English or history in Year 1 and commence American Studies in Year 2 and post-war American society in Year 3. Ten joint courses are also offered with American Studies that can also be taken in the Arts and Social Sciences. There is also a combined honours programme that offers American Studies with up to 11 subjects. A unique degree in Transatlantic Studies focuses on the USA and the EU in terms of international relations, and historical, geographical, economic and literary perspectives.

East Anglia* The preliminary programme in American and English Literature (two terms) covers literature, history and philosophy or linguistics plus options. The final honours programme is chosen at the end of the second term. There is a wide choice of honours programmes covering English and American literature, history, drama, film studies, linguistics and philosophy. In the American Studies course emphasis is on modern American cultural studies. Courses are also offered in American and English History, American History with Politics and American Literature with Creative Writing. (High research rating)

East London Anthropology is offered with North American Studies including a year in New Mexico.

Essex* The history, literature, culture, social and political structure of the United States are covered in the American (United States) Studies four-year course, with the third year spent in the US. Optional courses on American topics are available in the School of Comparative Studies and in the School of Social Studies. There is also a degree in Latin American Studies with options in history, politics, sociology, literature and the art of Latin America.

Glamorgan American Studies can be taken as a minor subject with a second subject.

Hertfordshire Joint and combined courses are offered with American Studies.

Hull All students on the American Studies course study American history and literature, film and the arts. Special honours students select one ancillary subject from a wide range on offer. The American Studies course lasts four years (with Year 2 in the USA). There are also 10 joint courses. The Department is very highly rated for its teaching provision.

Keele American Studies (three or four years) covers history, geography, literature and politics. Keele is noted for its dual honours courses with American Studies offered with 28 other subjects. (High research rating)

Kent American Studies is offered as a multidisciplinary course with a bias in history or literature. The third year of this four-year course, and also of the course in British and American Policy Studies focusing on economic, political and social issues, is spent in the United States. There is also a course in English and American Literature.

Lancaster* All American Studies students study English, history and politics in Year 1. The three-year course covers American history and literature. Year 2 is spent in the USA.

Leeds* A course is offered in Hispanic Studies and Latin American Studies.

Leicester* The American Studies course focuses on American literature, history and politics to 1945, with a supplementary subject taken in Year 1. The subject can also be studied within the Combined Arts programme with other subjects. There is an optional 4th year in the USA. Scholarships offered.

Lincoln A three-year course is offered and also joint honours programmes with English, Drama, Media Studies, Journalism and History.

Liverpool* Three-year and four-year courses are offered in Comparative American Studies and Latin American Studies.

Liverpool John Moores American Studies consists of a study of American history and culture to the present day. This is offered as a joint course with a choice of over 15 other subjects or as a major/minor or combined studies award.

London (Goldsmiths)* English and American Literature and Spanish and Latin American Studies courses are on offer.

London (King's)* American Studies is offered with a bias towards history and literature; American Studies is taken with a year abroad. There is also a joint course with Film Studies.

London (UCL)* A course is offered in Modern Iberian and Latin American Studies.

London Metropolitan American Studies covers American history, literature, film and politics. Study is possible in the USA. There is also a course in Caribbean Studies.

Loughborough* There is a degree course in English with a minor option in North American film and literature.

Manchester* Three-year courses are offered in American Studies and English and American Literature. With the option to study in North America. There is also a four-year course in American and Latin American Studies.

Manchester Metropolitan American Studies is offered as part of a joint honours and a Humanities and Social Studies programme. The course is based on the Crewe campus.

Middlesex Latin American Studies is part of the joint honours programme.

Newcastle* Latin American Studies is offered with Spanish and Portuguese.

Northampton Over 20 joint honours courses are offered with American Studies. Transfer to single honours courses is possible at the end of Year 1. There is also a course in American Literature and Film.

Northumbria A unique course is offered in British and American Cultures examining the similarities and differences between the respective countries. It draws on literature, history and film, the second year of the course being spent at Georgia State University.

Nottingham* The American Studies course covers history, literature, politics, music and the visual arts. Single honours students devote two-thirds of the course to American Studies and the remainder to a subsidiary course outside the department. There are optional modules on Canada and Year 2 can be taken in Canada or the USA. There are also joint courses with several subjects including English, Chinese Studies, History, or Latin American Studies. (High research rating)

Plymouth American Studies can be taken as part of the Combined Studies programme with English, History, Media Arts or Popular Culture, or as a single honours course.

Portsmouth Courses are offered in Latin American Studies with Spanish and in American Studies with English, History, or languages. There is an optional semester in US, Mexico or Brazil.

Queen's Belfast The American Studies course offers modules in the history, literature, politics and society of the USA.

Reading This American Studies course is taught in four departments (English, Film and Drama, Politics and History). Students spend a period of their studies in the USA.

Salford A course in English with American Studies is on offer.

Sheffield The American Studies course covers American history from the Revolution to the present day and American literature from the colonial period to the first half of the 19th century. During the first year, students take a third arts or social science subject, for example politics, geography, economics or a language.

Southampton Latin American Studies can be taken with Spanish.

Sunderland American Studies can be taken as a single or joint course offered with over 20 other subjects. Opportunities exist to spend one or two semesters in Year 2 at an American university.

Sussex* American Studies may be studied with an emphasis on literature and culture or history and politics. All students take complementary courses within the School of English and American Studies. This is a four-year course with Year 3 spent at a university in the USA. (High research rating)

Swansea Both single and joint honours courses offer the opportunity to spend a year at an American university.

Trinity St David (Lampeter) The American Studies course covers literature, history and cultural forms such as films and television. A unique course in Australian Studies is also offered, covering similar topics including the physical and human environment, history and literature.

Ulster American Studies with a semester in the USA covers literature, culture and film.

Warwick* Comparative American Studies students take two courses on themes and problems in North America, Latin America and the Caribbean, and a beginners' course in Spanish. Second-year students choose four options of which one must relate to North America and one to Latin America; two should be either historical or literary. Final courses are chosen from a range of options in this multidisciplinary course that covers politics, history, literature and film studies. The third year is spent at a university in USA, Latin America, Canada or the Caribbean.

Winchester American Literature is offered as a single, main, joint or subsidiary subject. American Studies can also be taken with Film or Literature. There is an optional exchange scheme with several American universities.

Wolverhampton American Studies is taken as part of an extensive Humanities programme with 15 joint options or as a specialist subject with one or two other subjects.

Worcester The American Studies course covers history, literature, film, music, drama and politics with the opportunity to study in the USA.

York St John American Studies can be taken with nine joint courses including Film Studies, Media, English Literature or History.

ALTERNATIVE COURSES
English Literature, Government, History, International History, International Relations, Latin American Relations, Spanish American Studies and Politics.

ANIMAL SCIENCES

(*indicates universities with the highest entry requirements)

SUBJECT REQUIREMENTS/PREFERENCES
GCE A-level: Biology, Chemistry required or preferred. **GCSE:** Mathematics usually required.

SUBJECT INFORMATION
Animal Sciences is a popular course in its own right and is often an appropriate option for those who fail to obtain a place in Veterinary Science. Courses cover a biological study of animals, reproduction and nutrition. Equine Studies has also become popular in recent years.

Aberystwyth After a common first year for all students one of three pathways can be chosen – production science, animal biology or equine science. Degrees in Equine Studies and Equine Science are also offered. A course is also available in Animal Behaviour, studying farmed and domestic animals with opportunities to observe animals, birds and sea life in their natural habitats.

Anglia Ruskin Animal Behaviour is offered as a three-year full-time degree or with Psychology or Ecology or Wildlife Biology. There are also similar courses in Animal Welfare and joint courses with Psychology.

Bristol* There are courses in Animal Behaviour and Welfare and a course in Veterinary Anatomy. See also **Biology**.

Bristol UWE Animal Science focuses on nutrition, anatomy and physiology and has options in Aquatic and Avian Studies. Degrees in Equine Science (and with Management) and Animal Behaviour and Welfare are also offered at Hartpury College.

Bucks New Courses are offered in Animal Behaviour Management including specialist areas in Animal Welfare Law and Training and Learning. Courses can be taken in Equine Sports Performance and Equine Industry Management. There is also a course in animal Industry Management covering various business practices.

Canterbury Christ Church Full-time or part-time courses are offered in Animal Science, with options in Ecology and Conservation in Year 3. There is also a focus on animal health and welfare.

Central Lancashire Equine Studies is offered at the nearby Myerscough College and focuses on management with optional routes in physiology or behaviour and welfare. There is also a course in Animal Conservation Science at the Penrith campus which includes the study of ecology and wildlife identification.

Chester The Course in Animal Behaviour includes theoretical studies and practical modules taken at Reaseheath College, Nantwich and Chester Zoo. There is also a course in Animal Management.

Cumbria The course in Animal Conservation Science covers ecology, animal behaviour, habitat, genetics and wildlife.

Exeter Two degree schemes are offered in Animal Behaviour, one with Biology. This is an interdisciplinary programme covering zoology, ecology, conservation biology, psychology and neuroscience.

Greenwich Degrees are offered in Animal Management and Equine Management.

Harper Adams (UC) Animal Science is offered with Agriculture. The BSc courses cover animal health, nutrition, behaviour and welfare.

Lancaster* Animal Sciences can be taken as a course option in Biological Sciences.

Lincoln Courses in Equine Science and Sport Science, Animal Behavioural Science and Animal Management and Welfare are offered.

Liverpool John Moores The Animal Behaviour degree covers the welfare, husbandry and conservation of animals. There is also a degree in wildlife conservation with extensive fieldwork and opportunities for work placement.

Newcastle* The Animal Science (Livestock Technology) course involves physiology, biochemistry, nutrition and reproduction and the health and welfare of livestock. Studies also cover the environmental concerns over the production of meat and other animal products. There is also a course in Animal Science (Companion Animal Studies) involving dogs, cats, horses and less common pet species.

Northampton There are degree courses in Equine Management including modules in event management. An Applied Animal Studies course is offered including modules in zoo animal management and conservation.

Nottingham Specialist topics in the Animal Science course include animal production, physiology and nutrition and environmental science (plants and animals). This is also offered with European Studies on a four-year course.

Nottingham Trent There are courses in Equine Sports Science, which also include a specialism in equestrian psychology, and separate courses in Animal Science, Animal and Zoo Biology and Wildlife Conservation.

Oxford Brookes Equine Science can be taken on a three-year full-time course.

Plymouth Animal Science can be studied with a bias towards Equine Studies, Animal Behaviour, Management and Welfare. There is also a course in wildlife conservation. Scholarships available.

Queen's Belfast Single and joint honours courses are offered in Social Anthropology. A wide range of modules can be studied in Year 3.

Reading The Animal Science course has a focus on farm animals with applications in biology and immunology to animal production. Final year options include captive animal management, equine management and wildlife.

Staffordshire A course is offered in Animal Biology and Conservation. Topics covered include wildlife, marine and field biology.

Stirling The course in Animal Biology covers conservation management. Ecology and fieldwork in Scotland and Switzerland. There is also a degree in Aquaculture.

Wolverhampton Courses are offered in Animal Biology and Behaviour, Animal Management and Equine Sport Performance.

Worcester See under **Biological Science**.

OTHER INSTITUTIONS OFFERING ANIMAL SCIENCE/EQUINE COURSES
Askham Bryan (Coll), Barony (Coll), Bishop Burton (Coll), CAFRE, Cornwall (Coll), Craven (Coll), Duchy (Coll), Guildford (CFHE), Huddersfield (TC), Leeds Park Lane (Coll), Myerscough (Coll), NESCOT, Royal (CAg), SAC, Sparsholt (Coll), Solihull (Coll), UHI Millennium Inst, Warwickshire (Coll), Welsh (Coll Hort), West Anglia (Coll), Writtle (Coll).

ALTERNATIVE COURSES
Agricultural Sciences, Agriculture, Veterinary Science, Zoology.

ANTHROPOLOGY AND SOCIAL ANTHROPOLOGY

(*indicates universities with the highest entry requirements)

SUBJECT REQUIREMENTS/PREFERENCES
GCSE: Grade A–C in Mathematics may be required.

SUBJECT INFORMATION
The study of anthropology will include some biology, some history and a study of the cultures, rituals and beliefs of humankind (ancient and modern) with extensions into art, kinship, family, religion, political and legal structures.

Aberdeen A new programme in Anthropology with close links with cultural history and sociology. Excellent collections at the local museum of national importance. The Anthropology course covers society, nature and cultural differences, the anthropology of religion and the anthropology of the North.

Birmingham* Anthropology is offered as a joint course with eight other subjects.

Bristol* A programme is offered in Archaeology and Anthropology, covering both biological and social aspects of the latter.

Bristol UWE The three year or four year sandwich course in Biological Anthropology includes the history of biology, human evolution, anthropology and genetics.

Brunel Anthropology is offered as a three-year full-time or four-year thin sandwich course. It can also be taken with Sociology or with Psychology. (High research rating)

Cambridge* The Archaeology and Anthropology course is multidisciplinary, covering the social sciences, natural sciences and the humanities by way of archaeology, biological anthropology and social anthropology, allowing specialisation in one of these disciplines after Year 1. The Archaeology course in theory and practice covers prehistory, the Roman Empire, the Ancient Near East, Africa and the Far East. Biological Anthropology involves human ecology and genetics and social anthropology, gender, urban and ethnic studies. There is also a course in Evolution and Behaviour, taken as part of the Natural Sciences course. (High research rating)

Dundee A degree in Forensic Anthropology introduces the student to anatomical and medical investigations of human remains.

Durham* Anthropology teaching and research focuses on social and biological anthropology (no previous knowledge is assumed). The former covers social institutions and cultures, with specialised studies in family, kinship, art, religion, ritual, political and legal structures. Biological anthropology involves the evolution of the species and ecology. There are also degrees in Human Sciences and Health and Human Sciences at the Stockton Campus and joint courses offered with Anthropology include Archaeology, Sociology. IT is also offered in the combined honours programme and in Natural Sciences. (High research rating)

East Anglia Anthropology is offered with Archaeology and Art History and can include a year in Australia or North America.

East London The unique degree in Anthropology links biological and social anthropology. A year in New Mexico is part of the degree with North American Studies.

Edinburgh* Social Anthropology courses focus on ritual, religion, family, marriage and the Third World, or alternatively on current issues such as environment, society and gender. At present there are five joint courses with Social Anthropology. (High research rating)

Glasgow* Anthropology is offered as a joint subject with a range of courses. Societies in Melanesia, Africa, Australia, South America and Indonesia can be studied. See also **Social Science/Studies**.

Hull Anthropology is offered as a joint honours course.

Kent The Anthropology course is offered, focusing on the biological, cultural and social processes that underlie the human experience in non-industrial and industrial societies. Combined courses with European languages are also offered. There are also courses in Medical Anthropology, Biological Anthropology and Social Anthropology (with languages or a year in Finland).

Lancaster* A course is offered in the Anthropology of Religion.

Liverpool* A new course is offered in Evolutionary Archaeology, developing from the course in Human Evolution. Topics covered include anatomy, psychology and human and animal behaviour.

Liverpool John Moores A course is offered in Forensic Anthropology focusing on the study of human remains for medico-legal purposes.

London (Goldsmiths) Anthropology courses, which can also be studied with Media or Sociology, cover a range of specialist studies including anthropological aspects of food, health, complex societies, European integration, art, sex, gender and psychology perspectives. (High research rating)

London (LSE)* Core courses are taken in social anthropology in each year of the course. In Year 1, students may take an additional course in economics, geography, government, history, international relations, law, politics or psychology. Anthropology is also offered as a joint degree with Law. (High research rating)

London (SOAS)* Anthropology and Sociology is offered with a range of other subjects including Economics, Geography, History and languages. Social Anthropology is offered with over 30 subjects including African, Asian and Oriental Languages. (High research rating)

London (UCL)* The Anthropology Department is unusual in covering all three branches of anthropology: biological, social and cultural material. Students study all three branches for the first two years, after which they may choose to specialise in one field or to combine courses from two or three branches. Combined honours are offered in Ancient History and Social Anthropology and Anthropology and Geography. (High research rating)

London Metropolitan A course is offered in Social Anthropology covering topics which include gender, cultures, beliefs, racism and identity.

Manchester* The Social Anthropology course follows a similar pattern and covers the same topics as other courses in this field, with departmental interests covering Africa and the Far East. A degree in Anthropology can be taken with Archaeology. (High research rating)

Oxford* Anthropology is offered as part of the Human Sciences degree and is also combined with Archaeology (see **Archaeology**). (High research rating)

Oxford Brookes* Anthropology is offered as a single or combined course with 40 other subjects. There are also opportunities to study abroad during the course.

Queen's Belfast* Social Anthropology can be taken as a single honours course, a joint or combined honours course or a major/minor course. Social Anthropology (a comparative study of society and culture) compares societies around the world. Topics include economics, relationships, politics, religious systems, modes of livelihood, perception and belief, marriage and the organisation of public life. (High research rating)

Roehampton Courses are offered in Biological and Social Anthropology, allowing students to focus on either topic with a wide variety of optional modules. Human Biosciences examines the central aspects of human biology, such as physiology, behaviour, evolution, disease and ecology. It may be studied as a single honours course or a combined course with Psychology or Sport Science. A three-year course in Anthropology is also provided.

St Andrews* The Social Anthropology degree provides a study of tribal and peasant societies comparing Western and non-Western cultures. Particular attention is given to Africa, India and the Americas. Social Anthropology can also be studied with a number of joint subjects. Scholarships available. (High research rating)

Southampton Anthropology is offered as one of four pathways in the Applied Social Science degree programme. Scholarships available.

Sussex* Anthropology is offered as a single or joint honours degree. Human sciences and joint degrees are offered in which equal amounts of time are spent on each subject or alternatively a minor subject may be chosen in which three quarters of the time is spent on Anthropology. Opportunities exist for placement overseas. (High research rating)

Trinity St David (Lampeter) The Anthropology course offers topics in contemporary human societies with an emphasis on the study of art and material culture including film and museum studies.

West London A degree offered in Human Sciences.

ALTERNATIVE COURSES
History, Psychology, Religious Studies, Sociology and Archaeology.

ARCHAEOLOGY

(*indicates universities with the highest entry requirements)

SUBJECT REQUIREMENTS/PREFERENCES
GCE A-level: For BSc courses Chemistry may be required. Latin or Greek may be required by some universities. **GCSE:** Mathematics or science usually required for BSc courses.

SUBJECT INFORMATION
It would be unusual for an applicant to pursue this degree course without having been involved in some basic fieldwork. Studies can cover European, Greek, Roman or African archaeology.

Aberdeen The course in Archaeology has a northern focus covering Scottish history and antiques and Scandinavia and Northern Europe. A distance learning programme is offered for students throughout Northern Scotland.

Bangor Archaeology is offered with History or Welsh History and focuses on British prehistory and archaeology. There is also a course in Heritage, Archaeology and History.

Birmingham* Archaeology and Ancient History are offered as single and combined courses, the latter focusing on the archaeology of Ancient Greece, Rome, Egypt and the Near East. There is a practical archaeology option in Years 2 and 3. Archaeology can also be studied with a range of other degree subjects with practical fieldwork being an important component of the degree. (High research rating)

Bournemouth The Archaeology course has an emphasis on practical archaeology. There is a strong vocational focus that includes financial, personnel and management skills. Archaeology is also offered with Forensic Science and Prehistory and there are also specialist degrees in Archaeology of Shipwrecks, and Roman Archaeology.

Bradford Six courses are offered. The Archaeological Sciences course has a strong applied science input and Bioarchaeology has a strong element in applied biology focusing on the human environment. Other courses focus on Forensic Science and Geography. There is a four-year sandwich course available. (High research rating)

Bristol* The course focuses on the practice, theory and history of archaeology and has a range of options covering European, Aegean and Ancient Mediterranean Studies. Practical units involve site visits, artefacts, environmental archaeology and heritage management. Courses in Archaeology and Anthropology or with Ancient History are also available. (High research rating)

Cambridge* Archaeology is studied with Anthropology. The choice between Archaeology, Biology or Social Anthropology is made in Year 2. (High research rating) (See Anthropology)

Cardiff* The Archaeology course focuses primarily on British, European and Mediterranean archaeology and involves 'hands on' experience in various archaeological techniques such as drawing, surveying and excavation. For students with an appropriate science background, particularly in chemistry, there is also a degree course in Conservation of Objects in Museums and Archaeology. There are also combined courses with, for example, Ancient History or Medieval History. Scholarships available. (High research rating)

Central Lancashire Archaeology is offered as a single or combined course with degree programmes in Archaeology and Environmental Management, Geography, History or Forensic Science.

Chester The degree is offered as a single, minor, major or joint course. There are regular field units with some modules involving a larger element of practical work.

Durham* The first year of the Archaeology and Anthropology course consists of a general introduction to the history and nature of archaeology for the prehistoric, Roman and early medieval periods. Single honours students in Archaeology also take an ancillary subject in the first year. The second-year course covers both scientific and practical techniques. Archaeology is also offered with Ancient History as a joint course and in the Social Sciences combined honours programme and as a part of the Natural Sciences programme. (High research rating)

East Anglia* Archaeology can be studied alongside Anthropology and Art History or alternatively with a year in Australia or North America.

Edinburgh* The Archaeology degree covers the early civilisations in Europe and the Near East. Joint courses are introduced in Year 3 and include Environmental Archaeology, or Archaeology with History or Social Anthropology.

Exeter* After a general introduction in Year 1, Archaeology students have a wide choice of options in Years 2 and 3 with substantial practical and field work. European study is also offered in Year 3 prior to completing the course in Year 4. There are also courses in which Archaeology is combined with History or Ancient History. There are opportunities for professional placement and study abroad.

Glasgow This Archaeology course is offered in the Faculties of Science, Arts or Social Science, the choice being dependent on the other subject students wish to study. The course covers British (and Scottish) archaeology from the earliest times to AD1000 and later, and European and Mediterranean areas. There is an emphasis on practical and scientific aspects of the study. See also **Combined courses**. (High research rating)

Hull The course introduces history, theory and method involving theoretical and practical studies. Several optional modules are offered by the departments of Geography and History.

See *University Degree Course Offers* (Trotman Publishing) for details of offers

Kent Classical and Archaeological Studies covers literature, art, philosophy, history and archaeology. As the course progresses, students specialise in their preferred interest.

Leicester* In the BA Archaeology and Ancient History course one additional subject is taken in Years 1 and 2. The study covers Europe, Western Asia, Africa, Australasia and the Americas and archaeological methodology. Ancient History, History and Geography are also offered with Archaeology and other joint degree programmes are also offered. Scholarships available. See also **Combined courses**. (High research rating)

Liverpool* The BA courses in Archaeology offer a broad programme of fieldwork and analysis. The BSc courses focus on laboratory work covering artifacts and environmental analysis. Archaeology also features in the Combined Arts, Science or Social Science programmes and can be combined with Ancient History, Anthropology, Art, Egyptology and Geography. (High research rating)

London (King's)* The Classical Archaeology course unit structure, covering the art and archaeology of Greece and Rome, allows great flexibility but all students undertake some study of Latin or Greek. (A beginners level course is an option.)

London (RH)* Courses are offered in Classical Archaeology and Environmental Archaeology with Geography.

London (SOAS)* Archaeology is offered under Asian and African specialisms combined with History of Art.

London (UCL)* Core courses in Year 1 of Archaeology (General) lead on to a choice of more than 80 courses covering prehistoric and Western, Asiatic, Greek and Roman and Medieval archaeology, Egyptology and conservation. The BA and BSc courses are common for the first two years then divide with the BSc offering a greater element of scientific analysis. (High research rating)

Manchester* The Archaeology course explores the period from Neolithic man to the Middle Ages covering British prehistory, African and Pacific archaeology and providing a general foundation in the subject. Courses are offered in Ancient History, and Arts History. Scholarships available.

Newcastle* Archaeology is based around three subject strands: prehistory, historical archaeology and theory and practice. It involves a comprehensive practical training including fieldwork, excavation, museum work, computing etc. There is also a joint course in Archaeology and Ancient History whilst Archaeology is also offered with other subjects in the Combined Studies programme.

Nottingham* Part I (two years) of the Archaeology course covers the methods used by archaeologists and a study of the development of civilisation in Britain and Europe over 11,000 years. Part II (third year) follows specialist studies in prehistoric, Roman, Medieval or European regional archaeology as well as historical buildings, numismatics and mathematical and computer applications in archaeology. Compulsory excavation takes place during vacations. Subsidiary language study is possible and six joint honours courses are available. Several joint courses are offered and a unique course in Viking Studies covering language, literature, geography, history, and art history.

Oxford* The course in Archaeology and Anthropology covers world archaeology and introduces anthropological theory. Topics include human evolution and ecology, social analysis and interpretation, cultural representations and beliefs and urbanisation. The geographical areas studied cover the Aegean, Middle East, Maritime South East Asia, South America, Africa and the Islamic world. A minimum of three weeks archaeological work is mandatory. There is also a course in Classical Archaeology and Ancient History. (High research rating)

Queen's Belfast* Archaeology (history of past human activities) can also be combined with Palaeoecology (the study of past environments) and courses in European prehistory and history from the

Middle Ages. Special attention is given to the British Isles and Europe, and Ireland. Single, joint and major/minor Archaeology courses are available. (High research rating)

Reading Prehistoric, Roman, and Medieval archaeology in Britain, Europe and the Mediterranean form the foundations of the BSc/BA Archaeology courses. Four-week training excavations take place during the summer vacation. Joint courses involve Classical Studies, History, History of Art, Italian and Chemistry. (High research rating)

St Andrews* Archaeology is offered with Ancient or Medieval History.

Sheffield* The Archaeology course provides opportunities for single honours students to focus on European archaeology at the beginning of the second year. Option courses are offered in the second and third years. Courses are also offered in Classical and Historical Archaeology, Archaeology and Archaeological Science. In addition there are nine joint courses. (High research rating)

Southampton* A flexible thematic Archaeology course is offered ranging from ancient Mediterranean studies to the archaeology of towns and cities. A wide range of options follows in Years 2 and 3, including ancient maritime trade and underwater archaeology. Scholarships available. (High research rating)

Swansea* Courses are offered in Egyptology and Anthropology, Ancient History and Classical Civilisation.

Trinity St David (Lampeter) The Archaeology course focuses on Palaeolithic to modern cultures. There are particular strengths in landscape, prehistoric, environmental and forensic archaeology. Archaeology is also offered together with joint subjects including Anthropology and with a focus on either Environmental or Practical or World Cultures.

Warwick* A course is offered in Classical Archaeology with Ancient History.

Winchester Ancient and Medieval Archaeology and Art is offered awaiting validation. There is also a course in Archaeological Practice and a more theoretical degree in Archaeology.

Worcester Several courses are offered combining Archaeology and Heritage Studies (BA or BSc) with one of 11 other subjects.

York* The Archaeology course is concerned with both archaeological method (including a significant practical element) and theory (with special courses on the interpretation of archaeological data). One main course is taken each term on single themes covering Europe from the Bronze Age onwards. There are opportunities to study a foreign language. The department has particular strengths in medieval history and medieval archaeology. Degree courses are also offered in Bioarchaeology and Historical Archaeology. (High research rating)

OTHER INSTITUTIONS OFFERING ARCHAEOLOGY COURSES
Peterborough (Reg Coll), Truro (Coll).

ALTERNATIVE COURSES
Ancient History, Anthropology, Art and Design, Classical Studies, Classics, Geology, History, History of Architecture, Medieval History, Prehistory and Social Anthropology.

ARCHITECTURE

(including **Architectural Technology** and **Landscape Architecture**)
(*indicates universities with the highest entry requirements)

SUBJECT REQUIREMENTS/PREFERENCES
GCE A-level: Mathematics or Physics may be required. **GCSE:** English and Mathematics.

SUBJECT INFORMATION
Institutions offering Architecture have very similar courses. An awareness of the relationship between people and the built environment is necessary, plus the ability to create and to express oneself in terms of drawings, paintings etc. Most Architecture schools will expect to see a portfolio of work, particularly drawings of buildings or parts of buildings.

Anglia Ruskin BSc courses in Architecture and Architectural Technology share common first-year modules that include design and technology, building construction, project management, urban studies and over 20 other options.

Bath* For the BSc in Architectural Studies (Faculty of Engineering), the first year is spent in university with Semester 2 and the summer terms spent in training. The course gives exemptions from Part I of the RIBA Final examination. The course leads on to the Master of Architecture degree but admission is not automatic as the minimum requirement is a second-class honours degree – second division. Bath has a joint School of Architecture and Civil Engineering with Architecture and Engineering students working together on joint projects. See also **Engineering** courses.

Birmingham City The School of Architecture is one of the largest in the country and draws strength from its association with the Departments of Planning, Landscape and Construction and Surveying. Following the three-year BArch course, a postgraduate diploma course gives complete exemptions from RIBA examinations. Architecture can also be studied with an emphasis on urban design, conservation or regeneration. Courses are also offered in Architectural Technology and Landscape Architecture.

Bolton The degree in Architectural Technology is accredited by the Chartered Institutes of Architectural Technologists and Building.

Brighton* The Architecture course provides a balance between environmental needs, technology and creative design. The programme develops through basic design and graphic skills, history, materials, and includes interior design and visits to European cities. The course in Architectural Technology (three-year or four-year sandwich) is basically a building course with a greater emphasis on design. There is also a three-year degree in Interior Architecture.

Bristol UWE The Architecture BA honours course is followed by the BArch course (the second undergraduate degree) which some students study on a part-time basis. The first part of the latter course is built around work placement and both are validated by the Royal Institute of British Architects. There are also courses in Architectural Technology and Architecture and Planning.

Cambridge* Architecture Parts IA and IB and II each lasting a year provide a basic training in architecture through design and studio exercises covering the history of European architecture. After the degree students normally take a further two years supervised office experience with RIBA Parts 2 and 3 examinations leading to registration.

Cardiff* The Architectural Programme is a two-tier scheme of study, first leading to a BSc in Architectural Studies in three years and then followed by two years of study (including one year practice) for the MArch degree. Visual communication, interior design, town planning and landscape design are included throughout the BSc course and opportunities exist for a specialist study in the BArch degree. There is a focus on design creativity integrated with technological and environmental concerns of modern architectural practice. The School of Architecture works in close liaison with the Town Planning Department in the fields of urban design, housing and landscape. Scholarships available. (High research rating)

Cardiff (UWIC) A course is offered in Architectural Design Technology which includes a study of building technology, materials and environmental studies. There is also a course in Interior Architecture.

Central Lancashire A three-year full-time course is offered in Architectural Technology covering building design and technology, with sponsored studentships on application. There is also a course in Architecture awaiting validation.

City* Full-time and sandwich courses combining Civil Engineering and Architecture are offered.

Coventry A course in Architectural Design Technology is offered, leading to a support career for architects.

Creative Arts Three courses are offered in Architecture, Architectural Technology and Interior Architecture and Design.

De Montfort The three-year Architecture course focusing on studio-based projects is followed by one year of practical study and a further two years leading to the graduate diploma. There is also a course in Architectural Design Technology and Production leading to qualification as an architect technician.

Derby Four courses are offered with Architectural Design. The course in Architectural Conservation covers architectural and technological skills and environmental conservation. Other courses cover Architectural Technology, a Built Environment (Architecture) Programme and also a range of joint courses.

Dundee Architecture is a five-year course that comprises three years leading to the BSc (Arch) followed by BArch after a further two years. A year of practical experience may be taken between the third and fourth years. Exchange programmes take place with seven European countries.

East London Environmental design, history, construction, conservation, law, the building industry and urban studies are topics covered in this standard Architecture course. The course is suitable for students with an arts-based background.

Edinburgh* A four-year course is offered in Architectural Design, leading on to an MArch course. There is also a degree in Architectural History.

Glamorgan A course is offered in Architectural and Heritage Conservation that includes a field course in conservation with the National Trust. There is also a course in Architectural Technology which can be taken as a joint or major/minor programme.

Glasgow Architecture is offered by the Mackintosh School of Architecture. The course leads to an ordinary or honours degree after which graduates study for the Diploma in Architecture for professional recognition. Civil Engineering is also offered with Architecture.

Gloucestershire The Landscape Architecture degree, accredited by the Landscape Institute, covers graphic expression, plant knowledge, site planning, landscapes, environmental impact assessment, landscape engineering and advanced horticulture.

Greenwich Architecture is a design-based course with strong visual studies and computing input. Architecture can also be studied with Landscape Architecture. There is a four year part-time course. Scholarships available. There is also a course in Garden Design.

Huddersfield Design, design technology, communication and context of design are the four main subject areas in the BA Architecture course. The Architecture (International) course is unique in the UK. A course of three years only, it is designed specifically to apply the principles of design on a worldwide basis and examines the architecture of developing countries. Extensive overseas fieldwork is part of the course. The course in Architecture runs parallel for Year 1, after which students decide their course route. There is also a course in Architectural Technology.

Kent* A BA degree (three years) followed by an MArch course (two years) was introduced in 2006. Both courses provide a thorough grounding in design, technology, law, and management aspects for those wishing to enter a career in architecture. There is also a degree in Interior Architecture and Design.

Kingston* The Architecture course has design as its principal core element. A particular feature of the course is the use of continuous assessment. Courses in Landscape Architecture and Landscape Planning and Historic Building Conservation are also available.

Leeds Metropolitan Architectural design is the main feature of the Architecture course, which is linked with building, design management, urban and landscape design and environmental control. Interior design and a study of Third World housing is also included. The graduate diploma course follows the three-year BA course. There are also courses in Landscape Architecture, Landscape Planning, Garden Art and Design and Architectural Technology.

Lincoln The Architecture course is structured around project-based design teaching covering technical, professional, human and social aspects and historical studies.

Liverpool* The Architecture course has a strong emphasis on design and has close links with building, civil engineering and civic design areas. Transfer to the new Design Studies BA is an option at the end of Year 1. (High research rating)

Liverpool John Moores The Architecture course involves design, history, theory, technology and practice and gives exemption from the RIBA Part I examinations. The postgraduate diploma exempts from the RIBA Part 2 examination. There is also a degree in Architectural Technology with an optional sandwich year.

London (UCL)* This three-year Architecture course for a BSc degree is largely based on design projects and provides a very broad academic education for those who are concerned with planning, design and management of the built environment. (High research rating)

London Metropolitan A three-year Architecture course is offered, focusing on design and urbanism. It is not a preparation for a career as an architect. There is however a separate degree for students aiming to enter the profession. There is also a course in Interior Architecture and Design.

London South Bank The Architecture Studies course includes design, information technology and history of architecture. There are also courses in Architectural Technology and Architectural Engineering.

Manchester* The three-year BA course in Architecture leads on to the two-year study for the Bachelor of Architecture degree. The course is predominantly design based. Field trips in the UK and abroad are compulsory and exchanges at BArch level take place in France, Germany, Spain and Italy.

Manchester Metropolitan This is a three-year full-time or four-year sandwich course in Architecture with design projects supported by studies in technical and administrative skills. There is also a course in Landscape Architecture.

Napier Courses are offered in Architectural Technology and Interior Architecture.

Newcastle* This three-year course in Architectural Studies covers the theory and history of architecture, building technology, studio design projects and environmental design. It is followed by a year's practical training leading on to a two-year course of advanced architectural design for the BArch degree. The course presents a realistic view of the environment of architecture and encourages students to develop a personal philosophy of design. It is strongly biased towards project work.

Northampton A degree is offered in Architectural Technology.

Northumbria* Managerial skills are included in the Architecture course. RIBA recognition for Part I is accepted. There is also a course in Architectural Technology.

Nottingham* A three-year BA course in Architecture is followed by two years to the BArch degree. A year of practical experience follows the BA course. The course is planned around project work investigating a wide variety of building problems and achieves a balance between art and technology and stresses the integration of technical work with projects but is without a strong scientific bias. There are also courses in Architectural and Environmental Engineering and Architecture and Environmental Design. (High research rating)

Nottingham Trent* A BArch degree in Architecture with RIBA Part I status is offered and also courses in Architectural Technology and Interior Architecture and Design.

Oxford Brookes* Architecture is a three-year project-based course supported by environmental and construction technologies, social sciences, history and philosophy. The course is highly rated by students. The Graduate Diploma course of two years follows with a year of practical experience. There are also courses in Interior Architecture – Design and Practice and joint programmes in Cities and Environment Design.

Plymouth* The Architecture degree (scholarships available) is a three-year full-time course followed by practical experience and two further years of study leading to a diploma. There is a possibility of study abroad. Courses are also available in Architectural Design with Digital Media, Architectural Technology and the Environment, and Architecture, Design and Structures, relating architecture to civil engineering.

Portsmouth The Architecture degree is based on design projects (50% of the course). The first year covers drawing techniques, user studies, planning and circulation, and environmental comfort. The second and third years focus on three themes: the house, urban residential and commercial buildings, and a public building – supported by history, drawing, computer-aided design, computing and construction. There is also a course in Restoration and Decorative Studies.

Queen's Belfast* Architecture (scholarships available) is a three-year course intended as a first degree for those wishing to take postgraduate studies and become professionally qualified architects. This typical course covers design and communication, building technology and professional skills.

Robert Gordon Architecture is a predominantly design course with units in information technology in Years 1 and 2. The course includes a one year salaried placement. There is also a four-year course in Architectural Technology.

Sheffield* The Architecture degree offers a balanced education, covering theory, design and professional experience. There are several options open to those who take the standard BA degree which, combined with practical experience, leads to exemptions from RIBA examinations. Work experience advised before application. There are also courses in Architecture and Landscape and Civil or Structural Engineering with Architecture. (High research rating)

Sheffield Hallam The Architecture and Environmental Design degree includes modules in environment and technology and urban design and landscape, and leads to RIBA accreditation. There is also a degree in Architectural Technology.

Southampton* A course is offered in Civil Engineering with Architecture.

Strathclyde* Architectural Studies can be studied alongside European Studies.

Ulster Degree courses are offered in Architecture and in Architectural Technology and Management.

West London Full-time and part-time courses are offered in Architectural Technology.

Westminster* The Architecture course is largely based on design project work and covers a study of architectural form and the physical, social and psychological needs of the user. There are also courses in Architecture (Interior Design) (Urban Design) and in Architectural Technology.

See *University Degree Course Offers* (Trotman Publishing) for details of offers

Wolverhampton Courses are offered in Architectural Technology, Architectural Studies plus another subject and Interior Architectural Design.

OTHER INSTITUTIONS OFFERING ARCHITECTURE COURSES
Blackpool and Fylde (Coll), Bournemouth (UC), Bradford (Coll), Dewsbury (Coll), Dudley (CT), Edinburgh (CA), Glasgow (SA), Hereford (CA), Leeds (CA), Menai (Coll), Pembrokeshire (Coll), Ravensbourne, UHI Millennium Inst, Wigan and Leigh (Coll), Worcester (CT).

ALTERNATIVE COURSES
Building, Building Surveying, Civil Engineering, Estate Management, Land Surveying, Landscape Architecture, Quantity Surveying and Town and Country Planning.

ART AND DESIGN

(see also **History of Art and Design**)
(*indicates universities with the highest entry requirements)

Abertay Dundee The degree course in Computer Arts (requiring previous studies in Art and Design) includes modules in Japanese with opportunities to study in Japan. There is also a course in Visual Communications and Media Design.

Aberystwyth* The three-year scheme in Fine Art begins with a broad visual education in Year 1, and in Years 2 and 3 allows the student to specialise in one or more from drawing, painting, printmaking, photography and book illustration. Fine Art can be studied with one of a range of subjects, including Art History, Film and Television Studies, Information and Library Studies, Mathematics, Museum and Gallery Studies, and Welsh History.

Anglia Ruskin BA Art degree courses are offered in Fine Art, Illustration, Printmaking, Graphic Design and Photography. There is also a course in Computer-aided Product Design.

Aston The university offers a number of programmes in Product Design, based in its School of Engineering. These cover Automotive, Engineering, Industrial, Medical, Product and Sustainable Product Design.

Bath Spa Practical degree courses are offered in Fine Art (Painting, Sculpture, Media), Graphic Design, 3D Design in Ceramics, Fashion and Textile Design and Creative Arts. Art can be combined with Dance, Drama and Music.

Bedfordshire Courses are offered in Graphic Design, Photography, Advertising Design, Fine Art, Illustration, Interior Architecture, Interior Design and Animation.

Birmingham City BA courses are offered in Design, Fine Art, Fashion Design, Textile Design (Embroidery) (Constructed Textiles) (Printed Textiles) (Retail Management), Three D Digital Design (Digital Product Design, Digital Spatial Design), Jewellery and Silversmithing, Visual Communication and Product Design (Furniture) (Industrial) (Design in Business).

Bolton All Art and Design degrees are modular and cover art and design, animation and illustration, fine arts, graphic design, photo and video and textile/surface design.

Bournemouth Design courses are offered in the School of Design, Engineering and Computing. These include Product Design and Interior Design. Courses are also offered in Computer-aided Product Design and Fashion and Textiles.

Bradford There are three courses in Design – Automotive Design Technology, Industrial Design and Product Design offered in the School of Engineering. The four-year course includes a paid industrial placement of one year.

Brighton The Critical Fine Art Practice course places equal emphasis on theory and practice and includes traditional drawing, painting or photography. There are also Fine Art Painting, Printmaking and Sculpture courses, Graphic Design, Illustration, Moving Image Photography, Product Design, Fashion Design (with Business Studies or Textiles) and Three Dimensional Design courses with specialisms in wood, metal, ceramics and plastics. (High research rating)

Bristol UWE Degree courses are offered in Fine Arts and Art and Visual Culture which share a common year with the decision on the degree of choice in Year 2. There are also degrees in Drawing and Applied Arts, Illustration, Animation, Fashion/Textiles and Graphic Design. There is also a Creative Product Design course with industrial placements. (High research rating)

Brunel* The Department of Design offers Industrial Design and Technology, Industrial Design Engineering and Product Design. Close links with industry exist for student placements.

Bucks New In addition to Fine Art, Graphic Arts and Creative Advertising, specialised studies are also offered in Ceramics and Glass, Design for Digital Media, Photography, Jewellery, Spatial Design, Product Design, Textiles (Fashion, Knit, Print) and Surface Design, and Three Dimensional Design. The university is also a leader in the UK in the field of Furniture Design and Furniture Conservation and Restoration.

Canterbury Christ Church Courses are offered in Fine and Applied Arts including, Ceramics, Painting, Printmaking, Sculpture and Studio Media and Drawing Technologies.

Cardiff (UWIC) Ceramics, Textiles, Fine Arts, Graphics, and Product Design courses are offered.

Central Lancashire The degree in Fine Art has major areas in painting, printmaking, sculpture and time-based media (film, video, animation). There are also courses in Fashion, Fashion Promotion, Advertising, Graphic Design, Animation, Audio Visual Media, Illustration, Industrial Design, Interior Design, Product Design, Jewellery and Surface Pattern with Crafts. Design Studies can also be taken with Fashion and Brand Promotion or Photography or Journalism. Fashion courses also include Styling, Marketing and Asian Fashion. There is also a new course in Antiques and Design Studies.

Chester Courses are offered in Fine Art, Graphics, and Photography which includes professional work placement.

Chichester The Fine Art programme includes textiles, painting, sculpture, media studies and printmaking.

Colchester (Inst) Courses are offered in Fashion and Textiles, Fine Art, Graphic Media and 3D Design.

Coventry The School of Art and Design offers courses in Consumer Product Design, Transport Design, Fashion Design and Fashion Accessories, Graphic Design, Art and Craft involving textiles, ceramics and metal and in Fine Art comprising painting, printmaking, sculpture, public art and art history. There is also a course in Contemporary Crafts.

Creative Arts The university has five campuses. UCA Canterbury – Fine Art, Interior Architecture. UCA Epsom – Fashion, Graphics. UCA Farnham – Advertising, Animation, Computer Games, Fine Art, Graphics, Interior Architecture, Photography, Product Design, Textiles for Fashion, 3D (Ceramics, Glass, Metal, Jewellery). UCA Maidstone – Graphics, Photography. UCA Rochester – Fashion, Product Design, Photography, 3D (Silverwave, Goldsmithing, Jewellery).

Cumbria Art and Design courses cover Animation, Applied Arts, Fine Art, Graphic Design, Illustration and Photography.

De Montfort Art and Design courses are offered in Animation, Fashion Design, Fine Art, Graphic Design, Footwear Design, Furniture Design, Interior Design, Textile Design, and Photography and Video.

Derby Courses are offered in Fine Art, Crafts and Joint honours Creative Design Practices, Fashion Studies and Textile Design.

Dundee (Duncan of Jordanstone Coll) After a general course in art and design, degree specialisations follow in Television and Imaging, Fine Art, Painting, History of Art or Design with specialisms in Printmaking, Jewellery and Metalwork, Drawing and Painting, Sculpture, Animation and Electronic Media Arts and Imaging. There are also courses in Textile Design, Interior and Environmental Design, Interactive Media Design and Innovative Product Design. There is also a course in Art, Philosophy and Contemporary Practice, with art occupying 60% of the teaching programme including studio projects. (High research rating)

East London Courses are offered in Fashion Design and/with Marketing, Fine Art, Graphic Design (Illustration, Photography, Printmaking), Product Design Futures, Printed Textiles and Surface Decoration, and Visual Theories.

Edge Hill The course in Animation focuses on the theoretical aspects of 2D and 3D digital animations and production techniques.

Edinburgh* The MA (Honours) in Fine Art is taught jointly by the University and the Edinburgh College of Art, with equal amounts of practical and academic work.

Falmouth (UC) Art courses include 3D Design, Fashion, Fine Art, Graphics, Interior Design, Textiles, Theatre Design and Photography.

Glamorgan A three-year full-time course is offered in Art Practice covering courses in ceramics, three dimensional studies, drawing, painting, fashion design and photography. Degree courses are also offered in Graphic Communication, Games Art and Animation, Interior, Product and Packaging Design, Animation and Design for Media.

Glasgow See **Engineering courses** for Product Design Engineering that is taught partly by the Glasgow School of Art, which also offers a BA in Design. This is a four-year honours course and has a common first year with the degree in Fine Art. Thereafter Design students go on to specialisms in Ceramics, Textiles, Visual Communication, Photography, Interior Design and Silversmithing and Jewellery. Fine Art students may specialise in Environmental Art/Sculpture, Painting/Printmaking or Photography.

Glasgow Caledonian Courses are offered in Interior Design, Graphic Design with Multimedia and Fashion Business and Marketing.

Gloucestershire A three-year full-time course in Fine Art leads to specialising in Painting, Photography or Video. Courses are also offered in Graphic Design and Animation, and Illustration.

Glyndŵr Specific degrees are offered in Fine Art, Graphic Design and Illustration with broad courses covering Creative Lens Media, Computer Arts and Decorative Arts.

Greenwich Courses offered include Fine Arts, Graphic Design, and Visual Art.

Heriot-Watt The School of Textiles and Design is located in Galashiels and the Scottish Borders. Six courses are offered in Fashion including Design for Industry, Textile and Fashion Design, Technology, Menswear, Womenswear, Marketing and Retailing and Communication. There are opportunities to study abroad.

Hertfordshire The Faculty offers degree courses in Applied Arts (ceramics, glass, textiles and jewellery), Fine Art (painting, sculpture, printmaking and photography), Model Design, Product Design, Graphics Design and Illustration, Digital Modelling, Digital Animation, Digital and Lens Media, Fashion, Industrial and Interior and Spatial Design.

See *University Degree Course Offers* (Trotman Publishing) for details of offers

Huddersfield Courses are offered in Fashion Design and Textiles, Advertising and Graphic Design, Illustration, Fine Art, Interior Design, and Product and Transport Design. The Contemporary Arts course includes Photography and Performance.

Hull Courses are offered in Design for Digital Media and Design and Technology.

Kent The Fine Art course is a theoretical course with practical studio work and options in photography. Visual and Performing Arts covers Art History and some Drama and Film Studies. There are also courses in Interior Design and Interior Architecture. See also **Film**.

Kingston The Design Faculty offers five main subject areas – Fine Art (painting, sculpture, printmaking, photography and computing), Graphic Design (communication media, moving image, animation, lettering, typography, packaging), Illustration (including animation and video), Interior Design, Product and Furniture Design and Fashion and Museums and Gallery Studies. There is also a course in Art, Performance and Digital Media, offering a range of skills including the moving image and music.

Lancaster* Creative Arts integrates creative work with art history of the 20th century and Art and Art History is largely concerned with art history with options in practical work. There is also a Creative Arts course offering four art forms – art, creative writing, music and theatre studies. Students choose two specialisms starting in Year 2. Scholarships available.

Leeds* The Art and Design course combines studio practice with a study of historic, technological and cultural aspects. The School of the Textile Industries provides a Textile Design programme in addition to Textile and Fashion Management. The Fine Art course offers a 50/50 balance of theory and practice. There is also a course in Design and Colour Technology. (High research rating)

Leeds Metropolitan In addition to the course in Art and Design, which covers most art specialisms, degree courses are also offered in Fashion, Fine Art, Graphic Arts and Design and Interior Design. There is also a Garden Art and Design course involving horticulture and planting design.

Lincoln Single subject degree courses are offered in Advertising, Animation, Fashion, Fine Art, Furniture Design, Decorative Crafts, Conservation and Restoration, Graphic Design, Graphic Illustration, Interior Design, and Museum and Exhibition Design.

Liverpool Hope The Creative and Performing Arts degree has options in sculpture and painting. There is a Design degree with options in textiles, product, design, silversmithing and jewellery ceramics, wood or metal, and a combined honours option leading to BA/QTS in Fine Art and Design.

Liverpool John Moores The Art School (founded in 1910) offers courses in Fine Art (painting and sculpture), Graphic Arts, Fashion and Textile Design, Interior Design, and Product Design and Digital Modelling.

London (Goldsmiths) Separate courses are offered in Art Practice and in Fine Art, the latter combining studio practice and contemporary critical studies with Art History. The Design Studies degree course is studio-based, covering all aspects of the practical and social aspects of design. In addition, a Design and Technology course offers Qualified Teacher Status at secondary level and there is also a degree course in Textiles. (High research rating)

London (UCL)* The Slade School of Fine Art places great emphasis on the creative and intellectual development of individual students. The Fine Art programme is 'taught by artists for the education of artists'. Students follow one studio discipline in painting, sculpture, fine art, or media (photography, printmaking, film, video and electronic media). A course is also offered in Italian and Design. (High research rating)

London Metropolitan three-year courses are offered in Fine Art, Design (Furniture and Product, Graphics) Textiles, Furnishing Design and Manufacture, Interior Design, and Silversmithing and Jewellery.

London South Bank There are courses in Digital Photography and Product Design, including Sports Products Design which is a four year sandwich course.

Loughborough Courses are offered in Design and Technology, Visual Communication (Illustration and Graphic Communication), Textile Design, Fine Art (Painting, Printmaking and Sculpture) and 3D Design New Practice comprising Furniture, Ceramics, Metalwork, Jewellery and Silversmithing.

Manchester* The Art and Archaeology of the Ancient World is offered as a three-year degree course. The Department of Textiles offers a wide range of courses including Design Management for Fashion Retailing, Textile Design and Management and Fibre Processing and Product Design. Fashion Retailing, Design Management and Textile Design courses are also offered which include business management with industrial experience and study abroad.

Manchester Metropolitan The Faculty of Art and Design offers degree courses in Design and Art Direction (with opportunities to study abroad), Illustration with Animation, Fine Art, Fashion (including embroidery, printed, woven or knitted textiles), Textiles, Interior Design, and Three Dimensional Design (involving wood, metal, ceramics and glass). There are also courses in Clothing Design and Technology, Fashion Buying in Retail, International Fashion Marketing, and Community and Contemporary Arts.

Middlesex Courses are offered in Design and Technology, Fashion, Fine Art, Printed Textiles, Product Design (Graphic Design and Illustration), Interior Architecture and Photography.

Napier Graphic Communications covers aspects of media studies, electronic information and graphic design. Courses are also offered in Design Futures, Interior Architecture and Consumer Product Design. Photography, Film and Imaging is also available.

Newcastle* A four-year Fine Art degree is offered by way of studio practice underpinned by historical and theoretical studies.

Newman (UC) Art and Design is available as a joint or minor course with another subject.

Newport Art and Design courses include Advertising, Games Design, Fashion, Graphic Design and Photography.

Northampton Courses are offered in Fine Art (Drawing and Painting), Graphic Communication, Fashion Illustration, Interior and Product Design and Textile Design.

Northumbria The Faculty of Art and Design offers courses in Fine Art, Fine Art and Conservation Science, Graphic Design, Design for Industry, Fashion, Fashion Marketing, Interior Design, Multimedia Design, Three Dimensional Design (Furniture and Fine Products), Transportation Design and Contemporary Photographic Practice.

Nottingham Trent The Faculty of Art and Design offers a very wide range of courses covering Furniture and Product Design, Design and Development: Landscape and Interiors, Interior Architecture and Design, Graphic Design, Fashion and Textile Management, Fashion Knitwear Design and Knitted Textiles, Decorative Arts (glass, metal, wood), Fine Art (sculpture, painting, video and photo-print), Photography, Textile Design and Theatre Design.

Oxford* The degree of Fine Art involves drawing and painting, printmaking and sculpture together with the history of art and anatomy. Most students have completed a foundation course prior to application, and entry is very competitive. (High research rating)

Oxford Brookes A degree course is offered in Fine Art introducing the student to a range of practices.

Plymouth Several Design courses are offered focusing on Illustration, Fashion, Textiles, Photography, Graphic Communication, Fine Art, Applied Arts (ceramics, glass and metals), Silversmithing and Jewellery, Media Arts, TV Arts, and Three Dimensional Design (product, furniture and interiors). (High research rating)

Portsmouth Communication Design, Illustration, Design for Fashion and Textiles, Photography, Fine Art, and Restoration and Decorative Studies are among the courses offered. Core studies in studio practice and history are undertaken by all students.

Queen Margaret A vocational and highly practical course is offered in Costume Design for stage, film and TV, with three placements throughout the country.

Reading* Four-year degrees in Fine Art and Art are offered with studio facilities for painting, wood, metal, plastics and printmaking, photography and video. A unique degree is also offered in Typography and Graphic Communication. Joint courses are also offered with the History of Art, Philosophy, Psychology, and Film and Theatre. (High research rating)

Robert Gordon Gray's School of Art offers courses in Design and Craft (Visual Communication, Textile and Surface Design, Fashion Design, or Three Dimensional Design (Ceramics, Glass or Jewellery), Design for Industry (Product Design, Graphic Design or Digital Media), Fine Art (Painting, Printmaking, Sculpture, or Photgraphic and Electronic Media) and Commercial Photography.

Salford Courses are offered in Design Studies, Advertising Design, Design Management, Graphic Design, Product Design and Development, Spatial/Interior Design, Visual Arts, Fashion Design (links with top fashion firms) and Sports Equipment Design.

Sheffield Hallam Degree courses are available in Contemporary Fine Art (Painting and Printmaking, Sculpture and Time-based Art), Graphic Design, Furniture Design, Interior Product and Transport Design, Packaging Design and Metalwork and Jewellery. There is also a broad course in Visual Culture. (High research rating)

Southampton* Courses are offered in Fine Art Practice and Theory (painting, printmaking and sculpture) Graphic Arts, and in Textiles, Fashion and Fibre (textile art and design). The courses are based at Winchester School of Art.

Southampton Solent Courses are offered in Creative Industries, Design Studies, Interior Design, Design Technology, Fashion, Fine Art Media, Graphic Design and Photography.

Staffordshire Degrees are offered in Fine Art, Design (Graphics, Animation, Electronic Graphics, Multimedia Graphics, Media Production, Photography, Product Design, Surface Pattern, Crafts, Glass and Ceramics), Design Management, Design Technology, Modern Art, Design and Visual Media, Product Design and Transport Design.

Strathclyde Product Design and Innovation is offered by way of a four-year course.

Sunderland The Art and Design BA offers 18 subjects. Two of these subjects (minimum) to a maximum of four are chosen in Level 1 and students progress in at least two subjects in Levels 2 and 3. The modules on offer are fine art, photography, ceramics, dance, drama and graphics. Degree courses are also offered in Advertising, Fine Art and Glass. There is also a teaching course in Design and Technology.

Swansea Metropolitan Fine Art, Graphic Design and Illustration and Surface Pattern Design courses are offered.

Teesside Degree courses are available in Fine Art Fashion and Textile Design, Graphic Design (including advertising, illustration and computer graphics), Interior Architecture and Design, Contemporary Three Dimensional Design, Product Design, Photography and Design Marketing.

Trinity St David (Carmarthen) Fine Art can be taken as a single honours course or jointly with English, Film Studies or Media Studies.

Ulster Courses are available in Fine and Applied Arts (painting, sculpture, performance, printmaking, lens-based media, history and theory, textile arts, ceramics, silversmithing and jewellery). Combined Studies available include graphic and product design, fine and applied arts, textile and fashion design and visual communication. Design, Graphic, Product and Interactive Design, Textiles and Fashion Design, Visual Communication and Technology and Design with the Diploma in Industrial Studies are also offered.

West London Courses are offered in Games Design and Development, Fashion and Textiles, Fine Art, Graphic Design, Interior Architecture, Illustration and Three Dimensional Studies.

West Scotland Design courses are offered covering Computer-Aided Design, Product Design and Design with Manufacturing Systems.

See *University Degree Course Offers* (Trotman Publishing) for details of offers

Westminster Courses are offered in Ceramics, Fashion, Graphic Information Design, Animation, and Mixed Media Art (photography, video, painting, printmaking, digital and web-based practices, performance art and media theory).

Wolverhampton Degrees are offered in a wide range of courses including Design and Applied Arts, Animation, Ceramics, Design for Interior Textiles, Glass, Computer-aided Design, Design, Digital Media, Fine Art, Furniture Design, Illustration, Graphic Communication, Figurative Sculpture and Modelling, Three Dimensional Design (wood, metals and plastics). There are also courses in Product Design focusing on Innovation and Technology.

Worcester The Art and Design course offers modules in Drawing, Painting, Graphic Design, Fine Art, Illustration, Textiles and Ceramics. There is a work placement in Year 3.

York St John The Product Design degree includes a work placement in Year 2.

OTHER INSTITUTIONS OFFERING ART AND DESIGN COURSES

Barking (Coll), Bishop Grosseteste (UC), Blackpool and Fylde (Coll), Bournemouth (UC), Bradford (Coll), Carmarthenshire (Coll), Central SchSpDr, Chichester (Coll), Cleveland (CAD), Colchester (Inst), Cornwall (Coll), Coventry City (Coll), Craven (Coll), Croydon (Coll), Dartington (CA), Dewsbury (Coll), Doncaster (Coll), East Lancashire (Coll), Edinburgh (CA), Exeter (Coll), Farnborough (UC), Glasgow (SA), Gloucestershire (Coll), Grimsby (IFHE), Havering (Coll), Hereford (CA), Hopwood Hall (Coll), Hull (Coll), Leeds (CA), Leeds Park Lane (Coll), LIPA, Liverpool (CmC), Llandrillo (Coll), Matthew Boulton (CFHE), Menai (Coll), Neath Port Talbot (Coll), NESCOT, Newcastle (Coll), North East Worcestershire (Coll), North Warwickshire (Coll), Northbrook (Coll), Norwich City (Coll), Nottingham New (Coll), Peterborough (Reg Coll), Ravensbourne, Richmond (American Univ), Rose Bruford (Coll), Rotherham (CAT), St Helens (Coll), Sheffield (Coll), Shrewsbury (CAT), Solihull (Coll), Somerset (CAT), South Nottingham (Coll), South Tyneside (Coll), Southport (Coll), Stamford (New Coll), Stockport (Coll), Stratford upon Avon (Coll), Suffolk (Univ Campus), Swindon (Coll), Truro (Coll), Tyne Metropolitan (Coll), UHI Millennium Inst, Uxbridge (Coll), Walsall (Coll), West Anglia (Coll), West Cheshire (Coll), West Thames (Coll), Westminster Kingsway (Coll), Wimbledon (CA), Wirral Metropolitan (Coll), Worcester (CT), York (Coll), Ystrad Mynach. Applications are sent direct to all other institutions.

ALTERNATIVE COURSES

All practical Art and Design courses. Archaeology, Architecture, Classical Civilisation, Communication Studies, Film Studies and Landscape Architecture, Media Studies and Performance Studies.

ASTRONOMY/ASTROPHYSICS

(*indicates universities with the highest entry requirements)

SUBJECT REQUIREMENTS/PREFERENCES

GCE A-level: Two or three science subjects. Mathematics and Physics important.

SUBJECT INFORMATION

These courses have a mathematics and physics emphasis. Applicants, however, should also realise that subject-related careers on graduation are limited. Astrophysics courses involve both physics and astronomy and are more difficult than single honours; students weak in mathematics and physics should avoid them.

Birmingham* Physics and Astrophysics is taken as a major theme in Year 3 by those with an interest in astronomy and astrophysics who wish to combine this with a training in basic physics. All Physics courses have a common Year 1 and 2. There are also programmes which include space research and particle physics with cosmology.

Bristol* Physics is offered with Astrophysics (also with industrial experience). Options are taken in astrophysics and in particle physics and astronomy alongside units common to the BSc Physics programme.

Cambridge* Astrophysics is offered as a third year (Part II) course in the Natural Science Tripos. See also **Biological Sciences**.

Cardiff* Physics with Astronomy is a four-year course designed for those aiming at less theoretical work and has an emphasis on astronomy and observational techniques. A four-year course in Astrophysics is also offered.

Central Lancashire Astrophysics degrees are offered on three year BSc and four year MPhys courses. Practical observations are made with Britain's largest optical telescope. Completion of the course leads to graduate fellowship of the Institute of Physics. Astronomy can also be taken with Mathematics. A part-time distance learning course in Astronomy is also offered (by way of direct application).

Durham* Three- and four-year courses are offered in Physics and Astronomy.

Edinburgh* The first two years of the Astrophysics course are largely similar to those for Physics students. In the third and fourth years the work is divided between astronomy and physics.

Exeter* Physics with Astrophysics can be studied over three or four years.

Glamorgan There are courses in Astronomy, and Astronomy with Space, Geology, Geography and Mathematics.

Glasgow Astronomy covers a study of the universe and the methods used in assessing distances, motions and nature of celestial objects. Later studies examine modern developments. Astronomy is also offered with Mathematics and Physics. No previous knowledge of Astronomy is required.

Hertfordshire In addition to degrees in Astronomy and Astrophysics, both are offered within the University's Combined Modular Scheme with an industrial placement option prior to the final year, or alternatively a year in Europe or North America. There is a well-equipped teaching observatory.

Keele Astrophysics can be taken as a dual honours course with over 28 other subjects.

Kent The three themes of Astronomy, Space Science and Astrophysics give this degree its name and it is taught by the Centre for Astrophysics and Space Science, which has a strong international reputation. There is also an option which includes a year in the USA.

Lancaster* Courses are offered in Astrophysics, Particle Physics and Cosmology.

Leeds* Physics with Astrophysics runs parallel to the Physics course during Year 1 and enables transfers between the Physics and the Physics with Astrophysics courses to be arranged up to the end of the first year. There is also a joint course with Mathematics.

Leicester* Courses are offered in Mathematics with Astronomy, Physics with Astrophysics and Physics with Space Science and Technology, or Planetary Sciences which includes solar physics and space flight dynamics.

Liverpool* The course in Astrophysics follows a common core with the Physics programme in Years 1 and 2 with one or two variations. Specialisms follow in Year 3. Astronomy is also offered with Physics.

Liverpool John Moores The four-year course is Astrophysics is a collaborative venture between John Moores and Liverpool University. The course covers physics, mathematics and computing. Some observational work is carried out at Jodrell Bank and at La Laguma University in Tenerife. There is also a course in Physics with Astronomy.

London (King's)* A course is offered in Physics or in Mathematics and Physics with Astrophysics.

London (QM)* The degree in Astrophysics offers a physics programme accompanied by specialised topics such as stellar and galactic structure and cosmology. In the Astronomy degree, physics and the principles and techniques of astronomy have equal emphasis in the first two years. Options in physics and observation and interpretational astronomy are offered in the third year. It is possible to study either subject as part of a joint honours degree with Mathematics.

London (RH)* Astrophysics is offered as a single honours course or with a three-year full-time degree course in Geology with Astrophysics.

London (UCL)* BSc and MSc courses are offered in Astrophysics, both with common structures in Years 1 and 2.

Manchester* Physics and Astrophysics is primarily a Physics course with specialist studies in astrophysics. There is also a course in Geology with Planetary Science.

Nottingham* Three- and four-year courses are offered in Physics with Astronomy, the latter leading to an MSc.

Nottingham Trent A three-year degree is offered in Physics with Astrophysics or Astronomy.

St Andrews* Astrophysics is offered as a five-year or a four-year degree course. The university has its own observatory.

Salford Four-year degrees in Space Technology and Physics are offered.

Sheffield Astronomy is offered with Physics and Mathematics.

Southampton* A course is offered in Physics with Astronomy either by way of one degree in both subjects (single honours) or two degrees in each subject (double honours). Mathematics with Astronomy is also available.

Surrey* Nuclear Astrophysics is available with Physics. There are also courses in Satellite Technology.

Sussex* Students taking the Astrophysics option spend about a quarter of their time on this subject and the rest on physics and undertake a fourth year project in Astrophysics.

York* Physics with Astrophysics covers courses on planetary science and stellar physics is taken in Year 2 and observational astronomy in Year 3.

ALTERNATIVE COURSES
Applied Physics or Physics, Computer Science, Electronics, Geology, Geophysics, Materials Science, Mathematics, Meteorology, Mineral Sciences, Oceanography, Optometry.

BIOCHEMISTRY

(*indicates universities with the highest entry requirements)

SUBJECT REQUIREMENTS/PREFERENCES
GCE A-level: Chemistry, usually supported by another science subject; Physics, Mathematics or Biology often preferred.

SUBJECT INFORMATION
Biochemistry is the study of life processes at the molecular level, involving animals and plants. There are also applications in human and veterinary medicine, biotechnology, environmental science, agriculture and forestry. (For research ratings see also **Biological Sciences**.)

Aberdeen After introductory studies, Biochemistry courses cover molecular aspects of biotechnology and genetics. Industrial placements are available for some courses and there are exchanges in Europe and North America.

Aberystwyth The Biochemistry scheme presents the subject very much from the biological perspective with modules covering genetics, medical biochemistry, genomics and bioinformatics. There are opportunities for some students to join the Year in Employment scheme in Year 2.

Aston Biochemistry is available as three-year full-time or four-year sandwich degrees with Economics or Marketing. A degree is also offered in Biological Chemistry.

Bath* Biochemistry is a three-year full-time or four-year sandwich course. Biochemistry is taken with chemistry, genetics and cell biology in the first year, together with plant and animal physiology and microbiology. Professional placement takes place in the third term in Years 2 and 3. The Department of Biology and Biochemistry has a range of training placements in Europe and the USA, although these cannot be guaranteed. Students can switch courses up to the end of Year 1.

Birmingham* Years 1 and 2 are common, leading to specialist studies in Year 3. An additional year can be spent in industrial research or study in France, Spain or Germany. See also **Combined courses**. (High research rating)

Bristol* A study of biochemistry and chemistry is the focus of Year 1 of the Biochemistry course, plus an optional unit that can bias your programme towards molecular biology, medical biochemistry or general biochemistry. In Year 2 other units include genetics, pathology, pharmacology, and physiology and specialist options follow in Year 3. Degrees are available in Biochemistry with Medical Biochemistry and Biochemistry with Molecular Biology and Biotechnology. Transfer to Biochemistry with Study in Industry may be possible at the end of Year 1. (High research rating)

Bristol UWE Applied Biochemistry can be studied with Molecular Biology. A three-year or four-year sandwich course is offered in Biological and Medicinal Chemistry.

Brunel See under **Biological Sciences**.

Cambridge* Biochemistry is offered in Year 2 of the course in Natural Sciences. The normal route for intending biochemists is to take Biology of Cells in Part IA and Biochemistry and Molecular Biology in the second year. See also **Chemistry**. (High research rating)

Cardiff* Biochemistry is taught as a modular course in the School of Biosciences. There is a common first-year course after which students make a choice. Separate degree courses are offered in Anatomy, Neuroscience, Physiology and Pharmacology. A four-year course including a year in industry is available.

Central Lancashire Biochemistry, and Biochemistry with Biology or Forensic Science are offered as three-year full-time degree courses. Biochemistry is also offered as part of the combined honours programme.

Coventry Biochemistry is a three-year full-time or four-year sandwich course, the latter with Year 3 in professional training or industry. A range of options is available in the final year. There is also a European option with concurrent language study in all years from French, German, Italian or Spanish *ab initio*. Biochemistry is also offered with Chemistry or Pharmaceutical Chemistry.

Dundee The Biochemistry course covers chemistry and biology in Year 1 and life sciences with other modules in Year 2 prior to embarking on a specialised biochemistry programme in Years 3 and 4. Biochemistry can also be taken with Pharmacology or Physiology. See also **Biological Sciences**. (High research rating)

Durham* First-year Molecular Biology and Biochemistry students follow courses in botany, zoology and chemistry, and go on to specialist areas that include genetics, virology and immunology.

East Anglia* There is an introduction to biochemistry, cell and molecular biology and genetics in the first year of the Biochemistry courses, allowing students, if they wish, to transfer to degree courses in

Biological or Chemical Sciences. In the second year, biochemistry and molecular biology are taken with a selection from microbiology, physiology, protein engineering and biotechnology. In the third year, students make a selection from a range of subjects. Biochemistry can also be taken with a year in Australia, New Zealand, Europe, Canada or the USA.

East London Biochemistry is a modular degree involving cell and molecular biology, genetics, medical and plant biotechnology. There is the opportunity to switch between courses in life sciences (your specialist course on entry is not binding).

Edinburgh* There is a common first year for all Biochemistry students entering courses in the School of Biology. See also **Biological Sciences**.

Essex Biochemistry students take a course in biosciences in Year 1 that leads to a degree course in Biochemistry in Years 2 and 3. At the end of the first year it is possible to take Biomedical Sciences including biochemistry with cell biology. Students obtaining good marks in Year 2 and a satisfactory UKCAT test are guaranteed interviews for graduate entry for a medical school place at Queen Mary Medical School. Full-time and sandwich courses are available.

Exeter* A course is offered in Biological and Medicinal Chemistry designed for graduates who wish to take advantage of new opportunities in the rapidly expanding field of biotechnology.

Glasgow* In the Biochemistry course an optional one-year placement is offered between Levels 3 and 4. Courses in Medical Biochemistry and in Environmental Biogeochemistry are offered. See also **Biological Sciences**. (High research rating)

Greenwich See under **Biological Sciences**.

Heriot-Watt A four-year full-time course in Biochemistry is offered and there is also a course in Chemistry with Biochemistry.

Hertfordshire See under **Biological Sciences**.

Huddersfield A modular course in Biochemistry is offered, of three or four years (which includes Year 3 in employment) and the final year with research into a major study of selected specialisms including immunology, biotechnology, genetic engineering and medical biochemistry.

Imperial London* Biochemistry is taught on a course unit system with specialisms in Year 3. Seven courses can also be taken including a year in industry or abroad. Biochemistry with Management (three-year or four-year courses) and Biotechnology programmes are also available. (High research rating)

Keele Biochemistry is taken as a dual honours subject with a second subject and carries an emphasis on human biochemistry and disease. A sandwich placement of a year in industry is offered at the end of Year 2. Biochemistry can be taken in combination with a choice from over 17 other subjects.

Kent Biochemistry can be studied as a three-year or four-year (sandwich) degree, with a bias towards biotechnology, cell or molecular biology, medical biosciences, microbiology or physiology.

Kingston The Biochemistry course covers chemistry, physiology and computing with other modules in the biology of disease, microbiology, pharmacology, immunology and medical biochemistry, which is also available as a degree course.

Lancaster* Biological sciences, chemistry and one other subject are taken in the first year of the Biochemistry course. Specialisation then follows in Year 2. Courses include a Year 2 option to study abroad. Biochemistry with Genetics or Biomedicines is also offered.

Leeds* Biochemistry, a modular programme within the School of Biological Sciences, gives great flexibility of choice. Specialisms at Level 3 include plant and medical options. Biochemistry can also be taken with Chemistry. There is also a degree in Biotechnology. Scholarships available. (High research rating)

Leicester* Biochemistry is offered as part of the Biological Sciences programme. Modules from Medical School courses are taken in the first and second years of the course in Medical Biochemistry. See also **Biological Sciences**. (High research rating)

Liverpool* Courses in Biochemistry and Biochemistry (Year in Industry) are offered, the latter introduces work placement following Year 2. The course includes computer skills and options in biotechnology, immunology and studies relating to cancer. See also **Biological Sciences**.

Liverpool John Moores The School of Biomolecular Sciences offers full-time or sandwich courses in Biochemistry with Microbiology or Forensic Science, and also Medical Biochemistry and Applied Medical Biochemistry. All programmes have an optional industrial sandwich year.

London (King's)* Biochemistry has a common first year with other subjects in the Life Sciences field. A course is also offered in Biomedical Science and can be taken by way of a sandwich course.

London (QM)* After a common first year in biological science, options are introduced in the second year of the Biochemistry degree course with reference to drug action and chemical pharmacology. Project work is a component of third-year studies. Courses with Biochemistry are offered together with Microbiology, or Forensic Science.

London (RH)* Students following degree courses in Biochemistry and Molecular Biology share a common first-year programme and have the option to change courses at the end of the year. The Biomedical Science course includes physiology and a hospital experience course in the summer vacation of the second year. Specialist courses include nutrition, birth control, disease and pollution.

London (UCL)* Biochemistry is offered as a three-year full-time degree. It is taken alongside Molecular Biology in Year 1, the courses dividing in Year 2; transfers are possible. A Biotechnology degree is also offered. There is also a course in Biochemical Engineering with work placements and study abroad opportunities. (High research rating.)

London Metropolitan A three-year full-time course in Biochemistry is offered, with options in pharmacology, immunology and pathology.

London South Bank Biochemistry is offered as a part of the Bioscience programme.

Manchester* Biochemistry is offered as a three-year degree course, or as a four-year course if studied with a modern language, or with industrial experience. Medical Biochemistry can also be taken with industrial experience. There is a modular course structure within the Faculty of Life Sciences that allows for early transfer. Students choose second- and final-year modules in keeping with their career aspirations. (High research rating)

Newcastle* The Biochemistry degree shares a common first year with Genetics and covers DNA synthesis and repair, immunology, virus and plant biology. Students may then change courses after Stage 1. A three-year full-time course in Biochemistry and Immunology is also offered. (High research rating)

Nottingham* In the first year of the Biochemistry and Biological Chemistry course students take biochemistry, chemistry and a third subject, usually physiology and pharmacology, languages or maths. In the second and third years the teaching is shared equally between the Departments of Biochemistry and Chemistry leading to specialisms in pharmaceutical and agrochemical science, enzyme technology and toxicology. BSc courses in Nutritional Biochemistry and Biochemistry and Genetics are also offered.

Nottingham Trent See under **Biological Sciences**.

Oxford* There is a four-year course in Molecular and Cellular Biochemistry. The fourth year involves a research project which may extend to other areas such as Clinical Biochemistry, Pathology and Pharmacology for some students in one of several European universities. (High research rating)

Portsmouth All students taking Biological Sciences follow a common course for the first three semesters. Specialisation in Biochemistry starts in the fourth semester. Biochemistry is also offered with Forensic Biology and Microbiology.

Queen's Belfast In the first year the Biochemistry course focuses on chemistry and includes a 16 week work placement period. After Level 1 the flexible modular system enables students to decide which special degree programme they wish to follow including Enzymology, Genetics and Physiology. The degree with Professional studies includes a 40 week placement period.

Reading* There is a focus on Biology and Chemistry in the first year of the Biochemistry course followed by a specialised subject choice. A range of option modules can be studied in each year. A course in Biotechnology is also offered. See also **Biology**.

St Andrews* Biochemistry is offered as part of the Biology programme, the final choice of degree being made at the end of Year 2.

Salford The Biochemical Sciences course is offered in the School of Biological Sciences with modules in biological science and biochemical science being shared. A final degree decision is made at the end of the first year. There is also a Biochemical Sciences course with study in the USA and Biochemistry can also be studied with Physiology.

Sheffield* Biochemistry students take core units in the main subject and biology modules in Year 1. Further studies lead to medical and industrial applications. Biochemistry can also be studied with Genetics and Microbiology and there are also degrees in Biological Chemistry and Medical Biochemistry.

Southampton* Biochemistry includes molecular biology, pharmacology and physiology. The structure of courses in the School of Biological Sciences is extremely flexible and allows students to transfer between various single and combined degrees in the second and third years. Scholarships available.

Staffordshire A three-year full-time course is offered in Biochemistry and Microbiology, involving biomedicine and medical microbiology.

Strathclyde Five joint honours degrees are offered in Biochemistry, Biological and Biomedical Sciences allowing students to combine two subject options or more specialist degrees and enabling a choice of career paths in industry or the public sector.

Surrey* Five degree courses are available: Biochemistry, Biochemistry (Medical) (Toxicology) (Neuroscience) (Pharmacology). All are common for the first two years, allowing interchange up to the end of the second year. These are four-year courses, with the third year consisting of professional training away from the university. In the fourth year, Biochemistry students select three options from a wide range of modules. Scholarships available.

Sussex* Biochemistry is taught in the School of Biological Sciences and provides the opportunity to pursue different specialisms in the subject. It is offered as a three-year or four-year sandwich course. There is an optional sandwich year in industry.

Swansea The degree scheme is made up of modules covering a broad spectrum of topics covering the biochemistry of medicine and pharmacology, and environmental and physiological aspects. Courses are also offered in Biochemistry with Genetics or Zoology. There is also a degree in Medical Biochemistry.

Warwick* A common first year in the Department of Biological Science allows entrants to Biochemistry the option to transfer to degree courses in Microbiology and Virology, Microbiology and Biological Sciences at the end of the year. Options in the final year include industrial biology, oncology as well as other subjects, for example business, music, languages.

West Scotland Biochemistry is offered only in a joint course with Applied Bioscience.

Westminster Biochemistry can be taken as a single honours course or with free choice modules in each year.

Wolverhampton Biochemistry is a three-year full-time or four-year sandwich course taught on the flexible modular system with one or two other subjects including Food Science and Molecular Biology. The course covers biology, microbiology and pharmacology. Biochemistry can also be taken with Biomedical Science, Food Science or Pharmacology.

See *University Degree Course Offers* (Trotman Publishing) for details of offers

York* Biochemistry, Chemistry and Biology students are taught together for the first part of the course. In the remaining two parts, Biochemistry specialisms include major practical courses in microbiology and biophysical techniques and biology as well as a range of selected optional subjects. Placements in industry or at a European university are optional in Year 3. Weekly tutorials for all students, in groups of four, are a distinctive and effective feature.

OTHER INSTITUTIONS OFFERING BIOLOGY COURSES
See under **Biology**

ALTERNATIVE COURSES
Agricultural Sciences, Agriculture, Biological Sciences, Botany, Brewing, Chemistry, Food Science, Geochemistry, Medicine, Microbiology, Nutrition, Pharmacology and Pharmacy.

BIOLOGICAL SCIENCES

(including **Biomedical Sciences**)
(see also **Biochemistry, Biology** and **Biotechnology**)
(*indicates universities with the highest entry requirements)

SUBJECT REQUIREMENTS/PREFERENCES
GCE A-level: Two or three subjects from Mathematics/sciences; Chemistry usually essential.

SUBJECT INFORMATION
In many universities the Department or School of Biological Sciences will offer a modular programme covering subjects such as biochemistry, botany, biotechnology, genetics, physiology and zoology. This type of programme usually offers a common first year for all students, allowing them to make a final choice of single or joint degree course in Year 2. In other universities Biological Sciences is offered as a single named subject.

Aberdeen* Students applying for Biological Sciences at Aberdeen have a range of options covering Biomedical Sciences, Genetics, Immunology, Microbiology, Neuroscience, Physiology, Plant Biology and Zoology.

Abertay Dundee Flexible programmes are offered in Biomedical Sciences (bursaries available to eligible students) and Biotechnology, the latter focusing on animals, plants and the environment. There are also degree courses in Forensic Sciences (professionally accredited) and Forensic Psychobiology.

Aberystwyth The Institute of Biological, Environmental and Rural Sciences offers courses including Animal Behaviour, Biochemistry, Biology, Bioinformatics, Genetics, Life Sciences, Marine Biology, and Zoology.

Anglia Ruskin Biological Science is a modular course in which two specialisms are chosen in Year 2 from Medical, Cell and Molecular Biology or Medical Biology and Microbiology. There are also degree courses in Biomedical Science and Forensic Science, which can be taken with Criminology, Biomedical Science or Psychology. Courses are also offered in Animal Sciences.

Aston See under **Biology**.

Bangor The School of Ocean Sciences, one of the largest in Europe, also offers degree courses in Oceanography, Ocean Science and Marine Biology, Chemistry, Coastal Water Resourses and Ocean Informatics. Paid clinical laboratory placements in Year 2 of the course in Biomedical Science. See also **Biology**.

Bedfordshire The course in Biomedical and Medical Sciences consists of specialist areas covering Genetics, Microbiology, Nutrition, Pathology, Pharmacology and Physiology. There is also a degree in Forensic Science.

Birmingham Over 20 specialisms in Biological Sciences follow a common first and second year taken by all students. These cover Animal Biology, Biotechnology, Environmental Biology, Genetics, Microbiology or Conservation Biology. There is also an option to study in Continental Europe or in industry. (High research rating)

Bournemouth The Biological Sciences course covers a wide range of topics including biology, chemistry, ecology, toxicology, evolution and anthropology. The course offers a mixture of laboratory and fieldwork.

Bradford Cellular Pathology, Cancer Biology and Medical Biochemistry and Microbiology or Pharmacology can be taken as specialised options in Year 3 of the Biomedical Sciences course. There is also a Clinical Sciences degree that offers entry for some students to Medicine at Leeds.

Brighton The Biological Sciences course offers modules in cell biology, biochemistry, ecology, environmental biology and human physiology. Two or three of these are chosen in the final year. There are also degree courses in Applied Biomedical Sciences and Human Ecology; students on the former are employed by the Regional NHS Laboratory during their course.

Bristol* The largest department in the UK offers three subjects in Year 1 alongside a subsidiary subject. Flexibility continues in Years 2 and 3 when the subjects offered include biology, botany, zoology, biology and geology or geography and psychology and zoology. There are separate degree courses in Anatomy, Biology, Botany, Cellular and Molecular Medicine, Human Musculo-skeletal Science, Neuroscience, Pathology and Microbiology, Physiological Science and Zoology. (High research rating)

Bristol UWE Courses can be followed in Applied Biomedical Sciences, Conservation Biology, Biological Sciences, Human Biology, Microbiology, Forensic Science and Genetics. There are sandwich courses with some placements in Europe, the USA and the Far East.

Brunel* The Bioscience field offers six courses in Biomedical Sciences, and with specialisms in Biochemistry, Forensic Science, Genetics, Human Health and Immunology. All courses have a sandwich placement.

Cambridge* The course in Natural Sciences is the framework in which most science subjects are taught at Cambridge. It offers options in Astrophysics, Biochemistry, Biological and Biomedical Sciences, Chemistry, Genetics, Geological Sciences, History and Philosophy of Science, Materials Science, Neuroscience, Pathology, Pharmacology, Physical Sciences, Physics, Physiology, Development and Neuroscience, Plant Sciences, Psychology and Zoology. The course is of four years duration with specialisation taking place from Year 3. (High research rating)

Canterbury Christ Church There is a course in Forensic Investigation with modules in policing, jurisprudence and a subject module from another department. The Biosciences degree offers specialisations in general biological science, environmental science or physical science. Studies cover animal health and welfare, anatomy, physiology, ecology and conservation and an individual study in Year 3.

Cardiff* In the Biomedical Sciences course specialisations are offered in Applied Biology, Anatomical Science, Biology, Biotechnology, Ecology, Genetics, Microbiology or Zoology in the second and third years. Anatomical Sciences, Neuroscience, Physiology are also offered. Scholarships available.

Cardiff (UWIC) Biomedical Science can be taken focusing on Biology, Forensic Toxicology or Sport.

Central Lancashire The Biological Sciences degree is modular offering studies in biology, genetics, biochemistry, physiology and pharmacology. There are also degree courses in Biomedical Science, Neuroscience, Forensic Science, Human Physiology and Microbiology which is also offered jointly with seven other subjects.

Chester Single and combined honours courses are offered in Biomedical Sciences. Courses are vocational leading to careers in industry and the health services.

Coventry Biological Sciences degrees are offered, including a study placement year in the UK or in Europe and an opportunity to specialise in several subjects in Year 3 including Biotechnology, Genetics and Biomedical Sciences. Courses in Forensic Science are also offered.

Cumbria A degree in Forensic Science has modules in evidence, criminal law, drugs and genetics.

De Montfort Several courses are offered including Forensic Science, Clinical Technology, and Medical Sciences.

Derby Courses are offered in Forensic Science with Criminology and Conservation Biology.

Dundee Twenty-two courses in Biological Sciences cover Biology, Biomedical Sciences, Microbiology, Pharmacology and Zoology. Degrees in Anatomical Sciences and Physiological Sciences are also offered and also a course in Sports Medicine.

Durham* All Biological programmes have a common first year leading on to specialisms in Biology, Cell Biology, Ecology, Plant Sciences and Zoology, all with or without industrial placement. This is also available as part of the programme in Natural Sciences and with Education Studies. Biomedical Sciences is also offered at the Stockton campus.

East Anglia* Biological Sciences are offered as three-year or four-year courses. Degree programmes in Ecology are offered covering climate change, pollution, intensive agriculture and ecosystems destruction. Courses are also offered in Australia, Europe and North America. Plant Biology, Microbiology and a Biomedicine degree are also available with the opportunity to steer one's degree to preferred specialities. Optional modules include drug design, career biology and human nutrition, diet and health.

East London A course is offered in Biomedical Sciences, with an optional sandwich placement. There are also degrees in Biomedical Sciences, Chemical Sciences, Immunology, Medical Biotechnology, Forensic Science and Clinical Physiology.

Edinburgh* The School of Biology offers degrees in Biochemistry, Biological Sciences, Developmental Biology, Biotechnology, Ecology, Genetics, Immunology, Infectious Diseases, Medical Microbiology, Molecular Biology, Neuroscience, Pharmacology, Physiology, Plant Science, Virology and Zoology. Students cover a broad curriculum in Year 1, taking up to six courses. Several combinations are possible, the final choice of subject being made at the end of Year 3. (High research rating)

Essex* In the first year students follow a pathway covering a range of subjects thus enabling a choice of degree to be made at a later stage. Degrees are offered in Biological Sciences, Genetics, Ecology, Marine and Freshwater Biology and Biodiversity and Conservation. Scholarships available. (High research rating)

Exeter* Single honours Biological Sciences students take core modules from cell structure and physiology, genetics, microbiology, biochemistry, animal physiology, plant physiology, animal biology, plant biology, biological investigation, animal and plant populations and human impact on the biosphere. Non-core biological options, such as geography, psychology, chemistry etc, can then be taken. Courses are also offered in Biological and Medicinal Chemistry, Human Biosciences and, in Cornwall, Conservation, Biology and Ecology.

Glamorgan Courses are available in Microbiology or Forensic Science.

Glasgow* Several specialist Biological Science subjects are offered by the Institute of Biological and Life Sciences that can be taken in Years 1 and 2 with other subjects in the Faculty of Science. Subjects covered include Anatomy, Aquatic Bioscience, Biomedical Science, Biomolecular Sciences, Genetics, Immunology, Microbiology, Neuroscience, Parasitology, Psychology and Zoology. In addition, degrees are offered in Pharmacology, Sports Medicine, Ecology and Marine Sciences.

Glasgow Caledonian Human Biosciences offers specialisation in Biomolecular Sciences, Microbiology or Physiological Sciences. There are degree courses in Biomedical Sciences (with work placement), Forensic Investigation, Food Bioscience and Microbiology.

Gloucestershire Biological Sciences and Animal Biology are offered as single and joint honours courses with work placement opportunities.

Glyndŵr Degrees are offered in Forensic Science and/with Criminal Justice. Part-time study is also available.

Greenwich Biosciences is a broad-based course offering specialisms in medical physiology, biological sciences, medical biochemistry, biochemistry or molecular biology. At the end of Year 2 it is possible to change to other life science degrees. It can be taken on a sandwich basis and combined with European study. Degrees in Biomedical Science and Forensic Science are also offered.

Heriot-Watt All courses in Biological Sciences follow a common core of subjects in Years 1 and 2. In addition Biological Sciences courses focus on Cell Biology, Food Science, Human Health or Microbiology. Applied Marine Biology, Biochemistry, and Brewing and Distilling are also offered.

Hertfordshire The School of Biosciences offers degrees in Applied Biology, Biochemistry, Biotechnology, Biological Science, Biomedical Sciences, Forensic Science, Microbiology, Molecular Biology and Physiology. Most Science courses offer a year in Europe or North America. Human Physiology and Pharmacology are offered within the Applied Biology course.

Huddersfield Courses are offered in Forensic and Analytical Science, Microbiology, Medical Genetics and Applied Science.

Hull Courses are offered in Aquatic Zoology, Biology, Human Biology and Marine and Freshwater Biology (including oceanograpy) with optional diving training, and Biomedical Science.

Imperial London* There is a very large Faculty of Life Sciences covering a range of courses in Biochemistry, Biotechnology, Biology, Biomedical Science, Microbiology, Ecology and Zoology.

Keele Biomedical Science is offered as a single honours course. Forensic Science can be taken with other subjects. See also **Biology**.

Kent The Department of Biosciences offers programmes of study in Biological Sciences, Biochemistry, Microbiology and Molecular and Cellular Biology. In all cases a sandwich degree or a year in Europe is an option, adding an extra year to the three-year degree. There are also courses in Conservation, Biomedical Sciences and Forensic Science. (High research rating)

Kingston Courses are offered in Biomedical Sciences and Forensic Science.

Lancaster* Biological Sciences is a very flexible modular course giving students a chance to tailor their own course. Specialisation begins in Years 2 and 3. There is also an option to study abroad. Biological Sciences is also offered with Biomedicine. A Biomedical Science course and two Ecology courses are also offered (one with a year abroad). (High research rating)

Leeds* Degrees in Ecology, Genetics and Human Genetics form part of the Biology programme. There are also degrees in Microbiology, Nanotechnology and Neuroscience, Physiology and Zoology. There is also a course in Medical Sciences for students interested in focusing on health careers. The Biological Science degree does not assume a strong background in chemistry. Scholarships available.

Leeds Metropolitan Biomedical Sciences can be taken with Microbiology, Physiology and Pharmacology.

Leicester* The School of Biological Sciences offers eight courses of three- and four-year duration; all with a common first year: the latter may involve a sandwich placement abroad. Courses focus on Biochemistry, Genetics, Microbiology, Physiology with Pharmacology or Zoology. There are also courses in Medical Bio-chemistry and Medical Genetics. See also **Combined courses**. Scholarships available. (High research rating)

Lincoln Courses are offered in Biomedical Science and Forensic Science. The former covers microbiology, pathology, biochemistry and immunology.

Liverpool* A large number of subjects are offered, with specialist studies being chosen in Year 3. Current specialisms in the Biological Sciences course include Biochemistry, Biology, Marine Biology, Biotechnology, Environmental Biology, Genetics, Microbiology, Tropical Disease Biology, Zoology and Biological and Medical Sciences.

Liverpool John Moores The Biomedical Science course has an optional sandwich year in employment. There is also a degree in Forensic Science.

London (King's)* The School of Biomedical and Health Sciences offers a flexible programme with a common first year, leading to a choice of specialist subjects in Years 2 and 3. These include Biochemistry, Biomedical Sciences, Human Sciences, Genetics, Neuroscience, Pharmacology and Physiology.

London (QM)* Course units are offered in Biological and Chemical Sciences leading to degrees in Biochemistry, Biology, Chemistry, Forensic Science, Genetics, Biomedical Science, Pharmacological Chemistry and Zoology.

London (RH)* The degree in Biomedical Science covers the study of disease, clinical diagnosis, immunology, neuroscience and the physiology of sport and exercise. Some special Year 3 options are taught at St George's. Scholarships available.

London (St George's) A study of a range of biological science subjects including physiology and pharmacology, which underpin medicine are studied in the Biomedical Science degree.

London (UCL) BSc and MSc Biological Sciences degrees are offered separating after the second year. There are also courses in Biomedical Science, Human Sciences and Neuroscience.

London Metropolitan Biological Sciences can be taken with Chemistry, Sports Science or Consumer Studies. Degrees are also offered in Biomedical Sciences, Medical Biosciences and Microbiology.

London South Bank The degree in Biosciences offers specialist studies in Biochemistry, Microbiology and Nutrition. The Applied Science course focuses on the biological sciences. There is also a degree in Forensic Science.

Manchester* The Faculty of Life Sciences offers a wide range of courses coupled with considerable flexibility to change direction as career plans develop. Subjects offered cover Anatomical Sciences, Biochemistry, Biology, Biomedical Sciences, Biotechnology, Cell Biology, Genetics, Life Sciences, Medical Biochemistry, Microbiology, Molecular Biology, Neuroscience, Pharmacology, Physiology, Plant Science, and Zoology.

Manchester Metropolitan Degrees available include Biomedical and Forensic Science, Physiology, Microbiology and Wildlife Ecology and Behaviour.

Middlesex A Biosciences course is offered which includes microbiology and immunology. There are also courses in Biomedical Science and Sports Biomedicine.

Napier The three-year or four-year sandwich course in Biological Sciences allows specialisation in Microbiology, Biomedical Science, Toxicology, Animal Biology and Human Biology.

Newcastle* Courses are offered in Biological Sciences (Deferred choice), in which the final choice of degree is made at the end of Year 1. Options include Genetics, Management, Medical Microbiology and Pharmocology. See also **Biology**.

Northumbria Biomedical Sciences is a three-year full-time or four-year sandwich course available as a single honours (including an optional year abroad) or combined with Chemistry. There are also degrees in Forensic Science, Biotechnology and Human Biosciences.

Nottingham* A three-year course is offered in Biotechnology, and in addition there are courses in Genetics, Food Microbiology, and Neuroscience. (High research rating)

Nottingham Trent The Biological Science degree has pathways in Biomedical Science, Biochemistry, Microbiology, Ecology and Pharmacology. Three Forensic Science degrees are also offered.

Oxford* The Honours School of Biological Sciences covers biochemistry, biology and physiological science. The essence of this course is flexibility and the choice exists of specialising in plant studies, animal studies, environmental biology or cell biology. A degree is offered in Human Sciences covering the biology of organisms, genetics and evolution, sociology and social anthropology and populations. In Years 2 and 3 there are several optional papers including psychology and languages. There is also a degree in Physiological Sciences.

Oxford Brookes Single and combined honours courses are offered in Biomedical Sciences, Biotechnology and Molecular Biology each with study abroad opportunities.

Plymouth Biological Sciences is a modular course covering ecology, plant science, microbial and cellular biology, human and marine biology. Specialisation can be delayed. Each area may be studied as a specialist degree or combined with other subjects. There are also courses in Human Biosciences and Biomedical Science. There is also an extensive range of marine subjects. Scholarships available.

Portsmouth Subjects taken in the first three semesters are common to all students. These are followed by a choice of pathways in Biology, Biochemistry, Environmental Biology, Genome Science and Forensic Biology.

Queen's Belfast* The Biological Sciences course provides an in-depth study of biochemistry, biological diversity, environmental biology, genetics and molecular biology and micro-organisms. In the final honours year, projects are offered in biochemistry, environmental biology, plant science, marine biology, genetics, microbiology and zoology. Degrees are also offered in Genetics, Microbiology and Biomedical Science, Physiology, Anatomy, Biomedical Sciences and Zoology. Scholarships available.

Reading* A whole range of modules cover Botany, Biomedical Science, Biotechnology (with industrial training) and Microbiology. Specialisation takes place in Year 3. See also **Biology.**

Robert Gordon Four year full-time degrees are offered in Biomedical Science, and Forensic Science with placements in Years 2 and 3.

Roehampton All areas of biology are covered in Year 1 of the Biological Sciences course. In Years 2 and 3, the main topics focus on human biology, organisms and ecology, and molecular biology and physiology. Biomedical Sciences is offered as a single honours subject, as is Zoology and Conservation Biology. Combined honours are offered in Biological Sciences, Biological Anthropology and Human Biosciences.

St Andrews* See under **Biology**.

Salford The Biological Sciences course has an applied biology emphasis and a common first year with Biochemical Science (which has a biochemistry emphasis). The final choice of course is made at the end of Year 1. Year 3 can be spent in industry or in the USA. There are also courses in Human Biology with Infectious Diseases and Physiology.

Sheffield* A wide range of courses is offered, including Biomedical Science, Microbiology and Genetics. All students follow the same course in Years 1 and 2, and specialise in Year 3. (High research rating)

Sheffield Hallam There is a course in Biological Sciences for Business and courses in Human and Forensic Biosciences.

Southampton* Biomedical Sciences has a common first year with other subjects in the School of Biological Sciences. Options can be taken in other subjects outside the field. Scholarships available. (See also **Biochemistry**.)

Staffordshire Biomedical Sciences, Biochemistry and Forensic Science courses are offered by way of a flexible modular system allowing for a change of degree at the end of Year 1.

Stirling Aquaculture, Ecology and Freshwater Science are offered as four-year degrees; Aquatic Science as a three-year course.

Strathclyde See under **Biochemistry**.

Sunderland The Biomedical Sciences degree focuses on human health and biology.

Surrey* The course in Biomedical Science includes biochemistry, physiology and pharmacology, with practical training in clinically relevant techniques. Optional subjects such as microbiology, nutrition and food science can also be studied. Courses involving Microbiology are offered with specialisms in medicine, food science and genetics. There are also Food Science and Biotechnology degrees.

Sussex* A course is offered in Biomedical Sciences covering genetics, neuroscience and cell biology. An optional sandwich year is also available. See also **Biology**.

Swansea The deferred choice allows Biological Sciences students to delay their choice of degree specialisation until the end of the first year, while the alternative course allows students to specialise in two areas of biological sciences, eg, biochemistry, genetics or zoology. There is also a degree in Medical Sciences which enables students to apply for graduate entry to medical schools. Courses are also offered in Clinical Physiology and Zoology.

Ulster There is a degree in Biomedical Science and an option to study abroad in Marine Sciences. See also **Biology**.

Warwick* Biological Sciences is a flexible course. Students opt for Biochemistry, Cell Biology, Biological Sciences, Environmental Biology, Biomedical Science, Biomedical Chemistry, Chemical Biology, Microbiology, or Virology. Opportunities exist for late decisions and transfers between courses. A good first class or upper second degree in biological sciences may admit students to the four-year medical degree at the Leicester Warwick Medical School.

West Scotland Courses are offered in Bioscience with pathways in Biochemistry, Environmental Science, Forensic Investigation, Immunology, Microbiology, Multimedia, Psychology and Zoology. There is also a course in Biomedical Science.

Westminster Biological Sciences subjects share common modules, with specialism possible in biomedical science, biotechnology, biochemistry, or microbiology. There is also a course in Biomedical Science.

Wolverhampton The Biological Sciences course with an optional third year in industry, enables students to specialise in specific areas of biotechnology, animal biology, microbiology, biochemistry, physiology, genetics, plant science and food science. These subjects can be taken as specialist subjects or as combined studies. There are also courses in Biomedical Science, Forensic Science, Genetics, Microbiology and Physiology.

Worcester After a common first year students choose a specialist pathway from Animal Biology, Biology, Ecology, Human Biology, Human Nutrition or Plant Science.

OTHER INSTITUTIONS OFFERING BIOLOGICAL SCIENCE COURSES
See under **Biology**.

ALTERNATIVE COURSES
Agriculture, Bacteriology, Biochemistry, Biology, Botany, Dentistry, Ecology, Environmental Sciences, Forestry, Medicine, Pharmacology, Pharmacy, Speech Science.

BIOLOGY

(see also **Biological Sciences**)
(*indicates universities with the highest entry requirements)

SUBJECT REQUIREMENTS/PREFERENCES
GCE A-level: Chemistry and another science, usually Biology. **GCSE:** Mathematics and English stipulated in some cases.

SUBJECT INFORMATION

Biology courses usually are more specialised than Biological Sciences with such options as aquatic biology, human biology, animal and plant biology. Many of these options are also offered on Applied Biology courses. (For research ratings see also **Biological Sciences**.)

Aberdeen A degree course in Biology is offered leading to a wide range of specialisations including Agriculture, Biology, Biotechnology, Environmental Science, Marine Biology and Zoology. Degrees in Biomedical Sciences, Conservation Biology and Ecology are also available.

Aberystwyth The Biology course will be of interest to those wishing to study molecular biology, cellular and physiological aspects of biology, with modules offered in genetics, plant physiology, microbiology and immunology. There are also degree courses in Marine and Freshwater Biology, Environmental Biology, Genetics, Microbiology, Life Sciences, Plant Biology and Zoology. Biology can also be taken with Sports Science.

Anglia Ruskin Courses are offered in Cell and Molecular Biology, Forensic Biology, Wildlife Biology, Marine Biology, Equine Studies, Ecology and Conservation, Genetics, Biomedical Science, Natural History and Zoology.

Aston* The Applied and Human Biology sandwich course emphasises human biology, reflecting the relevance of biology to medicine and human beings with the environment. The programme builds from a broad biological foundation into a selection of specialist options including a range of biomedical topics including immunology, medical biochemistry, pharmacology, and neurobiology. There are also additional degree courses in Cell and Molecular Biology, Human Biology, and Infection and Immunity. Business, Sociology, Psychology or Languages can also be taken with Biology.

Bangor Optional modules including languages, form part of the first year courses in the degrees in Biology, Molecular Biology, Cancer Biology (currently only four other courses in the UK), Ecology and Zoology with Animal Behaviour, Animal Ecology, Conservation or Marine Zoology.

Bath* A flexible programme is offered covering Biology and Molecular and Cellular Biology, and Biochemistry with three-year or four-year courses and placements in industry in the UK, Belgium, France, Finland or Switzerland are possible. (High research rating.) See also **Biochemistry**.

Bath Spa A very broad study of biology, covering a range of biological subjects including marine biology, environmental management and ecology.

Birmingham* Core subjects are offered in Year 1 of this Human Biology degree. The course is very flexible and students choose from a wide range of options in Year 3 including bacterial and viral diseases, genetics and neurobiology. An optional year in professional placement is also possible. There are also courses in Medical Sciences, Biomedical Materials, Science and Bioinformatics. (High research rating)

Bolton Three Biology pathways are offered in Animal Biology or Ecology and Conservation or in Molecular Sciences.

Bournemouth See under **Biological Sciences**.

Bradford See under **Biological Sciences**.

Brighton Courses are offered in Biogeography and Human Ecology. There is also a joint science programme in which Biology can be combined with Geography.

Bristol* Biology is offered as a single honours course and with Geology and Mathematics. There are also several Cancer Biology courses combined with Immunology and Virology with the option to study in industry as part of the courses. (High research rating.) A degree in Anatomy with optional units in biomedical sciences and human and veterinary anatomy.

Bristol UWE A degree is offered in Biology and IT in Science developing the theoretical and practical skills with the effective use of IT in science, data collection, interpretation and storage. There are also courses in Human, Sports and Conservation Biology.

Brunel* See under **Biological Sciences**. (High research rating)

Cambridge* The Biology of Cells and Organisms, is offered as Part I of the Natural Sciences Tripos. This is the framework within which most science is taught in Cambridge and includes the biological and physical sciences, materials and earth science and the history and philosophy of science. All students in Year 1 study three experimental sciences usually including one they have not met previously. In Years 2 and 3 specialised courses are followed in animal biology and cell and developmental biology. Courses are also offered in Biological Sciences with Education. (High research rating)

Canterbury Christ Church A broad study of the sciences leads to the degree in Environmental Biology.

Cardiff* There is a common first year for Biology and Applied Biology which covers cells, microbes, physiology, evolution, ecology, biological chemistry, maths, statistics and computing. Students then choose their special study in Year 2 leading to a degree in Applied Biology, Biology, Biotechnology, Ecology and Environmental Management, Genetics, Microbiology or Zoology. This is a three-year full-time or four-year sandwich course.

Central Lancashire A degree is offered in Medical Biology with core units in human physiology, genetics, microbiology and nutrition. Specialist areas include pharmacology, physiology, immunology and food microbiology.

Chester The Biology Department focuses on animal, behaviour, environmental, nutrition, ecology, human and biomedical aspects of the subject. There is also a degree course in Forensic Biology also in combination with such subjects as Psychology, Law, Biology or Criminology.

Cumbria There are courses in Conservation Biology and Forensic Science.

Derby Courses are offered in Biology (which can include a study abroad), Conservation and Chemical Biology. There is also a joint course with Zoology.

Dundee Students following the Biology course take a range of subjects in the first and second year science courses. They then proceed to an honours course in Biology, with modules available in botany, ecology, microbiology and zoology in the Department of Biological Sciences.

Durham* All departments in the Faculty of Science offer main, double main, main and subsidiary or subsidiary units that lead to single or joint honours degrees in Natural Science. The first year course in Biology includes genetics, biochemistry, animal and plant biology, physiology, ecology and behaviour. Further core subjects are taken in Year 2 and in Year 3 a modular scheme allows for considerable specialisation.

East Anglia* The School of Biology offers a wide range of courses covering Plant Biology, Cell Biology, Molecular Biology and Genetics and Microbiology. There is considerable flexibility in there programmes allowing students to specialise as their subject interests develop. There are also opportunities to study in Europe, North America or Australia. (High research rating)

East London Applied Biology has modules in genetics, microbiology, medical biochemistry and pharmacology.

Edge Hill The Biology degree has a strong practical base and covers plant and animal studies and marine communities. Residential field courses are free of charge. There is also a degree in Biogeography.

Edinburgh* See under **Biological Sciences**.

Glamorgan Biology is a three-year full-time or four-year sandwich course studying living organisms, their structure and survival mechanisms. Core modules include zoology, physiology, genetics, plant and animal diversity, and physiological ecology. Biology can be studied as part of a combined honours programme and there are degrees in Human Biology, and International Wildlife Biology.

Glasgow* A flexible course structure allows for late decisions on all specialist subjects. All students take three subjects from a wide choice in Year 1. Named degree subjects include Anatomy, Animal Biology, Biochemistry, Biomedical Sciences, Aquatic Bioscience, Genetics, Immunology, Marine Biology, Microbiology, Molecular and Cellular Biology, Neuroscience, Physiology, Parasitology, Plant Science, Virology and Zoology. Some courses involve work placements. (High research rating)

Glasgow Caledonian Human Biology is a multidisciplinary course with sociology and psychology.

Gloucestershire The degrees in Animal Biology and Biology both have optional year placements.

Heriot-Watt See under **Biological Sciences**.

Hertfordshire See under **Biological Sciences**.

Huddersfield The Biology course has optional work placements in Year 3. Final year options include immunology, medical biology and DNA technology. There are also courses in Human, Medical and Sport Biology. There are also separate degrees in Human and Medical Biology. Medical Genetics and Microbial Sciences also with optional placements.

Hull After taking Biology in Year 1 it is possible to transfer to degrees in Marine and Freshwater Biology, Aquatic Zoology with a Fisheries option, Biomedical Sciences and Biomolecular and Biomedical Science. There is also a course in Coastal Marine Biology. A Biology course is also combined with ornithology

Imperial London* The Biology department offers three-year courses in Biology, Biology with Management, Microbiology, Ecology and Zoology, and four-year courses in Biology with a year in Europe, management or research. All courses lead to the award of the BSc degree. (High research rating)

Keele* The Biology dual honours course offers modules in cell biology and biochemistry, behaviour and ecology, genetics, plant and animal physiology. There are also courses in Biomedical Sciences, Forensic Science and Neuroscience. There are also 29 subjects combinations in the dual honours programme including Human Biology.

Kent* The Biology degree may be taken with options in industry or study abroad. There is also a course in Forensic Biology with an optional year in industry.

Kingston The Biology degree enables students to follow a broad-based course in the biological sciences or to focus on environmental biology or biotechnology at Levels 2 and 3. There are also courses in Forensic and Human Biology.

Lancaster* Courses are offered in Cell Biology and Environmental Biology, the latter with possible placements in North America or Australia. Biology can also be taken with Geography and Psychology.

Leeds* A popular degree giving either breadth of study or the opportunity to specialise and change to Zoology or Ecology in Year 3.

Leeds Metropolitan The Biomedical Sciences programme has pathways in Health, Microbiology, Physiology and Human Biology.

Liverpool* The Life Sciences Unit scheme provides flexibility by enabling students to select a range of units related to the choice of degree including courses applicable to Medicine. Applied Biology is also available on a four-year sandwich course – students specialising in one of plant science, environmental biology, genetics, marine biology, zoology and molecular biology. See also **Biological Sciences**.

Liverpool Hope A combined honours course in Human Biology leads to a BA/QTS. Other popular combinations include Health and Psychology.

Liverpool John Moores Biology can be taken with an optional sandwich year.

London (King's)* Courses are offered covering Cell Biology (Biomolecular Sciences) and Human Biology (Human Sciences).

London (QM)* Courses include Biology, Biology with Psychology and Aquatic Biology. (High research rating.) See also **Biological Sciences**.

London (RH)* The School of Biological Sciences offers courses in Biology and Biology with Psychology. Geology is also offered with Biology.

London (UCL)* The course provides a broad and flexible Biology programme and also acts as an entry route for those who decide to transfer to more specialised degrees including Cellular and Molecular Biology, Environmental Biology and the Biology of Fertility and Embryo Development. (High research rating)

Loughborough Degree courses are offered in Human Biology and Ergonomics (Human Factors Design) which includes Psychology, Anatomy and Physiology.

Manchester* Biology is offered with industrial experience, a modern language or Science and Society, or as a single honours course. Biology is also part of the life sciences programme. (High research rating)

Manchester Metropolitan Biology is offered by way of a large number of joint courses. Human or Life Style Biology can also be taken as single honours degrees.

Napier Animal, Environmental, Forensic and Marine and Freshwater Biology are offered as three-year or four-year full-time courses or as five-year sandwich courses.

Newcastle* The wide range of Biology degrees offered includes: Animal Science (with options in companion animal studies or livestock technology); Applied Biology (with options involving biochemistry, microbiology and biotechnology); Marine Biology, and Zoology. Under a Biological Sciences deferred choice scheme, students can choose their final degree at the end of the first year.

Northampton Biology can be taken as a single honours subject and in addition there are over 20 joint courses in Biological Conservation. The Human Biosciences course covers genomics, neuroscience and health topics.

Northumbria Applied Biology (which can be taken jointly with Forensic Biology) is offered as a three-year full-time or four-year sandwich course with an emphasis on laboratory and analytical methods. There is also a course in Biology and Forensic Biology.

Nottingham* A comprehensive Biology course is offered covering microbiology, plant, animal and human biology plus a wide range of specialisms. Courses are also offered in Applied Biology, Biotechnology and Environmental Biology. (High research rating)

Nottingham Trent The course in Biology offers themes in living systems, clinical biochemistry, genetics, human systems and immunology. There are also courses in Animal Science and Biotechnology.

Oxford* Biology is taken as part of the course in Biological Sciences. The Human Sciences course open to science and arts applicants covers animal behaviour, ecology, populations and society and social geography.

Oxford Brookes* Degree courses are offered in Biology, Environmental Biology, Human Biology (with work placement) and Conservation Biology as a pathway in Environmental Sciences. All are offered as single or joint courses.

Plymouth The Biological Science course provides an overview of biological topics and includes options in biochemistry, microbiology, plant science and health and disease. There are also courses in Environmental and Marine Biology and Coastal Ecology, Toxicology, and Human Sciences.

Portsmouth After a common first three semesters, Biology students choose one of the elective streams leading to a range of named degrees including Environmental and Forensic Biology. See also **Biological Sciences**.

See *University Degree Course Offers* (Trotman Publishing) for details of offers

Queen Margaret Human Biology is a four year multidisciplinary course covering aspects of biochemistry, microbiology, health biology, nutrition, health psychology and sociology. The degree leads to a variety of scientific and health-related careers.

Queen's Belfast* A broad modular course in Environmental Biology is offered covering natural and human environments and providing pathways in Environmental Biology, Biological Sciences, Marine Biology and Paleobiology.

Reading* The Biological Science programme provides a wide range of modules allowing students to specialise in chosen fields covering biological subjects. Alternatively it is possible to change degrees to Biomedical Sciences, Biochemistry, Botany, Medical Microbiology or Zoology. See also **Biochemistry** and **Biological Sciences**.

Roehampton See under **Biological Sciences**.

St Andrews* After a broad first year, Biology students can specialise in one of eleven specialist areas, including biochemistry, human, animal and plant biology, cell biology, ecology, and genetics. (High research rating)

Sheffield* Several biology courses are offered with a modular format which enables the student to select from several subject specialisms with opportunities to study abroad. There are also degrees combining conservation, languages and archaeology. (High research rating.)

Sheffield Hallam A degree in Human Biology is offered with industrial placement in Year 3. The main focus lies in a study of human physiology leading to careers in healthcare and medical applications.

Southampton* Courses offered by the department are based on a unit structure with a common first year (units in cell biology, ecology, genetics and biochemistry) after which students can specialise. Courses are also offered in Marine Biology, Oceanography and Zoology.

Staffordshire All Biology students take core modules at Level 1 with transfers possible at the end of this stage. Courses offered include Biology, Human Biology, and Biology with Sport and Health or Forensic Science.

Stirling After an introductory course, students can proceed to specialist areas including animal physiology, plant physiology, ecology, marine and freshwater biology and aquatic science.

Strathclyde* See under **Biochemistry**.

Sussex* A broad range of biology courses are taken in Years 1 and 2 followed by specialist options in Year 3.

Swansea* First-year Biology students take two other subjects in the biological sciences as well as biology, or they may take botany, zoology and one other subject from geography, psychology, or mathematics methods. In the second year, course work covers genetics, biochemistry, cell and molecular biology, plant and animal biology. There is also a research project. The final year is devoted to a specialised area. Courses are also offered in Marine Biology and Environmental Biology.

Teesside Applied Biology and Forensic Biology are offered as full-time or sandwich courses.

Ulster The first year of the course in Biology is taken in common with degrees in Biomedical Sciences, Molecular Bioscience, Human Nutrition, and Food and Nutrition thus allowing transfers in Year 2.

Warwick* See under **Biological Sciences**.

West Scotland Environmental Biology is available with specialist studies in a wide range of subjects in Years 3 and 4.

Westminster Courses are available in Human and Medical Science and Forensic Biology.

Wolverhampton Animal Biology and Ecology and Applied Biology courses are on offer. Biology joint courses are also available with Computing, Psychology, Environmental Science, Geography and Business.

Worcester The course in Forensic and Applied Biology offers extensive practical training. Validation by the Forensic Science Society is being sought. See also **Biological Sciences**.

York* Five courses are offered, Biology, Molecular Cell Biology Genetics, Biotechnology and Ecology with option for a year in Europe or industry. First-year modules include genetics, evolution and ecology leading on to a choice of nine programmes. Students may also elect to transfer to the Biology with Education course at the end of Year 1. (High research rating)

OTHER INSTITUTIONS OFFERING BIOLOGY COURSES
Bishop Burton (Coll), Blackpool Fylde (Coll), Cornwall (Coll), Halton Riverside (Coll), Loughborough (Coll), SAC, St Mary's (UC), South Devon (Coll), Southport (Coll), Suffolk (Univ Campus), Truro (Coll), Warwickshire (Coll), Writtle (Coll).

ALTERNATIVE COURSES
Agriculture, Bacteriology, Biochemistry, Botany, Dentistry, Ecology, Environmental Health, Environmental Science, Forestry, Medicine, Microbiology, Pharmacology, Pharmacy, and Speech Science.

BIOTECHNOLOGY

(*indicates universities with the highest entry requirements)

SUBJECT REQUIREMENTS/PREFERENCES
GCE A-level: Chemistry usually required with two–three mathematics/science subjects.
GCSE: Mathematics grade A–C.

SUBJECT INFORMATION
Biotechnology is an interdisciplinary subject that can cover specialisms in agriculture, biochemistry, microbiology, genetics, chemical engineering, biophysics etc. (Courses in these named subjects should also be explored.)

Birmingham* Biotechnology is offered as a specialisation of the degree course in Biological Sciences.

Bradford An optional year in industry is offered to those choosing the degree course in Applied Biotechnology. Third year specialisms are linked to careers in the industry.

Bristol UWE The three or four-year course includes an optional placement year in industry in the UK or overseas.

Cardiff* The Biotechnology course covers most areas of biological science, and also aspects of medicine and agriculture. There are seven biological degrees, all served by the same broadly based first year, with the specialism in Biotechnology following in Years 2 and 3.

City A course is offered in Biomedical Engineering with Applied Physics.

East London The Medical Biotechnology course has a one-year industrial placement and involves a study of genetics and biology.

Edinburgh* A course in Biotechnology is offered as part of the Biological Sciences programme.

Glasgow* A multidisciplinary Biotechnology course covers micro-organisms, animals, plants and industrial and agricultural processes.

Hertfordshire Final-year courses in Biotechnology cover biochemistry, microbiology and molecular biology plus applied aspects such as industrial enzymology, fermentation and process technology.

Kingston Biotechnology is an option in the Biology degree.

Leeds* The Biotechnology course offers advanced studies in the biotechnology of medicine, chemical engineering, genetics and industrial and environmental microbiology, science, medical aspects of biotechnology and computer modelling, protein structure and drug design.

Liverpool* In the Microbial Biotechnology course 12 weeks are spent in industry. See also **Biological Sciences**.

Liverpool John Moores The three-year full-time or four-year Biotechnology sandwich course covers aspects of manufacturing techniques in agriculture and medicine, placing emphasis on the manipulation of micro-organisms and plants.

London (UCL)* Chemistry, cellular and molecular biology, microbiology, biological engineering and experimental biochemistry are studied in a common first-year programme in Biological Sciences. These strands carry on into Years 2 and 3 with a wide range of options, and a final-year research project is undertaken in one of these main areas.

Manchester* The course in Biotechnology provides a preparation for the commercial application of biological systems and can include a year of industrial experience.

Newcastle* The Biotechnology degree has a strong basis in biomolecular sciences including molecular biology, biochemistry, genetics and microbiology.

Northumbria The Biotechnology degree provides comprehensive coverage of scientific industrial applications.

Nottingham* The emphasis is on food production aspects of biotechnology. The degree can also be taken with a European placement following Year 2.

Oxford Brookes Single and combined honours degrees in Biotechnology are offered. Options include DNA technology, cell biology, immunology and virology.

Reading* The first-year course is the same for Biotechnology, Food Science and Food Technology, allowing for change between courses at the end of the year. The final year of the Biotechnology course covers industrial microbiology (fermentation, molecular biology, applied genetics and water and waste treatment), biochemical processes relating largely to food processes, and industrial management. A sandwich course is also available.

Surrey* Biotechnology is offered by way of three and four year programmes.

Swansea Students on the four-year course in Clinical Technology spend 50% of the time on paid hospital placements (salary currently £17,000). No fees are paid for this course.

Ulster There is a course in Biomedical Engineering.

Westminster The Biotechnology course draws on biochemistry, microbiology, genetics and biochemical engineering.

Wolverhampton Biotechnology is offered as a single subject degree, with an optional year in industry or as part of the Applied Sciences and modular degree scheme programmes with Microbiology or Pharmacology. There is a bias towards microbial and plant biotechnology.

ALTERNATIVE COURSES
Agriculture, Biological Science subjects, Genetics, Microbiology.

BUILDING

(including **Architectural Engineering** and **Building Services Engineering**)
(see also **Architecture** and **Property Management and Surveying**)
(*indicates universities with the highest entry requirements)

SUBJECT REQUIREMENTS/PREFERENCES
GCE A-level: Mathematics may be required. **GCSE:** English, Mathematics and science usually required.

SUBJECT INFORMATION
These courses involve the techniques and management methods employed in the building industry. This subject also covers civil and structural engineering and architecture.

Anglia Ruskin Several courses are offered including Building Surveying, Construction and Design, Construction Management, and Quantity Surveying.

Aston A common first year leads to a choice of degrees in Construction Management and Construction Project Management.

Birmingham See under **Architecture**.

Birmingham City The Construction Management and Economics course comprises a strong emphasis on building technology, construction management and cost control with supporting legal, social and economic subjects. There are also courses in Building and Quantity Surveying. See also **Property Management and Surveying**.

Bolton Several full-time and sandwich degree courses are offered, including Building Surveying and Property Management, Construction, Construction Management and Quantity Surveying and Commercial Management leading to qualification as a surveyor.

Bournemouth The Heritage Conservation course combines the elements of material science, environmental science, building conservation and archaeology with a study of cultural resource management. A wide variety of third-year options allows specialisation to suit individual interests.

Brighton The Building Studies course covers building technology, construction and management, conservation technology and business management. There are also degree courses in Building Surveying and Project Management for Construction and Construction Engineering and Management. See also **Architecture**.

Bristol UWE There are courses in Construction Management, Building Services Engineering and a modular degree in Building and Natural Environmental Studies in which there is an optional placement year in industry. There is also a course in Building Surveying. See also **Property Management**.

Central Lancashire The Department of the Built Environment offers courses in Construction Project Management, Facilities Management, Heritage Management and Building Services Engineering. See also **Property Management and Surveying**.

Colchester (Inst) The Construction Management degree specialises in commercial and site work.

Coventry Courses are available in Building Surveying, Building Services Engineering, Quantity Surveying and Construction Management, which can include industrial placement.

Derby There are three Built Environment courses with separate pathways in Architecture, Civil Engineering and Construction.

Glamorgan Courses offered include Construction Management, Architectural Technology, Quantity Surveying and Building Services Engineering. Sandwich courses with placements in industry are also available. See also **Architecture**.

Glasgow Caledonian The Building Services Engineering course covers electrical and computer technology, building law practice, lighting and air-conditioning engineering. There are also degrees in Construction Management, Fire Risk Engineering, Property Management, Building Surveying and Building Control. Scholarships available. See also **Property Management and Surveying**.

Glyndŵr A Building Studies degree has optional routes in Year 2 leading to Construction Management, Building Maintenance Management or Building Studies.

Greenwich The Building Engineering course has a strong focus on construction technology and building engineering design. A sandwich course option is available. Building Surveying, Construction Business Management, Construction Surveying Management and Quantity Surveying are also offered. Scholarships available.

Heriot-Watt Construction Management, Building Surveying, Building Economics, and Quantity Surveying and Architectural Engineering are offered. There is also a course in Urban Studies allowing transfer to other courses at the end of the year.

Huddersfield There is an optional sandwich course in Construction and Project Management and a course in Property Development which includes economics and marketing.

Kingston Courses offered associated with Building in the School of Surveying include Building and Quantity Surveying, Construction Management and Property Planning and Development.

Leeds Metropolitan The Construction Management course covers technological management, law, historic building and building conservation. Special studies include environmental science. Students spend Year 3 in industry; optional placements take place in the UK. Courses in Facilities Management, Building Control Engineering, Building Surveying and Quantity Surveying are also available.

Liverpool John Moores The Construction Management degree is a unique learning programme covering design and construction materials and management. There is also a course in Building Design, Technology and Management. See also **Property Management and Surveying**.

London (UCL) A degree is offered in Project Management for Construction covering building technology and business aspects. The course has a strong vocational focus. (High research rating)

London South Bank Construction Management offers an opportunity to study by way of subsidised four-day visits to a European city (previously Amsterdam, Barcelona and Berlin). After a common first year, decisions are made between Construction or Surveying courses. Architectural Technology, Building Services Engineering and Quantity Surveying are also offered.

Loughborough* Degree courses are offered in Construction Engineering Management and Commercial Management and Quantity Surveying, all students sponsored by a consortium of companies.

Napier Architectural Technology, Building Surveying and Construction and Project Management and Quantity Surveying are offered. There is also a course in Property Development and Valuation.

Newport A course is offered in Construction Engineering.

Northumbria Architectural Technology, Building Design Management, Building Project Management, Building Services Engineering, Building Surveying, Construction Management and Quantity Surveying courses involve a third year spent in work placement. There is also a course in Estate Management.

Nottingham* A course is offered in Sustainable Built Environment focusing on the design of energy-efficient buildings covering renewable energy, ventilation, lighting, acoustics, electricity and control.

Nottingham Trent Courses are offered in Construction Management, Planning and Property Development, Quantity Surveying, Building Surveying and Financial and Project Management in Construction.

Oxford Brookes The Construction Project Management degree covers technology, management, design, construction and the maintenance of buildings in this four-year sandwich course. Courses in Quantity Surveying and Real Estate Management are also available.

Plymouth Degrees in Construction Management and the Environment, and Surveying are offered as three-year full-time or four-year sandwich courses. Scholarships available.

Portsmouth Construction Engineering Management, Property Development and Building Studies are also offered. See also **Property Management and Surveying**.

Reading* The first and second years of the Building Construction and Management course are common with the courses in Quantity Surveying, Building Surveying and Construction Management, Engineering and Surveying. The course will appeal to students interested in building and civil engineering but who do not wish to undertake a highly mathematical and theoretical course and want to concentrate mainly on design. Scholarships available. (High research rating)

Robert Gordon Courses are offered in Construction Design and Management, Architectural Technology and Surveying, each course with work placements. See also **Property Management and Surveying**.

Salford Construction Management is a four-year scheme with two six-month placements in industry covering management studies and technology which form the core of the programme. There are also courses focusing on facilities, production and process management. Building Surveying, and Construction Project Management are also available. See also **Property Management and Surveying**. (High research rating)

Sheffield Hallam The Built Environment Foundation programme offers courses with a common first year. Final decisions are taken in Year 2, and lead to degrees in Architectural Technology, Construction Management, Building or Quantity Surveying and Construction Commercial Management.

Southampton Solent Courses are offered in Construction and Project Management with options in Business, Computing, Engineering, Environmental Management and Health Studies.

Swansea Metropolitan Courses are offered in Building Conservation Management and Construction Management. There is also a Quantity Surveying course awaiting approval.

Ulster The work experience period of 12 months is a compulsory part of the Building Surveying course. There are also degrees in Building Engineering and Materials, Construction Engineering Management and Quantity Surveying.

West London Degrees are offered in Quantity Surveying and Construction Management.

Westminster Full-time and part-time degree courses are offered in Building Engineering, Construction Management, Building and Quantity Surveying, Construction and Surveying and Architectural Technology.

Wolverhampton Construction Management is a broad-based course covering all the major topics required by a building engineer, with law, computing, management and language options. Industrial placement is optional. There are also courses in Building Surveying, Architectural Design Technology, Quantity Surveying and Computer-aided Design in Construction.

OTHER INSTITUTIONS OFFERING BUILDING COURSES

Bath (Coll), Blackpool and Fylde (Coll), Bradford (Coll), Cornwall (Coll), Dudley (CT), East Lancashire (IHE), Menai (Coll), SAC, Swansea (Coll), UHI Millennium Inst, Wigan and Leigh (Coll), Worcester (CT), Writtle (Coll).

ALTERNATIVE COURSES

Architecture, Building Services Engineering, Building Surveying, Civil Engineering, Estate Management, Land Economics, Quantity Surveying, Valuation Surveying.

BUSINESS COURSES

(including **Human Resources Management** and **Marketing Tourism**)
(*indicates universities with the highest entry requirements)

SUBJECT REQUIREMENTS/PREFERENCES

GCE A-level: Mathematics (or AS-level) required or preferred by some universities. Foreign language(s) required for some European or international courses. **GCSE:** English and Mathematics required.

SUBJECT INFORMATION

This is a very large subject area that may consist of courses in general topics (Business Studies or Business Administration), Management Science courses, which tend to have a mathematics emphasis, and more specialised fields that are covered by courses in Advertising, Consumer Science, Company and Public Administration, Financial Services (see also **Finance**), Industrial Relations, Organisation Studies, Retail Management and Travel and Tourism.

At HND level many institutions offer Business Studies courses with specialist streams as follows: accountancy, advertising, broadcasting/media, business administration, company secretaryship, computer studies, distribution, European business and marketing, fashion, food, health, horticulture, journalism, languages, law, leisure, marketing, media, personnel, printing, publicity, purchasing and tourism.

Aberdeen A degree in Management Studies includes marketing, public sector management, small business management and human resources management as electives at the honours level. In addition to a European Management Studies degree a unique course in Entrepreneurship and Marketing focuses on business development. Marine Resources Management covering fisheries and coastal planning is also offered.

Abertay Dundee The four year Business portfolio has a common first year followed by specialisations in Years, 2 and 3 in Chinese, Economics, Finance, Marketing, Law, and Spanish. There are also management courses in International Business, Human Resources, Tourism and Marketing.

Aberystwyth The Business and Management degree scheme of three years has core modules in marketing, business law, management accounting and human resources management in Years 2 and 3. There are also Welsh Medium electives focusing on the Welsh economy. A course in Marketing can be taken as a single honours scheme, or as a joint course. In addition there is a course in Tourism Management with the opportunity to study a modern language. (High research rating)

Anglia Ruskin Courses are offered in Business (with over 40 specialist options), Business Studies (with a 48 week placement in Year 3), Business Management Economics and International Business with language modules in French, German and Spanish, each with European programmes in Clermont-Ferrand, Berlin and Maastricht respectively, and the Netherlands. There is also a course in Human Resources Management and in Modern Business Applications with modules drawn from business studies, information systems and law and also Tourism and Marketing degrees.

Aston* The large Business School offers flexible sandwich courses on a modular basis. Single honours courses include Managerial and Administrative Studies, Human Resource Management, Marketing, Logistics and Transport Management, International Business and Economics and Management, joint courses in International Business with French, German or Spanish or with two languages, and major/minor courses. (High research rating)

Bangor Business courses are offered jointly with Economics, Marketing, a Modern Language, Finance and even Forestry. Other courses include Management, Social Administration, Finance, Banking, Accountancy, Leisure and Tourism.

Bath* The Business Administration course is a blend of practical experience and academic study in a four-year sandwich course. First-year core subjects include business economics, behaviour in organisations, accounting and some computing, statistics and law. The course continues with specialisms in finance, employee relations and marketing. Courses are also offered in International Management and Modern Languages – French, German or Spanish. (High research rating)

Bath Spa The Business and Management degree presents a diverse range of topics and includes an optional 10-month work assignment. There is also a course in Tourism Management.

Bedfordshire Full-time and sandwich courses are offered in Business Studies with specialist options in marketing, accounting and finance, international business, law, psychology and organisation behaviour. There are also courses in Human Resources Management and Tourism. In addition there are also degrees in Advertising, Marketing and Public Relations.

Birmingham* Courses are offered with a year in industry, in European Business and with Communications. The three-year specialist programme in Business Administration leads to a BCom degree and provides a window on the modern world of business. French, German, Italian, Japanese, Portuguese and Spanish and 12 engineering subjects are also offered with Business Studies. (High research rating)

Birmingham (UC) Marketing is offered with Hospitality, Events and Tourism. Salon Business and Spa Management are also offered.

Birmingham City Courses in the business field cover Advertising, Business Administration, Business Information Technology, Human Resource Management, Retail Marketing and International Marketing and Public Relations.

Bolton Full-time courses with some overseas placements are offered in Business Studies and Human Resources Management. There is also a degree in Marketing with options in communications strategy, management and buying behaviour and a course in Tourism Management.

Bournemouth* The Business Studies degree includes a 40 week paid placement in industry or commerce in the third year. There are 10 named Business programmes combined with a range of subjects including languages, Human Resource Management, Law and in addition an International Business degree, Public Relations and Retail Management courses and several Marketing and Tourism courses are also offered.

Bradford The Management Centre offers a degree programme in Business and Management Studies which provides a broad education with opportunities for later specialisations in accounting, human resource management, international business or marketing. There is also a course in Business and Law giving partial exemption from Law Society examinations. See also **Accountancy/Accounting**.

Brighton* Business Studies degrees (and also with Law, Marketing and Finance) are offered on a four-year sandwich basis while Business Administration is a three-year full-time course. International Business can be taken with French, German or Spanish while International Finance and Investment opens doors to stockbroking portfolio management and corporate finance. There are also degrees in Marketing, and Tourism.

Bristol Management is taken with Accountancy or Economics.

Bristol UWE A large number of courses are offered in Business. These include Business Studies linked with Financial Management, Accountancy, Marketing, Human Resources Management and Property. Also offered are International Business and Languages with placements in France, Germany or Spain and Business Mathematics combining business topics and mathematics. Modern language options support some of these courses.

Brunel* Courses are offered in Business and Management, with pathways in Accountancy, eBusiness Systems, and Marketing. Business Studies is also offered with Sports Sciences. There are also three-year and four-year (thick sandwich) courses in International Business, without a language requirement.

See *University Degree Course Offers* (Trotman Publishing) for details of offers

Buckingham Courses are offered in Business Enterprise or Management commencing in January for the former or July (a two-year course) with streams in Information Systems. Courses are also offered in Marketing with Media Communications, or Psychology. Scholarships available.

Bucks New In addition to the Business Management degree the subject is also offered jointly with advertising, sport, tourism, retail management and marketing. There are also specialised courses in Air Travel Management, Air Transport with Pilot Training, Airline and Airport Management, Advertising, Events and Festival Management, Human Resources Management, International Management, Marketing and Music Industry Management and Public Relations Management.

Cambridge* A one-year Management course is offered to students who have taken two or three years of another Tripos.

Canterbury Christ Church Courses are offered in Business Studies as a joint or combined honours degree, leading to pathways in Accounting, Advertising, Management, Business Computing, Logistics, Human Resource Management, Retail Marketing and Marketing.

Cardiff* A specialist degree scheme is offered in Business Management covering all the main areas relevant to business in Year 1 followed by 12 modules of selected specialist areas in Years 2 and 3. These include Human Resources, Marketing, Logistics and International Management. Courses are also available with French, Spanish and Japanese with Year 3 spent abroad. (See also **Accountancy/Accounting**, **Finance** and **Economics**.) Transport Management can be studied with Business Administration and there is also a course in Industrial Relations with Sociology. (High research rating)

Cardiff (UWIC) Business degrees include Accounting, Marketing, International Business and Retail Management.

Central Lancashire Over 15 courses are offered covering Advertising, Business, International Business, Business Information Technology, Public Relations and Marketing. Business is also offered as part of the combined honours degree course and there are also courses in E-Business, Human Resource Management, Retail Management and Chinese and Business. Several courses are also offered in Ecotourism, focusing on environmental development. Scholarships available.

Chester Courses are offered in Business Management, Advertising, Public Relations, Business Information Systems, Marketing Tourism and International Business.

Chichester The Business Studies course covers finance, marketing, human resources management and business law. Business Studies can also be taken with Information Technology.

City* The Business School offers courses in Business Studies and Management in which optional placements in the UK and abroad are offered in Year 3. The Management course is interdisciplinary and covers organisational behaviour, management of technology, international relations and marketing. A course in Air Transport Operations is also offered with pilot training. See also **Finance**. (High research rating)

Colchester (Inst) Four management courses cover Hospitality, Sport, Tourism and General Management.

Coventry There are courses in Business Studies and Business Administration with optional work placement. There are also courses in Advertising, Marketing, Tourism Management, Human Resource Management, Logistics, Events Management, International Business and Disaster Management. See also **Leisure, Recreation Management and Tourism** and **Sports Science/Studies**.

Creative Arts Marketing and Management courses cover Advertising and Brand Communication, Fashion Management and Fashion Promotion.

Cumbria The Business Studies programme includes Management Studies, Logistics, Marketing and Travel and Tourism.

De Montfort Courses are offered in Business, Business Studies (full-time joint honours), Business Enterprise, Human Resource Management, Arts Management, Advertising, Marketing and International Business.

Derby The Business School offers three year and four year (sandwich) courses in Business Studies, Business Management, Marketing and International Spa Management. Several business courses also offer pathways in finance, mathematics, human resources, and psychology.

Dundee The Business Management course focuses on Accounting and Financial Management in Years 1 and 2 with a wide range of options in Years 3 and 4 including languages, Human Resource Management and Accounting. Management forms part of courses in Engineering (civil and electronic), Environmental Studies and Accountancy. There are also courses that focus on Business Economics; International Business (BSc) is now available with studies including modern languages.

Durham (Stockton)* After a broad first year, Business students spend Years 2 and 3 choosing from a number of course modules including organisations, the Pacific Rim, strategy and international business. Courses are also offered in Management Studies with Chinese or Japanese or as part of the combined honours programme. Business Finance and Accountancy share a common first year with Business with options to change at the end of Year 1.

East Anglia* The Business Management degree programme provides a broad base with the opportunity to specialise, while the Business Finance and Economics course provides a focus for those aiming for careers in accountancy and finance. Management can also be combined with Accounting, languages, Biology and Mathematics. There are also courses in Business Information Systems and Statistics.

East London Business Studies courses are offered with a range of subjects covering business finance, human resource management, marketing, supply chain management, entrepreneurship and corporate social responsibility. There is also a course in International Business with placements abroad and courses in Events Management and Tourism, Human Resources Management, Marketing.

Edge Hill All students take a common first year after which it is possible specialise in Accounting, Human Resource Management, International Business or Marketing.

Edinburgh* The Business Studies course focuses on the management of organisations and covers strategic planning, employment relations, finance, marketing and technology. Languages, Accounting, Geography and Law are also offered with Business. (High research rating)

Essex* The Business Management course offers an in-depth study of the various aspects of the management of commercial and industrial organisations. Financial management subjects are taken in each year of the three-year course. Business Management can also be taken with French, German, Italian and Portuguese, and with Latin American Studies. There is also a course in Entrepreneurship and Business.

Exeter* The School of Business and Economics offers courses in Business and Management with Leadership that can also be taken with European Study in which students spend a year abroad. Three-year and four-year courses are also offered in Accounting or Economics and Finance.

Falmouth (UC) A comprehensive Public Relations degree is offered covering key aspects of the media. Advertising can also be studied.

Glamorgan A wide range of courses can be selected depending on personal preferences. They cover three-year and four-year sandwich courses including Business Management, Business Information Technology, Tourism Management, Human Resource Management, Marketing, International Business Studies and Fashion Promotions. Three-year full-time and four-year sandwich courses are offered.

Glasgow* Business and Management, which focuses on the practical and theoretical aspects of business, has options in small business management, applied managerial psychology and the art of influencing. There is also a course in International Business Administration. (High research rating)

Glasgow Caledonian Courses in Business Studies, International Business Studies with placements in Year 3 are offered followed by a wide range of specialisations in the final year. Business Economics, Information Management, Marketing, People Management, Consumer and Trading Standards, Public Management, Retailing, Tourism Management, Adventure Recreation Management, and Entertainment and Events Management are also available.

See *University Degree Course Offers* (Trotman Publishing) for details of offers

Gloucestershire The Business Management degree has pathways in Human Resource Management, Business Management, and International Business. There are also courses is Advertising, Tourism and Marketing. Other degree courses include Public Relations and Publishing.

Glyndŵr A common first year leads to a choice of degree in Business Management, Marketing or Human Resource Management. There is also a course in Law with Business. See also under **Accountancy**.

Greenwich Business is offered in a range of programmes. It can be taken on a full-time or sandwich basis, with French, German, Italian or Spanish. There are also courses in Advertising, Marketing (also with languages), and International Business, Human Resources Management and Events Management.

Harper Adams (UC) Courses on offer include Agri-food Marketing, Business Management, Food Retail and Food Supply Chain Management.

Heriot-Watt The School of Management courses include Management with Marketing or Human Resource Management or Operations Management or Business Law; Business and Finance and Business and Economics are also offered. There is also an International Management course with languages and study placements in France, Germany, Austria or Spain. Joint degrees in Business and Economics or Finance are also available.

Hertfordshire Courses are offered in Business Studies (including four-year sandwich courses), Airport Operations, Human Resource Management, Event Management, Tourism Management, Marketing, International Business and Management Science. Joint honours Business courses are also offered. Business Studies can be studied with Languages or Finance. Scholarships available.

Huddersfield Business Studies is offered as a three-year full-time course with an optional placement year in addition to Business Management. Business is also offered with Finance, Psychology, Journalism, Design, Law, Computing and International Business. There are also courses in Advertising and Marketing Communications, Marketing, Human Resource Management, Tourism and Leisure Management, and Logistics Management.

Hull From a broad base of economics, accounting and business information technology, the Business degree focuses on marketing, business law, international business and financial management. Other courses include International Business, Management, Public Relations, Marketing, and Financial Management. All courses share a common first year followed by specialisation.

Keele Management is offered as a single honours course whilst Business Management is a dual honours course with over 20 combinations in an interdisciplinary Social Science degree with a wide variety of specialist options. Twenty-eight dual honours courses are offered with Marketing, Human Resources Management and Management Science. (High research rating)

Kent Business Administration can be studied with a year in industry. Courses are also offered in Industrial Relations and Human Resource Management and in Business Studies or Business Economics.

Kingston* The Business Studies course covers all the main business areas including a foreign language and IT skills, and has links with American and European universities. Other courses include Business with Economics, Information Technology, Law, French, Spanish, Human Resource Management, International Business and Marketing. Several joint honours are also possible. Scholarships available.

Lancaster* Business Studies (also offered with study abroad) is a three-year degree programme providing a grounding in theoretical and practical aspects of business. Options include accounting and finance, business law, purchasing and international business. There is also a Management course including a Human Resources option and a Marketing course with Design, both including study abroad options. There are also degrees in Organisation Studies, Operations Management and Entrepreneurship, and European Management with Languages. (See also **Economics**) (High research rating)

Leeds* The Business School offers courses in Management Studies (economics, operations management, marketing, international marketing and business) and other courses covering Accounting, and Business Economics, with a wide range of joint courses. Courses are also offered in Human Resource Management, Transport Studies and in Textile and Fashion Management. (High research rating)

Leeds Metropolitan A wide range of full-time courses and sandwich courses are offered including Business, Business Studies with Languages, Retailing, Human Resources Management, Public Relations, Events Management, Marketing and International Business courses.

Leeds Trinity (UC) Business degrees can be taken with Enterprise, Finance, Management, Law or Marketing.

Leicester* The Management degree focuses on a wide range of management issues including business ethics, finance and economics with third year modules in retailing and marketing.

Lincoln 21 Business courses can be studied as a single subject or joint degree as a three-year or four-year course. Courses are also offered in Business Studies, European Business, Human Resource Management, Marketing and Public Relations. Eight Management courses are also offered in addition to separate Marketing and Advertising courses.

Liverpool* The Management School offers business programmes in Accounting, Languages, International Business, Marketing, E-Business, Human Resources Management.

Liverpool Hope Business can be studied as a single or combined honours course with a range of subjects relating to business including Marketing, Information Technology and Tourism.

Liverpool John Moores Business Administration, Maritime Business and Management and courses in Business and Business Studies are offered. The latter includes a full-time option with a choice of specialist route (marketing, purchasing, human resource management, finance or general management) being made in Year 2. The International Business Management course (Year 3 abroad) can be taken with French, Japanese, Chinese or Spanish. Other courses include Human Resources Management, Retail Estate Management and Business, Management Transport and Logistics, Marketing, Tourism and Leisure.

London (King's)* The Business Management programme covers all aspects of business including a foreign language option in Years 1 and 2. Some students take the opportunity to study in Canada, at the University of Toronto in Year 2. Management is also available with Computer Science, Engineering, French, Mathematics and Physics.

London (LSE)* A course is offered in Management (described as `an intellectually broad preparation for management drawing on economics, psychology and sociology'). There is also a course in Management Sciences with elements of accountancy, IT and operational research. The degree in Employment Relations includes psychology, sociology and anthropology.

London (QM)* Students taking Business Management can also take units from other subjects including Economics, Computer Science, Environmental Science, Materials, Politics, Technology, and languages. A course in Economics, Finance and Management is also offered.

London (RH)* Management is offered with several subjects as a major subject including Accounting, Economics, Marketing, Mathematics, International Business and European languages. Core courses in Management focus on the main functional areas of business covering finance, information systems and management skills in Europe and abroad.

London (SOAS) Management is offered with a range of languages including Arabic, Chinese, Hebrew, Urdu, Thai, Turkish and Vietnamese.

London Metropolitan Courses offered include single and joint honours degrees in Advertising and Marketing, Arts Management, Aviation Management, Business Enterprise, Business Information Technology, International Business, Human Resource Management, Events Management and Public Relations.

See *University Degree Course Offers* (Trotman Publishing) for details of offers

London South Bank The Business Studies or Business Administration courses cover advertising, consumer behaviour, international business, finance, industrial relations and marketing. There is also a course in Arts Management covering technology, performance and visual arts, with a placement and project involving setting up an arts company, theatre and events organisations. There are also courses in Business Information Technology, Human Resources Management, Marketing and Tourism.

Loughborough* Business courses cover a range of undergraduate degree programmes. Air Transport Management, Business Studies, Management, Sciences, Retail Management, Transport Management, Leisure Management and International Business. These courses came top in a survey of student satisfaction. There are also degrees in Publishing.

Manchester* There is a comprehensive programme of Business, International Business and Management courses with specialisms in Accountancy, Decision Science, Human Resources and Retailing, Marketing. There is also a Management and Leisure course. See also **Art and Design**. (High research rating)

Manchester Metropolitan A very wide range of courses lead to degrees in Business including Business Information Technology, Business Management, Marketing, Retailing, Enterprise, Human Resource Management, International Business, Business and Sport and Advertising.

Marjon (UCP) There are minor combined courses with Management in either Applied Sports Science or Outdoor Adventure.

Middlesex Business Studies and Business Administration can be studied as full- or part-time courses. Degrees are also offered with Marketing, Human Resource Management, and International Management.

Napier Business Management programmes are modular, giving considerable flexibility and also combined with Accountancy, Economics, Human Resource Management, Festival and Event Management, Languages, Marketing or Law. There is also an International Business course with a placement abroad.

Newcastle* Degree programmes in Marketing cover specialist areas such as accounting, marketing and production as well as general, theoretical fields such as economics and organisational behaviour. Degrees in Business Management and Marketing share a common first year, after which students can choose their degree. Business Studies can also be taken with Languages and there are several joint courses with Management.

Newman (UC) Management Studies can be taken as a major, joint or minor course with another subject.

Newport All business courses have a common first year enabling students to transfer to other business courses at the end of Year 1. Courses offered include Human Resources Management, Marketing and Transport Management.

Northampton A very large number of single and joint courses are offered including Human Resource Management, Advertising, Business Management, Events Management, Retailing and Logistics.

Northumbria* A wide range of degrees is offered in Business and both full-time and sandwich options are available. Specialisms are offered in Accounting, Advertising, Economics, Finance, Logistics and Supply Chain Management, Human Resource Management, Marketing, Tourism and International Business Management. There is also a course in Corporate Management.

Nottingham* The Management Studies degree offers core modules in management and organisations, strategic management and marketing, finance and accounting and economics for management. There are also courses in Finance and Accounting Management and in Industrial Economics. Joint courses can also be taken with languages and engineering. (High research rating)

Nottingham Trent The Business School offers courses in Management Studies, Financial Services, Business Studies (three years with supervised work experience), Business Management with pathways in Economics, Accountancy, Human Resources, and Marketing, International Business (with optional placements in Germany, France or Spain).

See *University Degree Course Offers* (Trotman Publishing) for details of offers

Oxford* The degree in Economics and Management offers an intellectual approach to both subjects and includes an accounting course and the roles of managers in the process of decision-making.

Oxford Brookes* A very large number of course combinations are offered in Business subjects. Including Business and Management, Business and Marketing, Business of Real Estate, and Economics, Finance, International Business and Tourism. Most courses have work placements or international exchanges.

Plymouth Business Administration (three years) and Business Studies (four-year sandwich) are the main courses focusing on the UK, while International Business and European Business includes modern languages (French, German, Italian and Spanish). There are also courses specialising in Business and Tourism, Marketing, Sports Management, International Business with Languages, Human Resources Management, Maritime Business and Shipping and Logistics.

Portsmouth* Business Administration/Studies courses provide a very wide range of modules in Year 2 including employee relations, company law, European business and marketing. There are also full-time and sandwich courses in Business Enterprise Development, Intenational Business Studies and European Business, in Human Resource Management (also with Psychology) and Marketing.

Queen Margaret Business Management, Consumer Studies, Marketing, Events Management, Tourism, Public Relations and Retail Business are all offered as single honours courses. Combinations of some of these subjects can be taken in the fourth year of the course.

Queen's Belfast* The degree in Management is a three-year course with final-year specialisms in human resource and operations management, marketing, international business, technology or public sector management. An optional placement year is available between years 2 and 3. The Management course with a modern language offers French or German (post A-level) or Spanish or Italian *ab initio*. There are also courses in Agribusiness Economics and Management, Business Information Technology and in Consumer Behaviour and Marketing.

Reading* A range of Business and Management courses is offered including Accounting and Management, Agricultural Business Management, Business Statistics and Business Analysis. International Management is also offered with French, German, and Italian. (High research rating)

Robert Gordon A range of Management courses is offered including Management with Finance, Marketing, Economics and Human Resource Management. There are also courses in Fashion Management, Retail Management, and International Business and Tourism Management.

Roehampton International Business, Retail Management and Marketing, Human Resource Management are offered as single honours courses. Business Management is offered as both a single and combined course with a range of other subjects including Computing Studies, Modern Languages, Sociology and Sport Science. There is also a degree course in Marketing and Multimedia.

St Andrews* Management is offered as a single or joint honours course. Topics covered include organisations and societies, management and society, public sector and human resource management, corporate finance and global business. (High research rating)

St Mary's (UC) Management Studies can be taken as a single or combined course. There is also a degree in Tourism Management.

Salford Business Studies students follow a common core in Years 1 and 2 and then choose specialised pathways in financial, marketing, human resource or quantitative business management, law or international business. There is also a European Business degree that includes a European language and Year 3 spent in Europe and degree programmes in Human Resources Management, Marketing, Financial Management and Leisure and Tourism Management.

Sheffield* The joint degrees in Management include consumer behaviour, human resources management, leisure management and information systems organisation. Business Studies can also be taken with a large number of engineering and technological subjects.

See *University Degree Course Offers* (Trotman Publishing) for details of offers

Sheffield Hallam Business Studies is offered as a three-year full-time or four-year sandwich course. Other sandwich courses include Business and Marketing, International Business Studies (also with languages), Marketing and Retailing and courses involving Business and Human Resource Management and Operations Management are also offered.

Southampton* The Management degrees offer modules in accounting, marketing, information systems, and languages. (High research rating)

Southampton Solent Business can be studied with a range of options including Psychology. Courses are also offered in Adventure Tourism, Advertising, Human Resource Management, Marketing and business aspects related to Maritime Studies, the Music and Arts industries.

Staffordshire A wide range of degrees can be taken including Business Studies, Business Management, Advertising, Human Resource Management, Marketing, International Business and Travel and Tourism. Joint courses can also be taken with Electronic Commerce.

Stirling The Business Studies degree includes the study of a foreign language. Optional courses include personnel management, industrial relations, employee training, European business, and venture management. There are also degrees in Human Resource Management, Marketing, Management Science, International Management Studies, Retail Marketing and Business Computing.

Strathclyde* For the BA Business course, students choose two principal subjects from accounting, business law, economics, finance, management science, mathematics and statistics, marketing, human resource management, modern languages and tourism. There are also courses in International Business and Modern Languages. (High research rating)

Sunderland A wide range of courses associated with business is offered. These include Business Administration, Business Studies, Public Relations, Marketing, Human Resource Management, Business, Retail, Enterprise and Management joint courses. Human Resources Management can be taken as a combined course.

Surrey* Several Business degrees are offered with sandwich placements. The degree in Retail Management covers accounting and business law, human resources and supply chain management and marketing. There are specialist options in the final year in fashion or food retail management, food and nutritional management, small business management and optional language modules. Business Management with either French or Spanish is offered as three-year full-time or four-year sandwich course. Chemistry with Industrial Management and Language and Business Culture is also available.

Sussex* Business and Management Studies offers core subjects plus pathways in Finance, Human Resources Management, Marketing and International Business.

Swansea* Courses are offered in Business Management Studies (or with Accounting). The modular courses provide maximum flexibility and cover all management schemes including International Business, European Schemes, or American or Australian Year Abroad Schemes. Scholarships available.

Swansea Metropolitan A vocational course in Business Studies enables students to specialise in Years 2 and 3. A broad course in Management is also offered. Human Resources Management and Marketing can also be taken.

Teesside Courses are offered in Business Management and Business Studies with the latter enabling students to spend one semester in a range of institutions in the USA or across Europe. Foreign languages, retail, marketing and public relations are specialist subject areas. Other courses cover International Business, Sport Management, Marketing and Retailing.

Trinity St David (Carmarthen) A broad course in Business Management is offered with exchange opportunities in Europe and USA. There are also degrees in Business Information Technology Management and Tourism Management.

See *University Degree Course Offers* (Trotman Publishing) for details of offers

Trinity St David (Lampeter) Business Management (marketing, finance and human resources management) is offered as a single honours degree, emphasising all transferable skills. It can also be studied with a range of subjects including Film Studies, Islamic Studies, Jewish Studies, Church History, Australian Studies, American Studies, and Welsh Studies.

Ulster Courses are available in Business Studies (and with specialisms in accounting, American business, business law, design, enterprise development, human resource management, management information systems, marketing and operations management). There are also Modular Business degrees with Advertising and Retail, languages, Marketing, Human Resources Management, Psychology, and a course in Consumer Studies.

Warwick* The Business School offers courses in Management (with engineering options), International Business or Business Studies and Accounting and Finance. Students taking Management may take a generalist programme or specialise in marketing operations management, personnel management, information systems or accounting. (High research rating)

West London Degree courses are offered in Business Studies and Management, Advertising with Marketing, Human Resources Management, Retailing, Event Management, Public Relations, Airline and Airport Management, and Tourism Management.

West Scotland Several Business courses are available including Business, Marketing, Human Resources, Enterprise Studies, Information Management and Events Management.

Westminster* The Business Studies degree programme comprises a general course or specialisms in finance, human resource management, information management, marketing and service industries. Business Management courses include financial services, retailing, human resources management or travel and tourism. There is also a degree in International Business with a study year abroad.

Winchester The Business Management programme has several specialisms including E-Commerce, Finance and Economics, Human Resource Management, Information Technology, Marketing and Public Service Management. There are also degrees in Tourism and Leisure Management. See also **Hospitality Management**.

Wolverhampton There are several joint combinations with Business Studies or Business Management, including E-Commerce, Marketing, Human Resource Management, Retailing, Entrepreneurship and Event Management available on three-year and, in some cases, four-year sandwich courses.

Worcester The Business Management course has an optional sandwich year with options is advertising, accounting, human resources management and marketing.

York* Courses are offered in Accounting, Business Finance and Management or in Management. Both have optional years in industry.

York St John Several business courses are offered including specialisms in Human Resource Management, Finance and IT.

OTHER INSTITUTIONS OFFERING BUSINESS COURSES
Askham Bryan (Coll), Barking (Coll), Bath (Coll), Birmingham (UC), Birmingham City, Bishop Burton (Coll), Blackpool and Fylde (Coll), Bradford (Coll), Bridgwater (Coll), Bristol City (Coll), Bristol Filton (Coll), Carmarthenshire (Coll), Chesterfield (Coll), Chichester (Coll), Cornwall (Coll), Coventry City (Coll), Craven (Coll), Croydon (Coll), Dearne Valley (Coll), Duchy (Coll), Durham New (Coll), Ealing (Coll), East Lancashire (Coll), East Riding (Coll), European (BusSch), Farnborough (UC), Gloucestershire (Coll), Grimsby (IFHE), Guildford (CFHE), Halton Riverside (Coll), Havering (Coll), Highbury (Coll), Holborn (Coll), Hopwood Hall (Coll), Lakes (Coll), Leeds Park Lane (Coll), Llandrillo (Coll), Manchester (CAT), Manchester City (Coll), Matthew Boulton (CFHE), Mid-Cheshire (Coll), Myerscough (Coll), Neath Port Talbot (Coll), NESCOT, North

East Worcestershire (Coll), North Lindsey (Coll), Northbrook (Coll), Norwich City (Coll), Nottingham New (Coll), Peterborough (Reg Coll), Regents (BusSch), Richmond (American Univ), Royal (CAg), SAC, St Helens (Coll), Sandwell (Coll), Sheffield (Coll), Solihull (Coll), South Essex (Coll), Suffolk (Univ Campus), Sunderland City (Coll), Tameside (Coll), Totton (Coll), Truro (Coll), UHI Millennium Inst, Uxbridge (Coll), Wakefield (Coll), Walsall (Coll), Warrington (Coll), Warwickshire (Coll), West Anglia (Coll), West Thames (Coll), Wigan and Leigh (Coll), Wiltshire (Coll), Worcester (CT), Writtle (Coll), York (Coll).

ALTERNATIVE COURSES

Accountancy, Banking, Economics and Insurance, in addition to the courses listed under **Subject information** at the beginning of this table.

CHEMISTRY

(*indicates universities with the highest entry requirements)

SUBJECT REQUIREMENTS/PREFERENCES

GCE A-level: Chemistry and another science usually required.

SUBJECT INFORMATION

There is a considerable shortage of applicants for Chemistry, which has very many career applications. These include oceanography (marine chemistry), agriculture and environmental work, colour chemistry, medical chemistry, pharmacy, pharmacology and polymer science. Refer to entries covering these subjects.

Aberdeen A broad course covering all aspects of chemistry is offered leading to degrees in Chemistry with New Materials Technology, Chemistry with Management Studies, Medicinal Chemistry, Environmental Chemistry and Chemistry with Modern Languages (French or German).

Anglia Ruskin Degree courses are offered in Chemistry, covering the full range of chemical topics, and in Medicinal Chemistry, which includes medical laboratory sciences and pharmaceutical chemistry.

Aston* The Chemistry and Applied Chemistry Programme emphasises industrial applications with placements and sponsorships. Scholarships available.

Bangor The broad modular Chemistry course can include industrial placement or a year in Europe in Year 3. There are also courses in Environmental Chemistry and Marine Chemistry in which students spend half of their time in the School of Ocean Sciences. (High research rating)

Bath* Courses are offered in Chemistry and Chemistry and Drug Recovery Education or Management. In all courses there is a common first year with the option to change degree programmes and placements which take place in industry, either in the UK or abroad. The final year provides the opportunity to choose from a range of options. There is also a Natural Sciences programme in which chemistry can be taken with another science subject in Year 1. (High research rating)

Birmingham* Core modules are taken in Chemistry with specialisations in several areas, including Analytical Science, Business Management and Psychology; major/minor combinations are possible. (High research rating)

Bradford Chemistry4 provides a choice of four employment pathways (pharmaceuticals, forensic, biotechnology and quality control/analytical) in Year 3 of this three- or four-year course. There is also a course is Chemical and Forensic Science which can also include a sandwich placement.

Brighton Pharmaceutical and Chemical Sciences can be studied either as a three-year full-time or four-year sandwich course. The course includes biology, biochemistry, chemistry and microbiology. The course in Analytical Chemistry with Business also has an optional placement year.

Bristol* Seven programmes are offered, all having a common first year and allowing transfer between courses during the first two years. Chemistry is taken in Year 1 with two other subjects from biochemistry, pharmacology, physics, geology, or computer methods. In Year 2, chemistry is taken with one other. The third year involves a research project from a range of options. Courses are offered involving study in Continental Europe and North America. There is also a degree in Chemical Physics. (High research rating)

Bristol UWE The degree in Forensic Chemistry covers biology, organic, inorganic and physical chemistry and genetics. DNA analysis and Interpretation of Forensic Evidence are compulsory modules.

Cambridge* Chemistry is offered as part of the Natural Sciences programme in which first-year scientists choose three sciences from the biology of cells, biology of organisms, chemistry, geology, materials and mineral sciences, physics and physiology, mathematics, quantitative biology, and elementary mathematics for biologists. The course is designed for those who wish to specialise in chemistry and also for those whose interests lie in subjects such as geology, biochemistry and pharmacology. (High research rating) See also **Biological Sciences**.

Cardiff* Degrees in Chemistry, Chemistry and Physics, and Chemistry with Bioscience or Chemistry with Industrial Experience (Year 3 in industry) or a Year Abroad are available. Optional modules in Year 1 of the Chemistry course include biochemistry, biology, geology, physics and languages. The MChem scheme follows the same syllabus in Years 1 and 2. (High research rating)

Dundee A BSc degree is offered in Pharmaceutical Chemistry.

Durham* The first year of the Chemistry honours course may be accompanied by a wide range of subsidiary courses (sciences, humanities languages). Common first-year courses provide maximum flexibility with opportunities for industrial placement, study abroad, joint honours courses and natural sciences. (High research rating)

East Anglia* The School of Chemistry offers a number of Chemistry programmes and the flexibility in the choice of units enables a range of scientific areas to be studied. Therefore the overall content of the degree programme depends to a large extent on the interests and strengths of an individual student. The Chemistry with a year in North America course extends over three years. For the Chemistry with a year in Europe course students study at a university in Denmark, France, Germany or the Netherlands during the third year of their course. Environmental or Pharmaceutical Chemistry are also available.

Edinburgh* Thirteen Degrees in Chemistry are offered with the options of a year abroad or a year of industrial experience. Scholarships available. (High research rating)

Glamorgan The Chemistry course includes physical, inorganic, organic and analytical chemistry with specialisms in Years 3 and 4 in pharmaceutical, agrochemistry and food chemistry. The study of a foreign language can be continued throughout the course. Several joint courses are offered along with Combined Science and Combined Studies programmes. There are also degrees in Forensic Science and Forensic Chemistry.

Glasgow* Chemistry is a broad course that provides a basis of the principles of chemical science in the early years and leads to special topics at honours level in the fourth year. Chemistry with Medicinal Chemistry, Forensic Studies Chemistry and Mathematics and Environmental Chemistry are also offered. (High research rating)

Glasgow Caledonian A course is offered in Chemistry with Information Technology and with instrumental specialisation in either environmental analysis or food analysis.

Greenwich Specialist courses within the Chemistry degree structure, either MSc or BSc, include biochemistry, microbiology, biotechnology, materials science, and chemistry in medicine and agriculture. Year 3 is spent in industrial placement, or in work and study in another EU country. There are also sandwich courses in Pharmaceutical Chemistry and Analytical Chemistry, and a range of joint courses.

Heriot-Watt Fifteen Chemistry courses are offered with the choice of degree being deferred up to the end of Year 3. There are options in Biochemistry, Computer Science, Materials, Environmental Economics, Forensic Science, Industrial Experience, Management, Pharmaceutical Chemistry and Education. Scholarships available. (High research rating)

Huddersfield A modular Chemistry course is offered, with options in Year 2 in chemical technology, forensic science, or biology. Similar options follow in Year 4 after work placement throughout Year 3.

Hull A range of BSc Chemistry courses (with paid industrial experience possible) follows a similar path in Years 1 and 2 allowing for transfer between degrees. Other honours programmes allow for combinations with, for example, French, German, Nanotechnology, Analytical Chemistry, Applied Chemistry, and Toxicology and Forensic Science. Scholarships available. (High research rating)

Imperial London* The Department offers 15 Chemistry courses including a three-year course in Chemistry and Management, four-year courses in Chemistry, Chemistry with Management with a Year in Industry, or Abroad (with language study) and Chemistry with either Medicinal Chemistry or with Languages. Scholarships available. (High research rating)

Keele Chemistry and Medicinal Chemistry are offered as dual honours courses with a large number of combinations. (High research rating)

Kingston Chemistry and Applied Chemistry include industrial placement throughout Year 3. The second year contains options in life sciences or petrochemicals. Courses in Medicinal and Forensic Chemistry and Chemistry with Business Management are also available.

Lancaster* Two courses in Environmental Chemistry are offered, one of which includes study abroad. The Environmental Science course combines aspects of geography, geology, chemistry and physics.

Leeds* Chemistry and Applied Chemistry, Medicinal Chemistry and Chemistry with Analytical Chemistry are all single-subject courses that have the same academic standing and a common first year; they are offered at BSc and MChem level and may be coupled with a year abroad or in industry. Leeds also offers a Colour and Polymer Chemistry degree. The course provides both a general degree of applied chemistry and specialised training in all aspects of dye chemistry, textile, paint and ink technology, photochemistry and spectroscopy, and carries professional recognition as a Chemistry degree. A wide range of joint courses is also offered. (High research rating)

Leicester* BSc (three-year) and MChem (four-year) Chemistry courses are offered. In Years 1 and 2 optional modules can be taken that include computing, environmental chemistry, industrial and polymer chemistry and management. In addition to the sandwich course, it is possible to spend a year in the USA or Europe or study Chemistry with Management, or Forensic Science. There is also a course in Biological Chemistry with the option to take a year in industry or the USA. Scholarships available. (High research rating)

Liverpool* In the first year, Chemistry can be taken with two non-chemistry courses. This is a very flexible chemistry programme with additional options in the second year including materials science, oceanography, archaeology, computer science, biochemistry or pharmacology. There are also degree courses in Chemistry with Nanotechnology, Medicinal Chemistry, Oceanography, or Business Studies. A year in industry is also an option. (High research rating)

Liverpool John Moores The School of Chemistry offers courses focusing on Medicinal and Analytical Chemistry.

London (QM)* A course is offered in Pharmaceutical Chemistry.

London (UCL)* For the degree in Chemistry, BSc and MSc students follow the same course for two years with the decision to choose the degree in Year 3. The course in Medicinal Chemistry includes biology, pharmacology, physiology and biochemistry. Chemistry can also be studied with Mathematics,

Management Studies or a European language, with 75% of the course chemistry and 25% the elected option. All courses may be taken as a three-year BSc or a four-year MSc. (High research rating)

London Metropolitan Biological and Medicinal Chemistry, and Chemistry with Forensic Science, Human Nutrition and Sport Science are all offered as three-year full-time degrees. There is also a degree course in Cosmetic Science.

London Univ Arts A degree course in Cosmetic Science in now offered.

Loughborough* Courses offered include Chemistry, and Chemistry with Analytical Chemistry, Business or Patent Law or Information Technology. All have three-year or four-year options with sandwich placements. (High research rating)

Manchester* A range of Chemistry courses is offered, including Chemistry with Forensic Science, or Medicinal Chemistry, Business Management or Patent Law. There are opportunities to study for a year in industry, Europe or North America. Three-year and four-year full-time courses are offered. (See the prospectus.) Scholarships available. (High research rating)

Manchester Metropolitan A large and flexible programme with Chemistry is offered with Study in Industry or in Europe (modern languages option in Year 1). Forensic or Pharmaceutical or Analytical Chemistry and over 20 joint courses are available. The Chemical Science course allows transfers to other Chemistry degrees after Year 1.

Newcastle* Chemistry is taken with modules in other subjects. A wide range of topics is offered in the final year, including languages, and there is an optional industrial placement in Year 3. Chemistry can also be taken with Medicinal Chemistry, Management or with study in North America or with Europe. Scholarships available. (High research rating)

Northumbria Applied Chemistry is a three-year full-time or four-year sandwich course with the industrial training period in Year 3 focusing on industrial applications. The MChem Chemistry course is designed for students interested in pursuing further research in the subject. Chemistry is also offered with Biomedical Sciences and Forensic Chemistry and there is a degree in Pharmaceutical Chemistry.

Nottingham* BSc and MSc Chemistry are modular courses with options in a wide range of subjects (scientific and non-scientific) in all years and the opportunity to transfer to the MSc (four-year) course at the end of the second year. There are also degrees in Chemistry and Molecular Physics, and Chemistry and Management Studies. There are also options to spend a research year in industry or an international study year. Scholarships available. (High research rating)

Nottingham Trent BSc and MChem Chemistry courses with placements are offered. Pharmaceutical and Medicinal Chemistry courses are offered along with the option to have a paid year in industry or abroad.

Oxford* A four-year Chemistry course is offered, covering inorganic, physical and organic chemistry, with the fourth year spent in a full-time research programme. All undergraduates attend a course in computing and their time is divided equally between chemistry lectures, practical work and preparation for tutorials and classes. Some opportunities exist for fourth year students to study in European or American universities. (High research rating)

Plymouth Courses are offered in Analytical and Applied Chemistry, with these specialisms being chosen in Year 3. Forensic and Medicinal Chemistry and Pharmaceutical Science are also available.

Queen's Belfast* The course is designed to provide a basic understanding of all the major aspects of chemistry, allowing some degree of choice in the final year of study. It is also possible to follow courses in Chemistry with study in Europe (France, Germany or Spain) and Medicinal Chemistry, and Forensic Analysis including a year in industry.

Reading* In Part I of the Chemistry course, students take three units of chemistry and three from a wide selection of other units. In Terms 3, 4 and 5, Chemistry students spend two-thirds of their time on chemistry and one-third on a subsidiary subject. Thereafter, their whole time is spent on chemistry, with equal emphasis on inorganic, organic and physical chemistry throughout most of the course, but with some specialisation in the third year. Chemistry can also be taken with Forensic or Medical Chemistry or with industrial placements in the UK or Europe. Scholarships available. (High research rating)

St Andrews* Basic studies in Chemistry occupy the first and second years, with certain subjects being obligatory. Modules are offered in chemistry and society, organic and biological chemistry and materials science. Placement years in industry are offered. Chemistry can be combined with a large number of other subjects including French, German or Spanish which can include a year abroad. (High research rating)

Sheffield* During the first year of the Chemistry degree, three unrestricted modules are offered (in other subject areas). Most students enrol for the four-year MChem course. There are also degrees in Chemistry and Enterprise Management, Mathematics and Informatics. There are opportunities to study in industry, in Europe, Australia, Japan and the USA. Scholarships available. (High research rating)

Southampton* The Chemistry degree is an extremely flexible course and serves as a basis for the study of physical, organic and inorganic chemistry. Other courses include Chemistry with Medicinal Sciences and with six month and one year placements. (High research rating)

Strathclyde* Chemistry and Applied Chemistry students take the same course in the first three years, after which there is an industrial placement of five or 12 months. The choice between degrees in Chemistry and Applied Chemistry is then made. There are also courses in Forensic and Analytical Chemistry, Chemistry with Drug Discovery and Teaching and Natural Sciences programmes. An MSci course in Applied Chemistry and Chemical Engineering is also offered. (High research rating)

Sunderland The Chemical and Pharmaceutical Sciences course provides a comprehensive understanding of pharmaceutical and chemical science, developed through extensive study of chemical and biological analysis. Emphasis is placed on the scrutiny of pharmaceuticals, together with drug design and formulation. Final-year specialisms include drug development, medical chemistry, forensic analysis, environmental analysis and food analysis. An optional sandwich year is available. Chemistry is also offered with a large number of other subjects in the joint honours programme.

Surrey* Chemistry is a modular course with special options such as forensic chemistry and computing. Ninety per cent of entrants take the four-year course with one year of industrial training, mostly in Europe, Canada, Australia and New Zealand. Courses in Medicinal and Computer Aided Chemistry are also offered. Scholarships available.

Sussex* A BSc course is offered, with an optional sandwich year in the UK or Europe. (High research rating)

Teesside The Applied Chemistry programme provides specialisms in environmental, forensic chemistry and biomedical science. There is also a degree in Forensic Chemistry.

Warwick* Considerable flexibility exists for first-year students to transfer between the courses in Chemistry (MChem and BSc) and Chemistry with Medicinal Chemistry. There are also courses in Chemistry with Management or Mathematics and in Biomedical Chemistry. (High research rating)

West Scotland The Chemistry course offers a broad study of organic, inorganic and physical chemistry. Optional industrial placement takes place in Year 3. There is also a course in Medicinal Chemistry with an optional placement in industry.

York* All Chemistry students, irrespective of their choice of degree course, follow the same first year (Part I) course that includes some maths, computing, biochemistry and physics. Part II includes more advanced chemistry studies and a choice of modules that lead to a degree in mainstream Chemistry, or Biological and Medicinal Chemistry, Chemistry Resources and the Environment, or Chemistry, Management and Industry. Students on the MChem course can spend their fourth year at York, in industry or in Europe. See also **Combined courses**. Scholarships available. (High research rating)

OTHER INSTITUTIONS OFFERING CHEMISTRY COURSES
Halton Riverside (Coll), South Devon (Coll), Staffordshire (Reg Fed).

ALTERNATIVE COURSES
Agriculture, Biochemistry, Botany, Ceramics, Chemical Engineering, Environmental Science, Pharmacology, Pharmacy.

CLASSICS

(including **Classical Civilisation/Studies**)
(*indicates universities with the highest entry requirements)

SUBJECT REQUIREMENTS/PREFERENCES
GCE A-level: Latin, Greek, a modern language may be required for certain courses.

SUBJECT INFORMATION
The literature, history, philosophy and archaeology of Ancient Greece and Rome are covered by these subjects. A knowledge of classical languages is not necessary for many courses.

Aberdeen Two courses are available in Latin: in either Language or introducing students to Roman Civilisation. The courses are only available at Level 1. In each case they are available for students with little or no previous knowledge of the subject.

Birmingham* There is a course in Classical Literature and Civilisation with options in art, religion, philosophy and archaeology. Classical languages are not required for this course.

Bristol* The course focuses on the Greco-Roman world with an emphasis on literature, philosophy, art and culture in the Department of Classics courses. Reading from the Latin and Greek (with beginners' courses) is an integral part of the course. Classical Studies is also offered with study in continental Europe for those proficient in a modern language. (This is a leading Classics department in the UK.) (High research rating)

Cambridge* Years 1 and 2 of the three-year course cover a study of Greek and Latin, the literature, history, philosophy, art, archaeology and architecture of classical civilisation. There is also a four-year course commencing with a preliminary year for students without Greek or Latin at A-level. Classics is an appropriate subject for anyone aiming to read another Tripos in their third year for example Archaeology and Anthropology, English, History, Law, Philosophy or Theology and Religious Stuidies. (High research rating)

Durham* There are three single honours courses, all with a common first year. The core of the Classics course is language, catering for students with A-levels in Greek and/or Latin, but also open to beginners. Language is optional in the Classical Past and Ancient History courses, the core being the cultural and intellectual history of Greece and Rome. (High research rating) Classics and Ancient History is also offered in the combined honours in Arts programme.

Edinburgh* In the Classics course a study is made of the Greek and Roman civilisations with equal amounts of Greek and Latin (including beginners' courses). Years 3 and 4 focus on Ancient History, Classical Archaeology and Classical Studies. Several degree options in classical subjects are also offered. (High research rating)

Exeter Courses in Classical Studies and Ancient History are available without any previous knowledge of Latin or Greek. There are courses in Classics, Ancient History and Latin and in addition English, French, Italian or Theology are also offered with Classical Studies.

Glasgow* The Classics course comprises Classical Civilisation. Knowledge of Greek or Latin languages is not required. See also **Combined courses**. (High research rating)

Kent Classical and Archaeological Studies is offered as a single or joint course, the latter with 15 subject options.

Leeds* The A and B Classics courses cover a study of Greek and Latin and classical literature. Students taking Greek from beginners level may choose Classics B course which involves an extra year. Classical languages, however, are not required for Classical Civilisation which is a broad study of the literature, language, history and art of Greece and Rome. There are also joint courses in classical literature, five in Roman Civilisation and four in Greek Civilisation. (High research rating)

Liverpool* The Classics course focuses on the study of ancient languages Latin or Greek. Classical Studies (no language involved) covers ancient history and classical archaeology. Classics is also available on the Arts Combined and the BA combined honours courses. (High research rating)

London (King's)* The Classics programme covers Classics for those wishing to study aspects of the classical world through reading texts in Greek or Latin and, alternatively, a study of culture and thought for those without a classical language. There are also courses in Classical, Byzantine and Modern Greek Studies and in Classical Studies. Latin and Greek are offered as joint courses. (High research rating)

London (RH)* The Classical Studies degree is particularly suitable for those wishing to give more time to archaeological, philosophical or other less language-oriented topics. Courses are also offered in Latin, Greek, and studies with Classical English, Drama, Italian or French or German. (High research rating)

London (UCL)* In the first year of the Classics course, Latin and Greek (prominent in all years) are provided at three levels – beginners, intermediate and advanced. Topics for detailed study include Greek philosophy, sculpture, drama and history, Roman Britain, law and history and Latin satire, elegy, late and medieval Latin, art and architecture. It is possible to take a degree in Greek with Latin or Latin with Greek. There are also other courses – in Ancient World Studies and in Archaeology, Classics and Classical Archaeology and Classical Civilisation. (High research rating)

Manchester* In the Classical Studies course a wide range of options is offered in Years 2 and 3, giving the opportunity to study Greek and Latin in all years. Joint courses with both subjects are offered. Degrees in Greek, Latin and Classics, Classics and Ancient History, Greek and English and Latin with English, Italian, French, Spanish and Linguistics are offered. (High research rating)

Newcastle* The Classical Studies course is varied and flexible and allows students to concentrate on areas and topics of particular interest to them such as art, archaeology, history and philosophy. No previous knowledge of Greek or Latin is required for entry. The Department is noted for its expertise in teaching the languages to beginners. The courses in Classics, Latin with Greek and Greek with Latin focus on language work in the first year. Later years are devoted to such areas as epic, drama and lyric with a wide range of options. Latin and Greek can also be taken as part of the Combined Studies programme. (High research rating)

Nottingham* The Classics (Latin and Greek) courses have an emphasis on language and literature. The focus of the honours Latin course is the world of Rome. The course in Classical Civilisation at honours level surveys the achievement of the Greco-Roman world without requiring a previous knowledge of Latin or Greek, which are studied in the first year. Ancient History is also offered with Archaeology and Latin. There are also joint courses with Classical Civilisation including English Studies, French, German and Philosophy. Scholarships available.

Oxford* The largest Classics department in the world offers two main Classics degrees (courses I and II), the former requiring Latin and/or Greek, while no experience of Latin or Greek are required for the latter.

Courses are also offered with English, Modern Languages and Oriental Studies. Scholarships available (High research rating)

Reading* Courses are offered in Classics (in which a fluent reading of Greek or Latin is required) Classical Studies and Ancient History. The main core of these courses lies in a series of options chosen from epic, drama, poetry, satire, the novel, history, art and philosophy. Ample opportunity exists for students to specialise or diversify in their chosen field. Joint courses are also available with Classical Studies. Entrance Scholarships available. (High research rating)

Roehampton Nine joint courses are offered with Classical Civilisation. It is also offered as a single subject.

St Andrews* Students studying Classics may specialise in Greek or Latin (language and literature) and, in addition, study ancient history, ancient philosophy or some other aspect of classical studies. There is a degree course in Classical Studies covering poetry, drama, satire, religion and art for which language study is not compulsory, while Latin and Greek are also offered as single and joint courses. There are also courses in Greek, Latin and Ancient History. (High research rating)

Swansea* The Department offers a wide range of courses in Classics, Classical Civilisation, Latin and Greek or Roman Studies, Ancient History and Medieval Studies and Egyptology. (High research rating)

Trinity St David (Lampeter) No previous knowledge of classical languages is required for Classical Studies, although students must take Greek or Latin as a Part I subject. The subject enables students to develop individual special interests covering literature, art, history, archaeology, philosophy and religion. The main emphasis of the Classics course lies in the study of languages and classical texts. Courses in Latin and Greek and Classical Studies are also offered. Scholarships available. See also **History**.

Warwick* Classical Civilisation covers the languages, literature, history, philosophy and archaeology of ancient Greece and Rome. There are also degree courses in Classical Civilisation with Philosophy, English and Latin Literature and in Classics. (High research rating)

ALTERNATIVE COURSES
Ancient History, Archaeology, Philosophy.

COMBINED COURSES

(including **Humanities**)
(*indicates universities with the highest entry requirements)

SUBJECT REQUIREMENTS/PREFERENCES
Varies depending on the course choice.

SUBJECT INFORMATION
In addition to providing single subject degree courses, many universities or their individual faculties now provide students with the opportunity to take two or three subjects throughout their studies. Specific examples of combined-subject courses are listed below.

Aston Two subjects may be studied from over 70 in the combined honours programme. Three and four-year courses are offered the latter with industrial and commercial placements.

Bath* A Natural Sciences programme is offered with Biology, Chemistry, Mathematics, and Physics by way of a three-year full-time or four-year sandwich course.

Bedfordshire The modular programme leads to a single major, major/minor or joint degree. Modules are taken, with up to a quarter of the programme in subjects outside the main study areas. One hundred and one subjects are offered. The university offers a Humanities programme in which students choose a joint degree at the end of Year 1.

Birmingham* The course in Natural Sciences covers biochemistry, biology, chemistry, computer science and earth science, mathematics and physics. Students take two major subjects and minor options, which can include languages. There are also 150 different joint honours combination.

Bolton Combined honours degrees are offered in seven major groups of subjects. Subjects are chosen on a major/minor basis in which two thirds of the course is taken in the major subject and one third in the minor choice.

Bradford A three-year course in Interdisciplinary Human Studies is offered in which specialisms are available in English, Philosophy, Psychology, Sociology. There is also a Combined Studies programme offering a choice of modules from 22 subject fields.

Brighton The Humanities degree focuses on historical, philosophical and social aspects of life in the modern world. There is also a similar course in Cultural and Historical Studies.

Bristol* 31 subjects are offered in the joint honours programme in which the two dozen subjects are studied in equal weight but with fewer options than in single honours programmes.

Cambridge* The Natural Sciences programme covers 25 subject options allowing for specialisation in Years 2 and 3.

Canterbury Christ Church A Humanities programme is offered covering Art and Design, English, History, Languages, Media, Music and Theology and Religious Studies.

Cardiff* In the BA degree scheme three subjects are studied in Year 1, followed in Years 2 and 3 by a study of one or two of these subjects. The BSc Econ degree allows students to choose up to six from 18 subjects in Year 1, followed in Years 2 and 3 by one of the subjects selected. Natural Science subjects are offered in the preliminary year.

Central Lancashire Over 70 subjects are offered, providing maximum flexibility in the choice of major, joint or minor subjects in the final year. Two subjects are chosen to be studied over three years; a third subject is taken in Year 1 only.

Chester A BA combined honours programme offers a choice of two subjects taken from 48 options.

Coventry Up to three subjects can be selected from nine options including languages with a year abroad. There is also a Humanities degree.

De Montfort. In the joint honours programme two subjects are taken from 30 options. Each subject is studied equally.

Derby Combined Subjects is a modular scheme in which 50 subjects are available, two or three being chosen on a major, joint or minor basis. There is also a very flexible degree in Applied Studies.

Durham* Students may choose two to four familiar subjects or start new subjects. In Combined Studies in Arts the combinations allow for a study of a mixture of arts subjects from Arabic, Art History, British Sign Language, Classics and Ancient History, English, French, German, Greek, Latin, History, Italian, Mathematics, Music, Philosophy, Russian, Spanish and Theology. Combined Studies in Social Sciences is a modular course enabling the student to choose subjects from Anthropology, Archaeology, Business Accountancy and Finance, Criminology, Economics, Education, Geography, Government, International Affairs, Management, Middle Eastern and Islamic Studies, Politics, Sociology and Sport. Natural Science is a flexible modular course with a choice from Astronomy, Biology, Chemistry, Computer Science, Earth Sciences (Geology and Geophysics), Mathematics, Physics, Psychology and Statistics.

See *University Degree Course Offers* (Trotman Publishing) for details of offers

East London There is a large number of combined honours degrees covering both joint and major/minor courses.

Edge Hill A large number of BA and BSc major/minor combinations are available and similarly joint honours courses.

Essex The Humanities degree scheme offers a wide range of options, following a foundation year, from Years 2 and 3. The main areas cover Sociology, History, Philosophy, Linguistics, Literature, Art History and Theory, Film Studies, Government, History of Art and Modern Languages. There is also a Politics, Philosophy and Economics course.

Exeter Combined and joint honours programmes are offered in addition to which there is a flexible combined honours scheme offering modules from a number of different fields.

Glamorgan In the Combined Studies programme up to six subjects may be chosen from a list of over 30. The choice can be reduced to three, two or one during Years 2 and 3. (See also **Social Science/ Studies**.) In the Combined Science programme two subjects are chosen from Astronomy, Biology, Chemistry, Forensic Science, Geology, Mineral Surveying, Geography or Sport Science. There is also a Humanities programme with 13 options and also major/minor courses.

Glasgow The General Humanities programme covers options in Ancient, Creative, Historical, Literary, Linguistic and Scottish studies. A Liberal Arts programme is also offered at the Dumfries campus. See also **Social Sciences**.

Gloucestershire The Modular Scheme offers a very wide range of joint honours courses.

Greenwich The Humanities programme enables students to study a range of subjects rather than specialising in one. Three options are chosen from over 30 courses. There is also an extensive list of combined honours degrees.

Heriot-Watt The Combined Studies course covering sciences, engineering and management comprises over 21 subjects offered as modules and awarded by credits. Students obtain the degree by way of achieving the required number of credits over three years.

Hertfordshire In the Humanities Scheme four subjects can be chosen (from 16 subjects). All four can be studied for three years (one being English History or Philosophy) or specialist studies can be selected in one or more of the four.

Huddersfield A flexible Humanities programme is offered allowing students to select modules from a wide range of subject fields including English, History, Politics and Sociology choosing a joint or major/minor subject scheme.

Keele Dual honours courses are offered with each subject taught in equal amounts. A Foundation Year is available for applicants without the necessary A-levels in eight Health subjects, 10 Humanities subjects and 20 Science subjects. Some single honours courses are offered.

Kingston A very wide range of courses includes 'classic' degrees in Computer Science and information systems along with those offering specialist modules such as digital imaging and network communications. There are single and joint honours degrees and opportunities for professional placements in industry.

Lancaster* There is a Combined Science course (22 subjects offered) in which students choose two science subjects plus one non-science, or three science subjects and Natural Sciences with a choice of five subjects. A study abroad option is included.

Leeds* The Cultural Studies course covers film, literature, music and the visual arts.

Leicester* Three subjects are chosen initially in the Combined Studies BA course: two of the three are studied for three years; the third subject is studied for two years. Sixteen subjects are offered, with certain subject combinations. The subjects include Ancient History, Archaeology, English, French, Geography, German, History, History of Art, Italian, Medieval Studies, Politics, Psychology, Pure Mathematics, Sociology and Spanish. In addition the combined honours Science course offers 13 option including Astrophysics, Geology, Genetics and Psychology whilst the Social Science course includes options in Law, Politics and Economics.

Lincoln There is a large number of study combinations at the Hull and Lincoln campuses.

Liverpool* Three subjects are chosen in the combined honours (BA) course, two being taken for three years. Over 30 subjects are offered (17 subject options) with some limitations on choice. In Combined Sciences two subjects are chosen, with a change in combination being possible at the end of Year 1. Modules in a third subject can be taken. For Combined Social and Environmental Sciences three subjects are taken in Year 1 with an introductory course in Social Sciences. In Years 2 and 3, two subjects are taken or alternatively one of several 'packaged' programmes designed in multidisciplinary pathways. Twenty-five subjects are offered.

Liverpool Hope An extensive combined honours programme is offered with over 30 subject options.

Liverpool John Moores The Integrated Credit Scheme offers a modular course structure in which students take a main subject plus electives from a very long list of subject topics.

London (Goldsmiths) The Social and Cultural Studies degree enables students to focus on a range of subjects covering anthropology, creative writing history, journalism, literature, media and communications, politics, psychology and sociology.

London (QM)* A Science and Engineering programme is offered with specialist options in eight subjects.

London (UCL)* Seven subjects are offered, in the Statistics, Computing, Operational Research and Economics programme and 20 alternative courses in the Modern Language group.

London Metropolitan Over 100 joint degrees are offered.

Manchester* In the Combined Studies two subjects can be combined chosen from 14 areas of study covring History, Philosophy, Social Sciences, Holocaust Studies, Languages, Linguistics, Classical Civilisation, Religious Studies, Sciences and the Built Environment. (See also **Economics**.)

Manchester Metropolitan In Combined Studies two subjects are chosen from over 15 options, and these are taught on a course unit system. Subjects include Business Studies, Drama, Science, Music, Sport and PE, Visual Arts and Writing. They can be taken as major, joint or in some cases minor combinations. There is also a joint honours programme. In the Humanities/Social Studies programme up to three subjects are chosen leading to a single honours or major/minor degree. Subjects offered include Economics, English, History, Modern Languages (French, German, Spanish), Philosophy, Politics, Social and Economic History or Sociology. There is also a varied course in Cultural Studies.

Marjon (UCP) Students take two subjects equally as a joint honours degree or as major and minor subjects.

Napier The university offers a Customised Programme with a wide range of vocational and academic subjects in which students plan their own course.

Newcastle* Combined Arts is a flexible and varied programme in which three subjects are chosen in Year 1 followed by two or three in Years 2 and 3. Thirty-one subjects are offered covering such areas as Accounting, Ancient History, Archaeology, Chinese, Classical Studies, Economics, Film Studies, Geography, History of Art, Japanese, English, Modern Languages, Politics, Music or Science. Combined Studies in Science offers modules from all Science departments (and elsewhere). Science subjects available include Astronomy, Biological Sciences, Chemistry, Computer Science, Software Engineering, Mathematics, Psychology and Surveying.

Northumbria Three subjects are taken from a choice of nine groups. Specialisation in two follows in Years 2 and 3.

See *University Degree Course Offers* (Trotman Publishing) for details of offers

Nottingham The BA degree in Combined Studies offers a range of flexible study options including Archaeology, Art History, Business, Creative Writing, English, History, modern languages and Music. A part-time course is also available.

Nottingham Trent In the Humanities course two main subjects are chosen from English, French, Geography, Heritage Studies, History, Languages, Media, and Psychology. Students also take a third main subject or a programme of special studies. Combined Studies in Science provides options in two subjects chosen from 10 options that include Sports Science.

Oxford Brookes* Combined Studies offers students who have already completed at least one year of full-time study the opportunity to follow a course designed by themselves: the course is of one or two years' duration. It is possible to spread the programme of study over two or more subjects from a wide choice of options.

Plymouth The Combined Arts scheme offers the choice of one subject, for example Art History, Contemporary History, English, Heritage and Landscape, Media Arts, Theatre Arts and Performance Studies, Visual Arts, Politics, Business Studies or Law.

Queen Margaret Twelve vocational subjects are offered in which applicants choose any two.

Queen's Belfast The BA joint course provides for the study of two equal subjects from Economics, Geography, History of Art, Human Geography, Linguistics, Modern Greek, Philosophy, Social Policy and Theology.

St Mary's (UC) Students can choose from a long list of combinations giving maximum flexibility to the choice of course.

Sheffield Hallam In Combined Studies two or three subject areas can be chosen, and within each area, a range of subject units can be selected. The subject areas comprise Computing and Management, Construction, Cultural Studies, Education, Engineering, Finance and Law, Health and Community Studies, Leisure and Food Management, Science and Mathematics, and Urban and Regional Studies. There is also a combined programme covering engineering subjects.

Southampton* The BSc Social Sciences course offers degrees in one subject or two subjects studied equally (combined or joint course). The academic year is divided into two semesters with students taking four courses in each semester. Part 1 provides a background in basic skills. Other units are chosen from a range of subjects including Accountancy, Biology, Economics, Geography, Law, Philosophy, Politics, Psychology and Sociology.

Strathclyde* Five subjects are taken in Year 1, later specialising in two in Arts and Social Sciences. There is also a Science programme.

Sunderland* Thirty subjects are offered to make up the combined subjects programme with major/minor, subjects (with an emphasis on one) or dual (two subjects, equal emphasis) programmes.

Teesside The course structure consists of major and minor subjects. Thirty-nine major subjects and 46 minor subjects are offered. In addition, there is a large number of specialist subjects.

Trinity St David (Lampeter) Three subjects are chosen from two options in the combined honours programme.

Warwick* The MORSE course offers Mathematics, Operational Research, Statistics and Economics with a choice of five subjects. The PPE course offers seven subject combinations.

West Scotland Over 30 subjects are offered on a combined degree scheme in which students select modules to suit their interests or career aspirations.

Westminster The combined honours programme has a choice of 15 subjects.

Wolverhampton Eighteen subjects are offered on the Applied Sciences programme and 65 subjects on the Combined degree course.

See *University Degree Course Offers* (Trotman Publishing) for details of offers

York[*] All students, irrespective of their degree subject, are offered the opportunity to study a foreign language in the 'Languages for All' scheme. First-year students take this course free of charge. The languages on offer include French, German, Spanish, Italian, Dutch, Russian, Japanese, Chinese (Mandarin) and possibly Arabic and Portuguese if there is a demand. A course is also offered in Philosophy, Politics and Economics.

OTHER UCAS INSTITUTIONS OFFERING COMBINED DEGREE COURSES
Bradford (Coll).

COMPUTER COURSES

(including **Information Technology**)
(see also **Engineering courses**)
([*]indicates universities with the highest entry requirements)

SUBJECT REQUIREMENTS/PREFERENCES
GCE A-level: Mathematics required in some cases.

SUBJECT INFORMATION
Programming languages, data processing, systems analysis, artificial intelligence, graphics, software and hardware are all aspects of these courses. Several institutions offer courses with languages and placements.

Aberdeen Single honours courses are available in Computing Science and Computing covering all aspects of programming. Topics include internet information systems, artificial intelligence, robotics, business computing, microprocessors and systems analysis. There is also a degree in Information Systems and Management. There are overseas exchanges and degrees with industrial placements.

Abertay Dundee Courses are offered in Computing and Networks, Computer Games Technology and Computing (Games Development) with strong contacts with the games industry. In addition there are courses in Information Systems and a degree in Computer Arts for those with an artistic interest in the new media industries. There is also a degree in Ethical Hacking and Counter-measures.

Aberystwyth A very flexible course is offered in Computer Science, with one third of the time in Years 2 and 3 studying modules in another subject. Courses are also offered in Software Engineering, Internet Engineering, Internet Computing and Artificial Intelligence, Computer Games, Information Management and Computer Graphics. All students are encouraged to spend a year working in the computing industry between Years 2 and 3. (High research rating)

Anglia Ruskin Modules in the Computer Science degree include systems modelling, artificial intelligence, programming, graphics, animation and visualisation, format languages and management. There are also four Internet Technology courses and several other specialised courses including Software Development, Computing and Gaming Systems, Computing with a Foreign Language, Multimedia Studies and Business Information Systems.

Aston[*] The Computing Science course has an emphasis on practice in programming languages and applications, data processing and systems analysis (no prior knowledge of computing is required). Artificial intelligence, graphics and software engineering are also part of the course. There are also degrees in Computing for Business and combined honours programmes.

Bangor The Computer Science degree covers all the key areas of the subject with particular specialities in computer graphics, artificial intelligence, data communications and business activities. The applications of computers in the marketing of goods and services and computers in industry and business are also offered respectively, with courses in Internet Systems and E-Commerce and Information and Communications Technology. The Creative Technologies course is one of the first of its kind and covers the applications of TV and radio, film and video. Scholarships available.

Bath* Studies cover a range of subjects both theoretical and practical, including computer science, software engineering, multimedia and human–computer interaction, with options in computer graphics and computer music, depending on career intentions. Courses are offered in Computer Information Systems, Computing with Mathematics, Business or a modern language including Chinese or Japanese for beginners. Four-year sandwich courses are available with placements in the UK or study abroad. (High research rating)

Bedfordshire Computing is offered in a large number of joint courses including Computer Networking, Graphics, Internet Computing, E-Business Management, Artificial Intelligence and Software Engineering.

Birmingham* The School of Computer Science offers several courses including Computer Interactive Systems, Artificial Intelligence, and Computer Science and Computer Studies combinations with one of a range of subjects including Business Studies, Arts subjects, Software Engineering and Civil Engineering. There are options to study in continental Europe. A course in Bioinformatics bridges the disciplines of biology and computing. See also **Combined courses**. Scholarships available. (High research rating)

Birmingham City Ten degrees with sandwich placements are offered by the School of Computing. These cover Information Systems, Computing, Software Engineering, Business Information Technology, Computer-aided Design, Computing and Electronics, Computer Networks and Security. Sandwich placements are offered in most subjects and E-Commerce.

Bolton A number of courses are offered, including Internet Communications, Business Software Development and Computer Technology and Computing.

Bournemouth A four-year sandwich course in Computing is offered, in addition to which there are courses in Business Information Systems and Business Information Technology. There is also a Software Engineering Management degree covering product development, with a 40-week placement in Year 3. In addition there are also courses in Multimedia Communications, IT Management and Applied Computing and Electronics. The University's Media School is the home to the National Centre for Computer Animation (NCCA) making it a leading centre for the study of computer animation.

Bradford A range of courses is offered including Computer Science, Computing and Information Systems, Internet Computing, Business Computing, Mobile Computing, Multimedia Computing, and Software Engineering. The four-year courses provide the opportunity for those wishing to have a year in industry. There are also courses in Computer Animation and Video Games Design.

Brighton The Computer Science programme has a common first year leading on to a wide range of courses including Business Information Systems, Computer Science and Software Engineering. Information and Technical Education Communication is offered by the same faculty, and there is a course in European Computing that enables students to qualify with a Diplome d'Etudes Superieurs Technologies d'Informatique after a final year in Paris.

Bristol* The curriculum adopts four main themes: software, hardware, applications and cross-disciplinary themes. BSc, MEng and MSc courses are offered including the opportunity to study in Europe. Throughout, there is a balance between theory and practice. Fourth-year options include artificial intelligence, databases, systems architecture and computer networks. A three or four-year course in Mathematics and Computer Science is also offered and a four-year course with Electronics. (High research rating)

Bristol UWE A wide range of courses is offered in Computer Science a number of which are three- or four-year sandwich courses. Other courses involve information systems, forensics, security, games technology and software engineering. Some overseas placements.

Brunel* Computer Science and Information Systems courses can be taken as three-year or four-year courses. The former focuses on the design and development of software, while the latter prepares students for the application of computing in commercial and industrial organisations. There are specialist routes is both degree programmes.

Buckingham A two-year course in Computing is offered starting in January or September. Several specialisms are offered in Year 2.

Bucks New Courses are offered in Computing, Mobile Computing and Network Management and Security. There are also courses in Multimedia Technology specialising in Animation, Games Design or Web Design and a course in Business Information Technology.

Cambridge* The first year of the Computer Science Tripos introduces basic principles. All students take the Mathematics course and one Natural Sciences subject. The second year covers core technologies and themes and the third year graphics, digital communication and artificial intelligence. Students from other subjects can change to Computer Science in their third year. (High research rating)

Cardiff* Computer Science is a broad course in Parts I and II, with modules on artificial intelligence, graphics, parallel computing, object-oriented languages and software engineering. The course in Computer Systems Engineering integrates with electronic engineering involving software and hardware pathways. Computing is offered with Physics or Mathematics. Scholarships available. (High research rating)

Cardiff (UWIC) Courses include Business Information Systems and Software Development.

Central Lancashire Fourteen computing courses are offered including Business and Computing, Computer-aided Design, Business Information Systems, Forensics, Computer Games Development, Multimedia Networks and Software Development. All are focused an vocational and practical skills.

Chester Computer Science is a broad course involving all aspects of the subject with a six-week work placement in Year 2. Several specialist courses are offered.

Chichester IT Management is offered as a full-time or sandwich course with professional placement. The programme can be taken as single or joint honours course. There are also joint courses linked with E Business.

City* There is a common first year for all courses taking specialist modules in your chosen course in Years 2 and 3. A one year placement is possible between Years 2 and 3. There are courses in Business Computing Systems, Computer Science and Artificial Intelligence, Distributed Systems, Games Technology, Music Technology, Informatics and Software Engineering.

Colchester (Inst) Computing Solutions degrees are offered specialising in Internet and Network Computing.

Coventry Twelve degree courses are offered including Computer Science, Computer Systems, Games Technology, Computer Network Communications and Creative Computing and Software Engineering with optional third year paid placements in industry.

Creative Arts (See also under **Art**) (UCA Farnham) Computer Games Design.

Cumbria There are courses in applied computing and in IT.

De Montfort The three and four-year sandwich course in Computer Science emphasises the uses and applications of the computer in commercial, industrial and scientific roles in the areas of software engineering and systems analysis and design. There are also courses in Multimedia Computing, Internet Computing, Business Information Systems, Software Engineering and Artificial Intelligence.

Derby The BSc Computing degree focuses on the practical and theoretical aspects of developing and maintaining software systems. Other courses cover Computer Networks, Games and Business programmes and Internet Computing.

Dundee After Years 1 and 2 in the Applied Computing course, which includes a subject of your own choice eg Accountancy, Psychology, Mathematics, students may proceed to an honours degree in Years 3 and 4. Several joint courses are also offered including Applied Computing and Financial Economics, Computing and Economics. Third-year options include software engineering, computer systems and internet programming. Scholarships available. (High research rating)

Durham* Three courses are offered – Computer Science, Computer Science (Europe) and Software Engineering. All have a common first year followed by the chosen specialisation. (High research rating)

East Anglia* The course in Computing Science aims to establish an appreciation of the theoretical foundations that underlie computing as a scientific discipline and to develop practical skills. Applied Computing comprises a study of computing and its applications, including computer graphics, commercial information systems and operational research. Business Information Systems aims to give a broad understanding of information system theory and technology. In the first year, courses in accountancy, mathematics, statistics and economics are followed. Computing for Computer Graphics and Computing for Business are also offered as three-year full-time courses, in addition to a range of other courses including Information Systems and Software Engineering, Computational Linguistics, and the opportunity to study for a year in North America or Australia or industry. A number of scholarships and bursaries are available. (High research rating)

East London Several courses are offered, including Computing, Information Systems and Software Engineering, Information Technology, Internet Technology, Games Development and E-Commerce.

Edge Hill Computing is offered with specialisms in business information technology, information and software systems. Students can also design their own course.

Edinburgh* BSc or BEng Computer Science courses are offered, depending on the student's preferences. The BSc courses focus on Computer Science which can be combined with Mathematics, Physics, Electronics, Artificial Intelligence or Management. The BEng courses in Software Engineering also have options in the same subject areas. (High research rating)

Essex Computer Science is a modular course in which eight foundation units are chosen in Year 1 leading to a choice of 16 degree courses including Computer Science, Artificial Intelligence, Artificial Intelligence and Robotics, Internet Technology or Software Engineering. There are also degrees in Computer Games and Internet Technology and Internet Engineering. (High research rating)

Exeter* Computer Science is a broad course comprising software development, artificial intelligence and hardware, and gives opportunities to debate the effects on society of new developments in computer science. Optional summer industrial placements contribute towards your degree. There is also a four-year course with industrial placement. Scholarships available. (High research rating)

Glamorgan The Computer Studies course is one of breadth and includes options to specialise in a chosen field. Other courses include Software Engineering, Information Technology, Internet Computing, Computer Forensics, Games Development, Mobile Computing and Multimedia Computing.

Glasgow* This highly rated research department offers courses in Computing that require no previous experience of computing. They are offered with a range of subjects such as Physics, Mathematics, Business Management, Physiology, Psychology and Statistics. An Arts and Media Informatics degree focuses on IT and digital media. (High research rating)

Glasgow Caledonian Computing is available as a four-year sandwich course with specialist schemes. Other courses include E-Business, Information Systems Development, Multimedia Systems, Games Development and Computer Engineering.

Gloucestershire The three year computing degree is essentially vocational and aims to equip students with a range of software development skills. There are also courses in E-Business, E-Marketing, Business Information Technology and Multimedia. There is optional work placement on the four-year course.

Glyndŵr There is a degree in Computer Games Development. Students are assessed by way of course work and the demonstration of competence in the delivery of practical work. Several computer courses are awaiting validation. Check with the university.

See *University Degree Course Offers* (Trotman Publishing) for details of offers

Greenwich Computing Science is a three- or four-year (sandwich) course involving business skills, data systems, computer information systems. Specialisms in the final year include information systems, software engineering, computer networking, multimedia and artificial intelligence. Courses are also offered in Software Engineering, Multimedia and Business Technology, Internet Systems and Games Development. In all there are 29 BEng and BSc courses offered in Computing.

Heriot-Watt No previous computing experience is required for the nine Computer Science courses. The four-year courses cover language theory, graphics, data processing and various topics in artificial intelligence. Computer Science courses are also offered with specialism in Information Technology, Software Engineering, Multimedia Systems, Artificial Intelligence and Human Computer Interaction. It is possible to transfer to other courses at the end of Year 1. (High research rating)

Hertfordshire A wide range of degree courses is offered covering Computing, Computer Science, Computer and Network Technology, Information Systems, Interactive Systems, Multimedia Communication and Software Engineering. Psychology with Artificial Intelligence is also offered and in addition a course in Software Systems for the Arts and Media. In addition the Computing joint honours programme has 12 optional subjects. Scholarships available.

Huddersfield A very wide range of courses is on offer, including Business Computing with Artificial Intelligence, and with Software Development, Virtual Reality Systems, Computing Science and Computer Games Programming. Many of these are four-year courses with Year 3 being supervised professional experience. Scholarships available.

Hull Several degree programmes are offered that cover Software Engineering, Internet Computing-IT Management, Computer Music, Games Development, Computer Systems Engineering, Computer Science, and Computer-aided Engineering. A complementary subject can also be studied. There is a common first year for all courses, after which students can choose their specialism or transfer to other courses.

Imperial London* The Computing Integrated Engineering Study Scheme offers a common two-year course leading to specialist courses in Artificial Intelligence, Computational Management, Software Engineering, and European Studies. (High research rating)

Keele The Computer Science course is designed to give students an understanding of the logical structure and organisation of computers and the theory and practice of computer operation and programming. Final-year options include software engineering (also a freestanding degree), communications, graphics and artificial intelligence. There are also dual honours programmes in Computer Science Creative Computing, Information Systems and Smart Systems.

Kent* A Computer Systems Engineering course is offered with a year in industry. There are also several joint honours courses in which computing can be combined with accounting, business, philosophy or film studies focusing on the application of computers rather than theoretical aspects of computer science. There is also a degree in Information Technology.

Kingston Several courses are on offer focusing on Computer Science with specialisms in Network Communications, Digital Imaging, Digital Microelectronics and also Information Systems with Multimedia and Business Information options. Other courses include Business Management, Mobile Computing and Software Engineering. Scholarships available.

Lancaster* The degree in Computer Science has a strong emphasis on practical computing with a balance between hardware and software aspects. A common first-year course leads to specialisms in Software Engineering or Multimedia Systems or Embedded Systems. There is also a study abroad option.

Leeds* The Computing course offers a broad range of opportunities relevant to the design of computer systems. Artificial Intelligence is also offered with Mathematics, Philosophy and Physics. A large number of Computer Science and Computing joint courses are offered and also degrees in Informatics and Information Systems. (High research rating)

Leeds Metropolitan Courses in Computing have a common first year, after which students select their degree specialisation from a general computing course or Computer Communications, Software

Development, Multimedia Systems, Database Systems or Artificial Intelligence. Business Computing and ICT are also offered.

Leicester* A three-year Computer Science course, accredited by the British Computer Society, can also be taken with Management or Mathematics or with a year in industry. There are also four-year courses to enable students to study in Europe. Scholarships available.

Lincoln A wide range of Computing courses is offered. All have a common core and courses include Games Production, Internet Computing, Computing and Cybernetics, Software Engineering and Information Systems.

Liverpool* Fourteen Courses are offered including Computer Information Systems, E-Business and Electronic Commerce Systems, Artificial Intelligence and Software Development. The Arts and Science Combined programmes also include Computer Science. A year in industry is also an option.

Liverpool Hope Single and combined honours courses are offered in Information Technology, and Computing with specialisation in Gaming Technology, Web Development or Computing Graphics.

Liverpool John Moores Computer Studies with four main themes can be studied (business information systems, computer systems, software development and systems analysis and design). Other courses include Computer Technology, Internet Computing and Software Engineering.

London (Goldsmiths)* Courses are offered in Computer Science or Computing and Information Systems, Internet Computing or Creative Computing. Industrial placements are arranged.

London (King's)* Computer Science courses have a mainly common first year. Thereafter the course unit system permits a large element of choice and leads to courses including Computer Science with Management or with Mathematics or Electronics. Courses involving a year in industry or a year abroad are also offered.

London (QM)* The Computer Science course emphasises the role of software. Years 1 and 2 cover the theory of program construction and software engineering. Project work and options follow in the third year, including computer graphics, multimedia and artificial intelligence. Computer Science is offered with Business Management and several other subjects and with industrial experience. (High research rating)

London (RH)* The flexibility of the course unit systems in Computer Science means that students are not committed to any particular course but may choose their course from year to year as their interests develop. Students may choose three main options including management, a year in industry, artificial intelligence. Scholarships available. (High research rating)

London (St George's) The degree in Biomedical Information is a healthcare information science and computing course providing experience of the interface between technology and health and patient care.

London (UCL)* All Computer Science degrees have a common core in Years 1 and 2. The first year gives a broad training (including programming) and mathematics with some optional courses, for example languages and psychology. BEng and MEng courses occupy Year 3. Information Management for Business is offered in the Faculty of Engineering. (High research rating)

London Metropolitan Computer Animation, Digital Media and Applications Development, Computer Networking and Computer Visualisation and Games are among the range of computing courses offered.

London South Bank The Computing course has a common first year with all other computing specialisms covering software design and development, business information technology, computer networks and multimedia technology. Specialisms in such areas as Business Information Technology, Computer-Aided Design, Digital Media Arts and Electronic Business follow in Year 2.

Loughborough* Three, four and five year MComp Computer Science courses are offered. After a broad introduction, specialisation is possible in database systems, networks and artificial intelligence, and many other areas. These courses came top in a survey on student satisfaction. Courses include Artificial Intelligence and Software Engineering, Computer Science, E-Business, Computing and Management, IT Management and Business. (High research rating)

Manchester* Five courses are offered in Computer Science including one with Business and Management. Courses are modular but a free choice of units allows for study in other subjects, for example languages, psychology and economics. Courses are also offered in Artificial Intelligence, Modern Telecommunications, Computer Engineering and Software Engineering. Check the prospectus. Scholarships available. (High research rating)

Manchester Metropolitan Computing courses allow students to build their own programme to suit their interests. Courses include Computation and Artificial Intelligence, Business Information Technology, Multimedia Computing and Software Engineering, Computer and Information Systems and Games Technology.

Middlesex Computing Science is offered as a three-year full-time degree and with optional work placement and courses are also offered in Business Information Systems, Computer Networks, Information Technology and Forensic Computing.

Napier A wide range of courses is available, including Computing, Computer-aided Design and Computing, Networks Computing, E-Business, and Electronic Computer Engineering, Information Systems and Software Technology.

Newcastle* First- and second-year courses of all Computing Science degrees are common for all students. This gives considerable flexibility for change of course, for example to or from joint honours, at the end of the first year. Courses with Computing Science include Economics, Mathematics and Statistics. Courses are also available in Information Systems with joint courses in Business Studies. (High research rating)

Newman (UC) Information Technology can be taken as a single, joint or minor course with another subject.

Newport The Computing degree covers the key elements including software development design and the implementation of computing systems.

Northampton. Computing course specialisms cover communications, computer studies, computer systems graphics, internet technology and software engineering. There are also 20 joint courses from which to choose.

Northumbria A very large portfolio of computer-based programmes is on offer. These cover Computer Games, Forensics, Computer Networks, Business, Software Engineering, Informatics, the Internet and Ethical Hacking. There is also a course in Information Studies, focusing on the organisation, retrieval, design and marketing of information. Scholarships available.

Nottingham* The Computer Science course involves software and hardware systems with a range of optional modules in each year. There are also courses in Computer Science and Management Studies, Artificial Intelligence, Robotics, and E-Commerce and Digital Business. (High research rating)

Nottingham Trent Courses include Computing (Visualisation), Computer Science, Business and Computing for Science, Information Communication Technology, Software Engineering and Information Systems.

Oxford* BA (three years) and MComp Sci (four years) courses are offered the decision being made in Year 3 as to the choice of degree. The Computer Science course provides a bridge between theory and practice, hardware and software. The first-year course is shared with Mathematics. Final year options include computer graphics, artificial intelligence and computer security. Scholarships available. (High research rating)

Oxford Brookes Computing Science is a three-year full-time or four-year sandwich course in software engineering design and programming with over 30 modules from which to choose in Year 2 of the course, thus giving maximum flexibility in the choice of specialisms. There are also courses in Communication Network Software Engineering and Multimedia Production. A large number of combined courses can be taken with these subjects.

Plymouth Computing Informatics is a four-year sandwich course. In Years 1 and 2 students cover programming, systems analysis and design and software production. In the final year an individual project is undertaken along with two optional courses. Nine degree courses are also offered including Computing, Computer Systems and Networks, Digital Art and Web Development and Information Technology. There are also joint courses with Geography, Geology and Mathematics.

Portsmouth A very flexible scheme is offered with a common first year for all courses, after which the final degree choice is made. Degree subjects include Computer Science, Computing Software Engineering, Digital Forensics, Internet Systems, Computer Animation and Games Technology, Creative Computing Technologies, and Computer Network Management and Information Systems.

Queen's Belfast* The aim is to produce graduates wanting to become software engineers although the course also covers programming and fundamental aspects of computer hardware in the first and second years. In addition to single honours courses, the subjects can also be taken in major/minor programmes. Courses in Business Information Technology, Computer Games Design and Development are also available. (High research rating)

Reading* The Computer Science degree offers a practical grounding in the subject but the course unit system allows great flexibility. Other courses include Applied Computer Science (with industrial placement), Information Technology, Computer Engineering, Robotics, Artificial Intelligence and Cybernetics. Scholarships available. (High research rating)

Robert Gordon The Computer Science course includes a one-year work placement. The Computing for Business course covers operations management, data communications and software engineering. Courses are also offered in Computing for Internet and Multimedia, Information and Business Systems and Graphics and Animation.

Roehampton Computing Studies can be studied as a single subject or combined with seven other options. There are single honours courses in Computing with Database Systems, Computing with Information Management and Computing with Web and Multimedia.

St Andrews* Courses are offered in Computer Science with 12 other subjects including Language and Management. Direct entry to Year 2 is possible with an appropriate academic background. (High research rating)

Salford The Computer Science course has a bias towards the software aspects of the subject and can be taken as a three-year full-time or four-year sandwich course. Courses in Business Information Systems, Software Engineering, E-Commerce Systems, Internet Computing and Mobile Computing are also available. Scholarships available.

Sheffield* Computer Science has an emphasis on theoretical principles and their applications. Computer Science can also be taken with Mathematics, modern languages and Physics. (High research rating)

Sheffield Hallam The Computing programme has a professional placement in Year 3 and focuses on business and IT systems. There is a foreign language option in Years 2 and 4.

Southampton* The BSc Computer Science course includes elements concerned with the engineering background to the design and application of computer systems, software and hardware in industry. Options in Year 3 include artificial intelligence, computer graphics, multimedia systems and programming language design. The MSc course includes work placements. Joint courses with Computer Science include Artificial Intelligence, Distributed Systems and Networks, and Image and Multimedia Systems. (High research rating)

Southampton Solent In addition to Computer Studies, several programmes are on offer in Computer Networks with options in Communication, Management and Web Design, Video Games, Digital Media, Software Engineering and Business Information Technology.

Staffordshire BSc honours courses are grouped into Business Computing and IT, Computing and IT, each providing a range of specialisms. In addition there is a large number joint courses covering Business Computing, Computer Games, Computer Graphics, Computer Science, Forensic Computing, Mobile Computing and Network Systems.

See *University Degree Course Offers* (Trotman Publishing) for details of offers

Stirling Computing Science covers artificial intelligence, programming, software engineering, communications and networks. 18 courses are on offer including modern languages (French or Spanish), Marketing and Psychology.

Strathclyde Computer Science is a four-year course to honours level or three years to a pass degree. In the first and second years courses are selected from programming, software design and artificial intelligence. The third year of the honours course covers communication and software development, with project work in Year 4. Other courses include Business Information Systems, Software Engineering, Computer Science with Law and Computer and Electronic Systems.

Sunderland Business Computing is a three-year full-time course or a four-year full-time extended course with a foundation year covering computer systems analysis and design and business studies. There are also degree courses in Computer Studies (and with joint courses), Computing, Information Technology, Business Computing, Forensic Computing, Software Engineering and Network Computing.

Surrey* The first two years of the Computer Science programme offer a wide range of modules and are followed by an optional placement in Year 3. Three- or four-year courses are offered in Computer Modelling and Simulation, Computer Science Engineering, and Computer Information Technology.

Sussex* The Computer Science degree includes the five core strands of programming, software engineering, computer systems, foundations and professional issues. There are options in web computing, computer graphics and animation, robotics and intelligent systems. Courses are also offered in Artificial Intelligence, Internet Computing and Music Informatics. (High research rating)

Swansea* There are several schemes involving Computer Science (which can also be taken with a language). In addition, there are several joint degrees with options in Geoinformatics, Physics and a language. Scholarships available. (High research rating)

Swansea Metropolitan All aspects of the computer industry are covered in the degree courses on offer. These include information technology, games, networks software and web development.

Teesside The Computer Science degree leads to specialisations in computer applications and computer science – while Business Computing focuses on the commercial world. Other degree courses include Software Engineering, Web Development, Visualisation, Business Information Technology, and Computer Games Design.

Trinity St David (Carmarthen) The BSc in computing focuses on practical skills in informatic systems and technology.

Trinity St David (Lampeter) Information Technology can be taken as a single or combined honours course. The emphasis is on how computers are used rather than on how they work. Topics covered include computer-aided learning, electronic mail, software engineering and word-processing. There is also a course in Business Information Technology.

Ulster Four-year sandwich courses are offered in Computing Science, Games Development, Software Systems and Computing with specialisms. In addition there are over 20 joint courses.

Warwick* BSc and MEng courses are offered. The first-year Computer Science course consists of four core courses covering programming, architecture, mathematics and professional aspects of computing. In the second year more advanced work in programming, languages and computer systems takes place. Third-year options include artificial intelligence and psychology, robot technology and computers in business. Courses also include Computer Systems Engineering and Computer and Business Studies or Management Science. (High research rating)

West London Six courses include Mobile Applications, Business Information Systems, and Computing Science and Network Management.

West Scotland Computing Science students choose their specialisms at the end of the first year. All programmes have a strong practical bias with team projects introduced from the first year. Other courses include Business Information Technology, Computer Games Technology, Computing Science, Digital Arts and Computer Animation, Information Systems and Software Engineering.

Westminster A large number of courses are offered covering Computer Science, Computer Systems Engineering, Computer Visualisation, Computer Communications and Networks, Computing, E-Business, Internet Computing, Multimedia Computing, Software Engineering and Design for the Digital Media.

Wolverhampton The Computer Science degree scheme allows specialisation in Multimedia Technology, Information Systems, Business or Software Engineering. All decisions can be delayed until Year 2. There are also several courses covering Multimedia Computer Games and The Web.

Worcester In addition to the Computing degree there are specialist degrees in Business Information Technology, Computer Networks, Computer Games and Web Development.

York* Computer Science is offered as a three-year full-time or four-year sandwich course, transfers being possible at the end of Year 1. About a third of sandwich placements are outside the United Kingdom, others being in industry. Other courses include Computer Science and Mathematics or with Embedded Systems. (High research rating)

OTHER INSTITUTIONS OFFERING COMPUTER COURSES

Bath City (Coll), Blackpool and Fylde (Coll), Bradford (Coll), Bridgwater (Coll), Bristol City (Coll), Carmarthenshire (Coll), Chichester (Coll), Coalville Stephenson (Coll), Colchester (Inst), Cornwall (Coll), Coventry City (Coll), Craven (Coll), Dearne Valley (Coll), Dewsbury (Coll), Doncaster (Coll), Dudley (CT), Durham New (Coll), East Lancashire (Coll), East Riding (Coll), Farnborough (UC), Gloucestershire (Coll), Grimsby (IFHE), Guildford (CFHE), Halton Riverside (Coll), Havering (Coll), Hopwood Hall (Coll), Hull (Coll), Lakes (Coll), Leeds Park Lane (Coll), Lincoln (Coll), Llandrillo (Coll), Manchester (CAT), Neath Port Talbot (Coll), NESCOT, North East Worcestershire (Coll), North Lindsey (Coll), Northbrook (Coll), Norwich City (Coll), Nottingham Castle (Coll), Nottingham New (Coll), Pembrokeshire (Coll), Ravensbourne (CAD), St Helens (Coll), Sheffield (Coll), Shrewsbury (CAT), Solihull (Coll), Somerset (CAT), South Cheshire (Coll), South Devon (Coll), South Essex (Coll), Southport (Coll), Staffordshire (Reg Fed), Stockport (Coll), Stourbridge (Coll), Suffolk (Univ Campus), Sunderland City (Coll), Swindon (Coll), Tameside (Coll), Truro (Coll), Tyne Metropolitan (Coll), UHI Millennium Inst, Uxbridge (Coll), Wakefield (Coll), Walsall (Coll), Warrington (Coll), Warwickshire (Coll), West Anglia (Coll), West Cheshire (Coll), West Thames (Coll), Worcester (CT), York (Coll).

ALTERNATIVE COURSES

Business Studies, Economics, Electrical and Electronic Engineering, Mathematics.

DENTISTRY

SUBJECT REQUIREMENTS/PREFERENCES

GCE A-level: Preference given to three subjects from science/mathematics. Chemistry usually essential.

SUBJECT INFORMATION

Courses in Dentistry cover the basic medical science, human disease and clinical dentistry. The amount of patient contact varies between universities. All dental schools stress that work shadowing and experience is essential beyond that of the ordinary patient.

Aberdeen The new course is based around a series of themes to meet the requirements of the General Dental Council. The school is in partnership with Dundee Dental School.

Birmingham* The Dentistry course lasts five years (with five terms of pre-clinical studies), biology forming an important part of the first year. A study of oral biology, and human and oral diseases continues through the course. Clinical studies begin in the sixth term and specialist studies at the start of the third year. Part of this clinical studies course involves attachments in oral surgery at local hospitals. Continuous assessment is an important feature of the final examination. There is also a course in Dental Hygiene and Therapy.

Bristol* A pre-dental course is offered (previous knowledge of chemistry and physics strongly advised). Features of the course include early clinical experience, integrated teaching and self-directed learning. Academically able students are encouraged to intercalate two years of extra study to obtain a BSc honours degree. Regular clinical placements take place from Year 1. (High research rating)

Cardiff* The Dentistry pre-clinical year (or two years for students without the preferred A-level combination) is undertaken at the Cardiff School of Biosciences. The course offers early contact with patients, teaching based on whole patient care, newly equipped areas for children and adult dentistry and an opportunity to pursue an intercalated BSc honours degree. In the final year there is an elective where students choose to work for at least six weeks in a medical centre, research unit or community practice anywhere in the UK or abroad. There is also a BDS foundation course.

Cardiff (UWIC) There is a course is Dental Technology.

Dundee* A pre-dental year is offered for those without science subjects at Scottish Highers/Advanced Highers or A-level, extending the length of the course to five and a half years. For students embarking on the four-and-a-half-year course the pre-clinical year (first professional year) covers anatomy, physiology and biochemistry. Practical experience in hospital commences in the third professional year. In the fourth and fifth professional years, students become responsible for patients' dental health. Intercalated degrees in a range of subjects including Forensic Medicine are offered. Ten medically related subjects can be taken by selected students on a one year course in Year 3. The Oral Health Sciences degree is unique to Scotland and provides a training in dental hygiene and therapy. Scholarships available.

Edinburgh* The Oral Health Science degree leads to a qualification in dental hygiene and dental therapy and provides a platform for those aiming for a graduate course is Dentistry.

Glasgow* The Dentistry course extends over five years. The first two years cover anatomy, physiology, pharmacology and also an environment, behaviour and health course. In April of the third year, students embark on the practical aspects of clinical dentistry with patients. Students who show a particular ability in basic science subjects may interrupt their dentistry course for a year and study for a BSc on a one-year or two-year course in one of 15 Life Science subjects.

Leeds* Clinical dentistry is introduced at the beginning of the course with the development of personal and professional skills. Community and practice-based education occur throughout the course. Child-centred and complex adult dentistry are introduced in Year 4 when optional courses are also offered. (High research rating)

Liverpool* As elsewhere in the UK, Dentistry is a five-year course divided into three phases covering basic medical sciences, human disease and clinical studies. The opportunity to take a one-year BSc is open to most students. There is a strong emphasis on basic medical sciences, preventive dentistry and dental clinical practice.

London (King's)* The first two years of the five-year BDS degree concentrate on the basic medical and dental sciences, with early patient contact. In the third and subsequent years more emphasis is placed on clinical dentistry, with supervised treatment of patients. Some students may opt to take the one-year BSc degree at the end of the second year. There is also a foundation course in Natural Sciences/Dentistry. (High research rating)

London (QM)* The BDS course lasts five years and the curriculum is organised in three phases: fundamentals of dentistry, clinical studies and vocational training. The opportunity to intercalate a one-year BSc degree is open to most students. (High research rating)

Manchester* Theory and practice are integrated in the dental course leading to enquiry-based learning with traditional lectures not forming a major part of the learning experience. There is also a pre-dental Foundation course open to those with arts subjects and one science subject at A-level. The Dental School is on the University campus. There is also a course in Oral Health Sciences. Clinical work with children and adults commences in Year 2. (High research rating)

Manchester Metropolitan* A three-year full-time or part-time course is offered in Dental Technology.

Newcastle* Dentistry has an introductory integrated five-term course in basic sciences and an opportunity for an intercalated science degree course. The Dentistry course lasts five years. Contact with patients occupies half of every day in the final three years. Purpose-built premises adjoin the city's major teaching hospital.

Plymouth The Peninsula Dental School (Universities of Plymouth and Exeter offer a four-year BDS course).

Portsmouth A three-year degree course is offered in Dental Hygiene and Dental Therapy.

Queen's Belfast* This is a patient-focused, student-centred course with the emphasis on learning. The majority of students are involved in Clinical Dentistry from the third year. There is an intercalated degree option in Year 3 leading to degrees in Anatomy, Biochemistry, Microbiology, Physiology and Pharmacology. Cadetships in the Dental Branch of the Armed Services can be obtained. A pre-dental course is also available for students not offering science subjects.

Sheffield The Dentistry course lasts five years. Students treat patients under supervision from the third year onwards. A special feature of the Sheffield course is the transitional training unit where final-year students work in an authentic working environment.

ALTERNATIVE COURSES
Anatomy, Biochemistry, Biological Science, Medicine, Nursing, Pharmacy, Physiology and Speech Therapy.

DRAMA, DANCE AND PERFORMANCE ARTS

(*indicates universities with the highest entry requirements)

SUBJECT REQUIREMENTS/PREFERENCES (DRAMA)
GCE A-level: English, Theatre Studies, Drama, a foreign language and History are relevant for some Drama courses. **GCSE:** English usually essential; Mathematics may be required. (Research ratings cover Dance, Drama and Cinematics.)

SUBJECT INFORMATION
Your choice of Drama course will vary depending on your preferences. For example, how much theory or practice do you want? It is worth remembering that by choosing a different subject degree course your interest in drama can be maintained by joining amateur drama groups. Performance Arts courses should also be considered, as well as courses offered by the stage schools. For Dance, be prepared for a study of the theory, educational, historical and social aspects of dance as well as practical studies.

Aberystwyth* The Drama Department (one of the largest in Britain) is characteristically a 'performing unit' but also offers an intellectually demanding course covering an historical perspective and a study of selected periods and playwrights. Film and TV studies (set, costume, lighting and sound, theatre administration and directing) are also covered in the course. Nineteen joint courses with Drama are also offered including Performance Studies and Scenographic Studies and Theatre Film and TV studies.

Anglia Ruskin A course in Drama is offered for students to study the subject from a practical or academic standpoint, or both. There are also joint course with English and Film Studies. There is also a Performance Arts degree covering drama and music.

Bangor There are courses in English with Theatre Studies and also in Theatre and Media Studies. The Media Centre at Bangor houses TV and radio studios used by the BBC and the students' radio Storm FM. There is also a parallel course in the Welsh medium.

Bath Spa Courses are offered in Dance (practical choreography), Drama (academic and practical), Performing Arts (production and performing).

Bedfordshire A three-year degree is offered in Performing Arts covering studies-based, practice-led contemporary dance, theatre and performance. There is also a course in contemporary theatre practice.

Birmingham* The programmes in Drama and Theatre Arts cover directing, playwriting, physical theatre, costume, stage management and lighting. (High research rating)

Birmingham City Three courses are offered in Acting with an emphasis on Performance, Community and Applied Dance Theatre, and in Stage Management.

Brighton Dance Theatre or Music with Visual Art courses link three areas of study: visual art, historical studies and performance and choreography. Students may specialise in one of these options.

Bristol* The Drama course covers the theory and history of dramatic literature and performance and has an introduction to practical aspects of dramatic art. The course includes radio, TV and film drama, playwriting and American theatre. Drama is also offered with English or a modern language (all these are highly competitive courses). (High research rating)

Bristol UWE Drama is offered as a single honours or joint honours course or with English and Education, Film Studies, Media, Applied Arts or Psychology. The Drama component is a balance between practical and theory.

Brunel* The main focus of the Modern Drama Studies course is on 20th century theory with a strong practical element and a work placement in Year 3. Drama and Music, Film and TV Studies, Screenwriting and English are offered as joint honours courses.

Bucks New The course in Performing Arts covers film, TV and stage work and dance.

Cambridge* See under **Education**.

Canterbury Christ Church The degree in Dance Education provides an in depth study of the subject with an emphasis on education. The Performing Arts Programme has pathways in Dance, Drama, Technical Theatre and Vocal Studies.

Cardiff (UWIC) The Dance course covers composition, choreography, staging and performance. There is also a Drama course for intending teachers.

Central Lancashire The Drama degree is mainly theoretical and is part of the combined honours programme. Related courses include English or Drama and Theatre Studies, Contemporary Theatre and Performance, Acting, Dance and Theatre Practice.

Chester The Dance course focuses on contemporary dance, with modules in choreography. A single or combined honours course in Drama and Theatre Studies is also offered emphasising practical work.

Chichester Courses are offered in Dance, Performing Arts and Drama. The Dance course has a core of choreography and performance whilst the latter includes performance, production, and teaching.

City The University validates the Dance Theatre degree at the Laban Centre and the Stage Management and Technical Theatre degree at the Guildhall School of Music and Drama.

Coventry There are courses in Dance and Professional Practice, Theatre and Professional Practice.

Cumbria A range of programmes includes Drama, Dance and Musical and Technical Theatre, Performance and Production and Performing Arts (Acting, Singing, Dancing).

De Montfort Performing Arts applicants indicate a choice of options between arts management, dance or drama. In addition there are degrees in Performing Arts, Arts and Festival Management, Dance and Drama.

Derby The Theatre Arts programme covers acting, directing, technical theatre, theatre in education, play-writing and production. There is also a degree in Dance and Movement Studies.

East Anglia* Drama is taught with a strong practical emphasis, supported by the theory and history of the subject. This is complemented by a close study of dramatic literature. Overall, the course has a distinctive vocational element. Courses are also offered in English Literature and Drama and in Scriptwriting and Performance. There is also a European Exchange programme.

East London Courses are offered in Dance and Theatre Studies, the latter involving both theoretical and practical studies.

Edge Hill Courses are offered in Dance and in Drama with Physical Theatre and Dance or with Music and Sound.

Essex Courses are offered in Drama and in Drama and Literature. Both courses have practical strands, and theoretical studies in theatre. The East 15 Acting School is also part of the university and offers professional training for those wishing to enter theatre, film, TV or radio. Courses in Acting, Community Theatre, Physical Theatre, Technical Theatre Studies and Stagecombat.

Exeter* The Drama course is based on a study of the medium of theatre from 'the inside' as a dramatic participant, rather than as a critic, and aims to explore and develop the physical and intellectual resources that are the basis of any serious creative acting and directing. The course also aims to develop drama-teaching skills through the Northcott Theatre and the local Theatre-in-Education. (High research rating)

Falmouth (UC) A wide range of courses are on offer including Dance (Choreography or Performance) Screen and Media Performance and Theatre Studies including Performance and Writing.

Glamorgan The Theatre and Media Drama course offers practical creative work and theory, with options in scriptwriting, world cinema, radio and TV drama. Theatre and Media Drama is also offered on combined honours, Combined Studies, Humanities and joint honours courses and there are courses in Lighting and Live Event Technology.

Glasgow Theatre Studies covers various aspects of the arts of the theatre including production, play construction and play spaces. It also deals with the place of the theatre in contemporary society and historical approaches to a play text. It is offered in combination with 30 subjects. (High research rating)

Gloucestershire A flexible course in Performing Arts has optional pathways in dance, drama and singing.

Glyndŵr The degree in Theatre and Performance covers practical skills, stage management, design as well as a study of dramatic literature. Special topics include mime, puppetry, mask work and improvisation.

Greenwich Drama is offered with options in Education, English, History, Philosophy or Politics. The Dance and Theatre Performance course is an intensive practical course and vocational training. The Modern American Drama course can be taken as part of a joint or combined honours degree.

See *University Degree Course Offers* (Trotman Publishing) for details of offers

Huddersfield Drama, Theatre and Performance courses provide opportunities to work with professional practitioners and to undertake a third-year project in an area of vocational interest.

Hull* The Drama course offers a study of drama in all its aspects – literary, historical, aesthetic and presentational – with equal stress on formal teaching and practical work. Performance Studies is also offered with Drama Music or Theatre. (High research rating)

Kent* The Drama and Theatre Studies course combines theoretical and practical studies involving acting, directing, community and educational theatre and management. Drama is also available as a joint subject with subjects such as Film Studies, History and French, German or Spanish. (High research rating.) There is also a unique course in creative events devising live events and covering practical and managerial aspects.

Kingston* Drama (practice, history and theory) is available as a single honours degree or as a joint honours course with a range of subjects including Psychology, Film Studies and Applied English Language and Literature. There are also single and joint degrees in Dance.

Lancaster* Theatre Studies covers all aspects of theatre and offers courses within it in acting, directing, playwriting, lighting and sound, set and costume design, theatre administration and TV drama as well as historical studies. The course can also be combined with languages and English Literature. (High research rating)

Leeds* Theatre and Performance provides opportunities for the study of Acting, Music Theatre, Performance Design and Arts Education. There is also a separate degree for those interested in Dance. Choreography is a major part of the programme.

Lincoln The three-year single honours Drama course includes acting, directing, dramatic theory and literature and theatrical history. There are opportunities for short work placements. There are separate degrees in Dance and Drama.

Liverpool Hope In addition to degrees in Dance and Drama and Theatre Studies, the Creative and Performing Arts degree has options in dance, performance skills and technical theatre.

Liverpool John Moores The Drama course focuses on practical skills and theoretical studies. Dance Studies covers performance, community dance, education and management.

London (Goldsmiths)* The Drama and Theatre Arts course provides a broad study of theatre, radio, film and TV as well as drama in the community. It has a good balance of practical experience and theatrical study. (High research rating)

London (QM)* Drama with English or Film Studies or a modern language are offered. The degree offers practical and theoretical studies.

London (RH)* Drama and Theatre Studies balances the theory and practice of drama which is considered from different perspectives and includes a two-year course on film. In the second year several options are offered including direction, TV and radio drama, scene design, music and theatre and electronics and sound. There is also an International Theatre degree with a year in Australia and joint courses with Languages and creative writing. (High research rating)

London Metropolitan The Performing Arts degree involves practical and theoretical studies in theatre and dance. Theatre Studies covers both theory and practice. Check the prospectus.

London South Bank A three-year Acting vocational course at the Italia Conti Academy of Theatre Arts is validated by the University. It is very intensive, with some 35 hours of classes each week as well as practical evening work.

Loughborough* The Drama course begins with practice in movement, speech and the art of acting and play construction plus seminars in drama and theatre. Television technique, lighting, sound, wardrobe studies, theatre practice and historical studies follow the project work in the third year. Throughout the course, theoretical studies support the practical aspects with historical and analytical elements of European and American Theatre. A programme with a study of English as a minor subject is also possible.

See *University Degree Course Offers* (Trotman Publishing) for details of offers

Manchester* Drama can be taken as a single subject or with Screen Studies or English Literature. It is primarily for the academic study of drama and is not an acting course. (High research rating)

Manchester Metropolitan Drama and Dance courses include Acting and at the Cheshire Campus, Dance and Contemporary Theatre and Performance.

Marjon (UCP) Drama is offered with six subjects including English Media or Education or as a single subject.

Middlesex Several specialist degrees are offered including Dance Studies, with specialisms in Dance Science, Community Dance, and Choreography. Drama courses involve practical skills, writing for the theatre and technical skills.

Newman (UC) Drama is available as a single, joint or minor course with another subject.

Newport The Performing Arts course focuses on acting and other drama activities.

Northampton Single and joint honours degrees are offered in Dance and Drama. There is also a separate Acting course: highly practical.

Northumbria The Performance course involves a study of styles and approaches in drama, integrating theory and practice. Performance-based modules involve sound, movement, music, song and visual imagery. There is also a Dance and Choreography course in partnership with Dance City, and a Scriptwriting and Drama joint course.

Oxford Brookes* Drama focusing on performance and history is offered with a wide range of subjects in the modular degree scheme including such subjects as Fine Art, Theology, Sports and Coaching Studies, and Music.

Plymouth Theatre and Performance is offered as a three-year course that focuses on theatre, dance, ritual, performance arts and community arts. There is also a separate degree in Dance Theatre.

Portsmouth The English and Drama combined honours course concentrates on the study of literary texts and their interpretation, and on practical and academic approaches to the study of various aspects of drama. Students are strongly encouraged to develop their skills in dramatic performance. Other courses include Drama with Creative Writing, or Performing Arts, Film Studies and Media Studies.

Queen Margaret The university offers a range of courses from the highly practical and vocational Acting and Performance degree to the theoretical Drama and Theatre Arts course. Other opportunities exist in costume design, lighting, sound and set design to Performing Arts Management.

Queen's Belfast* Drama is offered as a single, major/minor or joint honours course. Students in Stages 2 and 3 may focus their studies on the practical or academic aspects of drama.

Reading* The Film and Theatre course covers the history of the cinema and drama with practical work in drama, film and video. Courses in Theatre Arts Education and Deaf Studies and TV, Film and Theatre are also offered. (High research rating)

Roehampton Courses are offered in Drama, Theatre and Performance Studies and in Dance Studies. The Drama course covers performance studies, as well as modules including writing and approaches to directing in Years 2 and 3. Dance Studies includes modules in choreography, world music and dance criticism.

St Mary's (UC) Practical and theoretical studies followed in the Drama course. There are special studies in Applied Theatre, Physical Theatre or Theatre Arts.

Salford Performing Arts has an emphasis on live theatre and acting with media modules. The Media Performance course integrates elements of media production and performance and includes dance, singing, scriptwriting, directing and producing. There is also a new course in Contemporary Theatre Practice, focusing on 20th- and 21st-century theatre and performance studies.

Southampton Solent A course is offered in Performance, combining theory and practice in physical theatre. There is also a degree in Dance.

See *University Degree Course Offers* (Trotman Publishing) for details of offers

Staffordshire The degree in Drama Performance and Theatre Arts combines both theory and practice.

Sunderland A Performance Arts Studies degree offers study of more than one art form from dance, drama, music, performance or visual arts. Dance and Drama are also offered as part of the combined honours scheme.

Surrey* Dance and Culture is a three-year full-time or four-year sandwich course that encompasses both practical and theoretical studies of a wide variety of dance styles: African, Indian, Western classical ballet, and contemporary dance. In the third year students gain practical professional training in one of the following career areas: dance administration/management, anthropology/community work, criticism/media education, notation and reconstruction, resources and archive work, therapy. The degree in theatre studies covers performance and dance. (High research rating)

Sussex* Drama Studies can now be taken with languages, English and Film Studies. The course equips students with both theoretical and practical skills.

Swansea Metropolitan The Performance Arts course offers special studies in arts management, directing, acting and technical aspects of theatre production.

Teesside Courses are offered in Dance (both practical and theoretical studies) Performance and Events Production and in Performance for the Live and Recorded Media.

Trinity UC An 'intensive programme of practical study' is offered in the BA Acting degree. There is also a course in Theatre Design and Productions.

Ulster Drama is a broad course that offers specialist options in stage management, theatre technologies and administration, press, publicity and print. There is also a Practical Dance degree. Both degrees can be combined with several subjects.

Warwick* The main emphasis of the Theatre and Performance Studies course lies in a study of the modern theatre (the last 100 years). It also introduces dramatic skills in the first year leading on to the second and third years that allow students to specialise in either practical work or historical and analytical studies. Options include the moving image, marketing theatre and courses offered in the Faculties of Arts and Social Sciences. English and Italian are also offered with Theatre Studies. (High research rating)

West London Courses are offered in Acting, Dance and Drama.

Winchester In addition to the Drama Studies degree, a course is offered in Applied Theatre involving theoretical studies and practical skills in theatre and video production. There is also a course in Choreography and Dance with a strong focus on practical work and degrees in Performance Management and Performing Arts, Stage and Arts Management combining music, dance, theatre and management.

Wolverhampton Dance Practice and Drama are offered as single honours courses. Several joint courses are offered with both subjects.

Worcester A wide ranging practical course in Drama and Performance Studies can be taken as single or joint honours courses.

York There is a degree in writing, directing and performance.

York St John There is a Theatre course and a degree in Dance with specialisms in choreography or community dance.

OTHER INSTITUTIONS OFFERING DANCE AND DRAMA COURSES
Dance courses Bristol City (Coll), Chichester (Coll), Colchester (Inst), Coventry City (Coll), Dartington (CA), Doncaster (Coll), Exeter (Coll), Grimsby (IFHE), Hereford (CA), Hull (Coll), Leicester (Coll), LIPA, Liverpool (CmC), Newcastle (Coll), Northbrook (Coll), Nottingham New (Coll), Royal Academy of Dance London, South Devon (Coll), Staffordshire (Reg Fed), Suffolk (Univ Campus), Truro (Coll), Wakefield (Coll), West Thames (Coll).

Drama courses Bournemouth (UC), Central SchSpDr, Colchester (Inst), Dartington (CA), Doncaster (Coll), East Surrey (Coll), Farnborough (UC), Gloucestershire (Coll), Hereford (CA), LIPA, Liverpool (CmC), Manchester City (Coll), Matthew Boulton (CFHE), Newcastle (Coll), Northbrook (Coll), Nottingham New (Coll), Rose Bruford (Coll), Rotherham (CAT), Royal Welsh (Coll), St Helens (Coll), Shrewsbury (CAT), South Devon (Coll), Truro (Coll), UHI Millennium Inst, Wakefield (Coll), West Thames (Coll).

ECONOMICS

(*indicates universities with the highest entry requirements)

SUBJECT REQUIREMENTS/PREFERENCES

GCSE: Mathematics, English and a foreign language may be required.

SUBJECT INFORMATION

If you haven't taken economics at A-level be prepared for study involving some mathematics, statistics and, depending on which course you choose, economic and social history, industrial policies, the British economy and labour history, money, banking and regional economics.

Aberdeen The honours degree in Economic Science offers a wide choice of topics including financial management, regional labour economics, public policy and natural resources. In the honours programmes, students choose between Economic Science with a mathematical emphasis or Political Economy. Both programmes are offered as joint degrees. (High research rating)

Abertay Dundee The course in European Economy and Management has a common first year with the Business degree with options in business communication and Spanish studies. Scholarships available.

Aberystwyth A modular Economics course is offered consisting of core subjects and electives in a complementary subject, for example computing, accountancy, marketing, human resource management or small business management. A course in Business Economics is also offered.

Anglia Ruskin The Business Economics course has links with Denmark, Holland, Sweden and Finland (programmes taught in English) with placements abroad. Option modules include environmental and international economics, finance and human resources. Economics can also be studied as part of the combined honours course.

Aston* Economics and International Business is offered as a four-year sandwich course.

Bangor The Business Studies and Economics degree provides a broad business education with specialist studies in economic decision making. There is also a separate degree in Business Economics.

Bath* Economics is offered as a three-year or a four-year sandwich course with a one-year placement in industry or commerce worldwide. There is a choice of optional units each year. Joint courses with Economics are offered with Politics or International Development. Including optional placements in Year 3.

Birmingham* The Economics degree may be followed as a specialist subject or in combination with other subjects. Three compulsory modules are offered in the first and second years with two optional courses. Four options are offered in the third year. Courses are also available with French, German, Italian, Portuguese, Japanese or Spanish. A course in Money, Banking and Finance is also offered. Scholarships available. (High research rating)

Birmingham City Economics can be studied as a three year joint degree or as a four year sandwich course. Joint courses include Accountancy, Advertising, Business, Finance or Marketing. A course in International Management and Economics is also offered.

Bradford The Economics course places less emphasis than most on mathematics and has major electives in management, politics, sociology and psychology. Economics is also offered with International Relations, Marketing, Sociology and Psychology or with an emphasis on business or finance.

Brighton See under **Finance**.

Bristol* Tuition is given in economics and econometrics (use of statistical methods in economics), accounting, finance and management. There are several joint courses including Economics and Mathematics, Politics and Philosophy. There are also language options to support the course, which includes study in Continental Europe. (High research rating)

Bristol UWE Single and joint courses are offered with placements or study abroad in Europe or the USA. Students choose a specialist option in Year 2 and two further options in Year 3. There is also a specialist degree in the Economics of Money, Banking and Finance with an optional work placement year.

Brunel* Three courses are offered in Economics, Economics and Business Finance and Business Economics. All students take the same core modules at Level 1 before specialising in Years 2 and 3.

Buckingham The International Studies courses in Economics have three separate entry points – January, July and September. Courses are offered with Business and Law, Business Journalism, English Language, Information Systems, Politics and Languages. Scholarships available.

Cambridge* Economics Part I (Year 1) covers economics, economic history, politics and statistics. In Years 2 and 3, Parts IIa and IIb of the Tripos provide a sound understanding of the core of pure and applied economics, and the workings of economic systems and links with social and political issues. There is also a degree in Land Economy covering Law the Environment and Economics. It is also possible to combine Economics with another subject, transferring at the end of Years 1 or 2. See also **Property Management and Surveying** (Land Economy).

Cardiff The Business School offers courses in Economics and in Business Economics. Modules can be chosen from a wide range of subjects including accounting, management and a modern language (French or Spanish with Year 3 spent abroad). Economics can also be taken with Management, Politics, Sociology, Finance, Languages or a Humanities subject.

Cardiff (UWIC) Economics is offered as part of the business programme.

Central Lancashire Economics and Business Economics are offered as a single honours courses. There are also joint courses with Accounting and International Business.

Chester Economics can be taken as a single honours course or combined with appropriate subjects such as accounting, international development studies, politics, history, sociology or law.

City The Economics degree combines theory and real-world applications. There is also a course in Financial Economics. Optional placement years are available in both courses. Economics can be combined with Accountancy.

Coventry Four Economics pathways are offered. A common first year leads on to a specialised study in Part II in Economics, Business or Financial Economics or International Economics and Trade.

DeMontfort Courses are offered in Economics with Finance or Government each with a one year placement in industry or commerce.

Dundee In the Economics course the principles of economics are covered and their applications to current problems. It also emphasises the broad outlines of national and international economic issues. Over 20 MA and BSc degree courses are offered covering Economics, Financial Economics and Business Economics. (High research rating)

Durham Single and joint honours Economics students follow the same first-year course in economics. This allows flexibility in the choice of combined degree at the end of the first year, leading on to courses in Economics, Business Economics or Economics with French or Politics. There is also a course in PPE and a combined honours programme in Social Sciences.

East Anglia Economics students take a common programme of courses in the first two terms introducing economics, economic and social history, sociology, philosophy and politics. They then proceed to the honours programme. Economics can be taken with Accountancy, Business Economics, Philosophy, Politics and Economics. (High research rating)

East London Part I (first year) Economics offers a broad introduction, followed by Part II specialisms (second and third years). Continuous assessment accounts for up to 50% of the marks.

Edinburgh In the first two years of the single honours course a third of the work is economics, plus two other subjects. Courses in Economics include the study of economic theory and institutions, the organisation of firms and the banking world, and economic policy making. Eight joint courses are offered with Economics. (High research rating)

Essex Single honours Economics degrees are offered, including Management Economics, Financial and International Economics, and nine joint courses. A course in Philosophy, Politics and Economics and a four-year European exchange Economics course with French, German, Italian or Spanish are also available. (High research rating)

Exeter The first year of the Economics course covers a study of economics and statistics and two other social science subjects chosen from a list of options. More advanced studies continue along similar lines in the second and third years, when during the latter students choose a subject in which to specialise from a wide range of options including business techniques, management accountancy, investment and the economics of banking and financial institutions. There are joint courses in Business Economics and several courses that can also be taken with European Studies in which students spend Year 3 abroad. See also **Business courses**. (High research rating)

Glamorgan The Business Economics course is a specialist route on the BA Business Studies programme.

Glasgow Economics can be taken to general and honours levels as a single subject and also by way of a wide range of joint courses. Courses in Business Economics are also offered.

Glasgow Caledonian Major and joint honours courses in Economics are offered as part of the BA Social Sciences Programme.

Greenwich Students taking the Economics degree may choose options in international trade and financial markets, business economics and finance. Courses are also offered in Business Economics and Economics and Banking.

Heriot-Watt Six Economics courses are offered, including options in Business, Law, Marketing, Management, Marketing, Finance and Accountancy. There are opportunities to study abroad.

Hertfordshire The Economics Sandwich course provides a firm background in computing, quantitative methods and modelling. There is also a Business Economics degree with an optional year in industry. Economics is also offered as a joint subject from one other subject.

Hull All students taking the BSc (Econ) degree follow a largely common course and a definitive choice of specialism need not be made until the beginning of the second year. Various streams are offered including mainstream economics, business economics, finance and development, accountancy or economic history. Ten joint honours courses are offered. BA students choose their specialism in Year 3.

Keele Economics dual honours programme is taken with a second subject from 30 options. Final-year specialisms include finance, ecological economics, labour and public economics. A Business Economics course is also offered as a single honours degree. (High research rating)

See *University Degree Course Offers* (Trotman Publishing) for details of offers

Kent The Economics course has a strong European flavour and a European course enables students to spend a year in France or Spain. (High research rating)

Kingston The Economics degree is constructed around a set of core courses in each year. This enables students to select from a number of routes throughout the course. There are also courses in Applied, Global, Financial and Business Economics.

Lancaster The first year of the Economics course comprises an introduction to economics and economic history plus two other subjects. The third year offers students a choice of a number of specialised options including international trade, and business enterprise. The International Business course also has an economics focus. Economics can also be taken with Geography, International Relations, Mathematics, Politics or with study abroad.

Leeds The BA Economics programme is a generalist course focusing on the application of economics to a broad range of topics. Courses are also offered emphasising business and financial economics. Specialist modules can be taken in other business subjects and from other university departments including foreign languages. (High research rating)

Leicester Four degrees are available, in Economics, Business Economics, Financial Economics and Banking and Finance. All students share a common core of economic subjects that cover economic theory and its applications.

Liverpool The Economics course focuses on theoretical and applied economics backed up by mathematics and statistics and a wide range of options. Students on the BSc course can follow either a generalism pathway or a financial route. There is also a degree in Business Economics. Economics is also one of 16 subjects offered in the combined honours programme. (High research rating)

Liverpool John Moores The Business and Economics course offers modules in finance in organisations and an introduction to accounting. The Economics course focuses on political economy. Economics can also be studied with History or Politics. See also **Social Science/Studies**.

London (Goldsmiths)* Economics is offered with Politics in a three-year full-time degree and there is also a degree in Economics, Politics and Public Policy.

London (LSE)* Two single honours degrees are offered in Economics and Econometrics and Mathematical Economics. Economics can also be taken with Environmental Policy, Geography, Government, Mathematics, Philosophy or Social Policy. (High research rating)

London (QM)* A wide range of study options are offered covering all aspects of economics. There is also exchange programmes with Latvia, Italy, Spain and the USA. (High research rating)

London (RH)* The Economics course deals with all aspects of the subject including financial and industrial economics, economic and econometric and game theory and analytical political economy. Ten courses are also offered with economics as a major subject and there is a separate degree in Financial and Business Economics.

London (SOAS)* single or joint Economics courses are offered with a focus on Africa and Asia and their languages. Units are offered on developing countries, Japan, China and the Middle East. There are also courses in Development Economics and Financial and Management Studies.

London (UCL)* Degree courses with Economics are based on the course unit system and some courses can be chosen from other departments. A certains amount of maths is compulsory and an A-level A* is required. The single honours course provides specialisation in economics with an emphasis on economic policy. There are courses in Economics and Statistics, Philosophy and Economics, Economics and Business with East European Studies including a year abroad option. (High research rating)

London Metropolitan The single honours Economics course gives an in-depth knowledge of methods, theory and application in Economics. Other courses include Economic Studies, Financial and International

Economics and Politics, Philosophy and Economics. A Large number of joint courses are offered with Economics and Business Economics.

Loughborough* Economics may be offered as a single honours degree, or it may be taken with a minor subject (eg Geography, Politics, languages, Sociology, Social Policy) or in combination with Accounting, which is designed as a more vocational degree. The course aims to provide a balanced package of theoretical and applied studies with an exceptional range of options in the final year. There are also courses in Business Economics and Finance and International Economics. (High research rating)

Manchester* Economic and Social Studies at Manchester is designed to give you maximum flexibility and choice. Your can specialise in Accounting, Business Studies, Criminology, Finance, Economic and Social History, Economic Studies, Politics, Social Anthropology, Sociology and Development Studies. There is also a BEconSc (Hons) degree. Half of the course units being compulsory the remaining units being chosen from a range of options. (High research rating)

Manchester Metropolitan Over 50 joint courses are offered with either Economics or Business Economics.

Middlesex There are degrees in Business Economics, Business Economics and Statistics and Money Banking and Finance each with optional work placements. Special options can be chosen in the third year of each course.

Napier Two-year full-time courses are offered in Accounting and Economics and Business Economics.

Newcastle* A range of courses is offered by the Faculty of Social Sciences. In the first and second year of the Economics course students also choose one other subject from a list of options including accounting, law, history or a foreign language. The foreign language can continue in the second year and a range of specialised topics is offered in the third year. Other courses offered include Economics and Business Management, Financial and Business Economics and joint courses with Computer Science, Mathematics and Statistics. (High research rating)

Newport Economics is offered with Law; the latter offers several CPE exemptions enabling students to pursue a legal career.

Northampton Thirty joint honours courses are offered with Economics.

Northumbria* Economics is offered as a specialism within the Business degree. There is also a degree in Business with International Trade.

Nottingham* The first two years of all School of Economics degrees provide a basic foundation of theoretical and applied knowledge. Specialist options are chosen in Year 3. Economics is also offered with Philosophy, modern languages, with European Union Studies and with Chinese Studies. There are also courses in Industrial and International Economics. (High research rating)

Nottingham Trent A broad Economics course is provided with an introduction to politics in the first year, and options in politics, accounting and computing are available in the third year. There is also a Business Economics degree.

Oxford* In the first year of the Philosophy, Politics and Economics course, the three subjects are studied equally; in the second and third years, two or three subjects may be studied and also Sociology. There is also a course in Economics and Management that allows a choice from six subjects in Economics and two in Management or vice versa. Economics is also offered with History and with Engineering and Management. Scholarships available. (High research rating).

Oxford Brookes* Economics is offered as a four year (optional) sandwich course jointly with over 40 other subjects including Languages and science subjects. Business Economics can also be taken as a single honours subject.

Plymouth Joint courses are offered with Economics and in addition there are degrees in Financial Economics and International Business Economics.

Portsmouth* The Economics degree is an extremely flexible course that allows students to move between various Economics schemes in the Business School. These include Business Economics (which can also be studied with law), Applied Economics and Finance Banking and Economics each course with an optional work placement.

Queen's Belfast* A BSc (Econ) course occupies one-third of the first year and two-thirds of the course in subsequent years with modules in the economics of the workplace, the environment or the public sector and political studies opportunities exist for summer and year-long placements. The Faculty offers a very wide range of courses including Business Economics, Economics and Accounting or Economics with International Studies, Accounting, Finance, a Modern Language or Management.

Reading* For the First University Examination the Economics course has two parts. All students take units in mathematical economics and in economic theory. Optional subjects in the third years include money and banking, business economics, European urban and regional economics. Courses in Economics and Econometrics, Business Economics and European languages with Economics are also available. (High research rating)

Robert Gordon Management with Economics is offered as a four-year full-time degree.

St Andrews* Degrees are offered in Applied Economics, Financial Economics, and Economics, which can be studied singly or in combination with another subject including International Relations, Middle East Studies and Russian. Optional papers at honours level include financial markets, labour economics and industrial relations. (High research rating)

Salford This Economics degree has an applied focus. It offers the student a wide choice of optional areas including the pursuit of specialist streams in business economics, world economy and quantitative techniques. Courses are also offered in Business Economics, Business Economics with Gambling Studies, and Economics and Sports Economics.

Sheffield* For the foundation year, Economics students take micro economics and macro economics and additional modules in other subjects. Single and dual honours degrees offer considerable flexibility and several subjects can be combined with Economics including Accounting and Financial Management, Econometrics, Social Policy and Russian.

Southampton* Economics, mathematics and statistics are compulsory units in Year 1 with options in managerial systems, political systems and modern languages. Micro economics and macro economics follow in Years 2 and 3 with a wide range of options in each year. Economics is also offered with Actuarial Studies, Financial Accounting, Philosophy, Politics and Management Sciences. Scholarships available. (High research rating)

Staffordshire Economics, maths, statistics, politics and economic history are taken in the first year of the Economics course, plus sociology, international relations, accounting, geography or a language. These studies lead to a range of options in the second and third years that include managerial economics, poverty, income and wealth and the economics of sport and recreation. Economics courses are also offered with Actuarial Science, Management and Finance.

Stirling Economics can be taken as general, single or joint honours. Students follow a sequence of core courses covering all aspects of economics, with a choice of a number of options towards the end of the course. Stirling also offers a course in Politics, Philosophy and Economics. (High research rating)

Strathclyde The Economics course assumes no previous study of the subject and is presented in two major parts: consumers, enterprises and industries; and markets and governments. Business Economics degrees are also available. (High research rating)

Surrey* Business Economics courses focus on real world issues and are highly applied and vocational. In the first and second years a study is made of economics and related subjects including computing, maths, statistics, sociology, politics and history. The third year is spent on an industrial or commercial placement and the final year devoted to specialist topics chosen by the student. Opportunities exist for an exchange scheme in the USA for the students following the four-year course. There is also a programme in Business Economics and Finance with good employer contacts. (High research rating)

Sussex* The focus is on the practical application of economics and an analysis of contemporary issues and problems. Other courses include Management Economics with Development Studies and Economics and International Relations. (High research rating)

Swansea* Courses are offered in Business Economics (and with Accounting), Financial Economics and Economics. Joint honours courses are also available. (High research rating.) (See also under **Philosophy** for PPE)

Ulster Economics is a three- or four-year course with commercial placement in Year 3. The course offers modules from a wide range of options including international trade, small business and the economics of poverty. There are also eight joint modular courses.

Warwick* Economics degree courses are based on a core of courses in economic analysis, quantitative techniques and economic and social history. There is then considerable flexibility of choice available in the optional subjects taught within the Department including business studies, politics and international studies, law, accounting, industrial relations and marketing. There is the possibility to transfer to another Economics degree course at the end of Year 1. Other courses cover Industrial Economics, Economics and Economic History, Economics, Politics and International Studies and MORSE (Mathematics, Operational Research, Statistics and Economics – grade A in Mathematics required). (High research rating)

West Scotland The Economics course offers modules covering industrial, international, labour, public and social economics and economic techniques.

Westminster Business Economics can be studied as a specialism in Business Degrees. A combined honours programme includes Economics.

York* In the first year all Economics students are required to take four modules in Part I (economics, economic and social history, statistics and one other social science subject). Students who are undecided about their choice of course need not make the final decision until the end of the first year. During the first year there are no restrictions on transfers within the department. Part II (Years 2 and 3) also offers flexibility and a very wide choice of options. The university has one of the largest Economics departments in the UK and offers several joint courses. Changes to the modular scheme may affect degree programmes for 2011 so check with the department. (High research rating)

OTHER INSTITUTIONS OFFERING ECONOMICS COURSES
Bradford (Coll), European (BusSch), Oxford Ruskin (Coll), Richmond (American Univ), South Devon (Coll).

ALTERNATIVE COURSES
Accountancy, Banking, Business Studies, E-Commerce, Estate Management, Financial Studies, Marketing, Quantity Surveying, Valuation Surveying.

EDUCATION

(Teaching and Non-teaching Courses)
(*indicates universities with the highest entry requirements)

SUBJECT REQUIREMENTS/PREFERENCES
GCE A-level: In chosen major subjects. **GCSE:** English and Mathematics and Science.

SUBJECT INFORMATION

There are two types of courses under the title Education, those which cover the history, philosophy and theory of education and educational administration, which are not necessarily teacher-training courses, and those which are specifically designed for people wishing to enter the teaching profession.

It should be noted that students taking first degrees in National Curriculum subjects can, on graduation, take a one-year course leading to the Postgraduate Certificate in Education that will provide a teaching qualification. Grants are awarded for students taking these courses.

Aberdeen BA courses are offered in Secondary and Primary Education. Core courses cover the practice of education, expressive arts, language studies, mathematics, environmental studies, religious and moral education and information technology.

Aberystwyth The degree in Education explores the development of children and adolescents through learning and teaching. The course involves the psychology of learning and thinking, language and literacy, health and education and multicultural education. Education can also be studied with a choice of up to 22 other subjects.

Anglia Ruskin A Primary BEd course is offered in which students follow a course comprising mathematics, science, English, art or additionally with a modern language. Secondary BEd courses are offered in French and Science. Courses are also offered in Early Childhood Education and Education Studies.

Bangor BEd Primary courses are offered in Art, Design and Technology, English Literature, Geography, History, Mathematics, Music, Physical Education, Religious Studies, Science and Welsh (first and second language). There is also a Secondary Teaching course in Design and Technology and a second course focusing on Product Design, and a degree in Childhood Studies. Course are also offered in the Welsh medium.

Bath* The degree in Childhood, Youth and Education Studies is taught by staff from the department of Education and Psychology. There is an optional placement year in a professional setting. The degree in Education and International Development can be taken with a placement year. A course is also offered in Coach Education and Sports Development. See under **Sports Science/Studies**.

Bath Spa Two degrees are offered in Education Studies (focusing on Early Years) both leading to PGCE Primary and a third course in Combined Studies.

Bedfordshire Physical Education (Secondary) and Primary Education teaching courses are offered along with several Education specialities including child and youth and disability studies.

Birmingham* Psychology, Sociology, Philosophy and Social Policy are disciplines studied in the Childhood, Culture and Education degree. Education programmes are offered in Childhood Studies, English Language and Literature, Sport, and Physical Education.

Birmingham City A BA course is offered in Primary Education. Students choose one subject from Art, Design and Technology, Drama with English, English, Geography, History, Mathematics, Music, Science or Religious Studies with compulsory core subjects in mathematics, science and English. Education is also offered as part of the combined honours programme or with English Literature, History or Sociology. Degrees are also offered in Early Years and Early Childhood Studies.

Bolton Educational Studies can be taken in the Combined Studies programme. This is a non-teaching course focusing on educational issues. There is also a BEd degree is Technical and Vocational Education.

Brighton Courses offered in Primary Education (Early or Later Years), Upper Primary and Lower Secondary (Mathematics, Science, Design and Technology, Religious Studies, Geography, Physical Education, Information Technology, Science and English BA QTS). There is also a degree course in Education.

Bristol* There is a degree in Childhood Studies studying child development and service provision for children and their families. There is a degree in Deaf Studies with an emphasis on theory of British Sign Language. (High research rating)

See *University Degree Course Offers* (Trotman Publishing) for details of offers

Bristol UWE* Courses are offered in Primary Education and in Early Childhood Studies which includes child development, communication, behaviour, hearing and psychology. The Education Studies course focuses on systems, approaches and political aspects.

Brunel* A course is offered in Secondary Education (Physical Education) involving school experience in each year.

Cambridge* The Education Studies Tripos is divided into two main parts which offer studies in philosophy, psychology, history and sociology or in curriculum studies for students wishing to teach at primary or middle school levels. Subject options cover Biological Sciences, Classics, English and with Drama, Geography, History, Mathematics, Languages, Physical Sciences and Religious Studies.

Canterbury Christ Church Single, joint and combined courses are offered in Early Childhood Studies. Primary Teaching courses leading to Qualified Teacher Status, degree in Education Studies and courses in Physical Education and Maths Education at Secondary Level.

Cardiff* The Education degree places an emphasis on the social and psychological development of children from birth to adolescence and on national and international policies in education. Practical issues in teaching, learning and school management are also covered. (High research rating)

Cardiff (UWIC) Courses offered include Primary and Secondary Teaching, Education Studies and Youth and Community Studies.

Central Lancashire Education can be taken as a major, joint or minor degree programme or combined with Sociology or History. Courses are also offered in British Sign Language and Deaf Studies.

Chester Courses are offered in Education Studies and Teacher Education covering Early Years (3–7 years) or General Primary (5–11 years). There is also a course in Early Childhood Studies focusing on child development working with children and families.

Chichester Courses in Education include Adventure Education, Childhood Studies including health, child development and special needs. Teacher training courses are offered in Primary Education, Secondary and Physical Education.

Colchester (Inst) A BA Early Years course is offered.

Cumbria In addition to Primary and Secondary Education courses with specialist options ICT, English, Maths and RE, there are also several options covering outdoor education and leadership.

De Montfort An Education Studies degree new for 2010 is a child centred course. The joint degree can be taken with a national curriculum subject which allows students to go on to take a Postgraduate Certificate in Education.

Derby A BEd Primary course is available in which all students study core subjects (Mathematics, English and Science). Degrees are also offered in Early Childhood Studies and Education Studies (also joint courses).

Dundee A BEd course is offered in the Primary range (3–12 years). Elective subjects cover information technology, modern languages, science and Scottish studies. There is also a four-year degree in Community Education with a professional qualification.

Durham* A study of Education can be combined with Biological Sciences, English, Geography, History, Mathematics, Music, Philosophy, Sociology, Theology and Psychology (which is BPS accredited). An additional year leading to a Postgraduate Certificate in Education provides entry to the teaching profession.

Durham (Stockton) A BA(Ed) Primary Teaching (General) course is offered leading to QTS. It includes 32 weeks of school experience.

East Anglia The Educational Studies degree offers a flexible pathway enabling students to tailor their degree to their own interests. It involves a balance between theory and practical experience and a study of the whole field of education in the UK and abroad including modules in teaching, learning and assessment.

East London* A degree in Education and Community Development theory is offered with pathways in health, early childhood studies, special needs and playwork with youth studies. Other degrees include Community Studies, Early Childhood Studies and Education Studies.

Edge Hill BA Honours courses leading to QTS are offered in Primary Education with specialisms in Language, Communication and Literacy, Humanities, Creative and Expressive Arts, Foreign Languages, or Personal, Social and Health Education, Mathematics, PE and Science. There is also a course in Early Years Education and courses in Secondary Design and Technology, ICT, Mathematics and Science and Childhood and Youth Studies.

Edinburgh* A four-year BEd programme is offered that prepares students to teach in the 3–12 years Primary range. Basic subjects cover numeracy, language and literacy, environmental studies, expressive arts, religious and moral education and core education courses. A range of specialist options can be studied in Years 3 and 4. Other courses are offered in Design and Technology, Physical Education, Childhood Studies and Community Education. (High research rating)

Exeter* The degree in Education Studies enables students to choose a first degree in a relevant subject prior to proceeding to a qualification (PGCE) for both primary and secondary teaching. There is also a course in Child and Youth Studies, covering gender, creativity, citizenship, health and relationships. (High research rating) Sports Science and English are also offered with Education.

Glamorgan The courses in Early Years and Developmental Education cover psychological, educational and social perspectives. Education is also offered as part of the combined programme as a minor subject.

Glasgow* The Faculty of Education comprises departments of Curriculum Studies, Educational Studies, Religious Education and Adult and Continuing Education. There are teaching courses covering Primary, Religious, Technological, Music and Community Education.

Glyndŵr Courses focus on childhood care and education by way of degrees in Early Childhood Studies, Education Studies and Play and Playwork.

Gloucestershire Courses are offered in Early Childhood Studies, Education Studies and Nursery (Key Stage 1) and Primary Education (Early 3–7 and Later Years 5–11).

Greenwich Primary teaching courses leading to the BEd and BA Hons course leading to QTS are offered in English, French, Design Technology, Art and Early Years. Secondary education courses are available in Design and Technology. There is also a course in Childhood Studies.

Hertfordshire In addition to Primary and Secondary Education courses a degree in Education Studies presents a broad picture of educational issues.

Huddersfield For those wishing to work with children there is a Childhood Studies degree. For intending teachers there is an Early Primary Education course with QTS and a degree in Religion and Education.

Hull BA/BSc Primary courses are offered in Biology, English, Information and Communications Technology and Mathematics there are also courses in Education with Early Childhood Studies, Psychology or Urban Learning.

Keele Education Studies is offered as a dual honours subject with a choice of 28 other subjects.

Kent The course in Intellectual and Developmental Disabilities covers behaviour problems, learning disabilities, work-based learning and person-centred support.

Kingston BA courses are offered leading to primary school teaching in core subjects Art, Maths, Science, ICT and Humanities followed in Year 2 and 3 with specialisation.

See *University Degree Course Offers* (Trotman Publishing) for details of offers

Leeds* There is a course in Childhood Studies covering education, sociology and psychology.

Leeds Metropolitan Courses are offered leading to degrees in Childhood Studies, Primary Education (Design Technology, French, Maths, Spanish, English, History, PE) and Secondary Physical Education.

Leeds Trinity (UC) Primary teaching courses are offered in Early Years (3–7) and Junior Years (7–11). There are also courses is PE (Primary) and Childhood and Youth Studies and Education.

Lincoln A course is offered in Child and Youth Studies.

Liverpool* Mathematics or Science can be studied with Education.

Liverpool Hope Single and combined honours degrees are offered in Education Studies, Inclusive Education and Early Childhood Studies, focusing on early years education and childcare provision. A BA (QTS) Primary programme is also offered and there are single and combined honours degrees in Childhood and Youth Studies.

Liverpool John Moores Early Years, Primary and Secondary Education courses are offered and also Outdoor Education and Environmental Education and Sport Development and Physical Education.

London (Goldsmiths)* Education, Culture and Society leads to opportunities in education outside the school system as well as a range of other careers. (High research rating)

London (King's) Degrees are offered in Education with Mathematics, and modern foreign languages.

London Metropolitan Courses are offered in Early Childhood Studies, and also Education Studies with seven joint courses.

Manchester Metropolitan BEd Primary and Secondary courses are offered. In the Primary course one main subject is taken from Science, English, History, Information Technology, and Physical Education. BA/BSc Secondary courses are offered in Business, Communication Technology, Physical Education, Design and Technology and Mathematics. Over 24 other subjects are also offered with Education in the combined honours or joint honours programmes.

Marjon (UCP) Courses are offered in Early Years, Primary and Secondary (Maths or PE) Education all with QTS status. See also **Social Sciences**.

Middlesex A Primary programme is offered for the 5–11 age range. Modules are offered in English, Mathematics and Science. There are also degrees in Education Studies and Early Childhood Studies.

Newman (UC) Courses are offered in Early Years Education Studies, Education Studies, Theology for Education and Religious Education.

Newport Primary and Secondary education courses are offered, the latter involving Design and Technology, Mathematics and Science. There is also an Education degree and an Early Years Programme.

Northampton BA Honours courses leading to QTS in Early Years Education (3–8 years) and Primary Education (QTS General Primary) are offered along with joint courses in Education.

Northumbria Primary Education courses are offered concentrating on Early Primary (3–8 years) or Late Primary (7–11 years). There are also courses linked with Care and Education, Disability studies, and Health and Social Care programmes.

Nottingham Trent A specialist Primary Education course is offered with students taking modules in a wide range of subjects. Subject specialisations are available in English, Mathematics, Science, Art, Music, Design and Technology, Information Technology, Humanities, Physical Education and Early Years. There are also degrees in Early Years Psychology and Sport and Leisure Education with Education.

Oxford Brookes* A large number of courses are offered including Creativity and Arts in Education, International Education or Early Childhood Studies.

Plymouth General Primary courses are offered in Art and Design, Early Childhood Studies, English, ICT, Mathematics, Music, Physical Education and Science. There is also a course in Steiner Waldorf Education. Some work experience abroad in possible in the state of New York, Finland and Denmark.

Portsmouth Courses are offered in Early Childhood Studies and in Education with English or Languages.

Queen's Belfast* A four-year BEd course is offered for those intending to teach in primary schools. Alternatively, a PGCE course is available for graduates wishing to specialise in the secondary field. The BEd course takes place at either St Mary's or Stranmillis University College.

Reading* A BEd degree (Primary) is offered with Qualified Teacher Status with specialisms in Art, English, and Music. There is also a BA programme in Theatre Arts, Education and Deaf Studies.

Roehampton Primary Education courses are offered in Art and Design, Design and Technology, Early Childhood Studies, English, Geography, History, Music, Physical Education, Religious Education and Sciences. Courses in Childhood and Society and in Early Childhood Studies are also offered. A flexible programme in Education is offered as a single or combined course, with the opportunity to specialise in different aspects of education for young children to adults in a range of settings. Courses in Early Childhood Studies and in Childhood in Society are also offered as single or combined courses. There is also a Foundation degree in Supporting Learning and Teaching.

St Mary's (UC) There is a theoretical Study of Education and Employment with modules for those wishing to train to teach.

Sheffield Hallam Courses are offered in Education Studies and Primary (3–8 years and 5–10 years) teaching. There are also Secondary Education courses in Design and Technology, Maths and Science teaching.

Staffordshire Work placements are part of the degree in Early Childhood Studies.

Stirling Primary and Secondary courses are offered the former with two pathways in Languages and Environment.

Stranmillis (UC) Two BEd courses are offered in Primary and Post Primary Studies.

Strathclyde A Primary Education course is offered in which all students take core programmes in a range of subjects and select a range of elective programmes. A four-year course is also offered in Community Education. There are also courses leading to Maths and Science Teaching.

Sunderland Courses are offered in Primary Education with specialisms in ages 5–11 and in the Secondary sector covering Design and Technology, English, Geography, Information Technology, Mathematics, and Science. There is also a course in Early Childhood Studies.

Swansea There is a course in Early Childhood Studies.

Swansea Metropolitan Education can be studied as a social science with English, Psychology or Counselling. There is also an Education Studies course leading to a Primary teaching qualification.

Teesside A degree in Early Childhood Studies covers health and well-being, children's services and language and literacy.

Trinity St David (Carmarthen) Several Education courses are offered with combinations in English, Religious Studies and Social Inclusion. There is also an Early Years Education course. Primary Education QTS is also offered.

Ulster Education can be taken as a minor subject with 10 other subjects.

Warwick* There is a course in Early Childhood Studies (not a teacher training course) which covers the development and welfare of young children. Students wishing to teach the 3–8 age range can follow with a one-year course leading to a PGCE. (High research rating)

See *University Degree Course Offers* (Trotman Publishing) for details of offers

West Scotland A course in Primary Education is offered with students focusing on the main areas: Expressive Arts, Environmental Studies, Language, Personal and Social Education, Mathematics, Religious Studies and ICT. There is also a course in Childhood Studies.

Winchester Courses are offered in Education Studies and Education Studies (Early Childhood). When taken as combined degrees, these can be an excellent preparation for students wishing to take the Primary teaching qualification (PGCE). There is also a BA Primary Education programme.

Wolverhampton Primary Education courses focus on English, Mathematics and Science. There is also a highly specialised degree in Conductive Education directed at children and adults with motor disorders, and courses in Early Childhood Studies and Special Needs.

Worcester Primary Teaching courses with Early Years (3–7) and Later Years (5–11) specialisation are offered. There are also several joint honours courses with Education Studies.

York* Key themes of the Educational Studies course include literature and art, learning and education and primary education. An optional placement is offered in an educational service in or near York. Other courses include Sociology/Education and Language and Literature in Education. (High research rating)

York St John Eleven joint courses with Education Studies are offered and also a BA Primary Teacher Education (3–7 years or 5–11 years) course.

OTHER INSTITUTIONS OFFERING EDUCATION COURSES
Blackpool and Fylde (Coll), Bradford (Coll), Cornwall (Coll), Doncaster (Coll), East Lancashire (Coll), Farnborough (UC), Guildford (CFHE), Havering (Coll), Leeds Park Lane (Coll), Neath Port Talbot (Coll), Northbrook (Coll), Norwich City (Coll), Peterborough (Reg Coll), Royal Academy of Dance, South Devon (Coll), Southport (Coll), Truro (Coll), UHI Millennium Inst, Warrington (Coll), Warwickshire (Coll), West Anglia (Coll), Wigan and Leigh (Coll).

ALTERNATIVE COURSES
Occupational Therapy, Psychology, Social Policy.

ENGINEERING COURSES

(*indicates universities with the highest entry requirements)

ENGINEERING (GENERAL)/ENGINEERING SCIENCES

SUBJECT REQUIREMENTS/PREFERENCES
GCE A-level: Mathematics and Physics usually essential (except for Engineering foundation courses). **GCSE:** Grade A–C may be required in English, Chemistry or language for some courses. Mathematics essential.

SUBJECT INFORMATION
Engineering courses provide the opportunity to study two, three or four engineering specialisms and enable students to delay their choice of specialism. Mathematics and physics provide the foundation of engineering subjects. Several universities and colleges offer one-year foundation courses for applicants with non-science A-levels. Extended Engineering courses are available in institutions throughout the UK: in some cases courses are open to applicants without the normal science A-levels. After the initial foundation course they move on to the degree programme. Many sponsorships are available in engineering subjects.

See *University Degree Course Offers* (Trotman Publishing) for details of offers

AERONAUTICAL ENGINEERING

SUBJECT REQUIREMENTS/PREFERENCES
See under **Engineering (General)/Engineering Sciences**.

SUBJECT INFORMATION
Courses cover the manufacture of military and civil aircraft, theories of mechanics, thermodynamics, electronics, computing and engine design and manufacture.

CHEMICAL ENGINEERING

SUBJECT REQUIREMENTS/PREFERENCES
GCE A-level: Chemistry with Mathematics and possibly Physics. Check Biology for some university courses. See also **Engineering (General)/Engineering Sciences**.

SUBJECT INFORMATION
Courses are based on maths, physics and chemistry and lead to studies in energy resources, nuclear energy, pollution, petroleum engineering, bio-process engineering and biotechnology.

CIVIL ENGINEERING

SUBJECT REQUIREMENTS/PREFERENCES
See under **Engineering (General)/Engineering Sciences**.

SUBJECT INFORMATION
Specialist courses in this field may cover traffic and highway engineering, water and waste engineering, construction management, explosives and public health engineering. Essential elements in all courses, however, include surveying, design projects (for example Channel Tunnel, suspension bridges) and building technology. Aesthetic design may also play a part in the design of some structures (for example motorway bridges).

COMPUTER ENGINEERING

SUBJECT REQUIREMENTS/PREFERENCES
See under **Engineering (General)/Engineering Sciences**.

SUBJECT INFORMATION
The design and application of modern computer systems is fundamental to all these courses, which will also include electronic engineering, software engineering and computer-aided engineering. Several universities offer sufficient flexibility to enable final course decisions to be made in the second year. Applicants should note that many of these courses overlap with Computer Science and Electronic Engineering courses.

ELECTRICAL/ELECTRONIC ENGINEERING

SUBJECT REQUIREMENTS/PREFERENCES
See under **Engineering (General)/Engineering Sciences**.

SUBJECT INFORMATION

Options to specialise should be considered when choosing courses, so read the prospectuses carefully. In this field, options could include opto-electronics and optical communication systems, microwave systems, radio frequency engineering and circuit technology.

MANUFACTURING ENGINEERING

SUBJECT REQUIREMENTS/PREFERENCES

GCE A-level: Physics may be required, check prospectuses. See also **Engineering (General)/Engineering Sciences**.

SUBJECT INFORMATION

Manufacturing engineering is sometimes referred to as production engineering. It is a branch of the subject concerned with management aspects of engineering such as industrial organisation, purchasing and the planning and control of operations, and at the same time provides an overview of engineering design systems. Engineering personnel are key staff in most manufacturing firms. These courses are often combined with Mechanical Engineering or with Business/Management Studies.

MECHANICAL ENGINEERING

SUBJECT REQUIREMENTS/PREFERENCES

See under **Engineering (General)/Engineering Sciences**.

SUBJECT INFORMATION

All courses involve the design, installation and maintenance of equipment used in industry. Thermodynamics, computer-aided design, fluid mechanics and materials science are subjects fundamental to this branch of engineering. Many universities offer students the opportunity to transfer to other engineering courses in Year 2.

MINING ENGINEERING

SUBJECT REQUIREMENTS/PREFERENCES

See under **Engineering (General)/Engineering Sciences**.

SUBJECT INFORMATION

Mining Engineering covers geology, surveying and mineral processing and offers opportunities to enter careers in petroleum engineering as well as coal and metalliferous mining.

UNIVERSITY COURSE INFORMATION

Aberdeen There are 22 MEng and 26 BEng courses covering all the main Engineering disciplines. BSc courses are also available. Students have the opportunity to study abroad for a four-month period. Scholarships available.

Abertay Dundee Civil Engineering involves both practical and theoretical studies, with optional industrial experience in Year 3. Scholarships available.

Anglia Ruskin Degree courses are offered specialising in Integrated, Civil, and Electronics covering Audio Technology and Computer Science.

Aston* Courses in the School of Engineering are offered in Chemical, Electro-mechanical, Electronic, Mechanical Communications, Internet and Mechanical Engineering. There are several Product Design and Engineering Management courses. Most courses incorporate optional paid professional placements. Scholarships available.

Bangor The School of Electronic Engineering and Computer Systems offers a number of Electronics courses. The Computer Systems BEng course covers hardware, software engineering. The School has extensive industrial links leading to industrial placements. A degree in Music Technology is subject to approval.

Bath* The University offers several Engineering courses covering Computer, Communications, Chemical, Civil and Architectural, Electronic and Electrical, and Mechanical (Aerospace, Automotive, Innovation and Design, Manufacturing, Mechanical, Medical or Sports) Engineering. Full-time or sandwich courses are offered and language (French or German) options are available. Scholarships available. (High research rating)

Birmingham* There are five Schools of Engineering and courses on offer cover Chemical, Biomedical Engineering, Civil, Electronic and Electrical, Mechanical and Materials and Computer and Communications Systems Engineering. Three-year and four-year programmes are offered and in each discipline the first two years are common to both the BEng and MEng programmes. A year of industrial training at home or abroad is optional. Scholarships available. (High research rating)

Birmingham City The Faculty of Engineering offers a range of courses in Automotive Engineering, Electronic Engineering, Electronic and Audio, Communications, and Mechanical Engineering, Sound Engineering, Manufacturing Systems and Motorsport Technology, most offering sandwich placement.

Bolton Full-time and part-time courses are offered in various Engineering disciplines, including Aerospace, Automotive, Civil, Electronic and Computer, Mechanical and Motorsport Engineering.

Bournemouth Electronic Engineering courses include specialisms in Communication and Computer Systems and Robotics. There is also a Design Engineering programme with an optional placement in Year 3.

Bradford A range of Engineering disciplines is offered. These include Automotive, Civil and Structural, Electrical and Electronic, Mechanical and Medical and Clinical Technology, and Technology Management. Scholarships available.

Brighton A general programme in Engineering embraces a broad range of subjects combined with business skills and management. There are also specialist courses in other fields of engineering covering Aeronautics, Automotive, Civil, Environmental, Electrical and Electronic, Mechanical and Manufacturing Engineering, Product Design and Sports Technology. Courses are offered on a three-year full-time or four-year sandwich basis.

Bristol* Three-year (BEng) and four-year (MEng) courses are offered in Engineering Design, Aeronautical Engineering, Avionic Systems, Computer Systems, Civil, Electrical and Electronic and Electronic and Communications Engineering, Mechanical Engineering and Engineering Design and Engineering Mathematics. Several have the option to study in continental Europe. (High research rating)

Bristol UWE Degrees are offered in 13 Engineering disciplines: Aerospace Design, Aerospace Manufacturing, Aerospace Systems, Architecture and Environmental, Building Services, Civil, Computer Systems, Electrical, Electronic, Mechanical Engineering, Music Systems, Motorsport, and River and Coastal Engineering. There is also a broad BSc Engineering course and a degree in Robotics.

Brunel* Computer Systems Engineering, and Internet Engineering are offered in addition to which Electronic and Electrical Engineering can be studied with specialisms in Communications Systems and Renewable Energy Systems. There are also full-time and sandwich courses in Multimedia Technology and Design. There are also courses in Industrial Design, Product Design, Aerospace, Aviation (with Pilot Studies), Mechanical and Motorsport Engineering. (High research rating)

Cambridge* The four-year Engineering course is divided into Parts I and II, each of two years. Part I provides a broad education whilst in Part II (Years 3 and 4) specialisation begins in one of the following areas: Aerospace and Aerothermal Engineering; Civil, Structural and Environmental Engineering, Electrical and Electronic Engineering, Electrical and Information Sciences; Energy and the Environment; Engineering for the Life Sciences; Information and Computer Engineering; Instrumentation and Control; Mechanical Engineering. A degree in Chemical Engineering (a four-year course) is also offered, the first two years being spent studying either Engineering or Natural Sciences (the majority of students coming via the latter). There is also a two year Manufacturing Engineering course following two years of Engineering study. (High research rating)

Cardiff* The School of Engineering offers courses in Architectural, Civil, Civil and Environmental, Computer Systems, Electrical and Electronic, Manufacturing, Mechanical and Medical Engineering. There is also an Integrated Engineering course, a broad-based education covering electronic, electrical, manu-facturing and mechanical disciplines. The degree schemes cover MEng, BEng, and 'Year in Europe' courses. Scholarships available. (High research rating)

Central Lancashire Degrees are offered in Computer, Electronic, Computer-aided, Mechanical, Fire and Building Services Engineering and Motor Sports. Two other significant courses involve Fire Engineering and Fire Safety and Risk Management. Scholarships available.

City* Courses offered cover Aeronautical Engineering, Air Transport Engineering, Air Transport Operations with Pilot Training, Automotive and Motorsport Engineering, Biomedical Engineering, Civil Engineering and Civil Engineering with Surveying or Architecture, Computer Systems Engineering, Communication Systems Engineering, Electrical and Electronic Engineering, Energy Engineering, Mechanical Engineering and Multimedia and Internet Systems Engineering. Many courses have placements in Europe and North America and sponsorships may be offered.

Coventry The School of Engineering offers courses covering Automotive Engineering Design, Civil and Mechanical Engineering, Electrical and Electronic Engineering, Aerospace Systems and Technology and Motorsport Engineering. Disaster Management and Product and Industrial Design Engineering are also offered. Scholarships available.

Cumbria An Engineering degree is offered with pathways in Environmental, and Mechanical Engineering.

De Montfort Courses offered include Electronic, Mechanical and Mechatronic Engineering and Engineering Design.

Derby The School of Engineering offers courses in Electrical, Electronic, Mechanical and Motorsport Engineering, Music Technology with Audio Systems Design, Design Technology, and Product Design.

Dundee Courses are offered in Civil, Electronic and Electrical, Mechanical, Microelectronics and Photonics, and Engineering with options in Management. There are also courses in Electronics and Computing, Electronic Media and Renewable Energy. Scholarships available.

Durham* All MEng Engineering students take a common course for the first two years. In the third year, courses are available in Aeronautics, Civil, Communication, Computer, Electronic, Mechanical, Design Manufacture and Management or General Engineering. A BEng course in General Engineering is also available.

East Anglia* The Computer Systems Engineering course covers all aspects of hardware and software. Specialist courses in Year 3 include Advanced Digital Design, Computer Networks and Computer Architecture.

East London Full-time and sandwich courses are offered in Civil Engineering, Computing and Electronics, Electrical and Electronic, Communications, Control and Power Engineering and Product Design.

Edinburgh* The School of Engineering and Informatics offers degree courses in Chemical, Civil, Structural and Environmental, Electrical and Mechanical Engineering and Electronics. Students taking Engineering courses defer their choice of specialism until the second half of Year 1, or to the beginning of Year 2 or even Year 3. Two new degree programmes have been introduced in Electronics with Bioelectronics and Electrical Engineering with Renewable Energy. (High research rating)

Essex BEng, MEng or BSc courses are offered in Computer Engineering, Telecommunications, Electronic and Internet Engineering. Scholarships available. (High research rating)

Exeter* All General Engineering students attend the same classes for the first two semesters, followed by specialisation. Students choose from one of four specialist subjects – Civil, Electronic, Mechanical and Engineering and Management. The Camborne School of Mines also offers courses in Mining Engineering and Engineering Geology. Scholarships available.

Glamorgan Full-time sandwich courses are offered in Audio Technology, Aeronautical, Constructions Technology, Computer Systems, Civil, Electrical and Electronic, Mechatronic, Mechanical and Manufacturing Engineering. Scholarships available.

Glasgow* This School of Engineering teaches the five main branches of the subject: Aerospace Engineering with Avionics options; Civil Engineering, which can be combined with Architecture; Electronics and Electrical Engineering with options to specialise in Software Engineering or with a European or international emphasis. There are also courses in Mechanical Engineering (which also has a European option), Naval Architecture, Marine and Ocean Engineering, in which one can specialise in Fast Ship Design or Small Craft Design and Product Design Engineering. (High research rating)

Glasgow Caledonian Courses are provided in Computer, Building Services, Electrical Power, Electronic, Telecommunication, Environmental and Civil, Fire Risk, Computer-aided Manufacturing Systems and Mechanical Engineering.

Glyndŵr Various Engineering courses are offered including Automotive, Aeronautical and Mechanical, Electrical and Electronics, Avionics and Broadcast Engineering. Speciality degrees include Motorsport Design Management and Performance Car Technology and Product Design. The Renewable Energy degree focuses on Project Management in Year 3.

Greenwich The School of Engineering offers courses leading to Chartered or Incorporated Engineer status in Civil Engineering, Communications and Computer Systems and Software Engineering, Internet Engineering, Electrical and Electronic Engineering, Marine, Mechatronics, Engineering Product Design, Public Health, Mechanical and Automotive Engineering and Engineering with Business Management, which contains elements of automatic control, data communications and manufacturing engineering. (High research rating)

Harper-Adams (UC) Agricultural Engineering and Off-Road Vehicle Design are offered. The latter covers tractors, combine harvesters and fighting vehicles. Scholarships available.

Heriot-Watt Courses are offered in Automotive Engineering, Chemical Engineering, Architectural, Civil and Structural, Electrical and Electronic, Mechanical Engineering and Software Engineering, Microwave and Photonics, Materials Ocean Engineering, and Engineering with Management. Students taking Electronic and Photonic Engineering may also opt for a degree in Physics (during the course). Scholarships available. (High research rating)

Hertfordshire The Faculty of Engineering offers degrees in Civil, Electronic and Electrical, Manufacturing, Mechanical, Automotive, Aerospace, Computer-aided and Software Engineering. Engineering can also be studied with another subject in the Combined Modular scheme. Scholarships available.

Huddersfield Industrial training forms part of all Engineering courses, which include a Master of Engineering route via all Bachelor of Engineering courses. Options include Automotive and Motorsport Engineering, Chemical Computer Systems, Electronic, Mechanical, Software, and Manufacturing Engineering. Courses in Multimedia Design, Virtual Reality Design, and Music Technology, which involves acoustics and electronics, are also offered by the School of Engineering.

Hull All students follow a similar path of study with specialisms being chosen in Years 2 and 3. Courses are offered in Computer-aided Engineering, Electronics, Mechanical, Telecommunications Engineering and Design Technology. (High research rating)

Imperial London* The Faculty of Engineering offers Courses in Aeronautics, Bioengineering, Chemical Engineering and Chemical Technology, Civil and Environmental Engineering, Computing, Earth Science and Engineering Electrical and Electronic Engineering (with an option in Management), Materials or Mechanical Engineering. Many include the option to study abroad. (High research rating)

Kent The Electronic Engineering programme offers courses in Electronics and Communications, the latter covering radio and satellite specialisms and medical electronics. The course is highly rated by students. In addition there is a course in Computer Systems Engineering with the option of a year in industry.

Kingston Degrees are offered in Aerospace, Aircraft, Automotive Systems, Building Services, Civil (and Construction Management), Communication Systems, Mechanical and Motorcycle, Motorsport and Product Design Engineering. Scholarships available.

Lancaster* Several Engineering options are available covering Engineering (study abroad), Electronic Systems, Mechanical, Mechatronics and Nuclear. In collaboration with other departments, it is also possible to study Computer Systems Engineering. MEng and BEng courses with options to study in the USA or Canada are also offered.

Leeds* Engineering courses are offered in the following specialisms – Aeronautical and Aerospace, Architectural, Automotive, Chemical, Civil and Environmental or Structural, Communications, Computer, Electronics and Communications, Energy, Environmental, Fire and Explosion, Mechanical, Materials Science and Engineering, Product Design, Pharmaceutical Chemical Engineering, Mining, Medical and Safety Engineering. (High research rating)

Leeds Metropolitan Courses are offered in Civil, Electronic and Electrical, Manufacturing and Building Control Engineering.

Leicester* A broad-based general Engineering degree programme is offered, with a common first year covering mechanical and materials engineering, electrical and software engineering. The decision to specialise between mechanical and electrical cores is taken in Year 2, other courses include Aerospace Communications and Electronics, Software and Electronic Engineering, Electrical and Electronic Engineering, General Engineering, and Mechanical Engineering degrees. BEng and MEng courses are offered with sandwich courses offering placements in the UK and Europe or the USA. Scholarships available. (High research rating)

Liverpool* The Faculty of Engineering offers courses in Aerospace, Avionic Systems (with Pilot Studies), Civil and Environmental, Biomaterials and Materials Science, Metallurgy, Mechanical, Electrical and Electronic Engineering and Mechatronics. There is also a BEng course in Engineering that enables students to study Mechanical, Electrical and Materials Engineering. Scholarships available. (High research rating)

Liverpool John Moores The School of Engineering has a strong multicultural and international base. Most students are offered the opportunity to take an industrial placement during the course. Degree courses in the main engineering disciplines are offered: Broadcast, Civil, Computer, Electrical and Electronic, Mechanical and Marine, Mechatronics and Networks and Telecommunications Engineering. There are also courses in Nautical Science and Navigation and Marine Technology.

London (Goldsmiths) There is a BEng/MEng honours degree in Design and Innovation offered through the Engineering Dept of Queen Mary College.

London (King's)* Courses are offered in Telecommunication Engineering, Computer Systems and Electronics, Electronic Engineering Systems, Mechatronics, and Mechanical Engineering. Engineering offers a Management option while a year in industry is possible in Electronic Engineering. (High research rating)

London (QM)* The Department of Engineering offers a wide range of degree programmes covering Aerospace, Audio Systems, Computing, Biomedical, Design and Innovation, Engineering Science (and with Business Management), Internet, Telecommunications, Materials Science, Electrical, Medical and Electronic, and Mechanical Engineering. (High research rating)

London (UCL)* The Faculty of Engineering Sciences offers courses in Biochemical, Chemical, Civil, Computer Science, Electronic and Electrical, Engineering Information Management, Mechanical Engineering, Medical Physics and Naval Architecture and Marine Engineering. There are opportunities for sponsorship in a number of these areas as well as the opportunity to study abroad. (High research rating)

London Metropolitan The Electronics and Electronic Communications course has an optional German exchange. There is also a Polymer Engineering course for Business.

London South Bank Degrees are available in Architectural, Building Services, Civil, Computer, Electrical and Electronic, Internet and Telecommunications, Chemical, Mechanical and Mechatronic Engineering.

Loughborough* All Engineering courses (very highly rated by students) lead to professional recognition and are supported by well-organised industrial placements. Students can graduate in Aeronautical and Automotive, Chemical, Construction, Civil, Computer Systems, Electronic and Electrical, Manufacturing and Management, Materials and Management, Mechanical and Manufacturing, Engineering Systems, Engineering Physics. A BEng is also offered in Product Design and Manufacturing. Scholarships available. (High research rating)

Manchester* The School of Engineering offers BEng and MEng degree programmes in Aerospace, Mechanical, Chemical, Communication Systems, Civil, Computer Systems, Electrical and Electronic Engineering, Electronic Systems, Mechatronic, Materials Science and Petroleum. These studies will cover design, manufacture, research, development, marketing and sales. There are also courses in Engineering and Business. European placements are possible in some cases. Scholarships available. (High research rating)

Manchester Metropolitan Degree courses are offered in Electrical and Electronic Engineering, Communication and Electronic Engineering, Virtual Design in Engineering, Mechanical, Engineering, Engineering and in Automation and Control on full-time or sandwich course options. In addition, there are several specialised Technology courses including the media, special effects and robotics.

Napier Engineering courses offered include Civil Transportation and Timber, Communication, Electronic and Electrical, Computer, Energy and Environmental, Mechanical, Mechatronics, Polymer and Product Design Engineering, as well as Materials Technology and Sports Technology. Degree programmes share a common first two levels and up to the end of Level 2 transfer between programmes is possible.

Newcastle* The Faculty is one of the largest in the country and offers more than 30 Engineering degree programmes. These cover Chemical and Process Engineering, Civil and Environmental Engineering, Civil and Structural Engineering, Computer Systems, Electrical and Electronic, Marine Engineering and Technology, including Naval Architecture, Offshore Engineering and Small Craft Technology, Mechanical and Systems Engineering. Scholarships available. (High research rating)

Newport Engineering courses include Civil, Construction, Electronic, Electrical, Fire, Manufacturing and Mechanical.

Northumbria Building Services Engineering, Communication and Electronic Engineering, Computer-aided Engineering, Electrical and Electronic, and Mechanical Engineering are offered. There are also courses in Manufacturing Systems Engineering, Electronic Design Technology and Mechanical Design and Technology can also be taken. Scholarship available.

Nottingham* Over 30 courses are offered in Chemical and Environmental, Civil, Electrical, Electronic, Mechanical, Materials and Manufacturing Engineering. Scholarships available. (High research rating)

Nottingham Trent A course is offered in Civil Engineering.

Oxford* The Engineering Science degree integrates the study of the subject across several areas. The first year is common to Engineering Science and Engineering Economics and Management. In Years 3 and 4 specialisation takes place in one of six branches of Engineering in Mechanical, Civil, Electrical, Information, Chemical, or Biomedical Engineering. Scholarships available. (High research rating)

Oxford Brookes* Courses are offered in Automotive, Electronic Systems Design, Motorsport Technology, Manufacturing Technology, Telecommunications and Mechanical Engineering.

Plymouth Engineering courses are available in Civil, Civil and Coastal, Clinical Technology, Communication, Electronic and Electrical Engineering, Computer Systems, Robotics and Automated Systems, Composite Materials, Marine Technology, and Mechanical Engineering specialisms, in three-year and four-year sandwich courses.

Portsmouth Degrees are offered in Civil, Communication Systems, Construction, Computer, Electronic and Electrical, Mechanical and Manufacturing Engineering. There is also a BEng course in Engineering Geology and Geotechnics.

Queen's Belfast* BEng Engineering courses are offered in the following specialisms: Aerospace, Chemical, Environmental and Civil, Electrical and Electronic, Electronic and Software, Manufacturing, Mechanical Engineering and Product Design and Development. Four-year enhanced courses are offered in the same subjects with sandwich placements. Scholarships available. (High research rating)

Reading* Degrees are available covering Biomedical Cybernetics, Computer, and Electronic and Robotic and Systems Engineering. Four-year courses are offered in each of these disciplines. Scholarships available.

Robert Gordon In addition to BEng and MEng Engineering courses there are several degrees with specialisms including in Electronic and Electrical Engineering, Computer and Communications, Mechanical Engineering and Offshore Engineering. Scholarships available.

Salford Degree courses are offered in Acoustics, Aeronautical, Audio and Video and Broadcast Technology, and Civil, Digital Electronics, Mechanical, Software and Structural Engineering. Scholarships available.

Sheffield* Degrees are offered in Aerospace, Biomedical, Chemical, Civil, Computer Systems, Electrical, Electronic, Materials Science, Mechanical, Mechatronics, Software and Motorsport Engineering. (High research rating)

Sheffield Hallam Courses are offered in Computer-aided Engineering and Design, Electrical and Electronic Engineering, Environmental Engineering, Mechanical Engineering, Auto Engineering and Design Communications and Information Engineering.

Southampton* The large Faculty of Engineering and associated departments offer a wide range of BEng, BSc and MEng courses covering Acoustical, Aerospace, Civil, Environmental, Computer, Electrical, Electronic and Mechanical Engineering. Degrees in Ship Science, Naval Architecture and Engineering Management are also available. Scholarships available (Acoustics). (High research rating)

Southampton Solent In addition to Electronic and Mechanical and Marine Engineering, there is a course in Audio Technology.

Staffordshire Courses are offered in Auto Engineering, Electronic, Electrical and Forensic Engineering, Mechanical, Mechatronics and Network Engineering.

Strathclyde Forty-six BEng and MEng courses cover Aeromechanical, Architectural, Chemical, Civil and Environmental, Computer and Electronic Systems, Electronic and Electrical, Manufacturing, Mechanical and Sports Engineering, Offshore specialisms, Naval Architecture. Product Design and Prosthetics and Orthotics (see under Health) Engineering is also offered with Business Management. (High research rating)

Sunderland Automotive Engineering is offered, whilst the broad course in Engineering Design includes Electrical, Electronics and Mechanical Engineering.

Surrey* A large Engineering programme offers courses in Engineering Business Management, Chemical, Civil, Electronic, Aerospace, Media, Medical and Mechanical Engineering. Some courses are offered with a European language. Electronics courses comprise audio media engineering, digital broadcasting, mobile communications, radio frequency, satellite and systems engineering. There are also specialisms in offshore and maritime engineering, power/aerospace studies and information systems engineering. Scholarships available (Sound Recording). (High research rating)

Sussex* There is considerable flexibility between most Engineering degree programmes. MEng and BEng degrees are offered in the following Engineering courses: Computer Systems, Electrical and Electronic, Electronic and Communication, Mechanical and Automotive Engineering. Some courses can also be combined with European, North American and Business Studies. Scholarships available. (High research rating)

Swansea A large selection of Engineering courses includes Aerospace, Chemical and Biological Process, Communication, Civil, Electrical and Electronic, Environmental, Materials, Mechanical, Medical, Nanotechnology and Product Design. (High research rating)

Swansea Metropolitan Automotive Engineering is a special subject at the university. A design course is also offered. In addition other engineering courses cover civil, mechanical, motorsport, and manufacturing engineering.

Teesside Courses are offered in Chemical or Mechanical Engineering, Construction, Control and Process, Electrical and Electronic, Manufacturing, and Civil Engineering, also with Disaster Management.

Ulster Courses are available in the following disciplines: Civil, Electrical/Electronic and Mechanical Engineering. There is also a General Engineering course.

Warwick* BEng and MEng degree courses are offered in Auto, Civil, Electronic, Manufacturing, Mechanical and Computer Systems Engineering, and also in Engineering Business Management. The General degree in Engineering enables students to defer their choice of specialisation in one of the options above until the end of Year 1.

West London Courses are offered in Electronics, Mechatronics and Computer Systems Engineerng.

West Scotland There are three- and four-year courses in Mechanical, and Motorsport, Chemical, Civil Engineering and Engineering Management.

Westminster BEng courses are available in Digital and Mobile Communications, Electronic Engineering and Computer Systems.

Wolverhampton Courses are offered in Automotive Systems, Civil, Electrical and Electronic, Mechatronics, and Mechanical Engineering. A general Engineering course is also available.

York* Thirteen courses are offered including Electronic Engineering, Electronic and Communication Engineering, Computer Systems Engineering, Avionics, Business Management and Music Technology Systems. MEng courses are also available in Media Technology and Radio Frequency Engineering. Scholarships available. (High research rating)

OTHER INSTITUTIONS OFFERING ENGINEERING COURSES

Barking (Coll), Bath (Coll), Blackpool and Fylde (Coll), Bradford (Coll), Bristol City (Coll), Carmarthenshire (Coll), Chesterfield (Coll), Coalville Stephenson (Coll), Colchester (Inst), Cornwall (Coll), Doncaster (Coll), Dudley (CT), East Lancashire (Coll), Exeter (Coll), Farnborough (UC), Grimsby (IFHE), Havering (Coll), Highbury (Coll), Hopwood Hall (Coll), Lakes (Coll), Lincoln (Coll), LIPA, Llandrillo (Coll), Loughborough (Coll), Manchester (CAT), Mid-Cheshire (Coll), Myerscough (Coll), Neath Port Talbot (Coll), NESCOT, Northbrook (Coll), Norwich City (Coll), Nottingham Castle (Coll), Pembrokeshire (Coll), Ravensbourne, St

Helens (Coll), Sandwell (Coll), Shrewsbury (CAT), Sollihull (Coll), Somerset (CAT), South Cheshire (Coll), South Essex (Coll), South Tyneside (Coll), Staffordshire (Reg Fed), Stockport (Coll), Swansea (Coll), Tameside (Coll), Truro (Coll), Tyne Metropolitan (Coll), UHI Millennium Inst, Uxbridge (Coll), Warrington (Coll), Warwickshire (Coll), West Anglia (Coll), West Thames (Coll), Wigan and Leigh (Coll), Worcester (CT).

ALTERNATIVE COURSES
Architecture, Building, Chemistry, Mathematics, Physics, Surveying.

ENGLISH

(*indicates universities with the highest entry requirements)

SUBJECT REQUIREMENTS/PREFERENCES
GCE A-level: English **GCSE:** A foreign language may be preferred.

SUBJECT INFORMATION
English courses are an extension of school studies in literature and language and may cover topics ranging from Anglo-Saxon literature to the present day. Many courses will focus on certain areas such as the medieval or Renaissance periods of literature or English language studies. Admissions tutors will expect students to have read widely outside their A-level syllabus. (Sunday newspaper book reviews will give a useful introduction to contemporary writing.)

Aberdeen A major Department offering literature of the British Isles courses that involve the critical and historical study of British authors of all periods from the Middle Ages to the present day, courses cover English, Scottish, Irish and American literature. The English Language courses are concerned with the nature and development of the English language from the earliest period to the present day. English (Literature) is offered as a joint course with a choice from a wide range of subjects including Management Studies. A course in English and Scottish literature is also offered.

Aberystwyth English Literature focuses on different aspects of reading and writing about the texts of different periods, the genres of poetry, drama and the novel. In Part II topics explore the Renaissance and modern drama, the 20th century novel and poetry. Specialisation follows in a range of subjects, including Medieval and Victorian literature and 20th century British, Anglo-Welsh, American Literature and creative writing. There is also a degree in Creative Writing and English. Aberystwyth is also at the forefront for facilities in information and library studies and management and offers degrees in these subjects.

Anglia Ruskin The course strikes a balance between the study of leading writers (Wordsworth, Milton, Dickens etc) and less traditional areas such as modern science fiction. Modules include film and contemporary writers. There is also the option to take a course in practical writing. An English Language degree with Communication Studies is also offered. A Writing degree offers professional writing skills covering fiction, drama, radio and poetry.

Aston English language can be taken as a single, joint or combined honours subject. This is the only English course in the UK which includes a placement year. Opportunities to specialise in Business English, Legal Language or Teaching.

Bangor English degrees cover a wide range of subjects on all periods of English Language and English and American literature. In Part II of the course students select modules from a number of topics ranging from Old English to 20th century literature. Studies in creative writing and plays in performance, film studies, journalism, theatre studies and linguistics are also offered. There is also a broad course that covers literature, history and society, offered on a part-time basis. Bangor is an internationally recognised centre for work on Arthurian literature. English can be combined with Creative Writing, Film Studies, Journalism and Theatre Studies and in addition there are courses in Linguistics.

Bath Spa The English Literature course allows a wide choice of modules, some period based (17th century) others on modern topics and specialist subjects eg environmental, film etc. There is also a creative writing programme with strands in prose, poetry and scriptwriting.

Bedfordshire Courses in Creative Writing (and with Journalism) and English for Business are offered along with several English Language courses. Several journalism courses are offered.

Birmingham* Single honours students choose between literature and some language or literature and language equal. Joint honours students choose between all literature or all language. English can also be taken as a major or minor subject with American Literature or creative writing. (High research rating)

Birmingham City Twelve courses in English are offered in joint or minor programmes with creative writing, media, drama and psychology. There is also a degree in English and Drama.

Bolton English courses focus on literary studies. Courses are also offered in Creative Writing and Media Writing and Production.

Bournemouth The English and History degree is delivered at the University Centre in Yeovil.

Bradford A course is offered in Creative Writing which covers gender, ethnicity, popular culture, mass media, film and literature. There is also an English degree offering a range of genres and periods alongside social and cultural issues.

Brighton Several courses are offered in English Language, English Literature and Linguistics. There are also joint courses with Education, Sociology and Media. A broad course in Cultures, Histories and Literatures can also be taken.

Bristol* The English course focuses on English Literature from 1200 to the present day. A special subject from a very wide range of options is taken in each semester in Year 2. English is offered with Drama, Classical Studies and Philosophy. (High research rating)

Bristol UWE The English course focuses on a range of topics with additional modules offered in history, media studies, women's studies, modern languages and American literature. A complementary module can be taken in Year 1 in the humanities, psychology, sociology, international relations, politics, French, German or Spanish. There are also degrees in English Language jointly with several other subjects.

Brunel The English course emphasises personal response to English literature rather than a chronological historical survey. A wide range of options allows students to select choices of specialisms from poetry, creative writing, drama, fiction and literatures from across the world. There is also a degree in English with Creative Writing, a central feature of the English programme at Brunel and joint courses with Film/TV Studies, Drama and Music.

Buckingham English Literature is a two-year course offering a broad programme from Shakespeare, Romantic Literature and the Victorians to American literature, film studies and modern drama. English Language programmes are offered for overseas students. English Literature is also offered with Multimedia Journalism, French, Spanish, History and Psychology.

Bucks New Scriptwriting for film, TV and stage and creative writing degrees are offered.

Cambridge* The English degree offers a study of English literature from the Middle Ages to the present day. Literature is also studied in an historical and cultural context with comparisons offered as options in Anglo-Saxon, Early Norse, Welsh and Irish. Various options including classical and other literatures are offered in Year 2. In addition to English, applicants for the course are reminded that classics, modern languages and history are among the most relevant A-levels. There is also a degree in Linguistics. (High research rating)

Canterbury Christ Church The English course is unique in that a double degree is offered combining study in Canterbury with a year in Lille. There is also a course in English and Communication, Teaching English as a Foreign Language is a module in Year 3.

Cardiff* Part I of the English Literature course covers English literature, Medieval English and language and communications. In Years 2 and 3 nearly 100 modules of specialist themes are available. There are also courses in English Language Studies, Cultural Criticism, and Language and Communication. English Literature and Language Studies can also be taken with a humanities subject. (High research rating)

Cardiff (UWIC) English can be taken with Creative Writing, Drama or Popular Culture.

Central Lancashire English Literature is offered singly or combined with other subjects or as a joint course with Film and Media. The English Language Studies course covers English language with options in linguistics and literature. There is also a degree in English Literature and several joint courses with English can also be taken. In addition there are courses involving Linguistics, Communication and Popular Culture, American Literature, Theatre Studies and Creative Writing.

Chester Courses are offered in English Literature including American and Irish Literature and in creative writing exploring prose, journalism, poetry, reviews and essays.

Chichester English and English with Creative Writing are offered as single and joint courses with a range of subjects.

Coventry English is offered as a single or joint honours programme with six options. There is also a course with Journalistic Studies.

Cumbria A three year programme is offered in Creative Writing in addition to the English degree or joint degree which both provide a wide range of options in Year 3.

De Montfort The English course covers English literature and literature in translation as well as literature in a social context. English can also be taken with Media Studies. There is a separate creative writing degree.

Derby Students may take English as a full-time degree or major or joint subject. Creative Writing is also offered in the combined and single honours programmes.

Dundee All periods of literature are studied in the English course, from Chaucer to the present time. Modules are offered in film studies and creative writing. Eleven joint honours courses with English are available including English with Theatre Studies. (High research rating)

Durham* English Literature is a wide-ranging course focusing on poetry, drama and the novel in Year 1 with modules on selected themes. Years 2 and 3 enable students to follow their special interest. Joint courses are offered with History and Philosophy and the subject can be studied in combined honours in Arts. (High research rating)

East Anglia* The School of English Literature and Creative Writing offers flexibility to study a wide range of different but related courses including American and English Literature, English Literature and Drama. There are also courses in English Literature with Creative Writing, English and Comparative Literature, and Literature and joint courses with History, Drama, American Literature, Politics, Film, Philosophy and Art History. Degree courses in Linguistics are also offered. (High research rating)

East London English Literature is offered as a joint course with Linguistics, Cultural Studies, Law and History. There are also courses in English Language, Linguistics, Languages in Education and Creative and Professional Writing.

Edge Hill Courses are offered in English Language and Literature. Creative Writing is also available and can be taken with Drama, English, Film Studies History or Media. English can also be taken with Chinese Studies (Mandarin).

Edinburgh* Students follow courses in either English or Scottish Literature in Years 1 and 2 followed by courses of special interest in Years 3 and 4. English Language covers pronunciation and grammar and examines the historical background to language through Anglo-Saxon English, Medieval English, Elizabethan English and older Scots. Linguistics is also offered and also with Artificial Intelligence, Scottish Ethnology or Anthropology. There is also a Mind and Language degree combining Philosophy, Linguistics and Psychology and also degrees in English Language and History or Linguistics. (High research rating)

Essex* English Language and Linguistics is offered with options in linguistics and the role of language in society. It is possible to switch courses between language and linguistics. There are also degrees in English Language and Literature, Psycholinguistics, and a BA in Teaching English as a Foreign Language. Several Literature courses are also offered, including Comparative Literature and a course combined with Creative Writing.

Exeter* The English course provides a knowledge of the major texts, literary forms and periods of English literature and allows for considerable specialisations. The basic courses are the Renaissance, Shakespeare, the Restoration and the 18th century, and the 19th and the 20th centuries. In levels 2 and 3, specialisation takes place, with options including creative writing, American literature and post-colonial studies.

Falmouth (UC) English can be taken with Media Studies or Creative Writing. There are also three writing courses.

Glamorgan The English course covers language, literature and creative writing with options in language and society, women's writing and the writing media. There are separate courses in English Literature and English and Communication.

Glasgow* The English Language course covers the history of the language from the earliest times to the present day. Phonetics and grammar are included and there are specialist options including dialectology, sociolinguistics and Scots language. The English Literature course concentrates on the Romantic period with optional subjects covering the Renaissance period and European literature in translation in poetry, drama and prose. Scottish Literature is also offered. There are also courses in Comparative Literature and Linguistics.

Gloucestershire English Language and Literature are offered with an extensive range of joint courses with subjects ranging from Multimedia, Psychology and Film Studies to Modern Writing, Performance Arts and Wildlife Biology. There is also a course in Creative Writing.

Glyndŵr In addition to English degrees with options in History, Media Studies, Writing, Broadcasting and Journalism, there are special degrees in Writing and Media Communications.

Greenwich English is a broad course that includes Victorian studies, ideas in the modern world, American film and writing, drama in performance and video production. Electives include theatre studies and film studies. English is also offered with Creative Writing (part of the combined honours course), Media Writing, Modern Languages, Law and Legal Studies. There is also a degree in Linguistics.

Hertfordshire English is offered as part of the Humanities programme in which English Literature, and English Language and Communication can be studied as single, joint or combined honours subjects. Several courses are available in English Language Teaching and Creative Writing is offered in the combined honours programme.

Huddersfield The English courses cover language, literature and writing. Optional modules include language or literature, media studies, information technology, desktop publishing, creative writing and a European language. English is also offered with Creative Writing, Journalism and Modern Languages.

Hull* A modular course is offered in English language and literature that covers modern literature, criticism, medieval language and a subject from another department. A wide range of specialist options is available, in addition to which there are 15 joint honours programmes. A Creative Writing single honours course and joint courses are also offered with American Studies, English, Philosophy and Theology.

Keele* English is taken with a second subject from a choice of 30 subjects including American Studies, Law, Finance and International Relations. The course provides a good general grounding in literary criticism. English and American Literature is offered as a single honours subject.

Kent* The School of English offers a range of subjects. English and American Literature can be taken with a bias towards history, philosophy or politics. There is also a single and joint honours course in Comparative Literary Studies, with Drama, Film Studies or Philosophy whilst courses in English Language Studies can have options in History, Linguistics, Philosophy or Politics.

Kingston The emphasis of the English Literature course is on 19th and 20th century Anglo-American literature and women's writing; there is also the opportunity to study in Europe and America. There is also a course in Applied English Language and Linguistics and a range of joint English Language or Literature courses. Creative Writing is offered as a joint course with several subjects.

Lancaster* Courses in English Language, English Literature and Creative Writing can be taken, together with several joint options, including English Language and the Media, and English Literature and Languages. Some students spend part of the course in a European country or in the USA. Single and combined Linguistics courses are also available. (High research rating)

Leeds* A course in English language and literature is combined with an extensive range of options covering English, American and Commonwealth literature. Students have a choice from a list of over 70 options in Years 2 and 3. These courses are combined with 'core' courses that involve a study of English from the Middle Ages to the present day. English can also be taken with Theatre Studies. There is also an English Language programme and degree in Linguistics and Phonetics. (High research rating)

Leeds Metropolitan Courses are offered as three-year full-time study in English Literature and in English with History.

Leeds Trinity (UC) English can be taken as a single subject or with Film, History, Media, TV or Writing.

Leicester* English is a diverse and flexible course with lectures and small group teaching. A modular course is provided with a chronological approach to the major periods of English literature. Language is part of the curriculum in Years 1 and 2 and there is an optional year in Europe. English can be taken with Film Studies, Languages and History of Art. See also **Combined courses**. (High research rating)

Lincoln In addition to the single-subject English degree eight joint courses are offered in Media Studies, Politics, Drama, History, Journalism, Advertising, American Studies and Criminology.

Liverpool* English Language and Literature can be studied from its origins in the Anglo-Saxon period to the modern period, covering all the major literary and linguistic developments. Optional courses are available in the second and third years. There are also seven joint courses with English including Communication Studies, languages, History and Philosophy. (High research rating)

Liverpool Hope The English degrees enable students to study the foundations of both language and literature. A large number of joint courses are offered.

Liverpool John Moores There are three-year courses in creative Writing and English (Literature) with Journalism.

London (Goldsmiths)* All aspects of literature are covered in the English degree, including Shakespeare, Gothic literature, the Victorians, Caribbean women writers and the English detective story. English can also be studied with American Literature or History or Drama or Comparative Literature, Creative Writing, Drama or History.

London (King's)* English Language and Literature covers a study of language and all the major periods of English literature from Old English to the 20th century. Optional courses in the second and third years allow specialisation in such fields as American literature, creative writing, modern theatre and socio-linguistics. There is also a degree in Comparative Literature spanning nine languages and over 2500 years. (High research rating)

London (QM)* The English course covers the study of both English language and literature from the earliest periods to the present day, plus a wide range of options. English is also offered with Drama, Linguistics, History, a language or Hispanic Studies. Courses are also offered in Comparative Literature and Linguistics (High research rating)

London (RH)* The English course is common to all students for the first two terms, comprising literature, critical ideas, aspects or periods of literature and introductory language courses. This enables students to plan the remainder of their course to suit their own particular interests. Creative Writing, Drama, and European languages are offered with English. (High research rating)

London (UCL)* After the first-year foundation studies course, students are encouraged to build their own programme. There is an emphasis on one-to-one tutorials. A four-year course in English can be taken with Dutch, French, German or Scandinavia Studies. (High research rating)

London Metropolitan English Language Studies is a modular programme offered as a single or a joint degree or a minor subject. Courses in Creative Writing and English Literature are also available.

London South Bank The English degree covers literatures spanning American, Caribbean, African, Canadian and Australian texts as well as those of British origin. Film and detective fiction is included. There is also a course in Writing for Media Arts.

Loughborough* The English course concentrates on modern English literature starting with the Renaissance although there is an option in medieval literature. It also includes a wide range of subsidiary subjects in the second year including publishing and marketing, politics, languages and art history. English can also be taken with North American Film and Literature, Publishing and Sports Science. There is also a part-time English degree.

Manchester* Nineteen courses are offered involving English Language and Literature. The courses focus on language and the entire range of English literature. A large number of joint courses are offered with Drama, Languages, Philosophy and Linguistics. There is also a course in language, literacy and communication. (High research rating)

Manchester Metropolitan English is available as a single subject degree or with other subjects involving American Literature, Creative Writing or Film. (Subject to approval)

Marjon (UCP) Single and combined courses are offered in English Literature and combined courses with English Language and Linguistics or Creative Writing.

Middlesex Thirteen English courses are offered covering English Language, English Literature and Creative Writing.

Napier The English can be taken alongside communication, film, publishing and journalism.

Newcastle* All courses include compulsory and optional modules. The English Literature course has a firm basis in traditional literary areas, combined with a variety of options (including film, American literature, and the Russian novel). There is a variety of examination methods and an emphasis on small-group teaching. English Language and Literature is distinctive and occupies one-third of the student's workload in Year 1. Thereafter there is much freedom in the choice of options. English Language covers a wide range of approaches to the study of the English language – both historical and descriptive – and also Medieval English literature. Subsidiary subjects, eg psychology, computer science, can be taken in the English course. Several courses in Linguistics are also offered, and English can also be taken as part of the Combined Studies in Arts programme.

Newman (UC) English is offered as a single, joint or major course with another subject, creative writing and literature are available as minor subjects.

Newport Degrees are offered in Creative Writing and English Literature.

Northampton Degrees in English, English Literature, Creative Writing and American Literature and Films are offered as single courses and joint honours.

Northumbria There are two language programmes – English Language Studies and English which offers a study of the major phases of literature and its historical background from the medieval to modern periods. English can be studied with Creative Writing, Film Studies, History and Sociology. There is also a Scriptwriting course with Drama.

Nottingham The English Studies course covers the entire range of English literature from its beginnings to the 20th century and also Medieval and modern English language. English Studies can also be taken with, for example, Latin, Philosophy, Theology, Viking Studies and Hispanic Studies. There is also a unique course in Viking Studies covering language, literature, history and archaeology. (High research rating)

Nottingham Trent A flexible English course is offered with a free choice of areas of study from traditional English and colonial cultures. Linguistics, Heritage Studies, History and International Relations and Creative Writing can also be studied with English, and there is a wide choice of English and Communication Studies joint courses.

Oxford* The course in English Language and Literature covers the whole range of English writing from the beginnings to the present day. The first year covers Old English and Middle English literature and English literature 1832–1960, while the second and third years offer alternatives in a range of periods of literature, Shakespeare, English language, special authors and special topics. There is also a course in English and Modern Languages. (High research rating)

Oxford Brookes* English is offered as a study of language and literature with a wide range of specialisations including medieval, modern literature and theatre literature. Combined honours courses are also offered in English. There is also a degree in English and communication with modules in language, culture, communication, media, psychology and linguistics with an option to study for two semesters in Europe North America or Australia.

Plymouth English is offered jointly with a range of other subjects including Media Arts, American Studies, Creative Writing, History, and Popular Culture.

Portsmouth A very wide range of courses are offered including English and Creative Writing, English and English with Media Studies, History and Languages.

Queen's Belfast* Literature and Language courses are offered with over 30 specialist modules in Year 3 of the former. Major joint and minor courses are available. A course in Linguistics is also available.

Reading* Several individual units are taken in the English Language and Literature course, four of which are compulsory core subjects covering literature from the Elizabethan period to the mid-19th century. The remaining five courses are chosen from a long list of options. Other courses available, include English and Television and English and Classical Studies. See also **European Studies**. (High research rating)

Roehampton English Language and Linguistics, English Literature, Creative Writing can be studied in joint degrees with another subject from a wide choice. There is also a course in TESOL (Teaching English to Speakers of Other Languages).

St Andrews* Students proceeding to the single honours English degree may take several specialist topics, which include creative writing and speech writing. There are also 24 courses combining English with a second subject including Management, Psychology and Modern Languages. There is also a programme of English Language teaching. (High research rating)

Salford English Literature with English Language offers a study of both language and literature with an emphasis on the modern period (post-1750) literature and its connections with society, which are central to the degree. Courses are also offered with Journalism and Creative Writing.

Sheffield* English is offered as a dual honours with nine other subjects, including Modern Languages, Management and Music. (High research rating)

Sheffield Hallam The English Studies course covers literary studies (16th–19th centuries), linguistics and creative writing skills, English and American fiction, biography and autobiography and teaching English as a foreign language.

Southampton* The English degree introduces the major genres of English literature, after which students form their own course by choosing topics out of the whole range of English literature, from the medieval period to the present day. During the first year, English language and an additional subject may be taken from another department. English with Modern Languages and with History, Music or Philosophy are also offered. Scholarships available. (High research rating)

Southampton Solent English literature and English language are studied on a 50/50 basis with joint courses with Journalism, Screenwriting and Writing Popular Fiction and Writing, Fashion and Culture, which introduces students to the broad field of magazine journalism.

Staffordshire There is a degree in English Language and Literature, Creative Writing and Scriptwriting courses are offered.

Stirling A study of the novel, drama and poetry occupies the first three semesters of the English Studies course. Thereafter, in the next three semesters, studies focus on the literary tradition, critical theory, language and literature and Renaissance drama and the 19th century novel. During this time, and in the final year, a range of 18 options allows students to choose their own specialist areas to study. A degree in English Studies and Scottish Literature is also offered.

Strathclyde Single and joint courses are offered in English. There is also a Journalism and Creative Writing course which can be taken as a second subject.

Sunderland In the English single honours course a range of topics is on offer including 20th century literature and poetry and American literature. English can also be taken with Creative Writing, Drama, Film or Literature.

Surrey Several degree courses are offered in English literature and can be combined with Creative Writing, French, Spanish, Dance and Theatre.

Sussex* The English Language programme is one of considerable breadth and presents the subject in terms of intellectual, moral, religious, political, social and aesthetic contexts. The first term introduces the range of approaches to the study of English in addition to giving the student a choice of options. English literature is offered with English. English is also offered with languages and in English language teaching. (High research rating)

Swansea* In the English Literature syllabus, tragic drama, lyric poetry, theories and monsters (*Dracula* and *Frankenstein*) are studied in Part I. For single honours during Years 2 and 3 there are two core courses – literature from Chaucer to the present day and criticism – plus a choice of options. English Language is also offered in a wide range of joint courses including Welsh, Politics, European Languages and Geography. Language Studies courses are offered with subjects such as Latin, Ancient History and Italian.

Teesside Core modules in the English Studies course introduce English prose and poetry and creative writing. In the second and third years students construct their own programme, which includes historical periods, women's writing, drama and children's literature. English can also be taken with Creative Writing, Media or History.

Trinity St David (Carmarthen) English and Creative Writing joint courses are offered.

Trinity St David (Lampeter) The English Literature degree offers a wide range of courses from Anglo-Saxon Literature to Contemporary Drama. Courses in Modern Literature and Creative Writing can also be taken.

See *University Degree Course Offers* (Trotman Publishing) for details of offers

Ulster English is offered as a single honours course and as main and major subjects is combination with 25 other subjects.

Warwick* Degrees include English and European Literature, English and American Literature, and English and Creative Writing (which covers poetry, writing for the theatre, film, as well as an introduction to journalism). Students take the same modules in Year 1 before specialising. There are also several joint degrees including theatre studies and creative writing with English.

Westminster Joint degrees with English are offered in Creative Writing, International Relations, and Politics.

Winchester This is a wide-ranging programme covering old and new literature, creative writing and critical analysis. Courses are also offered in English Literature and English Language and also English with American Literature. A degree course in Creative Writing is also offered involving fiction, poetry, short stories, screen plays, features and film-writing.

Wolverhampton English can be taken in specialist, joint, major or minor programmes of study. The course covers Shakespeare, the novel, journalism and American literature. Degree courses in Linguistics and English, Creative and Professional Writing and English as a Foreign Language are also offered. There is also a course in British Sign Language.

Worcester Single and joint courses are offered in English and Literary Studies.

York* English can be studied as a single subject or in combination with seven other subjects, including History of Art, Philosophy or Politics. Single-subject students must take at least one course involving the study of literature in a foreign language. All students follow the preliminary course for one term before choosing their subject or subjects. Courses are examined by continuous assessment. Scholarships available. (High research rating)

York St John Courses are offered in English Literature, Language and Linguistics in addition.

OTHER INSTITUTIONS OFFERING ENGLISH DEGREE COURSES
Blackpool and Fylde (Coll), Burton (Coll), Dartington (CA), Doncaster (Coll), East Lancashire (Coll), Grimsby (IFHE), Havering (Coll), North Lindsey (Coll), Norwich City (Coll), Peterborough (Reg Coll), Suffolk (Univ Campus), West Anglia (Coll), Wigan and Leigh (Coll).

ALTERNATIVE COURSES
Combined Arts courses, Drama, Information Management/Sciences, Journalism.

ENVIRONMENTAL SCIENCE/STUDIES

(including **Ecology**)
(*indicates universities with the highest entry requirements)

SUBJECT REQUIREMENTS/PREFERENCES
GCE A-level: Sciences, Biology and Chemistry usually preferred. Geography may be required. **GCSE:** English, Mathematics and a science (often Chemistry) usually required.

SUBJECT INFORMATION
Environmental Science can cover a range of subjects with options to specialise that may include biology, geography, geology, oceanography or chemistry. Environmental Science/Studies could also involve town

and country planning or environmental health options, thus leading to two quite different careers. Environmental Health courses usually lead to qualifications as an environmental health officer.

Aberdeen The course in Environmental Science covers animal and plant biology, ecology, chemistry, geography and geology in the early years with a strong physics/chemistry/biology element in Years 3 and 4. Two specialist areas are also offered in physical science or ecology. There are courses in Pollution and Reclamation, Coastal Management, Immunology, Tropical Environment Science, and Wildlife Management. Aberdeen is also ideally situated for a study of marine environments and has a Marine Resource Management course.

Abertay Dundee The course in Natural Resources Management covers geography, environmental science, ecology and biology.

Aberystwyth Part I of the Environmental Science course covers physical and biological processes and support studies involving environmental chemistry and biology. These studies are extended in Year 2 with field modules covering mid-Wales, the Low Countries and the Rhine delta. Optional modules in Year 3 include freshwater biology, soil science and ecology. There is also a degree course in Environmental Earth Science, covering aspects of geology and oceanography, and a course in Water Science involving the hydrological cycle, resources, catchment dynamics and water quality and health.

Anglia Ruskin The course in Environmental Planning focuses on urban design and meets the requirements of the Royal Town Planning Institute.

Aston* Combined honours courses in Environmental Science and Technology involve sandwich placement or can be taken full time. Environmental Science can also be taken in conjunction with Construction Management and Transport subjects.

Bangor Access to the coastlines, forests and mountains of the Snowdonia National Park provide ideal opportunities for those following one of the eight courses covering environmental sciences, ocean sciences management, conservation, and marine ecology. Studying in Canada or Finland in Year 2 may also be part of the Forestry degree, whilst the four-year course includes work placement in the industry.

Bath Spa Geographical and biological issues are covered in the very flexible Environmental Science degree. Scholarships available.

Birmingham* Specialisation in four pathways (applied ecology, water in the environment, atmospheric processes and earth surface processes) follows a broad first-year Environmental Science course. There are also courses in Environmental Management and Environmental Geoscience.

Bolton The Environmental Studies degree covers conservation, pollution, planning, freshwater ecology and management. There is a professional placement module in preparation for a future career.

Bournemouth An Environmental Protection course is offered with options in river/water/waste management, health and industrial safety and coastal protection. It combines elements of material science, environmental science and monitoring technology with a study of management and legislative aspects of the protection of the environment. The Heritage Conservation course with professional placements focuses on architectural heritage, landscapes, education services and tourism. Courses are also available in Environment and Coastal Management and Environment Conservation Biology, Heritage Conservation and Tourism and Ecology and Wildlife Conservation.

Bradford Environmental Science is offered as a three-year full-time or four-year sandwich course. There are also courses in Environmental Management and Geography, and Environmental Geography.

Brighton The Environmental Sciences course involves a study of the human and physical environment, ecology, energy and pollution. There are also degrees in Environmental Hazards, covering geography, health, pollution and human hazards and Earth and Ocean Science, Environmental Biology and Ecology and Biogegraphy.

Bristol* See under **Geology**.

Bristol UWE The Environmental Science course has special options that cover ecology, toxicology, environmental biotechnology, pollution and waste management. There is an Environmental Health course leading to professional qualification as an environmental health officer. Other degree options include Environmental Management and Geography and Environmental Biology or Forensics and Health, Safety and the Environment.

Cambridge* Ecology can be studied in the Natural Sciences Tripos. The Land Economy course covers the Environment, Law and Economics. (See under **Property Management and Surveying**.)

Canterbury Christ Church The Environmental Science course covers the biological, chemical and physical aspects of the environment. There are also courses in Ecology and Conservation and in Environmental Biology. (High Quality Ratings)

Cardiff* A course in Ecology and Environmental Management follows a common first year covering seven biological sciences. There is also a course in Environmental Geoscience.

Central Lancashire The Geography and Environmental Management course covers geography, ecology, law, chemistry and planning. Scientific emphasis is provided in the three-year Environmental Science degree. There are also courses in Ecology and Environmental Hazards and Management.

Chester A combined honours course in Natural Hazard Management focuses on geography, geology and people.

Coventry The Environmental Health course covers food, health and safety and leads to professional status as an Environmental Health Officer.

Derby Environmental Science, Environmental Management and Global Hazards are available as three-year full-time degree courses. There are also courses in Third World Development and Conservation and Countryside Management.

Dundee The first year of the Environmental Science course covers global environmental processes, geography, geology and natural environmental systems. Second-year topics include eco-systems and resource monitoring and management while the third-year themes cover environmental geoscience, remote sensing and resource management. Courses in Environmental Management and Renewable Energy are also offered.

Durham* A course is offered in Environmental Geoscience.

East Anglia* An extensive range of courses and fieldwork opportunities are offered including Meteorology and Oceanography along with Environmental Sciences, Earth Sciences and Ecology with the opportunity to study in Europe, Australasia or North America or working in industry.

Edge Hill Environmental Science is a comprehensive course involving fieldwork in the UK and Mallorca and optional visits to Europe and the Far East.

Edinburgh* Ecological Science is divided into four degree programmes covering Conservation and Management, Ecology, Environmental Science and Forestry. It is possible to change degree programmes up till the end of the third year. Environmental Studies can also be studied alongside Economic and Social History.

Essex The course in Environment, Lifestyle and Health focuses on human disease, public health conservation and environmental issues. There are also degrees in Ecology and in Biodiversity and Conservation.

Glasgow* Courses are offered in Environmental Chemistry (reclamation, pollution, pesticides), Environmental Biogeochemistry (interactions of water in different environments) and Earth Science. A degree in Environmental Sustainability is offered at the Crichton campus in Dumfries.

Glasgow Caledonian In Year 3 of the Environmental Business Management course, students undertake a six-month placement. Specialist modules include waste management, water quality and urban regeneration.

Gloucestershire Environmental Science and Environmental Management can each be studied with work placements. There is also a course is Water Resource Management.

Glyndŵr Fieldwork, IT skills and a study of Geographical Information Systems are included in the Environmental Science degree. Tutorial support is available through the medium of Welsh.

Greenwich The Environmental Science course offers three options from a choice of 12 in Year 3 including geological and scientific topics, and planning and landscape issues. There is also a course in Ecology.

Harper Adams (UC) Countryside and Environmental Management courses are offered, the latter covering water quality, ecology and pollution. Scholarships available.

Heriot-Watt The Environmental Management and Planning course is a multidisciplinary programme with modules in coastal biology and offshore technology.

Hertfordshire Environmental Studies covers biological, physical and social aspects. In Year 2, environmental planning, landscape development and pollution issues are covered. Supervised work experience takes place in Year 3. There is also a course in Environmental Management which can include study abroad.

Hull The course in Environmental Science covers biology, geography and anthropology. There is also a degree in Ecology.

Imperial London* A course is offered in Environmental Geoscience. The course, which is part of the Geology programme leads to the Associateship of the Royal School of Mines. (High research rating)

Keele* The Applied Environmental Science dual honours course covers biology, geology and chemistry and is taken with Physical Geography. Over 20 dual honours combinations are possible.

Kent The course in Environmental Social Science covers anthropology, economics, law, social policy and sociology. Courses are also offered in Conservation including Wildlife Conservation.

Kingston Pathways in Environmental Science include ecology, conservation and resource management. Options include languages, business and human geography. Environmental Studies is offered with a range of subjects including Business Management. There are also degree courses in Natural History, Environmental Hazards and Disaster Management and Environmental Management.

Lancaster* The Environmental Science (ES) Department is a major centre in this subject field. Specialisation is introduced in the final year when a choice is made between aquatics and atmospheric systems, applied earth science or environmental assessment and management. Final-year topics include pollution, water resources management, earth science and geophysics. Degrees in Ecology, Earth and Environmental Science and Environmental Biology or Chemistry are also offered. (High research rating)

Leeds* Environmental courses are offered with variations in Business, Ecology, Energy Science, Conservation, Management and Sustainability.

Leeds Metropolitan The Environmental Health course involves five study areas, comprising environmental science, technology, management, the environment, methodology and practice. Topics include occupational health, food safety control and public health. Year 3 is spent in practical experience. The course leads to qualification as an environmental health officer.

Leicester* See under **Geology**.

Liverpool Hope Environmental Management is offered as part of a combined honours (BA/BSc) programme. Popular combinations include Geography, Sport Studies and Sport Development.

See *University Degree Course Offers* (Trotman Publishing) for details of offers

Liverpool John Moores Environmental Sciences is available as a three-year full-time or four-year sandwich course. It focuses on issues relating to geography, ecology and the social sciences.

London (King's)* Courses offered include Ecology, Environmental Health, and Environment and Society.

London (LSE)* The Environmental Policy course covers the natural environment, geography, economics and sociology. A second subject can be studied in Year 1. Final-year options include management, transport, urban planning or geography. There is also a course in Environmental Policy focusing on Economics.

London (QM)* Environmental Science is an interdisciplinary course offered by the Departments of Geography and Biology studying the natural environment, covering physical geography, geology, environmental biology and chemistry. There is some emphasis on marine aspects, for example oceanic, river and coastal environment, and marine biology. Specialisms include conservation, ecology management, chemistry and environmental quality. A course can also be taken with Business Management.

London (RH)* Courses are offered in Ecology and the Environment, Environmental Geology and Geography with Environmental Archaeology.

London (UCL)* Courses are offered in Environmental Geography, Environmental Biology and Environmental Geoscience.

Manchester* The Environmental Science degree programme enables students to specialise in their particular fields of interest within biology, earth sciences, chemistry or biology. The course in Environmental Studies offers similar topics but deals more with the relationship between humans and their environment Entrance scholarships available.

Manchester Metropolitan The Environmental Health course leads to a career as an environmental health officer. Courses are also available in Environmental Management and Environmental Protection, together with Environmental Studies and Ecology and Conservation. All courses provide links with North America.

Middlesex Courses are offered in Environmental Health, covering food safety, housing and health and safety.

Napier A BSc ordinary and honours course is available in Environmental Biology.

Newcastle* The Environmental Science course covers management, ecology, tropical environments and biological conservation. Courses are also offered in Countryside Management and Rural Studies.

Northampton A BSc course is available in Environmental Science with separate pathways in Climate Change, Landscape Ecology, and Wastes Management.

Northumbria* Environmental Management focuses on the sustainability of natural and human systems, eg wildlife, landscapes or industry. The Environmental Health degree leads to careers in food science and public health.

Nottingham* Degrees are offered in Environmental Biology and Environmental Science, focusing on the management of ecosystems. A wide range of options is offered in Year 3. (High research rating)

Nottingham Trent Courses include Environmental Biology, Environmental Health, and Environmental Science with Business, Environment and Wildlife Conservation or Countryside Management. Environmental courses cover ecology, conservation, countryside management and business.

Oxford Brookes* A large number of combined courses with Environmental Sciences can be taken as a BA or BSc degree. There are also single honours courses in Environmental Biology, and Conservation Biology.

Plymouth The Environmental Science degree course includes a study of environmental biology, chemistry, geology and the human environment, environmental management, food and water resources, pollution and land reclamation. Specialist pathways include environmental sustainability, environmental health, biodiversity and conservation, environmental change and marine conservation. There are also courses in Wildlife Conservation and several courses focusing on Marine Studies including pathways in merchant shipping, navigation and ocean exploration. Scholarships available.

Portsmouth The Environmental Science course is a blend of biology chemistry, physics and geology conservation. There is also a course in Marine Environmental Science with industrial placements and courses in Environmental Biology, Environmental Hazards, and Environmental Forensic Science and Environmental Health which can also be taken over six years on a part-time basis.

Queen's Belfast* For Land Use and Environmental Management, see under **Agriculture and related courses**. Environmental Biology is offered from Stage 0, and after Stage 1 students may transfer to pathways leading to degrees in Biological Sciences, Plant Science Genetics, Marine Biology and Zoology. See also **Town Planning and Urban Planning Studies**.

Reading* Environmental courses follow different themes. Part I prepares all students with a basic core of subjects and thereafter specialisms follow. Programmes offered cover biology, chemistry, earth science, geology or earth and atmosphere. Courses include Environmental and Countryside Management, Environmental Science or Forensics, and Applied Ecology and Conservation. (High research rating)

St Andrews* A four-year course in Environmental Biology and Geography is offered. There is also a single honours course in Sustainable Development, covering ecological, social, economic and environmental issues.

Salford Environmental Studies aims to provide a comprehensive understanding of environmental problems and professional practice. This is a four-year course giving full exemption from the examinations of the Institute of Environmental Health Officers. Environmental Management, Environmental Geography, and Wildlife Conservation courses are also offered.

Sheffield* The first year of the Environmental Science course covers geography, geology, environmental biology and ecology. A more specialised treatment of the subject follows in the second year while in the third year specialist areas include global change, hydrology and biology in the environment. There is also a course in Environmental Mathematics.

Sheffield Hallam Environmental Management is a four-year sandwich course with a European language option. The course involves environmental quality engineering, landscape management and water engineering. Other courses cover Environmental Studies and Environmental Conservation.

Southampton* Environmental Sciences is an interdisciplinary course comprising options from biology, geography, geology, chemistry and oceanography. Students have the opportunity to design their courses in groups of units. The groups cover the physical and the biological environments, chemistry and human sciences within the environment and water in the environment, hydrology and hydrobiology. There are also courses in Environmental Engineering. (High research rating)

Southampton Solent Environmental Studies with options in Tourism or Media Communications can be followed and in addition Coastal Conservation or Marine Environmental Science.

Staffordshire The degree in Environmental Conservation has a vocational emphasis with work placement opportunities.

Stirling Environmental Science focuses attention on the surface and near-surface environments of the earth. Part I covers the environmental systems, earth science and resources and the environment. Part II deals with climatology, resources, geomorphology, soils and vegetation, environmental management and computing. Final-year options include environmental hazards, remote sensing, pollution, rivers and tropical environments. Several joint courses are also offered. There is also a course is Environmental Science and Outdoor Education. The Primary Education course has an Environmental pathway.

Strathclyde The Environmental Health course deals with radiation and health, physics, law, pollution, occupational health and safety and is accredited by professional bodies in the UK. A course is also offered in Environmental Protection and Pollution Control.

Sussex* The Environmental Science course establishes the link between chemistry, biology and geography. The emphasis is on scientific investigation, although social and economic aspects are also considered. Ecology and Conservation is also offered. (High research rating)

Swansea* Environmental Biology can be taken as part of the Biological Sciences group of subjects.

Swansea Metropolitan Environmental courses can be taken focusing on scientific, legal, political and social aspects. Specialisation follows in BSc. routes after a common first year.

Ulster After a common first year for all Environmental Science students aiming for the ordinary and the honours degrees, Years 2 and 3 offer a choice between a study of geological aspects including natural resources and society's exploitation of them, or a course with a geographical emphasis. There are also courses in Environmental Health and over 20 joint courses in Environmental Science.

West Scotland Environmental Science is offered with Applied Bioscience. The course covers biochemistry and biotechnology and can be taken with a year's industrial placement.

Wolverhampton The course in Environmental Health provides training as an environmental health officer. There is an optional year's placement. There is also a degree in Environmental Science and Management.

Worcester There is a degree in Water and Environmental Management. The Environmental Management course focuses on the rural environment.

York* Courses are offered in Environmental Science, Environmental Geography and Environmental Economics and Management with specialisations taking place in Year 2.

OTHER INSTITUTIONS OFFERING ENVIRONMENTAL COURSES
Blackpool and Fylde (Coll), Cornwall (Coll), Farnborough (UC), Pembrokeshire (Coll), SAC, UHI Millennium Inst, Warwickshire (Coll), Writtle (Coll).

ALTERNATIVE COURSES
Agricultural Sciences, Agriculture, Applied Natural Sciences, Biological Sciences, Countryside Management, Earth Resources, Estate Management, Forest Resources, Garden Design, Geography, Geology, Landscape Architecture, Maritime Environmental Management, Meteorology, Ocean Sciences, Soil Science, Underwater Studies.

EUROPEAN STUDIES

(*indicates universities with the highest entry requirements)

SUBJECT REQUIREMENTS/PREFERENCES
GCE A-level: Two or three appropriate languages. **GCSE:** English for all courses and possibly Mathematics.

SUBJECT INFORMATION
European Studies is an increasingly popular subject and offers the language student the opportunity to study modern languages within the context of a European country (for example economic, political,

legal, social and cultural aspects). On these courses there is usually a strong emphasis placed on the written and spoken word. There are also European Business Studies courses available.

Aberdeen First-year European Studies students follow courses in modern and contemporary European history, comparative European politics and two languages from Gaelic, French, German and Spanish. Language study continues over three years. The third year is spent abroad. Courses in European Management Studies, European Languages, Twentieth Century Culture and European Cultural Studies are also offered.

Abertay Dundee The European Economy and Management programme is designed for holders of HND European Business or for European exchange students respectively.

Aberystwyth The four-year BA course in European Studies combines a European language (French, German or Spanish) with a study of European economic, political and legal institutions. There are also separate degree courses in European Languages, European History and European Politics.

Aston* The European Studies programme is a joint or combined honours course offering a choice between French or German and topics covering the history and development of the European Union, European law, current affairs and International Relations. European Studies is also offered with Business Administration, Public Policy and Management, and Sociology. There is a one year placement year following Year 2.

Birmingham* A course in European Politics, Society and Economics provides a broad study of European development.

Bristol UWE European Studies can be taken as a joint honours course with 25 other subjects.

Cardiff* European Union Studies offers an integrated four-year programme in which students choose one or two modern European languages (from French, German, Italian or Spanish with an option in Catalan) in the context of the contemporary political, economic, legal and social structure of Western Europe. Emphasis is placed on the practical (non-literary) aspects of language. The third year is spent in study abroad.

Central Lancashire A course in International Business Studies is offered.

Coventry European Law is offered with French, German, Italian, Russian and Spanish.

Dundee* During the first two years of the European Studies course, students normally take at least two courses from French, German, and Spanish. A two-year honours course in French, German or Spanish is compulsory for single honours students. In the third and fourth year five courses on Europe are chosen from a wide range of subjects. The whole or part of Year 3 may be spent in France, Germany or Spain.

East Anglia* The European Studies programme is one of the most flexible on offer, starting with a foundation year and progressing to a wide range of options including languages and exchanges with European universities.

Essex* European Studies is offered with a range of subjects including French, German, Italian, Spanish, and Politics and Economics. Beginners courses are possible and it is possible to transfer between courses.

Glamorgan The course on Modern Europe consists of a wide range of options; students build their own course.

Glasgow* A course in Central and East European Studies covers Russia, Poland, Hungary, Czech Republic, Bulgaria and Romania and deals with the geography and the social, political and cultural development of the areas. There is also a general humanities course in European Civilisation.

Hertfordshire The European Studies programme offers courses with 12 other subjects such as Business, Health Studies, Biology, Geography, Law, Sport Studies and Tourism.

Kent* A range of degrees in European Studies is available including specialisations in French, German, Spanish and combined languages.

See *University Degree Course Offers* (Trotman Publishing) for details of offers

Lancaster* The European Studies four-year degree scheme enables students to aim for a high proficiency in two European languages (from French, German, Italian or Spanish) of which one can be taken from beginners' level. Topics cover European ideas, regions, cinema and society. There is also a course in European Management with a foreign language.

Lincoln European Business Studies, European Marketing and European Tourism are offered.

Liverpool John Moores Three-year courses in European Studies are offered in which a Community language is taken with a study covering the history, politics, geography and economics of contemporary Europe. A four-year European Studies course includes a year in France, Germany, Italy or Spain.

London (Goldsmiths)* A four-year degree in European Studies is available which includes a European language and a broad study of cultures and politics.

London (King's)* The four-year European Studies Humanities course has a focus on politics, history, and the culture of modern Europe with French, German or Spanish pathways.

London (QM)* The course unit system enables European Studies students to select courses in French, German, Russian or Hispanic Studies, combined with at least two courses in linguistics and/or literature, and a wide choice of other subjects such as law, politics or mathematics. A year abroad is normally undertaken.

London (RH)* European Studies courses are offered with French, German, Italian and Spanish. Year 3 is spent in the relevant country. The final year consists of core courses in social sciences, international relations and a language.

London (UCL)* European Social and Political Studies is a four-year degree that combines the study of one or two European languages (from Dutch, French, German, Italian, Russian, Scandinavian languages and Spanish) with a chosen Humanities or Social Science specialisation including Anthropology, Economics, Geography, History, Law, Philosophy or Politics. The third year is spent abroad. Degree courses are also offered in East European Studies with Bulgarian, Czech, Slovak, Finnish, Hungarian, Polish, Romanian, Serbian, and Ukrainian.

London Metropolitan European Studies is offered as a joint honours course studied with subjects such as Economics, History, Law, Politics or Spanish. Courses are also available in European Business Studies and European Banking and Finance.

London South Bank The European Policy Studies degree covers European and British history and politics, European issues and international relations. French, German or Spanish language units are also available.

Loughborough* European and International Studies is a three-year course combining languages and social sciences with fluency in one or more European languages (French, German and Spanish).

Manchester* European Studies and Modern Languages offers French, German, Italian, Russian and Spanish, with one major language being studied and one at subsidiary level, plus the government and politics of Western Europe.

Manchester Metropolitan European Studies is offered as a joint course with several subjects including Business Mathematics, Computing Science, and Multimedia Technology, languages and communications.

Newcastle* Government and European Union Studies is offered as a four-year course. European Studies can also be studied with Chemistry with French, German or Spanish specialisation.

Nottingham* The Modern European Studies course is a four-year course with the third year being spent abroad. Taught jointly by the Departments of History and Modern Languages, it is designed to enable students to study aspects of modern European history, the contemporary societies and institutions in Eastern and Western Europe and at least two European languages.

Nottingham Trent There are several European Studies courses with a study of a language from beginners', intermediate or advanced level. Joint courses include Geography, History, International Relations or Politics.

See *University Degree Course Offers* (Trotman Publishing) for details of offers

Portsmouth* European Studies is a three-year course covering European history, culture and a specialist knowledge in chosen aspects of EU policy of a particular European country. Language study is optional. European Studies can be taken with International Relations, Law or languages.

Queen's Belfast* The European Studies course involves the study of one European language (French, German and Spanish). The course covers history and politics with language fluency, with a placement in Europe between Years 2 and 3.

Reading* In the European Studies degree one or two languages are taken from French, German and Italian, with minor studies offered in Spanish, Dutch, Swedish or Greek. Specialisms follow in language and culture, politics, history, economic and social studies. There is also a course in European Literature and Culture.

Southampton* The Contemporary Europe degree comprises a study of the history and politics of Europe and European Union institutions, with options in economics, history, law or politics. Two European languages are studied from French, German or Spanish. Portuguese is also offered as a minor language. Scholarships available.

Stirling European Studies is an integrated package comprising a modern European language (French, German, Spanish), European history and politics. European Social Policy and European Film and Media are also offered.

Sunderland European Studies is offered with a wide range of second subjects, including Business Law, History of Art and Design, Photography, Journalism, Management and Media Studies.

Sussex* There is a degree in International Relation and Contemporary European Studies. The latter can be taken as a joint degree or as a minor subject.

Ulster European Studies can be taken as a Combined Arts course combined with over 25 other subjects. The course covers Western and Eastern Europe.

ALTERNATIVE COURSES
European Business Studies, European languages, History, International Studies/Relations, Sociology.

FILM, RADIO, VIDEO AND TELEVISION STUDIES

(*indicates universities with the highest entry requirements)

SUBJECT REQUIREMENTS/PREFERENCES
GCE A-level: English, Media Studies. History may be required. **GCSE:** English usually required. Courses vary, so check prospectuses.

SUBJECT INFORMATION
Many of these courses are mainly theoretical and historical in approach, but may involve practical studies, the media in general and video work.

Aberdeen There is a course in Film and Visual Culture exploring all aspects of this art form in the 20th century.

Aberystwyth Film and TV Studies is a degree scheme covering aspects of history and analysis. Practical work in video production, scripting and editing is also included with the added advantage of access to the National Screen and Sound Archive for Wales.

Anglia Ruskin Film Studies is offered as part of the combined honours programme with History, Media, Communication, Technology, Drama, English and Sociology. Options include practical work with camcorder, video documentary and internet communications.

Bath Spa Over 20 subjects can be taken with Film and Screen Studies.

Birmingham City Film Production or Television Technology and Production are offered as a three-year full-time, four-year sandwich or as a five-year sandwich course with a foundation year.

Bolton The new Film and Media course covers a wide range of topics relating to the cinema and the use of film in the media.

Bournemouth* A three-year course is offered which has a short work placement in Year 2 and there is a one-year top-up degree course in Photography, Film and Television. There is also a three-year course in Scriptwriting for Film and Television.

Bradford Film studies is a largely theoretical course. 20% of the time is spent on practical work.

Bristol* See under **Drama, Dance and Performance Arts**.

Bristol UWE The single honours courses in Film Studies provide special studies in the field of documentary films, Hollywood and World Cinema. Joint courses are available with Media Studies, Drama and English.

Brunel* Single and joint honours courses are offered in Film and Television Studies, covering history, theory and practice in both video and still photography. Work placements are optional.

Bucks New The Film and TV Production course covers camera work, lighting, sound and editing. A creative production-based course is also offered in Digital Film Art. There is also a scriptwriting course.

Canterbury Christ Church The course in Film, Radio and Television Studies offers the opportunity to develop and practise production skills in each of the three media.

Central Lancashire Single and joint honours courses are offered in Film and Media Studies and involve the mass media, television, the press, cinema, advertising and photography. Other courses cover Film Production and Screenwriting.

Chester Film Studies is a combined honours degree. A single honours degree is being validated.

Creative Arts Courses are offered in Film Production and Video Arts.

Cumbria Film Studies (joint honours) has a theoretical approach to the subject.

De Montfort The Film Studies degree is offered as a joint course. The course is largely theoretical but there is a practical option to explore the techniques of video making. There is also a Film Studies, Photography and Video degree course and a Radio Production course.

Derby The course in Film and Video offers 75% practical work, while some work placements are offered in the Film and Television degree course. There are also Photography courses.

Dundee See under **English**.

East Anglia* Courses in Film and English Studies or American Studies are offered. There is also a course in Film and Television Studies with an emphasis on film history. Some practical work is also offered.

East London Courses are offered in Film and Video (Cinematics) Theory and Practice, and Film Studies taken with a second subject.

Edge Hill Courses are offered in Film Studies and Film and Television Production. There are also nine joint courses.

Essex* Film Studies is a broad course focusing on the social and historical aspects of the media. It is offered as a joint programme with History of Art, Literature or History and American Studies.

Exeter* The Film Studies course has an emphasis on European, Latin American and African cinema in addition to Hollywood. Joint courses with modern languages are also available. There are opportunities for practical film-making.

Glamorgan Courses are offered in Film Studies including scriptwriting and joint courses with TV and Set Design, Drama, Media and English.

Glasgow* The Film and Television course studies both cinema and TV as major forces within 20th century culture. An introduction to video techniques is available to students.

Gloucestershire The major, minor or joint course in Film Studies focuses on genre topics in film history and the Hollywood film industry. There is an optional placement period on the Film Management courses.

Greenwich Film Studies is subject to validations.

Hertfordshire* Three degrees are offered in Film and Television specialising in Fiction Documentary or Entertainment. There are also degrees in Screen Cultures with Media. There is also a course in Special Effects.

Huddersfield There is a course in Digital Film and Visual Effects Production.

Hull* Film Studies is part of a joint programme and focuses mainly on British and American cinema.

Keele* Film and American Studies can be taken as a single honours course.

Kent* The Film Studies single and dual honours course provides a theoretical study of film history and production. Practical photography, video and film modules are only available to single honours students.

Kingston The Film Studies course is theoretical and focuses on the history of film and contemporary European and American cinema. It can be studied with French or Spanish and other subjects.

Lancaster* The Film Studies course explores the links between theory and practice. It is not a vocational course preparing students for media. It is offered as a combined course with European languages, Philosophy, Sociology and English Literature.

Leeds* A three-year course is offered in Cinema and Photography with a practice-based study of both art forms supported by historical and critical analysis.

Leeds Metropolitan A course is offered in Film and Moving Image Production requiring a portfolio of art or film work.

Leeds Trinity (UC) In Years 2 and 3 the Film and TV course provides a range of options eg video production, radio broadcasting, broadcast journalism etc.

Leicester* Film Studies and Visual Arts comprises a study of the history of film and art.

Lincoln Several courses are offered with Film and TV Studies.

Liverpool* European Film Studies and Modern Languages offers students the opportunity to combine Film Studies with degree-level study in either one or two language areas from French, German or Hispanic Studies.

Liverpool Hope Film Studies is offered as a combined honours subject and combines theory and practice. The Film and TV Production degree combine practical and theoretical work.

Liverpool John Moores The Screen Studies course spans the histories and practices of film and television. It has a critical rather than creative approach.

See *University Degree Course Offers* (Trotman Publishing) for details of offers

London (King's)* Eleven courses in Film Studies are offered. The department has excellent facilities and lies in close proximity to the British Film Institute, the National Film Theatre and the Museum of the Moving Image.

London (QM)* Film Studies is offered jointly with Drama, languages and History. The course includes a wide range of options in Years 2 and 3.

London (SOAS) See under **Media Studies**.

London Metropolitan Film Studies is a single or joint honours course with practical modules. There are also courses in Film and Broadcast Production and in Cinematics.

London South Bank The Applied Science course focuses on the biological sciences and the food industry.

Manchester* Courses are offered in Film Studies which can be combined with Media and Cultural Studies, Creative Writing or Video. There are also courses in TV Journalism and Production.

Manchester Metropolitan Courses are offered in Film and Television Studies, Film and Media Studies, European Film and Contemporary Film and Video.

Middlesex The Film Studies course covers film theory, history and criticism. There are also 14 joint courses.

Napier Photography, Film and Imaging is available either as a three-year or four-year full-time course.

Newcastle* Film Studies can be taken with Modern Languages.

Newport A practical course in Documentary Film and TV is available.

Northampton There is a degree course in American Literature and Film. In addition to a study of the history, theory and cultural significance in the Film and TV degree.

Northumbria Film can be studied with English or the History of Modern Art and Design.

Nottingham* Film and TV Studies is offered with American Studies, Art History, Music, Cinemas, and Theology, French, German, Hispanic Studies, Russian.

Nottingham Trent There is a course in Design for Film and TV.

Oxford Brookes* Film Studies is a theoretical course as a single honours degree or can be taken with 16 other subjects.

Portsmouth There is a single honours course in Film Studies and combined programmes with Creative Writing or Drama.

Queen Margaret Film and Media combines a study of the industry with many specialisms including video production, documentaries, media management and world cinema.

Queen's Belfast* The Film Studies course is offered as a single, joint, major or minor subject. Students can specialise in creative practice, scriptwriting, cinematography or direction and production.

Reading The Film, Theatre and Television course integrates practical work, a critical study of film and theatre and the historical and cultural significance of television.

Roehampton Film can be studied as a single honours course or in joint degrees with another subject from a choice of 12, such as Journalism and News Media, Media and Culture. Roehampton runs partnership events with the British Film Institute.

St Andrews* Film Studies is a joint course with a strong bias in European film-making. Scholarships available.

St Mary's (UC) A theoretical course in Film and TV can lead to pathways in creative writing, media arts or sociology.

Sheffield Hallam Courses are offered in Film and Literature, History or Media Production, covering history and criticism with several options in photography or film production.

Southampton * A degree in Film covers European and US studies and some practical work. Students opt for specialist studies each year. Students have the option to take an alternative subject for 25% of the course.

Southampton Solent Courses are offered in Film Studies and Television Production. The Film, TV and Radio degree has a substantial element of practical work.

Staffordshire Courses are offered in Film Production Technology and Film, Television and Radio Studies, both involved largely with practical studies.

Stirling The focus on the two courses in Film and Media Studies and European Film and Media lies in the very wide range of options. In the latter students opt for either Media or Film.

Sunderland See **Media Studies**.

Surrey The Film Studies degree offers the study of audio visual media focusing on Film (theory and industry).

Sussex * The Film Studies course provides a foundation in film genre and theory and the range of film-making worldwide. It can also be taken with Languages, Drama, Music and English.

Swansea There is a degree in Screen Studies covering film and TV.

Trinity St David (Carmarthen) Film Studies can be taken with Creative Writing, English, Fine Art and Media Studies.

Trinity St David (Lampeter) The Film Studies course offers practical training with an academic approach to the subject. There is also a course in Film and Media Studies.

Ulster Film Studies can be taken with 18 other subjects.

Warwick * Five courses are offered – Film and Literature and Film with Television Studies and three Film Studies programmes. The first offers a study of English, European and American literature linked to aspects of film while the second provides wider coverage of film and develops TV studies.

West London Video Production courses are offered including Advertising with Video Production and Film, Video Production with Film Studies.

West Scotland The course in Film-making and screen writing is mainly practical and is available as either a three-year or four-year course.

Westminster The three-year Film and Television Production degree covers film-making, TV drama and documentary, screenwriting, film theory and criticism.

Winchester A theoretical Film Studies course is offered and also a large number of joint courses with Film and Cinema Technologies which includes cinematography, lighting and set design.

Wolverhampton The Film Studies degree can be combined with one or two other subjects from 10 options. The course focuses on production, language and aesthetics of the cinema with specialist options that include the British, French, Spanish and American cinema. There is also a practical course in Video and Film Production.

Worcester Courses are offered in Film Studies and in Digital Film Production.

York St John Courses are offered in Film and TV Production.

OTHER INSTITUTIONS OFFERING FILM/TV COURSES

Bournemouth (UC), Edinburgh (CA), Falmouth (UC), Grimsby (IFHE), Northbrook (Coll), St Helens (Coll), Bradford (Coll), Manchester City (Coll), Sunderland City (Coll), Cleveland (CAD), Cornwall (Coll), Croydon (Coll), Dewsbury (Coll), Exeter (Coll), Hereford (CA), Hull (Coll), Newham (Coll), Norwich (SAD), NESCOT, Sandwell (Coll), Solihull (Coll), South Cheshire (Coll), South Nottingham (Coll) Stockport (Coll), Suffolk (Univ Campus), Truro (Coll), Walsall (Coll), Warwickshire (Coll), Wiltshire (Coll).

ALTERNATIVE COURSES

Media Studies, Photography, TV and Video, Visual Communication.

FINANCE

(including **Banking** and **Insurance**)
(see also **Accountancy/Accounting**)
(* indicates universities with the highest entry requirements)

SUBJECT REQUIREMENTS/PREFERENCES

GCSE: English and Mathematics required.

SUBJECT INFORMATION

These are specialised courses leading to careers in banking, building societies, insurance companies, pensions funds etc. Major banks offer sponsorship. Most courses follow a similar curriculum; many Finance courses are combined with Accountancy.

Aberdeen The degree in Finance involves a broad study of aspects of accounting, corporate banking and personal finance, treasury and international management, and property investment. Part of the degree may be taken abroad.

Abertay Dundee This is a four-year course in the applications of finance and accounting in business.

Aberystwyth A broad course in Business Finance includes investment fundamentals, portfolio management and global finance.

Anglia Ruskin Degrees in Financial Services and International Financial Markets are offered.

Bangor The course in Banking and Finance provides a study of financial services and markets. Banking can be studied with a range of subjects including Mathematics, Accounting, Italian, Spanish, French and German.

Bedfordshire There are degrees in Business Studies (Finance and International Finance).

Birmingham* The Money, Banking, Finance course provides a study of the UK financial system and a sound grounding in law, accountancy, finance and economics.

Birmingham City Finance is offered as a joint degree of three years or with an additional year on a business placement after Year 2.

Bournemouth Financial Services, a four-year sandwich course, covers accounting, banking, financial management, insurance, marketing, building societies, money markets, business strategy and information technology. The third year is spent in commerce. There is also a European language option. Finance is also offered with Law.

Brighton The degree course (three-year full-time or four-year sandwich) in Finance and Investment covers both the UK and international economics. The course involves economics, corporate law and risk management. This course has a common first year with Economics and Finance. A transfer is possible in Year 2.

Bristol UWE Full-time and sandwich courses are offered in Economics, Money, Banking and Finance.

Brunel Business Finance is offered with Economics. Courses are also available in Finance and Accounting, Financial Computing and Financial Mathematics.

Buckingham A course in Financial Services is offered starting in January or July. It is aimed at students seeking careers in banking, finance, investment analysis and other financial services. Courses in Accounting and Financial Management, and Finance with Information Systems are also available.

Cardiff* Banking and Finance is an economics-based course that includes a training relevant to the practice of banking. Optional courses include accounting, management with a foreign language and a year spent abroad.

City* In the Banking and International Finance course economics, statistics, computer programming and introductions to law and accounting are studied with banking and international finance in the first year. There are options in two subjects to be chosen in the second and third years including French or German. Study abroad and work placements are an option. The degree in Investment, Finance and Risk includes international investment policies in Europe, North America and Japan. A course is also offered in Actuarial Science. See also **Mathematics**.

Coventry The Finance and Investment courses can be taken on a full-time or part-time basis. Finance can also be taken with Accountancy or Economics.

Dundee The Finance courses include financial economics and can also be taken with eight other subjects including Psychology, Political Science and German. See also **Accountancy/Accounting**.

Durham (Stockton)* A course in Business Finance covering economics, management, marketing and international money. It shares a first year with Accountancy and Business degrees with options to transfer at the end of Year 1.

East London There is a modular course in Finance, Money and Banking with options in asset pricing, political economy and corporate finance.

Essex Courses in Financial Management and Finance are offered, together with Mathematics and Accounting.

Exeter* Finance can be studied with Accounting and Economics. Both have a European study option.

Glasgow Caledonian Options on the Financial Services course include business management, social security, languages, insurance, banking, building societies, international banking and underwriting. There is also a course in Risk Management relating to insurance with topics involving fire, employee injury, pollution and computer fraud, and a four-year full-time course in Financial Mathematics.

Greenwich Banking can be studied with Economics. A degree in Finance and Financial Information Systems is offered and covers banking, insurance, securities and investments.

Heriot-Watt Several Finance courses are offered with specialisms in Business Law, Business, Economics and Mathematics. The courses receive accreditation from accountancy bodies.

Hertfordshire There is a three-year full-time or four-year sandwich course in Finance which covers business and international finance, global economy and taxation.

Hull Several courses are offered in Financial Management focusing on Business, Economics, Logistics or Marketing.

See *University Degree Course Offers* (Trotman Publishing) for details of offers

Keele The degree in Finance focuses on financial markets and can be combined with over 25 subjects including Languages, Management, Computer Sciences and Business Economics.

Kent The University offers one of the few courses in Actuarial Science.

Lancaster* Finance is offered as a three-year degree course and can also be taken in combination with Accounting or Economics.

Lincoln A course in Finance can be taken as a single subject or in combination, for example with Management, Public Relations, or Marketing.

Liverpool John Moores The course in International Banking and Finance covers economics, statistics, accounting and law, with final year options in personal finance, international economics, money and banking. There is a modern language option in Year 2.

London (LSE)* Finance is offered with Accounting and there is also a course in Actuarial Science.

London (QM)* Courses in Finance are offered with Mathematics, and Business Management or with Physics or Economics.

London (UCL)* Business Finance is offered with Engineering in three-year and four-year full-time honours degree courses.

London Metropolitan Courses are offered in Banking, Banking and Finance, and Financial Services.

London South Bank A three-year honours degree is offered in Financial Management which covers taxation, business law, auditing and information systems.

Loughborough* Banking, Finance and Management is a four-year sandwich course covering managerial, financial, legal and economic aspects of banking and finance. Optional subjects include French, German, computing, personnel work, marketing and economic history. Other courses offered include Financial Management or Financial Mathematics.

Manchester* A single honours course is offered in Finance, or it can be taken in combination with Accounting, Economics, Physics or Civil Engineering.

Manchester Metropolitan There are courses in Financial Services and Financial Sector Management.

Middlesex A course in Money, Banking and Finance is offered with optional industrial placements in Year 3.

Northampton The Financial Services degree covers banking, insurance, building society operations, fund management and treasury operations.

Northumbria A three-year degree is offered in Finance and Investment Management that covers economics, accounting, marketing, international finance and taxation.

Nottingham* A unique course is offered in Industrial Economics and Insurance and there is also a course in Finance, Accounting and Management.

Nottingham Trent An 'in company' Retail Banking degree is offered.

Plymouth International Financial Services is offered as a three- or four-year sandwich course.

Portsmouth Finance and Business is a three-year or four-year sandwich course covering building society and banking operations and the marketing of financial services. A degree is also available in International Finance and Trade.

Queen's Belfast* The course in Finance covers accounting, capital investment decisions, management of stock, debtors, company and international finance. Year 3 is a placement year in a financial institution in the UK or abroad. It can also be studied with French, German or Spanish.

Reading* Courses are offered in Finance and Investment Banking or Property Investment. Internships can be arranged during summer vacations.

Robert Gordon Management is offered with Finance.

Salford Property Management and Investment is available as a three-year full-time degree.

Sheffield Hallam A four-year sandwich course in Business and Financial Services is offered. Core subjects include economics, business accounts, international finance, financial and management accounting, quantitative analysis, information systems, financial institutions, law and marketing. There is also a degree in Banking with Finance.

Southampton* Finance is offered with Accounting, Mathematics and Economics.

Southampton Solent Degrees are offered in Finance with either Business Management or Entrepreneurship.

Staffordshire Degree courses are offered in Finance, and Business and Financial Economics.

Stirling Several courses are offered with Finance including French, Management, Law, Marketing, Sports Studies and Spanish. There is also a degree in Money, Banking and Finance. Semesters 1 and 2 focus on accounting. Study abroad in a European University is an option.

Strathclyde Finance is offered jointly with Management, Marketing, International Business and Mathematics.

Surrey The course in Financial Services Management is designed to match the needs of industry and can be taken to include a Professional Training year adding considerably to employmemt prospects.

Swansea* There is a Finance specialisation in the Business and Management Science programmes and there is also a degree in Actuarial Studies.

Teesside Accounting and Cybercrime is an option.

Ulster Finance and Investment Analysis is offered as a three-year full-time degree. There is also a Financial Services course.

Westminster A Finance pathway is available in the three-year Business degree and in the four-year Business Studies sandwich course.

OTHER INSTITUTIONS OFFERING FINANCE COURSES

Bradford (Coll), Cornwall (Coll), Dudley (CT), East Lancashire (Coll), European (BusSch), Grimsby (IFHE), Guildford (CFHE), Highbury (Coll), Hopwood Hall (Coll), Manchester (CAT), Manchester City (Coll), Newcastle (Coll), Northbrook (Coll), Norwich City (Coll), Nottingham New (Coll), Peterborough (Reg Coll), Regents (BusSch), Richmond (American Univ), Sandwell (Coll), Sheffield (Coll), South Essex (Coll), Suffolk (Univ Campus), Swindon (Coll), Truro (Coll), Warwickshire (Coll), Wigan and Leigh (Coll).

ALTERNATIVE COURSES

Accounting, Actuarial Studies, Business Studies, Economics and Retail Management.

FOOD SCIENCE

(including **Nutrition** and **Dietetics**)
(See also **Agriculture and related courses**)
(* indicates universities with the highest entry requirements)

SUBJECT REQUIREMENTS/PREFERENCES
GCE A-level: Sciences, usually including Chemistry and Biology. **GCSE:** English, Mathematics and a science.

SUBJECT INFORMATION
Biochemistry, microbiology, human nutrition, food processing and technology are components of these courses. The study depends for its understanding on a secure foundation of several pure sciences – chemistry and two subjects from physics, mathematics, biology, botany or zoology. Only students offering such a combination can be considered. Food Technology covers the engineering aspects of food processing and management.

Abertay Dundee Three courses are offered, all with common first and second years, leading to a choice of degree in Food and Consumer Science, Food Design and Technology or Food, Nutrition and Health. Opportunities exist for one-semester or year-long exchanges with students from a university in Toronto or on work placement.

Bath Spa The central theme of the Diet and Health course explores the impact of diet, nutrition and lifestyle on health. Food and Design focuses on food product development, whilst the Food, Nutrition and Consumer Protection and the Human Nutrition course emphasise food chain and nutritional issues.

Birmingham (UC) The Food Consumer Management Course includes food practice and demonstration. Marketing and Media can also be studied.

Bournemouth* The BSc Nutrition course includes a study of the molecular, physiological and biochemical aspects of nutrition, psychology, health promotion, public health, food production and safety. Students undertake a placement and project. (course under review)

Brighton* There is a degree in Marketing Food and Drink closely linked to the hospitality industry and also a unique course in Viticulture and Oenology involving all aspects of the wine industry.

Cardiff (UWIC) The four year Human Nutrition and Dietetics includes clinical training in Years 2, 3 and 4. There are also degrees in Public Health Nutrition with specialisms in Sports Medicine and Food Technology, and Consumer and Trading Standards. Scholarships available.

Chester Courses are offered in Nutrition and Dietetics, leading to the career of dietitian, and also a single honours course in Human Nutrition.

Coventry The Food Science and Nutrition course deals with food analysis, food safety and human nutrition. There is also a four year Dietetics course in which they seek 'strong interpersonal skills, adaptability and flexibility'.

Glamorgan The course in Nutrition, Food Science and Health includes food safety and processing, managing customers and suppliers, product development. The degree in Nutrition, Physical Activity and Community Health has a short placement in the community.

Glasgow Caledonian Year 1 of the Human Nutrition course includes sociology and information studies in addition to nutrition, physiology and chemistry. Community studies, management, food science and clinical dietetic studies follow. There are also courses in Food Technology, Food Bioscience, Applied Nutrition and Human Nutrition and Dietetics leading to professional qualification.

Greenwich The Human Nutrition degree includes options in medical biochemistry, immunology, and nutrition in sport and exercise.

Harper Adams (UC) Foods and Nutrition and Well-being and Food and Consumer Studies are both offered with a placement year in the industry. There is also a more business centred degree in Agri-Food Marketing with Business Studies.

Heriot-Watt The Food Science Technology and Management course combines biochemistry and microbiology with management topics. Nutrition, human resources, health and safety and marketing are also included. There is also one of the very few Brewing and Distilling courses available in the UK.

Hertfordshire A Dietetics degree in offered with placements throughout the course.

Huddersfield The Food and Nutrition course leads to technical management careers in the food and related industries. Specialisms include food processing, applied nutrition, food safety and food science. Courses in Food, Nutrition and Health, Diet and Health, and Food Science Technology Management are also offered. The Nutrition and Public Health degree can be taken over three years or as a four year sandwich course with a placement year.

Kingston The degree in Exercise, Nutrition and Health has an emphasis on sport and exercise with modules in physiology, sport and exercise and psychology.

Leeds* The Food Studies and Nutrition degrees include options to spend Year 3 in a salaried position in industry, or to study abroad in Europe (including spoken language training for six months followed by industrial placement) or a year at a university overseas eg USA.

Leeds Metropolitan There are three degrees focusing on Public Health one of which centres on Nutrition with an emphasis on the relationship between nutrition and nutrition-related health and disease.

Leeds Trinity (UC) The degree in Nutrition and Food includes two placements each of six weeks. The course covers health and well-being, food culture and behaviour, food safety and quality and community health. Nutrition can also be studied on the combined honours programmes with Psychology or Sport and Health Exercise.

Lincoln The Human Nutrition course includes a broad study of the sciences and covers biochemistry, anatomy, physiology and aspects of diet, health, diet-related disease.

Liverpool Hope Nutrition is taken as a combined honours degree with or with Health Promotion as a single honours programme. Other appropriate combined subjects could include Child and Youth Studies or Human Biology.

Liverpool John Moores The degree in Nutrition can be taken over three years or as a four year sandwich course. There are also degrees in Food and Nutrition and in Consumer Studies and Marketing. A specialised course in Home Economics is also offered.

London (Kings)* The BSc course is a modular programme with specialised options including, diet, disease, obesity and antioxidants and cancer. There is also a four year Nutrition and Dietetics course with clinical placements in Year 2, 3 and 4, leading to qualification as a dietician.

London Metropolitan The scientific emphasis of the course in Nutrition, Exercise and Health covers cell biology, biochemistry, human physiology and focuses on the importance of the links between nutrition and exercise. There is also a course in Food and Consumer studies.

London South Bank Food Design and Technology covers all aspects of the study of food including chemistry, hygiene, processing and preservation. There is also a degree in Food and Nutrition.

Manchester Metropolitan There are courses in Food Studies with a choice from Nutrition, Management, Marketing or Technology. The Human Nutrition course is subject to review. Check with the university.

Middlesex The Sport and Exercise Science course focuses entirely on sports nutrition with opportunities for work placement.

Newcastle* Students taking the four-year course in Food and Human Nutrition which includes a year's placement in Year 3 in the UK or abroad are able to take options in economics, marketing or a foreign language.

Northumbria In the Human Nutrition degree (three or four years) the fundamentals of biochemistry and physiology are studied in addition to the nutritional composition of foods and diets. There is also a degree in Food Science and Nutrition.

Nottingham* three-year courses are offered in Nutrition, Nutrition and Food Science (students are eligible to apply for a Northern Foods or Sainsbury's Scholarship) and Nutrition Biochemistry focusing on health and agriculture. There is also a four-year course leading to Master of Nutrition (Dietetics). Courses are also offered in Food Science and Food Microbiology.

Nottingham Trent The degree in Exercise, Nutrition and Health is subject to validation. Check with the University.

Oxford Brookes* Two courses are offered, Nutrition and Public Health Nutrition. Both courses have work experience modules and provide the opportunity in Year 2 for student to study abroad in Europe, the USA, Canada or Australia.

Queen Margaret The degree in Nutrition provides expertise in areas such as health promotion, clinical sciences, epidemiology, international health and research. The first two years are identical with the BSc in Dietetics however transfer from Nutrition into Dietetics is not normally possible.

Queen's Belfast* The Food Quality, Safety and Nutrition degree has a 16 week work placement period in Year 3 or a one year placement in the four-year course leading to qualification as a dietician.

Plymouth Problem-based learning features throughout the Dietetics degree of three years. Other courses offered include Applied Biosciences (Food and Nutrition), Experience Nutrition and Health, and Health and Social Care studies.

Reading* The Nutrition and Food Science course is taken over three years with a four year option involving professional placement in Year 3. Food science degrees are also offered with Business and with industrial training. Scholarships are available.

Robert Gordon four-year degree courses in Nutrition and Nutrition and Dietetics are offered with placements intergrated in Years 2, 3 and 4.

Roehampton The degree in Nutrition and Health is offered on a full-time or part-time basis. The course encompasses physiology and biochemistry as well as aspects of psychology and sociology which may influence food intakes.

St Mary's (UC) The Nutrition degree offers options in Clinical Nutrition, Obesity, Public Health Nutrition and Sports Nutrition.

Scottish (CAg) The degree in Food Technology covers quality, production and marketing.

Sheffield Hallam A degree is offered in Food and Nutrition. There is some emphasis on food quality, and technology and consumer studies and also focus health promotion in the community.

Surrey* Food Science and the Nutrition and Dietetics degrees are offered, the former on a three or four year basis. As with the Dietetics option the four-year degree courses include a year placement with an employer.

See *University Degree Course Offers* (Trotman Publishing) for details of offers

Teesside Food, Nutrition and Health Science is a three-year course with the option to extend it by including a professional placement in the UK of one year.

Ulster There is also a course in Consumer Studies and a course in Food and Nutrition (see also **Biology**).

West London Nutritional Medicine is offered as a part-time degree course lasting five or six years. The start dates are in October, February and June. Scholarships available.

Westminster A free choice subject module is offered in each year of the degree couse in Human Nutrition. Relevant topics include Public Health, Physiology and Psychology. There is also a course in Nutrition and Exercise Science.

Worcester Human Nutrition can be taken as a single, joint or major/minor course. It may be combined with other biological subjects or with most other subjects in the modular scheme eg Health, Psychology or Sports subjects.

OTHER INSTITUTIONS OFFERING FOOD STUDIES/SCIENCE COURSES
Bradford College, Suffolk (Univ Campus).

ALTERNATIVE COURSES
Biological Sciences, Biomedical Science, Food Science, Health Science, Psychology.

GEOGRAPHY

(* indicates universities with the highest entry requirements)

SUBJECT REQUIREMENTS/PREFERENCES
GCE A-level: Geography is usually the highest grade shown in the offers made. One or more science subjects may be required for BSc courses. **GCSE:** Mathematics often required for BSc courses.

SUBJECT INFORMATION
These courses cover the human, physical, economic and social aspects of geography. Each institution offers its own particular emphasis. Check the prospectuses for all courses, with particular attention to the specialist options in the second and third years.

Aberdeen Geography honours students have the opportunity to specialise in topics chosen from human, physical and environmental geography. In Level 2 courses are offered in Environmental Systems, Space Economy and Society, and Mapping. Student exchange programmes are also available. There are many joint courses.

Aberystwyth Degrees in Human and Physical Geography are offered in the Faculties of Arts or Science. Specialist modules can be taken in both physical and human geography courses. Several joint honours schemes link Geography with other subjects. There are also courses in Environmental and Earth Sciences. Scholarships available. (High research rating)

Anglia Ruskin The first year of the Applied Geography course is common to all students. In Years 2 and 3 students may construct their own programme of general or specialist topics chosen from over 20 modules. A work experience module allows students to spend a short period in industry or commerce.

Aston* A degree in Geographical Information Systems is offered in the combined honours programme that covers geography, computing and natural resource management.

Bangor A three-year course in Geography is offered leading to BA or BSc degrees with a specialist stream for those aiming to teach. There is an emphasis on practical work. Specialist BA streams are available in Planning, Housing, Transport and Environmental Management whilst BSc options include Oceanography, Agriculture and Atmospheres.

Bath Spa Human and Physical Geography are the main features of this degree. Both courses can be taken in as part of the combined award. There is also a course in Geographical Information Systems. School and voluntary placements are also organised. Scholarships available.

Birmingham* In the first year of the Geography (BSc and BA) courses, students cover human and physical geography. In the second year, single honours students choose three from five elective courses that determine the final degree and which include conservation, settlements, planning and resource management and physical geography. There is a free choice of options in Year 3. A wide range of joint courses is also offered and there is also a course in Geography and Urban and Regional Planning. (High research rating)

Bournemouth The Applied Geography course aims to focus on geographical skills related to real world issues covering resources, planning, countryside management and environmental matters.

Bradford Geography can be studied with Environmental Management or Archaeology or as a degree in Physical and Environmental Geography. Both are sandwich courses with a 40-week placement in Year 3. The flexible degree structure allows students to switch courses.

Brighton Human environmental and physical geography are offered at Level 1 of the Geography degree followed by specialist topics in Levels 2 and 3. These include water resources, medical geography and environmental studies. Geography can also be taken with Geology and with subjects in the joint Science field. A Biogeography course is also offered.

Bristol* The Geography course covers a wide range of geographical interests and related problems concerning the environment and the regions. After Stage I (first year), three different syllabuses are offered allowing specialisation in human and/or physical geography. Complementary subjects are offered as minor courses occupying one-third of Year 1. A course involving study in continental Europe is also offered. (High research rating)

Bristol UWE Both human and physical geography are covered in the Geography course with joint courses in environmental management, planning and tourism. Associated courses are also offered in Planning and Communities and Transport Planning.

Cambridge* Part IA of the Geography course covers physical, human and historical geography, environment and resources and geographical methods. In the second year (Part IB) there are options in human or physical and environmental geography. In the third year, four topics are chosen from a wide range of subjects. (High research rating)

Canterbury Christ Church Geography students can choose course specialisations from Human or Physical Geography or Planning and the Environment. There is a strong emphasis on regional geography and in Year 2 an opportunity to study in Canada.

Cardiff* The Marine Geography course focuses on the ocean as a maritime frontier and human beings' socio-economic relationship with the physical environment and the principles of maritime transport, the maritime industries and ocean and coastal management. Topics covered include geology, the ocean atmosphere, cartography, coastal hydrography and coastal zone management. The third year may be spent in industrial training. (High research rating)

Central Lancashire The BA/BSc Geography courses offer specialisms in physical, human, social and industrial geography or urban planning. There is a language option available. The subject is also offered on the combined honours programme and can also be studied with Sociology, and Environmental Management.

Chester Human and physical geography are key features of this course which includes geographical information systems and useful joint courses in Urban Studies and International Development Studies.

Coventry In addition to the BA programme, the BSc Geography course is a three-year or four-year sandwich course. A unique feature of this course is the third year spent in professional training in which students have placements related to geography such as hydrology, forestry, offshore surveying, marketing and transport, in the UK and abroad. Four geography modules are selected from a choice of 10 in the final year. There are also courses in Natural Hazards, Global Sustainability and climate change.

Cumbria Courses are offered in Geography covering Human and Physical Geography.

Derby The Geography course is offered with the option to study abroad. There are also pathways in Third World Development and International Relations.

Dundee The emphasis in the first two years of the Geography course is population geography, urban and regional development, physical geography and the evolution of Europe's landscape. In Year 3, students select from a range of physical, human and regional courses. A BSc course is also offered that includes a study of two other science subjects in Years 1 and 2. It is also possible to study Geography with Environmental Science.

Durham* The first-year courses in Geography cover human, physical and regional geography with field-work in the UK and abroad and practical classes. In the second and third years a choice of specialist options enables students to choose their own emphasis to the subject, either social or science research. Continuous assessment is used for one-third of the degree. Geography is also part of the Natural Sciences and combined honours programmes in social sciences. (High research rating)

East Anglia* Environmental Geography is combined with International Development Studies, a subject with a social science perspective focusing on social analysis, economics and the management of natural resources and the environment. There is also a degree in Meteorology and Oceanography, with options to study in Europe or North America. There is also a course in development studies covering international, social and environmental perspectives.

East London The University offers three-year full-time degrees in Geographical Information Science, and Surveying and Mapping Sciences.

Edge Hill Honours courses in Geography, Human Geography, Physical Geography and Physical Geography and Geology are offered. There is also a course in Geotourism focusing on environments, communities, culture and lifestyles.

Edinburgh* Geography may be studied as a natural science or a social science. The main distinction lies in the entry qualifications, which must include the basic sciences for the BSc course. There is a range of options including the economic and social landscape, disease and the environment and leisure studies. (High research rating)

Exeter* The undergraduate Geography programme extends over three years and offers alternative courses that lead to single or combined honours degrees in the Faculties of Arts, Science or Social Studies. There is a choice of field courses in the UK and abroad. Each student can therefore make his or her own specialist studies. Geography with European Study is a four-year course involving a year abroad. Some degree courses are taken at the Cornwall campus. Scholarships available. (High research rating)

Glamorgan The course in Geography gives both the human and physical aspects of the subject and includes the development of skills in Geographical Information Systems. Human Geography and Physical Geography are also available as single honours degrees. Work experience and some sponsorships for Welsh language students.

Glasgow* Physical and Human Geography are covered in Year 1, followed by the study of a major world area, statistics, computing and mapping. Geography may be studied in the Arts, Social Science or Science Faculties, and is available as a joint course with a wide range of subjects.

Gloucestershire Human Geography and Physical Geography are studied over three years. Nine other subjects are available in the joint degree programme, including Biology, Psychology and English.

See *University Degree Course Offers* (Trotman Publishing) for details of offers

Greenwich Geography students elect to follow the BA or BSc courses at the end of the first year. Options include environmental or natural resources management or human geography. Sandwich course students go on industrial or commercial work placements in Year 3.

Hertfordshire A broad Geography degree (including the option of a work placement) is available with specialism in human or physical geography. It is also offered as a sandwich course and with the opportunity to study in Europe or North America and as a joint degree with up to 15 subjects.

Hull A modular course leading to a BA (Human Geography) or BSc (Physical Geography) is offered. The first year is common to both courses. Some modules can be taken in other subjects. Geography is offered as a single or joint course with over 10 subjects including American Studies, Archaeology, History and Sociology. (High research rating)

Keele The Geography (single honours), Human Geography and Physical Geography (both dual honours) courses offer field courses in the UK, Europe and further afield. The courses are taken with a second subject from more than 20 options.

Kingston The Geography courses offer a choice of options in both human and physical geography. These include regional geography and geographical information systems.

Lancaster* All Geography students follow courses in human and physical geography and geographical techniques in Year 1. These, and environmental themes, develop in Years 2 and 3. There are also separate courses in Physical and Human Geography. Many of the courses have a strong applied theme, giving a broad picture of the social, economic and environmental problems. In Year 2 there is an option of teaching geography in a local school. Exchanges with the USA may be arranged. (High research rating)

Leeds* Courses in Geography cover both social and natural science interests with one or two subsidiary subjects. The former offers a wide range of options with particular strength in urban and resources studies, and with compulsory field weeks and visits to France in Year 2. The BSc course aims to provide a broad base in geography while emphasising the scientific study of the environment. This is reflected in the training provided in the field, laboratory and computing techniques. There is a wide choice of third-year options including hydrology, water quality, energy resources, soils, conservation, environmental risk assessment, climatic change, geomorphological modelling, fluvial and glacial processes. Geology or Transport Planning can also be studied with Geography. (High research rating)

Leeds Metropolitan Human Geography is offered, as a single honours course and also with Housing or Planning.

Leicester* The Geography course has a common first year for BA and BSc students. Thereafter the BA students follow a human geography course, and a bias towards physical geography exists for BSc students with a high degree of flexibility in option choice and specialisation. Year 1 supplementary subjects include archaeology, computer science, history and politics. A degree in Human Geography is offered whilst Geography can also be studied with Archaeology, Geology. Scholarships available. See also **Combined courses**. (High research rating)

Liverpool* Geography is offered as a BA or BSc course. Students follow first-year courses in physical and human geography and introduction to the planet Earth. Options are available in the first and second years. The science bias has a strong physical geography element. Archaeology, Biology or Management are additional options. Scholarships available. (High research rating)

Liverpool Hope The BSc Geography single honours course provides a mix of human, physical and environmental geography. Several combined honours combinations are also on offer.

Liverpool John Moores The Geography course combines modules from both environmental and human geography. The course has a vocational emphasis. There is a BSc course which covers both Human and Physical Geography.

London (King's)* Physical and human geography and geographical techniques are covered in the first year of the BA and BSc courses. With a European language option. Second-year and third-year students follow optional course units and present an independent geographical study. There is also a course in Development Geography.

London (LSE)* The BA Geography course focuses on human geography and the environment. There is also a course in Geography and Economics. (High research rating)

London (QM)* Geography is taught under the course unit system, enabling students to combine their own choice of geographical studies with a wide variety of other disciplines, for example economics, history, politics, geology, a modern language. The subject can be studied either as an arts or as a science subject. There are separate courses leading to BA, BSc or BSc(Econ) degrees with a wide range of joint courses. (High research rating)

London (RH)* Geography courses cover physical and human geography and involve the interactions between people and their natural, economic and social environments. In Years 2 and 3 students have a free choice in the selection of specialist courses and are encouraged to acquire career-related skills. There is also a course combined with Environmental Archaeology. (High research rating)

London (SOAS)* This is the only Geography degree course that is specific to regions of the world, namely Asia and Africa. Various joint honours combinations are also available with 10 other subjects. There is also a course in Development Studies and there are eight joint courses with Geography.

London (UCL)* BA and BSc degrees in Geography are offered in human and physical geography in the first year to integrate with international topics and environmental studies. Geography may be studied as either an arts or a science subject and all students have the same wide choice of options, designing their own second-year and third-year programmes. Geography may also be studied with Anthropology or Economics and there is also a course in Environmental Geography.

Loughborough* Modular programmes in human, physical and environmental geography are taken in the first year of the Geography course followed by a wide range of options in the second and third years. Subsidiary options can be taken from non-geographical subjects including languages. Geography can also be studied with Economics, Management, Sport Management and Sport Science. (High research rating)

Manchester* Geography courses are offered in both the Faculties of Arts and Sciences with a variety of subsidiary courses in Years 2 and 3. Geographical issues cover social, economic, historical and political topics, with 20 options in the final year. Geography can also be studied with Archaeology. (High research rating) or International Study with the possibility of studying abroad, worldwide.

Manchester Metropolitan Several courses can be taken including Human or Physical Geography. Similar programmes are offered in Geographical Information Science with study in North America. Geography is offered with several subjects in the combined honours programme.

Newcastle* Geography is offered in both the Faculty of Arts and Sciences. This is a modular course in which two modules can be taken from the Combined Studies or Arts programmes. Second-year and third-year courses offer similar optional and core topics. It is also one of the subjects in the Combined Studies programme. (High research rating) Geography can also be taken with Planning, Mathematics or Statistics.

Northampton A BSc degree can be taken as a single honours subject with pathways in human geography, physical geography and joint honours courses.

Northumbria The Geography BA/BSc course introduces human, environmental and physical geography. A wide range of options is available in the third year. Geography is also offered with Environmental Management or Sports Studies.

Nottingham* BA and BSc students follow a common first-year Geography course in human and physical geography and also a course in geographical information science. Specialised topics begin in the second year, including meteorology, industry and transport, environmental studies and geomorphology. Geography can also be taken with Chinese Studies, Business and the Environment and East European Studies. (High research rating)

Nottingham Trent A BSc degree in Physical Geography can be taken as a specialised study. Geography is taught at the Brackenhurst Campus.

Oxford* The first-year Geography course introduces human and physical geography, and offers optional subjects (ethnology, geomorphology, sociology, political history or plant ecology), from which one must be selected. During the second and third years three geography papers are common to all students and there are optional topics, depending on their geographical interests. (High research rating)

Oxford Brookes* Geography (BA or BSc) combined honours courses are offered with a very large number of other subjects and courses. A compulsory field course abroad takes place in Year 2.

Plymouth The BA and BSc courses include optional work experience for a year the latter with a further option to travel in Europe, the USA or Australia. There's also a course in Physical Geography and Geology.

Portsmouth The BA/BSc Geography honours degree is a single-subject, broadly based degree programme, offering a balance between both physical and human fields of interest. Degrees in Human and Physical Geography and Geographical Information Science are also offered.

Queen's Belfast* Human and physical geography are taken in the first year. In the second year courses vary depending on the type of degree course chosen. Regional geography is studied in the second and third years alongside modules including social, human, economic, urban or physical geography with an introduction to earth science.

Reading Geography is offered with specialisation in human or physical geography or both combined or as Geography and Economics combined in the Regional Science degree course. A rare course in Meteorology with scholarships available can also be taken.

St Andrews* Geography is taught in the Arts and Science Faculties, the first two years being common to all students. A system of teaching in small option groups follows for the next two years. Students may specialise in human or physical geography or may study groups of courses concerned, for example, with landscape processes, land and water resources. Some exchanges take place with European institutions.

St Mary's (UC) Geography is offered as a single or joint degree and provides an overview of physical, social, cultural and political aspects.

Sheffield* The first-year BA Geography course introduces human and physical geography followed by a choice between three streams in the second year. Two of these focus on physical geography (geomorphology, soil formation and vegetation), one on human geography (population and environmental resources). Selective specialisation takes place in the third year. The BSc course lays emphasis on physical geography throughout. Geography can also be taken with Mathematics, Politics, Sociology and Planning. (High research rating)

Sheffield Hallam A Human Geography course can be followed with options in urban, social and economic geography and modern languages. There are also degrees with Planning and Transport.

Southampton* The BA and BSc Geography courses provide a common broad foundation until midway through the second year. Thereafter students begin to specialise and have considerable opportunity to select courses in transport geography, urban development, environmental change, remote sensing and hydrology. Physical Geography can also be taken with Geology or Oceanography. Scholarships available. (High research rating)

Southampton Solent Courses in Geography with Environmental Studies or Tourism are offered and in addition there is a BSc course in Marine Geography and a large Maritime operations programme covering topics from shipping and port management to yachting.

Staffordshire The BA Geography course emphasises human aspects of the discipline while the BSc course focuses on environmental and physical subjects. There is a broad range of options in Years 2 and 3. There are also degrees in Geography with Mountain Leadership, Physical and Environmental Geography (highly rated by students) and two-year accelerated degrees.

Stirling Environmental Geography courses are offered as pathways in the Environmental Science programme.

Strathclyde The course specialises in Human Geography including population dynamics, society and nature and natural hazards. Joint courses are offered including German, Law, Psychology, Sociology and Human Resource Management.

Sunderland Geography is offered with over 25 other subjects including American Studies, Criminology, Business Studies, Human Resource Management and Journalism or as a single honours subject covering both human and physical geography. A career placement is offered for Geography students.

Sussex* The subject emphasis of the Geography course depends on the School chosen. It can cover environmental, social, physical or urban issues and historical geography, physical geography, resource development and geographical analysis. Twelve joint courses can be followed.

Swansea* Geography is offered in the Faculties of Arts, Science and Economic and Social Studies. The first-year course is common to all three Faculties and deals with human, physical, economic and social courses in the practice of geography, computing, four compulsory courses and a selection from a very wide range of options. There are 10 joint honours programmes with subjects including languages, Social Policy, Biological Sciences and Geoinformatics. Scholarships are available. (High research rating)

Ulster The Geography course covers human and physical geography and includes work experience or study abroad. Geography can also be taken as part of the a modular programme with over 20 subjects.

Westminster The Human Geography course includes specialisms in European, UK and Third World geography and is taken as part of the Social Science programme.

Wolverhampton The Geography BSc course offers topics in soil management, pollution, and the alpine environment, while the BA course focuses on Britain, the USA and Eastern Europe. There is a common first year for both degrees. Eleven joint courses are also on offer.

Worcester Courses can be taken in Physical and Human Geography with work placement opportunities.

OTHER INSTITUTIONS OFFERING GEOGRAPHY COURSES
Havering (Coll), Staffordshire (Reg Fed), UHI Millennium Inst.

ALTERNATIVE COURSES
Development Studies, Earth Sciences, Environmental Studies and Sciences, Estate Management, Town and Country Planning.

GEOLOGY/GEOLOGICAL SCIENCES

(including **Earth Sciences**)
(* indicates universities with the highest entry requirements)

SUBJECT REQUIREMENTS/PREFERENCES
GCE A-level: Two to three subjects from sciences/Mathematics usually required. **GCSE:** English and Mathematics required.

SUBJECT INFORMATION

Geology is the science of the earth. Topics covered include the physical and chemical constitution of the earth, exploration geophysics, oil and marine geology (oceanography) and seismic interpretation.

Aberdeen Geology is offered with Petroleum Geology and is designed for those whose career intentions are with the petroleum industry. Geoscience degrees are also available. Students are able to take one year of study at an overseas institution.

Aberystwyth A degree course in Environmental Earth Science is offered covering the fields of earth science and physical geography. There is also a course in Earth, Planetary and Space Science. Scholarship available.

Bangor For all degree programmes in Ocean Science including Geological Oceanography, students are sought with a good scientific background. In Year 1, all Oceanography students take core courses in ocean and earth science. In Years 2 and 3, the degree has a dominant oceanographic perspective. Courses in Coastal Water Resources, Ocean Informatics and Environmental Forensics are available.

Birmingham* Courses are offered in Geology, Resource and Applied Geology (including water resource management), Environmental Geoscience (pollution and hazards) and Geology and Archaeology or Geography or Biology. Core courses and specialisms in the chosen degree are offered in Years 2 and 3. (High research rating)

Brighton Geology is offered as a three-year course or with an optional placement year. It can also be taken combined with Geography.

Bristol* The Geology course in this leading research department is aimed at those who wish to practise geology professionally and the degree is regarded as the basic foundation for further training in industry or research. Two subsidiary subjects are taken. One other subject from the Faculty of Science is also taken in the first year with specialism in geology in Years 2 and 3. There is a strong emphasis on fieldwork and geological mapping projects. A degree in Environmental Geoscience is offered, concerned with issues such as global climate change, the disposal of toxic waste and population needs. MSc courses are offered with a study in North America or Continental Europe. (High research rating)

Cambridge* Geological Science is offered as part of the Natural Sciences course. Specialisation is possible in mineral sciences, mineralogy or mineral physics or chemistry, historical geology and subjects of interest to those aiming for oil exploration. (High research rating) See also **Biological Sciences**.

Cardiff* The Geology programme is open to those with no prior knowledge of geology. There is a strong fieldwork element and up to two modules per year can be taken possibly from other departments. Topics covered include the physical and chemical constitution of the earth, exploration geophysics and seismic interpretation, geological time and earth history. Courses in Environmental Geoscience, Exploration Geology, Earth Sciences, and Marine Geography are also offered; these are choices in Years 2 and 3.

Derby Geology is offered with pathways in Applied Geology or Environmental Hazards or with study abroad.

Durham* The first year of the Geological Sciences course introduces the basic principles and methods of geology and recent advances. Single honours students then continue through the second and third years with a study of special branches of the geological sciences, for example economic geology, lunar geology, geochemistry and geophysics. Geology is also offered as part of the Natural Sciences programme and there are also courses in Earth Sciences, Environmental Geoscience and Geophysics with Geology. (High research rating)

East Anglia* The Geophysical Sciences course applies mathematics and physics to a range of natural phenomena such as floods, earthquakes and other weather systems. There are also courses allowing study in continental Europe or North America or in industry.

Edinburgh* The foundation of geological and other subjects is laid down in Years 1 and 2 with specialised studies following in Years 3 and 4. Courses in Geology, Geophysics, Geology and Physical Geography and Environmental Geoscience are offered. Overseas field work takes place in Cyprus, Jamaica and Spain. (High research rating)

Exeter (Camborne School of Mines) Applied Geology, Engineering Geology and Geotechnics and Applied Geology are offered as three-year full-time courses. Training courses in Cornwall, Wales, Scotland and Spain. Excellent employment prospects.

Glamorgan Geology is offered as a single, joint or major/minor degree within the Applied Sciences scheme, or it can be studied as part of the combined degree course. The course, which can be taken with a sandwich year, includes minerals surveying and exploration.

Glasgow* The degree in Earth Science offers an extensive range of options and has close links with geography and environmental management. Geology can be studied with a second subject such as Astronomy, and there is a Geological Science course. There is also a four-year course in Environmental Biogeochemistry. (High research rating)

Greenwich The Geology course offers a wide range of vocational options including environmental monitoring, mineral deposits, economic development and conservation management.

Imperial London* The Department offers four-year MSci courses in Environmental Geoscience, Geophysics, and Geology and Geophysics. There are also three-year and four-year degrees in Geology. Scholarships available. (High research rating)

Keele Geology is offered jointly with over 30 subjects. No previous knowledge of geology is required. The course covers rocks, minerals, fossils, geophysics and computing. A single honours course in Geoscience is also available.

Kingston The courses in Geology and Applied Geology assume no previous knowledge of the subject. Fieldwork is an important element of the courses. The Earth Sciences course is a broad study covering rocks, air, water and life systems and there is also an Earth Systems course together with a four-year degree with a foundation year in Earth and Planetary Sciences.

Lancaster* The Earth Science and Environmental Science courses are integrated programmes covering land, weather, geographical and science topics. There are options to study in North America or Australasia.

Leeds* The first two years in Geological Sciences cover a basic training in geology and the principles of geophysics plus a first-year study of two other relevant sciences. In the final year, students choose the emphasis of their courses by selecting from a range of options that includes environmental geochemistry, global geophysics and engineering geology. Geophysical Sciences and Environmental Geology are also offered as three-year degrees or with an additional year in Europe or abroad. (High research rating)

Leicester* Nine courses are offered in the Geosciences programme with opportunities to study in Europe, USA or New Zealand. In the Geology course a supplementary subject is studied in the first year. Geology can also be taken with Geophysics, Palaeobiology and Geography.

Liverpool* A range of well-integrated courses in Geology and Geophysics can be followed in this Geology programme and there is a four-year course that includes a year in North America. Field courses take place in Scotland, Wales, Greenland and the Alps. Oceanography, Climate Studies and Earth Sciences courses are also offered. (High research rating)

Liverpool John Moores A three-year full-time course in Geology is offered with a four-year sandwich course option. Geography or Geology at A2 are preferred subjects.

London (RH)* Geology is offered as single or joint honours. The single honours course introduces geology, earth materials and earth structure. In the second and third years a selection of optional courses allows specialisation. These include such topics as marine geology, fossil fuels, mineral deposits and engineering geology. There are also courses in Geology with a year in industry or a year of international study and courses in Petroleum or Environmental Geoscience and Planetary Geology. Scholarships available. (High research rating)

London (UCL)* Geology is a broad-based three-year or four-year course covering all the major aspects of geological sciences. Introductory courses are available in maths, physics, chemistry or biology. Theoretical and practical skills are developed through the programme and students are encouraged to take a computing course. There are also courses in Planetary Science, Environmental Geoscience, Palaeobiology and Geophysics. The Department of Earth Sciences has the only Regional Planetary Image Facility of NASA images. (High research rating)

Manchester* The Department of Earth Sciences offers degree courses in Geology, Earth Sciences, and Petroleum Engineering. The common first year of the Earth Science course covers most aspects of geology and a basic training in physical science. Students select which stream to follow in the second year and have a choice of specialist options in the third year including Geochemistry, Geology and Environmental and Resource Geology. Geology can also be taken with Planetary Science or Geography. Entrance scholarships are offered. (High research rating)

Oxford* The first year of the four-year Earth Sciences course is designed to cater for students with a variety of A-level subjects (a good foundation is chemistry and physics with maths, geology or a biological subject). The course covers the main aspects of geology, geophysics and geochemistry. Scholarships available. (High research rating)

Plymouth Students who enter the Geology course are expected to have an interest in geology, but not necessarily previous geological experience or qualifications. The degree in Applied Geology follows the same programme as Geology in Stages 1 and 2 but leads on to specialist modules in Stage 3 including mining geohazards, engineering geology, and vulcanology. There are also degree courses in Geology with Physical Geography, Computing or Geography.

Portsmouth Fieldwork forms a major part of the Geology course. Throughout the three years, the practical work is continually assessed and makes up to 25% of the total assessment in each year. There is a clear emphasis on the economic significance and practice of geology. There are also courses in Earth Sciences, Engineering Geology and Geotechnics, Geological Hazards and Palaeobiology and Evolution.

St Andrews* The Geoscience degree provides training across the earth sciences, geology and physical geography and can be studied as a single honours degree or it is offered with several subjects including Spanish, French, or Management. There is also Environmental Geoscience.

Southampton* A Master of Geology degree with the option of a year in North America provides comprehensive training for those aiming for a career in earth sciences. In the first year, Geology students take five units in geology. These include geochemistry, map interpretation, mineralogy and petrology and palaeontology. More advanced studies on these subjects continue in the second year plus new topics such as geotechnics and geophysics, while third-year students choose options according to their interests. Geophysics, and Ocean and Earth System Science are also offered. There is also a degree in Geophysical Sciences with a common first year enabling students to transfer to degrees in Physics, Geology or Oceanography. Scholarships available. (High research rating)

ALTERNATIVE COURSES
Chemistry, Civil Engineering, Earth Sciences, Environmental Science, Geography, Mining Engineering, Soil Science, Surveying and Geophysics.

See *University Degree Course Offers* (Trotman Publishing) for details of offers

HEALTH STUDIES/SCIENCES

(including **Occupational Therapy**, **Optometry**, **Podiatry**, **Radiography** and **Physiotherapy**)
(see also **Nursing** and **Sports Science/Studies**)
(* indicates universities with the highest entry requirements)

SUBJECT REQUIREMENTS/PREFERENCES

These vary according to the specific course and university.

Aberdeen Core courses in the Health Sciences degree cover biology, psychology, statistics and sociology, environmental studies and community health. The degree can focus on health promotion, health services and research, health and nutrition or health and society.

Anglia Ruskin Courses in Optical Management, Ophthalmic Dispensing and Radiography are offered. The course in Complementary Medicine specialises in aromatherapy or reflexology. There is also a new course in Family and Public Health.

Aston* Degrees in Optometry and Audiology are offered with clinical placement in Year 3 and there is also a combined honours option in Health and Safety Management which focuses on the prevention of occupational accidents and ill-health.

Bangor A broad Health Studies course is offered covering care and counselling management and focuses on specific areas of practice with optional specialisation in nursing. These areas include mental illness, housing policy, personal social services, poverty and welfare law. In addition there is also a vocational course in Diagnostic Radiography and Imaging. See also **Nursing**.

Bath Spa The Health Studies degree offers a study of health issues related to social, cultural, economic and environmental factors. There is also a degree in Diet and Health focusing on nutrition, food safety and health promotion and a separate course in Food, Nutrition and Consumer Protection. Scholarships available.

Bedfordshire A course is offered in Health and Social Care focusing on community care and health education. There is also a degree in Sports Therapy.

Birmingham* Physiotherapy, a very popular course in all universities, comprises both university and clinically based modules. There is also a course in Dental Hygiene and Therapy.

Birmingham City Degree courses with placements are offered by way of the pathways Health and Wellbeing (Exercise Science) and (Individuals and Communities) and (Nutrition). There are also courses in Radiography and Radiotherapy, Speech and Language Therapy.

Bolton The Health Studies course focuses on the study of contemporary health issues relating to health care practice.

Bournemouth The Exercise Science course focuses on health and rehabilitation. There are also professional practice courses in Occupational Therapy and Physiotherapy.*

Bradford* Optometry, Occupational Therapy, Diagnostic Radiography and Physiotherapy are offered. Additional courses include Health and Social Care (part time) and Clinical Sciences, and also a part-time course in Dementia Studies.

Brighton* Several courses are offered including Physiotherapy, Podiatry, Health and Social Care (also with Social Policy, Psychology or Sociology), Acupuncture, Health Studies, Osteopathy and Occupational Therapy.

Bristol* A degree course in Deaf Studies is offered by the Faculty of Social Sciences. A BSc degree is also offered in Audiology to study the treatment of hearing loss and rehabilitation.

Bristol UWE Several Health Science courses are offered as well as Diagnostic Imaging, Occupational Therapy, Physiotherapy, Health, Safety and the Environment, Public Health, Radiotherapy and Mental Health.

Brunel* Degree courses are available in Occupational Therapy and Physiotherapy and Public Health Nursing.

Canterbury Christ Church The Health Studies degree is a joint or combined honours programme with options in health promotion, education or psychology, public health nutrition and holistic health promotion. There are also degrees in Operating Department Practice and in Occupational Therapy leading to professional practice. There is also a degree in Diagnostic Radiography.

Cardiff* The degree in Optometry leads to registration by the General Medical Council as with other courses in this subject. Courses are also offered in Occupational Therapy, Physiotherapy, Radiotherapy and Oncology and Diagnostic Radiography and Imaging. There is also a Diploma in Higher Education award in Operating Department Practice Education.

Cardiff (UWIC) Courses are offered in Podiatry, Speech and Language Therapy and Complementary Therapies and Dental Technology.

Central Lancashire A new course in offered in Strength and Conditioning covering biomechanical studies and psychology. The Health Studies degree covers politics, sociology, economics, philosophy, history and a study of health concepts and health service provision. The Stage 2 programme can focus on Community Health, Health Promotion or Health Policy and Management. Courses are also offered in Health Sciences, Complementary Medicine, Homeopathic Medicine, Herbal Medicine, Exercise Nutrition and Health and Public Health. There are also courses in Acupuncture and Herbal Medicine.

Chester Courses are offered in Human Nutrition, Health and Social Care and Nutrition, and Dietetics giving full professional status.

City* The university is a major provider of education and training in health-related subjects. Courses offered include Speech and Language Therapy, Optometry and Diagnostic Radiography and Radiotherapy and Oncology. There is also a degree in Human Communication which focuses on speech, language and hearing.

Coventry Health and Lifestyle Management is a theoretical course covering psychology, nutrition, exercise science and a background to the promotion and market research of health practices. Degrees are also offered in Dietetics, Occupational Therapy and Physiotherapy.

Cumbria Courses cover Health and Social Care, Health Improvement, Occupational Therapy, Physiotherapy, Diagnostic Radiography and Complementary Therapies.

De Montfort The Health Studies degree course provides a preparation for careers in health service administration, education and promotion. There is also a degree in Human Communication leading to a qualification in speech and language therapy and a vocational course in Audiology. Several Youth and Community courses are also offered.

Derby Courses are offered in International Spa Management, Spa Therapies. Health can also be studied with Information Technology, Diagnostic Radiography, Occupational Therapy and Complementary Therapies (Aromatherapy and Reflexology).

Durham* A course in Health and Human Sciences covers the biological sciences and cross-cultural approaches of social and cultural anthropology.

East Anglia In addition to the Community Healthcare degree, courses are offered in Occupational Therapy, Physiotherapy, Speech and Language Therapy.

East London The courses offered cover Health Studies, Health Promotion and Health Services Management, Public Health, Acupuncture, Herbal Medicine, Physiotherapy and Podiatry.

Edge Hill Work-based experience takes place in Year 3 of the course in Health and Social Well-being which focuses on community work. There is also a degree in Women's Health.

Essex The two courses which run in parallel are Health and Human Sciences and Social Psychology and Sociology. Both courses include elements of psychology with the latter offering a bias towards sociology. There are also courses in Clinical Physiology (Cardiology) and Adult and Mental Health Nursing.

Exeter* A course is offered in Diagnostic Radiography.

Glamorgan A four-year full-time course is offered in Chiropractic leading to professional registration. Degrees in Medical Sciences, and Nutrition, Food and Science and Health and Social Care are also offered.

Glasgow A Health and Social Studies course is offered at the Dumfries Campus.

Glasgow Caledonian Courses are offered in Diagnostic Imaging Science, Radiation Oncology Science, Optometry and Ophthalmic Dispensing, Occupational Therapy, Physiotherapy, Podiatry, Human Nutrition, (also offered with Physiology and Sport Science), Dietetics and Radiography.

Gloucestershire Work-based experience takes place in the Health, Community and Social Care honours course.

Glyndŵr A degree is offered in Chinese Medicine studying diagnostic and therapeutic skills. The course in Complementary Medicine includes massage, aromatherapy and reflexology. There are also degrees in Addictive Behaviours (Substance Use), Occupational Therapy and Occupational Health and Safety.

Greenwich In addition to the Health BSc, which focuses on health systems and management, courses are also offered in Osteopathy, Human Nutrition, Public Health and Complementary Therapies (General/ Aromatherapy/Stress Management) and Occupational Health.

Hertfordshire The first Paramedic Science with Paramedic Award degree with work placement is offered with topics ranging across biosciences, pharmacology, psychology, law, ethics and health promotion. Placements constitute 40% of the course. Degrees in Radiography (Diagnostic or Therapeutic), Radiotherapy and Oncology, Physiotherapy, Dietetics and Sport Therapy can be studied. Health Studies is also offered as a joint course.

Huddersfield Courses are offered in Health and Community Studies or Social Welfare, Nutrition, Occupational Therapy, Physiotherapy, Podiatry, Sports and Health Studies and Sport Therapy.

Hull The degree in Global Health and Disease covers world health issues, health service systems and some aspects of biological science.

Keele Degrees in Osteopathy and in Physiotherapy are offered the latter including a comprehensive clinical programme.

Kent A course is offered in Health and Social Care that will appeal to potential employees in the NHS, social service departments and to potential managers in the voluntary and private social and healthcare sector. There is also a Care Practice degree.

Kingston* Physiotherapy, Diagnostic and Therapeutic Radiography are studied at Kingston in Year 1 and at St George's for practical applications. In addition to a single honours course in Nutrition there is also a degree in Exercise, Nutrition and Health with an optional sandwich year. Acupuncture can be taken as a single honours degree.

See *University Degree Course Offers* (Trotman Publishing) for details of offers

Leeds The School of Health Care Studies offers single honours courses in Audiology, Diagnostic Radiography, Clincal Physiology, and Food Studies and Nutrition.

Leeds Metropolitan Courses in Health include degrees in Acupuncture, Physical Activity, Exercise and Health, Physiotherapy, Dietetics, Nutrition, Public Health, Complementary Therapies, and Clinical Language Sciences which leads to qualification as a speech therapist. (See also **Nursing**)

Leeds Trinity (UC) Health Promotion and Health Psychology courses are offered the latter covering stress, ageing and forensic psychology.

Lincoln The Health and Social Care course covers physical and social services, management and education and international health issues. There is also a course in Herbal Medicine leading to full professional qualification and also a degree in Acupuncture.

Liverpool* Courses are offered in Nursing, Orthoptics, Physiotherapy, Radiotherapy, Occupational Therapy and Diagnostic Radiography.

Liverpool Hope The Health degree has a strong foundation in health, sociology, psychology and geography. Nutrition can be studied on the combined honours programme or as a minor pathway leading to a postgraduate study in Dietetics. There is a separate degree in Disability Studies, and a single honours course in Health Nutrition and Fitness.

Liverpool John Moores The School of Health is a major provider of healthcare education in the UK. Courses include Health Studies and Public Health. A course in Nutrition is also offered.

London (King's)* A course is offered in Physiotherapy. (See also **Nursing**.) The Nutrition course shares the same syllabus as the degree in Nutrition and Dietetics except that the latter has a dietetic research project and a 28-week placement in Years 3 and 4. Scholarships available.

London (St George's)* Courses are offered in Diagnostic and Therapeutic Radiography and in Physiotherapy. See also **Computer courses** (Biomedical Informatics).

London (UCL)* There is a four-year course in Speech Sciences with clinical placements in London and the South East. A course is also offered in Audiology.

London Metropolitan The Health Promotion course combines psychological, consumer, social and communication aspects of health promotion. Courses are also offered in Herbal Medicinal Science, Human Nutrition and in Health and Safety covering economic, political and legal aspects.

London South Bank Diagnostic Imaging (Radiography), Occupational Therapy, Physiotherapy and several other Health courses are offered.

Manchester* A degree is offered in Speech and Language Therapy (four years) leading to professional registration. There are also courses in Audiology, Nursing, Optometry, and Oral Health Science.

Manchester Metropolitan Health Studies involves sociology, psychology, biology and health promotion with specialisations in management, public health, physiology and complementary therapy. There is also a full-time degree in Speech Pathology and Therapy and courses in Environmental Health, Nutrition and Physiotherapy.

Marjon (UCP) There is a Speech and Language Therapy course leading to professional registration. Tuition fees are paid by the NHS.

Middlesex Complementary Health courses predomimate with degrees in Herbal Medicine, Ayurveda and Traditional Chinese Medicine.

Napier A course is offered in Herbal Medicine (Phytotherapy).

Newcastle* Speech and Language Sciences covers anatomy, psychology, linguistics and child language and leads to qualification as a speech therapist. Clinical practice increases throughout the four years of the course.

See *University Degree Course Offers* (Trotman Publishing) for details of offers

Northampton Degrees are offered in Health and Exercise, and in Health Studies comprising biology, sociology, psychology and nutrition. Podiatry and Occupational Therapy can also be studied.

Northumbria The degree in Community Health Care Studies focuses on public health, healthcare and policy making and health promotion. Degrees are also available in Occupational Therapy, and Physiotherapy.

Nottingham* Courses are offered in Physiotherapy, Dietetics and Nutrition.

Nottingham Trent A four-year sandwich degree is offered in Health and Environment covering health and safety, law, food studies and housing.

Oxford Brookes* Opportunities exist to study Physiotherapy, Occupational Therapy, Osteopathy, Nutrition, Health and Social Care, and Public Health Nutrition.

Plymouth Courses are offered offered include Dietetics, Physiotherapy, Podiatry, Occupational Therapy and Health and Social Care Studies.

Portsmouth Degrees offered include Diagnostic and Therapeutic Radiography, Applied Medical Technology, and Clinical Physiology.

Queen Margaret* BSc courses cover Audiology, Diagnostic and Therapeutic Radiography, Dietetics, Health Psychology, Occupational Therapy, Physiotherapy, Podiatry, and Speech and Language Therapy all leading to professional status.

Reading* The degree in Speech and Language Therapy is a training course leading to speech therapy careers. There are also courses in Nutrition.

Robert Gordon* Courses in Occupational Therapy, Physiotherapy and Diagnostic Radiography are offered by the School of Health Sciences. Nutrition and Dietetics courses are also offered.

Roehampton Health and Social Studies is offered as a single honours course and the programme is available in both full and part-time mode. Health Studies is offered as a single honours course and a combined course with Early Childhood Studies. There are also courses in Nutrition and Health and Psychology and Health.

St Mary's (UC) Health and Exercise is a theoretical study of health promotion focusing on life style and behaviour.

Salford Several courses are available including Traditional Chinese Medicine (Acupuncture), Counselling, Complementary Medicine and Health Sciences, Diagnostic Radiography, Exercise and Health Sciences, Occupational Therapy, Sports Rehabilitation, Prosthetics and Orthotics, Physiotherapy and Podiatry.

Sheffield* A course in Speech Science is offered (leading to work as a speech and language therapist). Health and Human Sciences, and Orthoptics are also offered.

Sheffield Hallam A degree is offered in Community Health, involving social psychology and law, leisure, food, sport, fitness and training. There are also degrees in Occupational Therapy, Physiotherapy, Diagnostic Radiography, Radiotherapy and Oncology, and Human Bioscience.

Southampton* Courses are offered in Audiology, Occupational Therapy, Physiotherapy, Podiatry.

Southampton Solent There are courses in Health and Fitness Management and Fitness and Personal Training each with a six-week placement at the end of Year 1.

Staffordshire A course is available in Exercise and Health, which includes social aspects of health and illness and healthcare policy and management. There is also a degree in Sport and Exercise Nutrition.

See *University Degree Course Offers* (Trotman Publishing) for details of offers

Strathclyde There are courses in Speech and Language Pathology and also Prosthetics and Orthotics, a highly practical course dealing with clinical biomechanics and limb replacements.

Sunderland Health and Social Care offers a broad multidisciplinary study of health covering biological, psychological and sociological perspectives. There are also degrees in Community Health and in Podiatry.

Swansea A three-year degree in Audiology is supported with an NHS Bursary.

Teesside* There are courses in Diagnostic Radiography, Physiotherapy, Food, Nutrition and Health Sciences, Occupational Therapy, Social Work with Nursing and Physiotherapy.

Trinity St David (Carmarthen) There is a degree in Health Nutrition and Lifestyle with an exchange programme available in Year 2.

Ulster Courses are available in Health and Social Care Policy, Dietetics, Human Nutrition, Occupational Therapy, Optometry, Radiography, Physiotherapy, Podiatry and Speech Science.

West London There are courses in Health Studies, Sport, Health and Fitness Management.

West Scotland A three-year degree in Health Science covers public health, physiology and medical chemistry. The Health and Lifestyle course includes nutrition and stress management. There is also a course in Occupational Health and Safety.

Westminster Complementary therapy courses are available in Health Sciences, Human Nutrition, Naturopathy, Herbal Medicine, Nutritional Therapy, Homeopathy, Therapeutic Bodywork and Acupuncture. There is also a Complementary Therapies degree with options in aromatherapy, reflexology, Thai massage and sports massage. The University also validates courses at the British College of Naturopathy and Osteopathy in both these subjects.

Winchester A course in Health and Well-being is awaiting validation.

Wolverhampton Health Studies, Public Health Nursing, Rehabilitation Studies and a degree in Complementary Therapies are offered. The latter can follow a general course or alternatively there is a choice of a specialist route in Aromatherapy or Reflexology or both. There are also degrees in Conductive Education dealing with children with motor disorders and courses in Deaf Studies and British Sign Language.

Worcester Health courses are offered with pathways in Well-Being, Management Psychology and Science.

York St John Occupational Therapy courses can be taken.

OTHER INSTITUTIONS OFFERING HEALTH COURSES
Blackpool and Fylde (Coll), Bradford (Coll), Bristol City (Coll), Bristol Filton (Coll), British Coll of Naturopathy and Osteopathy, CAFRE, Chesterfield (Coll), Colchester (Inst), Cornwall (Coll), Duchy (Coll), East Lancashire (Coll), European School of Osteopathy, Exeter (Coll), Grimsby (IFHE), Hopwood Hall (Coll), Leeds Park Lane (Coll), Loughborough (Coll), Manchester (CAT), Neath Port Talbot (Coll), NESCOT, Newcastle (Coll), Norwich City (Coll), Sheffield (Coll), South Devon (Coll), Sunderland City (Coll), Truro (Coll), Tyne Metropolitan (Coll), UHI Millennium Inst, Wakefield (Coll), Walsall (Coll), Warwickshire (Coll), West Anglia (Coll), Wigan and Leigh (Coll), Worcester (CT), Writtle (Coll), York (Coll)

ALTERNATIVE COURSES
Biological Sciences, Biomedical Sciences, Dietetics, Food Science, Medical Sciences, Nursing, Nutrition, Sports Science.

See *University Degree Course Offers* (Trotman Publishing) for details of offers

HISTORY

(including **Medieval Studies**)
(* indicates universities with the highest entry requirements)

SUBJECT REQUIREMENTS/PREFERENCES
GCE A-level: History usually required.

SUBJECT INFORMATION
History is a very broad subject, with most courses covering British and European history. There is, however, a wide range of specialist topics on offer, for example American, Scottish, Welsh, Irish, East European and Far Eastern history.

Aberdeen The degree in History includes coverage of European and British history, medieval history and Scottish history. In Years 3 and 4, options cover a wide range of topics including Science and Religion, History of Medicine and the Holocaust. In addition, there is a course in Scottish Studies and also one in Celtic Studies covering literature, music, language and the Gaelic community. The degree in Cultural History covers social relations, resources, beliefs and values.

Aberystwyth A very wide range of single honours courses is offered including History, European and Welsh History and Medieval and Modern History. There are also 28 joint courses with History.

Anglia Ruskin British, European and American History is offered with a wide range of topics including American and Latin American History, Film Studies, English, Politics and War Studies. There is also a separate course in 20th Century European History.

Bangor A general introduction to the History course includes four modules covering early and modern history with modules from other subject areas. In Years 2 and 3 a range of specialist history topics can be taken including medieval, modern and British political history, archaeology, Renaissance art, Arthurian Britain and Celtic heritage. History courses are also offered with Archaeology, Film Studies, Journalism, Heritage Studies and Welsh History.

Bath Spa The degree in History is a modular course with a very wide range of options allowing students to choose their own field. There is also a degree in Cultural Studies.

Birmingham* History courses offered cover the range of studies from Ancient and Medieval History to Modern History. The former extend from the Classical World and its Western Medieval and Byzantine successors. Modern History offers a thematic approach from 1500 to the present day. There are also courses in Medieval Studies, East Mediterranean History, and in Economic and Social History. (High research rating)

Bolton The History degree focuses on modern history areas including British international, political, social and economic history.

Bournemouth The Heritage Conservation course covers all aspects of the historic environment including archaeology, buildings and landscape history, materials and environmental sciences. Sandwich placements in Year 3 are arranged.

Bradford Modern European History is offered including elements of political theory and international relations. There are also courses in History with Philosophy, Law or Politics.

Brighton The degree course in Cultures, Histories and Literatures covers critical traditions in Western thought, nation and identity, history, narratives and gender and local history. Culture forms include novels, newspapers, films and photographs. Modern History is also offered as part of the Humanities course. There are also courses in Globalisation: History, Politics and Culture, and Museum and Heritage studies.

Bristol* The course covers medieval and modern history in Europe and offers a wide range of specialised units. Language options are available in the first two years. History can be studied with French or German with a year abroad and there is also a degree in Economics and History. There is also a separate degree in Ancient History focusing on the Greek and Roman world. (High research rating)

Bristol UWE The History course focuses on Early Modern and Modern History covering British, European, Imperial, International, American and Women's History. Complementary modules in other subjects are offered. There is also a course in International History and Politics.

Brunel* The History course involves a core curriculum and optional modules with an emphasis on social, political, intellectual or cultural histroy. The courses offered covers British, European, American and Russian history. History is also offered with Politics.

Buckingham Two main paths can be followed in the History programme covering British History from the earliest times to the present day and International History from 1800. History is combined with French, Spanish, Politics, English Literature, Economics and the History of Art.

Cambridge* The History course offers a flexible timetable with a choice of five from 22 periods of history in Years 1 and 2. A wider range of courses can be taken in Year 3. (High research rating) Some students transfer to other subjects at the end of the first year, Law and History of Art being popular choices.

Canterbury Christ Church The History course covers Medieval and Early Modern History and a pathway in Archaeology. A wide range of options can be selected in Years 2 and 3. Joint and combined courses are possible.

Cardiff* The History course introduces medieval history and contemporary history. Specialist topics are offered in the second and third years covering British, European and Asian history. There are specialist degree courses offered in Welsh History, Ancient History and Ancient and Medieval History, and with Archaeology as well as various joint honours combinations. (High research rating)

Cardiff (UWIC) Modern History can be taken with English or Politics.

Central Lancashire The History course covers Britain and Europe and also focuses on North America and Asian History. Joint subjects include Law, Politics, Film and Media and American Studies. Other courses include Modern World History and History, Museums and Heritage. There are also joint courses with English Literature, Education, Law, Sociology and Politics. See also **Combined courses**.

Chester Single and combined honours courses are offered in History with options in world, American or British history. Popular combinations include Archaeology, English, Law and Theology.

Chichester History is a broad course covering a range of subjects including education, local history, the heritage industry, film, and early modern art.

Coventry The History course focuses on the 20th century. It can also be taken with Politics, English or International Relations.

Cumbria The History degree covers a range of historical subjects from the Romans to early modern and modern Britain, Ireland and America.

De Montfort A broad course in History is offered covering the period from the French Revolution to the modern world. Joint honours subjects include Education, Film Studies, Politics, and International Relations.

Derby History is offered as part of the Humanities programme and covers modern British, European and international history.

Dundee After Levels 1 and 2, History students follow their own preferences in the countries and periods they prefer. There are also courses in Scottish Historical Studies and a multidisciplinary degree in Transatlantic Studies.

Durham* The History course focuses on the history of the West from the fall of the Roman Empire. In the first year, all students read early European history from the fourth to the 11th century and later choose two courses from a selection of history topics. In the second and third year specialist topics are followed. There are also courses in Ancient, Medieval and Modern History, History with English Literature or Modern Languages or Education. It can also be taken under combined honours in Arts or Social Sciences. (High research rating)

East Anglia* The School of History offers courses in Modern History and European History with over 100 units offered, from Anglo-Saxon. A minor subject can be taken as one-third of the degree; subjects offered include English, Politics, Law and Languages. There are also courses in History and History of Art, Landscape Architecture and the History of Medicine. (High research rating)

East London The History course covers Britain and cultural imperialism and the development of British society from the 18th century.

Edge Hill History is offered as a single, major/minor or joint honours course with 11 other subjects. In the single honours course specialisation is possible in British political, social and economic history or in European or American history.

Edinburgh* History is a two-part course with the division coming at the end of the second year. In the first year, students take a course in modern British and European history, plus two other courses from history or social science subjects. Specialised history courses are chosen by the student in the third and fourth years. A range of History degree courses is offered, including Ancient, Architectural, Scottish, Medieval, European and Economic and Social History. (High research rating)

Essex This programme offers a comparative approach to History with an emphasis on the Modern period. Courses are also offered in Modern, Contemporary and Social History and there are joint courses with Politics, Criminology, Languages, Law and Geography.

Exeter* Single and a wide range of joint honours courses are offered including Cornish Studies and Contemporary Celtic Studies. There is also an interdiciplinary course in Historical, Political and Sociological Studies. Ancient History can also be taken with Archaeology. (High research rating)

Glamorgan The History course covers social, economic, political and cultural history covering British, Welsh, European and American history. There is also a course in Modern and Contemporary Wales.

Glasgow* The History course covers Medieval, Modern and Scottish History. Economic and Social History is also offered. There is also a degree course in a range of subjects which can be studied with Economic and Social History. Courses are also offered in Celtic and Celtic Civilisation. There is also a course in Scottish History. See also **Archaeology** and **History of Art and Design**.

Gloucestershire History is offered with a wide range of subjects including Creative Writing, Education Studies and Psychology.

Glyndŵr History degrees can be combined with English. Study themes cover Medieval Renaissance and Modern History.

Greenwich Early modern and modern British and European history are the main features of the BA History course. History can be combined with English, Politics or a foreign language or as part of the combined honours programme. These studies in Year 3 include magic and witchcraft.

Hertfordshire History is offered as a single honours subject and also with one of several subjects including Journalism, Publishing, Film, English, English Language and Communication, Literature and Languages.

Huddersfield The modular course in History covers Medieval, Modern, British, European and World history. History can also be combined with English, Journalism, Politics and Heritage, Media and Sociology.

Hull* The first year of the History degree has seven modules covering a range of periods and options in social, maritime and art history. A special subject is chosen in Year 3. There is also a course in 20th-century History and 18 joint courses. (High research rating). The department also incorporates Archaeology and the History of Art, providing opportunities to specialise.

Keele* History must be taken with a second subject (over 25 options). There are compulsory courses in Medieval Europe, Early Modern Europe and Modern Europe. Anglo-Saxon is offered as a subsidiary course. A large number of subjects are offered in combination with History and International History. (High research rating)

Kent* Courses include British History, European History (with one year in France or Germany) and History joint degrees including Drama, Film, Archaeology or Politics. There is also a course in the History and Philosophy of Art with a year abroad.

Kingston The History course has a focus on 19th and 20th century British, European and American history. Opportunities are provided to study an additional language and to study in Europe and America. History can also be studied with another subject, ranging from languages, History and Ideas, Journalism and Creative Writing to Criminology.

Lancaster* The History course offers a very wide selection of topics – medieval and modern history, British, European, American and Russian history. A Social History degree combining History and Sociology is also available. Some exchanges with the USA and with European universities are possible. Courses in Modern European History (subject to validation) and Medieval and Renaissance Studies are also offered. There are also 12 combined courses with History. Scholarships available. (High research rating)

Leeds* The size and structure of the School enables it to offer a very wide range of History options over the whole of European, British and world history, from ancient to contemporary. The International History and Politics course has no precise parallel in any British university at the moment; its purpose is to set the international events of the recent past firmly into their historical context. Taking the first-, second- and third-year courses together, all students will have studied international history from 1494 to the present day. Joint courses include Economic and Social History. (High research rating)

Leeds Metropolitan History is offered as a single honours degree or with Politics.

Leeds Trinity (UC) The course covers the Romans to the present day and British and World History.

Leicester* Two supplementary modules are studied from nine options in the first year of the History course, along with three history courses taken for two years in medieval, early modern and modern history. In the second and third years subjects are chosen from British, European (a year in Europe is an option) and non-European history. Other degree courses cover Contemporary History and combinations with Politics, English, Ancient History, Archaeology and International Relations. There is also a degree in Ancient History in which some scholarships are offered. See also **Archaeology**. (High research rating)

Lincoln In addition to a single honours History course covering historical skills, society and popular culture, there are joint courses with Politics, Journalism, Criminology, English, American Studies, Drama and Media Studies.

Liverpool* A broad-based History course enables students to develop their interests within a wide range of periods and geographical areas. These cover medieval history, modern history and 20th century Britain in Year 1 plus another subject. Students select options in Year 2 and follow a comparative course in Year 3. Ancient History is also offered with Archaeology, and there are also courses in Irish Studies and History, and Modern History and Politics and History with Languages. (High research rating)

Liverpool Hope The History degree is offered as a single or combined honours course. Popular combinations with the latter include Politics, Irish Studies, Theology and Religious Studies.

Liverpool John Moores History is offered as a single honours degree or in conjunction with other subjects including Human Geography, English, American Studies, Politics and Sociology. A study is made of British, European and non-European history (1700–present day). See also **Social Science/Studies**.

London (Goldsmiths)* History students take a compulsory course in concepts and methods, with a choice of three other foundation courses. In the second year they choose a selection of courses from a related discipline, and in the final year concentrate on a special subject. Other degree courses include History and History of Art, History of Ideas, Anthropology, Sociology or Politics.

London (King's)* History students can develop their interests in ancient, medieval or modern history in this course by way of a very large range of modules. Combined Studies courses in War Studies are offered with 12 subject choices. (High research rating)

London (LSE)* The School offers a range of historical studies including degrees in History, Economic History, Government and History, and International Relations and History. (High research rating)

London (QM)* The History course is aimed at those students who do not wish to specialise in any one period. The programme covers British, European and American history with options in other periods. Specialised subject areas are covered in other degrees. (High research rating)

London (RH)* In addition to the single honours course in History, courses are offered in Ancient and in Modern History and Politics, with an option to study in Europe. (High research rating)

London (SOAS)* Seven regional and thematic pathways are offered in the History course covering Africa, the Near and the Middle East, the Indian sub-continent, South East Asia, China and Japan and the modern Third World. Over 20 joint courses in Far Eastern languages are also offered. (High research rating)

London (UCL)* Courses include modules covering Ancient History, Medieval or Early Modern History and Modern History. A year abroad in North or Latin America can be taken and also history with a European language. There is also a degree course in Jewish Studies. (High research rating)

London Metropolitan History can be taken as a single or joint degree and covers British and European History.

Manchester* A broad History course includes options covering all the major historical periods. Other courses offered include Medieval Studies, Economic History and Economics, Modern History and History and Sociology of Politics. There are also opportunities to spend part of the degree studying abroad. (High research rating)

Manchester Metropolitan History courses focus on Modern and Medieval History.

Newcastle* In the first year of the History course a choice is made from one of two medieval European courses, one of several modern and contemporary history courses, two of four courses concerning historical method, and one course from a range of options. In the second and third years, studies can cover the history of Britain, Europe, and North America. There is also a course in Politics and History. History and Ancient History can also be taken as part of the Combined Studies Programme. (High research rating)

Newman (UC) History is offered as a single, joint or minor course with another subject. There is also a course in local History and Heritage.

Newport The History degree covers British, European and Global history sourcing information from film and media, literature and archaeology.

Northampton The university offers a single honours courses and a wide range of joint courses with History in addition to a degree in Heritage Management.

Northumbria The History programme offers a breadth of historical knowledge covering Britain, Europe and world history from the medieval period to the present day. History is also offered with Politics. A course in British and American Cultures is also available in which history topics are included.

Nottingham* The History course covers the period from AD500 to the present day and is offered as a single honours subject and also in a range of joint courses including Art History, Politics, Contemporary

Chinese Studies. There are also courses in Ancient History and there is also a unique course in Viking Studies covering language, history, literature and archaeology. (High research rating)

Nottingham Trent In the History course, foundation modules are taken in Medieval and Modern History leading to a wide range of units covering British, European and American history. History is also offered as a joint course with 14 other subjects.

Oxford* The Modern History course covers the history of the British Isles and European history. In the first year, students take papers in a period of British history, but thereafter there is considerable choice at all stages. Other degree courses offered include Ancient and Modern History, and joint courses with Economics, English, Politics, Modern Languages and the History of Art. (High research rating)

Oxford Brookes* The first year of the History course covers 1750–1850, followed in Years 2 and 3 with modules on British and European history from 1900. History can also be studied with other subjects in the modular degree scheme including Computing, Publishing, Theology and Leisure and Tourism. There is also a course in the History of Medicine.

Plymouth The History degree has an emphasis on British, American, European, Irish and imperial history from 1650 to the present day. There is also a wide range of History joint courses which include Popular Culture, English, Media Arts and Archaeology.

Portsmouth History is offered as a single honours course or can be studied in joint courses with Politics and English.

Queen's Belfast* Ancient History deals with Greek and Roman civilisation and its influence on the history and culture of the whole Mediterranean, the Near East and Europe. The Modern History course covers all periods except the ancient world. Although it covers Great Britain and Ireland, there are also modules on North America, China and Africa. Courses are also offered in Byzantine Studies (AD300–1500) and the History of Science. (High research rating)

Reading* In the first year, two themes are introduced in approaches and landmarks in history. This provides a foundation for the more specialised topics chosen in the third year, covering British and European history. Twenty joint courses are also offered.

Roehampton History can be taken as a single honours subject or in joint courses with subjects including Art History, Classical Civilisation, English and Philosophy.

St Andrews* An integrated single honours course in History is available for students who wish to take a degree course covering various types of historical subject matter. Specialist modules are taken from Ancient History, History or Scottish History. Courses are also offered in Ancient, Medieval, Modern and Scottish History. (High research rating)

St Mary's (UC) History can be studied as a single or joint honours courses with pathways in general History or in Modern, Early-Modern or Military History. There is also a course in Irish studies.

Salford A degree in Contemporary Military and International History is worth considering, which covers the period from World War I to the present day. There is also a programme leading to a degree in Contemporary History and Politics.

Sheffield* At Level 1 of the History course a study is made covering the period from the fall of Rome to the present day with options in European or American History. Options across these fields continue in Level 2 and special studies on selected themes follow in Level 3. Other courses include Archaeology and History, and International History and International Politics. (High research rating)

Sheffield Hallam The History course concentrates on the 19th and 20th centuries in Britain. History can also be studied with Criminology or English or Film.

Southampton* A general introduction in the first year of the History course covers both medieval and modern periods. Units available in the second year are: European and British history, economic, social, political, religious, intellectual and art history, and American civilisation. The third year is dominated by the study of a special subject. There are also eight joint courses with History. Scholarships available. (High research rating)

Staffordshire Courses in Modern and International History both as single or joint honours courses can be taken.

Stirling The History course covers British and European history from the 18th century and Scottish history from 1513. Specialist options are available as are opportunities to study in the US.

Strathclyde History is a principal subject in the Faculty of Arts and Social Sciences. From Year 2, students choose from a very wide range of history subjects and periods. (High research rating)

Sunderland History is offered as a joint honours course with subjects such as Comparative Literature, History of Art and Design, Media Studies, Photography and Psychology.

Sussex* The History degree is strong in early modern intellectual and contemporary history and enables students to explore a variety of subject areas alongside other subjects related to history. Degree courses are also offered in Contemporary and in Intellectual and Cultural History, and several joint courses are also available. (High research rating)

Swansea Specialist themes commence in Year 2 covering British, European and American history. In addition to single honours History, degrees are offered in Ancient and Medieval History, European History with a European language (English, Welsh, French, German or Dutch). Scholarships available.

Teesside The History course covers British, European and American history with a very wide range of optional modules. Degree courses are also offered in History with English, Media Studies or Politics. There are also courses in contemporary European History and Social and Cultural History.

Trinity St David (Lampeter) One other subject is taken with History in the first year. The second and third years cover British, European and American history. Courses are also offered in Ancient History, (scholarships offered), Ancient History and Archaeology, Ancient and Medieval History, Medieval Studies and Modern Historical Studies covering the Victorians, 20th-century Britain and the American Frontier.

Ulster History and Irish History may be taken as a single honours course or in combination with other subjects in the Humanities programme.

Warwick* Particular strengths include Renaissance, early modern British and European history. The history of medicine courses offered include History and Culture, Modern History, and Renaissance and Modern History.

Westminster History is taken as a course within Social Sciences focusing on economic, social and political history.

Winchester Courses are offered in History, and History and the Medieval or Modern World and a number of joint courses are on offer. Heritage Management is also available and places great emphasis on students' skills development and employability.

Wolverhampton History is a modular course covering 20th-century Europe, early modern England, women's history, British social history from 1530, the Americas post-1860 and the West Midlands from 1600. There are also degrees in War Studies and Applied Historical Studies.

Worcester The History degree offers a study of significant political and cultural movements of the recent past covering British, European and world history. Over 20 joint courses can be taken.

York* The courses in History offer study in depth and a wide range of individual choice throughout. Students study many types of history from a wide geographical and chronological range. Teaching is mainly by individual tutorial and small group seminar. Each student also undertakes an independent research project as well as a paper in historical methodology. History can be combined with English, Politics, Education, History of Art, Philosophy and French. (High research rating)

York St John Nine joint courses are offered.

OTHER INSTITUTIONS OFFERING HISTORY COURSES
Blackpool and Fylde (Coll), Bradford (Coll), Burton (Coll), East Lancashire (Coll), Havering (Coll), North Lindsey (Coll), Oxford Ruskin (Coll), Peterborough (Reg Coll), Richmond (American Univ), Suffolk (Univ Campus), Truro (Coll), UHI Millennium Inst, West Anglia (Coll) Wigan and Leigh (Coll).

ALTERNATIVE COURSES
Archaeology, Economic and Social History, International Relations, Politics and Public Administration.

HISTORY OF ART AND DESIGN

(* indicates universities with the highest entry requirements)

SUBJECT REQUIREMENTS/PREFERENCES
GCE A-level: No specific subjects required.

SUBJECT INFORMATION
Art History covers a very wide range of topics that involve a study of classical Greek and Roman art and architecture through to modern 20th century art and design. The main focus is usually on painting and sculpture with a specialised study of the European schools of painting. Some courses, however, diversify into textiles, furniture, ceramic design, photography and film.

Aberdeen The History of Art course provides a broad introduction to the history of painting, sculpture, architecture and the decorative arts from classical times to the modern period. There is a focus on the western European tradition and options in Latin American art.

Aberystwyth The university offers courses in Art History. Options range from the Renaissance to the present day including the history of graphic design and photography and art in Wales. There is also an unusual degree scheme in Museum and Gallery Studies that includes new technologies and changes in display and the management of collections.

Anglia Ruskin Year 1 of the Art History modules cover classical, Byzantine, Renaissance and modern topics. A later emphasis is on early medieval and European art. A period of study abroad is possible.

Birmingham* History of Art is offered as a single honours or a joint major/minor programme and covers Western art from the Renaissance to the present day. Part of the Easter vacation in Year 2 is spent abroad.

Brighton The History of Design, Culture and Society course specialises in the manufacturing and design aspects of modern industrial society and its beginnings from the 17th century. The History of Decorative Arts and Crafts course is a study of artefacts from 1880 to the present day in Britain, touching on 'exotic' and non-European art and design. The Visual Culture course combines studies in art and history with cultural studies and the history of visual communication including photography, advertising and fashion.

Bristol* The History of Art course provides a broad study of European and British art and architecture from the medieval period to recent 20th-century movements. There are opportunities to study abroad in Year 2 in the USA and joint degrees with languages (French, German, Italian, Russian, Portuguese and Spanish) are also offered.

Cambridge* History of Art is a flexible course covering areas from classical antiquity to modern art but aiming to foster a deep understanding of Western European art and architecture. There is a compulsory paper on the Display of Art in Year 3. (High research rating)

See *University Degree Course Offers* (Trotman Publishing) for details of offers

Central Lancashire There are combined courses in art history and visual culture. The course includes exhibition design and curatorship.

East Anglia* History of Art can be studied as a single course or with another subject such as Literature or History or with Archaeology, Anthropology with options to study in Australia or North America. (High research rating)

Edinburgh The History of Art and Architectural History course topics include the art, sculpture and architecture of the Western world from late antiquity to the present day. In Year 3 students are placed within a gallery or similar institution or undertake a major project eg, writing exhibition reviews or cataloguing works of art, Scottish painting and American art. Other courses include Fine Art and Architectural History. (High research rating)

Essex This non-practical History of Art course includes the European Enlightenment and the History of Architecture 1. This is followed by a study of Tuscan art from 1330 to 1500, 19th century or pre-Columbian art and architecture. Topics also include Russian art, industrial design and the fine arts in England. There are also degrees in the History and American Studies, and courses with Literature, Film and Modern Languages. (High research rating)

Glasgow First-year studies in the History of Art cover the Renaissance and the 19th-century periods. These are followed by short courses concentrating on aspects of modern art, medieval art and architecture and Scottish art. The third and fourth years are devoted to special studies on specific artists. Travel grants available.

Glyndŵr Artistic and Visual Art practice is a modular course on a 50/50 ratio between art theory and practice art modules.

Greenwich A course is offered in Arts, Gallery and Heritage Management, largely focusing on business activities.

Hull History of Art is offered as a minor subject or as a joint course with Drama, English, History and Theology.

Kent* Part I of the History and visual culture course covers history, media and genres, followed in Part II by historical studies and special options. There is also a multidisciplinary course in the Visual and Performed Arts. (High research rating)

Kingston The History of Art, Design and Film course involves four main study areas – art, architecture, design and film. There is also a course in Visual Culture focusing on the impact of art on contemporary society.

Lancaster* History of Art is offered with Art. There is also a single or joint degree in Museum and Gallery Studies focusing on the presentation of artefacts and works of art.

Leeds* There are courses in the History of Art and Museum Studies, the latter covering country house and museum collections and a study of the decorative arts. (High research rating)

Leicester* History of Art is offered as a three-year course or over four years including a year in Europe. Practical art classes are available. Combined degrees can include History, Archaeology and languages. Scholarships available.

Lincoln The course in Conservation and Restoration covers drawings, photography and the decorative arts.

Liverpool John Moores The History of Art and Museum Studies course involves collaboration with the Tate Liverpool and focuses on a practical as well as theoretical framework involving the organising and designing of exhibitions.

London (Courtauld)* This specialist degree in the History of Art covers classical, Byzantine, medieval, Renaissance, early modern and contemporary art. (High research rating)

See *University Degree Course Offers* (Trotman Publishing) for details of offers

London (Goldsmiths)* The History of Art course covers techniques and technologies in Year 1 followed by a choice of different approaches in Years 2 and 3.

London (SOAS)* History of Art is offered as a single honours subject and also with Archaeology or with an emphasis on Asia, Africa and Europe. Joint courses with several other subjects can be selected. (High research rating)

London (UCL)* History of Art single honours students take two course units in either anthropology, history or philosophy to support their studies. The course focuses on Western art with specialised studies following in Years 2 and 3. Joint courses are offered with Dutch, French, German, Italian, Philosophy, or Spanish. There is also a course in History of Art and Materials Studies involving conservation. (High research rating)

London Metropolitan Courses are offered in Art and Design History with specialisms in Sociology, Textiles, Communications, Design, Interior Design or Marketing. The Conservation and Restoration course has work placements in leading galleries and museums.

Manchester* History of Art is offered as a single subject or with another subject including a modern language and Archaeology. There is also a course in Visual Cultures exploring all aspects of the visual media. Scholarships available. (High research rating)

Manchester Metropolitan History of Art and Design is a modular degree programme looking at art, architecture and sculpture, three dimensional design and communication arts (graphics, photography and film).

Middlesex History of Art and Architecture is offered as a joint honours course with subjects such as Media and Cultural Studies, Film Studies and European Languages.

Newcastle* History of Art is offered as part of the Combined Studies in Art degree (previous experience of the subject preferred).

Northampton The History of Art can be taken as a joint course with over 20 other subjects.

Northumbria* The History of Modern Art, Design and Film course provides a broad introduction and is followed by a choice of main themes covering such topics as architecture, conservation, film or arts management. The course in Visual Culture focuses on 20th-century visual culture including film and TV, photography, architecture, design, fashion, advertising and fine art.

Nottingham The Art History degree focuses on painting, sculpture and graphic arts, photography and architecture in western Europe from classical times to contemporary art. Joint courses are offered with Classical Civilisation, English and German.

Oxford* In Year 1, the History of Art course covers visual culture, Renaissance art to postmodernism, classical art and an extended essay on a building, object or image in Oxford. In Years 2 and 3, seven elements are taken involving the whole field of Western art from classical times to the present day.

Oxford Brookes* History of Art (focusing on Western Art – 19th–20th century) is offered as a single or joint honours course. (High research rating)

Plymouth Art History is offered as part of the Art and Design programme with Fine Art and also as a single honours course.

Reading* The course in History of Art and Architecture covers Western art and architecture with options to specialise in the history of painting, sculpture or architecture. Joint courses are also offered. (High research rating)

Roehampton Art History is offered as a single or combined honours course with subjects such as Classical Civilisation, History, Journalism and News Media, Photography.

Sheffield Hallam The course in Art and Visual Culture involves history, theory and management. The programme covers a study of fine art, photography, film and TV, architecture and arts organisations.

Southampton Solent There is a unique course in Fine Arts Valuation.

See *University Degree Course Offers* (Trotman Publishing) for details of offers

St Andrews* First-level courses in Art History cover the Renaissance and art in Britain from the early Middle Ages to the 19th century. This is followed by a study of European art from 1800 and the Modern Movement. Students then select specialist studies from a range of 25 modules. Over 20 joint courses are offered. (High research rating)

Sunderland History of Art and Design is offered as a three-year full-time joint honours course with over 30 subjects.

Sussex* Art History focuses on Western art from Byzantium to the Renaissance to the present day, with attention to the arts of China and India. A study of special periods takes place in Year 2 and options in several specialisms are available in Year 3 including museum studies. Joint courses are offered with Modern Languages, Cultural Studies, Film Studies, History, and Archaeology. (High research rating)

Swansea Metropolitan Joint courses in Art History are offered with English, Psychology and Visual Arts.

Warwick* History of Art is a wide-ranging course covering the history of architecture from Gothic to the present day and the major periods of the history of art. A wide choice of options are offered throughout the course. (High research rating)

York* In Year 1 History of Art students choose papers from the history of art, English and history. The course is modular with topics covering early Christian and Byzantine art, medieval art, Italian art, the English country house and modernism. (High research rating)

ALTERNATIVE COURSES
All practical Art and Design courses, Archaeology, Architecture, Classical Civilisation, Communication Studies, Film Studies, Landscape Architecture.

HOSPITALITY MANAGEMENT

(including **Hotel and Catering Management, Tourism and Events Management**)
(see also **Leisure, Recreation Management and Tourism**)
(* indicates universities with the highest entry requirements)

SUBJECT REQUIREMENTS/PREFERENCES
GCSE: English and Mathematics usually required plus a foreign language for International Hospitality Management courses.

SUBJECT INFORMATION
All courses provide a comprehensive preparation for entry into hotel, catering, tourism and leisure industries.

Anglia Ruskin* A three-year full-time course is offered in Residential Agency Management.

Birmingham (UC) There is a year's paid placement as part of the Hospitality and Food Management course. Courses in Culinary Arts Management and Events Management are also offered.

Bournemouth* There are courses in Hospitality Management and Hospitality Business Development with 40-week placements in the industry in Year 3 in the UK and overseas.

Brighton* The International Hospitality Management degree has an optional placement in Year 3 and provides students with the opportunity to study languages. There is also a degree in Marketing, Food and Drink.

Buckingham The International Hotel Management and Business Studies course starts in January and lasts two years. All students take a hotel operations management course in a Swiss hotel school.

Cardiff (UWIC) There are courses in Hospitality, Events and Tourism Managements.

Central Lancashire Hospitality and International Hospitality Management are four-year sandwich courses taught jointly with Blackpool and the Fylde College, providing management education for those wishing to enter the hotel and leisure industries. The third year is spent on sandwich placement in the UK or worldwide overseas. There are also courses in Event Management and Sports Event Management both with options for a one year placement in the industry.

Canterbury Christ Church A course in Events Management covers entertainment and the arts, cinema, tourism and leisure marketing, heritage and festivals.

Chester The Events Management course covers groups playing in local venues to Chester Races. Field units further afield and a six week work placement are part of the course.

Derby Two courses are offered in Events Management one of which is combined with tourism. Courses are also offered in Culinary Arts, Hospitality Management (joint honours) and International Spa Management.

Glamorgan The course in Event Management covers the social and cultural aspects of tourism and the leisure industry as well as practical work experience. There are separate courses in tourism.

Glasgow Caledonian The Hospitality Management course covers food, sales, marketing, restaurant management, languages, tourism and travel.

Gloucestershire Hospitality Management is offered with a range of subjects in the modular degree scheme including Events Management and Tourism Management. There is a compulsory placement for honours Event Management students.

Hertfordshire A degree is offered in Event Management with an optional year in work placement.

Huddersfield The Hospitality Business course leads to either Hospitality Management with Tourism and Leisure, or to International Hotel Management. In both cases Year 3 is spent on work placement in the UK or overseas. There is also an Events Management sandwich course.

Leeds Metropolitan The three-year full-time or four-year sandwich course in Hospitality Business Management covers all aspects of the industry – food and accommodation studies, tourism, European business, management and manpower studies, finance, law and business policy. A non-language route is available. Other relevant courses include Events Management and Sport Event Management and Conference and Exhibitions Management.

London Metropolitan* There is an International Hospitality Management course including a foreign language, and a combined honours course offered with Business. Events Management and International Tourism Management are also offered.

Manchester Metropolitan Hospitality Management covers operations management (catering and accommodation) and includes management and business, which are the core subjects in Years 1, 2 and 4. Industrial placement occupies the third year. There is also a course in International Hospitality Management with language options (French, German and Spanish) and other courses in Licensed Retail Management, Culinary Arts and Events Management.

Middlesex Hospitality Management is offered as a three-year full-time HND top-up course.

Napier Hospitality Management is a modular course that includes options and electives. A foreign language is included. Particular emphasis is given to personal development and transferable skills. There is a strong information technology resource base. There are also courses in Festival and Event Management with Languages, Tourism, Hospitality and Human Resources Management.

Oxford Brookes* There is a four-year single honours course in International Hospitality Management with industrial placements abroad.

Plymouth Hospitality Management is a modular programme that includes hospitality, the consumer, food and beverage services, front office and accommodation services. There is also a four-year sandwich course in International Hospitality Management with French, German, economics and accounting modules. Optional industrial placements available following Year 2. There are also courses in Cruise Management, Events Management and Tourism and Hospitality Management.

Portsmouth* Hospitality Management is either a three-year full-time or a four-year sandwich course with industrial experience taking place in Year 3. The course covers catering and accommodation studies, behavioural science, personnel work, law, marketing and finance. Similar courses emphasise tourism or marketing. The degree can also be combined with Tourism.

Queen Margaret Courses are offered in Hospitality and Tourism Management, International Hospitality Management and Events Management. A £1000 busary is offered to high scoring students at the end of Year 1.

Robert Gordon International Hospitality Management is offered as a three-year or four-year full-time course. There is also a course in Events Management.

Salford Hospitality Management is a modular course sharing units with, for example, Tourism and Leisure Management degree courses. The course includes 12-week placements with some options to work abroad.

Sheffield Hallam Hospitality Business Management with Conference and Events or the International Option share a common first year with the BSc course in Hospitality Business Management and with the BSc course in Hospitality Business Management with Culinary Arts. The courses are accredited by the Hotel and Catering International Management Association.

Strathclyde Hotel and Hospitality Management courses cover hotel operations with options in tourism, food and beverage, and leisure management and planning. In the first and second years, one class is normally chosen from business-related subjects such as marketing, business law, computing and accounting and finance.

Surrey* Courses with a worldwide reputation are offered in International Hospitality Management (four years) and International Hospitality and Tourism Management with placements in the UK and abroad.

Ulster International Hospitality Management and Tourism Management are four-year sandwich courses that covers food and accommodation studies, tourism, accounts and marketing. A foreign language is taken in Year 1 and becomes optional in Years 2 and 3. There are also four-year sandwich degrees in International Hospitality Studies with languages.

West London The Hospitality Management course covers the business environment, operations (food/beverage/wines/spirits/room division) and includes information technology and accounting. There are also courses in Culinary Arts Management, Hospitality Management and Food Studies, International Hotel Management and Restaurant Management. Scholarships available.

Winchester Event Management is studied in the context of leisure, business and tourism.

Wolverhampton Courses are offered in Hospitality and International Management, Entertainment Industries Management, and Event and Venue Management.

See *University Degree Course Offers* (Trotman Publishing) for details of offers

OTHER INSTITUTIONS OFFERING HOSPITALITY COURSES

Bedford (Coll), Blackpool and Fylde (Coll), Bradford (Coll), Bristol City (Coll), Chichester (Coll), Colchester (Inst), Cornwall (Coll), Doncaser (Coll), Ealing (Coll), East Lancashire (Coll), European (BusSch), Grimsby (IFHE), Guildford (CFHE), Highbury (Coll), Leicester (Coll), Llandrillo (Coll), Liverpool (CmC), Loughborough (Coll), Menai (Coll), Neath Port Talbot (Coll), Newcastle (Coll), North East Worcestershire (Coll), North Lindsey (Coll), Norwich City (Coll), Nottingham New (Coll), South Devon (Coll), Stratford upon Avon (Coll), Suffolk (Univ Campus), Tameside (Coll), UHI Millennium Inst, Walsall (Coll), Warrington (Coll), Warwickshire (Coll), Westminster Kingsway (Coll), Wigan and Leigh (Coll), Worcestershire (Coll), York (Coll).

ALTERNATIVE COURSES

Consumer Sciences, Consumer Studies, Dietetics, Events Management, Food Science.

INFORMATION MANAGEMENT AND LIBRARY STUDIES

(* indicates universities with the highest entry requirements)

SUBJECT REQUIREMENTS/PREFERENCES

GCE A-level: Subject requirements may apply to joint courses. **GCSE:** English, Mathematics and occasionally a foreign language.

SUBJECT INFORMATION

This subject area involves the study of information systems. These cover retrieval, indexing, computer and media technology, classification and cataloguing.

Abertay Dundee Information Systems is offered as a four-year honours degree and shares a common first year with Business Computing and Information Technology. Main areas of study include databases, networks, the internet, knowledge management and business engineering.

Aberystwyth This leading department offers courses in Information and Library Studies by way of 15 specialist joint subjects. There is also a unique course in Historical and Archival Studies in addition to courses in Museum and Gallery Studies.

Bradford Information and Communication Technology can be taken with a range of subjects including business, marketing, media and law.

Brighton Core subjects in the Library Studies and Information course focus on the library and community, knowledge and records, and library management; heavy use is made of computing and media technologies. There is also a choice of specialist studies from media resources, bibliographical studies and computer studies, electronic publishing, newspaper publishing, school libraries and picture archives. Short practical placements in this three-year course take place each year. An Information Management course is offered. It gives a business context for the organisation, retrieval and management of information.

Central Lancashire There is a course in Museums and Heritage.

Chester The Information Systems Management course is offered by the Department of Computer Science.

De Montfort The BSc in Information Systems Management equips students to observe, manage, process, analyse, present and evaluate information. It focuses on databases, information systems and quantitative modelling.

Gloucestershire Optional placements are offered on the Information Technology course.

Huddersfield A four year sandwich course in ICT is offered, also with Criminology.

Kingston Museum and Gallery Studies is offered as a single honours course.

Liverpool Hope The Management of Information course is a single honours programme.

London (UCL)* Some Information Management course subjects should not be confused with library studies. This Information Management has core courses in computer science, management and information. Options include digital business, e-commerce law for managers, and languages.

Loughborough* The Information Management course is offered with computing or Business Studies and is accredited by the Chartered Institute of Library and Information Professionals. It covers informatics, statistics, accounting, financial management, databases, systems modelling, knowledge management, electronic media and strategic management. There is an optional placement in Year 3. Scholarships available. (High research rating)

Manchester Metropolitan Information and Communications is a modular course, which is recognised by the Library Association, and offers the basic core subjects covering management, information systems, retrieval and information technology. Special studies in Year 3 provide flexibility to cover areas of special interest to students. These include working in academic, business and commercial communities. Students are required to undertake two periods of placement, each of five weeks' duration. Courses in Information and Communications, and Information Management are also offered.

Napier Information Management is offered with Business Studies in three-year and four-year full-time or four-year and five-year sandwich courses.

Newman (UC) Information Technology can be taken as a single, joint or minor course with another subject.

Northumbria Several courses in Information Technologies are offered as three-year full-time or four year sandwich programmes. There are also courses in Communication and Public Relations and in Publishing. Scholarships available.

Sheffield* Information Management is offered as a single subject course or with Accounting and Financial Management or Business Management. (High research rating)

Stirling A full-time and part-time degree is offered in Information Systems.

West Scotland Information Management is offered as a three-year or four-year full-time course or four-year or five-year sandwich degree.

Wolverhampton Business Information Management is a modular course with a bias towards business and management and human factors over purely technical design. Information Systems and Technology are also offered.

OTHER INSTITUTIONS OFFERING INFORMATION COURSES
Blackpool and Fylde (Coll), Bradford (Coll), Bristol City (Coll), Carmarthenshire (Coll), Cornwall (Coll), Craven (Coll), Croydon (Coll), East Lancashire (Coll), Havering (Coll), Hopwood Hall (Coll), Lincoln (Coll), Llandrillo (Coll), Neath Port Talbot (Coll), NESCOT, Newcastle (Coll), Northbrook (Coll), Nottingham New (Coll), Pembrokeshire (Coll), Peterborough (Reg Coll), Richmond (American Univ), Shrewsbury (CAT), South Essex (Coll), Staffordshire (Reg Fed), Swindon (Coll), Truro (Coll), UHI Millennium Inst, Warrington (Coll), Warwickshire (Coll), West Anglia (Coll), Wirral Metropolian (Coll).

ALTERNATIVE COURSES
Communication Studies, Cultural Studies, Information Science, Information Systems, Publishing and Technical Communication.

LANGUAGES

(* indicates universities with the highest entry requirements)

SUBJECT REQUIREMENTS/PREFERENCES

GCE A-level: French and German courses: the chosen language is almost always required at A-level (or equivalent). Spanish courses: most universities require the language at A-level (or equivalent) although some offer Spanish courses *ab initio*.

Aberdeen In addition to the European Studies course, degrees are offered in French, German, and Hispanic and Latin American Studies. Gaelic is taken in the Celtic Studies programme and courses are also available in Latin. There are also courses in Language and Linguistics, European Languages and Twentieth Century Culture, and the Languages and Literature of Scotland. (High research rating – Fr/Span)

Aberystwyth Single and joint honours courses are offered in French, German, Italian and Spanish. There is also a European language degree scheme that combines the study of any three languages (two at major level, one at minor level) from French, German, Italian or Spanish. A degree scheme combining Modern Languages with Business Studies has also been introduced. Courses are also offered in Celtic Studies, Irish and Welsh. (High research rating – Span)

Anglia Ruskin French, German and Spanish are offered. Courses are offered in two languages or, alternatively, students may study one language or with a second subject.

Aston* French and German can be studied as honours degrees or half programmes with Spanish. Courses are also offered in European Studies, Translation Studies, International Business and International Relations.

Bangor The School of Modern Languages offers honours degrees in French, German, Spanish, Italian and Welsh. There are one, two and three language courses available and several joint courses with non-language subjects. Welsh language courses are also available, including one with Media Studies and Creative Writing.

Bath* The course in Modern Languages and European Studies focuses on high-quality spoken and written language learning combined with units devoted to cultural studies and the politics and society of individual countries in Europe as a whole. Equal weighting is given to two languages from French, German, Italian, Russian and Spanish, the last four also being offered *ab initio*. A year abroad is compulsory. There is also a course in European Language and Politics. Scholarships available.

Birmingham* French, German, Italian, Russian, Spanish and Portuguese are offered and, in the Hispanic Studies course, Galician and Catalan. There are also degrees with Modern Languages and European Studies. (High research rating – Fr/Ger/Span)

Bradford A non-degree Languages for All programme is offered to all students wishing to study French, German, Spanish, English (EFL) or Arabic.

Brighton Modern language degrees are available in French, German, Italian and Spanish.

Bristol* Single and joint courses can be followed in Czech, French, German, Italian, Portuguese, Spanish or Russian. The Modern Languages programme allows for a study of two of these languages with the possibility of a third (Catalan in Year 1). (High research rating – Fr/Span)

Bristol UWE French, Chinese and Spanish can be studied in joint honours courses. French and Spanish are also offered with Law.

Brunel French and German are offered with Engineering, Law, and Mathematics. The Language Centre also provides courses in French, German, Italian and Spanish to prepare students for living and studying abroad by way of option modules as part of their degree course.

See *University Degree Course Offers* (Trotman Publishing) for details of offers

Buckingham Courses are offered in French and Spanish.

Bucks New French, Italian and Spanish can be taken with Business Management, Human Resources Management, Marketing and International Management.

Cambridge* Classical, Modern and Medieval and Oriental Language courses are offered. Greek and Latin are taken as part of the Classics course while the Modern and Medieval Languages Tripos offers a high level of linguistic training in two languages. The languages available are Dutch, French, German (including a course for beginners), Modern Greek, Italian, Portuguese, Russian and Spanish. Classical Latin or Classical Greek may be combined with any one of these languages. Languages from the Faculty of Asian and Middle Eastern Studies are available in Arabic, Chinese, Hebrew, Japanese and Persian. Also, there is the unique course in Anglo-Saxon, Norse and Celtic covering history, languages and literature. (High research rating – Fr/Ger/Ital/Span)

Canterbury Christ Church French can be taken as a joint or combined subject.

Cardiff* French, German, Italian, Japanese, Spanish and Welsh are offered as single or joint honours courses. Hispanic Studies and Portuguese can be taken and there are options in Ancient Greek and Classical Hebrew. There is also a flourishing school of Welsh. Modern languages are also offered with Accounting, Banking, Business Administration, Business Economics, Economics, Japanese and Law. (High research rating – Fr/Ger/Ital/Span)

Central Lancashire Degree courses are offered in Chinese, French, German, Japanese and Spanish. In addition, some languages can be studied by way of Languages with Tourism or International Business and Law (French or German) and also on the Modern Languages degree in which two languages are chosen. There are also courses in Asia–Pacific Studies and Islamic studies.

Chester Courses are offered in French, German and Spanish which include an introduction to European studies and cinema. Placements abroad take place between Years 2 and 3. It is also possible to study two of these languages.

Coventry Modern Language programmes offer French and Spanish (not *ab initio*). There are optional placements of one year.

De Montfort French, German and Spanish joint or combined honours courses are available and these languages are available in the European Studies degree or in the Law degree.

Derby The Modern Languages degree allows for a study of two out of three languages from French, German or Spanish.

Dundee French, German or Spanish will be taken in Year 1 with two other subjects in Years 1 and 2. Specialised language studies follow in Years 3 and 4.

Durham* The modern languages offered are French, German, Russian and Spanish (all post A-level), with beginners' courses in Arabic, Italian, Russian and Spanish, and options in Croatian and Serbian for Russian students. Catalan and Persian are also available. (High research rating – Fr)

East Anglia* Four year Modern Language courses are offered in French and/or Spanish. In addition Translation and Media can be taken with Languages and there are also courses with Management Studies, Spanish with International Development and Translation and Interpreting with double honours languages.

East London French and Spanish are offered with Linguistics in the combined honours programme.

Edinburgh* Language courses are offered in Arabic, Celtic, Chinese, French, German, Greek, Italian, Japanese, Latin, Persian, Portuguese, Russian, Sanskrit Scandinavian Studies (Danish, Swedish, Norwegian) and Spanish. (High research rating – Fr/Ger). There is also a Modern Language degree (two subjects).

Essex A number of modern language courses are on offer at various levels, including French, German, Italian, Portuguese, Russian and Spanish. These courses are highly regarded by students.

Exeter* Courses are offered in French, German, Italian, Latin, Russian and Spanish. Arabic is also available. Several joint courses are available with European Language including French and Latin, and German and Drama. (High research rating – Fr/Ger/Span)

Glamorgan Welsh and Spanish can be taken as part of Combined Studies programmes.

Glasgow* Czech, French, German, Greek, Italian, Latin, Polish, Portuguese, Russian, Hispanic Studies, Spanish and Slavonic and East European Studies are offered. There are also courses in Gaelic and Celtic. (High research rating – Fr)

Greenwich French, German, Italian and Spanish are offered as part of the combined honours programme. Certificates are offered in Japanese and Chinese.

Heriot-Watt The university is one of the leading centres in the UK for the training of interpreters and translators. The courses involve intensive language training with complementary studies in administration, politics, economics, current affairs and international organisations. Joint language courses are offered in combinations with French, German and Spanish.

Hertfordshire Degrees in French, Spanish, Chinese, Italian and German are offered as part of joint or combined courses.

Hull Combined language programmes are offered with French, German, Italian and Spanish. Subject to availability, it may be possible to study Arabic, Chinese, Japanese, Dutch and Portuguese. There is also a minor course in Translation Studies. (High research rating – Fr/Span)

Keele French is offered as part of the dual honours programme with 28 subjects. (High research rating – Fr)

Kent French, German, Italian and Spanish single and joint honours courses are offered.

Kingston Languages offered cover French and Spanish in single honours courses or in joint courses with up to 20 subjects.

Lancaster* French, German, Italian and Spanish Studies courses are offered, combined with a large number of other subjects. (High research rating – Fr/Ger/Ital)

Leeds* Courses offered include Arabic, Chinese, French, German, Greek, Italian, Japanese, Latin, Portuguese, Russian, Spanish and Hispanic and Latin American Studies. (High research rating – Fr/Ital/Span)

Leeds Metropolitan Courses in French, German and Spanish can be taken. There are also several joint courses including combinations with Marketing, Public Relations, Tourism and Business.

Leicester* The School of Modern Languages offers French, German, Italian and Spanish. There are also courses in Modern Languages and with Management with a year in Europe. (High research rating – Fr/Ger)

Lincoln Applied courses are offered in any two Languages from Spanish, French or German. (See also **European Studies**)

Liverpool* The Modern European Languages course offers three languages in Year 1 from French, German, Spanish and a beginners' language from Catalan, Irish, Italian or Portuguese. There are also courses in Hispanic Studies and Latin American Studies. Scholarships available. (High research rating – Fr/Ger/Span)

Liverpool John Moores French, Spanish, Chinese and Japanese are offered as joint courses on the four year International Business degree course focusing on language skills.

London (Goldsmiths)* French, German and Spanish are offered in a range of combinations. Latin American Studies can be taken with Spanish.

London (King's)* A wide range of single and joint honours courses is offered in French, German, Hispanic Studies and Portuguese, and Brazilian Studies, Turkish and Modern Greek, as well as the classical languages of Greek and Latin. (High research rating – Fr/Ger/Span)

London (LSE)* French, German, Russian and Spanish languages are offered relating to a specific interest in one of the social sciences.

London (QM)* Language options include French, German, Hispanic Studies and Russian. These can be taken as single or joint courses and with History, Drama, Economics, Geography, European Studies or Film Studies. (High research rating – Fr/Ger/Span)

London (RH)* Languages are offered in French, German, Greek, Italian, Latin, and Spanish. There are also major/minor degrees in modern languages and another subject. (High research rating – Fr/Ital)

London (SOAS)* The School offers the widest range of African and Asian languages in the UK. These cover Amharic (Ethiopia), Hausa (Niger, Ghana, Cameroon), Somali (Horn of Africa, Djibouti, Ethiopia), Swahili (East Coast of Africa, Tanzania, Kenya), Yoruba (Nigeria), Zulu (South Africa), Chinese (Modern and Classical), Tibetan, Japanese, Korean, Ancient Near East, Arabic, Hebrew, Persian, Turkish, Georgian, Bengali (Bangladesh, West Bengal) Gujarati (North West India), Nepali (Nepal, Sikkim), Pali (Classical Middle Indo-Aryan), Panjabi (Panjab), Sanskrit (Classical Indian), Sinhalese (Sri Lanka), Tamil (South India), Urdu (Pakistan), Burmese, Indonesian, Malay, Tagalog (Philippines), Thai and Vietnamese. Linguistics is also offered as a single or two subject degree.

London (UCL)* Language courses are offered in Dutch, French, German, Greek, Hebrew, Italian, Latin, Polish, Russian, Swedish, Danish, Norwegian, Icelandic, Finnish, Yiddish, Hungarian, Romanian, Serbian, Croatian, Spanish, Ukrainian, Czech, Bulgarian and Slovak. The degree in languages and culture includes the study of a main and second languages. Linguistics is also offered. (High research rating – Fr/Ger/Ital/Span)

London Metropolitan French and French Studies are offered as joint subjects. There is also a course in Applied Translation Studies.

Loughborough* Apart from the European Studies course combining French, German and Spanish, there are several degree programmes with a substantial input of these languages. These involve Banking, Economics, International Business, Management Sciences, Politics and Retail Management.

Manchester* A single honours degree can be taken in Arabic, Chinese, French, German, Greek, Hebrew, Italian, Japanese, Latin, Russian, Persian, Portuguese, Spanish, Turkish, Hispanic Studies and Middle Eastern languages. Scholarships available. (High research rating – Fr/Ger/Span)

Manchester Metropolitan Language courses are offered in French, German, Italian and Spanish. There are over 20 degree courses covering Business, Economics and Engineering in which options in languages are available.

Middlesex Modern Languages are offered with French, and Spanish (single and joint honours), German, Italian (joint honours) aimed at developing a high level of proficiency in one or two of three languages. Modern Languages are also offered with Journalism, Marketing, Philosophy and Translation. There are also two publishing courses.

Newcastle The Modern European Languages degree covers French, Chinese, German, Japanese, and Spanish. Some joint honours subjects can be taken alongside other courses such as Business, European Studies, Politics, Chemistry and Engineering. (High research rating – Fr)

Northampton Degrees are offered in French or German.

Northumbria Degrees are offered in French, German and Spanish as well as in a large number of joint courses in the Modern Language or in Contemporary Language Studies programmes in which one language or two languages can be combined with either Nation Studies or Business.

Nottingham* Portuguese single and joint honours degrees are offered in Chinese, Dutch, French, German, Ancient Greek, Hispanic Studies, Latin, Russian, Spanish and Serbian and Croatian Studies. There is also a unique course in Viking Studies covering language, literature, history and archaeology. (High research rating – Fr/Ger/Span)

Nottingham Trent joint courses are on offer with Chinese (Mandarin), French, German, Italian and Spanish.

Oxford* Courses are offered in Modern Languages (two languages), European and Middle Eastern Languages and Modern Languages and Linguistics. There is also a course in History and Modern Languages. The range of languages offered is considerable and the Modern Language course covers French, German, Medieval and Modern Greek, Italian, Portuguese, Russian (not beginners' Russian), Spanish and Czech (with Slovak). The course in European and Middle Eastern Languages involves Arabic, Hebrew, Persian or Turkish and the Oriental Studies options cover Arabic, Chinese, Egyptology, Hebrew, Japanese, Jewish Studies, Persian, Sanskrit and Turkish. Modern languages can also be studied with Linguistics. (High research rating – Fr/Ger/Ital/Span)

Oxford Brookes* There is a single honours course in Japanese with a year in Japan and a BA combined honours programme in French Studies and similar language courses in French, Japanese or Spanish which can be added as a minor subject to a major subject.

Plymouth French, German and Spanish are offered with Modern Language degrees as major or minor subjects (two to be chosen).

Portsmouth Degrees are offered in Applied Languages in which two languages are chosen from French, German, Spanish and English as a Foreign Language. There are options in translation theory and practice in Year 2. Degrees are also available in Languages and International Relations, Journalism, American or European Studies.

Queen's Belfast* Courses are offered in French, German, Spanish, Portuguese and Celtic (including Irish, Scottish Gaelic, Welsh and Cornish). (High research rating – Fr/Span)

Reading* Single and joint honours courses are offered in French, German and Italian. (High research rating – Ital)

Roehampton French, Spanish and English are offered as main foreign languages in a new four-year programme with Year 3 as a year abroad. They are offered as single and combined honours courses with a range of other subjects. There is also a degree course in Translating and Interpreting between French, Spanish and English and in TESOL (Teaching English to Speakers of Other Languages.)

St Andrews* Courses are offered covering Arabic, French, Greek, Hebrew, Latin, German, Italian, Russian and Spanish can be taken from scratch or as a useful second language. (High research rating – Fr/Ger/Ital/Span)

Salford The Modern Languages programme offers a choice of two or three languages from French, German, Italian, Spanish or Portuguese, which can also be taken with Translation and Interpreting Studies. There are vocational courses with paid industrial placements in the EU. Scholarships available.

Sheffield* A wide range of languages may be studied including Bulgarian, Catalan, Chinese, Czech, Dutch, Japanese, Korean, French, German, Hispanic Studies, Polish, and Russian. (High research rating – Fr/Ger/Span)

Sheffield Hallam French, German, and Spanish can be taken with International Business Studies, Marketing or Tourism.

See *University Degree Course Offers* (Trotman Publishing) for details of offers

Southampton* Degrees in French, German, Spanish and Portuguese are offered, mainly as joint courses. In addition there is also a four-year. Modern Language degree offering a choice of three languages which include Chinese, Japanese and Russian.

Southampton Solent* Joint courses are offered in Chinese, French, German, Italian, Spanish and English as a foreign language, subject to demand.

Stirling Degree courses are offered in French and Spanish as single or joint honours courses. Two languages can also be studied with several other subjects.

Strathclyde Degrees are offered in French, German, Italian, and Spanish. Any two of these subjects are chosen for the Modern Languages programme. (High research rating – Fr)

Surrey Language courses focus on contemporary language in business, culture and society and cover French, German, Russian and Spanish.

Sussex* French, German, Italian, and Spanish are available in several joint courses. (High research rating – Fr/Ger)

Swansea* French, German, Greek, Italian, Latin, Russian, Spanish and Welsh are offered as major languages with a large number of joint courses in each case. Catalan can also be taken alongside Spanish with Business Studies. There are also courses in Language and Communications (linguistics, journalism, political etc) and in Translation. (High research rating – Ger/Span)

Trinity St David (Lampeter) Arabic, Greek (Ancient), Latin and Welsh are offered on a range of courses. There is also a course in Chinese Studies.

Ulster French, German, Irish and Spanish are available in the Combined Arts course and as joint courses with other subjects. A study of language is also possible in the Language and Linguistics degree.

Warwick* Single honours and joint courses are offered in French, German Studies and Italian. (High research rating – Fr/Ger)

West Scotland Language degrees are offered in French, German or Spanish.

Westminster Degrees are offered in Arabic, Chinese, French, German, Spanish, and Translation Studies. For all students at the university there is a 'languages for all' scheme in which language study can continue throughout their courses. There are also courses in Professional Language Studies.

Wolverhampton Language courses cover British Sign Language (English), and Deaf Studies, French, German, and Spanish.

York* French and German and Spanish joint courses are offered and also a course in Modern Languages and Linguistics. The university also offers a 'languages for all' scheme enabling any student to continue the study of a language. There are also courses in Languages and Linguistics and Linguistics jointly with English, Maths or Philosophy.

OTHER INSTITUTIONS OFFERING LANGUAGE COURSES

Blackpool and Fylde (Coll), Doncaster (Coll), East Lancashire (Coll), European (BusSch), London (Inst/Paris), Northbrook (Coll), UHI Millennium Inst.

ALTERNATIVE COURSES

English, Linguistics.

LAW

(*indicates universities with the highest entry requirements)

SUBJECT REQUIREMENTS/PREFERENCES
GCE A-level: Good grades in languages for courses combinded with a foreign language. **GCSE:** English. The National Admissions Test for Law (LNAT) may be required.

SUBJECT INFORMATION
Law courses are usually divided into two parts. Part 1 occupies Year 1 and introduces the student to criminal and constitutional law and the legal process. In order to gain exemption from the Common Professional Examinations students must have studied a number of core subjects. These are constitutional and administrative law, contract, criminal and land law, laws of tort, equity and law of trusts and European Union law. Thereafter many different specialised topics can be studied in Years 2 and 3. The course content in most Law degrees is very similar, although students not intending to practise in Scotland are recommended to limit their applications to universities south of the border.

Aberdeen* Topics covered in the first year include constitutional law, legal systems, contract, civil liberties, delict and computing. Over 40 honours options are offered including European law, and international law. In addition, there are degrees in Law and French, German, Spanish and Belgian Law and with European Studies. The course offered in Legal Studies does not qualify students to enter the legal profession. (High research rating)

Abertay Dundee A BA Law degree is offered accredited by the Scottish Law Society. It has a strong practical focus, business and business law being important features of the course. In addition there is a course in European Business Law covering business law of the United Kingdom and one other European Union country, European Union law, a European language (Spanish), commercial property and employment law, international trade and dispute settlement.

Aberystwyth* The LLB scheme is offered for those wishing to concentrate entirely on law while a broader course is offered in the BA degree by way of a 'major' in Law plus a 'minor' in another subject. LLB and BA degrees in Law are also offered with a European language – French, German or Spanish (not for beginners), with opportunities to study abroad. There are also courses in Criminal European, Public and Business Law, Human Rights and in Criminal Law.

Anglia Ruskin The Law degree is under revision. An integrated LLB/LPC degree is also planned for students seeking to qualify as a solicitor.

Aston The Law with Management programme is a qualifying Law degree focusing on business skills.

Bangor* The Law degree addresses the Welsh, British, European and global dimensions of contemporary legal developments. There are also courses in Law with Accountancy, Business, Criminal Justice, Social Policy, Media Studies and modern languages.

Bedfordshire An LLB degree is offered whilst Law can also be taken with Accountancy, Criminology and Management.

Birmingham* The Law course aims to provide thorough grounding in the main areas of English law in addition to the vocational training. Core subjects taken in the first two years provide students with exemptions from certain professional examinations should they wish to practise law. European Union law is a compulsory second year (Part I Finals) course. The third year offers a wide range of subjects including law and medicine, Japanese law, human rights and international law. Other degree courses offered by the Faculty of Law include Law with French or German and Law with Business Studies. (High research rating)

Birmingham City The Law course aims to provide a broad-based legal education sensitive to the social, economic and political contexts of modern society. Students have the opportunity to take part in simulated legal disputes by way of moots, mock trials and 'clinical' legal exercises. An emphasis is placed on the wide range of options available in Years 2 and 3, which includes medicine, ethics and law, company, consumer and European Union law and also press and broadcasting law. There are also courses in Law with American Legal Studies, Criminology and Legal Practice and Business Law.

Bolton An accredited course providing students with a thorough grounding in the discipline of Law. A part-time course is available.

Bournemouth* The four year LLB Law degree with a professional placement (40 weeks) in Year 3 offers a range of specialist Law options in Year 4. The theme of the European Union is taken in Year 2. A study of information technology for lawyers and accounting is also offered. This is a four-year course, with a year in professional practice. Taxation and law courses are also available.

Bradford* The LLB course enables graduates to apply for exemption from the Common Professional Exams and, if successful, proceed directly to training as lawyers in England and Wales. Law can also be taken with Business, History or politics.

Brighton* Law is offered with Accounting and Business Studies and Business Administration.

Bristol* The three-year course includes up to 10 mandatory units taken in Years 1 and 2 to meet the requirements for exemption from the Common Professional Examination. Optional units include criminology, women and the law, and medical and family law, human rights and UN law. Six programmes of study are offered and at the end of Year 1 it is possible to transfer from the LLB course to European Legal Studies. Law can also be studied with French, German or Chemistry or with study abroad.

Bristol UWE* This is a comprehensive Law course comprising four law subjects in the first year and five in the second year, with an option to take one or two non-law subjects, for example forensic science, accountancy and modern languages (one language taken). Additional subjects are taken in the third year along with a number of options. There is a course in European and International Law in which three languages are studied and nine months are spent in France, Germany or Spain. Commercial Law is also available, whilst Law can also be combined with Criminology, French or Spanish.

Brunel* Three-year and four-year Law courses are offered. For the latter, students spend three periods of approximately 20 weeks each year in law-related work placement. The study of law is placed in a wide context, and in Year 1 a small number of non-law modules are taken. (High research rating)

Buckingham The Law course, lasting two years, starting in January or July, comprises the six essential core subjects – public law, criminal law, contract, tort, land law and law of trusts – plus three other legal subjects. Law is also offered with Business Finance, Economics, English Language Studies, Management Studies, French, Spanish and Politics. There is also a part-time course. Scholarships available.

Bucks New LLB (Hons) courses are offered in Law and Business Law. Leading to exemption from the academic stage of qualifications as a solicitor or barrister.

Cambridge* The emphasis in the Law course is on principles and technique although, as in other courses, many students do not intend to practise. While the courses focus mainly on English law, the law of the European Union and French law can be studied. The sociological aspects of law such as jurisprudence and sentencing and the penal system are covered. Exchange schemes exist with universities in France, Holland, Germany and Spain. (High research rating)

Canterbury Christ Church Law is offered as a single honours LLB course in addition to which there is a Legal Studies course offered within the joint or combined honours programme.

Cardiff* The Law degree scheme is designed to give students a wide choice of subjects to suit their professional interests. The first year consists of standard core subjects, contract, tort, the legal system, constitutional and administrative law. This is then followed in the second and third years with a choice of eight courses from a list of over 20 options including maritime law and international trade and finance. Law can also be taken with French, German, Welsh and Politics. Scholarships available. (High research rating)

Central Lancashire Law is offered at both Preston and Carlisle. Second- and third-year options include copyright and trademark law, media law and medicine and the law. Students have the opportunity to go on placements with local solicitors and abroad. Joint honours degree courses are offered in Criminology, Business, Politics, Psychology, and Human Rights. Scholarships available.

Chester Core subjects are offered to fulfil the requirements for a Qualifying Law Degree, covering contract, land, European Community, constitutional and administrative law, crime and tort. Students achieving a 2:2 are guaranteed a place on the Legal Practice Course.

City* Core subjects are studied in the first two years of the Law course, followed in Year 3 with a choice from a range of options that currently includes company law, media law, family law and public international law. There is also a course in Law which can be combined with other subjects.

Coventry Three-year and four-year Law courses are offered, including Law with French, Spanish Business and International Studies.

Cumbria In addition to the seven foundation subjects required for legal professional purposes there are a number of taught options including media, medical, human rights and family Law.

De Montfort The Law course is a qualifying degree recognised by the Law Society and the Bar. In addition to the comprehensive legal education, students take either sociology throughout Years 1 and 2, or a foreign language (French or German) throughout the three years of the course. The School of Law promotes the use of computer-assisted learning. Joint courses are also offered with Criminal Justice and there is a single honours course in Law and Human Rights.

Derby An LLB course is offered with foundation areas of European Union law, contract, tort, criminal, constitutional, land law and trusts. In the final year students may specialise in Business Law, International Law or Social and Public Law. Law can also be taken with Criminology.

Dundee* This unique course offers two main streams – Scots Law and English Law. Since many of the subjects are common to all students both courses lead to qualifications as a lawyer in Scotland, England or Northern Ireland. There are also degrees in English Law and Accountancy, and English or Scots Law with History, Philosophy, Politics or Modern Languages. Scholarships available. (High research rating)

Durham* Core courses in the first year of the Law course leading to the examination (preliminary honours) at the end of the first year cover contract, tort, UK and EU constitutional law and civil liberties. Eight full subjects are then taken in the second and third years from 20 law topics or nine non-law subjects. There are courses on international, European and French law as well as English law. Although students on the single or joint honours degree courses can obtain exemption from the Common Professional Examination, the courses are intended as an education rather than professional training. (High research rating)

East Anglia* The preliminary programme of the Law course (Year 1) covers criminal, constitutional and land law. The honours programme (Years 2 and 3) in Part I covers a study of the laws of contract, tort, trusts and one optional subject. Part II comprises administrative law and four optional subjects. Degree courses in Law with German or French Law and Language, European Legal Systems and the American Legal System are also offered.

East London Compulsory subjects are taken in Years 1 and 2 of the Law course, with a range of options offered in Years 2 and 3 that give the necessary exemptions from professional examinations. Topics include medicine and law, European Union law, pension funds and international law. There are also courses in Law with American Law or French Law or with European Legal Systems.

Edge Hill The degree course in Law gains exemption from the Legal Practice course and Bar Finals. Law can also be studied with Criminology or Management.

Edinburgh* In the first year of the Law course compulsory subjects include the Scottish legal system, contract, family and constitutional law. It is also possible to take a course outside the Law Faculty, for example French, German, History. The decision to follow the honours courses is taken at the end of the second year when the required courses for those wishing to enter the profession will have been taken. In the third and fourth years further professional courses and options are taken. There are exemption from stages of professional training. Students wishing to practise in England and Wales are recommended to apply to law schools south of the border. (High research rating)

Essex* The Law course is in three parts each covering one year. The Law Qualifying Examination is taken at the end of the first year, and Parts I and II of the Final LLB at the end of the second and third years. In the second year it is possible to take a non-law subject as an option. There is also a degree in English and French Laws with Year 3 abroad and also Law with an International Exchange. Several academic departments also combine to offer degrees in Human Rights. (High research rating)

Exeter* In the first year of the Law course three modules are taken including European Union law. Examinations take place at the end of each year, LLB Parts I and II being taken at the end of the second and third years. The LLB (European) is a four-year course covering French or German law which includes French and German languages and a year spent abroad. There is also a course in Law and Society allowing students to study both Law and Sociology.

Glamorgan Law is taken as a modular semesterised course. Options are available in Years 2 and 3 and include languages, environmental law, international trade, patent law and criminology and social justice. Courses in Criminal Law, Commercial Law can also be taken. The award is a qualifying law degree.

Glasgow* Ordinary (three-year) and honours (four-year) Law courses are available. A wide range of degrees is available that can give appropriate exemptions from professional examinations. The Scottish legal system and Scottish law occupy an important place in the first-year course. Law can also be studied with language (French, German and Spanish) in addition to the legal systems of these countries. Students wishing to qualify in England or other member states of the EU need to pass additional examinations. (High research rating)

Glasgow Caledonian Law (accredited by the Law Society of Scotland) and Business Law are offered as four-year full-time degrees.

Gloucestershire The LLB course is a qualifying law degree and includes options in criminal, medical, employment and family law. There is a two year fast track course.

Greenwich BA and LLB course are offered. Law is also offered with 12 other subjects as a combined degree.

Hertfordshire* The Law course offers several interesting third year options including medical law, cyber law, company and international law. Joint honours courses are offered with a choice of 14 subjects. Scholarships available.

Huddersfield There is a Law (Exempting) course enabling students to qualify as a solicitor by incorporating the legal practice course in Years 3 and 4 (subject to an appropriate training contract). Degree courses are also offered in Law and Accountancy and Business Law.

Hull The first two years of the Law course introduce legal techniques and the English legal system. A significant emphasis is placed on the law relating to the European Union. Years 2 and 3 include options in more than 20 subjects including information technology law, government law, international law, American public law, Admiralty law and media regulation. Suitable students may spend their third year abroad in France, Germany, Belgium or Holland, which extends their course to four years. Law is also offered with French and German Law and Language.

Keele* Law and Law with Criminology or Politics can be taken as single honours (also dual honours) courses. The Law course qualifies for exemption from the Law Society Common Professional Examination. (High research rating)

See *University Degree Course Offers* (Trotman Publishing) for details of offers

Kent The Law course is designed to enable students to gain the necessary exemptions from the Law Society examinations. Other Law courses include English and French/German/Spanish/Italian Law, European Legal Studies (which includes a year in Europe), Law and International Law. There is a law clinic enabling students to practise law under the supervision of solicitors. (High research rating)

Kingston* All the major aspects of law are covered in this Law course with a wide choice of subjects in the final year. These include revenue and family law, the law of international trade, EU, medical, and welfare law. Law with French Law, Business, Criminology, Politics, Commercial Law and International Law are also offered. Scholarships available.

Lancaster* Part I of the Law course introduces the principles of law and provides a detailed study of constitutional and administrative law. Part II covers eight units in law and a free ninth unit course. The units cover various aspects of law and some are compulsory to comply with the examinations of the Law Society. A course in European Legal Studies is also on offer with a year abroad between Years 2 and 4 and there are courses in Law and Criminology and International Law.

Leeds* Four compulsory subjects are taken in the first year of the Law course and five in Years 2 and 3, with optional subjects chosen from a wide range of topics. Courses are also offered in Criminal Justice and Criminology, and Law with Accountancy, French or Management. (High research rating)

Leeds Metropolitan Core subjects of the Law course give exemptions from professional legal examinations for the Bar and Law Society. Law can also be studied with Criminal Justice.

Leicester* Students on the LLB course taking certain options are guaranteed a place at the College of Law on graduation. There are also courses in English and French Law and Law with French Law and Language. (High research rating)

Lincoln The LLB Law course is a qualifying degree giving professional exemptions. Joint honours courses are also offered with Politics, Business, Criminology or Finance.

Liverpool* The first year of the Law course (Intermediate) covers the core courses of criminal, constitutional law and an introduction to English law and EU law. Final Part I covers the second year with three compulsory subjects – tort, land law and equity – plus one optional subject. The third-year course (Final Part II) provides a wide range of options from which students select five subjects. Law and Business Studies can also be studied with modules in resources management, banking and commercial law.

Liverpool Hope The BA combined honours Law degree covers some of the key aspects of law including business law, criminal law, European law and UK parliamentary decision-making.

Liverpool John Moores The course in Law (LLB) is the standard qualifying Law degree. There is also a joint degree with Criminal Justice.

London (King's)* The Law course provides a grounding in the basic areas of legal knowledge, methods and technique in the first two years and permits a greater degree of specialisation in the final year. The course is highly rated by students. King's also offers English and French or American or Australian or German Law. There is also a course in European Legal Studies. (High research rating)

London (LSE)* Public law, the English legal system, contract and tort and property law are studied for the Intermediate examination at the end of the first year of the Law course. Parts I and II follow in the second and third years and include compulsory and optional subjects. Anthropology and Law is also offered. (High research rating)

London (QM)* A leading law department offers a standard law course with over 30 options in Year 3. There are also courses in English and European Law and Law with German. (High research rating)

London (SOAS)* The Law course is unique, instruction comprises English law subjects, including those required for professional purposes, and also aspects of law relating to a particular region in Asia or Africa, and comparative law. The second and third years involve eight courses chosen from 12 options. A course in Art with Archaeology and Law is also offered.

London (UCL)* The large Law faculty offers an LLB course with specialist areas covering labour law, media and communications law. Law is also offered with French, German, Hispanic or Italian Law or with another legal system (Australia, Singapore or Hong Kong). See also **European Studies**. (High research rating)

London Metropolitan The Business Law and LLB Law degrees are recognised by the Bar and the Law Society as giving full exemption from the academic stage of professional education. A Legal and Economic Studies degree is offered in conjunction with the Université René Descartes in Paris. There is also a course in International Law and International Politics.

London South Bank The Law course is recognised by the Law Society and the Council of Legal Education. It aims to develop the student's skill in the use of legal materials and their relation with the social environment. Optional units include company law, housing law, women and the law, medical law and ethics.

Manchester* Law students wishing to become solicitors graduating with a lower second class degree are guaranteed a place at a branch of the College of Law to do the legal practice course. A very wide range of options (32), including trade, the media, journalism, planning, child and labour law, can be chosen in Years 2 and 3 following a study of the basic subjects in Year 1. Accounting and Law, Politics and Law, and English Law and French Law are also available. (High research rating)

Manchester Metropolitan The first 'qualifying' year of the Law course is made up of basic legal subjects followed by a series of options that are chosen in Years 2 and 3. A degree course in Law with French is also offered when students take Year 3 in Europe. Courses in Law and Trading Standards and in Consumer Protection (Consumer Law) are also available. A large number of joint courses with Legal Studies are offered.

Middlesex The Law course involves compulsory law subjects which, with a wide range of options, lead to exemption from professional examinations. Law is also offered with Business.

Napier A broad legal education is offered in the BA Law course with the opportunity to study other subjects (European languages, business and management, information management and managerial finance). Accounting and Law is also available. The LLB course is accredited by the Law Society of Scotland.

Newcastle* This is a flexible Law course with constitutional and administrative law, land law, contract and tort, and judicial process in the first two years. Two options in the second year are followed by five options in the third year and these include international law and European Union law. Throughout the course there is an emphasis on the relationship between law and other social sciences, with a special optional course in law and economics. Law can also be taken with French and also as part of the BA combined studies programme.

Northampton A very large number of joint degrees with Law are offered in addition to an LLB qualifying Law degree.

Northumbria* The LLB degree is taken in three years or four years for students wishing to be exempt from the barristers or solicitors vocational awards.

Nottingham* BA and LLB courses are offered and students can defer their final choice until their arrival at the University. The LLB follows the traditional route of four compulsory courses in the first year, followed by compulsory and optional subjects in the second and third years. In the BA course, legal subjects are studied in each year along with two subsidiary non-law subjects. Law can also be studied with French or German. (High research rating)

Nottingham Trent* The qualifying LLB degree in Law is offered as a three-year full-time and four-year sandwich course with paid placements with a law firm in Year 3. The last six and nine months respectively of each course are spent in practical training in a solicitor's office at the end of Year 1 and during Year 3. Both courses give exemptions from professional examinations. There is also a sandwich course in Law.

Oxford* Three-year and four-year Law courses are offered, the latter with one year of Law Studies in Europe. The courses are identical except that after Year 2 students on course II may study in a university in France, Germany or Italy studying French, German or Italian Law or in the Netherlands studying European and International Law. (High research rating)

Oxford Brookes* Law (single or combined honours courses) is a flexible degree scheme within the modular degree course. By taking a prescribed combination of modules, students may obtain exemption from the first stage of the Law Society professional examinations. Law is also offered as a combined course with subjects including Accounting, Molecular Biology, Business, Japanese Studies, Publishing and Telecommunications.

Plymouth The LLB course offers the basic course subjects required for professional practice. Options in Year 3 include maritime law, employment law, the media and computer law. Courses are also offered in Law with International Relations, Criminal Justice Studies, Politics, Sociology and Business. There is also a course in Maritime Business with Maritime Law.

Portsmouth Degrees are offered in Law with Business, Accounting, Criminology, French, European Studies and International Relations.

Queen Margaret Law can be taken with Economics, German (four-year course) and Politics.

Queen's Belfast* Students study the law as it relates to Northern Ireland (similar to English Law) and are offered courses in European Union and Community law and the sociological aspects of the subject. Law can be taken with Politics and Accounting and there are courses in Common and Civil Law with French and Spanish.

Reading* The Law course is modular and 12 modules are taken for the First University Examination. Thereafter the course comprises the traditional compulsory and optional subjects leading to qualification through the Law Society or Bar Council. Law with Legal Studies in Europe is also offered.

Robert Gordon The BA Law and Management course combines both areas with language options offered in Years 2, 3 and 4. There is a 24-week placement for home students. There is also an LLB Law degree. Students with the BA degree may transfer to the LLB course in Year 3.

Salford An LLB course is offered, whilst Law can also be studied with Business and Management Studies.

Sheffield* In the first year, Law students take courses in contract, property and public law and an introduction to law and the legal system. This leads to the Intermediate examination. Thereafter there is considerable freedom of choice in planning the programme of study for the final two years. For those students not aiming for a law career it is possible to transfer to the BA Law course. Law is also offered with Criminology or with French, German or Spanish.

Sheffield Hallam LLB courses are offered and in addition there are joint courses with Business, or Criminology. There is also an Socrates exchange programme with European institutions and a joint programme with the university of Paris leading to a Maitrise en Droit Francais.

Southampton* The LLB course consists of a core of seven compulsory subjects studied in the first and second years, together with a wide range of optional subjects. These range from admiralty law and carriage of goods by sea to law and medicine, environmental law and EU law, including legal French, medical ethics and law, and information technology law. There are also degrees in European and International Legal Studies. (High research rating)

Southampton Solent A qualifying law degree can be taken singly or jointly with Business Management, Criminology, European studies or Human Resource Management. There is also a separate degree in Commercial Law.

Staffordshire All Law students follow a common course of compulsory subjects in the first year together with criminal law or accounting and finance or a language. They may continue these options in the second and third years. Several specialist options can also be taken including Business Law, Human Rights, and Sports Law. Advisory work in the field of social studies can be studied on the LLB Advice Work degree.

See *University Degree Course Offers* (Trotman Publishing) for details of offers

Stirling An LLB programme is offered whilst BA Law is offered with Business Studies, Economics, Finance, Human Resource Management, Sports Studies, Social Policy, Sociology, Marketing, Politics or Languages. A single honours Business Law course is also available.

Strathclyde The Law course (which focuses on Scottish law) includes law and legal processes, public law and Scottish law. Mercantile and criminal law are combined with Scottish law in the second year, with a choice of options in the second and third years that include forensic medicine, law and computers, international law and criminology. Law can also be taken as part of the Arts and Social Science degree. (High research rating)

Sunderland The LLB course has options in Employment, Environmental, Medical and International Law. Business Law is also offered with a range of subjects including Management, Marketing and Media Studies. The degree is recognised by the Bar and Law Society.

Surrey* Law is offered with French, German, Spanish or Russian Law. Courses have opportunities for legal work placements. Scholarships available.

Sussex* Law course students are examined in Law and also in contextual subjects taught within their Schools of Studies. The degree carries exemption from the Bar and Law Society examinations. Other Law courses offered include languages, Contemporary European Studies, American Studies and International Relations.

Swansea* All Law students follow a first year with four compulsory law modules and two non-law modules. Five law and one non-law modules are taken in Years 2 and 3. Law is also offered with other subjects including Politics, Psychology, Spanish and Welsh, and courses in Legal Studies are also available.

Teesside As well as the core subjects of a standard Law degree, all students take a course in business studies running through the three years of the course. European law is also compulsory. Other courses offered include Law with Criminology and Law with Politics.

Ulster Law is offered as a single honours degree or with 14 other subjects including Criminology, Economics, Politics, languages and Business Studies.

Warwick* Three-year and four-year Law courses are available. Both types of course allow the student to choose 'full' or 'half' courses in a wide range of legal subjects. In the four-year course second-, third- and fourth-year students may take up to a total of four non-law subjects. Law is studied in the context of wider social, political and theoretical practice – with expertise from 'all around the globe'. There is also a four-year course in European Law that requires students to have a good knowledge of French or German. Three-year courses combining Law with Sociology or Business Studies are also offered. (High research rating)

West London The LLB course provides a traditional legal education with a wide range of options in Years 2 and 3 including European Union law, public international law, medicine and the law, civil liberties and the government and politics of Britain. It is recognised by the Bar and Law Society. Criminology courses are also offered with New Media Journalism and Sociology.

West Scotland Law is offered as a single honours or jointly with Politics.

Westminster The seven compulsory law subjects required to gain necessary exemptions from professional law examinations are taken in Years 1 and 2 of the Law course with additional options in Years 2 and 3. Other courses include Commercial Law, European Legal Studies, and Law with French, Law and Solicitor's Exempting.

Winchester The LLB Law course is awaiting validation. Check with the university.

Wolverhampton The Law course is approved by the Law Society and the Bar Council for exemption from Law Society Final examinations. It covers the required compulsory core subjects plus a wide range of options from which seven must be chosen in Years 2 and 3. In the first year, students take one course from accounting, economics, politics, sociology, literature or psychology. Language options and European placements are possible. There is also a BA course in Business Law.

See *University Degree Course Offers* (Trotman Publishing) for details of offers

York A new Law course (LLB) has been introduced comprising three streams: Foundation, Law and Society and Law and Practice.

OTHER INSTITUTIONS OFFERING LAW COURSES
Bradford (Coll), Croydon (Coll), Doncaster (Coll), East End (BusColl), East Lancashire (Coll), European (BusSch), Exeter (Coll), Grimsby (IFHE), Holborn (Coll), Newcastle (Coll), Nottingham New (Coll), Oxford Ruskin (Coll), Peterborough (Reg Coll), Regents (BusSch), South Devon (Coll), Staffordshire (Reg Coll), Truro (Coll), Warrington (Coll), Warwickshire (Coll), Worcester (CAT).

ALTERNATIVE COURSES
Government, History, International Relations, Politics, Social Sciences, Social Studies, Sociology.

LEISURE, RECREATION MANAGEMENT AND TOURISM

(See also **Hospitality Management**)
(*indicates universities with the highest entry requirements)

SUBJECT REQUIREMENTS/PREFERENCES
GCSE: English and Mathematics and for some courses a foreign language.

SUBJECT INFORMATION
Courses in these subjects are generally quite similar. However, the applicant should note the specialist options offered, for example recreation management, countryside management and heritage studies.

Abertay Dundee Tourism Management is offered as a four-year. course. The degree examines the subject from economic, sociological, cultural and geographical standpoints.

Anglia Ruskin Courses are offered in Leisure and Tourism with modules/specialist studies in management, heritage or with an international focus.

Bangor The Leisure and Tourism Resource Management course offers modules in both English and Welsh. Compulsory and optional modules are taken throughout the course including the study of a European language. Specialist topics include sports, hospitality management, heritage management, travel, environment and amenity and leisure sociology. There is also a course in Heritage Management.

Bedfordshire* A Leisure Management degree is available and modules are also offered in Marketing and Finance. There are also Sport Tourism and Travel and Tourism degrees.

Birmingham* A unique course is offered in Sport and Leisure Facilities Design.

Birmingham (UC) The Adventure Tourism Management course involves studies in commerical and risk management, options include modern languages, sports international and nature tourism.

Bournemouth The Leisure Marketing course offers modules in accounting, leisure planning and marketing. Tourism Studies, a four-year sandwich course, covers all aspects of the industry; final-year options include tourist attractions and financial management. There is a European language option throughout the course. Several tourism courses can also be followed.

Brighton* Leisure and Sport Management is offered in which social, scientific and management subjects are studied within a European orientation. The Leisure and Sports Studies course focuses on leisure policy. There are European language options. The Travel Management course covers travel geography, operations and retail studies. There is an industrial placement in Year 3. There are also courses in Tourism Management and International Tourism Management with language studies in French, German or Spanish.

Bucks New Two courses are available in International Travel and Tourism including one with Air Travel and a second in Tourism in the 21st century.

Central Lancashire International Tourism Management is a four-year sandwich course with a placement abroad in Year 3. Other courses are offered in Tourism or Leisure Studies with Business and there are several courses involving outdoor leadership, recreation and education.

Chichester A course is offered in Tourism covering rural, sport, events and heritage studies.

Coventry The Coventry Business School offers courses in Leisure Management, with an optional study in Europe, and Tourism Management with an optional industrial placement in Year 3.

Cumbria Courses are offered in Adventure with Media, Recreation Management or Travel.

East London Courses are offered in Leisure, Hospitality and Tourism and in Travel Management. Third World Development and Tourism and Travel are two subjects offered in the three-subject BA/BSc combined honours degree. A degree in Tourism and Travel with Marketing is also available.

Edinburgh* Sport and Recreation Management is offered as a three-year or four-year full-time degree.

Glamorgan The Leisure and Tourism Management or Sports Management courses cover information technology, financial operations and marketing plus a range of specialised topics including tourism, sport and transportation systems.

Glasgow Caledonian Courses in Leisure Management, Tourism, International Travel Management and Adventure Recreation Management are offered.

Gloucestershire Leisure Management is offered with a wide range of subjects in the modular degree scheme. Courses also include Adventure Leisure Management, Leisure and Sport Management and Events Management.

Greenwich Courses are offered in Tourism Management with French, German or Spanish, Tourism and Heritage Management and Events Management.

Harper Adams (UC) The courses include Adventure Recreation Management, Tourism and Leisure Management.

Hertfordshire A large number of joint courses in Tourism are offered, including Tourism and Management Sciences, and Tourism and Human Resources.

Huddersfield Tourism and Leisure Management is offered as a three-year full-time or four-year sandwich degree. Tourism and Leisure are also part of the Hospitality programme.

Hull Sport and Leisure Management, Tourism Management and Sport, Leisure and Tourism Management as three-year or four-year full-time degrees.

Kingston* A course is offered in Leisure Property Development.

Leeds Metropolitan Courses are offered in Leisure and Sports Studies or Recreation and Tourism Management.

Lincoln Single and joint courses are offered in European and International Tourism which cover topics including the travel industry, tourism in the UK and Europe, economics, marketing and heritage management. There is an optional year in industry and a choice of Languages from French, German or Spanish.

See *University Degree Course Offers* (Trotman Publishing) for details of offers

Liverpool Hope Leisure and Tourism can both be taken as part ot the combined honours programme.

Liverpool John Moores The Tourism courses includes data management, accounting, economics, marketing, consumer studies and personnel management. Joint courses in Languages are offered including Japanese.

London Metropolitan Courses are offered in International Tourism Management, International Leisure and Tourism Management, and in Events and Sports Management.

Loughborough* Sport and Leisure Management is offered as a three-year full-time or four-year sandwich course. There is also a course in Physical Education, Sports Science and Recreation Management. Geography can also be studied with Sports and Leisure Management in a four-year sandwich degree.

Manchester Metropolitan Tourism Management can be studied as a single honours degree and is also offered with 28 other subjects.

Marjon (UCP) Single and combined courses can be taken with Outdoor Adventure.

Middlesex International Tourism Management is available with 11 other subjects.

Napier Tourism Management is offered with Languages or Human Resource Management. Courses are also offered in Festival and Event Management.

Oxford Brookes* Leisure and Tourism Planning is available as a single honours course with several joint degrees in Tourism.

Plymouth Courses are offered in Tourism Management, and International Tourism Management.

Portsmouth* Leisure Management and Marketing links leisure with business activities.

Robert Gordon International Tourism Management course offers 28 weeks of paid placement at the end of Year 2 and options in Languages.

Roehampton A BSc is offered in Sport, Leisure and Culture.

Salford Leisure and Tourism Management is a three-year full-time course that covers sport, recreation, tourism and health promotion, and includes languages with options for a placement in Europe. There are also courses in Leisure Management, and in Hospitality and Tourism Management.

Sheffield Hallam Courses are offered in Leisure Events Management with Outdoor Recreation and Tourism with Hospitality Management.

Staffordshire Degree courses are offered in Sport and Leisure Management and Travel and Tourism Management.

Strathclyde Tourism is offered in several joint courses.

Sunderland Large numbers of joint courses with Tourism are on offer.

Swansea Metropolitan Courses are offered in Leisure, Tourism and International Tourism Management.

Teesside The degree in Leisure Management offers specialist studies in sport, media or heritage, following a common core of studies. There is also a course in Tourism.

Trinity St David (Carmarthen) A broad course in Outdoor Education is available which includes work placement.

Trinity St David (Lampeter) Cultural Tourism is available with 16 other subjects.

Ulster Hotel and Tourism Management, Leisure, Events and Cultural Management and Sport, Exercise and Leisure are offered.

See *University Degree Course Offers* (Trotman Publishing) for details of offers

West London Courses are offered in Travel and Tourism Management.

West Scotland A BA full-time and sandwich degree in Tourism is offered at the Ayr campus. There is an optional work placement and specialist studies that include travel operations, hospitality management, arts and entertainment and European languages. There is also a BA course offered in Events Management.

Westminster* Courses in Tourism are offered with options in planning, travel and business.

Winchester Leisure Management provides a broad study of leisure at local, national and international levels and is combined with a range of related management options. There are also several courses in Tourism Management. See also under **Hospitality Management**.

Wolverhampton Tourism Management and Leisure Management joint degrees are offered.

York St John Tourism Management is a stand-alone degree with work placements in Year 2 and as an alternative it can be taken with a Marketing option.

OTHER INSTITUTIONS OFFERING LEISURE COURSES
Cornwall (Coll), Craven (Coll), Duchy (Coll), East Lancashire (Coll), Grimsby (IFHE), Halton Riverside (Coll), Liverpool (CmC), Loughborough (Coll), Northumberland (Coll), Norwich City (Coll), Nottingham New (Coll), SAC, Sheffield (Coll), Solihull (Coll), Somerset (CAT), Southport (Coll), Staffordshire (Reg Fed), Suffolk (Univ Campus), Truro (Coll), UHI Millennium Inst, Warwickshire (Coll), Wirral Metropolitan (Coll).

ALTERNATIVE COURSES
Amenities Management, Arts Management, Facilities Management, Hotel Management, Leisure Boat Design, Physical Education, Sports Studies. Materials Science/Metallurgy/Materials Engineering

---

MATERIALS SCIENCE/METALLURGY/ MATERIALS ENGINEERING

(*indicates universities with the highest entry requirements)

SUBJECT REQUIREMENTS/PREFERENCES
GCE A-level: Two or three science/mathematics subjects required for most courses. **GCSE:** Science/ mathematics subjects. **Brunel** Grades A–C in Physics and Chemistry if not offered at A-level. **Swansea** Predominantly grades A and B.

SUBJECT INFORMATION
This is a subject that covers physics, chemistry and engineering at one and the same time! From its origins in metallurgy, materials science has now moved into the processing, structure and properties of materials – ceramics, polymers, composites and electrical materials. Materials science and metallurgy are perhaps the most misunderstood of all careers. Thus applications for degree courses are low and offers are very reasonable. As with other careers in which there is a shortfall of applicants, graduate employment and future prospects are good.

Aberdeen A course is offered in Mechanical Engineering with Materials.

Birmingham* Courses are offered in Mechanical and Materials Science, Metallurgy/Materials Engineering, Materials Science and Technology and Biomedical Materials Science (artificial hip joints, heart valves, contact lenses etc). There is also a course in Sports Science and Materials Technology. (High research rating)

See *University Degree Course Offers* (Trotman Publishing) for details of offers

Cambridge* A course in Materials Science and Metallurgy is offered as part of the Natural Sciences course. In the second year, it is accompanied by two other physical sciences prior to a specialist third, and possibly fourth, year. (High research rating) See also **Biological Sciences**.

Heriot-Watt Textile studies, clothing studies and management are covered in all years of the Textile Technology course with marketing and quality evaluation. Several Textile courses are offered including Textile Science.

Imperial London* The Department offers three-year BEng courses in Materials Science and Engineering, Materials with Management, and Materials with a year abroad, and four-year courses in Aerospace Materials, and Materials Science and Engineering. Students are encouraged to gain practical experience during two summer vacations; some are spent abroad. There are also opportunities for industrial sponsorship. A course in Biomaterials and Tissue Engineering is also offered. (High research rating)

Leeds* Materials science is taken with maths, physics and computing in the first year of the Materials Science and Engineering course. The study continues in the second year with applied maths and statistics and engineering design. Materials science and engineering form the core of the third-year subjects. Courses are also offered in Materials Science and Engineering, Biomaterials, and Sports Materials Technology. (High research rating)

Liverpool* Mathematics, computing, corrosion and oxidation are common core courses for the Materials Science course. The Materials Science and Materials Engineering courses follow the same programme in Years 1 and 2. There are also courses in Aerospace Materials, Biomaterials Science and Engineering, Materials Chemistry and Materials Engineering and Metallurgy. Scholarships available (High research rating)

London (QM)* The course in Materials Science and Engineering provides a bridge between pure and applied sciences and covers polymers, biomaterials, metals and ceramics. There are also courses in Biomedical, Aerospace, Dental and Environmental Materials Science. (High research rating)

London (UCL)* History of Art with Material Studies is offered as a three-year full-time course.

London Metropolitan* Three-year degree courses are offered in Polymer Engineering and in Polymer Science.

Loughborough* The Materials Engineering programme allows students to develop either Materials Engineering or Business Management options in the final year. There is an optional third year in Europe or in industry. There are also courses in Automotive Materials. Scholarships available. (High research rating)

Manchester* The Materials Science programme focuses on engineering aspects whilst the Biomedical Materials Science programme can be taken with or without industrial experience. The Biomedical Materials Science course covers cell structure, anatomy, tissue interaction and drug release systems. There are also courses in Textile Sciences and Technology. Entrance scholarships. (High research rating)

Manchester Metropolitan There is a degree course in Dental Technology.

Napier A four-year sandwich course in Polymer Engineering is offered with 12 months' supervised work experience between Years 2 and 4. The course covers the most recent developments in the subject including liquid crystal polymers, flame-retardant materials and recycling.

Newcastle* Mechanical and Materials Engineering is offered in a four-year full-time degree and there are courses in Materials and Process Engineering. Scholarships available.

Northampton The University has always been one of the main centres for the study of Leather Technology.

Nottingham* A course is offered in Biomedical Materials Science that allows students to specialise in cell biology, materials design and processing and pharmaceutical applications. (High research rating)

Oxford* The study of the Science of Materials is interdisciplinary, involving the physics and chemistry of solids and their engineering applications. The course lasts four years and the final year involves research in the department or in industry leading to the thesis. This subject area is undersubscribed. A degree course is also offered in Materials, Economics and Management that has a common first year with the previous course. Scholarships available. (High research rating)

St Andrews* Courses are offered in Materials Science (with a one year industrial placement) and Chemistry with Materials Chemistry.

Sheffield* In this Materials Science and Engineering course options exist in ceramic science, polymer science, glass and metal science: these subjects are also offered as specialist degrees. Admission can also be by way of Physical Sciences since final degree course decisions between Materials Science or Physics or Chemistry can be delayed. Courses in Metal Science, Ceramic Science, Glass Science, and also Polymer Science and Engineering are also offered. (High research rating)

Southampton* Courses are offered in Aerospace Materials and in Textile Fashion and Fibre.

Staffordshire Design Technology for Ceramics is a comprehensive study of ceramic materials manufacture and design at a leading centre in the United Kingdom.

Strathclyde There is a course in Mechanical and Materials Engineering.

Swansea* Scholarships are available in the Materials Science and Engineering course, in which specialist topics include polymer engineering, micro electronics, materials technology and failure analysis. The course is also offered with a year in North America. A course in Resistant Materials Design is also offered. (High research rating)

Wolverhampton A four-year sandwich course in Materials and Quality Engineering involves a study of manufacturing processes with metals and non-metals.

OTHER INSTITUTIONS OFFERING MATERIALS COURSES
Bradford (Coll), Hull (Coll), Warwickshire (Coll)

ALTERNATIVE COURSES
Aerospace Materials Technology, Biomedical Materials Science, Chemistry and Applied Chemistry, Engineering Design, Geology, Geophysics, Materials Engineering, Mechanical, Mining and Production Engineering, Mineral Exploitation, Paper Science, Physics and Applied Physics, Polymer Chemistry, Polymer Science, Textiles and Wood Science.

MATHEMATICS

(including **Statistics**)
(*indicates universities with the highest entry requirements)

SUBJECT REQUIREMENTS/PREFERENCES
GCE A-level: Mathematics subjects, normally the highest grade in the offers made. **GCSE:** English often required.

SUBJECT INFORMATION
Mathematics degree courses are an extension of A-level Mathematics, covering pure and applied mathematics, statistics, computing, mathematical analysis and mathematical applications. Research ratings below include Pure and Applied Mathematics and Statistics unless otherwise indicated.

Aberdeen Students can aim to choose between focusing their attention on Mathematics or spreading their interests to combine it with other subjects.

Aberystwyth Mathematics is offered as a modular course for students wishing to specialise in Pure or Applied Mathematics or Statistics. It is possible to delay the final choice of specialisation until the end of Year 1. The course in Financial Mathematics draws together modules in economics, accounting, business law and mathematics. A wide range of joint courses can be taken including Mathematics with Education, Welsh History, European Languages, Fine Art and Applied Mathematics. Statistics can be studied with another subject including Computer Science, Geography, Accounting and Finance and Applied Mathematics.

Anglia Ruskin Mathematics is offered on over 30 combined courses including Business, Law, Internet Technology, and Language. There are also joint courses with Statistical Modelling and courses in Mathematics and Computing and Business Mathematics.

Aston There is an emphasis on Applied Mathematics relevant to business, industry and computing in addition to combinations with Economics and Languages. There are sandwich placement opportunities and a Qualified Teacher Status option.

Bath* In the School of Mathematical Sciences a number of three-year and four-year courses all with a common first year are offered covering Mathematics and Statistics, with some transfers possible at the end of Year 1 to pathways in pure and applied mathematics, probability and statistics. There are four-year courses with a job placement or study abroad. Mathematics can also be studied in the Natural Sciences programme. (High research rating)

Birmingham The Mathematical Science courses offer a broad framework of subjects with a wide choice of specialisms in Year 3. An additional year of Computer Science is possible. Joint courses with Business Management, Philosophy, Psychology, Sports Science or an Arts subject are possible and there is also a degree in Mathematical Economics and Statistics. Scholarships are available. (High research rating)

Bolton The degree offers a broad education in mathematics with a teaching module for those aiming to work in the profession.

Bradford There is a course in Computational Mathematics with a Foundation year in information for applicants with non-standard qualifications.

Brighton A BSc Mathematics course is available with over 15 options in the third-year including mathematics, statistics and operational research, and an optional placement year. Joint courses are also offered with Computing, Management, or Business, Finance.

Bristol* A particular feature is the flexibility of the Mathematics course structure at every undergraduate stage with most of the programmes having a common structure in the first year. Students may transfer from joint honours to single honours, either at the end of the first year or at the end of the second year. Students may also choose to spend one-third of their time on subjects outside the Mathematics Department in either or both of their second or third years, for example computer science, psychology, economics or philosophy. This is particularly useful for students moving into the business world who may wish to study economics in their final year. Mathematics can also be taken with Statistics. (High research rating)

Bristol UWE Mathematics is a modular programme covering mathematics, statistics and computing. Modern language options, finance and economics and study in Europe or America are also involved. There is also a separate degree in Statistics.

Brunel* The Department of Mathematics and Statistics caters for all possible interests with a wide range of courses that includes Mathematics, Mathematical and Management Studies and with Statistics, Mathematics and Computer Science and Financial Mathematics. These courses are also offered on a sandwich basis, which leads to a high proportion of successful graduate employment placements. (High research rating)

Cambridge* In Part IA of the Pure and Applied Mathematics Tripos there are two options: (a) Pure and Applied Mathematics; and (b) Mathematics with Physics. In Part II there is a choice of alternatives that lead either to practical applications of the subject or to research applications. About 10% of students change from mathematics each year having taken option (b) above and change to physics. (High research rating)

Cardiff* The core modules are taken by all Mathematics students in Year 1 with the opportunity to change degree programmes at the start of Year 2. The Mathematics course allows students to specialise in pure or applied mathematics or statistics. The Mathematics and its Applications course provides opportunities for specialisation in several branches of the subject. Mathematics can also be taken with Operational Research and Statistics, Computing and Physics, while Pure Mathematics can also be taken with a Humanities subject. Scholarships available.

Central Lancashire The BSc course in Mathematics provides an excellent foundation in modern mathematics covering statistics, applicable mathematics, computing and programming. Mathematics can also be taken with Education, Psychology, Business Information Systems and Statistics.

Chester Single and combined honours courses are offered involving Pure and Applied Mathematics, Statisics and Operational Research.

Chichester Mathematics is offered as a teaching programme for the Key Stages 2 and 3 (7–14 age range).

City* The Mathematical Sciences course gives an excellent grounding in mathematics, statistics and computer science, with options in finance and economics, statistics and computing in Years 2 and 3 leading to specialist degrees. Good opportunities exist for transfer across courses. There is an optional third year in industry or abroad. See also **Actuarial Sciences**.

Coventry Courses focus on the applications of mathematics in engineering, finance, computing, business and statistics.

Cumbria A unique course is offered in Mathematics with Workplace Applications and modules in business, information technology, and education.

Derby Mathematical Studies and Mathematics with Education follow similar courses at the outset before specialisms are decided. Mathematics and Computer Studies is also offered with an industrial placement.

Dundee Schemes are offered in which students can take Mathematics for one year only, or to honours level. The Department teaches a broadly based mathematics syllabus in Levels 1 to 3 leading on in Level 4 to a set of options. Fifteen joint courses in Mathematics are offered and, additionally, further joint courses in Statistics. Scholarships available.

Durham* Maths courses cover Pure and Applied Maths and Statistics with optional modules e.g. finance, education arts and social science. The BSc and M.Maths courses are common with the choice being made later.

East Anglia* The course unit system gives considerable flexibility for studying Mathematics. The preliminary programme in Mathematics includes two compulsory units and one optional unit. By taking certain optional units students may then choose to follow one of several joint courses in Mathematics (with Computing, Economics, Environmental Sciences, Management, Meteorology or Statistics) or single honours Mathematics. The second and third years are planned on a unit system, allowing students further flexibility in the choice of options. A four-year degree programme also offers a year in continental Europe, Australia or North America. There is also a course in Biomathematics. (High research rating – Pure/App)

Edinburgh* The first two years of the Mathematics course cover pure mathematics (mainly in the Faculty of Arts) and applied mathematics (Faculty of Science) and two other courses in science, arts or social sciences. The third and fourth years specialise in mathematics with a wide range of options in the fourth year. There are degrees in Mathematics and Statistics, Applied Mathematics and Mathematics with Management or Music. Scholarships available. (High research rating)

Essex Students follow common first-year courses that can then lead on to degrees in Mathematics or Mathematics with Accountancy, Computing and Management or with a teaching qualification. Scholarships available.

Exeter* Most first-year modules are common to all single honours courses. Transfers to other courses are possible from Year 2. There is a wide range of degrees including combinations with management, languages, physics and finance and accounting.

Glamorgan Mathematics is offered as part of several degree programmes. The BSc Mathematics course can be taken as a four-year sandwich option, giving it a strong vocational emphasis. There are also courses in Financial and Computing, and Mathematical Sciences.

Glasgow* The Mathematical Sciences course involves the study of three disciplines: maths, statistics and computing science. There is also a degree course in Mathematics and Applied Mathematics. Joint courses include Astronomy, Computing Science, Business, Physics or Music and Statistics. (High research rating)

Glasgow Caledonian A course is offered in Mathematics for Business Analysis with a period of industrial placement in Year 3. Courses are also offered in Financial Mathematics and Mathematics for Computing.

Greenwich Several full-time and sandwich courses in Mathematics are offered, covering Mathematics, Statistics, Computing and Decision Science.

Heriot-Watt Nine courses are offered in Mathematics including Actuarial Mathematics and Statistics with options in computer science, economics, finance, education, nanoscience, physics, languages and management. Late transfers to other degrees in Mathematics are possible. Scholarships available. (High research rating – App)

Hertfordshire The main feature of the Mathematics course is that a choice may be made between a broad BSc course in Mathematics or more specialised courses in Computing/Mathematics, Financial Mathematics or Mathematics with Qualified Teacher Status at the end of Year 1. Mathematics is also offered in the Modular Degree Scheme.

Imperial London* 12 courses are offered with considerable flexibility to transfer between courses and between BSc and MSci options including Applied Maths, Statistics, Computer Science and a year in Europe. (High research rating)

Keele Mathematics can be taken as a single honours course or in combination with one from over 15 other subjects. In the first and second years the principal course covers pure and applied mathematics and statistics, while the third year offers a wide choice of topics, depending on the student's interests. A degree in Statistics is also offered. (High research rating – App)

Kent Three-year programmes are offered in Mathematics, Financial Mathematics, Business Mathematics and in Mathematics and Statistics, all of which may be taken with a year in industry.

Kingston Courses in Mathematical Sciences and Actuarial Mathematics and Statistics are offered along with Statistics and Medical Statistics degrees, including joint honours options. Scholarships available.

Lancaster* Courses are offered in Mathematics, Mathematics and Statistics and with Operational Research. A course is also offered in Financial Mathematics with the option to study in North America or Australia for a year.

Leeds* The School of Mathematics is one of the largest in the country. Flexible degree schemes are offered, including opportunities to study in Europe. Study of non-mathematical subjects is possible along-side Mathematics. The Mathematics course is for those wishing to concentrate on maths (with up to two non-maths modules). Mathematics Studies allows more time to be spent on non-maths subjects (including management, physics, chemistry, economics, geography, music and English), with the choice of a BSc or MMaths at the end of Year 2, and European options in both. Courses are also offered in Mathematics with Finance and also in Statistics. (High research rating – App/Stats)

Leicester* BA, BSc and MMaths courses are offered in Mathematics and Computational Mathematics and Mathematics with Computer Science. Astronomy or Management are also offered. Modules in French and German can be taken and there is an opportunity to study in Europe or the USA.

Liverpool* Over 20 courses are available in Mathematics, the Department also being responsible for courses in Statistics and Computing. Core studies form the basis of first-year programmes followed by specialisation in Years 2 and 3. Computer science can be studied alongside Mathematics in Year 2. Mathematics can be studied with Ocean and Climate Studies, Finance, Education, Statistics and Management. Mathematics is also offered as part of the combined honours programme for students with or without A-level Mathematics. (High research rating – App/Stats)

Liverpool Hope Mathematics is offered as a BA QTS degree for teaching in schools or as part of the Education Studies programmes.

Liverpool John Moores The course in Mathematics, Computing and Statistics aims to provide a broad programme across the three fields. Professional placement takes place in Year 3. Business Mathematics is also offered as a four-year sandwich degree and there is also a course Mathematics and Statistics for Industry.

London (King's)* The Mathematics curriculum is flexible and allows for a change of direction according to ability and interest. Specialist mathematicians in their third year follow courses of their own choice from a range of options in pure and applied mathematics and mathematical physics. Computer Science, Management, Astrophysics, Physics and Philosophy can also be taken with Mathematics. (High research rating – Pure/App)

London (LSE)* Mathematics is offered with Economics and there is also a course in Business Mathematics and Statistics. The latter has a common first year with Actuarial Science. (High research rating – Stats)

London (QM)* The School of Mathematical Sciences embraces pure mathematics, probability and statistics, astronomy and computing, joint degrees are also offered involving other departments. A course unit system is in operation that enables students to choose from a large number of courses, both within mathematics itself and also combining mathematics with another subject including Discrete Mathematics, Mathematical Sciences and Statistics. Mathematics can also be studied with Management, Languages and Physics.

London (RH)* Mathematics can be taken on its own or with a range of options. There is also a course in Mathematics with Statistics. (High research rating – Pure)

London (UCL)* A range of courses, including Astronomy, Economics, Statistical Science and Theoretical Physics, is offered with Mathematics and some sponsorships are possible. Small group tutorials and computer-assisted learning are important features of this course. There are over 30 options in Years 3 and 4. There are several Statistics degree courses. (High research rating)

London Metropolitan There are single and joint degrees in Mathematics, Statistics and Mathematical Sciences. Which includes statistics and operational research.

Loughborough* BSc and MMaths programmes are common over Years 1 and 2. All students study calculus, linear algebra, applied mathematics, mathematical modelling and probability and statistics. Courses include Mathematics, Mathematics and Accounting, Business, Actuarial Science or Language, Financial Management, and Mathematics with Computing, Economics or Management. Scholarships available. (High research rating – App)

Manchester* Three-year and four-year courses are offered with modules taken in subjects from other departments. Modern languages, Management, Philosophy and Statistics are offered in joint courses with Mathematics. There is also a course in Mathematics, Statistics and Operational Research. (High research rating – Pure/App)

Manchester Metropolitan In addition to a very flexible degree course in Mathematics, Business Mathematics can be taken with a wide range of subjects.

Napier Business Mathematics, and Business Studies with Operations Management are offered as three-year or four-year courses.

Newcastle* The Mathematics course structure allows students to defer their choice of final degree course until the end of Year 2. In addition a significant amount of time can be spent studying a minor subject eg. accounting, music, languages. There are degrees in Statistics, Mathematical Sciences and several joint Mathematics and Statistics honours combinations. Opportunities exist to take non-mathematical options including accounting, economics, computing and languages. Changing between the various degrees offered by the Department is a routine matter at the end of the first and second years. Scholarships available. (High research rating – App/Stats)

Northampton A large number of joint courses are offered with Mathematics.

Northumbria The course in Mathematics is a strongly vocational three-year or four-year programme with Year 3 spent on optional placement in industry or commerce. Mathematics is also offered as a joint honours course with Business Management.

Nottingham* Mathematics is a flexible course in which students take optional modules in statistics and pure and applied maths in the first year, in addition to mathematics. Transfer is possible between single and joint courses. Mathematics can also be taken as a joint honours course with six other subjects, including Engineering, Philosophy, Management Studies, Economics and Computer Science. Scholarships available. (High research rating)

Nottingham Trent The Mathematics degree covers mathematics, statistics and computing. Sport Science and Computer Science can also be taken with Mathematics and there is a course in Computing Sciences and Financial Mathematics.

Oxford* The three-year course in Mathematics is designed for students who require a sound analytical and numerical training. The four-year option leads to advanced research areas. There is a common first year for both courses. In addition Mathematics is offered with Statistics, Computer Science or Philosophy. Scholarships available. (High research rating)

Oxford Brookes* Mathematics is offered jointly with a wide range of subjects. Mathematical Sciences is a broad course including computing and statistics. A range of courses with Statistics and Business Statistics is also available.

Plymouth Five Mathematics courses are offered including combinations with Statistics, Education, Computing and Finance. Applied Statistics can also be taken with Management Science.

Portsmouth Several Mathematics courses are on offer, including Mathematics for Finance or Management or with Computing or Statistics.

Queen's Belfast* Three departments teach Applied Mathematics, Pure Mathematics, Statistics and Operational Research. All courses and all students register initially for Mathematics. Thereafter, depending on the student's interest and progress, transfers can take place to the other three specialisms at the end of Year 1 and from the BSc to the MSc course. Scholarships available.

Reading* Ten courses are offered in Mathematics, Applied Statistics, Mathematical Studies, Computational Mathematics plus several courses involving Statistics. For each degree there is a set of compulsory units and optional units. Students taking Mathematics also take a third subject in the first year that could include computer science, statistics, physics or meteorology.

St Andrews* The three departments – offering courses in Mathematics, Pure Mathematics, Applied Mathematics and Statistics – co-operate within a very flexible course structure. Mathematics can be studied as an Arts or Science degree, and combined with a range of subjects including, for example, Psychology, Logic and Philosophy of Science, languages, Scottish History and Hebrew. Two routes may be followed with a four-year MMaths 'accelerated' course or a BSc/MA degree with 40 options. Scholarships available. (High research rating)

See *University Degree Course Offers* (Trotman Publishing) for details of offers

Sheffield* The single honours degree in Mathematics provides a balance between pure and applied mathematics and statistics in all years. Mathematics is offered with a number of second subjects including Astronomy, Philosophy, Physics, Languages and Economics. (High research rating – App/Stats)

Sheffield Hallam The three main strands of Mathematics cover modelling, analysis and statistics. Mathematics, information technology and statistics are taken in Year 1. There are placement options in Year 3. Courses in Applied Statistics, Mathematics, Mathematics with Computer Applications and Business Modelling and Management are also offered.

Southampton* A common first year for Mathematics students includes calculus, geometry, mechanics, statistics and computing, followed in Years 2 and 3 by a wide range of options. This enables students to build a course best suited to their interests and needs. There are also degrees with Mathematics including Languages, Astronomy, Statistics, Management Sciences and Actuarial Studies. Biology, Computer Science and Operational Research are also available.

Staffordshire Joint courses are offered in Mathematics and Computing Engineering subjects.

Stirling The Mathematics and its Applications course includes statistics and provides graduates with a strong base for many careers. A range of subjects can be studied with Mathematics including Modern Languages, Environmental Science, Psychology and Management Science.

Strathclyde Mathematics students are offered a range of single and joint honours courses involving Mathematics and Statistics, Computer Science, Accounting, Economics, Finance and Management. A flexible modular structure allows students to tailor their own courses. A course in Mathematics with teaching is also offered. (High research rating)

Sunderland A teacher-training course (11–18 years) is offered in Mathematics.

Surrey* The Mathematics programme covers a broad range of mathematical subjects, with all students following the same lecture course for the first two terms, after which there is some degree of specialisation. The programme is unusual since it offers an optional year of industrial or professional experience for all students. Mathematics may be studied with Statistics, Computing Science, Music, Business or Management, and there is a course in Financial Mathematics. (High research rating – Stats)

Sussex* The Mathematics course provides a broad mathematical education. The degree structure is based on a core of mathematics combined with another subject. Second subjects include Computer Science, Economics, Education and Management Studies. Scholarships available. (High research rating – Pure/App)

Swansea There are several Part I courses in Mathematics. For non-specialists the Part I course in mathematical methods includes practical training in the use of computers. Part II courses include both single and joint honours courses including Applied Mathematics and Pure Mathematics. Mathematics is also offered with Sport Science and with a language (French, German, Italian, Spanish or Welsh) and with Management Science or a year abroad. Scholarships available.

Warwick* A number of Mathematics degree courses are offered, including Mathematics with Economics, Business and Philosophy and Mathematics, Operational Research, Statistics and Economics (MORSE), as well as several joint honours combinations. Depending on individual choice, the Mathematics programme contains 75% mathematics in Year 1 and between 50 and 100% in Years 2 and 3. The balance is made up from an extensive range of options. Statistics degrees are offered with Mathematics and the MORSE course. (High research rating – Pure/Stats)

West Scotland Mathematical Sciences is a three-year or four-year (sandwich) course covering a wide variety of mathematical topics – numerical studies, computing, statistics and operational research. Psychology and Computing can also be studied with Mathematical Sciences.

Winchester A teacher-training course in Mathematics is aimed at the Primary age range.

Wolverhampton Mathematical Sciences can be studied by way of degree courses in Applied Sciences and Modular Degree Schemes. There is also a degree course in Mathematical Business Analysis that includes accountancy, business law, pure mathematics and statistics, marketing and a language, and a BSc in Mathematical Business Analysis and Statistical Sciences.

York A balanced foundation of general mathematical knowledge occupies the first year of Mathematics courses, with flexibility for course transfer. The second and third years provide a wide choice of options including Mathematics with a year in Europe or in industry. Joint honours courses include Mathematics with Economics, Philosophy or Physics or Statistics, Education, Linguistics and Computer Science. (High research rating – Pure)

OTHER INSTITUTIONS OFFERING MATHEMATICS COURSES
Staffordshire Univ. Fed.

ALTERNATIVE COURSES
Accountancy, Actuarial Studies, Astronomy, Computing, Engineering, Management Science, Meteorology, Operational Research, Physics, Statistics.

MEDIA STUDIES

(including **Communication Studies**, **Journalism** and **Photography**)
(*indicates universities with the highest entry requirements)

SUBJECT REQUIREMENTS/PREFERENCES
GCE A-level: Language requirement for appropriate language course. Communication Studies, English and Media Studies may be preferred. **GCSE:** English and Mathematics often required.

SUBJECT INFORMATION
Check prospectuses carefully since subject content differs considerably between universities. Media courses generally focus on radio, television, journalism and the effects of the media on society.

Communication Studies courses are not necessarily a training for the media but extend to management, international communications, design and psychology. The courses listed here are those with the title 'Communications' and the reader is strongly advised to recognise the distinction that different universities and colleges give to this title and to research the courses carefully.

Abertay Dundee Media, Culture and Society is a theoretical study of the media focusing on social and political issues and the emerging possibilities of new media technology.

Aberystwyth A Media and Communications Studies course offers both theory and practice in both traditional and new media including film, journalism and the information society.

Anglia Ruskin Communication Studies is offered as a joint course with English, French, German and Spanish. There is also a Media Studies degree involving radio, TV, video and film. (High research rating)

Bangor The BA in Creative Studies enables students to pursue a variety of related subject areas including Creative Writing, American Literature and Culture, Film Studies, Theatre Studies, Media and Journalism or to combine modules from these programmes. These subjects are also offered as separate degrees.

Bath Spa The Creative Media Practice course offers a choice of two options from interaction design, digital photography, music technology, media production for TV and radio, PR and marketing for publishing and script-writing for TV and radio. There is also a degree in Media Communication.

Bedfordshire The Media Practices (Mass Communications) course covers marketing and public relations. There are also courses in Journalism, Public Relations and Media and TV Production.

Birmingham The Culture, Society and Communication (Europe) degree has some modules in media, culture and communication. The course involves the study of a modern language.

Birmingham City Media and Communication courses have specialisms in culture and society, journalism, multimedia, media photography, public relations, radio production and television and video. There is also a separate course in Television Technology and Production with a sandwich placement and Multimedia Technology.

Bolton The Media Writing and Production course covers screenwriting and digital video production with work in film studies.

Bournemouth* The Multimedia Journalism course involves news and feature writing, radio and TV journalism, shorthand, and information technology. Specialist options cover sport, politics and the arts. Other Media courses include Interactive Media Production, Television Production and Scriptwriting for Film and Television. There are also courses in communications with media, advertising and marketing and a Public Relations degree.

Bradford The Media Studies course offers options in several subjects including music technology, animation, film and TV. Courses cover technical, social and cultural aspects.

Brighton The media studies degree covers visual communication, marketing video and film with work placements in the industry. Education or Sociology can also be taken with Media Production. There is also a Communication and Digital Media course that introduces the underlying technologies of the media industry, and courses in Editorial Photography, Sport Journalism, and Media Studies.

Bristol UWE The Cultural and Media Studies degree is not a vocational course but focuses on the social sciences. There are also courses in Media Practice, Animation, Photography and Marketing Communications as a joint course. (High research rating)

Brunel* A course is offered in Communications and Media Studies – course focusing on the social aspects of the media and new communications and information technologies. A quarter of the course involves practical work. A rigorous and demanding course in Journalism is also offered.

Buckingham Two-year degrees are offered in Media and Communications for EFL/ESL overseas students. There is also a degree in Journalism.

Bucks New Practical courses include Creative Writing, Radio and TV Production, Advertising and Journalism.

Canterbury Christ Church The Media and Cultural Studies programme is a theoretical study of print media, broadcasting, popular music, cinema and the arts. Courses in Journalism and Communication Studies are also offered.

Cardiff* In one of the largest Media departments in the UK the Journalism, Film and Media course is a theoretical scheme with some practical work aiming to provide an understanding of the media industries and of mass communications in society. There is also a course in Language and Communication, which emphasises the study of language as a means of human communication.

Central Lancashire* The Journalism course also covers radio and television skills. There is a foreign language option. This well-established course is aimed at those wishing to become professional journalists and introduces the broader study of related areas such as law, politics and history. There are also courses in Moving Image, Media Technology, TV Production, Sports Journalism and International Journalism. There is also a degree in Communication and Popular Culture. See also **Combined courses**.

Chester Several media programmes are offered, including Journalism and Media Studies with specialisations in Radio, and Television Production. There is also a course in Communication Studies which covers the media, sociology, politics, management and public relations.

Chichester Courses are offered in Media Production (including media writing and design) and Media Studies (marketing, advertising, film and news culture).

City* The Journalism course emphasises practical journalism – City is one of the leading centres in the UK. A four-year course is offered with a school of journalism abroad. First-year students take a vocational language course (French, German or Spanish). Journalism can also be combined with Sociology, Economics or Psychology or Contemporary History. Media Studies is offered with Sociology.

Coventry A course in Communication, Culture and Media offers modules in film, television, photography, journalism, public relations and video. There are also courses in Media Production and Journalism.

Creative Arts Courses are offered in Journalism focusing on fashion, leisure, motoring, music and sport.

Cumbria There are courses in Journalism with Contemporary Culture, Creative Writing or Film Studies, Communication and Media studies and also a Media Production degree.

De Montfort Year 1 of the Media and communication course focuses on close analysis of media texts including advertisements, news stands, films and television programmes. Options in Year 2 include film studies, video production and photography (for single honours students) and a study of journalism, television, multimedia and the Internet. Students can also choose to study French or Spanish as part of their degree. Other courses include Audio Recording, Journalism, Radio Productions and Video and Animation Production, Media Production and Media Technology, Journalism and Broadcast Technology.

Derby Three-year full-time courses are offered in Media Production, Media Writing, Broadcast Media, and Film and Television Studies.

Dundee The Media Arts and Imaging course cuts across art and design, studying cultural expression. Courses are also offered in television and imaging by way of degrees in Animation, Illustration and Digital Screen Art.

East Anglia* A broad course is offered in Society, Culture and the Media which covers social studies and political aspects. It is not a professional or technical media course.

East London The courses in Media Studies and Multimedia cover aspects of the media including film, print, recorded music and the TV industry. Specialisations include electronic publishing, 3D graphics and video production. Other courses include Communication Studies and Journalism and Journalism with Creative Writing.

Edge Hill Courses are offered in Journalism, and in Media specialising in advertising, film and TV or music and sound. There are also joint courses in Media with Drama, Creative Writing, English or Film.

Essex Courses are offered in Language and Communication, Multimedia Production and Internet Technology, in Film Studies and in Sociology, Culture and the Media.

Falmouth (UC) Up to 60% of the course is spent on practical work on the course in Journalism.

Glamorgan The degree in Media Communications offers a theoretical study of the media. Courses in Media Production, Media Practice, Media Technology, Multimedia Studies, Journalism, Radio and TV, and Multimedia Technology are also offered.

See *University Degree Course Offers* (Trotman Publishing) for details of offers

Glasgow Film and Television Studies is a theoretical study of the cinema and TV in the 20th century.

Glasgow Caledonian Communication and Mass Media covers psychology, sociology, print design, writing, public relations, advertising, video production and marketing. There are also courses in Multimedia Technology and Journalism.

Gloucestershire Courses are offered in Advertising, Journalism, Radio Production, Media Communications, and Photojournalism with optional work placements.

Glyndŵr Two overlapping Courses are offered by way of Studio Recording and Performance Technology and Radio Production and Communication. There are also courses in Media Studies and Media Communications and in Broadcasting and Journalism.

Greenwich The Media Culture and Communication course covers communication studies, media studies, cultural studies and options in each of the three years. Courses are also offered in Media Writing, Creative Writing, Television Production Technology and Applied Photography. Courses are also offered in Journalism, Public Relations and Marketing.

Hertfordshire Courses are offered in Media Cultures, Mass Communications, Film, Journalism, and Media Technology or Production and Film and TV. Joint honours courses are also offered with Journalism and Media Cultures.

Huddersfield Journalism and Media can be taken with options in film, music, radio and sport. There is also a course in Digital Journalism whilst English can also be taken with Media.

Hull The course in Media, Culture and Society includes several specialist modules including screen writing, Hollywood and TV narrative.

Keele A dual honours course is offered in Media, Communications and Culture focusing on theoretical issues. 25 subjects combinations are available.

Kent The new Journalism degree includes history, politics and law, learning radio and TV skills. There are opportunities for work placements.

Kingston Several joint courses are offered with Media and Cultural Studies including Creative Writing, Media Technology, Film, Journalism and Television Studies.

Lancaster* The course in Media and Cultural Studies is largely theoretical, covering such topics as anthropology, language and social life, visual representation, media and marketing.

Leeds* The very popular Broadcast Journalism course is aimed at those seeking a career in the industry. Communications Studies is also taken at degree level and four electives are taken in Years 1 and 3 from another subject area. Courses are also offered in New Media, Journalism and TV Production. (High research rating)

Leeds Metropolitan Media and Popular Culture is a theoretical course. There are also courses in Communication Management and Journalism.

Leeds Trinity (UC) Journalism is offered also with Public Relations and Media Studies, also with Marketing.

Leicester* The Communications, Media and Society course is multidisciplinary, covering all aspects of the media, with modules in radio and TV production. Media Studies can be taken with Sociology or Psychology.

Lincoln Media, Culture and Communications is a theoretical study of TV, film, radio and print. There is also a course in Journalism which can also be taken jointly with eight other subjects. Other courses involve Media Production or Technology.

Liverpool* Communication Studies is offered with English and Business Studies, and as part of the BA combined honours programme. The course is theoretical in emphasis and includes topics on TV analysis, popular music, public media and the politics of language. There are also courses in European Film Studies with a modern language.

Liverpool Hope Media (single or combined courses) is a highly vocational programme covering TV, film, radio, digital photography, marketing, PR, print journalism and web design.

Liverpool John Moores The Media and Cultural Studies is a theoretical courses covering cinema history, TV, pop music, journalism, photography and advertising. There are also vocational courses in Journalism, International Journalism and Broadcast Technology.

London (Goldsmiths)* The Media and Communications course combines media practice and communication theory. The media element involves TV, radio journalism, video graphics and animation, photography, creative writing and scriptwriting. Other courses offered combine Media with Communication, Anthropology, Sociology and International Media. (High research rating)

London (King's)* Film can be studied with languages, Classical Studies, American Studies and Geography. Short courses in Film are also organised.

London (QM)* Courses are offered in Journalism and Contemporary History, Literature with Film Studies.

London (RH)* The Media Arts course covers both theory and practice and includes screen drama, screenwriting, documentary, creative sound and film and TV production. There is also a separate degree in Film and TV studies with an emphasis on Hollywood, UK TV and European Film.

London (SOAS) The Global Film and Media courses focues on Asia, Africa and the Middle East.

London Metropolitan Mass Communications is offered in a range of courses including Media Studies, Politics and Sociology. There are also joint courses in Media Studies with work placement in Year 3.

London South Bank The Media and Society course covers history, politics and sociology of the mass media. One-quarter of the course involves practical workshop experience. Media studies can also be taken as a joint course.

Loughborough The Communications and Media Studies course examines the social, political and economic impact of communication and the media. Publishing with English is also available. These courses came top in a 'student satisfaction' survey.

Manchester* Media, Culture and Society, and 10 joint courses with Film Studies are now on offer.

Manchester Metropolitan Courses are offered covering Media Technology and Television Production. A course is also offered in Communications. It covers sociology and psychology and a language. Specialisms include interviewing and counselling. There is also a course in Writing for Film and TV.

Marjon (UCP) There are single honours courses in Media Production, Sports Media and Media Writing and combined and single courses with Media Studies.

Middlesex Media and Cultural Studies covers sociology, politics, history and economics and there is also a course in Publishing and the Media. More practical courses include Media Writing, Journalism, Advertising and Public Relations.

Napier A very vocational course in Journalism is available for students totally committed to a career in this field. Students are prepared for careers in specific areas in the Communication course, eg advertising, public relations, marketing. The emphasis is on personal communication skills. It is not a Media Studies course. Communications and Publishing Media are also offered.

Newcastle* Media, Communication and Cultural Studies covers the study of communication from the psychological, sociological, managerial and cultural aspects.

Newman (UC) Media and Communication is offered as a minor or joint course with another subject.

Northampton A very large number of joint courses in Media Studies are offered including a course in Journalism.

Northumbria* There are courses in Media Production enabling students to specialise in scriptwriting, film/video production or animation, Advertising and Journalism.

Nottingham* Film and TV studies can be taken with French, German, Hispanic Studies and Russian. The International Media and Communication course is a theoretical study of global communications and can be taken with French, Russian, German or Spanish.

Nottingham Trent Broadcast Journalism covers studio practice and microphone technique. Practical studies take place with Central TV Midlands, radio and BBC Midlands. There is also a course in Communication Studies covering linguistics, psychology and sociology, and courses in Media and Cultural Studies.

Oxford Brookes* Publishing Media is offered in combination with over 40 subjects including Computer Systems, Multimedia Systems and Music. A Media Technology degree is also offered providing a study of electronics as applied to the media industry and there are also courses in Communications, Media and Culture or languages.

Plymouth The Media Advertising course covers theory and practice in the fields of photography, film and video. There are also courses in Media Practice and Society and Science and the Media.

Portsmouth Courses are offered in Media Studies, with a range of subjects including Journalism, Drama and Creative Writing. There are also several courses with Journalism.

Queen Margaret The Media courses of three or four year duration offer a study of the media industries with specialist media topics in Years three and four.

Queen's Belfast A course is offered in Cultural and Media Studies. It is interdisciplinary in character and involves studies in anthropology, sociology, politics and aspects of the media including film and music. There is also a degree in Film Studies.

Robert Gordon Publishing Studies with Journalism covers all aspects of publishing including editing, word-processing, bookselling and distribution. There is also a degree in Corporate Communication with Public Relations. Work placements and study abroad opportunities exit.

Roehampton Courses are offered in Journalism and News Media with an academic rather than a vocational bias. There is also a broader study of the media by way of the degree in Media and Culture.

St Mary's (UC) There is a practical and theoretical course in Media Arts.

Salford Courses are offered in Journalism and Broadcasting Studies, Communication and Cultural Industries and in Journalism, Audio Video and Broadcasting Technology, TV and Radio and Media Performance and Theatre Studies.

Sheffield* The Journalism Studies course covers theoretical and practical aspects of reporting and sub-editing and includes radio work and special journals.

Sheffield Hallam Media Studies offers a study of mass media from social, political and economic aspects. Journalism and radio reporting also feature in the course. There is also a separate Journalism degree. Communication Studies balances theory and practice in a range of media topics. Other degrees include Public Relations and Film and Media Production.

Southampton Solent Students in Year 2 of the course in Journalism may specialise in print or broadcast journalism and may take part in an exchange scheme in a European country. There are also courses in Digital Media, Sport Writing, Film and TV Studies, Media Technology and Communication.

Staffordshire There are degrees in Journalism, Media Studies, Film Production, and Music Broadcasting.

Stirling Journalism is offered and also Film and Media Studies which concentrates on the critical and theoretical work based on film, television, radio and the press. A limited amount of practical work is available. Students may choose to specialise in Film or Media. Over 20 joint courses are offered.

Sunderland There are degrees in Journalism, TV, Radio, Public Relations, Video and New Media. The Media Studies course is also offered as a joint honours programme and covers the social and historical aspects of mass media, radio, video, computing and photography with options in American film, British cinema, radio and print journalism. Over 40 joint courses are offered, also with Photography.

Surrey* Media Studies is offered either as a three-year full-time or four-year sandwich course focusing on TV, radio, print and the internet. Media can also be combined with languages, Dance and Music.

Sussex* A theoretical course in Media Studies is offered with Sociology, Cultural Studies and Modern Languages. A practical course is offered in Media Practice and Theory. (High research rating)

Swansea Media Studies (theory and practice) can be taken as a single honours course or with languages including Welsh. There is also a Public and Media Relations degree and a course in Language and Communication.

Swansea Metropolitan Media topics are covered in courses involving video and documentary video studies, design for advertising, photo journalism and digital media.

Teesside In addition to a broad Media Studies degree, technologies covered in the Multimedia course include virtual reality, networking, the Internet, computer games, medical computing and knowledge-based systems. There are also degrees in Radio and TV Production.

Trinity St David (Carmarthen) Media Studies can be taken with Creative Writing, English, or Fine Art.

Trinity St David (Lampeter) Media Studies is offered as a single honours subject or with a range of subjects in the joint honours programme. Topics covered include TV, video, photography, journalism and the popular music industry.

Ulster Media Studies is a modular course, designed to promote a critical understanding of mass media (film, TV, radio, photography and the press). Students spend one-third of their time on practical projects. In addition there are several Communications courses with joint subjects including Advertising, Counselling and Public Relations.

Warwick* Film and Television Studies covers history, Hollywood, the silent cinema, and TV studies.

West London Degree courses are offered in Advertising, Journalism, Radio Broadcasting, Media Studies Photography and Public Relations.

West Scotland Three degree courses are offered in Broadcast Production (theoretical and practical), Journalism and Broadcast Journalism.

Westminster Media Studies covers mass media in society and the ways in which it is managed and financed. There are pathways in public relations, journalism, medical journalism, radio and TV broadcasting. Courses in Photography can also be taken. (High research rating)

Winchester The Media Studies course is an academic degree focusing on cultural studies and media practices. A work placement opportunity exists in Year 3. There are also courses in Journalism, and Media Production.

Wolverhampton Media and Communication Studies is a broad study of the media, its management and impact on society. Some opportunities exist for practical work and the subject can be combined with two or three others. There is also a course in Journalism and Editorial Design involving reporting, page layout and design and some photography. Other courses include Broadcasting and Journalism, Creative Advertising, Marketing and Public Relations.

See *University Degree Course Offers* (Trotman Publishing) for details of offers

Worcester There are courses in Advertising, Public Relations and Journalism with joint pathways in English, Politics, American and Film Studies and a theoretical Media and Cultural Studies degree.

York St John Media is offered as a single honours course or with English.

OTHER INSTITUTIONS OFFERING MEDIA COURSES

Blackpool and Fylde (Coll), Bournemouth (UC), Bradford (Coll), Bristol City (Coll), Chesterfield (Coll), Coalville Stephenson (Coll), Colchester (Inst), Cornwall (Coll), Croydon (Coll), Durham New (Coll), Ealing (Coll), East Lancashire (Coll), East Riding (Coll), Exeter (Coll), Farnborough (UC), Grimsby (IFHE), Guildford (CFHE), Hereford (CA), Highbury (Coll), Hopwood Hall (Coll), Hull (Coll), Liverpool (CmC), Llandrillo (Coll), Neath Port Talbot (Coll), NESCOT, Newcastle (Coll), North East Worcestershire (Coll), North Warwickshire (Coll), Northbrook (Coll), Norwich City (Coll), Peterborough (Reg Coll), Plymouth (CAD), Ravensbourne, St Helens (Coll), Sheffield (Coll), Somerset (CAT), South Devon (Coll), South Essex (Coll), South Leicestershire (Coll), South Nottingham (Coll), South Tyneside (Coll), Staffordshire (Reg Fed), Stratford upon Avon (Coll), Suffolk (Univ Campus), Swansea (Coll), Swindon (Coll), Truro (Coll), Tyne Metropolitan (Coll), Walsall (Coll), Warwickshire (Coll), West Cheshire (Coll), Wiltshire (Coll), Wirral Metropolitan (Coll), Worcester (CT).

ALTERNATIVE COURSES

Advertising, Communication Studies, English, Politics, Psychology, Public Relations, Publishing.

MEDICINE

(*indicates universities with the highest entry requirements)

SUBJECT REQUIREMENTS/PREFERENCES

In almost all cases, three A-level grades are expected including A* grades, with Chemistry at A-level normally required, plus one or two other science subjects. If only two sciences are offered, then a third 'rigorous' academic subject should be included in the choice of A-levels. Some medical schools also stipulate subjects at AS-level. Pre-medical courses do not require science A-levels: contact medical schools for their requirements.

SUBJECT INFORMATION

Candidates are required to limit their applications to four choices and submit their UCAS forms by 15 October and applicants to Oxford, Cambridge and the Royal Free and University College Medical School are required to take the Biomedical Admissions Test. All courses will offer the same components leading to a career in medicine. Many medical schools have moved away from an emphasis on lectures and factual learning to a system based on acquiring appropriate skills and understanding as well as knowledge. This system is referred to as the 'New Curriculum', which introduces communication, problem solving and more directed self-learning. While there is a core curriculum of knowledge, the first three years integrate scientific and clinical experience, and there are fewer formal lectures and more group and individual work.

For outstanding students without science A-levels some pre-medical courses are available. Thereafter for all, a period of pre-clinical studies leads on to clinical studies. Intercalated courses of one year leading to a BSc are also offered and elective periods abroad in the final years can sometimes be taken. All courses are very similar in content. Other courses in the medical field include Dentistry, Nursing, Pharmacy and Pharmacology, Biological Sciences, Microbiology, Genetics, Anatomy, Physiology, Medical Sciences (a branch of biological science), Physiotherapy, Occupational Therapy, Osteopathy, Chiropractic, Podiatry and Radiography.

Deans of medical schools have decided unanimously to adopt a policy of 'no detriment' for applicants to Medicine who list one non-medical course on the UCAS application. However, applicants should know that if they receive four rejections for Medicine and accept an offer for a non-medical course, they are not officially allowed to change their decision and attempt to re-open negotiations with medical schools if they achieve higher A-level grades than expected.

When selecting applicants, admissions tutors first look for evidence of academic excellence, not just for its own sake but because a medical course is long and demanding, and the ability to apply oneself and to survive is extremely important. Secondly, a longstanding interest in medicine is always an advantage, together with evidence that the applicant has a well-rounded personality, a wide range of interests, imagination, research potential, and is socially aware. A year out is also becoming an asset with some medical schools. A history of mental illness – even the mildest form – can be a bar to entry, and students' physical and mental stability is often under review. The confidential report from the applicant's school is very important. In addition to A-level applicants, most medical schools have a small annual intake (four–eight) of graduates (usually dental or science). Early applications are advantageous and very serious consideration is given to the overall GCSE grades achieved. The fact that applicants have four choices does not mean that they will receive equal consideration from all the institutions named on their UCAS application. In Medicine this is especially so: applicants receiving one or two offers will often be rejected by other medical schools. Therefore medical applicants receiving even one offer and three rejections have little cause for concern, since any other offer they might have received would have demanded the same, or very similar, high level of attainment.

Letters have been received from medical schools indicating that they continue to receive applications from candidates who are not predicted by their schools to achieve grades above DDD. They stress the futility of such applications.

Aberdeen* Phase 1 covers the fundamentals of medical sciences followed in Phase 2 by the principles of clinical medicine. Clinical Teaching and Patient contact from Year 1. An intercalated BSc Medical Sciences degree is offered with placements across the Highlands and Islands.

Birmingham* A curriculum based on student-centred learning and teaching combines the basic sciences and clinical experiences. The modular system of learning enables students to focus on their personal preferences. Courses leading to a BSc in Anatomical Studies, Medical Biochemical Studies, Pharmacology or Physiology are offered to promising students. Medical students who have attained honours or distinction standard at the end of the second year may take an extra year leading to a BSc in Medical Sciences which is also a stand-alone degree of four years with a year in industry. (High research rating)

Brighton* Brighton and Sussex Medical School students are members of both universities. The course offers an integrated programme of academic and clinical experience with students working with patients from the first term. From Year 3, students are based at the Royal Sussex County Hospital in Brighton. Experience of Medical Practice in different medical settings in the UK or abroad takes place in Year 4.

Bristol* The majority of applicants embark on the five-year course which is divided into three phases, with early patient contact in the first two terms. Each year 40% of students intercalate in a Medical Science or Humanities Subject. Bristol operates a European Credit Transfer scheme with 14 other schools in which a student may spend not less than three months in a participating medical school. A preliminary year of study in available for students without science A-levels. (High research rating)

Cambridge* The course of study in Medical Sciences falls into two periods, the two- or three-year preclinical period spent in Cambridge and the clinical course of three years and one term in the Cambridge Clinical School at Addenbrooke's Hospital. About half the students however choose to go to other medical schools, usually Oxford or London. Some students may devote the third year of the pre-clinical course to reading one of a variety of subjects for Part II of the Natural Sciences or Medical Science Tripos leading to a BA degree, before embarking on the clinical course. Applicants are required to take the BMAT test. (High research rating)

Cardiff* Students have direct patient contact from Year 1, the science curriculum extending throughout the course. A core course occupies approximately 75% of the curriculum and student-selected components form the rest, enabling students to explore topics to greater depth. The pre-medical course of six years is available for those without the required A-level subjects.

Dundee* A pre-medical course is available for those students who do not have the necessary science qualifications. The Medical course is 'problem-orientated, student-centred and community-based'. Promising students may, after the second year, take a one-year in-depth course leading to a degree in Anatomy, Biochemistry, Biomedical Engineering, Forensic Medicine, Human Genetics, Microbiology, Psychology, Pathology, Pharmacology or Physiology. Dundee also offers special modules such as Sports Medicine and Human Rights and Travel Medicine. (High research rating)

Durham (Stockton)* The university is now jointly offering a five-year medical course through Newcastle University. The first two years of study take place at the Stockton campus after which students are based at NHS regional centres in the North East. It is designed to provide a broad medical education leading to later career specialisation. Much of the learning is 'case-led', involving the presentation of a patient case. See under **Newcastle** (to which applications are made).

East Anglia* The course includes clinical and life sciences as well as socio-economic aspects (eg sociology, psychology, epidemiology, management, health economics, law and ethics). Clinical presentations will be grouped into units of learning based on body systems. Students will spend a substantial part of each year gaining clinical experience with patients.

Edinburgh* A six-year course with a pre-medical year is offered. In the five-year course, Years 1 and 2 cover principles for practice, Year 3 introduces clinical medicine, Year 4 focuses on the process of care and Year 5, preparations for practice. Important vertical themes in the curriculum include clinical skills, public health, pharmacology and therapeutics and the psychological aspects of medicine. (High research rating)

Exeter* See under **Peninsula Medical School**.

Glasgow* The MBChB programme introduces clinically-based exercises from Year 1. Learning takes place in small groups. Studies involve care and vocational modules and attachments.

Hull* The Hull-York Medical School was established in 2003 to offer a standard medical programme leading to entry to the medical profession. Years 1 and 2 are based in either Hull or York but all students follow the same course. In Years 3, 4 and 5 the groups combine to follow a programme of community- and hospital-based study in centres in East and North Yorkshire.

Imperial London* The course consists of three main elements that run throughout five of the six years. These are the scientific basis of medicine, doctor and patient, and early clinical experience from the first year. The final phase of the course consists of three senior rotations designed to prepare you for your final written and practical examinations. (High research rating)

Keele* The five year course has five themes, which run through the course: (a) scientific basis of medicine (b) clinical communication (C) individual communication and population health (d) quality and efficiency in health care and (e) ethics, personal and professional development. There is also a Health Foundation year.

Leeds* The course has three main phases – 'Preparing for clinical practice' (Years 1, 2 and 3), 'Clinical practice in context' (Year 4) and 'Becoming a doctor' (Years 5 and 6).

Leicester (Leicester and Warwick Medical School (LWMS))* The five-year medical course is divided into two phases. Phase 1 – Foundations, clinical skills, medical sciences, social and behavioural medicine, learning how to learn, learning to integrate. Phase 2 – Developing skills, organising learning, the elective, preparing for the house officer (pre-registration) year, testing skills, intercalating year and life after medical school. See also **Warwick**.

Liverpool* The main themes of the medical course focus on problem-based learning and cover structure and functions in health and disease, individuals and society, public health and professional practice.

Clinical skills are introduced in Year 1. A problem-solving approach is used with small-group teaching support.

London (King's)* The integrated programme of study in Medicine comprises basic medical science and clinical teaching over the first four years including special study modules in medical and non-medical areas (for example arts subjects). Students are encouraged to take an intercalated BSc degree course of one year after the end of the pre-clinical period. Subjects offered include Anatomy, Biochemistry, Pharmacology and Physiology. A foundation course in Natural Sciences (Medicine) is offered for candidates with no science A-level background. The course covers chemistry, biology, physics and maths and successful completion guarantees a place on the medical degree. (High research rating)

London (QM)* The curriculum for the five-year course at Barts and the London Medical School is based on five stages: fundamentals of medicine, systems in health, disease, specialities, integrated clinical studies and preparation for practice. A student centred teaching approach is used introducing early patient contact from the first term. (High research rating)

London (St George's)* The MBBS has been designed to enhance the integration between scientific and clinical disciplines and to develop self-directed learning skills.

London (UCL)* The degree is organised in three main phases: science and medicine (Years 1 and 2), science in medical practice (Years 3 and 4) and preparation for practice (Year 5). Promising students can take an additional year at the end of their pre-clinical course to take a BSc degree. (High research rating)

Manchester* The curriculum is organised around problem-based learning and incorporates early patient contact from Year 1. Intercalated degrees are available after either Year 2 or Year 4 leading to BSc. From Year 3, students are assigned to one of four major teaching hospitals. A pre-medical programme is available for students without science subjects and a European Studies option enables students to study abroad for part of the Medical course. (High research rating)

Newcastle* Phase 1 (two years) of the medical course is taken either at Newcastle or Stockton. Students come into contact with patients at the start of the course, being attached to a family doctor and accompanying them on some of their rounds. Clinical applications are emphasised throughout the course alongside basic sciences. Students not taking science subjects may apply for the pre-medical course. See also **Durham**.

Nottingham* The medical course is fully integrated and includes early patient contact. It covers a two-year study of basic medical sciences (Years 1 and 2) and a special medical sciences course (Year 3) lasting one year and leading to the BMedSci degree. Clinical practice takes place during Years 3, 4 and 5. This is followed by clinical practice lasting 26 months, which includes the last term of the third year.

Oxford* The course in Medicine lasts six years. The pre-clinical course lasts three years. This is followed by the clinical course, which is based in the John Radcliffe Hospital. A significant part of this course is examined by continuous assessment. (High research rating)

Peninsula Medical School* The Medical degree is awarded jointly by the Universities of Exeter and Plymouth where students spend Years 1 and 2, with the remainder of their course in different locations in Cornwall and Devon. The course covers life and human sciences, clinical skills, public health and professional development, with patient contact commencing in Year 1.

Queen's Belfast* A one-year pre-medical course is available for five students without the necessary science qualifications. (The course is likely to be phased out in 2011.) An integrated five-year course (system based and student centred) is offered linking the basic sciences with clinical experience (the latter from the second semester). Students achieving high marks in the second MB examination can take a one-year course leading to the BSc in Anatomy, Biochemistry, Medical Genetics, Medical Microbiology, Pathology or Physiology.

See *University Degree Course Offers* (Trotman Publishing) for details of offers

St Andrews* Medical Sciences is a three-year degree course and leads to the ordinary degree of BSc in three years or to an honours degree in four years. Studies cover molecular biochemistry, human anatomy and human physiology. Half of graduates progress to a clinical place at Manchester University Medical School to follow the three-year clinical course, the remainder have a place at one of the four medical schools in Scotland, almost a third at Edinburgh. (High research rating)

Sheffield* There is a foundation science year in Medicine for those who do not have the required combination of A-level subjects. The medical course aims to integrate the basic and clinical sciences and to cultivate in students a desire for intellectual curiosity and to equip students with the essential personal and professional skills. The three main stages of the course cover basic sciences (Stage 1), acquisition of clinical skills (Stage 2), and the refinement of skills (Stage 3). (High research rating)

Southampton* The first three years of the course are planned as a single exercise with integrated teaching programmes. In addition, there are courses in psychology and sociology, and patient contact in the early stages either in the hospital or the home. The first clinical attachments take place in the third year. The course is highly rated by students. The Medical School does not normally interview applicants. (High research rating)

Sussex* See under **Brighton**.

Swansea The Medical Sciences degree has elective modules in biological sciences, clinical sciences, the philosophy and social sciences of medicine and the history or literature of medicine. The course can lead to the graduate entry scheme for Medicine.

Warwick* Warwick Medical School is the only all-graduate medical school in the UK.

York* See under **Hull**.

ALTERNATIVE COURSES
Anatomy, Biochemistry, Biological Science, Dentistry, Nursing, Pharmacy, Physiotherapy and Speech Therapy.

MUSIC

(*indicates universities with the highest entry requirements)
(Scholarships are offered by most institutions)

SUBJECT REQUIREMENTS/PREFERENCES
GCE A-level: Music is usually the highest grade in the offers made.

SUBJECT INFORMATION
Theory and practice are combined in most of these courses to a greater or lesser extent. The menu of options is varied – choose with care!

Aberdeen Music is offered in the MA and BMus degree programmes Topics covered include musical history (Baroque, classical and 19th century), composition, style and performance. Opportunities exist for study abroad. Music Studies is also offered as the minor part in several major/minor degrees including Religious Studies, Divinity, Celtic and Philosophy.

Abertay Dundee The degree in Creative Sound Production aims to develop skills in music industry knowledge and general business awareness. It involves the study of production techniques for drama, radio, film and animation.

Anglia Ruskin Subject areas in Music include practical and historical studies, electronic music and recording techniques, jazz, rock and pop music and arts administration, and music teaching. There are also degree courses in Creative Music Technology and Audio and Music Technology. Music can also be taken with Drama and English. The performance Arts degree covers, Drama and Music.

Bangor BA and BMus courses are offered. The Department is active in the following areas: music history, composition, performance and interpretation, music and society (world music, Celtic music), popular culture and music in Western society, music technology including electro-acoustic composition. The degree in Music Technology is subject to approval.

Bath Spa In addition to the Music degree, which includes classical, jazz, musical theatre and world music, programmes are offered in Creative Music Technology and Commercial Music.

Birmingham* The Music course provides a wide general grounding in musicology (music as an academic discipline). Studio composition and performance at the same time offer each student the opportunity to develop special interests. Keyboard skills are covered in the first and second year and there is also an introductory course in electro-acoustics and studio techniques. The university has a strong music tradition enhanced by the music life of Birmingham. (High research rating)

Birmingham City The Music course is offered at the Birmingham Conservatoire and provides the opportunity for specialisation and diversification. The principal study may be in any orchestral instrument including jazz and pop instruments. All students study the principles of teaching his or her instrument or voice. Options include early music, chamber music, folk, jazz, electronic and world music. There are also Music Technology courses. A BMus course in Jazz incorporates a Postgraduate Certificate in Education.

Bournemouth The Music and Audio Technology course focuses on the application of hardware and software technologies to create music. There is a 40 week placement in Year 3.

Bradford A course in Music Technology is offered with Media Studies.

Brighton The course in Music Performance and Visual Art utilises the visual art/music interface with close links between dance, theatre and music. There is also a Digital Music degree in which music is studied relating to computers and electronic instruments, and a course in Music Production.

Bristol* The two main aims of the Music course are to give a wide understanding of the European musical tradition from medieval times to the present day and to enable students to develop their own individual interests in historical, creative and practical fields. The modular syllabus allows for an extensive choice of options. There are also Music and Language courses (French, German and Italian) with Year 3 spent abroad. (High research rating)

Bristol UWE Music Systems Engineering is a three-year or four-year course focusing on electronics, computing and engineering, with options in manufacturing, business and language. There is also a course in Creative Music Technology with a sandwich placement and a course in Audio and Music Technology.

Brunel* Single and joint honours courses are offered in Music, with a special focus on 20th century and contemporary music encompassing Western classical, jazz, rock/pop and world music. Music is offered with Film and Television Studies, English and Drama, and there are also courses in Sonic Arts introducing music technology as a creative tool. Other courses cover Musical Composition and Contemporary Music and Performance.

Bucks New Courses can be followed in Audio and Music Technology, Music Industry Management (with Artistic Development, Digital Media, Live Production, Marketing and Studio Production), Music Production and with Lighting Design.

Cambridge* Performance has an important place in the Music course and is one of several aspects of study in which music is covered in a very broad syllabus, giving weight to the appreciation and history of the subject as well as practical techniques. (High research rating)

See *University Degree Course Offers* (Trotman Publishing) for details of offers

Canterbury Christ Church The Music degree covers performance studies, written musicianship, critical studies and ensemble and practical musicianship. There are also courses in Commercial Music, Music Industry Management and Music Production.

Cardiff* The Department of Music aims to provide a musical education that achieves an equal balance between theoretical and practical studies and the pursuit of vocal and instrument study. The BMus degree (the most specialised) enables students to offer another subject, for example modern languages, in Part I. The BA scheme includes Music and two other subjects in Year 1. A second-year placement in a European university is possible through the Erasmus-Socrates scheme. There are also courses in Cultural Criticism/Music and Music/Welsh. (High research rating)

Central Lancashire Courses are offered in Music Practice, Music Production and Music Theatre which includes a music audition. Most applicants sing at their audition.

Chester A theoretical study of Popular Music (Performance) with practical options involving live perform- ance, musicianship, improvisation and digital recording. There is also a course in Commercial Music Production at the Warrington campus.

Chichester The Music degree has four strands – Performance and Direction, Composing, Arranging and Improvising, Style and Genre, History and Culture. There are also courses in Musical Theatre, Performing Arts, Commercial Music.

City* The Music course is concerned with music in today's multicultural and technological society and is intended to bridge the gap between music as 'art' and music as 'science'. Topics include the psychology of music, an electro-acoustic studio project, Afro-American and popular music, music therapy, perform- ance and sound recording. Conservatoire-standard practical and instrumental tuition is provided in collaboration with the nearby Guildhall School of Music and Drama. (High research rating)

Coventry A course in Music Composition and Professional Practice is offered that includes performance and administration. There is also a course in Music Technology covering sound and acoustics, recording technology and music analysis and composition.

Cumbria Music can be taken with Contemporary Culture, Creative Writing or Technical Theatre. There are also degrees in Musical Theatre Performance, Popular Music and in Performing Arts (Acting, Dancing, Singing).

De Montfort A joint or combined degree in Music Technology can be taken. The course covers creative projects (digital music and sound), studio techniques, sound recording, audio engineering, musicianship and performance. The subjects can also be taken with Moving Image or Performance.

Derby There are courses in Popular Music and Music Technology which is also offered with either Music Production or Audio Systems Design.

Durham* The Music course aims to provide a wide and critical knowledge of music and to develop the basic skills. Provision is made for students to develop their own special interests, with flexibility in the third year for specialisation. Options include electro-acoustic compositions, ethno-musicology and palaeography. Music, which is also part of the combined honours in Arts course, is also offered with the Education Studies programme.

East Anglia* A central programme is followed in Music involving the study of musical style in the Western tradition, orchestration and development of aural skills. Later options are performance, compo- sition, conducting, history and criticism of music. Practical sessions are common and students pursuing the performance option receive private tuition. Music can also be taken with Mathematics or Computing or Technology.

East London Music Culture, Theory and Production is offered as a comprehensive study of performance and composition. There is also a degree in Popular Music.

Edinburgh* Music is a three-year or four-year honours course. In each year the curriculum is broadly divided between composition, history and practical studies. Options are introduced in the third year and include electronic music but also cover music technology and acoustics. There is also a BMus course in Music Technology. (High research rating)

Falmouth (UC) Popular Music and a BA in Music are offered with options in Performance, Composition and Music Technology.

Glamorgan A BSc course is offered in Music Technology involving practical electronics and business practices. The Sound Technology degree covers acoustics and sound for radio and TV. There is also a degree in Popular Music.

Glasgow* This MA degree is for students with some musical ability and an interest in cultural aspects. The BMus course is for those aiming for a career in music at ordinary (three years) or honours (four years) level and includes performance on the piano, organ, any orchestral instrument or voice (every student must have the ability to play the piano), writing from dictation and harmony. Courses in Electronics and Education with Music, are also offered.

Gloucestershire The course in Popular Music covers history, music production and creative work and a study of the music industry and professional practice. There is also a Music and Media Management degree.

Greenwich A degree in Entertainment Technologies and Music Production is offered to school leavers. There is a Creative Production and Technology course for students who have completed a HND in Music and who intend to pursue careers in the music industry.

Hertfordshire Courses are offered in Composition and Technology, Sound Design Technology and Entertainment Industry Management, which has three pathways in studio production, entertainment industry and the classical music industry. There are also over 15 joint courses with Electronic Music.

Huddersfield In Year 1 of the Music course equal weight is given to performance, composition and the history of music. In Year 2, students choose two of these subjects as their major areas of study, with the third subject being their minor study. In Year 3 two subjects are chosen – a major and a minor. The course encourages increasing specialisation throughout its three years. Music is offered with Drama, Journalism, History, Modern Languages or English. There are also Popular Music degrees and degrees in Creative Music Technology and Music Production and Sound Recording. (High research rating)

Hull The first year of the Music course is devoted to an intensive basic course in harmony, counterpoint, history, set works, analysis and aural work and the performance. In the second year, students select their special option. In the final year there is a choice between church music, passion and oratorio, and the symphonic tradition. Instrumental tuition in one instrument is provided. Music is offered with six modern language subjects. There are also courses in Creative Music Technology, Jazz and Popular Music and Performance Arts and Drama. (High research rating)

Keele Music or Music Technology must be taken as a single honours course or with a second subject from a choice of over 15 options including Educational Studies, American Studies, languages, International History, Neurosciences, Japanese and Business Administration. Specialisation is offered in European and American 20th century music. Pathways are offered in musicology, performance, non-Western music and composition. (High research rating)

Kent The course in Music Technology combines music and computer technology exploring sound design in the context of new media applications.

Kingston Two alternative Music courses are offered. One concentrates on performance, theory and musicianship, and complementary studies such as psychology, world music and music technology. The other is more concerned with music and technology, and covers electronic music, recording technology and business studies. (The Gateway School of Music Technology, based at Kingston, has recording facilities on site.) There is also a course in Live Arts (Art, Music and Performance).

Imperial London* A four-year BSc course is offered in Physics and Studies in Musical Performance.

Lancaster A BA (Music) course is offered, to enable students to develop their artistic and intellectual potential. There is also a Music Technology degree with options in sound recording, electronic music and computer music. The BA in Popular Music Studies is offered jointly with the Department of Media, Film and Cultural Studies. (High research rating)

Leeds* The Music course is designed with topics common to all students in the first year (analysis, aural training, counterpoint, harmony, and historical studies). From the second year it is possible to concentrate increasingly on one of four main options – performance, notation, composition, or history and criticism. Throughout the course there is a balance between theoretical and practical, academic and vocational aspects of music, irrespective of the options taken. There are also courses in Popular and World Musics Performance, Music Multimedia and Electronics, and joint courses with languages. (High research rating)

Leeds Metropolitan Courses are offered in Creative Music and Sound Technology, Music Technology, Performance and Production.

Lincoln Computer music and sound design are two of the modules in the Audio Technology degree.

Liverpool* The three-year Music course strikes a balance between academic and practical work. Musical history is central to many of the complementary studies in style, composition, analysis, orchestration and practical musicianship with pathways giving a popular or classical emphasis. During the first year of the single honours course all students take an additional subject of their choice. There is also a Music/Popular Music BA degree. Proficiency in performing is not absolutely necessary. (High research rating)

Liverpool Hope A large number of combined courses with music are offered in which students can specialise in popular or classical music. BA (QTS) students specialise in the latter.

Liverpool John Moores A very broad course in Popular Music Studies includes some work experience. There is also a course in Audio and Music Production.

London (Goldsmiths)* The Music course aims to develop music skills and associated areas of study. There is a strong emphasis on the study of contemporary music, electronic music and advanced musical analysis. There is also a course in Popular Music Studies. (High research rating)

London (King's)* Music can be studied as a single honours course or in combination with Applied Computing or German (a four-year course with a year spent abroad). The BMus course aims to provide students with a knowledge of the history and theory of music, composition and techniques of analysis. The Department does not offer instrumental or singing instruction which are usually studied through the Royal Academy of Music. (High research rating)

London (RH)* Music can be offered as a single or combined honours course. The course offers a detailed study of the historical, theoretical and practical aspects of music with a wide range of second- and final-year options including practical and performance work. (High research rating)

London (SOAS) The Music course has a strong focus on Asian and African music. The programme includes vocal and instrumental performance, although to a lesser extent in joint rather than single honours courses. (High research rating)

London Metropolitan In addition to the course in Event Management and Music and Media Management the university offers courses in the repair of musical instruments. There are also courses in Music Technology and Education.

Manchester* The aim of the Music course is to give students a thorough grounding in the theoretical, practical and historical aspects of the subject. The final year is spent in performance analysis, history and criticism. Drama is also offered with Music. (High research rating)

Manchester Metropolitan A very large number of combined courses are offered which include Music, Popular Music, Music Studies and Sonic Arts.

See *University Degree Course Offers* (Trotman Publishing) for details of offers

Marjon (UCP) The course in Live Music provides a programme of study focusing on performance technology and media work.

Middlesex There are courses in Music (Composition and Performance) and Jazz with modules in music publishing and business, also Music and Arts Management, and Sonic Arts.

Napier The Music course allows students to take a principal study (either instrument, voice or composition) and core academic studies. There is also a three-year or four-year degree in Popular Music.

Newcastle* Practical tuition takes place throughout the Music course, which also covers the history of music, compositional techniques, acoustics, electro-acoustic music and, in the first year, a subsidiary subject. Courses in Folk and Traditional Music and Popular and Contemporary Music are also offered.

Newport There is a degree in Creative Sound and Music offering courses in practice performance media and business.

Northampton The Popular Music degree includes a study of the music industry.

Northumbria A Performance degree is offered which has courses on music available.

Nottingham* The Music course is wide ranging and offers the chance to specialise at an early stage. The course covers both practical and historical studies as well as offering options in such topics as the music of the Middle and Far East, electronic music and the music of the 20th century. Philosophy is also offered with Music. (High research rating)

Oxford* The purpose of the Music course is not simply to offer professional training but to produce musicians who are proficient in the technique of the art and its history and criticism. It is a broadly based course which still allows students the opportunity to specialise as they proceed through the course. (High research rating)

Oxford Brookes* Music is offered with over 40 subjects (including Film, Psychology, History and English) or as a single honours course. There is also a course in Sound Technology and Digital Music and Sound and Media Technology.

Plymouth Sound and Music Production can be taken as single honours subject. Music is offered as a stand-alone subject and with Education Studies, and in the General Primary teaching course.

Queen's Belfast* The BMus course provides a thorough grounding in Western music from medieval times to the present day, together with keyboard skills, conducting, history, electro-acoustic music, compositional technique and styles. There is a flexible course structure in Years 2 and 3 that enables students to choose their own options in practical work, as well as 20th century and electronic music. The BA course is taken with one or more other subjects. There are also degrees in Music Technology and Ethnomusicology. (High research rating)

Roehampton Music is offered as a single honours subject or with a second subject, including Art History, Dance Studies, Health Studies, Sport and Popular Culture, Education and Psychology. The Music course focuses on technology, composition, performance and music therapy with the opportunity to specialise in one of these areas.

Salford The Music course focuses on performance, composition and history. Popular Music and Recording and Audio, Video and Broadcast Technology courses should be considered.

Sheffield The broad-based course Music aims to develop practical as well as academic interests. Two non-music modules are also studied in the first year. A wide range of options provides students with the chance to specialise. Music is also offered with East Asian Studies, Chinese Studies, Hispanic Studies or Korean Studies. A three-year degree in Traditional Music with Folklore Studies is available. (High research rating)

Southampton* History, analysis and composition are integrated throughout this Music course. The history of Western music is studied from the Middle Ages to the present day. In Years 2 and 3 students choose historical periods for special emphasis, along with a considerable choice of other topics ranging from madrigals to jazz. Acoustics, French, German, Management and English are also offered with Music. (High research rating)

Southampton Solent Five music courses cover popular and electronic music, music promotion, journalism and performance. There are also courses in Sound and Music Technology and Outside Broadcast Production Operations.

Staffordshire The Creative Music Technology degree focuses on audio recording, acoustics, multimedia, and the design of auditoriums and recording studios. Courses are also offered in Music Technology and Management. Some students spend a year in USA.

Strathclyde Applied Music offers three specialised routes – music teaching, community music and music and business.

Sunderland Music is offered with a wide range of subjects, including Business Law, European Studies, Journalism, Management, Education, and Psychology.

Surrey* The Music course is taken by students who have a particular interest in performance, conducting, composition or musicology. French and German may be studied but are not part of the degree programme. Music and Sound Recording (Tonmeister) is followed by those whose main concern is with the theory and practice of recording and the reproduction of music (a year is spent in industrial training in a studio, with a manufacturer or broadcaster). Creative Music Technology prepares students for careers in the contemporary and computer-based music industry. (High research rating)

Sussex* Music is also offered with Film Studies, Cultural Studies and with French, German, Italian or Spanish. Performance can be taken as an option in Years 2 and 3 providing students hold the Grade VIII music qualification. (High research rating)

Teesside Three-year full-time or four-year sandwich courses are offered in Digital Music and Music Software Development.

Ulster The BMus course combines academic study with practical training on one or two instruments. Music can also be taken in a Modular framework with other subjects.

West London The BMus course focuses on popular music performance. There are also courses in Music Technology, Music Performance and Composition, Popular Music and Applied Sound Engineering.

West Scotland Commercial Music with work experience and Music Technology are offered as three-year full-time degrees. The latter includes computer technology, recording, editing in the fields of audio and video production.

Westminster Commercial Music is a unique course that combines the production of commercial music based on rock and pop with a strong grounding of business, law and cultural studies. (High research rating)

Winchester Courses can be taken in Music Theatre.

Wolverhampton Music may be studied as a specialist award or as a joint, major or minor programme. Practical experience is offered over a range of instruments, singing and keyboard. Modules cover multi-track recording and computers, popular or non-European music. A Popular Music specialist degree is also available and there is also a course in composition and song writing.

York* The Music course is designed to enable students to explore music from various aspects and is concentrated in a series of projects, in which students are able to work at their own pace. Projects cover history and musicological topics, written techniques, analysis and composition, solo and ensemble performance, electronic and computer music. (High research rating)

York St John Music can be studied with Art, Design and Education. There is also a course in performance.

See *University Degree Course Offers* (Trotman Publishing) for details of offers

OTHER INSTITUTIONS OFFERING MUSIC COURSES

Bath (Coll), Blackpool and Fylde (Coll), Central SchSpDr, Colchester (Inst), Coventry City (Coll), Dartington (CA), Doncaster (Coll), Durham New (Coll), East Surrey (Coll), Exeter (Coll), Great Yarmouth (Coll), Grimsby (IFHE), Havering (Coll), Hereford (CA), Hull (Coll), Leeds (CMus), Leeds Park Lane (Coll), LIPA, London (RAcMus), London (RCMus), London (TrCMus), Manchester (CAT), Manchester (RNCM), Manchester City (Coll), Mid-Cheshire (Coll), Neath Port Talbot (Coll), Newcastle (Coll), Newham (Coll), NESCOT, North East Worcestershire (Coll), North Lindsey (Coll), Northbrook (Coll), Norwich City (Coll), Nottingham Castle (Coll), Nottingham New (Coll), Ravensbourne, Rose Bruford (Coll), Rotherham (CAT), Royal Scottish (AMD), Royal Welsh (Coll), St Helens (Coll), South Downs (Coll), South Essex (Coll), South Tyneside (Coll), Staffordshire (Reg Fed), Stratford upon Avon (Coll), Suffolk (Univ Campus), Truro (Coll), UHI Millennium Inst, Wakefield (Coll), West Anglia (Coll), West Thames (Coll), Wiltshire (Coll), Worcester (CT).

ALTERNATIVE COURSES

Acoustics, Anthropology courses, Band Musicianship, Drama and Theatre Studies courses, Electronic Music, Music and Sound Recording, Music combined courses, Music Technology, Performance Studies, Popular Music and Recording courses.

NURSING

(including **Midwifery**)
(see also **Health Studies/Sciences**)
(*Higher offer)

SUBJECT REQUIREMENTS/PREFERENCES

GCE A-level: Two to three subjects may be required. **GCSE:** English, Maths and a science subject. All applicants holding firm offers are required to provide documentary evidence that they have not been infected with hepatitis B.

SUBJECT INFORMATION

Nursing courses, usually covering the social sciences as well as practical work, lead to state registration in the chosen specialism. Financial support is given by way of a means-tested bursary and all tuition fees for student nurses are paid by the Department of Health. This list does not include diploma courses or degrees for already qualified and registered nurses.

Abertay Dundee Nursing and Mental Health Nursing are offered as pre-registration courses integrating academic studies with clinical experience. A degree is also offered in Mental Health Nursing with opportunities to undertake work-based learning.

Anglia Ruskin There is a common element of Nursing for all specialised areas that cover nursing fields in Child, Adult, Mental Health and Learning Disabilities areas. There is also a BSc Midwifery degree course.

Bangor The same Nursing course is followed by diploma and degree students, the latter having extra assignments requiring higher marks. After a common foundation programme of 18 months, branch programmes are offered in Adult, Child, Mental Health and Learning Disability Nursing. There is also a course in Midwifery with theoretical studies taking place in Wrexham and Bangor.

Bedfordshire Obstetrics, midwifery, the midwife practitioner, women's health, ethics and law are all covered in the Nursing degree. Specialisation is offered in Adult, Children's and Mental Health Nursing. A Midwifery course is also provided.

See *University Degree Course Offers* (Trotman Publishing) for details of offers

Belfast* This is a three-year course leading to registration as a nurse with the Nursing and Midwifery Council. In Years 2 and 3 students choose to specialise in one of the branches of nursing – Adult, Children's, Mental Health or Learning Disability.

Birmingham* The Nursing course involves a common foundation in Years 1 and 2 and consists of biological, social and medical sciences along with clinical placements with choice of specialism being made at the end of the first year. More clinical placements and specialised studies continue in Years 3 and 4. Specialist studies in Adult, Child or Mental Health Nursing commence in Year 2. An overseas elective period is also available.

Birmingham City Degree courses are offered in Midwifery and Nursing, the latter with specialist studies in Adult, Mental Health, Child Nursing and Learning Difficulties.

Bournemouth Clinical Nursing and Midwifery (Advanced Diplomas in both subjects and a degree in the latter) are both three-year courses and include five clinical placements. Clinical Nursing students decide whether to seek registration in Adult, Learning Disabilities, Mental Health or Child Health Nursing. See also **Health Studies/Sciences**.

Bradford A BSc Hons course in Midwifery Studies is offered and there is also a three year BSc in Nursing Studies with options in Adult, Child or Mental Health nursing.

Brighton The BSc degree in Nursing covers has pathways in Adult, Children's and Mental Health. Practice placements take place in the United Kingdom, Holland or Spain (with language studies). There is also a BSc course in Midwifery.

Bristol UWE Three-year degree programmes are offered at Diploma of Higher Education and degree level leading to Adult, Children's, Mental Health Nursing or Learning Disabilities. There is also a degree in Midwifery and a range of specialist degrees covering Palliative Care, Emergency Care and Child Health.

Bucks New The nursing degree has specialist avenues in adult, child and mental health nursing. Courses are taken at the Uxbridge campus.

Canterbury Christ Church Courses are offered leading to Adult, Child and Mental Health Nursing. There is also a course in Midwifery.

Cardiff* The Nursing course covers Adult, Children's or Mental Health Nursing (to be stipulated on the application form). Elective periods of study take place abroad. A course in Midwifery is also offered.

Central Lancashire The Midwifery course leads to full registration and involves clinical placements covering 50% of the course. A Nursing (pre-registration) course is offered focusing on Adult Nursing, Mental Health or Paediatric Nursing. There are also degrees in Herbal or Homeopathic Medicine and Child Health.

Chester The BSc Nursing degree has branch programmes in Adult, Child Health, Learning Disability and Mental Health. There is also a degree in Midwifery.

City* Nursing is part of a modular scheme (50% practice based) that includes psychology, sociology and philosophy. Selection of a major study can be deferred to the end of the first year. The total period of study involved is four years and four months. Specialisms cover Adult, Mental Health and Children's Nursing. A degree course in Midwifery is also offered.

Coventry Specialisation covers Adult, Child and Mental Health Nursing. A three-year course in Midwifery is also offered.

Cumbria There are degrees in Nursing (Adult and Mental Health) and Midwifery.

Derby BSc (Hons) Nursing courses are offered, specialising in Mental Health Nursing. In addition there are degrees in Community Practice and in Public Health.

De Montfort Nursing courses are offered with specialisms in Adult, Children's, or Mental Health Nursing. Degree courses in Midwifery, Community Health Nursing and Health Studies are also available.

Dundee Bachelor of Nursing and Diploma of Higher Education courses are offered. They cover nursing, applied biological sciences, applied social sciences, applied healthcare ethics, care management and health promotion. The degree course provides specialism options in Adult, Child and Mental Health Nursing. A Degree programme is also offered in Midwifery.

East Anglia* Three-year Nursing degree courses are offered and lead to Adult, Child and Mental Health Nursing and Learning Disability specialisms. There is also a degree in Midwifery.

Edge Hill Courses are available in Adult, Children's and Mental Health Nursing, in Learning Disabilities and in Midwifery.

Edinburgh* The four-year Nursing course enables graduates to qualify for registration in General or Mental Health Nursing. Clinical practice is integrated with theoretical teaching throughout the four years and the whole of the third year is spent in hospital training. Students are also introduced to the wider social, economic and organisational issues in healthcare. Supporting courses can be selected from a very wide range of subjects in the Faculties of Social Sciences, Arts and Science.

Essex See under **Health Studies/Sciences**.

Glamorgan Degrees are offered in Adult, Child, Learning Disabilities and Mental Health Nursing. There is also a degree course in Midwifery.

Glasgow* The common Nursing foundation programme also includes a community care scheme. Adult, Children's Nursing, Learning Disabilities and Mental Health Nursing are covered by this course.

Glasgow Caledonian Nursing Studies is a broad course preparing graduates for employment in a variety of healthcare settings. There is also a Midwifery course and a diploma leading to Operating Departments Practice.

Glyndŵr There are Pre Registration courses in Adult and Mental Health Nursing, and Community Nursing degrees in Children's, District, General Practice and Health Visiting. See also under **Health Studies/Sciences**.

Greenwich Several Nursing courses are offered with specialisms in Midwifery, Adult, Mental Health and Children's Nursing. Two courses are offered in Health and Learning Disabilities. There is also a degree in Midwifery. See also **Health Studies/Sciences**.

Hertfordshire The Nursing degree covers Mental Health, Adult and Child Nursing. Pre Registration Nursing, Health Visiting and Paramedic and Midwifery courses are also available. See also **Health Studies/Sciences**.

Huddersfield After a basic course in Year 1, the Nursing degree offers specialisms in Adult and Child Nursing, Learning Disabilities and Mental Health. Midwifery and Midwifery Studies are also available.

Hull Nursing is a four-year programme of theoretical and practical work leading to a BSc degree in Mental Health, Children's, Adult and Learning Disability Nursing. There is also a BSc Midwifery degree lasting 78 weeks. A Diploma course of three years leads to Adult, Children's, Mental Health or Learning Disability Nursing.

Keele Adult, Children's, Mental Health and Learning Disability are the specialisms on the Nursing degree. A course in Midwifery is also offered.

Kingston A BSc course is offered in Nursing.

Leeds* A Midwifery course is offered that leads to registration and there is also a BSc programme in Adult and Child Nursing.

Leeds Metropolitan A three-year Nursing course provides a foundation in nursing, and natural and social sciences in Year 1. In Years 2 and 3 students develop their technical skills, including nursing in adult and mental health areas. A course in Midwifery is also offered.

Lincoln A three-year course (each year of 45 weeks) leads to a qualification in Adult Nursing.

Liverpool* The Nursing degree is a three-year course leading to the degree (BNurs), with opportunities to specialise in district nursing, health visiting, clinical nursing, research or cancer Nursing.

Liverpool John Moores The three-year Nursing degree covers Child, Adult, Learning Difficulties and Mental Health Nursing. The Midwifery course is divided between theory and practice and includes options in the management of professional practice, law and ethics.

London (King's)* Nursing Studies focusing on Adult and Children's Nursing is based on three main areas of study – the biological, medical and social sciences. A substantial amount of practical work forms an integral part of the course (80 weeks in total) through St George's School of Nursing. Graduates qualify as Registered General Nurses at the end of the course. Courses are also available for qualified nurses in Midwifery and Community Nursing. There are also courses in Physiotherapy and Midwifery Studies.

London South Bank Nursing courses cover Mental Health, Child Care, Adult Health and Learning Disabilities.

Manchester* The BNurs degree course (covering Adult, and Mental Health Nursing) has a strong theoretical basis of nursing and midwifery practice, together with aspects of behavioural, social and biological sciences. There is also a degree in Midwifery. (High research rating)

Middlesex Special features of the four-year Nursing course lead to Adult, Mental Health or Children's Nursing. Clinical experience can be taken anywhere in the UK or abroad. A three-year full-time course in European Nursing is offered, introducing European nursing methods. Diploma and degree courses in Midwifery can also be taken.

Napier Nursing courses are offered in Adult, Child, Mental Health and Learning Disability specialisms. There is also a degree in Midwifery.

Northampton There are courses covering all aspects of nursing in addition to which there is a Midwifery degree.

Northumbria Nursing Studies is offered with specialism in Child, Mental Health, Learning Disabilities or Adult Nursing. There is also a Midwifery Studies course leading to registration.

Nottingham* The Master of Nursing (MN) course leads to a qualification in nursing and a professional qualification. The four-year course has a strong research foundation and provides pathways in Adult, Mental Health, Learning Disabilities and Child Nursing. There is also a pre-registration degree (shortened) in Midwifery.

Oxford Brookes* Nursing is offered with specialisms in Adult, Children's, Mental Health and Learning Disabilities. There is a Midwifery course and a specialist distance learning Nursing degree. Other courses include Mental Health Nursing and specialist courses for those with nursing experience.

Plymouth The three-year full-time Nursing course leads to specialisms in Adult and Child Nursing.

Queen Margaret A four-year Nursing degree is offered with a period of clinical practice. Some students may be entitled to a bursary in Years 1 to 3.

Queen's Belfast* The BSc Nursing course offers specialisation in Adult, Children's, Learning Disability and Mental Health Nursing in Year 2. There is also a BSc Midwifery degree.

Reading Nursing courses of a specialised nature are limited to health and social care practitioners.

Robert Gordon This four-year Nursing course has a common foundation programme followed by specialist studies in Adult, Children's or Mental Health Nursing.

Salford The three-year Nursing course provides programmes in Adult, Child and Mental Health Nursing. There are also three-year degrees in Midwifery and in Professional Studies in Nursing and Social work.

Sheffield* BMedSci courses are offered in Nursing (Adult, Children's, Mental Health and Learning Disability Nursing). A Midwifery course is also available.

Sheffield Hallam Three-year courses in Nursing Studies are offered with specialisms in Adult, Child, Mental Health Care Nursing and Learning Disability.

Southampton* Nursing degrees in Adult or Child Nursing, Mental Health and Learning Disabilities are available and a degree in Midwifery is also offered. Scholarships available.

Staffordshire Courses in Nursing focus on Adult, Child and Mental Health Nursing. There is also a degree in Midwifery Practice.

Stirling* The BSc Nursing degree covers Adult, Mental Health or Learning Disability branches.

Surrey* Nursing Studies degree courses lead to Child, Adult and Mental Health Nursing. There is also a Midwifery course. (High research rating)

Swansea Nursing students in Wales are paid by a bursary from the NHS Wales Bursary Scheme. It is not means tested. The course covers Adult, Child and Mental Health Nursing, prior to which a common foundation course is offered. There is also a Midwifery degree.

Teesside There are courses in Nursing specialising in Adult, Child, Mental Health and Learning Disabilities and also in Midwifery.

Ulster Years 1 and 2 and the final year of the Nursing course are suitable for students aiming for an Adult Nursing or Mental Health qualifications. Thirty-six units are studied, with both theory and practical placements in every year of the course. Theoretical units cover biological sciences, behavioural sciences (psychology and sociology), research and nursing.

West London Degree courses are offered in Mental Health, Child Health and Adult Health Nursing and also in Midwifery.

West Scotland Midwifery and Nursing courses (Adult and Mental Health) are offered at various campuses (Ayr, Dumfries, Hamilton or Paisley).

Wolverhampton Three-year courses are offered in Nursing and Midwifery.

Worcester Midwifery is offered as a three-year degree course and also Nursing in Adult, Child, Mental Health and Learning Disabilities.

York* Degrees are offered in all four branches – Adult, Children, Mental Health and Learning Disability. There is also a three year Midwifery Practice degree.

OTHER INSTITUTIONS OFFERING NURSING COURSES
Suffolk (Univ Campus), York (Coll).

ALTERNATIVE COURSES
Anatomy, Biochemistry, Biological Sciences, Biology and Applied Biology, Environmental Health, Health and Community Studies, Occupational Therapy, Physiotherapy, Psychology, Radiography, Social Administration and Speech Therapy.

PHARMACOLOGY

(including **Toxicology**)
(* indicates universities with the highest entry requirements)

SUBJECT REQUIREMENTS/PREFERENCES

GCE A-level: Two to three science subjects; Chemistry usually required. **GCSE:** English and Mathematics.

SUBJECT INFORMATION

Pharmacology is the study of drugs and medicine in which courses focus on physiology, biochemistry, toxicology, immunology, microbiology and chemotherapy. Pharmacologists are not qualified to work as pharmacists.

Aberdeen Pharmacology is offered as a Biomedical Science degree, in which there are no first- or second-level courses in Pharmacology. Level 3 comprises four units of study covering all aspects of the subject. Level 4 enables the student to make a study in depth of selected aspects, including Pharmacology or with Toxicology, and to carry out an extensive research project.

Bath Pharmacology is a three-year full-time course or a four-year sandwich course in which the third year is spent on industrial placement. In the first year the core subjects are cell biology, physiology, pharmacology and pathology, chemistry and computing skills. The second year develops these subjects more fully, and in the final year pharmacology is combined with a research project. Transfers are possible between the three- and four-year courses up to the end of Year 2. (High research rating)

Birmingham Pharmacology can be taken as part of the degree in Medical Science.

Bristol* Subjects covered in the Pharmacology course include chemistry, anatomy and biochemistry. In the second year, pharmacology is taken with anatomical science, biochemistry or physiology and one other course, and in the final year, pharmacology is studied throughout the year. There is a strong research base involving neuropharmacology and cell signalling with training in a wide variety of modern techniques. The MSci course includes a year in industry. (High research rating).

Cambridge* Pharmacology is offered as part of the course in Natural Sciences. It is accompanied by two related sciences in the second year (see under **Biological Sciences**). (High research rating)

Cardiff* The first year of the Pharmacology course deals with chemistry, biochemistry and physiology, pharmacology, and toxicology. In Part II, practical experience is combined with theory in a number of specialised areas, which include an insight into the philosophical implications of drugs and society.

Central Lancashire Pharmacology is offered with Physiology.

Coventry The course in Medical and Pharmacological Sciences focuses on a study of pharmacology and physiology and applications in medicine. It can be taken with a year in professional placement.

De Montfort See under **Chemistry**.

Dundee The Pharmacology degree begins in Year 2 after a first year in allied sciences with biology or chemistry, and is taken as a single honours or joint honours with Biochemistry or Chemistry. During the third year two courses are taken – pharmacology of systems and pharmacology of drug action. The rapidly developing area of neurosciences features strongly in Year 4. Four-year full-time degree courses are also offered in Pharmacology and Physiological Sciences and Biochemistry and Pharmacology. See also **Biological Sciences**.

East London The first year of the four-year sandwich course in Pharmacology is taken in common with Applied Biology and Medical Biotechnology, and transfer between courses is possible. Second-year students take pharmacology, human physiology and biochemistry. The third year is spent in industrial training. Fourth-year students take pharmacology and toxicology and undertake a research project. Toxicology and Pharmacology can also be taken as extended degrees.

Edinburgh* Biology and physiology are taken by all students specialising in Pharmacology. Pharmacology and three other subjects are taken in Year 3 and pharmacology is studied throughout in Year 4. See also **Biological Sciences**.

Glasgow* Pharmacology students enter the honours course after studying biology, chemistry and related subjects for the first two years. Students may register for a degree with a work placement in research or industry in the UK or abroad.

Glasgow Caledonian Specialist studies in Pharmacology are chosen in Year 2 after a common first year with students aiming for Food Bioscience, Microbiology and Cell Biology.

Hertfordshire Pharmacology is offered as a three-year full-time or four-year sandwich course and there are also options for a year in North America or Europe.

Imperial College* Pharmacology and Transitional Medical Science is offered with a year in industry.

Kingston Pharmacology is offered as a three-year full-time or four-year sandwich course. Final-year topics include toxicology, drug development and biotechnology in healthcare. Joint courses are also offered.

Leeds* Pharmacology is a broad scientific course as opposed to an applied study and is taken with physiology and biochemistry in the first year. This is common to all students who can delay their choice between single or combined courses until the end of Year 1. There are also four combined honours Pharmacology degree courses offered with Biochemistry, Chemistry, Physiology and Management Studies.

Liverpool* Pharmacology is studied as part of the Life Science scheme. A basic core of units is studied followed by a choice of other units to suit the student's interests. At Liverpool the emphasis is given to the physiological, biochemical, toxicology and clinical aspects of pharmacology. There are also three-year full-time and four-year sandwich courses in Chemistry with Pharmacology. (High research rating)

London (King's)* A single honours degree is offered in Pharmacology and also a joint degree with Physiology. In the first two years the focus is on physiology, biochemistry and pharmacology. In the third year, specialist topics include toxicology, immunology and environmental pharmacology. See also **Biological Sciences**.

London (UCL)* Pharmacology is the study of how drugs work. Students take physiology, chemistry, cellular and molecular biology, and pharmacology in their first year. A range of advanced courses in the final year allows students to concentrate on particular aspects of the subject and undertake a research project. (High research rating)

London Metropolitan A single honours course is offered in Pharmacology.

Manchester* Five courses are offered in Pharmacology, including joint courses with Physiology with Industrial Experience and with a Modern Language; one with industrial experience is also offered.

Manchester Metropolitan A three-year full-time or four-year sandwich course is offered in Physiology with Pharmacology.

Napier Toxicology is offered as a three-, four- or five-year course and there is also a degree in Immunology and Toxicology.

Newcastle* Pharmacology is a modular course with a wide range of biological sciences studied in Stage 1. More advanced topics of pharmacology follow in Stages 2 and 3 covering anti-cancer drugs, cardiovascular pharmacology and toxicology. There is also a degree in Physiology. See also **Biology**.

Nottingham Trent Pharmacology is offered with Physiology and with Neuroscience. See also **Biological Sciences.**

Portsmouth The Pharmacology course has a common first year with Biomedical Science. This is a three-year full-time or four-year sandwich course and includes a study of physiology, biochemistry and chemistry to support studies in pharmacology. Overall the course has a biochemical focus towards modern pharmacology with an emphasis on pharmacology in all three years.

Queen Margaret Applied Pharmacology is a three year single honours degree. The course covers medical microbiology, health psychology, clinical science, nutrition and neuroscience.

St Andrews Pharmacology is offered with Chemistry.

Sheffield* Pharmacology is studied in a joint department with Medicine and located in the Royal Hallamshire Hospital, thus the student is able to relate the scientific and clinical aspects of the subject.

Southampton* The Pharmacology degree is based on both physiology and biochemistry and looks at the design of drugs and their biological effects. A one year placement is possible.

Strathclyde* In the Biochemistry and Pharmacology degree course, physiology and chemistry are taken in the first year with biochemistry and pharmacology, followed by advanced studies in biochemistry and pharmacology in the second and third years. Final-year modules include drug development, mammalian toxicology, psycho-pharmacology and immuno-haematology. A four-year full-time degree is offered in Immunology and Pharmacology and there is also a degree involving industrial placement.

Sunderland Pharmacology is offered as a full-time, sandwich or extended degree. There are also courses in Chemical and Forensic, Pharmaceutical Sciences.

Surrey* Pharmacology and Toxicology are offered as a pathway in the three-year full-time or four-year Biochemistry degree.

Ulster A three-year degree without work placements is offered in Pharmacology.

Westminster Pharmacology can be studied in a joint three-year degree with Physiology.

Wolverhampton A three-year course is available in Pharmacology focusing on immunology, human physiology and microbiology and also a Pharmaceutical Science degree.

ALTERNATIVE COURSES
Agricultural Sciences, Biochemistry, Biological Sciences, Chemistry, Dietetics, Food Science and Pharmacy.

PHARMACY
(including **Pharmaceutical Sciences**)
(* indicates universities with the highest entry requirements)

SUBJECT REQUIREMENTS/PREFERENCES
GCE A-level: Two to three science subjects. Chemistry usually required. **GCSE:** English, Mathematics and a science subject.

SUBJECT INFORMATION
All Pharmacy courses are very similar and lead to qualification as a pharmacist who may then work in hospitals or private practice. All the Pharmacy degree courses listed below lead to an MPharm degree. They are all of at least four years' duration. Programmes are fully accredited by the Royal Pharmaceutical

See *University Degree Course Offers* (Trotman Publishing) for details of offers

Society. In order to practise as a fully qualified pharmacist an additional pre-registration year must be completed, supervised by a registered pharmacist, followed by passing the Society's professional examinations. Pre-registration experience is an integral part of Pharmacy courses and leads to Membership of the Royal Pharmaceutical Society of Great Britain. **Pharmaceutical Science courses do not prepare students for careers as pharmacists.**

Aston* The Pharmacy course covers the basic sciences and includes communication skills and computing in Year 1. In Year 2, pharmacology occupies one-third of the total time along with pharmaceutical and medicinal chemistry. In Years 3 and 4, a core course includes chemotherapy, disease mechanisms, toxicology and professional practice. There is an emphasis on professional studies and patient-oriented care.

Bath* Pharmacy is a four-year full-time course introduced by basic studies in biology, human biology, pharmaceutical chemistry and physical pharmacy. Pharmacy practice takes place in the second year and third years with clinical pharmacy being the focus in Year 4 leading to the MPharm degree. (High research rating)

Bradford* The course in Pharmacy includes two six-month practical training periods in two different areas of practice in the third and fifth years as part of this five-year sandwich course. There is also a four-year full-time course. Both courses satisfy the training and registration requirements for practice as a pharmacist. A degree in Pharmaceutical Management is also offered involving marketing, human resource management and language options (French, German or Spanish).

Brighton The Pharmacy degree covers microbiology, clinical pharmacology, legislation, marketing management, computing and statistics. In Years 3 and 4, core subjects involve chemotherapy, pharmaceutics, and an opportunity is provided to gain work experience in hospital and in community pharmacy. There is also a course in Pharmaceutical and Chemical Sciences covering chemistry, biology and biochemistry.

Bristol UWE The three-year full-time course in Pharmaceutical Sciences offers three options in the final year from bioinformatics, drug delivery, toxicology, nuclear medicine, phytomedicine, synthetic chemistry and genome analysis. A fourth year with work placement is also possible.

Cardiff* The Pharmacy course with an intake of 120 students each year is divided into four main divisions: pharmaceutical chemistry and pharmacognosy (natural products, synthetic drugs and their effects on living tissues); pharmaceutics (design, production and control of all medical preparations); and clinical pharmacy (the law and practice of pharmacy). All subjects are covered in each year of the four-year course. (High research rating)

Coventry Pharmaceutical Sciences, with or without a study in Europe, prepares students for laboratory careers but not pharmacy.

De Montfort A degree is offered in Pharmacy in which pharmaceutical science subjects are taken in Years 1 and 2. In Years 3 and 4 a number of elective topics are offered combined with pharmaceutics, pharmacy and clinical studies. A degree course is also offered in Pharmaceutical and Cosmetic Science.

East Anglia* The four-year degree in Pharmacy covers pharmaceutical chemistry, physiology, genetics and pharmacy practice, leading to the MPharm degree and full professional registration. Professional placements take place in the community, in hospitals and in industry. There are also degrees in Pharmaceutical Chemistry, Biomedicine and Biological and Medical Chemistry.

Greenwich An MPharm degree at the Medway School of Pharmacy is offered leading to full registration in Pharmacy. The degree in Pharmaceutical Sciences lays a foundation in chemistry, biology, physiology, product formation and process technology, with mathematics and computing. Further studies include micro-organisms, drug testing, pharmacokinetics and quality assurance. Professional recognition is available for the Pharmaceutical Sciences course which can be taken as a four year sandwich course.

Hertfordshire Pharmaceutical Sciences, with or without a year in Europe or North America, or work placement is offered as a three- or four-year course.

Huddersfield A Pharmacy degree is offered and also a course in Pharmaceutical Science can be studied as a three-year full-time course or with industrial placement for one year.

Hull* Courses are offered in Pharmaceutical Science with optional industrial experience.

Keele The Pharmacy course can include a Foundation year for those without science A-levels.

Kent* The Medway School of Pharmacy offers an MPharm degree, which includes placements in hospitals and in the community.

Kingston A range of three-, four- and five-year full-time and sandwich courses is offered in Pharmaceutical Science, with options available for placements in industry. At the end of Year 1 students may be considered for transfer to the MPharm course at King's College London.

Liverpool John Moores The accredited four-year Pharmacy course includes study of the scientific basis of therapeutics, dosage form design, medicinal chemistry and quality control, pharmacy practice and veterinary pharmacy. There are also courses in Pharmaceutical Science.

London (King's)* The Master of Pharmacy course commences with a four-week pharmacy orientation course. This is followed by an integrated programme covering 'the Principles of Pharmacy', 'Pharmacy and Therapeutics' and 'Pharmacy into Practice'. (High research rating)

London (School of Pharmacy)* Pharmaceutical chemistry, pharmaceutics and pharmacology are studied in Year 1 of the Pharmacy course; all these subjects are developed in Year 2 with a study of drug development with microbiology and chemotherapy. In Years 3 and 4 students take courses in drug design and testing, and clinical pharmacy, and visit hospitals; they also specialise in one elective subject. (High research rating)

London Metropolitan Pharmaceutical Sciences is offered as a single honours course. A one-year placement or six-week placements occupy part of the course.

Manchester* A standard Pharmacy course is offered that leads to full qualification of the MPS to work as community, hospital or industrial pharmacists. A Foundation year is also offered. (High research rating)

Medway School of Pharmacy See under **Greenwich** and **Kent**.

Northumbria* Pharmaceutical Chemistry involves the design, preparation and metabolism of drugs. The course is offered as a three- or four-year programme.

Nottingham* In the MPharm Pharmacy course the main subjects taught are pharmaceutics, pharmaceutical chemistry and pharmacology. In each of the two summer vacations, students are encouraged to take posts in some branch of pharmacy, the Department assisting students to find suitable posts. The course is biased towards careers in industry, hospital pharmacy and research. Scholarships available. (High research rating)

Nottingham Trent Courses can be taken in Pharmacology with Medical Science.

Portsmouth* The first-year foundation courses in Pharmacy cover pharmaceutical chemistry, physiology and biochemistry. Advanced and professional studies plus electives follow in Years 3 and 4. A three-year full-time course in Pharmaceutical Sciences is also offered.

Queen's Belfast* In the first year of the four-year course students are introduced to pharmacy, physiology, dispensing and aspects of microbiology. These lead on to a study of the traditional subjects (pharmaceutics, pharmacology and pharmaceutical chemistry). Topics are included that reflect the pharmacist's wider role as a member of the healthcare team and involve visits to hospitals, health centres and industrial pharmacy.

Reading* Entrance scholarships are available for applicants to the M. Pharm. degree at Reading (visit www.rdg.ac.uk/student finance, for details). Professional experience is gained by way of short placements during Years 2 and 3.

Robert Gordon The Pharmacy course develops the scientific basis of pharmacy through the study of pharmaceutics, pharmacology and pharmaceutical chemistry. It also develops the application of this knowledge to practical situations and the communication skills necessary to perform competently as part of the healthcare team in the clinical situation.

Sheffield Hallam Three- or four-year courses are offered in Pharmaceutical Sciences, which covers chemistry, biomedical sciences and pharmacology.

Strathclyde* This accredited degree provides several themes throughout the course including pharmacology, physiology and pharmaceutical practice and care.

Sunderland In the Pharmacy course a knowledge of the action and uses of drugs is achieved by a study of pharmaceutical chemistry, pharmaceutics and associated subjects. These studies are combined with ancillary computer appreciation, maths and statistics. Optional modules include drug information handling, clinical pharmacy, toxicology, health education and quality control. A course is also offered in Chemical and Pharmaceutical Sciences.

Ulster An MPharm degree in offered leading to professional recognition.

West London A unique course is offered in Ayurvedic Studies. This course covers the fundamentals of pharmacology and toxicology along with the history and philosophy of Ayurveda and the language of Sanskrit.

West Scotland Based on the chemical and biological sciences, the degree in Pharmaceutical Sciences can be taken with work experience in industry.

Wolverhampton A four year MPharm course in Pharmacy has practice placements in Years 1, 2 and 3.

ALTERNATIVE COURSES
Biochemistry, Biological Sciences, Chemistry and Pharmacology.

PHILOSOPHY

(* indicates universities with the highest entry requirements)

SUBJECT REQUIREMENTS/PREFERENCES
GCE A-level: No specific subjects required. **GCSE:** English and Mathematics. **Aberdeen, Dundee, Edinburgh, Glasgow, St Andrews** English, Mathematics or a science and a foreign language. **Oxford, Cambridge** Grade A in most subjects preferred. **Sussex** Grade B in a foreign language.

SUBJECT INFORMATION
Philosophy is a logical rigorous study of the most fundamental and general problems that arise in human thought. Contemporary philosophy covers political, educational, psychological, aesthetic and religious issues. Some reading of the works of the leading philosophers is recommended before applying for the courses.

Aberdeen The single honours course in Philosophy provides a grounding in the history of the subject and an understanding of its contemporary development. Topics cover political, social, moral, scientific and religious philosophy. Joint courses are offered with a range of options including languages, Physics, Sociology, Anthropology and Psychology. The history of philosophy is a key element in the course.

Anglia Ruskin Metaphysics, aesthetics, moral and political philosophy are covered in the single honours degree. Philosophy can also be taken with Drama, English and Film Studies. There is an opportunity to study for one semester in the USA.

Bath Spa Philosophy and Ethics can be taken as a major, joint or minor component with another subject eg. English, Sociology, History.

Birmingham* Central areas of philosophy including ethics, logic, moral, political philosophy and the philosophy of the mind are studied in the first year of Philosophy. These courses provide a basis for later and more advanced studies in Kant's philosophy, analytical philosophy, ethics and visual arts. Optional courses are also available in the second and third years when students design their own programme. Joint courses are offered. (High research rating)

Bolton Career planning and development and work-based learning are special features on the Philosophy course. Core and option modules are offered in each year of the Philosophy course.

Bradford Philosophy can be studied in conjunction with the degree course in Interdisciplinary Human Studies (see under **Combined Courses**) or with English or Sociology.

Bristol* The Philosophy course aims to present a thorough understanding of contemporary philosophical issues (political, psychological, linguistic and aesthetic) and provides a grounding in the subject covering philosophy in antiquity and from the 17th century onwards. Course choices and specialised topics give students considerable freedom to select those areas of philosophy that are of particular interest to them. Transfer from any one of the 15 joint courses to the single honours course may be possible in Year 2 depending on aptitude and departmental numbers. (High research rating)

Bristol UWE Philosophy is offered as a joint honours course with over 12 other subjects.

Cambridge* The Philosophy Tripos is divided into three parts, each taking one year. In the first year a study is made of logic, ethics and metaphysics, followed in the second year by a choice of two subjects from the philosophy of science, aesthetics, politics and experimental psychology (which includes some lab work). A range of options in Part II (third year) allows for a closer study of topics studied in the first two years. Philosophy of Science can be studied with History in the Natural Sciences Tripos. See under **Biological Science**. (High research rating)

Cardiff* No previous knowledge of philosophy is required for the degree in Philosophy, which begins with the practical relevance of political and moral philosophy and the theory of knowledge in Part I. In Part II the main branches of philosophy are covered, with a wide choice of courses available. Joint courses are also offered in Social Philosophy, and Applied Ethics, and another Humanities subject, the History of Ideas and Philosophy and a range of other subjects.

Central Lancashire Modules in critical and creative thinking, consciousness, freedom and value form part of the degree in Pure and Applied Philosophy. Philosophy is also offered as part of the combined honours programme as a joint or minor course with English Literature, Health Studies, Politics, Sociology or Religion and Culture.

Cumbria The course in Philosophy and Ethics covers such issues as business, media and medical ethics.

Dundee The Philosophy course covers the history of philosophy in the first two years, ethics, moral problems and other specialised studies. General courses follow on continental philosophy and other options including the philosophy of religion (Christian or Indian), aesthetics and the philosophy of science, European politics and history, international relations and fine art. This is an innovative department which also offers a course in Art, Philosophy and Contemporary Practices.

Durham* Philosophy can be studied as a single honours course, a joint course or in the combined honours Arts or Social Science or Natural Sciences programmes. All students take a common first-year course. In the second and third years of the honours course students choose from a wide range of topics. A course in Philosophy, Politics and Economics is also offered. (High research rating)

East Anglia Single and joint courses are offered with considerable flexibility. The courses have an emphasis on the links between Philosophy and other subjects in the humanities and social sciences and over 20 modules are offered covering art, science, religion, history, the leading philosophers and mental health. Joint courses can be taken with History and Politics.

Edinburgh* A first-year course in philosophy is taken by all students on all Philosophy courses, which has options in aesthetics and general philosophy, the history, logic and philosophy of science, metaphysics and moral philosophy. This continues in the second year with options to take courses in sociology and politics while in Years 3 and 4 specialisation begins. There are five joint courses with Philosophy also a degree in Mind and Language covering philosophy, linguistics and psychology.

Essex In the Philosophy course, the main topics covered include the introduction to philosophy and logic, reason and experience and 20th-century continental philosophy. Other specialisms involve the philosophy of religion, the arts, law, literature, rights, Freud and psychoanalysis and ethics. There is also a course with an international exchange. (High research rating)

Exeter* A large number of combined honours courses are offered in Philosophy including options with modern languages in which a year is spent abroad. Ohter programmes also allow for a year of study in Europe, North America and Australia.

Glamorgan The course in Philosophy and Contemporary Thought includes topics such as ethics, logic, 'green' political thought, healthcare, and modern European philosophy. Philosophy can also be studied with Politics, Psychology and English Studies. Philosophy can also be taken as a minor or joint course.

Glasgow* Philosophy is studied within the Social Science programme and includes general and moral philosophy and the work of the leading philosophers. A very large number of joint courses are also offered including Celtic Civilisation, Scottish Literature, Polish, Computing, Anthropology, Mathematics and Management Studies. The honours course contains 20 core and optional papers.

Greenwich The Philosophy course covers aspects of the western philosophy tradition from the Greeks to the present day including literature, political science and language. Philosophy is also offered with, for example, Business, Psychology, Mathematics, Education, Creative Writing and Law.

Hertfordshire Philosophy can be taken as a minor subject in the Combined Studies programme and also as a major or single honours course in the Humanities modular scheme. Computing, Psychology, Law, and Journalism and Media Cultures can be studied with Philosophy.

Hull The first two terms of the Philosophy course are devoted to an introduction to the subject – its history, methods and problems. Over the next six terms, courses are taken in epistemology (theory of knowledge), moral philosophy and metaphysics. Students then choose courses to develop their own interest. Seventeen joint honours courses are also offered, and also Politics, Philosophy and Economics. (High research rating)

Keele Philosophy can be taken with a choice of over 20 dual honours options, including Mathematics, Educational Studies, Politics, English and Psychology. The course aims to develop the student's analytical and critical abilities. Final-year options include the philosophies of mind, religion and politics.

Kent* After an introduction to Philosophy in Part I, core courses in Part II cover moral philosophy, theory of knowledge, logic and social philosophy, aesthetics and ancient philosophy. Options courses are also offered as specialised studies in the second and third years, and also the opportunity to spend a year abroad. Philosophy can be studied in 14 honours programmes, including Business Administration, Drama, Religious Studies, Social Anthropology, European Languages, Computing and Social Behaviour.

Kingston History of Ideas joint courses are offered.

Lancaster* Two other subjects are taken with Philosophy in Year 1. These are followed in Years 2 and 3 with a range of options covering various aspects of philosophy. Philosophy is also offered with Religious Studies and there is also a PPE course. Exchange programmes with European and American universities are possible.

Leeds In Year 1 of Philosophy two philosophy courses are taken (introduction to ethics and reason and argument) plus two other subjects. In Years 2 and 3 courses include the history of ancient, medieval and modern philosophy, ethics and social philosophy and logic. Philosophy can be combined with 20 other subjects including Artificial Intelligence, Chemistry and History. Second-year logic is taught with the assistance of computers. (High research rating)

Liverpool* The Philosophy course provides a solid foundation in core areas of western analytical philosophy and involves ethics, epistemology and logic plus another subject in the first year. The non-philosophy subject can be continued in the second year along with a further compulsory philosophy topic. In the third year, students choose areas of special interest to them taken from a wide range of options.

Liverpool Hope Philosophy and Ethics can be taken as a single or combined honours programme.

London (Heythrop)* Philosophy students follow courses in logic, epistemology, metaphysics, ethics or political philosophy and the history of philosophy, as well as two courses from a wide range of options, and produce a dissertation on a special topic. Philosophy may be combined with Theology or Religion and Ethics or Psychology.

London (King's) Five compulsory subjects are taken through the Philosophy course – logic and methodology, Greek philosophy, modern (17th/18th century) philosophy, ethics or political philosophy, epistemology and metaphysics. Students also choose two options from a wide range including aesthetics, religion, language, science and the philosophy of the mind as well as a study of the great philosophers. Philosophy can also be taken with languages, Mathematics, Physics, Religion or War Studies. (High research rating)

London (LSE)* Philosophy, Logic and Scientific Method focuses on commitment to clarity of expression and argumentative rigour and the links with the social and natural sciences. Several 'outside' options are offered including anthropology, economics, history, linguistics, politics, psychology and sociology. The courses offered are in Philosophy and Economics and Philosophy, Logic and Scientific Method. (High research rating)

London (UCL)* First-year Philosophy students attend introductory courses in logic and methodology, epistemology and metaphysics, Greek philosophy, modern philosophy, and ethics or political philosophy. These studies continue in the second and third years with a wide range of subject options. Philosophy can also be taken as a joint subject with Economics, Greek, or the History of Art. (High research rating)

London Metropolitan The Philosophy course provides a wide coverage of topics with Level 2 and 3 units including the philosophies of language, science and technology, artificial intelligence and virtual reality, para-psychology, psychoanalysis, war, law, ethics, art and gender. Courses in Ethics are also offered and there are programmes in Politics, Philosophy and Economy with specialist options.

Manchester* Philosophy is a broad course covering the main subject topics such as the philosophy of modern religion, modern political thought, psychology, law and a language. Philosophy is also offered with Politics. (High research rating)

Manchester Metropolitan Philosophy is offered as single, joint and combined honours programmes and can be studied with, for example, Sport, Cultural Studies, Marketing, Health Studies and Drama.

Middlesex Philosophy can be taken as a three-year full-time degree or as a joint honours programme with Religious Studies, a Modern Language, Translation or English Literature. It also forms part of the Fine Art and Critical Theory course.

Newcastle* There is a course in Philosophical Studies – Knowledge and Human Interests, which can be taken as a single honours course or as part of the Combined Studies (BA) Programme.

Newman (UC) Philosophy course with either Theology or with Religion and Ethics can be taken as a minor course with a second subject.

Newport Religious Studies and Philosophy can be taken with Creative Writing, Sports Studies, History or Psychology.

Northampton Fifty-six joint courses are offered with Philosophy.

Nottingham The Philosophy course provides a rigorous training in analytical philosophy. The department's strengths include metaphysics, mind and language. Subsidiary subjects can also be taken from other departments and optional choices form the major part of the third year. Scholarships available.

Oxford* Philosophy is offered as part of several joint courses that share a common structure. For the course in Philosophy, Politics and Economics, all three subjects are studied equally in Year 1. In Years 2 and 3, all three subjects can be continued or two main subjects can be chosen. Philosophy is also offered on its own or with Theology, with nine options in Modern Languages, or with Mathematics, Physics, Physiology or Psychology. (High research rating)

Oxford Brookes* Philosophy can be studied as a single subject or with a range of joint subjects including Anthropology, Molecular Biology, European Culture and Society, Fine Art, Mathematics, Psychology, Sociology and Theology.

Queen's Belfast* Philosophy can be studied as a single, joint or major/minor subject or in conjunction with other subjects including Scholastic Philosophy, Theology, Sociology, Psychology and Ancient History. In both cases a study is made of the works of leading philosophers over the last 2500 years, on debates relating to truth, proof, meaning and value, science, aesthetics and law.

Reading* Philosophy offers modules in logic and theory of knowledge and moral philosophy – subject centred rather than author centred. Thereafter, other courses follow, covering a range of specialisations that could include the philosophy of law, language, mind, science, religion or logic. A year abroad is spent by students combining Philosophy with a modern language. (High research rating)

Roehampton Philosophy is offered as a single or combined honours course with subjects such as Classical Civilisation, History, Human Rights and Theology and Religious Studies. Years 2 and 3 provide a choice of modules in the main areas of philosophy such as ethics, metaphysics and moral and political philosophy.

St Andrews* Degree courses are offered with Philosophy as both single and joint honours in the Faculty of Arts or Science. Programmes of study in Year 1 include reasoning and argument, knowledge and learning, logic, morals and political philosophy, with more specialist topics following in subsequent years. Scholarships available. (High research rating)

St Mary's (UC) The Philosophy degree draws on Christian, Islamic, Jewish and Indian traditions.

Sheffield* Philosophy in Year 1 is organised around the self, knowledge, ethics, religion, society, existentialism and science. A generous system of optional courses provides a wide choice of specialist subjects in Years 2 and 3. (High research rating)

Southampton* Single and combined Philosophy honours courses are offered, the latter available with Economics, English, Politics, French, German, Film, History, Mathematics, Politics or Sociology. The course is planned (as are most others in this subject) on the assumption that entrants know little about the subject.

Staffordshire The main focus of the Philosophy course lies in modern European philosophy. A range of other subjects can be studied with Philosophy, including Film Studies, Law, Journalism, Sociology, Modern History and Legal Studies.

Stirling Philosophy is taken with two other subjects in Part I with semesters in introduction to philosophy, the justification of behaviour, and the scope and limits of knowledge. Part II involves logic and language, rationalism and empiricism and a choice from a wide range of options. Combined Studies courses are also offered with 14 subject choices including Film and Media Studies, Politics and Japanese Studies. A course is also offered in Politics, Philosophy and Economics. (High research rating)

Sussex* Students specialise in two of the central areas of moral and political philosophy – modern continental philosophy and analytical philosophy. (High research rating)

See *University Degree Course Offers* (Trotman Publishing) for details of offers

Swansea The three core disciplines, Philosophy, Politics and Economics are strongly represented throughout the course, unlike the 'pick and mix' programmes offered by some other UK universities.

Trinity St David (Lampeter) Western and many facets of Eastern philosophy can be studied on three-year and four-year Philosophy courses. Options include mathematical logic and foundations of mathematics. There is a range of courses in Philosophical Studies.

Warwick* Philosophy can be offered as a single honours or a joint course with Mathematics, Literature, Psychology, Computer Science, Classical Civilisation, or Philosophy, Politics and Economics. In Year 1, students wishing to broaden the scope of their degree can take courses in other subjects, for example economics, film studies, French studies, history, history of art, mathematics, politics.

Winchester The course in Ethics and Spirituality is studied within Theology and Religious Studies and can be taken as part of a combined honours degree.

Wolverhampton The Philosophy course covers ethics, law, logic, philosophy of science, political philosophy and the philosophy of the mind. Religion, feminism, ecology and history also feature. A three-year full-time or four-year sandwich course in Human Rights is also offered.

York* A single honours and a range of integrated courses can be studied on an 'Equal' basis in which Philosophy is taken with English, French, German, History, Linguistics, Sociology, Mathematics and Physics. A Politics, Philosophy and Economics course is also offered. See also **Combined courses**.

ALTERNATIVE COURSES
Psychology, Religious Studies, Social Sciences.

PHYSICS

(including **Applied Physics**)
(*indicates universities with the highest entry requirements)

SUBJECT REQUIREMENTS/PREFERENCES
GCE A-level: Mathematics and Physics usually required. See prospectuses for foundation courses.

SUBJECT INFORMATION
There is a considerable shortage of applicants for Physics courses, which means that there is a likelihood of some courses being discontinued: check with the university. Many courses have flexible arrangements to enable students to follow their own interests, for example circuit design, microwave devices, cosmology, medical physics and solid-state electronics. (Research ratings below also include **Astronomy**.)

Aberdeen The Physics (Natural Philosophy) course starts with a broad introduction at Level 1, including astronomy, the physical universe, mechanics, electricity and magnetism, with practical studies in physical computing. In Level 4 specialisms are offered in statistical or biomedical physics, neuroscience and optical engineering. Physics is also available with Geology, Gaelic, Mathematics and a number of other subjects.

Aberystwyth Honours courses are offered in Physics and physics-based courses with specialisation in other areas, for example Planetary and Space Physics, or Atmospheric Physics. Part I of these courses includes similar modules that allow for specialisation in Year 2, ranging from optics and nuclear physics through astronomy, stars and galaxies to meteorology and global warming, depending on degree choice.

Physics with Business Studies (two-thirds Physics, one-third Business Studies) is also offered. There is also a degree in Space Science and Robotics.

Bath* Physics is a three-year full-time or four-year enhanced sandwich course, the latter having a placement year in industry in the third year, possibly in some European countries. Several degrees are offered in which all students follow a common course for the first two years with final choices between the BSc or MPhys courses and study abroad or full-time university study in Years 1 or 2. There are about nine applications per place. (High research rating)

Birmingham* The first two years are common to both BSc and MPhys degrees, and cover basic physics and maths, after which a study of the major areas of physics continues with a wide choice of options allowing considerable flexibility for students to build their own course. Personal tutorials and small-group teaching take place throughout the three years of the course. Physics can also be taken with Astrophysics, Particle Physics and Cosmology, Space Research, Nanotechnology and Theoretical Physics or in Europe (France, Germany, Italy, Spain or Portugal). (High research rating)

Bristol* Physics is a mathematically oriented course with core subjects being taken in the first and second years. In the third year, students choose from a wide range of options. The Physics first year is so arranged that students can transfer from joint courses to single honours courses and also transfer between the BSc and MSci at the end of Year 1. Languages are offered as an additional feature of the course and several complementary subjects can be taken including geography, psychology or philosophy. An MSc with Astrophysics is also offered, as are courses in Chemical Physics. (High research rating)

Cambridge* Physics is offered as part of the course in Natural Sciences. (See under **Biological Sciences**.) Mathematics is also an important component of physics in the first and second years. A first-year course is also available in both the Computer Sciences and Mathematics Triposes. (High research rating)

Cardiff* First-year studies in Physics include physics and another science subject (astrophysics, chemistry, computing, geology or mathematics). Transfer to another degree in a similar field is possible at the end of the year. In Years 2 and 3 the course is physics based with the option to specialise in chemistry, solid state electronics, engineering physics, computational physics, medical physics or astrophysics. Courses are also offered in Medical Physics, Mathematics, Computing and Physics with Astronomy.

Central Lancashire The first year of the Physics course provides a firm foundation in applied physics, mathematics, laboratory and IT skills. At the end of the year, students choose from applied physics, physics/astronomy or physics, or applied physics with another subject on a combined honours programme. Astronomy is also offered with Physics.

Coventry There is a course in Industrial Physics. It has a mathematical bias and a strong practical emphasis.

Dundee Bsc and MSci courses in Physics are taken with mathematics and engineering and one other subject in Years 1 and 2, with a single honours or joint honours course following in Years 3 and 4. Physics can be studied with 10 other subjects. There is also an extensive Physical Sciences degree programme taught by the departments within the School of Engineering whilst close links exist with the Medical Physics Department at the University Teaching Hospital.

Durham* Physics (BSc/MEng) is designed to prepare people in the understanding and use of knowledge and techniques in any branch of physics. There are also full-time and sandwich courses in Computational Physics. A transfer to other Physics courses is possible at the end of Year 1. In addition to joint honours courses there are programmes involving Physics and Astronomy, Natural Sciences and Theoretical Physics. (High research rating)

East Anglia* Chemical Physics is offered and courses in Environmental Sciences give opportunities for a year in Europe or North America.

Edinburgh* Physics students take the subject in each of the four years with options in nuclear physics, optical imaging, electronics and computing and meteorology. The second-year course in mathematical physics is aimed at students whose interests lie in the more theoretical aspects of the subject. There are also courses in Computational Physics, Astrophysics. Meteorology or Music can also be taken with Physics. (High research rating)

Exeter* Five courses are offered with Physics, covering Astrophysics, Biomedical Physics, Quantum Science and Laser Technology, with the opportunity to study in Europe, Australia, New Zealand and North America. The first year is common to all courses, allowing transfers to other courses in Year 2. There is also a four-year Physics with professional placement degree. (High research rating)

Glasgow* Core courses are studied by all Physics students, with specialised courses in the final year. Technological applications in laser physics, micro-electronics and semiconductor physics and devices can be followed in the single honours course. Courses are also available in, for example, Chemical Physics and Physics with Astrophysics, Mathematics, Business and Management, Music and Electronic Engineering. (High research rating)

Heriot-Watt The first year of the four-year course is common to all Physics degrees, with elective options in other subjects such as business or languages. Physics is developed in Year 2 and specialised pathways follow in Years 3 and 4 covering Computational and Engineering Physics, Photonics and Lasers, Environmental Science and Mathematics. (High research rating)

Hertfordshire An optional sandwich year or study abroad is offered on each of the Physics courses which include Physics and Astrophysics with Scientific Computing.

Hull The first two years are common to all courses followed by specialisms in Physics and Applied Physics, Astrophysics, and Physics with Laser Science. Scholarships available. (High research rating)

Imperial London* The Department offers three-year BSc courses in Physics and Physics with Theoretical Physics, four-year BSc and MSci courses in Physics, and Physics with a Year in Europe or with Studies in Musical Performance. (High research rating)

Keele Physics can be taken with a second subject from 17 options including Business Administration, Music Technology, and Media Communications and Culture. The course covers concepts of both classical and modern physics.

Kent The Physics course allows considerable flexibility and enables students to defer their choice between Physics and other degree programmes in the Faculty until the end of the first year. Physics can also be studied with Astrophysics, Forensic Science, Astronomy and Space Science.

Lancaster* Separate Physics degree schemes are possible, including Computational Astrophysics and Cosmology, and Physics with Partical Physics, Space Science and Theoretical Physics. There is also an option to combine Physics with study in North America. Scholarships available.

Leeds* Mathematics is taken in the first two years of the Physics course. At the end of the first year there is the opportunity to transfer between Physics courses (eg Physics, Physics/Astrophysics). Core subjects include atomic and quantum physics, nuclear physics, thermodynamics and electronics. Optional subjects include low temperature, polymer and theoretical physics, astrophysics, geophysics, computing and medical imaging. Courses in Meteorology, Nanotechnology and Atmospheric Science and in Theoretical Physics are also offered. (High research rating)

Leicester* Physics, Physics with Astrophysics, Physics with Space Science and Technology or with Planetary Science, or Nanoscience and Technology can be studied. Specific core subjects are studied in all three degrees, supplemented by a wide range of optional courses. An optional year in Europe is offered. Courses are also offered in Experimental Physics. (High research rating)

Liverpool* Several Physics courses are offered in addition to the single honours programme. These include Mathematical Physics and Physics of Ocean and Climate Studies. Students opting for Physics and Mathematics can study these subjects equally or defer a choice between the two until the end of the first or second year. There are degree courses in Astrophysics, Physics and Astronomy, Geophysics and Medical Applications. (High research rating)

Liverpool John Moores Physics with Astronomy is available as a three-year full-time honours course. This is a joint course with the Physics Dept. of Liverpool University.

London (King's)* The Physics course gives a thorough grounding in the concepts and techniques of physics and the essential elements of mathematics and computing. The course unit structure provides for a wide choice in the second and third years. Five joint honours combinations are also available including a year abroad and, for example, Physics with Medical Applications, with Astrophysics, Mathematics or Management. (High research rating)

London (QM)* The flexibility of the course unit system in Physics, and the wide range of options in the final year, allows students to change their choice of course as their interests develop. In addition to Physics, Theoretical Physics and Astrophysics courses there are also joint courses including Physics and the Environment, and Mathematics with Astrophysics or with Medical Applications. (High research rating)

London (RH)* All Physics courses have a common first year and provide a wide range of classes from applied physics and theoretical physics topics. Further options are courses in astrophysics, microcomputer electronics, management studies or music, and a possible third year out in an industrial or government laboratory preceding a final fourth year. Astrophysics, Particle Physics, Applied Physics and Physics with Music are among the courses offered. (High research rating)

London (UCL)* Study is based on the course unit system in which Physics students can select units appropriate to their interests. Courses offered include Astrophysics, Astronomy, Medical Physics, Planetary Science and Theoretical Physics. (High research rating)

London South Bank The Integrated Science course focuses on the physical sciences.

Loughborough Three-year and four-year full-time and sandwich Physics courses are offered, the latter being either with industrial training or an MPhys. Breadth of studies continues through to the final year, and there are optional courses in French or German, management or environmental science in Years 1 and 2. Industrial placements abroad are a feature of the course, which is highly rated by students. Three-year and four-year courses are also available in Engineering Physics, Physics with Mathematics, Sports Science and Physical Education, Management or Computing. A course in Quantum Information and Computation is also offered.

Manchester* There are several Physics courses, including Physics with Astrophysics, with a wide range of options including several from the Mathematics Department. Physics can also be combined with Business and Management, Theoretical Physics, Photonics, Philosophy or with a study in Europe, while the four-year Master's course involving study in Europe includes language tuition and exchange arrangements with France, Germany, Italy, Spain and Belgium. (High research rating)

Nottingham* In the Physics degree all single and joint honours students take physics, maths and a third subject. This allows for flexibility for transfers between single and joint courses at the end of the first year. Other courses offered include Physics with Astronomy or a European Language or with Nanoscience or Astronomy. Chemistry and Molecular Physics and Mathematical Physics can also be studied. (High research rating)

Nottingham Trent Five degrees in Physics are offered, and other degrees including Astronomy and Physics covering Astrophysics, Forensic Application, Quantum and Cosmological Physics and Forensic Applications.

Oxford* The first year of the Physics course is equally divided between maths and physics, with an introductory course in computing. At the end of Year 1, it may be possible to transfer to another degree course in the Mathematical and Physical Science Division. The second year covers all the main areas of modern physics. In the final year there is a choice of options including atomic physics, nuclear physics, modern laser physics, and astrophysics. Physics is also offered with Philosophy. Scholarships available. (High research rating)

Queen's Belfast* Courses in Physics and Theoretical Physics are offered. Physics can also be studied with Applied Mathematics, Astrophysics and Computer Science, with opportunities for an extended study in

Europe. All students take a common course in Level 1 after which they can choose which Physics degree course they wish to follow, or proceed to a degree in another science subject. (High research rating)

St Andrews* Courses include Physics with Astrophysics or Photonics and Theoretical Physics. The final choice between BSc and MPhys can be postponed until the third level. Institute of Physics bursaries worth £1000 are available. (High research rating)

Salford The first year of the Physics course covers subjects ranging from electricity and magnetism to atomic and nuclear physics. Industrial training in Year 3 is considered very important and leads on to a comprehensive study of solid state physics in the final year. A number of Physics joint courses are available including Physics with Space Technology, Acoustics, languages, Lasers and Aviation or Pilot Studies with opportunities to study in Europe or North America.

Sheffield* A broad course in Physics is offered covering both theoretical and experimental aspects including electronics. Physics can be studied with Astrophysics, Mathematics, Medical Physics and Enterprise Management. There are opportunities to study in North America or Australasia. (High research rating)

Southampton* Most of the core course material occupies the first two years, leaving the final year for a selection of advanced topics. These include lasers, cosmology, solid state and advanced quantum mechanics. Options in other scientific subjects can also be taken (chemistry, biology, electronics, geology and computation). Physics courses with Astronomy, Oceanography and Space Science and Nanotechnology are also available. Scholarships available. (High research rating)

Strathclyde* The first year is common to all courses and provides a foundation in physics, mathematics, electronics, computational physics and experimental measurement. Students may then take a further two years to complete one of the honours degree courses or transfer to the MPhys degree or a BSc award. A BSc course in Physics with Teaching is also offered. (High research rating)

Surrey* In addition to the BSc and MSci Physics single honours course, Physics can be taken with Satellite Technology, Finance or Nuclear Astrophysics. All BSc programmes can be taken as a three-year course or a four-year course including a period of professional training at a research laboratory or in industry in the United Kingdom, Europe or North America. Students have access to excellent computing facilities and well-resourced teaching laboratories. Optional modules in a broad range of topics are available in all academic years. There is also a degree in Space Technology and Planetary Exploration with hands-on experience in space-engineering. (High research rating)

Sussex* Physics can be studied as a three-year BSc or a four-year MPhys honours course. Both provide a wide range of options in addition to the core subjects, and give students the opportunity either to specialise in a single science strand or to sample a variety of maths and science topics. Other Physics courses include Physics with Astrophysics, Astronomy and Forensic Science.

Swansea Courses are offered in, for example, Physics, Physics with Particle Physics and Cosmology with Mathematics, Sports Science and Nanotechnology. In the core course common to each degree there is an intensive study of the main branches of both classical and modern physics, which is continued beyond Level 1. This is supplemented by one of the specialised courses appropriate to the chosen degree. (High research rating)

Warwick* A central core of physics and mathematics is taken by all Physics students, ensuring flexibility and freedom of choice in the courses that follow in the second and third years. Mathematics and Physics, and Physics and Business Studies courses are also available. (High research rating)

West Scotland Physics is part of the Science and Technology degree scheme which offers students maximum flexibility in their course specialisms. An optional sandwich placement is included. Courses include Physics with Medical Technology or with Multimedia, and Technological Physics.

York* A common first-year course allows for considerable flexibility to change courses. For those not fully committed to a particular course, this enables students to leave their final choice of course until the end of the first year. Other courses include Physics with Business Management, Physics with Astrophysics and Physics with Philosophy. (High research rating)

OTHER INSTITUTIONS OFFERING PHYSICS COURSES
South Devon (Coll).

ALTERNATIVE COURSES
Astronomy, Astrophysics, Computing, Electronics, Geophysics.

POLITICS

(including **Government**, **International Relations** and **Peace Studies**)
(*Higher offers)

SUBJECT REQUIREMENTS/PREFERENCES
GCE A-level: Foreign languages for courses with a language option. History or English may be required.

SUBJECT INFORMATION
Politics courses have become increasingly popular in recent years and usually cover the politics and government of the major powers. Through the degree courses on offer it is possible to study the politics of almost any country in the world.

Aberdeen The course in Politics and International Relations covers Europe and the comparative politics of the USA and Britain and political theories and behaviour. At Level 3 options include Scottish politics, the French party system, interior groups and electoral systems. (High research rating)

Aberystwyth A course in International Politics is offered with a House of Commons or Welsh Assembly Placement Scheme and there is also an exchange programme with European, Canadian and American universities. In addition, there are courses in Political Studies, International Relations, European Politics, Peace Conflict and Security and joint courses with International Politics that include strategic studies, intelligence studies and military history. (High research rating)

Anglia Ruskin Politics is available on the combined honours course with Philosophy and Sociology. The course covers American and European politics.

Aston* Politics is offered as a single honours or combined honours programme. The course combines history and politics with a strong present-day focus. A placement year is included.

Bangor Political and Social Sciences is offered as a three-year course, which includes modules in psychology, economic and social issues, European and American topics.

Bath* Politics is offered as a joint course with Economics, the main focus being on politics. Three and four year schemes are offerred in Politics and International Relations whilst Politics can also be studied with French, German, Italian, Russian and Spanish.

Birmingham* The first year of the Political Science course consists of two social science courses (a political option must be chosen). In the second and third years, students take either political theory or political analysis, with a choice of options from British, European, American and Comparative European Politics. Courses in International Studies are also available, together with courses in Politics, and Political

Science, Political Economy and International Relations with languages or Economics. There is also a degree in War Studies.

Bradford Peace Studies and Politics provides opportunities to specialise in conflict resolution, international relations and defence and security studies. There are also courses in Conflict Resolution, Peace Studies and International Relations and Security Studies.

Brighton Politics can be studied alongside Psychology, Criminology, Social Policy or Sociology.

Bristol* Previous study of politics is not necessary for this degree course, which offers a very wide range of specialisms. The course includes a study of political institutions in specific countries and in world politics. It can be studied with modern languages – French, German, Italian, Portuguese, Russian or Spanish – and with Philosophy, Sociology, Economics, Social Policy or Theology. (High research rating)

Bristol UWE Politics (joint honours) is part of the Social Science undergraduate modular programme. The course covers west European, British and world politics, political philosophy and justice. There is a modern language option in Year 1 of the Politics course. A degree in International Relations is also offered which can be combined with a variety of subjects including History and Politics.

Brunel* Politics and International Politics are offered including joint courses with History, Economics and Sociology. Work placements are arranged in local and national government and abroad.

Buckingham Two-year courses in Politics can be taken with Economics and Law. A wide range of options is offered in the Economics and Law programmes. A course in International Studies is also offered.

Cambridge* Politics, Psychology and Sociology (PPS) is a distinctive course among social science degrees due to the range of subjects and choices available. In few other institutions are politics and international studies, social and developmental psychology (in contrast to experimental psychology) taught on the same course.

Canterbury Christ Church The Politics and Global Government course offers an overview of national, international and global political developments. There is a separate course in International Relations and Politics.

Cardiff Part I of the Politics course covers the foundation of western political theory, electoral systems, party systems, and internal and international war. Part II offers a number of optional subjects including European Union policy and the comparative systems of Britain, France, Germany, Italy, Sweden and USA. Politics is also offered with a range of subjects including Modern History, Economics and Sociology and there is a degree in International Relations with European Politics.

Central Lancashire Politics is offered as part of the combined honours programme and can be taken with History, Philosophy or Social Policy.

Chester The International Development Studies course focuses on socio-economic, political, cultural and environmental aspects, exploring the Third World and comparisons between rich and poor, urban and rural and contemporary and historical. A Politics course in being validated.

City* The International Politics degree includes global policy-making, and inter-governmental organisations such as the United Nations, the European Union and the World Bank. A wide range of elective modules is offered in each year of the course.

Coventry Politics joint honours courses can be studied with History, International Relations and Politics. There are also separate programmes in International Relations and International Studies including long ranges.

De Montfort The degree in Government and Politics covers British and Global Politics including module on the government, public sector topics and health care. A course in International Relations in also offered.

Derby Courses are offered in Third World Development and in International Relations and Global Development.

Dundee Politics is offered as a single or joint honours course with nine subjects in the Arts and Social Sciences or combined honours programmes. The course covers British, European and Third World politics and has a wide range of options including Scottish politics. There are also courses in International Relations that can also be combined with American or European Studies, or History and courses in European Politics and Geopolitics.

Durham* All first-year Politics students take an introduction to politics course followed by a further eight courses, two of which may be taken from other subject areas, usually within the Faculty of Social Sciences. Politics can be taken with a year in Europe or in combined honours. Courses are also available in PPE and with Sociology, Philosophy, Economics and a year in Europe.

East Anglia The Politics course is extremely flexible allowing students to customise their course. There are currently over 20 specialised modules from which to choose ranging from Russian and American Politics to Conflict Resolution and Big Brother. Courses in European Studies and International Relations are also available. There are opportunities for parliamentary and other internships.

East London The Politics course includes a study of politics in its social and economic settings, political theory and historical ideas, government in Britain and other European countries, the law, human and civic rights and local government. There are also courses in International Third World Development and International Politics.

Edinburgh* The Politics degree course offers an introduction to political theory, British government and administration. In the third and fourth years, options are offered in European politics, political parties and the politics of the former Soviet Union, eastern Europe, the USA and Africa. Politics is also offered with Persian and Arabic in addition to a range of other subjects. There is also a degree in International Relations. (High research rating)

Essex The Department of Government offers a wide range of courses in two main degrees, Politics and International Relations and Politics. Over 30 specialist options are available covering world politics, democracy and human nights. Twelve other joint courses are also available. (High research rating)

Exeter* Single honours Politics students take courses in all branches of the subject. Opportunities to study in Europe, USA, Canada or Australia. Courses are offered in a range of subjects including Economic and Political Development, Philosophy and Political Economy and International Relations with optional work placement projects. (High research rating)

Glamorgan The course in Politics covers governments and governance, international relations, political leadership and global politics.

Glasgow* The Politics course is distinctive in concentrating on ideas and ideologies, liberalism and socialism while looking at political institutions, parties and pressure groups. Political organisations' behaviour in the United Kingdom and the USA is studied as well as the former Soviet Union, Spain, Nigeria, Latin America, Africa and Germany. (High research rating)

Greenwich The Politics course focuses mainly on British and European politics and aspects of society. Business, Law, Legal Studies, languages, Economics and Life Sciences can also be studied with Politics. There is also a course in Political Communication.

Huddersfield The Politics course involves British government and politics, European politics, international relations, Third World politics and American politics. In Year 1, four modules from other subjects can be taken, for example economics, business studies, history and a modern language. (Highly rated by students.) In addition there is a degree in International Politics. Politics can also be studied with Contemporary History, Sociology, Law and Media.

Hull An imaginative and broad Politics programme, allowing several specialist options from the single honours course, is provided. Politics and Politics, Philosophy and Economics or Law are also offered. There is also a course in International Relations, a four-year course in British Politics and Legislative Studies, and European Government and Politics. There is also a course in Globalisation, Governance and War and Security Studies. (High research rating)

Keele Politics can be taken as a single or dual honours subject with over 25 courses including Philosophy, Economics, History and Sociology. There is also a course in International Relations. (High research rating)

Kent The Department offers two main programmes – Politics, Politics and International Relations, also with French, German and Italian and an optional year in Finland, Japan or the Czech Republic. Other courses include British and American Policy Studies, European Politics, Industrial Relations, Human Resource Management and War Studies.

Kingston The Politics course is offered as a single honours course or as part of the modular scheme that offers a choice from more than 15 subjects including Journalism, Psychology and languages. There are special options in American, Irish, German and African history and exchanges in Europe and America. There is also a course in International Relations.

Lancaster In the first year of Politics with International Relations, students take politics (including British and American government and international relations) and two other subjects, for example law, religious studies, history, economics. In Years 2 and 3 a wide range of political topics is covered including political thought, government, comparative politics, international relations and strategic studies. Other degree courses include Global Politics, Peace Studies and International Relations and European Politics, Society and Culture.

Leeds* In the first year of the Political Studies course, compulsory subjects cover the introduction to politics and British government and explanation in political science. Second-year subjects cover foreign governments and comparative government in the USA, France, China, India and Pakistan; modern political doctrines; and political and social history. A wide range of final-year optional subjects is available. Politics and Parliamentary Studies is a unique course involving five months working as an intern in a Congress member's or senator's office in Ottawa or Washington DC, and a similar period in the House of Commons. There are also courses in European Politics, Politics and Parliamentary Studies, International Development and International Relations.

Leeds Metropolitan Relevant courses include Global Development, Peace Studies, International Relations and joint courses with Politics.

Leicester* Politics is offered as a single honours course with an opportunity to spend a second-year semester in Europe or the subject can be studied with English or languages. Courses in International Relations (or with History) are also available. (High research rating)

Lincoln The single honours degree in Politics covers all aspects of British politics and government and introduces international politics in the USA and Middle East. It can be taken as a joint honours course with eight other subjects. There are also degrees in International Relations with Politics and Social Policy.

Liverpool* The Politics course covers British politics in Year 1 and, later, western European, Russian, American, Latin American and South American politics. Special subjects include the media, immigration and environmental politics. Communication Studies, International Business, International Politics, Modern History and Philosophy can all be studied with Politics.

Liverpool Hope The course covers British politics, political ideas and the politics of international relations. In Year 3, a study is undertaken of American and European politics. There are also several joint courses in both Politics and Peace Studies.

Liverpool John Moores The Politics course covers the politics of the European Union, eastern Europe, the UK and south east Asia.

London (Goldsmiths)* Politics is offered with Economics, International Studies or Public Policy, or as a single honours subject. European politics, political ideas and public administration also feature in the course.

London (King's)* A BA programme in War Studies can be followed either as a single honours course or as one of nine joint courses. The subject focuses on the impact of war on human society from ancient times to the present day. (High research rating)

London (LSE)* The first-year Government course covers an introduction to the study of politics and political theory. Years 2 and 3 offer courses in the politics and government of another country. Options in other subjects are offered each year. International Relations courses are also offered. There are also courses in Government and Economics and Government and History. (High research rating)

London (QM)* The Politics course focuses on specialisation in modern western political institutions, theory and ideas. There are also several joint honours programmes including Russian or French or German, Hispanic Studies, Business Management, and Economics.

London (RH)* Politics can be taken as a single honours or joint honours subject with Economics, International Relations, Music or languages. All first year students take a common package of courses leading to optional courses in Year 2.

London (SOAS)* Single subject and Joint degree Politics students all take an introduction to political study and comparative politics focusing on Africa and Asia. Students then follow a programme with an increasing optional element. Courses taught at SOAS stress the issues and problems more specific to the non-European world, but the opportunity exists to choose courses at other colleges within the University. Politics is also offered with a wide range of African and Far Eastern languages. (High research rating)

London (UCL)* Politics and East European Studies is offered as a three-year full-time degree. Compulsory courses are taken in Years 1 and 2 in politics, government and international relations. (High research rating)

London Metropolitan Politics is offered as a single or joint subject. Other parallel courses include International Relations, Peace and Conflict Studies, Public Administration and Politics, and Governance and Law.

London South Bank The International Politics course provides a sound understanding of contemporary political issues covering a wide range of social science subjects and political issues in Europe, the USA and the Third World.

Loughborough* Three-year and four-year Politics and International Relations courses are available with minor subjects in Economics, Social Policy, French, German, Spanish, Sociology, Social Psychology or English. The Politics element provides a thorough grounding in political science with particular reference to western and eastern European states, the European Union, the USA and the former Soviet states. Language students may opt to spend the third year in, for example, France or Germany. Politics may also be studied with Economics or International Studies.

Manchester* The Department of Government is one of the largest in Britain, enabling students to build a good foundation in the study of politics covering Anglo-American, European and international politics, with opportunities to specialise in the final year. Politics can be studied with Development Studies, Business Studies, International Relations and there is also a degree in PPE. (High research rating)

Manchester Metropolitan A three-year Politics course covers politics, sociology, social administration and economics. Politics is also available with Cultural Studies, European Studies, Information and Communications, Public Policy and other subjects. There are also courses in Public Management Studies, International Politics and Public Services.

Middlesex Degrees in Political and International Studies covering aspects of the subject across the world are offered as single or joint courses.

Newcastle* The Politics course covers British politics, world politics, introduction to democratic politics and political ideas together with one or two from a range of other subjects including languages, history, law and psychology. In Stages 2 and 3 the focus is on political studies that cover western Europe, Africa, East Asia, the USA and China. Politics can also be studied with History, East Asian Studies (includes a year in the Far East) or Social Policy. There is also a degree in Government and European Union Studies that includes language study as part of the course (French, German Spanish or Portuguese) and involves a year abroad. (High research rating)

Newport A four-year course is offered in Political Studies.

Northampton Politics is offered as a single or joint course in addition to degrees in Third World Development.

Northumbria The Politics course covers British politics, political institutions and behaviour and international relations. Sociology, Social Policy, Criminology and Media Studies are also offered with Politics.

Nottingham* This degree concentrates on three key areas wirhin the study of politics: comparative politics, political theory, and international relations. A wide selection of optional modules allows you to specialise in a variety of different areas, such as the European Union, British politics, the government and politics of the USA, terrorism and security, and globalisation. There is also a degree in European Politics and an MSc in International Relations.

Nottingham Trent Politics is studied as a three-year single honours programme, and is also offered with International Relations, Geography, Psychology, Sociology, and History. There are also several courses in International Relations.

Oxford* Politics is offered with Philosophy and Economics or with History. Scholarships available. (High research rating)

Oxford Brookes* Politics is offered with over 40 separate subjects including Telecommunications, Sociology, and Philosophy. There is also a wide range of International Relations courses.

Plymouth The Politics course can be taken as a single honours, major or minor subject. It largely covers British and European politics but provides options in the politics of eastern Europe and Third World issues. The subject is also combined with Sociology, Law, Criminal Justice Studies and International Relations. There are also over 15 joint courses with International Relations.

Portsmouth In the first year, Politics is studied alongside economics, modern history, political thought and current politics. In Years 2 and 3 core courses are accompanied by options. There are also degrees in International Relations with Politics, History and languages.

Queen's Belfast* All students take four basic courses – politics of Britain and Ireland, Contemporary Europe, world politics and politics in a media culture. In Years 2 and 3 students choose from over 25 modules covering all aspects of the subject. Politics can be studied with another subject from a wide range including International Studies, Irish and Celtic, Law, Social Policy, Modern History and Psychological Studies. There is also a course in International Studies emphasising conflict resolution, and European integration. (High research rating)

Reading* The degree course in Politics and International Relations covers the politics of the United Kingdom, the USA, former Soviet states, Africa and northern, southern and western Europe. There are also courses in Modern History with Politics and with International Relations. Entrance scholarships are available.

Robert Gordon Politics can be taken with Management.

Roehampton Human Rights is offered as a single or combined honours course with a range of subjects such as Criminology, Philosophy, Modern Languages, Social Anthropology.

St Andrews* Degree courses are offered in International Relations either as single or joint honours courses. Programmes of study include Themes in 20th-century International Relations, Power and Violence and Peace and Governance in World Politics.

Salford Politics can be taken with Contemporary History, Journalism, Criminology and several other subjects.

Sheffield* The Politics course introduces British politics, moving on to international politics and political ideas. Specialised modules follow at Level 3. There are also courses with East Asian Studies, International History, International Relations, and International Politics. (High research rating)

Sheffield Hallam The course focuses on politics, political structures and recent developments on a UK, European and global scale.

Southampton* All Politics students in the Social Sciences faculty take an introductory first-year course in politics and may also take a course in international studies. In Years 2 and 3 students become progressively more specialised and may opt for such topics as arms control. Politics and International Relations or Languages, Philosophy or History are also offered. (High research rating)

Staffordshire Single and joint courses are offered in International Relations with options in War Peace and Terrorism.

Stirling The first three semesters (Part I) introduce the practical and theoretical aspects of politics and survey different political systems. Part II is designed to develop analytical skills and there are courses in nationalism, political philosophy and environmentalism. There is also a course in Politics, Philosophy and Economics and a separate degree in International Politics and also joint courses including Politics and Business Studies, Psychology or Sociology.

Strathclyde Politics is offered as part of the Arts and Social Studies programme. Honours students select from a wide range of options in Years 2 and 3. (High research rating)

Sunderland Politics can be taken jointly with a wide range of subjects including American Studies, Criminology, Health Studies, Marketing, Media Studies, Photography, Gender Studies and Public Relations.

Surrey* Students are able to choose from four programmes, each sharing a common first year and thereafter choosing Politics, Politics with Citizenship, International Studies or Policy Studies.

Sussex* Politics is available as a single honours course and in combination with 10 other subjects including International Relations, which is also available as single honours and in other joint courses. Students are increasingly encouraged to become independent and self-directed learners. (High research rating)

Swansea* A degree in Politics and International Relations is offered, leading to specialist studies in Years 2 and 3. There are also several joint courses in both these subjects. (High research rating) (See also **Philosophy** for PPE)

Ulster The degree in International Politics can be taken with 12 other subjects. There is also a Politics degree also with combinations.

Warwick* The courses in Politics have been designed to cater for a wide range of interests. There is an optional third year in an overseas university. As well as the single honours degree, Politics may be combined with Economics, History, Philosophy, Sociology, French, or International Studies and there is a course in Philosophy, Politics and Economics.

West Scotland Law is offered as a full-time course taken as part of the Social Sciences programme. British, European, American and Scottish politics are covered.

Westminster The Politics course covers British, American and European politics. It involves four core modules and more than 12 options. Politics can also be studied with Arabic or Chinese. Courses are also available in International Relations. There are also options in the combined honours programmes.

Winchester The Politics and Global Studies course focuses largely on international issues.

Wolverhampton Politics can be taken as part of the modular degree programme. The main focus is on British, European and American politics, and degrees include Politics and American Studies or English or History or Social Policy or Media and Communication Studies. War Studies and Politics is also offered.

Worcester Over 12 courses are offered including several focusing on People and Power.

York* A wide spectrum of subjects is covered in the degree course in Politics. These include the major governmental systems of Britain, western Europe, America, the middle East, China, Japan and the former Soviet Union. Subject strengths include Third World and British politics and political philosophy. Politics can also be studied with Economics, Education, English, Social Policy, Sociology, Philosophy and History. Philosophy, Politics and Economics is also offered. See **English**, also **Combined courses**. (High research rating)

OTHER INSTITUTIONS OFFERING POLITICS COURSES
East Lancashire (Coll), European (BusSch), Richmond (American Univ), Staffordshire (Reg Fed), Truro (Coll), Worcester (CT).

ALTERNATIVE COURSES
Economic History, Economics, Government, History, International Relations, Public Administration, Public and Social Policy, Social Administration, Social Sciences, Social Studies, Sociology.

PROPERTY MANAGEMENT AND SURVEYING

(including **Housing Studies**)
(see also **Town Planning and Urban Planning Studies**)
(* indicates universities with the highest entry requirements)

SUBJECT REQUIREMENTS/PREFERENCES
GCSE: English and Mathematics required, and for some institutions a science subject (for professional body registration).

SUBJECT INFORMATION
Surveying is a very broad subject (and career) that includes several specialisms, for example building surveying, quantity surveying, land valuation surveying and architecture, which could also be considered as alternative courses. Most courses cover very similar topics and lead to professional qualifications, giving exemptions from the examinations of the Royal Institution of Chartered Surveyors.

Aberdeen Degrees are offered in Property (covering finance, economics and management, valuation and investment) and Property and Spatial Planning. Both degrees are accredited by the Royal Institution of Chartered Suryeyors (RICS). There is also a course in Rural Surveying.

Anglia Ruskin The range of programmes includes, Building Surveying, Real Estate Management, Property and Surveying, Quantity Surveying and a degree in Housing.

Birmingham City There is a four-year course in Construction Management and Economics that includes professional experience. Course topics include construction studies, measurement and cost studies, economics, quantitative methods and law. The major strength is the application of information technology throughout the course as a tool for problem solving and information management. Courses are also offered in Building Surveying and Estate Management Practice, the latter with full accreditation by the RICS, and in Housing.

Brighton The first and second years of the Building Surveying course will cover building performance, built environment, building surveying practice and the professional environment. The third year is spent on supervised professional experience and the final year will cover building design, rehabilitation, asset management and two options, including a dissertation.

Bristol UWE Quantity Surveying and Commercial Management is a four-year sandwich course with professional placement in the third year. Topics include construction technology and measurement, contract and legal studies. Final-year studies cover construction services, building construction and civil engineering. Maximum exemptions are afforded graduates from relevant professional body examinations for this and the Building Surveying course. There are also courses in Business in Property and Property Management and Investment, Property Development and Planning and Real Estate (Valuation and Management).

Cambridge* The Land Economy course covers environment, law and economics and is concerned with the use of land and property and with the protection of the environment. Students take courses in law and economics relating to the ownership, exploitation, planning and protection of land, and explore the issues raised. The degree gives full exemptions from RICS examinations.

Central Lancashire Courses are offered in Building Surveying, Construction Project Management and Quantity Surveying all of which can be taken with an industrial placement of one year.

City* Real Estate Finance and Investment is designed to meet the needs of qualified specialists in the field of property, finance and investment, law and taxation. Valuation is studied throughout the course, along with building design and construction, company structure and planning. The course has an optional placement year and professional body recognition. See also **Engineering courses**.

Coventry Building Surveying is a three-year or four-year (sandwich) course in the built environment. There is a language option with possible placement in France, Germany and Spain.

East London A course in Surveying and Mapping Sciences covers environmental science and information technology, sea surveying and land and property law.

Glamorgan Several courses are offered leading to professional qualification. These cover Quantity or Building Surveying, Property Management and Valuation and Real Estate Management.

Glasgow Caledonian The Quantity Surveying course includes a six-month period of supervised work placement with private offices, contractors and local authorities. Property Management and Development is also offered.

Glyndŵr The Estate Management degree covers both natural and built environments with options in housing, planning and surveying. The Estate Agency course involves the investment and marketing of property. There is also a degree in Housing Studies.

Greenwich The Building Surveying course can be studied on a three-year full-time or four-year sandwich basis. The main subjects cover construction technology, design, economics of land and building, law and management. Quantity Surveying is a three-year full-time, four-year sandwich or five-year part-time course with topics focusing on construction technology, measurement, law and economics. Professional practice on the sandwich course comes in Year 3. It has professional body recognition, as is the case with the degree in Estate Management. There is also a degree in Housing Studies.

Harper Adams (UC) The Rural Property Management degree includes a placement year following Year 2.

Heriot-Watt This four-year Building Surveying course covers building technology, building economics, building appraisal and surveying, and gives exemptions from several professional institutes' examinations. In the first two years of the Building Economics and Quantity Surveying course, building technology, mathematics, economics and legal and business studies are included. Quantity surveying studies begin in the second year and continue to the end of the final (fourth) year. Professional and industrial practice are also included. In its first two years the Estate Management course involves a study of building technology, economics, urban appraisal and legal and business studies. In the third year, legal and planning studies and urban sociology are introduced and continued in the fourth year with building maintenance and a research design project.

Kingston* The third year of this four-year Quantity Surveying sandwich course is spent in professional placement. Basic economic theory and the principles of law lead on to applications in building work in Years 1 and 2. Other studies cover construction technology and measurement. Exemptions from relevant professional body examinations are gained on graduation, similarly with the courses in Real Estate Management, Property Studies, Property Planning and Development and Building Surveying.

Leeds Metropolitan The Quantity Surveying course provides a thorough understanding of all aspects of quantity surveying and building economics. Distinct themes include measurement and contractual procedures, cost price, and various supporting studies. Year 3 is spent in professional practice. There is professional body recognition. A course in Building Surveying is also offered. (See also Building.)

Liverpool Years 1 and 2 in the Building Surveying course provide a solid foundation in the subject, which is followed by a year in professional practice. Year 4 develops the theme of 'Building Life Cycle Management' (building maintenance design and production). There is professional body recognition.

Liverpool John Moores Quantity Surveying is a three-year full-time or four-year sandwich course. Industrial training takes place in the third year of the four-year course, which includes economic, quantitative and legal studies and construction management. There are exemptions from professional body examinations. There are also courses in Building Surveying, Property Management and Real Estate Management.

London South Bank Building Surveying is a three-year full-time or four-year sandwich course with Year 3 being spent in supervised professional attachment. Subject areas cover construction, quantitative, economic, legal and management studies. Professional body exemptions are gained on graduation. The course should not be confused with Building Services Engineering. Quantity Surveying is a four-year sandwich course with Year 3 being spent in professional placement. The course is based on three main areas: (a) technological studies, (b) economic studies, and (c) legal studies. The degree gives professional body exemptions. A three-year degree course in Housing is also offered.

Loughborough* The Commercial Management and Quantity Surveying programme, sponsored by major contractors, covers construction technology, law, economics, management and professional practice.

Napier Courses are offered in Estate Management, Building and Quantity Surveying.

Northumbria* Quantity Surveying is a four-year sandwich course with professional placement in Year 3. There is also a European route with one year of work and study abroad. Core subjects follow the set pattern prescribed by the Royal Institution of Chartered Surveyors for exemptions from their examinations. Courses are also offered in Building Surveying and Estate Management.

Nottingham Trent Estate Surveying is one of several pathways in the Department of Surveying. The course involves the core subjects of land economics, law, land use planning, property management and valuation, communication and building technology. Courses are also offered in Building and Quantity Surveying, Real Estate Management, Planning and Property Development.

Oxford Brookes* The Real Estate Management course is designed primarily for those students aiming to become chartered surveyors in the general practice division. The curriculum focuses on subjects based on valuation, building technology, town planning, economics and law. This is a very popular course.

Portsmouth* The three-year Quantity Surveying course covers in depth all the aspects of quantity surveying practice under the three main themes – economics, technology and the environment. The course also introduces new themes for future development in the field such as computer use, cost planning and design management. Financial management is an important feature of the course. There are also courses in Property Development and Property Marketing, Design and Development accredited by the Royal Institution of Chartered Surveyors.

Reading* There are four themes that run through the programmes: development and planning, investment and finance in property, urban property management and valuation, and rural studies. These programmes are highly integrated. This gives you the opportunity to move between the programmes easily in your first or second year, when you may still not be certain which aspect of property or planning most appeals to you. The courses offered cover Real Estate, Investment and Finance in Property Real Estate and Urban Planning and Rural Property Management.

Salford Building Surveying is a four-year sandwich course and incorporates elements common to the degree course in Quantity Surveying. There are three main study areas: professional, management and construction studies, leading to project work in the final year. Quantity Surveying is a four-year sandwich course, the third year being spent in approved professional experience. Construction technology is taken throughout Years 1, 2 and 4, with other aspects of science and design. Other subjects include management, finance and applied economics and mathematics and computing. A course is also offered in Property Management and Investment.

Sheffield Hallam Building Surveying is studied in common with Construction Management and Quantity Surveying, with transfers being possible at this stage. Years 2 and 4 cover construction technology, building services, law, economics, building surveying, design and refurbishment. The third year is spent in professional placement. Urban Land Economics covers land administration, economics, valuations, planning and building. This is a four-year course in which the third year is spent in professional training. Other courses offered include Business Property Management, Property Development and Property Studies and Housing Management.

Southampton Solent The Property and Development course focuses on construction, surveying and building management.

Ulster Surveying is offered with specialisms in Building and Quantity Surveying and there are also courses in Housing Management and Planning and Property Development and Investment.

West Scotland There is a joint degree in Real Estate Management which can be taken with Law or Marketing.

Westminster Degree courses in Building and Quantity Surveying are offered, giving professional body exemptions from examinations. Similarly, the degree in Urban Estate Management also gives exemptions from RICS examinations. There are also courses in Property in Business and Leisure Property.

Wolverhampton A degree in Building Surveying is offered and there are also degrees in Surveying and Property Asset Management validated by the RICS.

OTHER INSTITUTIONS OFFERING PROPERTY COURSES
Royal (CAg).

ALTERNATIVE COURSES
Accountancy, Architecture, Building, Civil Engineering, Housing, Structural Engineering, Town Planning and Urban Studies.

PSYCHOLOGY

(including **Behavioural Science**)
(* indicates universities with the highest entry requirements)

SUBJECT REQUIREMENTS/PREFERENCES

GCE A-level: One or two science subjects may be required for BSc courses. **GCSE:** English, Mathematics and/or a science may be required.

SUBJECT INFORMATION

Psychology is an ever-popular subject, covering studies in development, perception, learning, personality as well as social and abnormal psychology. (It is not training to enable you to psychoanalyse your friends!) **NB** All courses approved for future training as psychologists are listed in the publications of the British Psychological Society, St Andrews House, 48 Princess Road East, Leicester LE1 7DR.

Aberdeen The honours course in Psychology is recognised by the British Psychological Society and after Levels 1 and 2 there is a wide range of options available including biopsychology, developmental psychology, memory, social psychology and health behaviour. There are opportunities for study abroad.

Abertay Dundee The four year Behavioural Science course integrates the study of psychology and sociology with specialised options that include health, sociology, psychology, and human rights. There are opportunities for work placement in Year 4. There is also a course in Forensic Psychobiology and a Psychology degree covering biology, cognitive development and social psychology.

Aberystwyth Psychology is offered as a single honours programme or as joint honours degree schemes with 10 other subjects.

Anglia Ruskin Psychology can be taken as a single or a combined honours subject. The course covers social, health, developmental and forensic psychology. Joint courses are offered with Criminology, Law and Music.

Aston* The Human Psychology course is an applied programme with three-year and four-year sandwich courses. Students on the four-year course spend a year on work experience. Its emphasis is on the study of human behaviour and the underlying mental processes, with final year options in child, clinical, occupational and social psychology, psychology in organisations and consumer psychology. Psychology is also offered as part of the combined honours programme.

Bangor* The range of academic specialisms within the School currently enables students to choose from modules as varied as clinical and health psychology, psychology of addictive behaviours and infant development, consumer psychology, cognitive neuroscience and language. In addition to being one of the top seven REA 5* departments in the UK, the school has a number of prestigious research centres including the Wolfson Centre for Cognitive Neuroscience, the Centre for Experimental Consumer Psychology and the Bangor Centre for Developmental Disabilities. (High research rating)

Bath* The Department of Psychology offers a BSc course in Psychology focusing on cognitive developments and health and social psychology. Compulsory industrial placements in Year 3 are worldwide in clinical, occupational, educational or research settings.

Bath Spa The course in Psychology provides an introduction to the scientific study of human behaviour with an emphasis on 'real world' applications.

Bedfordshire The Psychology course has core modules in social, cognitive and developmental psychology and specialisms in counselling, child, sport and clinical psychology. In Year 1 an elective subject from another department can be taken, for example languages, anthropology or sociology. During Years 1 and 2, core subjects in psychology are taken. Other courses include Applied Psychology (a vocational degree with a one year placement), Health Psychology, Psychological Studies and Psychology with Criminology or Criminal Behaviour.

Birmingham* The Psychology course provides a scientific study of behaviour in all its aspects related to developmental and child psychology, perception, learning, social, abnormal psychology and neuropsychology. In the final year, students choose from a number of options in contemporary psychology including forensic and clinical psychology. Psychology can also be taken with Modern Languages, Chemistry or Mathematics. (High research rating)

Birmingham City Business Psychology can be studied in joint honours degrees with Advertising, Management, Human Resource Management, Retail Marketing, Public Relations and Criminal Justice. Psychology and Sociology is also offered. There is also a course in Criminal Justice combined with Psychology.

Bolton Work placements are offered on the Psychology degree, which includes modules in social, development, abnormal psychology and mental health. There are specialisms in Counselling, Sport and Exercise Psychology and Criminological and Forensic Psychology.

Bournemouth The Psychology and Computing course offers a study of human factors, social psychology, human-computer interaction and language. In addition there is also a new Psychology degree.

Bradford Specialisation takes place in Year 3 in this Psychology degree, in such subjects as Forensic or Evolutionary or Neuroscience. Psychology can be taken with Crime or Management Psychology.

Brighton There are courses in Applied Psychology and Sociology or Criminology. An additional conversion course needs to be taken for students wishing to become psychologists.

Bristol* The emphasis in the Psychology course is on both human and animal behaviour. Courses in the first two years provide a basis for specialisation in the third year and cover perception, learning, motivation, personality, social and physiological psychology. One additional subject is taken from another department in the first year and one additional subject in the second. Psychology is also available with either Philosophy or Zoology. A single honours degree in Neuroscience is also offered, studied alongside anatomical science and physiology. There is also a degree in counselling (offer CCC). (High research rating)

Bristol UWE The degree in Psychology is a joint honours programme and is accredited by the British Psychological Society. Various specialist modules are offered including Social, Health, Biological and Applied Psychology. Psychology is also offered with Forensic Science or Sports Biology.

Brunel During the first and second years of the Psychology course a broad approach is taken which covers the core areas of cognitive, biological, social, abnormal and development psychology. Options including autism, ageing, mental health and speech are offered in Year 3. Brunel offers an integrated sandwich course with three placements. Psychology is also offered with Anthropology and Sociology.

Buckingham The two-year programme in Psychology includes cognition and perception and social psychology in Year 1 and specialist subjects in business, developmental and clinical psychology in the Year 2 degree programme. Psychology can also be taken with Business Studies, English Language Studies, English Literature, French, Information Systems, Media, Socio-legal Studies, Spanish or Marketing.

Bucks New Psychology can be taken as a single honours degree and jointly with Criminology, or Sociology. There is also a degree in Sports Psychology.

Cambridge* Experimental Psychology can be taken in Part B of the Natural Sciences course (see under **Biological Sciences**) with two other subjects. Students concentrate on a single subject in Year 3. Psychology also features in the Politics, Psychology and Sociology degree (see under **Politics**) and those taking Psychology papers in Part II qualify for registration with the British Psychological Society. (High research rating)

Canterbury Christ Church Psychology is offered as a single or combined degree programme. Final year modules include the psychology of education or work or the therapeutic process. There is also a degree in Sport and Exercise Psychology.

Cardiff* The Psychology degree is a modular course in which six double modules focus on social, biological and cognitive psychology in Year 1. In Part II (second and third years) core courses and options are taken, including social and occupational psychology, abnormal psychology and clinical and counselling psychology. Final-year options lead to vocational and professional areas of work. There are also joint courses in Psychology and Criminology, which includes forensic psychology, and Education or Physiology with Psychology. (High research rating)

Cardiff (UWIC) The course is accredited by the British Psychological Society.

Central Lancashire The first, and much of the second, year content is common to both Psychology and Applied Psychology courses. In the third year, Applied Psychology students take organisational psychology and a techniques course, as well as six options and a project in an applied field. Psychology students take eight options from a wide range and also complete a project. The decision as to which course to follow is taken at the end of Year 1. Psychology is also available on the combined honours programme with a choice from eight other subjects and there are also courses in Forensic Psychology, Neuropsychology, Health Psychology, Neuroscience, and Sport Psychology or in joint courses with Business, Education, Law or Forensic Sciences. There is also a course in Counselling and Psychotherapy.

Chester The Psychology degree is approved for those wishing to become psychologists. The course emphasises the importance of practical work involving interviewing, observation and experimentation with modules in specialist fields. There is also a vocational course in counselling taken as part of the combined honours programme.

City* Psychology is studied as a three-year degree course and involves cognitive and social psychology, learning, and clinical and abnormal psychology. Specialist subjects include, health psychology and psychology abnormal and clinical.

Coventry A modular course in Psychology is offered with a focus on developmental, biological and social psychology and health. There are also courses with Criminology, Counselling and Sport Psychology.

Cumbria The Applied Psychology degree includes options in forensics, health, community and sport.

De Montfort This is a comprehensive psychology course covering human communication, language development, developmental, social, educational, clinical psychology and counselling. Psychology is also offered as part of the joint/major/minor degree schemes and can be taken with Applied Criminology, Health Sciences and Clinical Psychology.

Derby The course in Psychology leads to registration as a chartered psychologist. Child, cognitive and social psychology are studied in Year 1. Options in Year 3 include the psychology of emotion, criminology, sexuality and gender, psychotherapy, vision and psycholinguistics. Psychology can also be taken with Counselling Studies.

Dundee Students gaining a 2:2 degree will have satisfied the requirements of the BPS and can specialise in clinical, counselling, educational, forensic, health and occupational psychology. Psychology is also offered with 19 other subjects, including Business Economics, and Marketing, Geography and Applied Computing and Politics. (High research rating)

Durham* A course in Applied Psychology at Stockton focuses on everyday issues such as health, education and neuropsychological rehabilitation. The BSc Psychology degree at Durham covers cognitive, biological, social, developmental and abnormal psychology and perception. Psychology is also offered as part of the Natural Sciences and Social Sciences and Arts combined honours programmes. (High research rating)

East Anglia* The Psychosocial Sciences course (highly rated by students) draws upon psychology and perspectives on human behaviour.

East London The Psychology course is recognised by the BPS and covers mental health, counselling and families. Options include occupational psychology, health psychology, media and communications. Psychology can also be studied with Criminology, Biology or Health Studies. Degrees in Psychosocial Studies are also offered.

Edge Hill A broad introduction to Psychology takes place in Year 1 with electives being chosen in Years 2 and 3 depending on the student's particular interests and career objectives.

Edinburgh* A general introduction to Psychology in Year 1 is followed by a mainly experimental and biological programme in Year 2. (Entry to the honours course is then conditional on obtaining grades A or B in psychology in Year 2.) Compulsory core subjects in Year 3 combine with a range of options such as social psychology or animal behaviour. A wide range of options continues in Year 4. Research methods and analysis are included in the first three years. There is also a degree in Mind and Language comprising philosophy, linguistics and psychology.

Essex The schemes are identical for both BA and BSc courses in Psychology. Options taken in Year 2 dictate the final degree. The course has an emphasis on cognitive science, linguistics and the social sciences, except for compulsory options in mathematics and computer science in the latter. There are also courses in Developmental and Social Psychology. (High research rating) (See also under **Health Sciences**)

Exeter* Single honours Psychology courses are available in the Faculties of Science and Social Studies although the syllabus is much the same in both, only ancillary subjects being different. The course covers the whole field of psychology – comparative, physiological, social and abnormal – with students being introduced to clinical and other applications of the subject. There is a relatively high practical component to the course and considerable freedom in the choice of options. (High research rating)

Glamorgan A course in Psychology (leading to registration) is taken on a three-year full-time basis. Psychology is also available in the Humanities programme. Options include abnormal, educational, and occupational psychology and counselling. Degrees are also offered in Developmental and Sport and Child Psychology.

Glasgow* Computation techniques, abnormal and developmental psychology and cognitive science are included on the Psychology course. Psychology can be studied with other subjects including Islamic Studies, Czech, Celtic Civilisation, English Literature and Hispanic Studies. See also **Social Science/Studies**. (High research rating)

Glasgow Caledonian There is a wide range of options in this Psychology course, which has an emphasis on small-group teaching. Modules are offered in abnormal, health, and forensic and occupational psychology.

Gloucestershire The Psychology course provides a broad course for further training as specialist psychologists, 12 joint courses are also offered.

Greenwich A course is offered in Psychology and Psychology with Counselling. The courses are accredited by the British Psychological Society leading to registration for those holding a second class honours degree.

Heriot-Watt The course in Applied Psychology (recognised by the BPS) focuses on its uses in education, work and organisations, health and mental health, sport and crime.

Hertfordshire The Psychology course provides a grounding in all the major areas of psychology. In Year 3 six optional courses are offered. Courses in Counselling and altogether a range of 12 Psychology joint courses are also offered.

Huddersfield The Behavioural Sciences course offers a firm grounding in psychology and sociology with an applied focus. Third-year options include health and illness, organisational behaviour, decision processes, culture and illness. A broad Psychology course is offered and in addition it is also possible to take degrees in Criminology, Counselling Studies, Criminal and Community Justice and Police Studies.

Hull In Year 1 all Psychology students study core psychological theory, followed in Year 2 by social, developmental, biological, and cognitive psychology and a course in clinical psychology. In Year 3 students choose their specialisms, which include occupational, educational, health, clinical and counselling psychology. There are seven joint courses, including Psychology with Counselling, Anthropology, Criminology, Occupational Psychology and Sports Science. Scholarships available.

Keele Psychology and Applied Psychology are taken with a second subject. Over 25 joint courses are offered including Forensic Science, Management Science, Mathematics and Educational Studies. Specialist Psychology areas include clinical and occupational psychology, special education and personal relationships. There is also a degree in Neuroscience.

Kent Psychology, Social Psychology, and Applied Psychology courses provide a broad base from which to specialise. Clinical psychology features largely in some programmes. Psychology can be taken with Law, Anthropology and Sociology.

Kingston Psychology is offered as part of the modular course with a choice of some 10 other subjects including languages (French, German or Spanish), Criminology, Journalism and Creative Writing.

Lancaster* Developmental, cognitive biopsychology and social psychology are taken in the first year of the Psychology course with two other subjects. Second- and third-year studies include cognitive, social and neuropsychology. Two other courses are also taken, one in each year. Some exchanges with the USA are possible. Other courses include Psychology in Education or Statistics. (High research rating)

Leeds* In the Psychology course, four major areas are covered – social psychology, learning and biological psychology, cognitive psychology and developmental and clinical psychology. Electives are offered in educational and occupational psychology. Music, Philosophy, Sociology and Management Studies can be studied with Psychology, and there is also a degree in Cognitive Science. (High research rating)

Leeds Metropolitan Psychology is offered as a single or joint honours course, the latter with Forensic Biology, Criminology, Politics or Sociology. There is also a course in Applied Counselling.

Leeds Trinity (UC) The Psychology degree (BPS accredited) covers social, cognitive and biological psychology. Psychology can also be taken with Nutrition and Health and with Sport and Exercise.

Leicester* In the Psychology programme, courses are taken covering the biological bases of behaviour, cognitive psychology – learning, language, thinking – and in abnormal, social and developmental psychology. A supplementary subject can be taken in Years 1 and 2. There are also Psychology courses with Languages, Neuroscience, Biology and Sociology. See also **Combined courses**.

Lincoln In addition to the single honours Psychology course, joint courses are offered with Criminology, English, Health Studies, Marketing, Child Studies, Social Policy and Clinical Psychology.

Liverpool* In Year 1 of the Psychology course psychology is introduced, along with psychological statistics and methods and practical work. In Year 2, psychological themes include biological, abnormal, developmental and cognitive psychology. In Year 3, five courses are taken from about 12 options including clinical or health psychology and artificial intelligence. A course in Psychology with Clinical Psychology is also offered.

Liverpool Hope The BSc Psychology single honours degree confers eligibility for registration with the British Psychological Society. There is also a Sport Psychology degree. Combined courses are also offered.

Liverpool John Moores The Applied Psychology course offers modules that include social problems and client rehabilitation and care. There are also options in counselling, criminal behaviour and mental health. A joint course in Psychology and Biology is also available. There are also courses in Forensic Psychology and Criminal Justice and Business Psychology.

London (Goldsmiths)* The Psychology degree is a laboratory-based programme studied through course units, which allows considerable flexibility in what can be studied. In addition one or two courses are taken from other science subjects. Final-year options focus on vocational applications or intellectual curiosity and include occupational and social psychology and the psychology of language. (High research rating)

London (Heythrop) Psychology is offered with Philosophy or Theology. The latter course covers the social, developmental and cognitive aspects of the subject.

London (LSE)* Social Psychology is not offered as a degree but can be taken as outside options in many other subjects offered by the school.

London (Queen Mary) The course focuses on a natural and experimental subject with a large range of core and module options from the biological sciences.

London (RH)* The Psychology syllabus in years 1 and 2 covers both theoretical and experimental work on a whole range of topics. These include psychometrics, psychopathology, social and developmental psychology and animal behaviour. Individual differences, occupational health and social psychology are among several options offered in the third year. Psychology can also be taken with Biochemistry, Biology, Mathematics or Music. (High research rating)

London (UCL)* Psychology is taken as part of the BSc programme in which students make up their course by combining any prescribed subjects with elective subjects chosen according to their interests. Those wishing to enter careers as psychologists are recommended to take the single honours course. (High research rating)

London Metropolitan The three-year degree in Psychology offers specialisation in Year 3 that includes applied, health, child and social psychology. Other courses include Business Psychology, Applied Psychology and Sports Psychology.

London South Bank Psychology is offered as a single honours degree course and covers biology, social sciences and philosophy. It also focuses on the psychology of language and abnormal psychology. It can also be studied with a second subject, for example with Child Development, Clinical Psychology and Sexuality. There is also a course in Evolutionary Psychology focusing on the interface between the biological and psychological sciences.

Loughborough* The Psychology, and Psychology with Ergonomics courses qualify for professional status. Students choosing the four-year programme spend Year 3 on a placement in an approved occupation relevant to their degree. There are also courses in Social Psychology (a study of people in relation to others) and Human Sciences. (See under **Biology**.)

Manchester* A wide range of options can be taken in Year 3 of this comprehensive Psychology course, with particular reference to applied psychology practice 'in the real world'. There is also a wide range of joint subjects offered with Psychology. (High research rating)

Manchester Metropolitan Various aspects of the study of psychology are covered in the Psychology course, which has two major units – social and individual psychology and cognitive psychology. Psychology can also be taken with a large number of subjects including Speech Pathology, Health Studies, Childhood and Youth Studies, Crime Studies and Visual Arts.

Middlesex The three-year full-time or four-year sandwich course in Psychology includes biological, social and developmental psychology and the opportunity for work placements. Psychology can also be taken with Counselling Skills, Criminology, Human Resource Management or Marketing.

Napier Psychology is offered as a single honours subject or as a joint honours with Sociology.

Newcastle* In Stages 1 and 2 of the Psychology course, students receive a broad foundation in the major areas of experimental psychology – abnormal, developmental, social and psychological as well as animal behaviour, learning and language. Two other subjects, which can include languages, are taken in the first year, and three major and three minor subjects from a range of psychology options are taken in

Stage 3. Final-year options include clinical and occupational psychology and the psychology of health. It is possible to take a BSc Psychology degree that differs slightly in putting more emphasis on intelligence, perceptions and cognition and quantitative methods. (High research rating)

Newman (UC) Psychology is available as a single or major course with another subject. There is also a joint or minor course in Social and Applied Psychology.

Newport The Psychology course covers cognitive, social, health, counselling and sport aspects of the subject.

Northampton The Psychology degree is accredited by the BPS for further training as a psychologist.

Northumbria A general introduction to Psychology takes place in the first year of the course, followed by more specialised areas. These include social psychology, artificial intelligence, behaviour, health and illness, and dyslexia and word recognition. (No animal experiments.) Psychology with Sports Science or Criminology are also offered.

Nottingham* Central topics of the Psychology degree include social and developmental psychology, and biological and cognitive psychology. In Year 3 there is a wide range of options, including clinical and occupational psychology, child development, and computer applications. There is a considerable emphasis on applied psychology in this course, in which there is an optional year of work experience. There are also courses in Psychology and Neuroscience and Psychology with Philosophy. (High research rating)

Nottingham Trent This is a broad Psychology course with specialist options in health psychology, criminology, criminal justice, aggression and violence and abnormal psychology. Psychology with Sociology, Sport Science, Criminology and with Educational Development are also offered.

Oxford* Experimental Psychology is a study of psychology as an experimental science and covers the whole range of research – human experimental psychology, animal and physiological development, behaviour and linguistics. The course in Psychology, Philosophy and Physiology (PPP) allows students to specialise in two of these subjects. (High research rating)

Oxford Brookes* Psychology is offered as a single subject or jointly with over 40 other subjects including Anthropology, Business Statistics, Educational Studies, Complementary Therapies, Intelligent Systems, Human Biology and Music.

Plymouth The broad-based Psychology course introduces students to a range of topics including cognition, learning, motivation, psychopathology and social development and applied psychology. There are special facilities for work in clinical psychology, and psychological and social psychology. This is a three-year course with an optional sandwich year (subject to a successful application to transfer to the four-year course). Other courses include Psychology with Criminal Justice Studies, Sociology, Psychology, and Law.

Portsmouth* Introductory courses in the first year of the Psychology degree lead on to a range of specialist topics, including developmental psychology of childhood and adolescence, social and physiological psychology, the psychology of hypnosis, language, criminology, clinical psychology and social problems and politics. The course emphasises human behaviour, and the final year contains options in applied psychology and counselling. There is also a course in Forensic Psychology with topics covering cyber crime, interviewing and offender profiling. Psychology can also be studied with Human Resource Management, Marketing, Criminology and English.

Queen Margaret Psychology can be taken jointly with Sociology or Media. There is also a degree in Health Psychology combining behaviour with health.

Queen's Belfast* Psychology is offered in the Faculties of Arts, Science and Economics and Social Science, but the content is identical in each case – the major differences lie in the modules available. The flexibility of the course structure enables students to make the final decision on the choice of subject at the end of the first year. Emphasis is laid on practical and experimental work throughout the course. Final-year options include sports psychology, psychology at work, neurobiology and behaviour, child educational and clinical psychology. Courses include Drama or Social Policy or Politics with Psychological Studies.

Reading* The basic subject matter of modern psychology is studied during the first four terms of the Psychology degree. This is followed by a choice of 26 special options in the final year, covering a wide range of topics including clinical and neuropsychology and social, industrial and organisational psychology. Psychology can also be taken with Childhood and Ageing; Mental and Physical Health, Art, Biology or Philosophy. Entrance scholarships are offered. (High research rating)

Roehampton Psychology is offered as a single or combined honours course which qualifies graduates for graduate membership of the British Psychological Society. In Year 2 there is a focus on cognitive, social and development psychology, along with personality psychology and abnormal behaviour. In Year 3 there is a supervised, year-long research project and also the opportunity to study a range of optional modules such as autism and criminal and forensic psychology. There is also a degree course in Psychology and Counselling and in Psychology and Health.

St Andrews* Psychology can be offered in the Faculties of Arts and Sciences. Decisions to specialise are made in Year 3. Single and joint honours are available in both Faculties. Joint courses, and 'with' degrees are also offered – those degrees with other subjects having two-thirds of the time spent with psychology and one-third with the second subject. (High research rating)

St Mary's (UC) The Psychology course and the major route in the combined programme are accredited for registration by the British Psychological Society.

Salford A single honours course in Psychology is offered, with an emphasis on the application of theory and skills, together with Psychology Studies and Counselling Studies or Health Sciences. There are also modules in educational and forensic psychology.

Sheffield* Introductory modules cover biological, social and developmental psychology, neuroscience and psychological disorders. Specialist studies are chosen in Year 3. Courses are also available with Philosophy and in Human Communication Sciences. (High research rating)

Sheffield Hallam* Psychology specialisms are offered in social, behavioural and developmental psychology including communication disorders and mental health. Psychology can also be taken with Sociology or Criminology or Law.

Southampton* Psychology students follow three courses in psychology in Year 1 – introduction to psychology, the biological bases of behaviour and motivation, emotion and abnormal psychology. Practical work is an important component of the course. Specialisation takes place in Years 2 and 3 covering such topics as language, perception, criminal behaviour, education, amnesia and pain. Courses in Psychological Studies and Criminology are offered within the Applied Social Sciences Programme. Scholarship available.

Southampton Solent In addition to a single honours Psychology degree there are four pathways. Education, Counselling, Criminology Behaviour and Health Psychology.

Staffordshire This broad Psychology course provides options in health, neuropsychology, crime and counselling. Other courses include Psychology with Criminology, Counselling, Child Development and Sociology.

Stirling Psychology is introduced as a biological and social science. Other studies include learning, clinical and abnormal psychology, and the social and cognitive development in infants and young children. Part II covers psychological methods, animal behaviour, social psychology, perception and performance, clinical and counselling psychology, and occupational psychology. Psychology can also be studied with, for example, Film and Media Studies, Marketing and Politics. (High research rating)

Strathclyde Psychology is offered as a single or joint honours course with a range of subjects including Human Resource Management, Politics, Sociology and Languages. Joint courses are not accredited for qualification as a psychologist.

Sunderland In addition to the fundamentals of psychology and research methods there is a wide choice of options on the Psychology course, covering motivation, the emotions, abnormal child development, counselling, death, dying and bereavement, and health psychology. Psychology is offered with a wide range of courses including Gender Studies, Journalism, Business and Management, and Media Studies.

Surrey* Psychology is a four-year sandwich course in which the third year is spent in professional placement. These placements are in hospitals and clinical schools, social survey companies, personnel and occupational guidance services, industry and commerce. A sandwich course in Applied Psychology and Sociology is also offered that covers most areas of human behaviour, both individual and social. (High research rating)

Sussex* Students interested in Psychology are taken from both arts and science backgrounds. A variety of degree programmes is offered with a common core of subjects, allowing students to specialise later. These cover Applied, Developmental or Social Psychology. Degrees with Cognitive Science, Neuroscience and Sociology are also available.

Swansea* Psychology is offered by the Faculties of Arts, Science and Economic and Social Studies. In all faculties in Part I there is a range of lecture courses, including the biological bases of behaviour for arts and science students. In Part II students take, and have the choice of, a very wide range of topics, with the opportunity to specialise in biological, social or applied aspects of the subject. Psychology is offered with languages (including Welsh), Computer Science, Criminology, Economics and Law. (High research rating)

Swansea Metropolitan The Counselling and Psychology course offers special studies in such topics as health and well-being, learning, behaviour and occupational psychology.

Teesside The Psychology course provides a broad theoretical and practical base, together with computer skills, and is taught on the flexible modular system. Options include counselling, occupational psychology, and neuropsychology. Other courses include Psychology with Forensic Psychology, Counselling and Criminology.

Ulster The Psychology degree leads to specialisation in clinical, counselling, occupational and health psychology. There is also a separate degree in Social Psychology.

Warwick* In Year 1, Psychology students are introduced to the foundations of psychology and take an optional subject from a range of possibilities in science, mathematics, social sciences or humanities subjects. Core courses in Year 2 covering personality, psychopathology, perception, action, memory and language are followed by a choice of four courses from 10 in the final year.

West London Psychology is offered in the Humanities programme. It can be studied in combination with another subject or a specialist route giving eligibility for graduate membership of the British Psychological Society. Psychology is also offered with Criminology and Counselling and Health.

West Scotland The BSc course in Psychology is awaiting validation.

Westminster The Psychology course covers cognitive, social, developmental and abnormal psychology as well as units in statistics and computing and options in management and healthcare. Courses are also offered in Cognitive Science and Neuroscience.

Winchester The course is approved by the British Psychological Society and explores all aspect of human behaviour. Opportunities to specialise commence in Year 2. There are several joint courses from which to choose.

Wolverhampton After a broad introductory first year, Psychology students choose seven out of 10 optional modules such as social psychology, personality and abnormal psychology, human–computer interaction or counselling and group work. They also complete an individual project and have the opportunity to combine studies with one or two other subjects. Psychology courses include Deaf Studies, Counselling Psychology, Business, Geography, Marketing, Special Needs and Education Studies.

Worcester The Psychology course has a practical emphasis with final year options in eleven subjects. There is also a course in Business Psychology.

York* The Psychology course places particular emphasis on psychology as an experimental science and academic discipline. It attempts to avoid any strong bias in favour of – or against – any specific field or approach within psychology.

York St John The BSc course in Psychology is accredited for registration for a career as a psychologist. The BA course has less emphasis on statistics and biology and is not accredited. There is also a single and joint programme in Counselling Studies.

OTHER INSTITUTIONS OFFERING PSYCHOLOGY COURSES
Bradford (Coll), Burton (Coll), Cornwall (Coll), Duchy (Coll), East Lancashire (Coll), Grimsby (IFHE), Havering (Coll), Llandrillo (Coll), Norwich City (Coll), Richmond (American Univ), Somerset (CAT), Staffordshire (Reg Fed), Suffolk (Univ Campus), Truro (Coll), Welsh (Coll Hort), Warwickshire (Coll), Wigan and Leigh (Coll), West Anglia (Coll).

ALTERNATIVE COURSES
Advertising, Business Studies, Computer Science and Artificial Intelligence, Education and Teacher Training, Human Resources Management, Social Administration and Social Studies/Science.

RELIGIOUS STUDIES

(including **Biblical Studies**, **Theology** and **Divinity**)
(* indicates universities with the highest entry requirements)

SUBJECT REQUIREMENTS/PREFERENCES
GCE A-level: Religious Studies may be preferred; check institutions. **GCSE:** English, Mathematics or a science may be required. For teacher training, English, Mathematics and Science.

SUBJECT INFORMATION
Religious Studies courses cover four degree subjects – Religious Studies, Divinity, Theology and Biblical Studies. The subject content of these courses varies and students should check prospectuses carefully. They are not intended as training courses for the church ministry; an adherence to a particular religious persuasion is not a necessary qualification for entry. (A-level Religious Studies is an acceptable second or third A-level for any non-scientific degree course.)

Aberdeen Degrees in Divinity, and Religious Studies are offered, the latter covering topics in Judaism, Christianity, Islam, Buddhism and Hinduism. The degree in Divinity covers Church history, history of religions, Hebrew Bible, New Testament and theology. (High research rating)

Bangor Degree courses are available in Theology and Religious Studies and are offered in English and Welsh. In Part I of the Theology course there are introductory courses in the Old and New Testaments, Church history and doctrine and the history and philosophy of religion. These topics continue in Part II, in addition to which students take four other courses from the list prescribed for the Biblical Studies degree programme. The Religious Studies course combines Biblical studies with topics covering 20th century Christianity, theological ethics and Judaism.

Bath Spa The Study of Religions course explores religious ideas and practices and their influence on the world. Twelve joint courses are available.

Birmingham* A very flexible Theology and Religious Studies course is offered, focusing primarily on Christianity but offering programmes on other major religions. Core courses cover introductions to Biblical Studies, Christian Theology and Christian History. Second- and third-year options include a range of Biblical subjects, for example Hebrew, Greek texts, the Gospels and New Testament theology. Theology can also be taken with Sociology and Philosophy. There is also a degree in Islamic Studies. (High research rating)

Bristol* The course in Theology and Religious Studies has a strong focus on the study of religion both in the contemporary world and in the past. The basic subjects taught are Biblical studies, Jewish studies, Christian history and theology with an emphasis on the early, medieval and modern periods. In Years 2 and 3 the course continues with interfaith studies, Biblical studies, religion and gender, the New Testament, Judaism, Islam, Buddhism and Hinduism. Language options include Greek, Hebrew, Arabic, Latin and Sanskrit. (High research rating)

Cambridge* The Theology and Religious Studies Tripos is taken in two parts. Part I is taken after one year and Part II after a further two years. The Part I course, with no specific course requirements, provides for a wide variety of interests – Biblical, historical, philosophical and comparative, and students choose four out of 14 papers. Part II builds on the foundation laid by the Part I course and includes modern theology, the philosophy of religion, the history of Christian life and thought, and comparative religion (chiefly Indian religions and Judaism). Homerton College also offers Religious Studies for those aiming for a teaching qualification at Primary level. (High research rating)

Canterbury Christ Church The Religious Studies course covers world religions, religious movements and the Great Books, followed in Years 2 and 3 by a wide range of options. There is also a course in Theology. Previous study of religions is not required.

Cardiff* The Religious and Theological Studies course comprises a study of major faiths past and present, language and text theology and optional topics, including the history of the early Church, the Crusades and Welsh history and religious literature. For the course in Theology, students cover the Holy Scriptures, the Old and the New Testaments, Christian doctrine, ethics, and Church history. There are beginners' courses in Greek, Hebrew and Sanskrit, and practical theology involving fieldwork. A third pathway now covers Indian religions and includes Buddhism, Hinduism and Jainism, including Sanskrit language and texts. (High research rating)

Central Lancashire Ten courses are offered in Religion, Culture and Society including combined courses with Education, Philosophy, Politics, Archaeology, Sociology and Islamic studies.

Chester The courses in Religious Studies and Religion and Culture engage with religions such as Islam, Hinduism, Judaism and Christianity as well as modern religious movements. There is also a Theology degree exploring traditional ideas and concepts in the modern world.

Chichester The Theology degree covers Biblical studies, ethics, philosophy, worship and medical and professional ethics.

Cumbria The Religious Studies degree introduces a wide range of world religions. There is also a course is Contemporary Theology covering historical, Biblical, doctrinal and political issues.

Durham* The Theology course provides a broad study of the subject ranging from Biblical studies and Christian theology to Jewish studies and the sociology and anthropology of religion. Theology is also offered with Philosophy, Education Studies and in the combined honours programme in Arts. (High research rating)

Edinburgh* Divinity focuses on Christianity, its orgins, historical development and its global spread. There is also an MA course in Religion Studies.

Exeter* The Theology course provides an introduction to the subject by way of Old Testament studies (history and literature), the theologies of Paul and John and the development of Christian doctrine. Other modules include New Testament, Greek, Hebrew, Biblical texts, the synoptic gospels, modern theology, Christian ethics, Islam and Church history.

Glasgow Two degrees are offered leading to Bachelor of Divinity (BD), General (focusing on the study of Christianity) and Ministry (a vocational course). The former is wide ranging and interdisciplinary, covering religious beliefs and practices. There is also an MA degree in Religious Studies with specialist studies in Islam, Eastern Religions, Philosophy, Literature, Theology, Women's Studies and Holocaust Studies. The BD and MA degrees are recognised teaching qualifications in Religious Studies. A degree in Religious and Philosophical Education is also offered. (High research rating)

Gloucestershire There is a course bringing together the study of three subject areas by way of the degree in Religion, Philosophy and Ethics which is also offered as a joint course with other subjects.

Greenwich The programme in Theology and Religious Studies is offered as part of the combined honours course.

Hertfordshire Religious Studies is offered as part of the Primary Teaching Programme while a Study of Religion can be taken as a minor option in the combined honours degree.

Huddersfield The degree in Religion and Education is a study of major world religions and educational issues.

Hull Courses are offered in Theology and also Theology, Slavery and Liberation providing a basis for a broader study of religion. Other courses include Religion, Religion and Educational Studies, and Religion, Media and Culture; joint courses are also offered. (High research rating)

Kent Religious Studies is offered at single and joint honours levels. Topics include applied theology, Biblical interpretation, mysticism, and religious experience. A wide range of modules gives the course considerable flexibility with options in science, philosophy, psychology or theology and their impact on religion.

Lancaster* In Year 1 the Religious Studies course covers Western and Indian religions, the Bible, the Koran, Judaism and the philosophy of religion. Two other subjects are also taken. In Years 2 and 3, in which there are 40 option modules, the main studies include Judaism, Christianity, Islam, Hinduism, Buddhism and philosophy. Exchanges with the USA are possible. Other courses include Anthropology of Religion and Ethics, Philosophy and Religion. (High research rating)

Leeds In Year 1 of the Theology and Religious Studies course there is an introduction to Christian theological tradition, ancient Middle Eastern religion, New Testament Greek, early Indian religions or another subsidiary course. In the second and third years, students choose from a range of options. The course tends to stress the contemporary and 'lived' aspects of religions rather than their classical and theoretical aspects. Twenty-three joint courses with Religious Studies are also on offer, including Arabic and Islamic Studies, Jewish Civilisation, Theology and Religious Studies. (High research rating)

Leeds Trinity (UC) This study of World Religion includes topics relating to philosophy and ethics and theology. There are work placements each year to explore career options.

Liverpool Hope The degree in Theology and Religious Studies is offered at single and combined honours levels, with Philosophy and Ethics strongly recommended in the latter.

London (Heythrop)* Degree courses are offered in Theology, Philosophy and Theology, Philosophy, Religion and Ethics, Psychology and Theology and Abrahamic Religions (Islam, Christianity, Judaism) at this small college, yet it is one of the largest schools of theology in the United Kingdom.

London (King's)* Religious Studies and Theology degrees follow the course unit system. After a common first term, students decide on the core units they will take. Courses cover the philosophy of religion and ethics and studies of Christianity, Islam and Judaism. (High research rating)

London (SOAS)* Specialising in the religions of Asia and Africa the three-year degree in the Study of Religions is taken as a joint course with a choice of over 40 subjects, including African and Asian languages. (High research rating)

Manchester* Study of Religion and Theology is a broad-based course providing an introduction to the different approaches of this field. These cover historical, theological, psychological, anthropological, philosophical and sociological aspects. There are also pathways focusing on Jewish Studies, Biblical Studies, South Asian Studies and Religion and Society. There is also a separate degree in Islamic Studies and Muslim Societies. (High research rating)

Middlesex The courses in Religion in Context are offered as joint courses with Media Studies, Education, Philosophy and Psychology.

Newman (UC) Religious Education is offered with a major course in Education Studies for those aiming for teaching or education careers. There are also courses in Theology.

Newport A BA degree in Religious Studies embraces all the main religious.

Nottingham The Theology course introduces a study of the Old Testament, Christianity and Faith and Practice of Islam. Years 2 and 3 provide a wide choice of specialist options. (High research rating)

Oxford* The Theology course provides an informed and critical understanding of the Old and New Testaments, of the historical development of the role of the Church and the contemporary meaning of the Christian faith. A large range of options includes the philosophy of religion, ancient and modern Church history, Christian ethics, textual criticism and Biblical Hebrew. Theology may also be studied with Philosophy. (High research rating)

Oxford Brookes* Religion and Theology can be studied as a first or second subject in a wide range of joint degrees. Three-year full-time degrees are also available in a range of combined subjects, including Philosophy, Education, Youth Studies and Applied Theology, Anthropology, Psychology and Sociology.

Queen's Belfast* Queen's University is free from association with any religious denomination. Degrees in Theology (non-denominational) and Divinity are offered with a common curriculum in Year 1 in which a study of languages (Greek or Hebrew) is possible.

Roehampton Theology and Religious Studies is offered as a single or combined honours course which explores the multi-faceted nature of the subject. Topics range from Biblical themes, world religions, philosophy of religion and mythology. There is also the opportunity to study the languages of sacred texts such as Greek, Hebrew, Latin, classical Arabic, Sanskrit. There is also a Foundation degree in Ministerial Theology.

St Andrews* Biblical Studies and Theology can be taken as Arts or Divinity subjects. Within the Bachelor of Divinity (BD) course an honours subject or group may be chosen from among Old or New Testament language and literature, ecclesiastical history, divinity and practical theology. There are also separate joint degree courses in a range of subjects including Greek, Latin or History with New Testament, Theological Studies and Languages with Biblical Studies or Hebrew. (High research rating)

St Mary's (UC) The degree in Theology and Religious Studies covers Biblical studies, world religions and contemporary world issues.

Sheffield* In Year 1, Biblical Studies is combined with a wide-ranging survey of Biblical history, languages and literature. Years 2 and 3 cover Old and New Testament texts, broader areas of Biblical history, literature and theology. Students also take one or two unrestricted options. (High research rating)

Stirling The Religious Studies degree offers religion, myth and meaning, ethics and society, and Indian religions are taken in Part I (the first three semesters). In Semesters 4–6 all students take one course in Biblical studies and one in historical and philosophical studies. There are also options in Part II, along with eastern religions and new religious movements.

Trinity St David (Carmarthen) Several courses are offered including Religious Studies, Religious Education and Christianity and Community Studies. Scholarships available.

Trinity St David (Lampeter) Several courses are offered, including Religious Studies, Religious History, Islamic Studies, Divinity, Theology, Anthropology and Religion, and Religion, Ethics and Society. (High research rating)

Winchester The course in Theology and Religious Studies examines aspects and traditions of the major religions by way of single or combined honours programmes. There are also a number of joint courses with Ethics and Spirituality. (See also **Philosophy**)

Wolverhampton A degree in Religious Studies can be taken as a single or combined degree course with subjects such as Early Childhood Studies, Human Rights, Philosophy and Education Studies.

York St John Christan Theology and Theology and Religious Studies courses are offered as single or joint courses.

OTHER INSTITUTIONS OFFERING RELIGIOUS STUDIES COURSES
Havering (Coll), Nazarene (Theol Coll), UHI Millennium Inst.

ALTERNATIVE COURSES
History, Philosophy, Psychology, Social Studies.

SOCIAL SCIENCE/STUDIES

(including **Criminology**, **Social Policy** and **Social Work**)
(see also **Law** and **Sociology**)
(* indicates universities with the highest entry requirements)

SUBJECT REQUIREMENTS/PREFERENCES
GCSE: Usually English and Mathematics; a science may be required for some courses.

SUBJECT INFORMATION
These courses are a good vocational preparation for careers in the social services. A wide range of topics is covered, for example housing policy, health services, mental illness, the family and prisons. New social work degrees are being introduced, which replace the Diploma in Social Work. Check with institutions and with the General Social Care Council (www.gscc.org.uk) and on www.socialworkcareers.co.uk. (Research ratings are shown for **Social Work**.)

Aberdeen The course in Gender Studies covers women, power and society 1800–1918, gendering violence and the women's movement in 20th-century Britain.

Abertay Dundee The Social Science programme has Year 3 options including psychology, sociology, economics, health, management and sport development. A degree in Criminology is also offered with options in Sociology, Law and Psychology.

Anglia Ruskin A degree is offered in Criminology, covering forensic science, law, politics, crime and the criminal justice system. In addition there is a degree in Housing with modules in housing development, policy and law and also Social Work and Social Policy programmes.

Aston* Public Policy is offered with Management as a joint or combined honours programme with placement year opportunities.

Bangor The course in Health and Social Care involves a study of social policy, housing, poverty and family welfare and includes the opportunity to spend a semester abroad as part of the degree. There is also a course in Criminology and Criminal Justice which enables graduates who are interested in careers in law or the police to proceed from the degree to the Common Professional Examination or the Postgraduate Diploma in Law or to a graduate training programme with the police.

Bath* Courses are offered in Social Sciences, and Social Work, and Social Policy with optional units in economics, politics, psychology and languages. The courses in the Department of Social and Political Sciences are highly flexible and it is often possible to move from one programme to another at the end of the first year.

Bedfordshire The Applied Social Studies course is a vocational course preparing students for work in the social services and covers criminology, social policy, sociology, psychology. There are also courses in Social Work, Child and Adolescent studies, and Youth and Community Studies.

Birmingham* The Social Policy course covers politics, policy making, sociology, economics, psychology and urban studies. There is a range of specialist modules on offer covering healthcare, housing, criminology, ageing and society studies. There are also courses in Public and Social Policy, and Management and Social work. (High research rating)

Birmingham City A degree in Social Work is followed by the Diploma which is recognised for professional purposes. There is also a three-year course in Criminal Justice and Policing, or with Psychology, or Criminology. There is also a unique course in Criminal Investigation.

Bolton The Community Studies course includes modules in ethnicity and race, housing problems and mental illness. Work placement takes place in local community groups.

Bournemouth The Social Work degree covers children and young people, adults, mental health, social exclusion and law. There is also a course in Community Work.

Bradford There are courses in Social Work and Social Policy. There is also a course in Applied Criminal Justice Studies, a vocational course with a 33 day placement in Year 2.

Brighton The degree in Social Science covers social psychology, criminology, health and criminal justice. Courses in Criminology, Health and Social Care and Social Work are also offered. There is also a course in Applied Social Sciences based in Hastings.

Bristol* The Social Policy degree provides a broad picture of historical and contemporary issues leading to options in criminology, poverty, urban studies and violence to women. There is also a course on Childhood Studies which includes options in psychology and youth justice. (High research rating)

Bristol UWE Courses are offered in Public Health and Social Work, and in Housing Management, which has elective topics in the history of architecture, urban conservation and safer communities.

Brunel* The BA degree in Social Work includes modules in professional social work skills, theories and methods, law, social policy, social welfare and child observation. All students have to complete a 100-day practical placement. Specialist routes are offered in work with Adults or Children and Families. There are also courses in Youth Work.

Bucks New Courses are available in Police Studies, Criminology, Social Work, Public Services and Psychosocial Studies.

See *University Degree Course Offers* (Trotman Publishing) for details of offers

Cambridge* See under **Politics, Psychology** and **Sociology**.

Canterbury Christ Church Courses are offered in Social Work and Police Studies, the latter offered in conjunction with the Kent Police. There are also courses in Child and Youth Studies and in Applied Criminology.

Cardiff The Social Sciences degree scheme provides full degrees and half degrees in Education, Sociology, Social Policy and Criminology. (High research rating)

Cardiff (UWIC) Courses offered include Housing, Health and Social Care, Social Work and Community Education.

Central Lancashire Degree courses in Criminology, Deaf Studies and joint British Sign Language, Human Rights Race and Ethnic Studies and Social Policy are offered on the combined honours and joint programmes. The University offers a unit degree scheme that includes courses from economics, psychology and sociology.

Chester A Social Work programme is offered at the Warrington campus leading to a career in the profession. Courses are also offered in Counselling and Criminology which explores crime and punishment, discipline and deviance, mental health and crime and legal issues.

Chichester The Social Work course involves social policy, mental health and welfare, and child and adult services.

City* The University offers a unit degree scheme that includes courses from economics, psychology and sociology.

Coventry The Criminology degree focuses on the social aspects of crime and the workings of the police, sentencing and prisons. There is also a social work course with placements and degrees in Youth Work and Community Studies.

Cumbria A large Social Sciences programme includes criminology, family studies, policing, community arts and youth studies.

De Montfort The Social Studies programme offers degrees in Community and Criminal Justice, Social Work, Criminology and Youth Studies.

Derby Courses are offered in Applied Community and Youth Studies, Crime and Justice, Criminology (including joint courses), Applied Social Care, Social Work and Public Services Management.

Dundee After an introductory course the selection procedure for entry to the Social Work degree takes place at the end of Year 2. There is also a Community Education course with a professional qualification.

Durham* The criminology course covers crime, deviance, social control and criminal justice in society. Modules cover organised crime, punishment and forensic science.

East Anglia* A course in Psychosocial Studies is offered that explores childhood, adolescence, interpersonal skills, lifestyles and human relationships. There is also a degree in Social Work. (High research rating)

East London An extended Social Sciences degree covers power, crime, city life, government, and law. Students take two or three subjects in Year 1, specialising in Years 2 and 3. Courses are also offered in Criminology (with Psychology, Law, Sociology, Business and Criminal Justice), Social Work, Psychosocial Studies, Public Administration and Community Service and Enterprise.

Edge Hill There is a degree in Social Work leading to professional qualification. 200 days of practice placement takes place on the course, assessed as part of the degree.

Edinburgh* Fifteen subject departments are involved in undergraduate teaching in the Faculty of Social Sciences. The BSc (Social Science) is an eight-course degree in which students choose groups of courses depending on their particular interests. Courses include accounting, archaeology, architecture, business studies, Canadian studies, economic and social history, economics, geography, nursing studies, politics, psychology, social policy, social anthropology, social work and sociology. There are also degrees in Social Policy and Social Work. (High research rating)

Essex* The degree in Social Science Theories and Methods combines the expertise of the Departments of Government, Sociology and Economics and provides a flexible scheme of topics from these and other subject areas including human rights. A Human Rights degree is offered with Law, Politics, Sociology or Philosophy.

Glamorgan Social Science programmes include Community Regeneration, Criminology, Police Sciences, Public and Emergency Services and Sociology. There is also a degree in Social Work.

Glasgow The MA in Social Sciences spans a large number of subject areas (27). In addition degrees in Community Learning and Development and Public Policy are offered, the latter focussing on the major social policy issues of the day. Applicants for the Social Work degree apply through Strathclyde University; the degree is also available at Glasgow's Crichton Campus in Dumfries where a Liberal Arts Programme is also offered.

Glasgow Caledonian In Years 1, 2 and 3 of the Social Sciences degree six, five and four choices are made respectively, from economics, a foreign language, geography, history, politics, psychology and sociology. There is a degree in Social Work with placements in Years 2 and 3 and a course in legal studies and criminology.

Gloucestershire Degree courses are offered in Community Development, Social Work, Criminology and Local Policy focusing on the role of government.

Glyndŵr The degree in Public and Social Policy focuses on the werfare services including social and environmental aspects, drugs, youth problems, chile abuse and community care. Social Work and Youth Studies degrees are also offered.

Greenwich Courses covered by the Social Sciences include criminology, and social care with social work studies. There are also degrees in Youth and Community Studies, Social Work, Criminal Justice and Social Care and Criminology and Criminal Psychology.

Hertfordshire A course is offered in Social Work which provides professional registration with the General Social Care Council. An employment-based course is also possible (subject to employer's support).

Huddersfield There are courses in Criminology, Health and Community Studies and Police Studies and Youth Work. A three-year course is also offered leading to a degree and a Diploma in Social Work. The degree in Social Sciences covers Sociology, Politics, Psychology and Criminology. (High research rating)

Hull This is a multi-disciplinary social science department covering Criminology, Sociology, Anthropology, Gender Studies, Public Sector Management, Public Policy, Social Work and Social Policy.

Keele A degree in Criminology is offered with 27 other dual honours subjects and there is also a single honours course in Social Work.

Kent Degrees are offered in Social Policy, Social Work and Sociology. Course in Criminology and Criminal Justice Studies are also offered as single and joint honours programmes. Close links exist with criminal justice agencies.

Kingston Courses are offered in Social Work, Criminology and Human Rights.

Lancaster* Criminology students choose one other subject form the Faculties of Arts and Social Sciences. The Social Work course has a 20 week placement in Year 2. (High research rating)

Leeds* There is a Criminal Justice and Criminology course with a range of topics covering criminal law, punishment and society, crime prevention and community safety. Courses are also offered in Social Policy and Social work.

Leeds Metropolitan Social Work and Community Development and Youth Studies is offered in addition to several Social Science options.

Leicester* A course is offered in Criminology, covering the penal system, policing, terrorism, probation, punishment the courts and all issues relating to crime and justice.

Lincoln Courses are offered in Social Science, Social Work and Child and Youth Studies, and Criminology with joint subjects in Forensic Investigation, Politics and International Relations.

Liverpool* Courses in Criminology and Criminology with Sociology are offered in addition to the Social Sciences combined honours programme.

Liverpool Hope Courses are offered in Social Care and Social Work. The degree in Criminology (single and combined courses) runs parallel with Sociology and Psychology in Years 1 and 2, with options in Year 3. The Applied Social Science focuses on Sociology and Psychology.

Liverpool John Moores Degrees are offered in Applied Social Studies, Criminal Justice, Security and the State, Social Work, Childhood and Adolescent Studies and Youth Work.

London (Goldsmiths) A three-year Social Work degree is open to students over 18. There are also courses in Applied Social Studies, Community and Youth Work.

London (LSE)* Social Policy is offered with Economics, Sociology, Government or Criminology, in addition to the single honours course. (High research rating)

London (RH)* A BSc course is offered in Social Work with 200 days of supervised practice. There is also a course in Criminology and Sociology.

London Metropolitan A degree is offered in Public Administration and Social Policy dealing with political institutions, legal processes and the theory and practice of social organisations. Social Policy and Social Research can also be taken as a joint course. There is also a single honours degree in Social Work.

London South Bank Social Policy is offered as a single subject BSc course or with subjects including Politics, Psychology and Tourism. There are also several courses in International Social Policy, and courses in Criminology, and Social Work.

Loughborough* A course is offered in Criminology and Social Policy examining current theories and the problems of society.

Manchester* The Social Work course is integrated into the School of Nursing and Midwifery, providing the opportunity for interdisciplinary learning. There are also several courses linked with Social Sciences.

Manchester Metropolitan Courses are offered in Social Work, Criminology, and Childhood Studies and Youth and Community Work.

Marjon (UCP) Courses are offered in Children, Welfare and Society or Community Practice, Community Work, or Children's Physical Education.

Middlesex Courses focus on Policing, Criminal Justice and Criminology which can also be combined with Psychology or Sociology. There is also a Social Work course.

Napier The Social Sciences course offers core subjects in psychology, British society and economics. It later focuses on various aspects of social problems including welfare, education, organisations and health.

See *University Degree Course Offers* (Trotman Publishing) for details of offers

Newcastle* Social Studies provides a degree in Social Policy and Social Anthropology and covers most fields of importance in contemporary sociology. A degree is also offered in Social Work.

Newman (UC) A course is offered in Working with Children, Young People and Families as a single, joint of major course.

Newport Community and Youth Work, Social Work, Criminal Justice and Counselling Studies are offered.

Northampton Courses are offered in Criminology, Social Welfare, Social Work and Social and Community Development.

Northumbria The Social Work course has an emphasis on practice and experience in different welfare settings. A Criminology course can also be taken with Sociology.

Nottingham* A course is offered in Social and Cultural Studies covering political and social issues under debate in Britain, Europe and North America.

Nottingham Trent Courses are offered in Social Work, Youth Studies and Health and Social Care.

Oxford Brookes* The Social Work course is highly rated among students. There are also courses in Youth Studies and Community Work.

Plymouth There is a combined Social Science degree and courses in Health and Social Care Management, Social Work, Public Services, International Social Justice and Criminology.

Portsmouth Courses are offered in Social Work and Criminology with Criminal Justice, Forensic Science or Psychology.

Queen's Belfast* The Social Policy course covers citizenship, the family in European society, health and social care, penal policies, and aspects of poverty, politics and protest. There are also courses in Social Work, Criminology and Gender Studies. (High research rating)

Reading* A Social Work degree is offered via the Bursary Scheme or employer-sponsored.

Robert Gordon In the three-year BA Social Work degree course entry in Year 2 is possible for applicants with appropriate qualifications. There is also a flexible course in Applied Social Sciences with several options in social issues eg Psychology, Police Work and Health.

Roehampton Social Policy and Administration is offered as a BSc honours degree. It is also available as the first or second subject in the combined honours programme with such subjects as the Social Science of Sport, Sociology and Theology. Combined courses are also offered with Criminology.

Salford Degrees in Social Policy are offered with core modules in sociology and psychology and a wide range of options. There are also courses with Criminology and Counselling.

Sheffield* A degree is offered in Social and Political Studies, crossing both boundaries. It offers special topics including crime and deviance, ageing and society, social values, the European Union, east and central European democracy and territorial politics. There is also a degree in Social Policy and Sociology. (High research rating)

Sheffield Hallam There is a Social Sciences programme and several Criminology courses which include criminal justice, law, policing and psychology. There are also courses in Social Work and Youth Studies.

Southampton* Social Work can be taken as a sandwich course. Applied Social Science includes four pathways with options in anthropology, criminology and psychology. Scholarships available.

Southampton Solent Social Work and Criminology single honours courses are offered.

Staffordshire There is a Social Work degree with a 90 day placement.

Stirling Courses are offered in Social Work, Sociology and Social Policy. (High research rating)

Strathclyde Two Social Work courses are offered, one with a Residential Child Care pathway.

Sunderland Courses are offered in Health and Social Care, Criminology and Community Studies.

Sussex There are three- and four-year full-time or part-time courses in Social Work.

Swansea* Criminology is offered with Psychology or Social Policy. There is also a degree in Early Childhood Studies. Single honours courses are also offered in Social Policy and Social Work.

Swansea Metropolitan Public Administration and Public Services degrees cover finance, law, criminology, leisure, the emergency services and community work.

Teesside The Social Studies degree covers sociology, politics, public administration, economics and social policy, with an option in nursing. There are also degrees in Youth Studies with either Criminology or Psychology, Crime Scene Science (with placements), Crime and Investigation and Death Investigation.

Trinity St David (Carmarthen) There are several courses involving Social Inclusion and also a degree in Community Development.

Trinity St David (Lampeter) The course in Voluntary Sector Studies covers psychology, working with the homeless, experiencing disability and the management aspects of volunteer groups.

Ulster There are courses in Social Policy, Social Work and Community Work.

West Scotland There is a Social Sciences degree with a common first year. Students make a final choice of degree subject in Year 3 from Social Policy, Psychology, Sociology, Politics or Economics. There is also a degree in Criminal Justice.

Westminster Criminal Justice is a three-year full-time course with a free option module in Year 2 taken from anywhere across the university.

Winchester The Social Studies degree leads on to careers in social services, health services, schools, day centres and residential homes. A work placement is built into the second year of the course.

Wolverhampton Courses in Criminal Justice, Social Policy, Special Needs, Deaf Studies and Conductive Education should be considered.

Worcester There are courses in Social Work and also Social Welfare covering most social issues.

York The course in Applied Social Science follows the same programme as that in Social Policy in Year 1. Thereafter over 15 optional subjects are available, giving maximum flexibility to subject choice. (High research rating)

OTHER INSTITUTIONS OFFERING SOCIAL SCIENCE COURSES
Bradford (Coll), Cornwall (Coll), Dewsbury (Coll), Durham New (Coll), East Lancashire (Coll), Havering (Coll), Llandrillo (Coll), Norwich City (Coll), Oxford Ruskin (Coll), South Devon (Coll), South Essex (Coll), Suffolk (Univ Campus), Stockport (Coll), Sunderland City (Coll), Solihull (Coll), Somerset (CAT), Staffordshire (Reg Fed), Truro (Coll), UHI Millennium Inst, Wiltshire (Coll), Wigan and Leigh (Coll), Wirral Metropolitan (Coll), Worcester (CT), York (Coll).

ALTERNATIVE COURSES
See under **Sociology**.

See *University Degree Course Offers* (Trotman Publishing) for details of offers

SOCIOLOGY

(see also **Social Science/Studies**)

SUBJECT REQUIREMENTS/PREFERENCES
GCSE: English and Mathematics usually required.

SUBJECT INFORMATION
Sociology is the study of societies in general, both in Britain and abroad. Elective subjects offered will include industrial behaviour, crime and deviance, health and illness.

Aberdeen A highly rated department offering a course which covers topics in social life interaction, structures and institutions. Thereafter a study is made of self and society, modern lifestyles, work, sex and gender, poverty, housing and also European and Scottish issues.

Abertay Dundee The Sociology degree offers a study of both sociology and psychology along with computing and research methods. A specialised study of sociology commences at the end of the second year, when it is possible to transfer to either Psychology or Behavioural Science. Fourth year work placements are possible for sociology students.

Anglia Ruskin* More than 30 modules are offered in the Sociology degree (which can also be studied as part of its combined honours course) ranging from capitalist societies, science and technology, politics, popular cultures and class inequality to educational problems, race, deviance, health and illness and understanding crime. There is also an opportunity to spend a semester in Sweden.

Aston Sociology is offered as a single, joint or combined honours course with a number of subject options including Biology, Business Administration, Computer Science, Human Psychology, Public Policy and Management and Telecommunications. Some courses have sandwich options.

Bangor Each year of the Sociology course consists of core modules and a choice of optional subjects such as law, poverty, media and culture, mental illness, criminology etc. Sociology can also be taken as a joint subject with up to 17 other subjects.

Bath* In each year of the three-year Sociology course some subjects are stipulated, and in Years 2 and 3 subsidiary subjects (psychology, history, politics, philosophy and economics) are offered. There is also a course specialising in Human Resource Management, with a compulsory placement year.

Bath Spa Sociology is a flexible degree programme offering a range of modules which include topics related to business, health, psychology, education and the media.

Birmingham* The Sociology course offers a range of pathways focusing on politics, social policy, social history, work, youth studies, criminology and the media. (High research rating)

Birmingham City Sociology is a modular course of three years allowing students to select courses with options in Social Policy, Cultural and Media Studies, Psychology and Urban Studies.

Bolton Sociology is now offered as part of a joint or major/minor course.

Bradford The course in Sociology is one of the options in the Interdisciplinary Human Studies programme, also combining philosophy, psychology and English in Year 1. There is also a degree in Social Work, Sociology and Social Policy.

Brighton Sociology is offered with Social Policy, Community History and English Literature.

Bristol* In the first year of the Sociology course students choose two additional subjects from the Faculties of Social Sciences and the Arts. There are joint programmes combining with Philosophy, Social Policy, Politics and Theology. Sociology can also be taken with study abroad.

Bristol UWE Sociology is part of the Social Science undergraduate modular programme in which it can be taken as a joint honours course with several other subjects including Psychology and Criminology.

Brunel Three-year full-time and four-year thin sandwich courses are offered with a wide range of topics related to theory, methods and specialisation in aspects of British and international societies. Sociology can also be taken with Politics, Media Studies, Psychology or Anthropology. (High research rating)

Bucks New Sociology is offered as a single honours degree or jointly with Criminology or Psychology.

Cambridge Sociology is offered as part of the course in Politics, Psychology and Sociology (PPS); see under **Politics**.

Canterbury Christ Church Sociology is offered with Social Science as a single, joint or combined honours degree.

Cardiff* Sociology and the social structure of modern Britain are covered in Part I of the Sociology course, with studies in social change and developmental research methods, communist regimes, the mass media, women and the welfare state and the sociology of Wales as Part II options. Sociology can be taken as a joint subject with Social Policy (also a single honours subject), which is concerned with social problems such as housing, ageing, crime and health. (High research rating)

Cardiff (UWIC) Sociology can be taken with Popular Culture or Criminology.

Central Lancashire Sociology is offered in the combined honours course and also as a single honours subject in which students can follow courses in history, politics, race and ethnic studies and others in Year 1.

Chester The single and combined honours degrees provide a flexible curriculum offering a range of choices.

City Sociology can be taken as a major within the Social Sciences programme. The course includes applied sociology, race and society, mass communications, the sociology of work and industrial relations. Joint courses with Criminology, Media Studies, and Psychology can be taken. (High research rating)

Coventry In addition to a single honours course, Sociology can be taken with Psychology or Criminology. All courses can involve a year's work placement.

De Montfort Media, gender, race, politics, health and illness are all included in this typical Sociology course.

Derby A modular course in Sociology is offered that covers a diverse range of contemporary topics.

Durham* Sociology can be taken as a single honours subject focusing on social control and change, or within the combined honours degree, or with Law, Politics or Education.

East Anglia* Optional units in the Sociology course include art, media studies and social politics.

East London Sociology courses make use of the East London location for research studies.

Edge Hill Sociology can be taken as a single subject or with Childhood and Youth Studies, English, History or Criminology.

Edinburgh* Sociology, the discipline which examines the relationship between individuals and society, is offered as a single honours course or with Social Anthropology, Politics, South Asian Studies or Economic History. (High research rating)

Essex* There are four courses focusing on Sociology, including combinations with Criminology, Media Studies and Humanities. All include modules in sociology and the modern world. The BA degree in sociology can be taken with options in such areas as politics, sociology, psychology, history, philosophy and literature. (High research rating)

Exeter* Sociology is a modular course in which a range of topics is chosen, with further options taken from other subjects in the social sciences. There is also an opportunity to spend a year in a European country, the USA, Canada and Australia.

Glamorgan An honours degree can be taken in Sociology with a wide range of options in Year 3. It is also offered as part of the degree in Social Sciences with the option to study abroad.

Glasgow* Sociology is studied within the Faculty of Arts and Social Sciences. The study covers issues arising from the social relations of work, family, community and market, and from the distribution of wealth and power. Anthropology is included as part of the course. (High research rating)

Glasgow Caledonian See under **Social Science/Studies**.

Gloucestershire The degree in Sociological Studies includes social policy and the welfare state, disability, race, and a broad study of modern societies.

Greenwich The Sociology degree covers sociological debates, comparative sociology, sociological skills and reasoning, and science in society in Year 1. Options are available in such subjects as asylum seeking, racism, gypsies in contemporary Europe and drug use.

Huddersfield The Sociology degree covers the study of child abuse, education and psychiatric disorders. There is also a degree in Sociology and Criminology.

Hull* Degrees are offered in Sociology or with Social Anthropology with an option to focus on Development Studies, Danish, Dutch, Spanish, or Gender Studies. Five joint honours courses are also offered.

Keele Sociology must be taken with a second subject in the Dual honours programme.

Kent A single honours course is offered. In Part II, core courses are taken, including social analysis of industrial societies and research practices in sociology, as well as optional third-year courses such as the sociology of politics, education, knowledge, sex, gender and the family.

Kingston The single honours Sociology course is organised around three themes: sociological research, theory and the comparative analysis of societies. Modules include mass media, health, film, and spirituality. A course in Women's Studies is also available. Joint courses are also offered.

Lancaster* In the Sociology course, Year 1 includes two options from the sociology of class and gender, power and capitalism plus two other subjects. In Years 2 and 3 these subjects can be continued with additional topics such as deviance and social control, education and society, health and illness, the sociology of sport, popular culture and race. Sociolinguistics focuses on aspects of sociology and anthropology. Some exchanges with the USA are possible. Scholarships available. (High research rating)

Leeds* In the first year of the Sociology degree social, intellectual and cultural trends in the 19th and 20th centuries are studied together with computing skills. Social processes and institutions form the core subjects in Year 2, and in Year 3 options are taken from a wide range of topics from which students are asked to choose two for further research. (High research rating)

Leeds Metropolitan Sociology is offered as part of the Social Sciences programme or as a single honours subject.

Leicester* The Sociology course concentrates on sociological issues from Year 1. A wide range of modules provides flexibility for the student to focus his/her interests. Sociology can also be taken with

Archaeology, English, French and Psychology. A semester may be spent at a university in Europe or the USA. (High research rating)

Liverpool* Students are able to build their own degree course along chosen theories. In Year 2 one or two of five specialist pathways are chosen including crime and deviance, gender and law and ageing and society.

Liverpool Hope A wide range of options is offered in Years 2 and 3, including the sociology of religion, media, deviance, health and medicine, crime and justice, politics and feminism.

Liverpool John Moores The Sociology course involves the structure of modern society, racial divisions, health, education and the Third World. Joint courses are also offered with Applied Psychology, Criminology, History, Media and Politics.

London (Goldsmiths) Sociology core courses cover theory, methods of research and social structure. In addition, optional courses are offered in the sociology of health and race, sex and gender, culture and communications, philosophy and politics. Sociology is offered with Cultural Studies and Politics.

London (LSE)* One of the largest departments of Sociology, LSE offers a Social Policy and Sociology course planned on a unit system with core courses in sociology, social structure, statistical analysis and sociological theory. Year 3 students choose from over 12 options covering health, politics, psychology and population studies. (High research rating)

London Metropolitan Applied Sociology is offered as a joint honours degree programme. A course is offered in Social Work and there are several Criminology courses.

London South Bank Sociology is offered with several subjects including Accountancy, Gender Studies, Marketing and Psychology. There are also joint courses with Citizenship Studies.

Loughborough* The honours course in Sociology allows students to take modules in other subjects as career interests develop. (High research rating)

Manchester* Students may take either the BSocSci degree in Sociology or follow the BA (Econ) route, which allows specialisation in Sociology in Years 2 and 3. Sociology is also offered with Business Studies, Social Anthropology, Criminology, Economics, Politics and Development Studies. (High research rating)

Manchester Metropolitan Sociology can be taken as part of the Humanities or Social Studies programme.

Marjon (UCP) Sociology is offered as a combined course with six other subjects including English, Media or Drama.

Middlesex In the Sociology degree, topics cover the family and society, health, religion and crime. A one-year placement is offered in Year 3. Sociology can also be taken with Criminology, Politics or Psychology.

Napier Sociology can be taken with Psychology.

Newcastle* The Sociology course combines the fields of sociology and social anthropology. There is also a joint course with Politics.

Newport The Sociology degree covers the key issues in society including crime, society and social problems, social justice and social exclusion.

Northampton Sociology is offered as a single or joint honours course.

Northumbria Sociology is a broad-based course emphasising sociological aspects but including the related disciplines of economics, history, psychology and philosophy with course units covering class, gender and race. Sociology is also offered with English and Criminology.

Nottingham* The Sociology course aims to develop an awareness of the workings of social groups and organisations and to understand the theories and evidence about social and political problems. In addition to core courses, students select options each year from a range of subjects including the sociology of religion, education, industry and politics, race and minority groups and ideologies and social movements. There is also a course in Sociology with Film Studies.

Nottingham Trent Sociology covers contemporary areas such as sexualities, religion, spirituality, food and culture. It is also offered with Politics.

Oxford* It is possible to specialise in Sociology as part of the course in Philosophy, Politics and Economics.

Oxford Brookes* Sociology is offered as a joint course only with a wide range of second subjects including Law, languages, Criminal Justice Studies, International Relations, and Social Research.

Plymouth The Sociology course can be taken in single honours, major or minor programmes. It offers a range of specialised studies covering feminist thought, the Third World, the media, education, health and illness, religion, management and work. Several joint courses are offered.

Portsmouth Social theory, analysis and statistics, politics and economics are included in the first-year course in Sociology. Joint courses are also offered in Criminology, Media Studies, Psychology and Politics.

Queen Margaret The course covers the complexity of the social world, examining production and consumer cultures, the effects of the media and the place of the individual in society.

Queen's Belfast* Sociology is a broad course (single, joint, combined or major/minor honours) focusing on the study of individuals and the society in which we live. There is a wide range of modules in fields involving both theoretical and practical issues. (High research rating)

Roehampton Sociology is available as a full-time or part-time single or combined honours course, with a choice from 13 other subjects in the combined honours programme. Years 2 and 3 include courses in areas such as health and social policy, illness, the sociology of mental health, tourism and education. There are opportunities for placement with voluntary organisations.

St Mary's (UC) Sociology is offered as a single honours course or can be combined with a choice from fourteen other subjects.

Salford The Sociology programme has modules covering the sociology of management, pop music, politics and contemporary Britain. There are also courses with Cultural Studies, Criminology and Journalism.

Sheffield* The Level 1 modules of the Sociology course cover sociology and social policy with specialisms appearing in Levels 2 and 3. Several unrestricted units are offered as modules in Years 2 and 3. Sociology is also available with Economics, Geography, History and Japanese in the dual honours programme.

Sheffield Hallam Sociology topics cover social inequality, crime, the family and employment.

Staffordshire The Sociology course offers a combination of specialist aspects of sociology and related sciences including social psychology. Human geography, economics, law and international relations are options in Years 1 and 2, and a wide range of options is offered in Year 3. There are also degrees in Social Work and in Advice Work and Law.

Stirling A common first-year course is offered for the degree course in Sociology and for Social Policy and Social Administration. Students make their choice of degree programme, including combined courses, at the end of Year 1. The Sociology programme is built around a core course in theory and methods with options to suit the student's field of interest.

Strathclyde Sociology is a four-year course with an introductory first year covering social class, the family, education, work, sexual division, the media and deviance. In the next two years there is a range of options such as women and work or modern sociological theory. The final year is spent on a research seminar, a dissertation and two classes from a range of options.

Sunderland The degree in Sociology offers a broad picture of British and global society covering such topics as politics, history, media studies, and cultural studies, health factors, race, work, leisure and criminology.

Surrey* Sociology is a three-year course or a four-year course with a year spent in professional training in industry, commerce or the public sector. Sociology is also offered with Applied Psychology and Social Research. There is also a course in Sociology, Culture and New Media, which explores print, digital, broadcast and mobile phone technology. The course in Criminology and Sociology studies the nature of crime and deviance and possible solutions. (High research rating)

Sussex* The main emphasis of the Sociology course is on sociological theory, independent critical work, the opportunity for specialist studies in contextual courses and the practical approach to planning and conducting research. Sociology is offered in three schools and half of the time is spent on courses in these schools in addition to sociology itself. (High research rating)

Teesside Sociology is a modular course with specialisms in sport sociology, mental health, employment problems, crime, education and an option in languages. Psychology can also be combined with Sociology.

Ulster The emphasis in the second year covers contemporary industrial societies with Third World themes, and a variety of options follows in Year 3. There is also a modular programme with Politics and Criminology.

Warwick* The aim of the Sociology course is to provide students with an insight into theoretical sociology, methods of social research and the problems of the society in which we live. In Year 1, in addition to sociology courses, students choose an option from a course in applied social studies, economics, education, history, languages or psychology. More than 30 different options are available in Years 2 and 3. Sociology can be taken with French, History, Law or Politics. (High research rating)

West London Courses can be taken in Sociology combined with Health Studies, Human Sciences, and Psychology.

West Scotland Sociology is offered as part of the Social Sciences programme.

Westminster The Sociology degree has options in criminology, politics, history, international relations, race and ethnicity, health and illness, feminism and medicine.

Wolverhampton Sociology is offered as part of the modular degree scheme and covers British social life, health, old age, parenting and counselling.

Worcester The Sociology course offers themes in social welfare, criminal justice, gender and race.

York* The Sociology course provides a wide structural choice of subjects and perspectives. It may be taken as a single subject or in combination with Economics, Economic and Social History, Politics, Philosophy, Education or History. There are no compulsory courses in Years 2 and 3 and no examinations – only essays. See also **Combined courses**. (High research rating)

OTHER INSTITUTIONS OFFERING SOCIOLOGY COURSES

Bradford (Coll), Burton (Coll), Colchester (Inst), Cornwall (Coll), Doncaster (Coll), East Lancashire (Coll), Grimsby (IFHE), Havering (Coll), Norwich City (Coll), Oxford Ruskin (Coll), Richmond (American Univ), South Essex (Coll), Suffolk (Univ Campus), UHI Millennium Inst, West Anglia (Coll), Wigan and Leigh (Coll). See also **Social Science/Studies**.

ALTERNATIVE COURSES

Anthropology, Communication, Government, History, Politics, Psychology, Social Administration, Social Policy, Social Studies/Science, Social Work.

See *University Degree Course Offers* (Trotman Publishing) for details of offers

SPORTS SCIENCE/STUDIES

(including **Physical Education**)
(* indicates universities with the highest entry requirements)

SUBJECT REQUIREMENTS/PREFERENCES

GCE A-level: A science subject may be required (see separate courses). **GCSE:** English and Mathematics and often a science subject; check prospectuses.

SUBJECT INFORMATION

These are very popular courses and are increasing in number. Ability and involvement in sport are obviously important factors.

Aberdeen The programme in Sports and Exercise Science commences at Level 2 after a year following a course in biology and chemistry. In the final year, three specialist courses are offered: in the physiology of exercise, sports performance and nutrition. There is also a Sport and Leisure Management course with options in sociology, psychology and economics, and a course in Sport and Society that includes aspects of health and fitness and the prevention of disease.

Abertay Dundee At the end of Year 2 the Sport and Exercise programme leads to options in Sport and Exercise Science, Sport Coaching, Physical Activity and Health, Sport and Exercise, Sport Development and Strength and Conditioning. There are also separate Sports degrees with Nutrition, Management or Psychology.

Aberystwyth The Sport and Exercise Science degree follows three themes – psychology, physiology and biomechanics, which are studied in Years 1 and 2. Year 3 consists of specialist modules.

Anglia Ruskin Courses are offered in Sports Science and Sport, Health and Exercise with an option in Advanced Coaching Skills.

Bangor Sport, Health and Physical Education (SHAPE) includes sport psychology, health promotion, information technology and counselling. It is a 'theory' and 'practice' course. The same Department also offers courses in Sports Science with options to Specialise in Outdoor Activities, Physical Education or Psychology.

Bath* A three-year and a four-year sandwich degree is offered in Sports Performance, and Sport and Exercise Science. There is also a highly selective degree (11 applications for each place) in Coach Education and Sports Development, in which industrial placement is an option in Year 3 and also a degree in Sports Engineering.

Bedfordshire Health and Fitness Management covers general health, coaching, sports psychology and leisure management and is offered as a single honours or joint honours course. There is a very wide range of courses in sports subjects including Sport Studies, Management, Physical Education and Sports Therapy.

Birmingham* Sport, Physical Education and Community Studies is offered as a three-year full-time course. The degree is non-vocational although many graduates proceed to teacher training (sporting ability not essential). The degree in Sport and Materials Science focuses on sports equipment design. Courses are also offered in Sport Management, Applied Golf Management Studies and Sport and Exercise Science. Scholarships available.

Bolton Courses are offered in Sport and Leisure Management, Sport Development, Sport Rehabilitation and Sport Science and Coaching, the last two courses requiring PE or a science subject.

See *University Degree Course Offers* (Trotman Publishing) for details of offers

Bournemouth Courses are offered in Sport Development and Coaching, bringing together aspects of management and coaching, and sports management (Golf) both with industrial placement in Year 3.

Brighton The courses in Sport and Exercise Science have a common first year and options in Year 2 when a six months exchange is possible in mainland Europe, Canada or the USA. There is also a Physical Education degree leading to a teaching qualification. Other courses include Sport and Leisure Management, Sport Coaching, Equine Sports Performance, Sport Journalism. See also **Leisure, Recreation Management and Tourism**.

Bristol UWE Sports Biology, Sports Coaching, Sports Business Management, Sport Biomedicine. Sport Studies and Sport Therapy demonstrate the strength, scope and facilities in this department.

Brunel* At Level 1 a broad Sport Sciences course is followed by specialisms in Levels 2 and 3. Students can choose a non-teaching or a teaching route with a study of physical education modules. Other Sport Science courses focus on Management and Development, Coaching, Human Performance and Physical Education. Sport Sciences can also be taken with Business Studies or Geography.

Bucks New Sport can be taken with Coaching Science, Golf Studies, Rugby Studies or Football Studies. In addition courses are offered in Sport Broadcasting and Motorsport.

Canterbury Christ Church Courses are offered in Physical Education and Sport and Exercise Science, in Sport and Exercise Psychology or Exercise Science and Sport and Leisure Management.

Cardiff (UWIC) Degrees are offered in Biomedicine and Nutrition, Coaching Exercise, Physical Education and Management.

Central Lancashire Core subjects in the Sport Science degree cover biomechanics, physiology and information technology. Optional studies follow in Years 2 and 3. There are also courses in Sports Psychology, Football and Society, Outdoor Leadership, Public Relations, Sport Therapy and Sports Coaching Technology and Management.

Chester Sport and Exercise Sciences is offered at Chester and Sport Development and Management at the Warrington campus.

Chichester Several degrees in Sport are offered including Exercise and Health Science, Sports Coaching Science, Sport Psychology, Sport Exercise Science and Sport Therapy. There is also a degree in Physical Education and Teaching.

Coventry Sport and Exercise Science is offered, with specialist studies in Year 3. Other courses include Sport Development, Sport and Marketing and Management and Sports Therapy.

Cumbria A very wide range of Sport degrees is available covering coaching, exercise therapy and management.

De Montfort The Sports Studies course covers psychology and physiology, as well as sociological and philosophical sporting issues. Degrees in Adventure Recreation, Sport and Exercise Science and Sport, Media and Culture are also available.

Derby A three-year degree is offered in Sports Science and there is a wide range of Sports Studies courses covering Therapy, Education and Psychology, Sport and Outdoor Recreation Management and Adventure Tourism.

Dundee A degree is offered in Sports Biomedicine. In addition to biological topics the course also covers psychology and the design and administration of coaching programmes.

Durham* The course in Sport covers social issues, sport development and psychology, coaching and performance, and health and rehabilitation. Students have the opportunity to take part in community-based sports activities.

East London Courses in Sport and Exercise Science, Fitness and Health, Sports Coaching and Sports Development are offered. They share a common first year with specialisation taking place in Years 2 and 3.

Edge Hill Courses include Sport and Exercise Science, Sports Development, Sports Studies and Sport Therapy and there also are two Coaching courses.

Edinburgh* Courses are offered in Applied Sport Science, and Sport and Recreation Management, the former emphasising scientific aspects of sport, the latter with a 10 week placement with leading sports organisation.

Essex* The Sport and Exercise Science degree covers biology, biochemistry, physics and psychology with a focus on coaching and training. This degree and the joint programme with Biology have a strong practical component. There are sports bursaries for competing athletes.

Exeter* Exercise and Sport Science covers anatomy, biomechanics, physiology, psychology and sociology, teaching, learning, leadership, communication skills, coaching sport and exercise. There are opportunities for some specialisation in Years 2 and 3. There is a generous sport scholarships scheme.

Glamorgan The Sports Science course prepares students for the sports and leisure industry. There is a bursary scheme for top sports applicants. There are also degrees in Sport Psychology and Science and Rugby enabling students to gain Welsh Rugby Union coaching qualifications. Several joint courses with Sports Science are offered, and there are also courses in Sports Studies and Sports Technology and Sport Management.

Glasgow* A degree in Sports Medicine is offered in addition to Sports Science. It is also possible to study Physiology with Sport Science and with Nutrition.

Glasgow Caledonian A course is offered in Sport Management, covering community sport and recreation, sports policy and tourism.

Gloucestershire Coaching Exercise Sciences, Development, Education and Sport Sciences are some of the specialisms offered with a wide range of subjects in the modular degree scheme, including Tourism Management, Business Administration and Performance Arts.

Greenwich The Sports Science course covers human movement, the sociology of sport, sport physiology, computing, nutrition and performance. Sports Science is also offered with Professional Tennis or Football Coaching. Courses in Exercise Physiology, Fitness Science and Sports Development can also be taken.

Heriot-Watt The course in Sport and Exercise Science allows students to transfer and with a specialism in Psychology in Year 2.

Hertfordshire The Sports Therapy course includes psychology, physiotherapy, sports injury and treatments. Three-year Sport Studies and Sport and Exercise Science courses are also available.

Huddersfield There are several Sports degrees with specialisation in Coaching, Therapy, Exercise Science, Psychology and Promotion and Marketing.

Hull Joint degrees in Physical Education and Sports Science are offered with Psychology or Management. There are also courses in Sport and Exercise Management, and Sports Coaching and Rehabilitation. Scholarships available.

Kent* Sports Therapy, Health and Fitness includes health promotion, sport rehabilitation and event management. Other courses focus on Exercise Management and Psychology.

Kingston* Sports Science is offered as a three-year full-time course or as a four-year extended degree that includes a foundation course. A course in Sports Analysis and Coaching is also available.

Leeds* Sports and Exercise Science and Physiology are offered covering biology, physiology, psychology and sports specialisms. There are also courses in Sports Science (outdoor activities) and Sports Materials Technology.

Leeds Metropolitan Sport and Exercise Science is a modular course taken in the School of Leisure and Sports Studies, sharing Year 1 with Physical Education and Sport and Recreation Development. Other Sport courses cover Exercise and Fitness, Physical Education, Leisure and Recreation. The university is a leader in the field of sport courses.

Leeds Trinity (UC) Special options with sport include Health, Exercise and Nutrition, Sport Development, Journalism, and Psychology.

Lincoln Sport and Exercise Science, Sport Development and Coaching, and Equine Sports Science are offered as three-year degree courses.

Liverpool Hope Degrees are offered in Sport Psychology, Sport Studies and Sports Management.

Liverpool John Moores Sports Science covers research methods (including statistics), coaching and applied sports science. Topics include physiology, health science, psychology and recreational management. Science and Football, and Applied Sport Psychology are also offered.

London Metropolitan Several courses are offered, including Sport Psychology, Management and Development, Nutrition, Product Design, Therapy and Coaching.

London South Bank Three-year courses are offered in Sport and Exercise Science, and Sports Product Design.

Loughborough A leading University in this field offering a range of Sports Science and Management courses. A course is also offered in Sports Technology covering equipment design, ergonomics and includes industrial training.

Manchester Metropolitan Sport, Exercise and Coaching is a multidisciplinary course with opportunities to specialise in Exercise and Health or Performance Excellence. Other courses include Sports Writing, the Psychology of Sport and Outdoor Studies.

Marjon (UCP) Several courses are offered including Sport Science, Coaching, PE and Sport Development.

Middlesex Opportunities for work placements exist in the course in Sport Rehabilitation and Injury Prevention. Other courses include Psychology, Sport Nutrition and Sport Biomedicine.

Napier Sport and Exercise Science is offered as a three-year or four-year full-time degree. There is also a course in Sports Technology.

Newman (UC) Sport Studies is offered as a single, joint or minor course.

Newport Sports courses are offered with Exercise, Therapy, Community Studies, Coaching and Psychology.

Northampton Courses are offered in Sport and Recreation Management, Sport Studies and Sport and Exercise Science.

Northumbria* There are three programmes in which students can 'build' their studies around individual interests and strengths – Applied Sport Science or Sport Management, Coaching or Sport Development. There are also courses in Sport Studies with Geography or Psychology.

Nottingham Trent Sport and Exercise Science, Sport Science with Management, Psychology or Equine Sports Science are available.

Oxford Brookes* Courses in Sport and Exercise Science and Sport Science and Coaching Studies courses are available with study abroad options in Europe, USA, Canada and Australia.

See *University Degree Course Offers* (Trotman Publishing) for details of offers

Plymouth A unique course in Applied Marine Sports Science is offered that covers sailing and navigation, diving and surfing. There are also courses in Sport Therapy, a teacher training course in Physical Education and courses in surf science and ocean yachting.

Portsmouth The Sports Science course offers students the opportunity to participate in sport and obtain a variety of coaching awards. The scientific elements of this course include physiology, nutrition and psychology. There are also courses in Sports Development and Water Sports Science.

Robert Gordon Sport and Exercise Science is offered as a four-year full-time course with a work placement in Year 3.

Roehampton Sport and Exercise Science is a single honours course studying sport from a scientific and a cultural perspective. It allows focus on specific areas of personal interest or the study of a broad range of sport topics. Sport Science is offered as a combined course with one of Business Management, Computing, Human Biosciences or Journalism and News Media. There is also a single honours course in Sport Psychology and a Foundation degree in Sports Coaching and Practice.

St Mary's (UC) Courses are offered in Sport Science, Sports Coaching, Rehabilitation and Strength and Conditioning Science.

Salford A Sports Rehabilitation programme is available dealing with sports injuries and the psychology of sport. Hospital placements and overseas placements are included in the course. Exercise and Health Sciences and Sports Equipment Design and Development are also offered as degree courses, the latter under the Product Design programme.

Sheffield* The Sports Engineering degree focuses on the designs of sporting equipment and is an extension of the Mechanical Engineering programme.

Sheffield Hallam The Sports Studies degree programme offers Sport and Exercise Science, Sports Development and Coaching, Sport Management and Sport Equipment Development. There is a common first year for all these degrees and the opportunity to change at the end of the year.

Southampton* The course in Sport Management and Leadership involves commercial aspects, sponsorship and health and safety. Sport Studies covers scientific aspects of sport, exercise and physiology.

Southampton Solent Courses are offered in Sport Development and Marketing, Sport and the Media, Sport Studies and Business and Football Studies with Business. There are also Water Sports and Outdoor Adventure Programmes.

Staffordshire A range of sport courses is offered, including Sport and Exercise Science, Coaching courses and joint courses with Nutrition and Psychology and courses with options to study biology, psychology, leisure management and nutrition.

Stirling A course in Sports Studies is available covering physical education, psychology, medicine and management. Sports Studies can also be studied with, for example, Business Studies, Psychology, Finance or Human Resource Management.

Strathclyde* Courses cover Outdoor Education and Sport and Physical Activity, Sport and Exercise Science or Sports Engneering.

Sunderland The Sports courses include exercise sciences and development, coaching and sport studies. There are also opportunities to study abroad without a language barrier.

Swansea* The modular degree in Sports Science is centred around physiology, biometrics and psychology leading to specialisms in exercise and health, diet and nutrition, and sports coaching.

Teesside A range of courses is offered focusing on Sport and Exercise including Sports Therapy, Outdoor Leadership with specialisms in Coaching Science, Applied Exercise Science and Psychology.

See *University Degree Course Offers* (Trotman Publishing) for details of offers

Trinity St David (Carmarthen) A degree in Physical Education includes work placements and an exchange scheme in the USA. There is also a degree in Health and Exercise with Sport Studies.

Ulster During the first two years of the Sport and Exercise Sciences degree, students undertake an analysis of sport and leisure from both theoretical and practical perspectives. These include individual performance, psychology, interpersonal relations, issues in sport and vocational studies. At the end of Year 2 students can apply for a degree with a Certificate in Education or a degree with a Diploma in Industrial Studies. There are also degrees in Sport Studies and Sports Technology.

West London There are courses in Exercise Physiology and Nutrition, Sport Science and Medicine, Health and Exercise Science and Physical Activity and Health.

West Scotland Exercise and Health, Sport Coaching, Sports Development are offered.

Westminster Sports and Exercise Science is a three-year degree and includes physiology, nutrition and psychology. Degrees are also available in Nutrition and Exercise Science and Physiology.

Winchester Courses are offered in Sports Science, Sports Studies and Sports Development. They are offered as single or combined programmes.

Wolverhampton Sport Studies can be taken as a specialist award, joint, major or minor subject and covers a wide range of topics from community recreation and games performance to coaching, dance and European leisure policy. There are also courses in Sport and Exercise Science, Sports Coaching and Physical Education.

Worcester Courses are offered in Sport Therapy, Sport and Exercise Science, Business Management, Sports Studies and Sport Coaching Science.

York St John Courses are offered in Sport Performance, Sport, Society and Development and Sport Science and Injury Management.

OTHER INSTITUTIONS OFFERING SPORTS COURSES
Basingstoke (CT), Bath (Coll), Bishop Burton (Coll), Blackpool and Fylde (Coll), Bridgwater (Coll), Bristol Filton (Coll), Carmarthenshire (Coll), Colchester (Inst), Cornwall (Coll), Dearne Valley (Coll), Doncaster (Coll), Duchy (Coll), East Lancashire (Coll), Exeter (Coll), Farnborough (UC), Grimsby (IFHE), Hopwood Hall (Coll), Hull (Coll), Leeds Park Lane (Coll), Lincoln (Coll), Llandrillo (Coll), Loughborough (Coll), Manchester (CAT), Mid-Cheshire (Coll), Myerscough (Coll), NESCOT, Newcastle (Coll), North East Worcestershire (Coll), North Lindsey (Coll), North Warwickshire (Coll), Norwich City (Coll), Pembrokeshire (Coll), SAC, St Helens (Coll), Sheffield (Coll), Shrewsbury (CAT), South Cheshire (Coll), South Downs (Coll), South Essex (Coll), South Nottingham (Coll), Southport (Coll), Staffordshire (Reg Fed), Suffolk (Univ Campus), Sunderland City (Coll), Truro (Coll), Tyne Metropolitan (Coll), Wakefield (Coll), Warwickshire (Coll), Welsh (Coll Hort), Wigan and Leigh (Coll), Worcester (CT), Writtle (Coll), York (Coll).

ALTERNATIVE COURSES
Anatomy, Biology, Human Movement Studies, Leisure Studies, Physiology, Recreation Management and Sport Studies.

TOWN PLANNING AND URBAN PLANNING STUDIES

(* indicates universities with the highest entry requirements)

SUBJECT REQUIREMENTS/PREFERENCES

GCE A-level: Economics and Geography are appropriate. **GCSE:** English and Mathematics.

SUBJECT INFORMATION

Courses in Town Planning, which are all very similar, lead to qualification as a member of the Royal Town Planning Institute (RTPI). Courses usually include a year out. (Students should check with universities.) This is an ideal course for the geographer. The employment prospects for graduate planners have undergone a remarkable transformation in recent years. There is now a considerable shortage of planners in view of the increased demand by local authorities and the private sector. Increasingly consultants, developers and other property-related organisations, such as major retailers, are employing qualified Planning graduates, with the result that demand is far outstripping supply. In response, the Planning schools have increased their intakes but there would appear to be a significant shortage for the foreseeable future.

Additionally, the 3+1 format of courses provides an opportunity for students who are well trained in environmental matters to leave such courses after three years with an honours degree, but without the necessity of completing the Diploma in Town Planning (DTP) for professional qualification. There are also increasing job opportunities for such students.

Aberdeen A range of Planning-related degrees is offered including Environmental Planning, Planning and Development and Rural Planning and Economic Development. (High research rating)

Anglia Ruskin The Environmental Planning course is a modular programme leading to options in housing, leisure or design.

Aston* A three-year full-time or four-year sandwich degree is offered in Transport and Environmental Planning.

Bangor The Environmental Planning and Management course covers rural, urban and coastal environments and is offered in English and Welsh. The course includes two professional placements of one month.

Birmingham* Two courses are offered in Urban and Regional Planning, one combined with Geography and the other with Public Policy, Government and Management in addition to which there is a joint course in planning.

Brighton There is a three-year or four-year sandwich course in Urban Conservation and Environmental Management and a course in Urban Studies with an optional placement.

Bristol UWE Town and Country Planning is a three-year degree course, plus a further two years of practical experience, leading to membership of the Royal Town Planning Institute. There are also courses in Planning with Transport, Planning and Communities.

Cardiff* City and Regional Planning is a five-year sandwich course providing a comprehensive study of all aspects of town planning, including environmental design, economics, industrial development, social structure, urban land use and transportation planning. It includes a two-year sandwich course leading to the Diploma in Town Planning, which gives the necessary exemptions from the examinations of the

Royal Town Planning Institute and the Chartered Institute of Transport. Compared with other courses, Cardiff puts particular stress on social science approaches to planning and on analytical and computing skills. There is also a degree course in Geography and Planning. (High research rating)

Chester The course in Urban Studies has strong employer links and good opportunities for work placement. It covers urban regeneration, community renewal, planning, housing, tourism and the environment.

Dundee Town and Regional Planning is a four-year course providing a broad study leading to two areas of specialised study – in either conservation and design or environmental policy and practice. Final-year options include building conservation, heritage management and European urban conservation. Socrates-Erasmus contacts with the Netherlands. Planning is also offered with Economics or Geography.

Glamorgan Courses are offered in Transport and Environmental Sustainability.

Greenwich The three-year full-time or four-year sandwich degree in Housing Studies includes units in urban design. The programme gives full exemption from the Institute of Housing examinations.

Heriot-Watt Urban and Regional Planning is a four-year full-time or a five-year course with a sandwich year spent in practice between the second and third years. All aspects of planning are covered in this course, which leads to a BSc degree and full exemption from the final professional examinations of the RTPI. Students may graduate after three years' full-time study with a BSc ordinary degree.

Kent* Urban Studies (Social Policy) course reviews the problems of towns and cities and the various processes (political, economic, geographic and social) with a bias towards sociology or economics or social policy. There is also a course in Urban Regeneration.

Kingston* Property Planning and Development is offered as a three-year full-time or four-year sandwich course.

Leeds Metropolitan Urban and Regional Planning is a three-year full-time course. The first two years provide a broad foundation of town planning studies leading on to options of employment policy, urban planning and social welfare, leisure, recreation and tourism, and transportation.

Liverpool* The Environment and Planning (MPlan) course focuses on urban and regional planning, urban design and environmental planning. There are also courses in Town and Regional Planning and Urban Regeneration. (High research rating)

Liverpool John Moores The course in Urban Planning lasts three years but can be extended to four years for an Advanced Diploma in Planning.

London (UCL)* Two three-year courses are offered: Urban Planning, Design and Management*, and Urban Studies, both sharing a common first and second year. The final choice of degree is made in Year 3.

London South Bank Urban and Environmental Planning and Housing Studies degrees are offered.

Manchester* The four-year BA course in Town and Country Planning includes a one-year course leading to the degree of Bachelor of Planning. The latter is recognised by the Royal Town Planning Institute, giving exemptions from their examinations. One semester of the course can be taken in a university abroad. There are also courses on City and Regional Planning and Environmental Management.

Newcastle* Town Planning is a five-year sandwich course including one year of professional experience between the third and fifth years. The course carries full exemption from the examinations of the Royal Town Planning Institute. The degree can be followed by a two year certificate in Town Planning Practice and Diploma in Town Planning. There is also a three-year full-time degree in Geography and Planning. (High research rating)

Nottingham Trent A three-year or four-year sandwich degree is offered in Planning and Property Development, and there is also a three-year course in Design, Development and Regeneration.

Oxford Brookes* Two degrees, Cities – Environment, Design and Development, and City and Regional Planning, are offered as single honours courses. The former is also available as a combined course.

Queen's Belfast The Environmental Planning course can lead to a one year Master's course with specialism in either Spatial Regeneration or Urban and Rural Design. Level 1 runs jointly with the BSc course in Architecture. Subsequent studies involve both design and the social implications of the planned environment.

Reading* The four-year full-time course in Land Management also leads to a Diploma in Planning. (High research rating)

Sheffield* Urban Studies and Planning covers three major subjects studied in Year 1 – urban studies, the design of urban areas and one of economics, social history, geography, politics or sociology and social policy. In the second and third years, 10 compulsory subjects are studied, and four options from within the Faculty of Architectural Studies, such as housing or comparative studies or urbanisation. Courses are also offered in Landscape Architecture with Planning and Urban Studies. (High research rating)

Sheffield Hallam A Planning Studies course leading to a degree and a Diploma in Town Planning is offered. It also has a transport pathway that leads to a separate degree in Planning and Transport. Planning is also included in the BA honours courses in Geography (Urban) degree.

Westminster One of the degrees in Architecture focuses on Urban Design.

ALTERNATIVE COURSES
Architecture, Development Studies, Geography, Housing, Landscape Architecture, Social Administration, Sociology, Transport.

VETERINARY SCIENCE/MEDICINE

(see also **Animal Sciences**)
(* indicates universities with the highest entry requirements)

SUBJECT REQUIREMENTS/PREFERENCES
GCE A-level: Three subjects in mathematics/science subjects, Chemistry essential. Check prospectuses.

SUBJECT INFORMATION
These are very popular and academically demanding courses for which some work experience prior to application is obligatory. Every course has much the same content, but check with prospectuses for all courses.

Bristol* The first three years of Veterinary Science cover the pre-clinical stage and include the basic sciences (anatomy, biochemistry and physiology) with animal management, breeding and genetics. Years 4 and 5 are the clinical years and include veterinary medicine and surgery, pathology, public health and animal husbandry. The course is highly regarded by students. Degree courses are also offered in Veterinary Cellular and Molecular Sciences, in Veterinary Nursing and Bioveterinary Science. (High research rating)

Bristol UWE The degree in Veterinary Nursing Science includes 70 weeks of work placement and leads to the RCVS qualification. This course and that of Veterinary Practice Management take place at Hartpury College, Gloucester.

Cambridge* In the first and second years, students read for Part IA and Part IB of the Medical and Veterinary Sciences Tripos, with both parts including veterinary anatomy and veterinary physiology, pathology and pharmacology. Part II enables students to make a study of a single subject in depth such as applied biology, biochemistry, genetics, psychology and zoology. The three years that follow the pre-clinical course include 26 weeks' practical experience with a vet in practice. All applicants must take the BMAT test. (High research rating)

Central Lancashire A full-time or sandwich course is available in Veterinary Nursing linked with Myerscough College a few miles from the University.

Edinburgh* The curriculum of the Veterinary Medicine course falls into three interrelated main parts. The first (pre-clinical) covers the biology and chemistry of the animal body, and the second (para-clinical studies) deals with the nature of disease, diagnosis and treatment. Thirdly, students can interrupt their studies for a year to take an intercalated degree in Biochemistry, Neuroscience, Veterinary Biological Sciences or Microbiology. The degree is validated in the USA enabling students to practise in North America. (High research rating)

Glasgow* In the first two years (the pre-clinical period) of the Veterinary Medicine course, studies cover anatomy, biochemistry, physiology and animal management. The third year (para-clinical studies) covers pathology, bacteriology, virology, parasitology, animal husbandry and nutrition. The fourth and fifth years initially include lectures but are largely clinical, with practical lessons in medicine, surgery and pathology. Applicants are expected to have spent time working on a dairy farm and in a veterinary practice. Selected candidates may be admitted to an intercalated BSc degree course in one of eight subjects. (High research rating)

Liverpool* In Year 1 of the five-year Veterinary Science course, the structure and development of the animal body are studied. Animal husbandry, management, disease processes and disease-producing organisms are studied in Years 2 and 3. In Years 4 and 5, subjects include drugs, their actions and uses, clinical pathology, food hygiene, preventive and clinical medicine, surgery and reproductive studies enabling students follow their own special interests. A six-year course including an intercalated one-year honours degree is also offered. There is also a course in Bioveterinary Science. Scholarships available. (High research rating)

London (RVC)* Years 1 and 2 of the BVet Med course at the London campus are the pre-clinical years that introduce aspects such as anatomy, physiology, animal management and husbandry. In Year 3 students commence clinical studies involving pathology, toxicology, body systems and hygiene, and veterinary medicine in Year 4; 26 weeks of vacation study takes place in a veterinary practice, followed by rotations in small animal medicine, equine medicine and farm animal medicine. There is also a Veterinary Gateway programme for students wishing to reach the required entry standard and a Veterinary Nursing degree. (High research rating)

Nottingham* A School of Veterinary Medicine and Science is based on the Sutton Bonington campus, 10 miles south of the university. The five-year Veterinary Science course is divided into three stages, in Years 1 and 2 learning about normal animal care studies, Years 3 and 4 involving professional skills and the final year practising clinical skills. There is also a Pre-Veterinary Science course leading to a four-year course in the West Indies.

Surrey* The degree in Veterinary Biosciences focuses on animal health and disease. There are opportunities for professional placements.

INSTITUTIONS OFFERING VETERINARY NURSING COURSES
Askham Bryan (Coll), Barony (Coll), Brighton, Duchy (Coll), Greenwich, Harper Adams (UC), Lincoln (Biovet Sci), Middlesex, Myerscough (Coll), Napier, Nottingham Trent, Warwickshire (Coll), West Anglia (Coll), Worcester.

ALTERNATIVE COURSES
Agricultural Sciences, Animal Sciences, Biological Sciences, Medicine, Nutrition, Pharmacology.

Deciding what career path to follow after leaving university or college is an important issue for you – and your parents. Unfortunately there's not much information available to prove that one university is better than another in helping you. Your professors and lecturers certainly do not consider it their main responsibility to find you work! That's your problem, they will say, pointing you in the direction of the University Careers Service.

If you do want a steer in the right direction, then it's very interesting to note that students who have been on sandwich courses, in which they have spent time with an employer, seem to be more successful than others in obtaining full-time employment on graduation. The likelihood is that if you impress an employer while you are on work placement he or she will often offer you a job when you've completed your degree.

Research done among employers about graduate employment and what they seek shows that they invariably say 'intelligence and transferable skills'. In other words, bright young people who can be trained to do a job, who can 'communicate' with people, write reports, work in a team and perhaps use a computer or speak a foreign language.

Finally, remember that three, four or more years will elapse between the time you leave school and graduation day when you leave university, and your ideas about your future career will develop and change. So it's not absolutely important to decide on a future career before commencing a degree course.

However, it is useful to read through the information below, provided by Surrey University Careers Service. This gives you some insight into graduate destinations and careers.

BIOLOGY GRADUATES

Microbiology (Biotechnology)
Employment

Appleton Woods, Birmingham	Technical Sales
Unknown research company, Guildford	Microbiologist

Further study

Staffordshire University	MSc Journalism
Surrey University	PhD Charcoal Absorption

Microbiology (Medical)
Employment

NHS, Chertsey	Biomedical Scientist
NHS, Exeter	Assistant Technical Officer
Pfizer, Sandwich, Kent	Contract Packaging Coordinator
Robens Centre for Env and Public Health, Guildford	Technician
Roche Products, Welwyn Garden City	Drug Safety Associate
Royal Free Hampstead NHS Trust	Clinical Scientist and MSc
Sanofi Aventis, Kingshill, Kent	Clinical Projects Assistant
UK Trade Partners International, Guildford	Administration

Further study

King's College London	MSc Infectious Diseases – Microbiology
Sheffield University	PhD Microbiology

Surrey University   PhD Molecular Microbiology
Surrey University   PhD Poultry Contamination

Microbiology (Molecular)
Employment
Hog's Head, Weymouth   Team Leader
Surrey University, Guildford   Research Officer

Further study
Royal Veterinary College   PhD Mycobacterium Tuberculosis

Molecular Biology
Employment
Family business   General Building

Further study
Essex University   MSc Biotechnology
Oxford University   DPhil Zoology

BUSINESS GRADUATES
See under **Economics**.

CHEMISTRY GRADUATES
Analytical and Environmental Chemistry
Employment
CL Associates, Wokingham   Assistant Environmental Scientist
Sainsbury's, London   Sales Assistant

Further study
Edinburgh University   PhD Analytical Geochemistry
Surrey University   PhD Environmental and Analytical Chemistry

Biochemistry
Employment
Co-op, Grayshott, Surrey   Store Manager
Martindale Pharmaceuticals, Brentwood   Pharmacy Technician
MDS Pharma Service, Sittingbourne, Kent   Analyst
Merck Sharp and Dohme, Harlow   Research Scientist
National Bacteriology Laboratory, London   Medical Technical Officer
Procter & Gamble, Egham, Surrey   Package and Device Researcher
Shire Pharmaceuticals, London   Hospital Sales Specialist
Unknown finance company, London   General Administration
Unknown scientific recruitment consultancy   Consultant

Further study
Oxford University   PhD Genetics
Surrey University   MSc Toxicology
Surrey University   PhD Neuroendocrinology

Biochemistry (Medical)
Employment
Allery Therapeutics, Worthing   Junior Development Scientist
Barclays, Wimbledon   Bank Officer
Moorfields Eye Hospital, London   Clinical Physiology Technician
Tenovus, Cardiff   Volunteer Charity Shop Assistant

Further study

Surrey University	MSc Chemical Research
Surrey University	MSc Clinical Biochemistry
Surrey University	MSc Toxicology (2)
Surrey University	PhD Sleep Research
Other non-UK institution	PhD Sleep/Endocrinology

Biochemistry (Pharmacology)

Employment

Boots Chemist, Guildford	Healthcare Assistant

Further study

Nottingham University	PhD Biomedical Sciences
Surrey University	PhD Molecular Toxicology

Biochemistry (Toxicology)

Employment

Analytical Unit, St George's Hospital, London	Analytical Biochemist
Aventis Pasteur MSD, Maidenhead	Pharmacovigilance Coordinator
CMR International, Epsom, Surrey	Analyst
Environment Risk Mgt Authority, New Zealand	Adviser
Lonza Biologics, Slough	Protein Purification Development
Southend General Hospital	Healthcare Assistant
Unknown sales and deliveries company, Taunton	Sales and Deliveries

Further study

Edinburgh University	PhD Reproductive Sciences
Liverpool University	BVSc Veterinary Science
Surrey University	MSc Social Research Methods
University College London	PhD Genetics
Warwick University	MBCHB Medicine

Chemistry

Employment

Milward Brown, Warwick	Operational Research
Natural Resource Management, Bracknell	Chemical Analyst
Pharmorphix, Cambridge	Scientist
PricewaterhouseCoopers, London	Computer Security
Procter & Gamble, Surrey	Laboratory Manager
West Berkshire Council, Newbury	Event Organiser

Further study

Imperial College	PhD Biological Chemistry
University College London	MSc Computer Science

Chemistry for Europe (Germany)

Further study

Kingston University	MA Marketing

Chemistry with Management Studies

Further study

Bath College of HE	PGCE Chemistry/Science

Computer-Aided Chemistry

See under **Computing**.

COMPUTING GRADUATES

Computer-Aided Chemistry
Employment

IDBS, Guildford	Helpdesk Adviser
IDBS, Guildford	Software Tester
Information Resources, Bracknell	International Account Analyst
Logica CMG, Leatherhead	Consultant
Perkin Elmer, Beaconsfield	Software Engineer
Spring Recruitment, Guildford	Software Testing

Further study

Birkbeck College	PhD Crystallography
Imperial College	PhD Biological Chemistry
University of Southampton	PhD Bioinformatics

Computer Modelling and Simulation
Employment

Eli Lilley, London	Security Analyst
GAME, Guildford	Retail Supervisor
GO London, London	Voluntary Worker
National Grid, Wokingham	Power Systems Engineer

Computer Science and Engineering
Employment

Fujitsu Siemens Computers, Bracknell	Application Developer
Nortel, Maidenhead	Telecommunications Engineer

Computing and Information Technology
Employment

Accenture, London	Analyst
Altius Consulting, Houston, USA	Consultant – IT Business Intelligence
Antal International, London	Trainee Recruitment Consultant
Applied Business Consultancy, Lightwater	Software Developer
ARINC, Crawley	Internet Developer
Bank of New York Europe, London	Support Analyst
BDO Stoy Hayward, Reading	Insolvency Administrator
Branksome Restaurant, Bournemouth	Waitress
BT, Hemel Hempstead	Project Manager
BTF Holdings plc, Wallington	Managed Service Engineer
Cerillion Technologies, London	Graduate Developer
Continuing Education and Training, Croydon	MIS and Funding Support Officer
DTI, London	Database Engineer
Dune, London	Sales Adviser
General Medical Council, London	Change Management Assistant
Homebase, Newton Abbott	Customer Service Assistant
IPT, Bracknell	Database Manager
J P Morgan, Bournemouth	Business Analyst
KPMG, London	Information Technology Adviser
Logica CMG, Cardiff	Computer Analyst
Logica CMG, London	Software Designer
LUMH, Christian Dior Perfumes, Surrey	Purchase Ledger Clerk
Milkround.com, London	Web Designer
NPower, Hull	Billing Analyst
Qinetiq, Malvern	Research Scientist
Queen's Road Takeaway, Weybridge	Counter Assistant
Reading PCT	Data Analyst

Riley's, Guildford — Bar Staff
Schroeders Investment Management, London — Graduate Trainee
Screen Pages, Wisley, Surrey — Web Designer
Surrey University — Trainee Communications Analyst
Surrey University Students' Union — Entertainments Provider
Symbol Technologies, Berkshire — Information Services Support Engineer
Syzygy, London — Web Developer
Wyevale, Staffs — Management Trainee

Further study
Canterbury Christ Church University — PGCE Secondary ICT
Surrey University — MSc Information Systems
Surrey University — MSc Internet Computing

CREATIVE AND EXPRESSIVE ARTS GRADUATES
Dance and Culture
Employment
Artsites Birmingham — Acting Training and Education Manager
Back to Health Chiropractic Clinic, Guildford — Chiropractic Assistant
Chamber of Commerce, Manchester — Sales Coordinator
East London Dance — Project Coordinator
essexdance, Chelmsford — Project Coordinator
King Edward VI School, Suffolk — Teacher of Dance
King's College School, Guildford — Teaching Assistant
Ludus Dance Agency, Lancaster — Project Manager
Other private body in the UK — Dance Instructor
Self-employed — Dance Teacher – Ballet

Further study
Brighton University — PGCE Dance
Reading University — PGCE Primary
Other private body in the UK — PGCE Dance

Music
Employment
Allied Irish Bank, Northampton — Banking
AQA, Surrey — Marker
Centrepoint, London — Trust Fundraising Assistant
Chichester College of Arts, Science and Technology — Learning Support Assistant
County Music Centre, Guildford — Trumpet Teacher
Guildford County School, Guildford — Community Arts Manager
Musical Associates UK, Tring, Herts — Box Office Manager
Parsons Mead, Ashstead — Music Leader
Philharmonia Orchestra, London — Project Manager, Education Department
Royal College of Music, London — Registry Assistant
St John's, Smith Square, London — Box Office Assistant
SF2, St Albans — Administrator
Sheargold Pianos, Cobham, Surrey — Assistant Manager
Social Services, Guildford — Team Assistant
Surrey County Arts — Peripatetic Music Teacher
Surrey County Council, Guildford — Mentor
Victoria Library, London — Library Assistant
Youth with a Mission, Sussex — Volunteer
Unknown finance company — General Office/Clerical Work
Self-employed — Singing Teacher/Professional Singer

Further study

Cambridge University	MPhil Development Studies
Cambridge University (Homerton College)	PGCE Secondary Music
Canterbury Christ Church University	Unknown course
Reading University	PGCE Secondary Music
Royal Holloway and Bedford New College	MMus
Surrey University	MMus (2)
Sussex University	PGCE Music
Trinity College of Music	Dip Music Performance
Other private body in the UK	MA Composition for Film and Screen

Music and Sound Recording

Employment

AMEC, London	Office Administration
BBC, London	Sound Engineer
Data Connection, Enfield	InterOp Engineer
EMI Abbey Road Studios, London	Runner
Eurocom Developments, Derby	Sound Designer
Focusrite, High Wycombe	Operations Controller
Freelance	Sound Editor
IBF, London	Audio Operator
Music Department, London	Music Editor
Strong Room Recording Studio, London	Sound Engineer
Technical Earth, London	Technical Sales Support
Townhouse, Chiswick	Assistant Engineer
Self-employed	Freelance Music Teacher
Self-employed	Recording Engineer and Assistant
Self-employed	Sound Engineer (2)

DANCE GRADUATES
See under **Creative and Expressive Arts**.

ECONOMICS GRADUATES
Business Economics with Computing
Employment

Adecco, Borehamwood	Finance Assistant
Alliance Capital, London	Performance Analyst
Allianz Cornhill, Woking, Surrey	Assistant Underwriter
Bank of New York, London	Finance
Bloomberg, London	Sales Consultant
Deloitte Touche Tohmatsu, London	Analyst
Equion FM, London	Assistant Commercial Manager
European Patent Office, The Hague	Patent Administration
Exel, Croydon	Trainee Project Manager
First Choice Travel, Crawley	E-Commerce Trainee
Gulf Bank, Kuwait	Trainee Banking Executive
Hayden Financial Services, Guildford	Administrator/Trainee
Haymarket Publications, London	Sales Executive
Hewitts, Hemel Hempstead	Software Testing
Lehman Brothers, London	Analyst
Marie Curie Cancer Care, Mill Hill	Shop Assistant/Manager
Misys International Banking Systems, Wimbledon	Trainee Accountant
Rainbow Trust, Leatherhead	Special Projects Assistant
South Oxfordshire District Council	Temporary Administrative Assistant
State Street Bank, London	Currency Broker

UBS, London	Compliance Officer
UBS, USA	Operations Analyst
Family business	General Management
Self-employed	Researcher
Unknown restaurant, Wallington	Restaurant Management

Further study

Middlesex University	PGCE Primary
Nottingham University	MSc Economics
Reading University	MSc Finance
Surrey University	MSc Business Economics and Finance
Surrey University	MSc International Business Management
Surrey University	MSc Marketing Management
Warwick University	MSc Economics

Economics
Employment

AIG Global Investment (Europe), London	Portfolio Assistant
Avaya, Guildford	Sales Coordinator
Chiropractic Service, Spain	Chiropractic Manager
Euro RSCG, London	Purchase Ledger Clerk
Home Office, Croydon	Administrative Officer
HSBC, London	Graduate Trainee
Macmillan Cancer Relief, London	General Administration
National Australia Bank, London	Finance and Credit Analyst
www.soldoutgig.com	Founding Director

Further study

Brunel University	PGCE Mathematics
Imperial College	MSc Environmental Technology
University of Kent at Canterbury	MSc Economics
Loughborough University	MSc Finance and Management
Nottingham University	MSc Economics and Econometrics
Queen Mary and Westfield College	MSc Finance and Investment
Warwick University	MSc Economics
Other public body in the UK	MSc Economics and Finance

ENGINEERING GRADUATES
Aerospace
Employment

St Saviour's Church, Guildford	Volunteer Worker

Further study

Cranfield University	MSc Aerospace Vehicle Design
Surrey University	PhD Composite Materials

Chemical Engineering
Employment

BP, Aberdeen	Operations Engineer
Foster Wheeler Energy, Reading	Graduate Process Design Engineer
Hall & Woodhouse, Hayward's Heath, Sussex	Chef
Mariner's Hotel, Farnham	Manager
Pegram Associates, Sunbury	Structural Engineer

Further study

Surrey University	PhD Water Desalination
UMIST	MSc Environmental and Process Design
University College London	MSc Mathematics

Civil Engineering
Employment

AMEC	Civil Engineer
AMEC, Grimsby	Site Engineer
Dorey, Lyle & Ashman, Guernsey	Structural Engineer
Hyder Consulting, Guildford	Design Consultant Engineer
Hyder Consulting, Guildford	Geotechnic Engineer
Mouchel Parkman, West Byfleet	Graduate Engineer
Penten Group, Clapham	Site Engineer/Project Manager
Scott Wilson, London	Graduate Engineer
Tony Gee and Partners, Surrey	Research Engineer
Trant Construction, Guernsey	Site Engineer
WSP Development, Hertford	Graduate Engineer
Unknown civil engineering firm, London	Engineer

Further study

Surrey University (2)	MSc Structural Engineering
Surrey University	MSc Water and Environmental Engineering

Civil Engineering with Computing
Employment

Capita Symonds, East Grinstead	Hydraulic Modeller
Kier Group, Havant	Graduate Engineer

Further study

Imperial College	MSc Environmental Engineering

Civil Engineering with European Language
Employment

Atkins Water, Derby	Graduate Engineer

Electronic and Electrical Engineering
Employment

Accenture, London	Graduate Trainee – IT
AWE, Aldermaston	Electronic Engineer
Hoare Lea Consulting Engineers, London	Graduate Electrical Engineer
Motorola, Basingstoke	Applications Testing
Mouchel Parkman, Byfleet, Surrey	Project Management
Page Aerospace, Sunbury	Development Engineer

Further study

Surrey University	MSc Management

Electronic Engineering
Employment

Astrium, Portsmouth	Systems Engineer
Atkins Transport, Ripley, Surrey	Administrative Assistant
BBM Electronics, North Cheam	Design Engineer
BT, Scotland	Analyst
Dstl, Farnborough	Graduate Engineer
Hockway, Redhill	Proposals Engineer
Holy Cross Hospital, Haslemere	Charge Nurse

Home Office, Croydon	Asylum Support
Michigan State University, USA	Video Coordinator
MOD, Bristol	Graduate Trainee
Philips Electronics, Southampton	Electronic Engineer
Qinetiq, Malvern	Communications Engineer
Rayleigh Instruments, Essex	Electronics Engineer
Silvertech, Horsham	Graduate Engineer (2)
Silvertech, Horsham	Graduate Trainee Engineer
Sony, Basingstoke	Graduate Engineer
Tecton, Eastleigh, Hants	Electronic Engineer
Unknown company	Network Administrator

Further study

City University	BEng Electronic Engineering
Nottingham University	MSc Entrepreneurship Science and Technology
Surrey University	MSc Satellite Communications
Surrey University	PhD Cognitive Science
Surrey University	PhD Computer Vision
Surrey University	PhD Electronic Engineering
Surrey University	PhD Machine Intelligence
Surrey University	PhD Nanotechnology
Surrey University	PhD Semiconductor Electronics

Electronic Engineering with European Language
Employment

IPS GmbH, Krefeld, Germany	Export Sales Assistant and MSc
Vision Security Group	Security Officer

Electronics and Computer Engineering
Employment

Dixons, Kingston Upon Thames	Sales

Engineering with Business Management
Employment

Alfa Laval, Camberley, Surrey	Technical Sales Engineer
Eaton-Williams Group, Kent	Junior Bid/Project Engineer
Schindler, Sunbury, Middlesex	Trainee Estimator

Further study

Surrey University	MSc Biomedical Engineering

Engineering with Business Management and French
Employment

DML, Plymouth	Graduate Trainee

Mechanical Engineering
Employment

Bentley Motor Cars	Engineer
Delphi, Gillingham	Development Engineer
EADS Astrium, Portsmouth	Manufacturing Engineer
ERA Technology, Leatherhead	Mechanical Engineer
Frazer-Nash Consultancy, Dorking, Surrey	Engineer
Harding Auto Services, Woking, Surrey	Service Manager
Instron, High Wycombe	Graduate Engineer
Littlebrook Power Services, Dartford	Engineer
Metronet SSl, London	Graduate Trainee
Mott MacDonald, Croydon	Graduate Fire Safety Engineer
Naston, Surrey	Engineer

Noble Denton, London	Engineer
Production Engineering Solutions, Guildford	Managing Director
Rolls-Royce, Bristol	Graduate Trainee
Siemens Industrial Turbomachinery, Lincoln	Graduate Mechanical Engineer
Sucome Design and Technology, Guildford	Principal Engineer
Surrey University Students' Union	VP Education and Welfare
Surrey University Students' Union	VP Sports
Sutton and Merton Primary Care Trust	Clerical Officer

Further study

Reading University	MSc Mathematical Modelling
Strathclyde University	MEng Naval Architecture & Marine Engineering
Surrey University	MSc Materials
Surrey University	MSc Technology Management
University College London	MSc Marine Engineering

Mechanical Engineering with French
Employment

Urbis Lighting, Basingstoke	Lighting Design Engineer

Mechanical Engineering with Mechatronics
Employment

Scott Wilson Railways, Swindon	Electrification Engineer

Further study

Surrey University	PhD Biomedical Engineering

HEALTHCARE GRADUATES
See under **Medical and Health**.

HOSPITALITY AND TOURISM GRADUATES
Hotel and Catering Management
Employment

Caprice Holdings – The Ivy, London	Chef in Pastry Kitchen
Davy's Wine Bars, London	Trainee Assistant Manager
Foster MacCallum International, Farnham, Surrey	Research Quality Manager
Four Seasons Hotel, Dogmersfield, Hampshire	Graduate Trainee (2)
Haven Holidays, Bordeaux, France	Telesales
Insight HR and Management Consultancy, West Sussex	HR Coordinator
Jumeirah International Hotel, London	Banqueting Floor Manager
Lidl UK, Hampshire	District Manager
Marriott Hotels, Newcastle	Management Trainee
Pennyhill Park Hotel, Bagshot, Surrey	Accounts Assistant
Pizza Express Restaurants, Stamford	Assistant Restaurant Manager
Premier Labellers, Harwich	Receptionist/Administrative Assistant
Queen's Moat House Hotel, Harlow	Assistant Reception Manager
Robert Hale International, Guildford	Consultant
Sainsbury's, Eastbourne	Sales Assistant
Sodexho UK and Ireland	Graduate Executive Trainee
Thistle Hotels, North London	Meeting and Events Coordinator
Unknown hotel services, Hartley Whitney	Researcher

International Hospitality and Tourism Management
Employment

Adecco, Belgium	Recruitment Consultant Hospitality
Akiko Design, Guildford	Sales Manager
Fiat Dealership, Ware	Sales Representative

Holiday Inn Express, Stansted	Food and Beverage Manager
Hyatt Regency, Paris	Hotel Management Trainee
Ilyssion Hotel, Rhodes	Floor Manager
Inter Group, Farnham, Surrey	Assistance Coordinator
K West Hotel and Spa, London	Marketing Sales and Internet Coordinator
Korean Air, Heathrow	Staff Supervisor and MSc
MOD – Royal Logistic Corps	Staff Officer
Office for National Statistics, Titchfield	Telephone Unit Interviewer
Pathway Resourcing, Sutton, Surrey	Recruitment Consultant
Pineapple Marketing, London	Sales and Marketing Executive
Sheffield Insulators, Cardiff	Branch Administrator

Further study

Aston University	MSc Business Studies

International Hospitality Management
Employment

Myhotel Bloomsbury, London	Assistant Manager
toptable.co.uk	Customer Service Agent

Management and Tourism
Employment

Blunsdon House Hotel, Swindon	Reception Manager
British Airways, Gatwick	Customer Service Agent
British Airways, Heathrow	Marketing Executive
British Midland International, London, Heathrow	Customer Service Agent
Claire's Accessories, Guildford	Store Manager
Department of Education and Skills, London	Tribunal Assistant
East Surrey Hospital, Redhill	Nurse Bank Coordinator
Enterprise Rent-a-Car, Camberley	Graduate Trainee
First Choice Travel, Luton Airport	Cabin Crew
Haymarket Publishing Group, London	Operations Coordinator
Kelly Services, Guildford	Trainee Consultant
Lastminute.com, Camberley	Credit Controller
Lunn Poly/Thomson Travel, Walton on Thames	Assistant Manager
Moda in Pelle, Guildford	Assistant Manager
NatWest Bank, Haslemere	Cashier
NatWest Commercial Banking, London	Business Analyst
Pendragon, Weybridge, Surrey	Marketing Coordinator/Personal Assistant
Poole Council, Dorset	Management Trainee
Selfridges, London	Supervisor
Tardis Group, London	Researcher
Unwin Brothers, Woking	General Administration
Virgin Atlantic, Heathrow and Gatwick	Cabin Crew
W H Smith, Epsom, Surrey	Assistant Manager
Unknown wine warehouse, Thanet	Sales

Further study

Surrey University	MSc Business Management

LANGUAGES GRADUATES
Combined Languages
Employment

First Choice, Brighton	Tour Coordinator
German Embassy, London	Consular Assistant
VTec Electronics, Abingdon	Consumer Service Administrator
Wordbank, London	Project Manager

Further study

Southampton University	PGCE Primary Education with French
Other non-UK institution	Portuguese

French and Economics with International Business

Employment

Atlas Translations, London	Administration and Marketing Officer
British Army	Army Officer
City Broker & Profile, London	Account Executive
HSBC, Southampton	Management Trainee
Marine Ventures, Reading	Administration
Marks & Spencer, Guildford	Sales Assistant
Progressive Recruitment, Wimbledon	Recruitment Consultant
Robert Hall International, London	IT Support Executive
Thomson Financial, London	Helpdesk Executive

Further study

University of East London	PGCE Early Years Education
Westminster University	MA Diplomatic Studies

French and European Studies

Employment

Constance Spry, Farnham	Operations Manager
Corporate Executive Board, London	Administrative Research Associate

French and Law

Further study

Other private body in the UK	Graduate Diploma in Law

German and Economics with International Business

Employment

Channel Express (Air Services), Bournemouth	Aircraft Fleet Planner
Pattern, Richmond, Surrey	Project Coordinator
Unknown shipping company	Cost Accountant
Various educational organisations, Berlin	Teacher

Further study

Other non-UK institution	MSc Management Science

German and European Studies

Employment

Tradeweb, London	Associate Client Representative

Further study

Loughborough University	MSc International Management
Other non-UK institution	MA Sustainable Tourism

Languages and Business Culture in Europe

Employment

Corporate Venue Solutions, Malvern	Administrative Assistant

Linguistic and International Studies

Employment

Greene King, Guildford	Assistant Manager
Perduco Recruitment, London	Recruitment Consultant

Further study
Surrey University | MA Swedish Translation
Other private body in the UK | Graduate Diploma in Law

Russian and Econometrics with International Business
Employment
Moscow Times, Russia | Journalist
Stemcor Group, London | Trainee Trader

LAW GRADUATES
Law and European Studies
Employment
Ashfords Solicitors, Exeter | Conveyancing Assistant
Bristol City Council | Housing Officer
British Transport Police | Police Constable
Inland Revenue, Farnham | Clerk
Treasury Solicitor, London | Administrative Officer and LPC

Further study
London University – Senate Institutes | Legal Practice Course
Nottingham University | Legal Practice Course
Surrey University Roehampton | PGCE Religious Education
University of the West of England | Legal Practice Course
Other private body in the UK (7) | Legal Practice Course
Other public body in the UK (2) | Legal Practice Course
Other non-UK institution | Legal Practice Course
Other non-UK institution | LLM International Law

Law and French
Employment
Lexis Nexis Butterworths, Croydon | Senior Accountant Manager

Further study
University of Manchester | Bar Vocational Course

Law and German
Employment
Barnham Primary School, Sussex | Teaching Assistant
Inland Revenue, London | Fast Streamer
Popleston Allen, Nottingham | Paralegal

Further study
Other private body in the UK | Legal Practice Course

Law and Russian
Employment
Bircham Dyson Bell, London | Paralegal

Further study
Nottingham University | Legal Practice Course

MANAGEMENT AND TOURISM GRADUATES
See under **Hospitality and Tourism**.

MATHEMATICS GRADUATES
Mathematics
Employment

2nd Byte, Godalming, Surrey	Operations Administrator
Allianz Cornhill, Guildford	Statistician
Bracknell Forest Borough Council	Assistant Personnel Officer
HSBC, Bracknell	Management Training Scheme
Insolvency Service, Chatham	Insolvency Support Assistant
Jaguar/Land Rover, Solihull	Finance Analyst and CIMA
KPMG, London	Trainee Auditor and ACA
Lehman Brothers, Haywards Heath	Mortgage Accountant
Lloyds TSB, London	Assistant Manager
Mid-Kent College, Chatham	Administrator
MMA Insurance, Reading, Berks	Statistical Analyst
Office for National Statistics, London	Local Government Compiler
Oxford University	Development Assistant
Post Office, Aldershot	Postmaster
Sesame, Oxford	Applications Adviser
TRL, Wokingham	Associate Scientist

Further study

Oxford University	PGCE Mathematics
Southampton University	MSc Statistics and Medicine
Surrey University	PhD Mathematical Biology
Surrey University	PhD Mathematics
York St John University College	PGCE Secondary Mathematics

Mathematics and Computing Science
Employment

Deloitte Touche Tohmatsu, London	Associate Accountant and ACCA
Department for Education and Skills, London	Statistical Officer
Dual Corporate Risks, London	Finance Assistant and ACCA
Eli Lilly, Basingstoke	Business Affiliate Innovator
Hanover Park, HomeLet, Croydon	Compliance Assistant
J P Morgan Chase Bank, Bournemouth	Securities Lending Clerk
Metronet, London	Accounts Payable Clerk
SAP, Middlesex	Junior Consultant
UBS, London	IT Consultant

Further study

Surrey University	MSc Mathematics

Mathematics and Statistics
Employment

Barclays Bank, Poole, Dorset	Business Analyst
Barclays Bank, Poole, Dorset	HR Assistant
GE Capital, Leeds	Credit Analyst
One Railways, Braintree	Ticket Office Clerk
WS Atkins, Epsom, Surrey	Transport Planner

Further study

Exeter University	PGCE Secondary Mathematics
Institute of Education, University of London	PGCE Secondary Mathematics
St Mary's College	PGCE
Surrey University	PhD Astrodimensions

Mathematics and Statistics with European Languages
Employment

Neilson, Andorra	Administrator

Mathematics with Business Studies
Employment

Air Miles, Crawley	Statistician
Claytons, London	Junior Facilities Administrator
Friends Provident, Dorking	Pensions Administration
Future Publishing, Bath	Business Services Analyst
GlaxoSmithKline, Brentford	Administrative Assistant
Home Office, Croydon	Research Officer
KPMG, London	Finance Assistant/CIMA
University of Leeds	Senior Clerk Financial Aid
MFC Bank, Winkfield, Berks	Credit Risk Analyst
Opta Sports Data, London	Production Manager
Premium Credit MBNA Europe, Epsom	Accounts Administrator
PricewaterhouseCoopers, London	Assistant Consultant
Scott Wilson, Basingstoke	Management Accountant and ACCA
University of Southampton	Market Research/Mgt Information Analyst
Surrey University	Assistant Planning Officer
UnumProvident, Dorking, Surrey	Business Performance Analyst and CIMA

Further study

Surrey University	MSc Astrodynamics

Mathematics with European Languages
Employment

Kodak, Hemel Hempstead	Bilingual Accounts Payable Clerk/CIMA

MEDICAL AND HEALTH GRADUATES
Clinical Practice (Surgical)
Employment

NHS, Chichester, West Sussex	Staff Nurse

Health and Social Care
Employment

St Richard's Hospital	Research Nurse and BSc

Health Care (DipHE)
Employment

Ashford and St Peter's NHS Trust, Chertsey	Midwife
Ashford and St Peter's NHS Trust, Chertsey	Nurse
Ashford and St Peter's NHS Trust, Chertsey	Staff Nurse
Beacon Centre, Guildford	Nurse
East Surrey Hospital, Redhill	Specialist Nurse
Epsom and St Helier NHS Trust, Carshalton	Modern Matron and BSc
Frimley Park Hospital NHS Trust	Midwife
Frimley Park Hospital NHS Trust	Midwife and BSc
Frimley Park Hospital NHS Trust	Nurse
Frimley Park Hospital NHS Trust	Sister CCU
Frimley Park Hospital NHS Trust	Staff Nurse
NHS, Fleet, Hampshire	Sister
NHS, Guildford	Macmillan CMS Palliative Care and BSc
NHS, Reading	Staff Nurse
NHS, West Sussex	Staff Nurse

Royal Surrey County Hospital NHS Trust, Guildford	Midwife
Royal Surrey County Hospital NHS Trust, Guildford	Ward Sister
Surrey and Sussex NHS Trust	Clinical Nurse Specialist and BSc
Surrey and Sussex NHS Trust, Crawley	Senior Charge Nurse
Surrey and Sussex NHS Trust, Redhill	Community Midwife
Surrey and Sussex NHS Trust, Redhill	Midwife

Further study

| Surrey University | BSc Hs ICU Nursing |

Integrative Counselling
Employment

Dix Belgravia, Guildford	Marketing Executive
Freelance	Engineering Consultant
Let's Link, Oxted, Surrey	Project Manager
NHS, Bournemouth	Counsellor
Surrey Care Trust, Surrey County Council	Connexions Personal Adviser
Surrey Oaklands NHS Trust	Senior Team Leader
Self-employed	Counsellor

Midwifery
Employment

Ashford and St Peter's NHS Trust, Chertsey	Midwife (2)
East Somerset NHS Trust, Yeovil	Midwife
East Surrey Hospital, Redhill	Midwife
Frimley Park Hospital NHS Trust	Community Midwife
Frimley Park Hospital NHS Trust	Midwife (3)
Frimley Park Hospital NHS Trust	Senior Staff Nurse
NHS, Frimley, Surrey	Midwife
NHS, Kingston, Surrey	Midwife
Royal Surrey County Hospital NHS Trust, Guildford	Midwife (3)
Royal West Sussex Trust, Chichester	Midwife
St Peter's Hospital, Chertsey	Midwife (2)
St Richard's Hospital, Chichester	Midwife (2)

Nursing Studies
Employment

Abraham Cowley Unit, Chertsey	Senior Staff Nurse
Blackwater Valley PCT, Guildford	Community Nurse
Frimley Park Hospital NHS Trust	Staff Nurse
NHS, London	Staff Nurse
St Richard's Hospital, Chichester	Staff Nurse
Surrey Oaklands NHS Trust, Epsom	Senior Staff Nurse

Nursing Studies (Adult Nursing)
Employment

Abraham Cowley Unit, Chertsey	Staff Nurse
Ashford and St Peter's NHS Hospital, Chertsey	Staff Nurse (4)
Ashford and St Peter's NHS Hospital, Chertsey	Student Midwife and BSc
Bart's Hospital, London	Staff Nurse
BUPA Hospital, Birmingham	Staff Nurse
Crawley Hospital	Nurse
East Elmbridge Mid-Surrey PCT, Surrey	Community Staff Nurse
East Surrey Hospital, Redhill	Staff Nurse (2)
East Surrey PCT, Redhill	Community Staff Nurse (3)
Epping Hospital, Essex	Staff Nurse
Epsom and St Helier NHS Trust	Nurse

Frimley Park Hospital NHS Trust	Intensive Care Nurse
Frimley Park Hospital NHS Trust	Staff Nurse (9)
Frimley Park Hospital NHS Trust	Student Midwife and BSc
Great Western Hospital, Swindon	Staff Nurse
Guildford and Waverley PCT, Farnham	Staff Nurse
Guildford and Waverley PCT, Surrey	Community Nurse
James Padget NHS Trust, Great Yarmouth	Staff Nurse
John Radcliffe Hospital, Oxford	Staff Nurse
Kent and Sussex Hospital, Tunbridge Wells	Staff Nurse
Kingston Hospital, Surrey	Staff Nurse
Kingston Hospital, Surrey	Staff Nurse and BSc
Mount Alvernia Hospital, Guildford	Staff Nurse
New Support Options, Farnham	Senior Support Worker
NHS, Camberley	Senior Staff Nurse
NHS, Camberley	Staff Nurse
NHS, Chertsey	Staff Nurse
NHS, Epsom	Staff Nurse
NHS, Frimley, Surrey	Post Reg Student Midwife and BSc
NHS, Guildford	Staff Nurse
NHS Professional, Guildford	Bank Nurse
NHS, Redhill	Staff Nurse
NHS, Sutton	Staff Nurse
NHS, Warrington, Cheshire	Staff Nurse
NHS, West Drayton	Staff Nurse
Nuffield Hospital, Guildford	Staff Nurse
Queen Alexandra's Hospital, Portsmouth	Staff Nurse
Redwood Hospital, Redhill	Staff Nurse
Royal Berkshire Hospital, Reading	Staff Nurse
Royal Marsden Hospital, Sutton	Staff Nurse
Royal Surrey County Hospital, Guildford	Student Midwife and BSc
Royal Surrey County Hospital NHS Trust	Adult Nurse
Royal Surrey County Hospital NHS Trust	Bank Staff Nurse
Royal Surrey County Hospital NHS Trust	Nurse (2)
Royal Surrey County Hospital NHS Trust	Staff Nurse (7)
Royal Surrey County Hospital NHS Trust	Staff Nurse and BSc
Royal Sussex Hospital, Brighton	Staff Nurse
Royal West Sussex NHS Trust, Chichester	Staff Nurse (3)
St George's Hospital, London	Staff Nurse
St Helier Hospital, Carshalton	Staff Nurse
St Peter's Hospital, Chertsey	Staff Nurse (5)
St Richard's Hospital NHS Trust, Chichester	Staff Nurse (7)
Surrey and Sussex Healthcare	Staff Nurse
Surrey and Sussex Healthcare Trust, Redhill	Staff Nurse (5)
Surrey and Sussex NHS Trust, Crawley	Nurse
Surrey and Sussex NHS Trust, Crawley	Staff Nurse (2)
Surrey Health and Woking PCT, West Byfleet	Community Nurse
Surrey Health PCT, Woking	Community Staff Nurse
Surrey Health PCT and Woking Area	Community Staff Nurse
Surrey PCT, Ashford	Community Nurse
Swindon and Marlborough NHS Trust	Staff Nurse
Western Sussex Intensive Care, Bognor Regis	Community Nurse
Worthing Hospital	Staff Nurse

Further study

Surrey University	BSc Midwifery
Surrey University	Diploma Adult Nursing

Nursing Studies (Child Nursing)
Employment

Children's Trust, Tadworth, Surrey	Staff Nurse/Care Assistant
East Surrey Hospital, Redhill	Staff Nurse
Frimley Park Hospital NHS Trust	Staff Nurse
Kings Lynn and Wisbech NHS Trust	Staff Nurse
NHS London	Paediatric Nurse
North London NHS Trust	Children's Nurse
Royal Surrey County Hospital NHS Trust	Children's Nurse
Royal Surrey County Hospital NHS Trust	Recovery Nurse
Surrey and Sussex Healthcare Trust, Redhill	Nurse (child)
Surrey and Sussex Healthcare Trust, Redhill	Staff Nurse

Nursing Studies (Learning Disabilities)
Employment

Aspects and Milestones, Bristol	Assistant Home Manager
Berkshire Healthcare Trust	Community Nurse
Eversleigh Group, Crawley	Home Manager
NHS Lothian PCT, Edinburgh	Staff Nurse
Post Office Cottage Care Home, Chichester	Learning Disability Nurse
Robina, Surrey	RNLD Nurse
Unknown learning disability home, Redhill	Learning Disability Nurse

Nursing Studies (Mental Health)
Employment

Avon and Wiltshire Mental Health Authority, Bristol	Staff Nurse
Berkshire Healthcare Trust	Staff Nurse
Blackwater Valley PCT, Guildford	Community Nurse
Blenheim Group, England	Mental Health Nurse
Care Perspectives, Norfolk	Staff Nurse
Conifers CMHT – Surrey Hants Borders	Community Psychiatric Nurse
NHS Trust, Chichester	Staff Nurse
North Essex Mental Health Partnership, Clacton	Staff Nurse
NW Surrey Mental Health Partnership Trust, Ashford	Team Nurse
NW Surrey Mental Health Partnership Trust, Chertsey	Community Nurse
NW Surrey Mental Health Partnership Trust, Chertsey	Staff Nurse
NW Surrey Mental Health Partnership Trust, Staines	Deputy Manager
NW Surrey Mental Health Partnership Trust, Woking	Ward Manager
Oxleas Health Trust, Bromley	Staff Nurse
Royal Surrey County Hospital NHS Trust	Community Practice Nurse
South London & Maudsley Trust	Primary Nurse and BSc
South London & Maudsley Trust	Staff Nurse
Surrey Hampshire Borders NHS Trust	Registered Mental Nurse
Surrey Hampshire Borders NHS Trust, Aldershot	Community Psychiatric Nurse
Surrey Hampshire Borders NHS Trust, Guildford	Senior Staff Nurse
Surrey Hampshire Borders NHS Trust, Guildford	Staff Nurse
West London Mental Health Trust, Ealing	Staff Nurse
West Sussex Health and Social Care Trust, Chichester	Staff Nurse
West Sussex Health and Social Care Trust, Horsham	Staff Nurse
West Sussex Health and Social Care Trust, Worthing	Staff Nurse
Unknown hospital, London	Staff Nurse

Nutrition
Employment

Addenbrooks Hospital, Cambridge	Bank Services Officer
Ealing Education Business Partnership	Project Administrator for Work-related Learning

Institute of Naval Medicine, Hants   Nutritionist
Leatherhead Food International   Scientific Adviser
Manchester University   Research into Arthritis
Marks & Spencer, Southampton   Sales Assistant
Nation Water Treatments, UK   Technical Sales Representative
Oxygen Health Club, Penzance   Nutritionist
Poole Borough Council, Dorset   Licensing Assistant
Reed Employment, Croydon   Recruitment Consultant
Safeway Stores, London   Sales Assistant
Sainsbury's, Cobham, Surrey   Sales Assistant

Further study
Canterbury Christ Church University   Unknown course
London Metropolitan University   MSc Human Nutrition
London School of Hygiene & Tropical Medicine   MSc Public Health Nutrition
Sussex University   PGCE Science 11–18

Nutrition and Food Science
Employment
Campden & Chorleywood Food Research Association   Senior Research Officer and PhD
JAS Bowman & Sons, Herts   Development Baker
Princes Foods, Chichester, Sussex   New Product Development

Further study
Glasgow University   PhD Absorption and Metabolism

Nutrition/Dietetics
Employment
Basingstoke General Hospital   Dietitian
Children and Families Court Advisory Service, Taunton   Administrator
Churchill Insurance, Peterborough   Temporary Office Clerk
Darent Hospital, Dartford   Dietitian
Frimley Park Hospital NHS Trust   Dietitian
Hull and East Yorkshire NHS Trust   Dietitian
Kingston NHS Trust   Dietitian
Maidstone Weald PCT, Tunbridge Wells, Kent   Dietitian
Mansfield Hospital   Dietitian
Newbury & Community PCT, Reading   Dietitian
NHS, Boston Hospital   Dietitian
NHS, Chelmsford   Dietitian
NHS, Leicester   Dietitian
NHS, South Wales   Dietitian
NHS, Southampton   Dietitian
NHS, Swansea   Dietitian
NHS, Warrington, Cheshire   Dietitian
NHS, Worthing   Project Support
Portsmouth Hospitals Trust   Dietitian
Royal Berkshire Hospital, Reading   Dietitian
Royal Cornwall Hospital NHS Trust, Truro   Dietitian
Royal Glamorgan Hospital   Dietitian
Royal Sussex County Hospital, Brighton   Dietitian
Sheffield Teaching Hospital   Dietitian
Southend Hospital   Dietitian
Western Sussex NHS Trust, Chichester   Dietitian
Wirral Hospital NHS Trust   Dietitian

Further study
Brighton University   MSc Diabetes

MUSIC GRADUATES
See under **Creative and Expressive Arts**.

NURSING GRADUATES
See under **Medical and Health**.

NUTRITION GRADUATES
See under **Medical and Health**.

PHYSICS GRADUATES

Physics
Employment

Bookshelf, East Sussex	Book Cataloguer
Burgess Hodgson, Canterbury, Kent	Trainee Chartered Accountant and ACA
Gamma Associates, Laindon, Essex	Assistant Research Analyst
Hann Tucker Associates, Woking, Surrey	Assistant Acoustic Consultant
MOD, Andover	Administration
Qinetiq, Hants	Research Scientist
Sports Marketing Survey, Wisley, Surrey	Research Executive

Further study

Hertfordshire University	PGCE Secondary Science
Surrey University	MSc Radiation and Environmental Protection
Surrey University	PhD Physics

Physics with Computational Modelling
Further study

Westminster University	MSc Software Engineering

Physics with Finance
Employment

Halliburton KBR, Sutton, Surrey	Information Management
ICSA Software International, London	IT Support Consultant
Impey & Co, Cambridge	Trainee Chartered Accountant and ACA

Physics with Management Studies
Employment

Police Training Centre, Bramshill	Assistant Directorate Accountant

Further study

University College London	MSc Geographical Information Science

Physics with Medical Physics
Employment

Institute of Cancer Research, Banstead	Data Manager
Zenith Staybrite, Guildford	Show Home Consultant

Physics with Nuclear Astrophysics
Employment

Boots, Guildford	Sales Assistant
HFC Bank, Sutton, Surrey	Customer Account Manager and MSc
Medisend, Oxford	Laboratory Work
Mouchel Parkman, West Byfleet, Surrey	Administrator
Norwich Union, Worthing	Office Clerk
Royal Navy, Nuclear Dept, HMS Sultan	Senior Lecturer
Touchbase, London	Account Manager

Further study

Cambridge University	PhD Astrophysics
Cranfield University	MSc Aerospace Dynamics
Surrey University	MSc Radiation and Environmental Protection (2)

Physics with Satellite Technology
Employment

BSkyB	Platform Operative Support Engineer
Data Integration, London	Trainee Network Engineer
Home Office, Guildford	Freelance Security Consultant
Qinetiq, Farnborough	Remote Sensing Scientist
SSTL, Guildford	Satellite Technologist

Further study

Surrey University	MSc Radiation and Environmental Protection
Surrey University	PhD Quantum Physics
York University	PhD Experimental Nuclear Astrophysics
Other non-UK institution	PhD Nuclear Structure Physics
Other non-UK institution	PhD Physics

PSYCHOLOGY GRADUATES
Applied Psychology/Sociology
Employment

Halmer Recruit, Walton on Thames	Office Support
Heart of Kent Hospice, Maidstone, Kent	Commodity Fundraiser
KPMG, Birmingham	Department Secretary
Logic Group, Fleet	HR Assistant
Mencap, Alton, Hants	Carer
National Centre of Policing Excellence, Hants	National Injuries Database Assistant
New Look, Weymouth	Buying Administration
NHS, Herts	Secretary/Receptionist
NHS, Nottingham	Health Audit Officer

Integrative Counselling
See under **Medical and Health**.

Psychology
Employment

Billericay, Brentwood and Wickford PCT, Essex	Mental Health Worker
Bloomberg, London	Global Customer Support Representative
Boots Opticians, Cambridge	Customer Sales Adviser
Bristol General Hospital	Researcher
Burnley College, Lancs	Human Resources Administrator
Burton Day Nursery, Christchurch	Pre-School Nursery Nurse
Children's Adolescent Services, Bexleyheath	Behavioural Support Worker
Colgate Palmolive, Guildford	Dental Accounts Support
Croydon Primary Care Trust	Office Administrator/VDU Operator
DSMRU Headley Court, Surrey	Cognitive Rehabilitation Therapist
East Sussex County Healthcare NHS Trust	Assistant Psychologist
Forward, London	Planner
Freshfield Care, Seaford	Private Health Carer
Great Ormond Street, London	Assistant Psychologist
Guildford and Waverley PCT, Guildford	Health Care Assistant
Guildford College	Register Data Administrator
HMV, Guildford	Sales Assistant
Individual Care Services, Redditch	Support Worker

Institution of Civil Engineers, London	Group Coordinator
Intake, Southampton	Residential Practitioner
John Wiley, Chichester	Publishing Assistant
Learning Skills Council, Bournemouth	Personal Assistant
Liaise Loddon Basingstoke	Positive Support Manager
Lloyds Bank, London	HR Assistant and CIPD
MacMillan Publishing Company, Basingstoke	Coordinator
MOD, Gloucester	Occupational Psychologist
Monsoon Accessories, Canterbury	Sales Assistant
NHS Croydon	Assistant Psychologist
NHS East Kent	Recruitment Officer
NHS London	Treatment Centre Administrator
NHS Shrewsbury	Assistant Psychologist
North Lincolnshire PCT	Mental Health Worker
Pearson Education, London	Sales Representative
Red Lion, East Grinstead	Bar Manager
Royal Hospital for Neurodisability, Putney	Rehabilitation Assistant
Sainsburys, Godalming	Retail Management Graduate Trainee
St Peter's Hospital, Chertsey	Voluntary Healthcare
Shell International, London	Learning Consultant
Sony, Weybridge	HR Coordinator
Standard Life Healthcare, Guildford	HR Administrator
Surrey Police, Guildford	Administrator
Surrey University, Guildford	Researcher
Trade and Connections, Bromley	Futures Trader
United Kingdom Young Autism Project, Crawley	Tutor
Which?, London	Business Research Assistant
Self-employed	Professional Athlete
Unknown call centre, Guildford	Operator
Unknown company	Office Skills
Unknown hospital for adults, Guildford	Assistant Research Psychologist
Unknown law firm, London	Marketing
Unknown management consultancy	Trainee/Associate Consultant

Further study

Leeds University	MA Religion and Public Life
South Bank University	PG Dip Careers Guidance
Surrey University	MSc Forensic Psychology (3)
Surrey University	MSc Health Psychology
Surrey University	MSc Occupational and Organisational Psychology
Surrey University	MSc Occupational Psychology
Surrey University	MSc Social Psychology (2)
Surrey University	PhD Social/Clinical Psychology
Surrey University	PsychD Counselling Psychology

Psychosocial Interventions
Employment

Surrey Hampshire Borders NHS Trust	Community Psychiatric Nurse

RETAIL GRADUATES
Retail Management
Employment

Accessorise, Guildford	Assistant Manager
Army, Farnborough	Master Data Manager
Boots, Horsham	Retail Manager

Chichester Hospital, Sussex	HR Database Administrator
Claire's Accessories, Aldershot	Assistant Manager
Early Learning Centre, Eastleigh	Assistant Manager
Elizabeth Arden (UK), London	Visual Merchandising
Employment Tribunal Service, Bury St Edmunds	Tribunal Clerk
Enterprise Rent-a-Car, Basingstoke	Management Trainee
Enterprise Rent-a-Car, Crawley	Trainee Manager
Etam, London	Trading Assistant
Faith, Camberley	Store Manager
Fortnum & Mason, London	Trainee – International Division
Homebase, Surrey	Assistant Merchandiser
House of Fraser, Camberley	HR Administrator and CIPD
House of Fraser, Croydon	Sales Manager Lingerie and Childrenswear
House of Fraser, Guildford	Personnel Administrator
John Lewis, High Wycombe	Management Development Trainee
John Lewis, Reading	Sales Assistant
Lidl UK, Kent	District Manager
Luminar Leisure, Preston	PA to Head of Estates Management
Marks & Spencer, Camberley	Trainee Commercial Manager
Marks & Spencer, Exeter	Section Manager
Ministry of Defence, London	Civil Servant
New Look, Weymouth	Trainee Manager
Pantiles Nurseries, Surrey	Management Trainee
PRG-Schultz, London	Audit Development Manager
Siemens Traffic Control, Poole	Graduate Accountant and CIMA
Surrey University	HR Assistant
Surrey University Students' Union	President
Tesco, Addlestone	Retail Manager
Tesco, Gatwick	Graduate Trainee
Tesco, Sandhurst	Management Trainee
Virgin Megastore, Birmingham	Trainee Manager
Virginware, Reading	Store Manager
Waitrose John Lewis Partnership	Graduate Trainee
Waitrose, SE England	Graduate Trainee
Woolworths, Crawley	Assistant Manager
Woolworths, Sutton	Assistant Manager
Unknown architectural practice, Guildford	Marketing Officer

Further study

University of Westminster	MA Marketing Communications

SOCIOLOGY GRADUATES

Applied Psychology/Sociology
See under **Psychology**.

Sociology
Employment

AQA, Guildford	Administrator
Atlas Capital, London	Receptionist/Secretary
Camden Council Services, London	Family Support Worker
Capita, Maidenhead	Consultant
Centrex, Bramshill Police College	Assistant Crime Analyst
CMS Cameron McKenna, London	Marketing Assistant
Downsend School, Epsom	Teaching Assistant
Dunnes Stores	Section Manager
Employment Plus, Guildford, Surrey	Driver's Mate

Equazen, London	PR Assistant
Heal & Son, Guildford	Sales Assistant
Intercall, Bracknell	Internal Account Manager
ITT Industries, Basingstoke	HR Administrator
Kent County Council, Maidstone	Marketing/Promotions
Long Island Products, London	Administrative Assistant
M&J Seafood, London	Sales Administrator
Mole Valley District Council, Dorking, Surrey	Helpline Assistant Recycling
Mountbatten Internship, New York	Intern
Net Benefit, London	New Business Sales Executive
NOP World, London	Trainee Research Executive
Pierse Contracting, Surrey	Personal Assistant
Reed Employment, Welwyn Garden City	Office Administration
Southern Trains, East Croydon	Human Resources and CIPD
Sure Start Whitley, Reading	Parent Participation Worker
Surrey University Students' Union	Sabbatical Students' Union VP
Thanet Youth Offending Team, Kent	Office Temp
TNS, London	Graduate Trainee
Transport for London	Service Analyst

Further study

Goldsmiths College	PGCE Secondary
Manchester University	Unknown MSc
St Patrick's School, Farnborough	Graduate Teaching Programme
Surrey University	PhD Sociology
Surrey University Roehampton	PGCE Primary
Other private body in the UK	Graduate Diploma in Law
Unknown establishment	Diploma in Beauty

TOURISM GRADUATES

See under **Hospitality and Tourism**.

APPENDIX 1
DIRECTORY OF UNIVERSITIES AND COLLEGES

DIRECTORY OF UNIVERSITIES AND COLLEGES

SECTION 1 UNIVERSITIES

Listed below are universities in the United Kingdom that offer degree and diploma courses at higher education level. Applications to these institutions are submitted through UCAS unless otherwise stated. See the UCAS *The Big Guide – University and College Entrance* for a full list of courses (see **Booklist**).

Aberdeen: *The University of Aberdeen, King's College, Aberdeen, Grampian, Scotland AB24 3FX. Tel 01224 272090; www.abdn.ac.uk*

Abertay Dundee: *University of Abertay Dundee, 40 Bell Street, Dundee, Scotland DD1 1HG, Tel 01382 308000; www.abertay.ac.uk*

Aberystwyth: *Aberystwyth University, Old College, King Street, Aberystwyth, Ceredigion SY23 2AX. Tel 01970 622021; www.aber.ac.uk*

Anglia Ruskin: *Anglia Ruskin University Chelmsford Campus, Bishop Hall Lane, Chelmsford, Essex CM1 1SQ. Tel 0845 271 3333; www.anglia.ac.uk*

Arts London: *(University of the Arts London, 65 Davies Street, London W1K 5DA. Tel 020 7514 6000; www.arts.ac.uk) Four Colleges of Art and Design (Camberwell, Chelsea, Central St Martins (inc Byam Shaw) and Wimbledon) also the College of Communication and the London College of Fashion.*

Aston: *Aston University, Aston Triangle, Birmingham B4 7ET. Tel 0121 204 4444; www.aston.ac.uk*

Bangor: *Bangor University, Bangor, Gwynedd, Wales LL57 2DG. Tel 01248 351151; www.bangor.ac.uk*

Bath: *The University of Bath, Cleverton Down, Bath, Somerset BA2 7AY. Tel 01225 383019; www.bath.ac.uk*

Bath Spa: *Bath Spa University, Newton Park Newton St Loe, Bath, Somerset BA2 9BN. Tel 01225 875875; www.bathspa.ac.uk*

Bedfordshire: *University of Bedfordshire, Luton Campus, Park Square, Luton, Bedfordshire LU1 3JU. Tel 01582 489286; www.beds.ac.uk*

Birmingham: *The University of Birmingham, Edgbaston, Birmingham B15 2TT. Tel 0121 414 3344; www.bham.ac.uk*

Birmingham City: *Birmingham City University, City North Campus, Franchise Street, Perry Barr, Birmingham B42 2SU. Tel 0121 331 5000; www.bcu.ac.uk*

Bolton: *Bolton University, Deane Road, Bolton, Lancashire BL3 5AB. Tel 01204 900600; www.bolton.ac.uk*

Bournemouth: *Bournemouth University Lansdowne Campus, Ist Floor Melbury House, 1–3 Oxford Road, Bournemouth BH8 8ES. Tel 01202 524111; www.bournemouth.ac.uk*

Bradford: *The University of Bradford, Richmond Road, Bradford, West Yorkshire BD7 1DP. Tel 0800 073 1255; www.brad.ac.uk*

Brighton: *University of Brighton, Mithras House, Lewes Road, Brighton BN2 4AT. Tel 01273 600900; www.brighton.ac.uk*

Brighton and Sussex Medical School: *BSMS Teaching Unit, University of Sussex, Brighton, East Sussex BN1 9PX. Tel 01273 643528; www.bsms.ac.uk*

Bristol: *University of Bristol, Senate House, Tyndall Ave, Bristol BS8 1TH. Tel 0117 928 9000; www.bristol.ac.uk*

Bristol UWE: *University of the West of England, Frenchay Campus, Coldharbour Lane, Bristol BS16 1QY. Tel 0117 965 6261; www.uwe.ac.uk*

Brunel: *Brunel University, Uxbridge Campus, Uxbridge, Middlesex UB8 3PH. Tel 01895 265265; www.brunel.ac.uk*

Buckingham: *The University of Buckingham, Hunter Street, Buckingham MK18 1EG. Tel 01280 820313; www.buckingham.ac.uk*

Bucks New: *Buckinghamshire New University, High Wycombe Campus, Queen Alexandra Road, High Wycombe, Buckinghamshire HP11 2JZ. Tel 08000 565660; www.bucks.ac.uk*

Cambridge: The University has 31 colleges located throughout the city. Colleges Lucy Cavendish, Murray Edwards (formerly New Hall) and Newnham (women only); the following admit both men and women undergraduates: Christ's, Churchill, Clare, Corpus Christi, Darwin, Downing, Emmanuel, Fitzwilliam, Girton, Gonville and Caius, Homerton, Hughes, Jesus, King's, Magdalene, Pembroke, Peterhouse, Queens', Robinson, St Catharine's, St John's, Selwyn, Sidney Sussex, Trinity, Trinity Hall, Wolfson. Clare Hall and Darwin admit only graduates. *Enquiries should be addressed to the Tutor for Admissions, ... College, Cambridge or to the University of Cambridge, Cambridge Admissions Office, Fitzwilliam House, 32 Trumpington Street, Cambridge CB2 1QY. Tel 01223 333308; www.cam.ac.uk*

Canterbury Christ Church: *Canterbury Christ Church University, Canterbury Campus, North Holmes Road, Canterbury, Kent CT1 1QU. Tel 01227 782900; www.canterbury.ac.uk*

Cardiff: *Cardiff University, Cardiff, Wales CF10 3XQ. Tel 029 208 74000; www.cardiff.ac.uk*

Central Lancashire: *University of Central Lancashire, Preston PR1 2HE. Tel 01772 201201; www.uclan.ac.uk*

Chester: *University of Chester, Parkgate Road, Chester CH1 4BJ. Tel 01244 511000; www.chester.ac.uk*

Chichester: *University of Chichester, Bishop's Otter Campus, College Lane, Chichester, West Sussex PO19 6PE. Tel 01243 8160002. www.chiuni.ac.uk*

City: *City University, Northampton Square, London EC1V 0HB. Tel 020 7040 5060; www.city.ac.uk*

Coventry: *Coventry University, Priory Street, Coventry CV1 5FB. Tel 024 7688 7688; www.coventry.ac.uk*

Creative Arts The University has five colleges – three in Kent (Canterbury, Maidstone and Rochester) and two in Surrey (Epsom and Farnham). *University for the Creative Arts, Enquiries Service, Falkner Road, Farnham, Surrey GU9 7DS. Tel 01252 892883; www.ucreative.ac.uk*

Cumbria This new university (2007) was created by the merger of St Martin's College and Cumbria Institute of the Arts. There are campuses in Ambleside, Carlisle, Lancaster, Penrith and London. *University of Cumbria, Fusehill Street, Carlisle, Cumbria CA1 2HH. Tel 01228 616234; www.cumbria.ac.uk*

De Montfort: *De Montfort University, The Gateway, Leicester LE1 9BH; Tel 0116 255 1551; www.dmu.ac.uk*

Derby: *University of Derby, Kedleston Road, Derby DE22 1GB. Tel 01332 590500; www.derby.ac.uk*

Dundee: *University of Dundee, Nethergate, Dundee, Scotland DD1 4HN. Tel 01382 383000; www.dundee.ac.uk*

Durham: Colleges Collingwood, Grey, Hatfield, St Aidan's, St Chad's, St Hild & St Bede, St John's, St Mary's, Trevelyan, University, Van Mildert. **Society** St Cuthbert's. A 12th undergraduate college, Josephine Butler, opened in October 2006. Some courses are offered at the Queen's Campus, Stockton (Stephenson and John Snow Colleges). *(Durham University, University Office, Old Elvet, Durham DH1 3HP. Tel 0191 334 2000; www.dur.ac.uk)*

East Anglia: *The University of East Anglia, Norwich NR4 7TJ. Tel 01603 456161; www.uea.ac.uk*

East London: *University of East London, Docklands Campus, 4–6 University Way London E16 2RB. Tel 020 8223 3000; www.uel.ac.uk*

Edge Hill: *Edge Hill University, St Helens Road, Ormskirk, Lancashire L39 4QP. Tel 01695 575171; www.edgehill.ac.uk*

Edinburgh: Three main sites in and around city centre. *The University of Edinburgh, Old College, South Bridge, Edinburgh, Scotland EH8 9YL. Tel 0131 650 1000; www.ed.ac.uk*

Essex: *The University of Essex, Wivenhoe Park, Colchester, Essex CO4 3SQ. Tel 01206 873333; www.essex.ac.uk*

Exeter: *University of Exeter, Streatham Campus, Northcote House, Exeter, Devon EX4 4QJ. Tel 01392 661000; www.exeter.ac.uk*

Glamorgan: *The University of Glamorgan, Treforest, Pontypridd, Mid-Glamorgan, Wales CF37 1DL. Tel 0800 716925; www.glam.ac.uk*

Glasgow: *The University of Glasgow, University Avenue, Glasgow, Strathclyde, Scotland G12 8QQ. Tel 0141 330 2000; www.gla.ac.uk*

Glasgow Caledonian: *Glasgow Caledonian University, City Campus, Cowcaddens Road, Glasgow, Strathclyde, Scotland G4 0BA. Tel 0141 331 3000; www.gcal.ac.uk*

Gloucestershire: *University of Gloucestershire, The Park, Cheltenham, Gloucestershire GL50 2RH. Tel 0844 801 0001; www.glos.ac.uk*

Glyndŵr University *Plas Coch, Mold Road, Wrexham, Clwyd, Wales LL11 2AW. Tel 01978 290666; www.glyndwr.ac.uk*

Greenwich: *University of Greenwich, Old Royal Naval College, Park Row, Greenwich, London, SE10 9LS. Tel 0800 005 006; www.gre.ac.uk*

Heriot-Watt: *Heriot-Watt University, Edinburgh Campus, Edinburgh, Lothian, Scotland EH14 4AS. Tel 0131 449 5111; www.hw.ac.uk*

Hertfordshire: *University of Hertfordshire, College Lane, Hatfield, Hertfordshire AL10 9AB. Tel 01707 284800; www.herts.ac.uk*

Huddersfield: *The University of Huddersfield, Queensgate, Huddersfield HD1 3DH. Tel 01484 422288; www.hud.ac.uk*

Hull: *The University of Hull, Admissions Office, Cottingham Road, Hull, East Yorkshire HU6 7RX. Tel 01482 346311; www.hull.ac.uk*

Hull York Medical School The Medical School is a partnership between the Universities of Hull and York, with teaching facilities on the main campuses of both universities. *Admissions Section, University of York, Heslington, York YO10 5DD. Tel 0870 124 5500, www.hyms.ac.uk*

Imperial London: *Imperial College London, South Kensington, London SW7 2AZ. Tel 020 7589 5111; www.imperial.ac.uk*

Keele: *Keele University, Keele, Staffordshire ST5 5BG. Tel 01782 732000; www.keele.ac.uk*

Kent: *The University of Kent, Canterbury, Kent CT2 7NZ. Tel 01227 764000; www.kent.ac.uk*

Kingston: *Kingston University, River House, 53-57, High Street, Kingston-upon-Thames, Surrey KT1 1LQ. Tel 020 8417 9000; www.kingston.ac.uk*

Lancaster: *Lancaster University, Lancaster LA1 4YW. Tel 01524 65201; www.lancs.ac.uk*

Leeds: *The University of Leeds, Leeds LS2 9JT. Tel 0113 243 1751; www.leeds.ac.uk*

Leeds Metropolitan: *Leeds Metropolitan University, Civic Quarter, Leeds LS1 3HE. Tel 0113 812 0000; www.leedsmet.ac.uk*

Leicester: *University of Leicester, University Road, Leicester LE1 7RH. Tel 0116 252 2522; www.le.ac.uk*

Lincoln: *University of Lincoln, Brayford Pool, Lincoln LN6 7TS. Tel 01552 882000; www.lincoln.ac.uk*

Liverpool: *The University of Liverpool, Liverpool L69 3BX. Tel 0151 794 2000; www.liv.ac.uk*

Liverpool Hope: *Liverpool Hope University, Hope Park, Liverpool L16 9JD. Tel 0151 291 3000; www.hope.ac.uk*

Liverpool John Moores: *Liverpool John Moores University, Roscoe Court, 4 Rodney Street, Liverpool L1 2TZ. Tel 0151 231 5090; www.ljmu.ac.uk*

London – Birkbeck: *Birkbeck College, University of London, Malet Street, London WC1E 7HX. Tel 0845 601 0174; www.bbk.ac.uk*

London – Institute in Paris: *University of London, Institute in Paris, Department of French Studies, 9–11 rue de Constantine, 75340 Paris Cedex 07. Tel 00 331 44117383; www.ulip.lon.ac.uk*

London – Courtauld Institute of Art: *Courtauld Institute of Art, University of London, Somerset House, Strand, London WC2R 0RN. Tel 020 7848 2645; www.courtauld.ac.uk*

London – Goldsmiths College: *Goldsmiths, University of London, Lewisham Way, New Cross, London SE14 6NW. Tel 020 7919 7171; www.gold.ac.uk*

London – Heythrop College: *Heythrop College, University of London, Kensington Square, London W8 5HN. Tel 020 7795 6600; www.heythrop.ac.uk*

London – King's College (King's): *King's College, University of London, Strand, London WC2R 2LS. Tel 020 7836 5454; www.kcl.ac.uk*

London – Queen Mary (QM): *Queen Mary, University of London, Mile End Road, London E1 4NS. Tel 020 7882 5555; www.qmul.ac.uk*

London – Royal Holloway (RH): *Royal Holloway, University of London, Egham, Surrey TW20 0EX. Tel 01784 434455; www.rhul.ac.uk*

London – Royal Veterinary College (RVC): *Royal Veterinary College, Camden Campus, Royal College Street, London NW1 0TU. Tel 020 7468 5147; www.rvc.ac.uk*

London – St George's: *St George's, University of London, Cranmer Terrace, Tooting, London SW17 0RE. Tel 020 8672 9944; www.sgul.ac.uk*

London – School of Economics and Political Science (LSE): *London School of Economics and Political Science, Houghton Street, London WC2A 2AE. Tel 020 7405 7686; www.lse.ac.uk*

London – School of Oriental and African Studies (SOAS): *School of Oriental and African Studies, University of London, Thornhaugh Street, Russell Square, London WC1H 0XG. Tel 020 7637 2388; www.soas.ac.uk*

London – School of Pharmacy: *The School of Pharmacy, University of London, 29–39 Brunswick Square, London WC1N 1AX. Tel 020 7753 5800; www.pharmacy.ac.uk*

London – University College (UCL): *University College London, University of London, Gower Street, London WC1E 6BT. Tel 020 7679 2000; www.ucl.ac.uk*

London Metropolitan: *London Metropolitan University, Admissions Office, 166 Holloway Road, London N7 8DB. Tel 020 7133 4200; www.londonmet.ac.uk*

London South Bank: *London South Bank University, 103 Borough Road, London SE1 0AA. Tel 020 7815 7815; www.lsbu.ac.uk*

Loughborough: *Loughborough University, Loughborough, Leicestershire LE11 3TU. Tel 01509 263171; www.lboro.ac.uk*

Manchester: *The University of Manchester, Oxford Road, Manchester M13 9PL. Tel 0161 275 2077; www.manchester.ac.uk*

Manchester Metropolitan: *The Manchester Metropolitan University, All Saints Building, All Saints, Manchester M15 6BH. Tel 0161 247 2000; www.mmu.ac.uk*

Middlesex: *Middlesex University in London, The Burroughs, London NW4 4BT. Tel 020 8411 5555; www.mdx.ac.uk*

Napier: *Edinburgh Napier University, Craiglockhart Campus, Edinburgh, Lothian, Scotland EH14 1DJ. Tel 0845 260 6040; www.napier.ac.uk*

Newcastle: *Newcastle University, 6 Kensington Terrace, Newcastle upon Tyne NE1 7RU. Tel 0191 222 5594; www.ncl.ac.uk*

Newport: *University of Wales Newport, Caerleon Campus, Lodge Road, Caerleon, Newport, Wales NP18 3QT. Tel 01633 432432; www.newport.ac.uk*

Northampton: *The University of Northampton, Park Campus, Boughton Green Road, Northampton NN2 7AL. Tel 0800 358 2232; www.northampton.ac.uk*

Northumbria: *University of Northumbria, Newcastle City Campus, Ellison Place, Newcastle upon Tyne NE1 8ST. Tel 0191 232 6002; www.northumbria.ac.uk*

Nottingham: *The University of Nottingham, University Park, Nottingham NG7 2RD. Tel 0115 951 5151; www.nottingham.ac.uk*

Nottingham Trent: *Nottingham Trent University, Burton Street, Nottingham NG1 4BU. Tel 0115 941 8418; www.ntu.ac.uk*

Oxford: Colleges Balliol, Brasenose, Christ Church, Corpus Christi, Exeter, Hertford, Jesus, Keble, Lady Margaret Hall, Lincoln, Magdalen, Manchester (mature students only), Mansfield, Merton, New, Oriel, Pembroke, Queen's, St Anne's, St Catherine's, St Edmund Hall, St Hilda's (women only), St Hugh's, St John's, St Peter's, Somerville, Trinity, University, Wadham, Worcester. **Private Halls** Campion Hall (men only), Greyfriars, Regent's Park, St Benet's Hall. *(Enquiries should be addressed to The Tutor for Admissions, ... College, Oxford, or to The Oxford Colleges Admissions Office, Wellington Square, Oxford OX1 2JD. Tel 01865 270000; www.admissions.ox.ac.uk)*

Oxford Brookes: *Oxford Brookes University, Headington Campus, Gypsy Lane, Headington, Oxford OX3 0BP. Tel 01865 741111; www.brookes.ac.uk*

Peninsula College of Medicine and Dentistry: *Peninsula Medical school, The John Bull Building, Research Way, Plymouth, Devon PL6 8BU. Tel 01752 437444; www.pms.ac.uk*

Plymouth: *The University of Plymouth, Drake Circus, Plymouth PL4 8AA. Tel 01752 600600; www.plymouth.ac.uk*

Portsmouth: *The University of Portsmouth, University House, Winston Churchill Avenue, Portsmouth PO1 2UP. Tel 023 9284 8484; www.port.ac.uk*

Queen Margaret: *Queen Margaret University, University Drive, Musselburgh, Edinburgh. EH21 6UU. Tel 0131 474 0000; www.qmu.ac.uk*

Queen's Belfast: *Queen's University, Belfast, University Road, Belfast, Northern Ireland BT7 1NN. Tel 028 9097 2727; www.qub.ac.uk*

Reading: *The University of Reading, Whiteknights, PO Box 217, Reading, Berkshire RG6 2AH. Tel 0118 987 5123; www.rdg.ac.uk*

Richmond American International University: *Richmond American International University in London, Queens Road, Richmond, Surrey TW10 6JP. Tel 020 8332 9000; www.richmond.ac.uk*

Robert Gordon: *The Robert Gordon University, Schoolhill, Aberdeen, Grampian, Scotland AB10 1FR. Tel 01224 262000; www.rgu.ac.uk*

Roehampton: *Roehampton University, Erasmus House, Roehampton Lane, London SW15 5PU Tel 020 8392 3232; www.roehampton.ac.uk*

St Andrews: *The University of St Andrews, College Gate, St Andrews, Fife, Scotland KY16 9AJ. Tel 01334 476161; www.st-andrews.ac.uk*

Salford: *The University of Salford, Salford M5 4WT. Tel 0161 295 5000; www.salford.ac.uk*

Sheffield: *The University of Sheffield, Western Bank, Sheffield, South Yorkshire S10 2TN. Tel 0114 222 2000; Medical School Tel 0114 271 3349; www.sheffield.ac.uk*

Sheffield Hallam: *Sheffield Hallam University, City Campus, Howard Street, Sheffield, South Yorkshire S1 1WB. Tel 0114 225 5555; www.shu.ac.uk*

Southampton: *The University of Southampton, University Road, Southampton SO17 1BJ. Tel 023 8059 5000; www.soton.ac.uk*

Southampton Solent: *Southampton Solent University, East Park Terrace, Southampton, Hampshire SO14 0YN. Tel 023 8031 9000; www.solent.ac.uk*

Staffordshire: *Staffordshire University, College Road, Stoke-on-Trent, Staffordshire ST4 2DE. Tel 01782 292753; www.staffs.ac.uk*

Stirling: *The University of Stirling, Stirling, Central Scotland FK9 4LA. Tel 01786 473171; www.stir.ac.uk*

Strathclyde: *The University of Strathclyde, 16 Richmond Street, Glasgow, Scotland GI 1XQ. Tel 0141 552 4400; www.strath.ac.uk*

Sunderland: *University of Sunderland, Chester Road, Sunderland, Tyne and Wear SR1 3SD. Tel 0191 515 2000; www.sunderland.ac.uk*

Surrey: *The University of Surrey, Guildford, Surrey GU2 7XH. Tel 01483 689305; www.surrey.ac.uk*

Sussex: *University of Sussex, Sussex House, Brighton, Sussex BN1 9RH. Tel 01273 606755; www.sussex.ac.uk*

Swansea: *University of Wales, Swansea, Singleton Park, Swansea, Wales SA2 8PP. Tel 01792 205678; www.swan.ac.uk*

Swansea Metropolitan: *Swansea Metropolitan University, Mount Pleasant Campus, Swansea, Wales SA1 6ED. Tel 01792 481000; www.smu.ac.uk*

Teesside: *Teesside University, Middlesbrough, Tees Valley TS1 3BA. Tel 01642 218121; www.tees.ac.uk*

Trinity St David Carmarthen Campus: *The University of Wales Trinity St David, Carmarthenshire, Wales SA31 3EP. Tel 01267 676766; www.trinity-cm.ac.uk*

Trinity St David Lampeter Campus: *The University of Wales Trinity St David, Ceredigion, Wales SA48 7ED. Tel 01570 422351; www.lamp.ac.uk*

Ulster: *University of Ulster, Coleraine, County Londonderry, Northern Ireland BT52 1SA. Tel 087 0040 0700; www.ulster.ac.uk*

Warwick: *The University of Warwick, Coventry, Warwickshire CV4 7AL. Tel 024 7652 3723; www.warwick.ac.uk*

West London: *University of West London, St Mary's Road, Ealing, London W5 5RF. Tel 0800 036 8888; www.tvu.ac.uk*

West Scotland: *University of the West of Scotland, Paisley Campus, Paisley, Strathclyde, Scotland PA1 2BE. Tel 0141 848 3000; www.uws.ac.uk*

Westminster: *University of Westminster, 309 Regent Street, London W1B 2UW. Tel 020 7911 5000; www.westminster.ac.uk*

Winchester: *University of Winchester, Winchester, Hampshire SO22 4NR. Tel 01962 841515; www.winchester.ac.uk*

Wolverhampton: *The University of Wolverhampton, Wulfruna Street, Wolverhampton, West Midlands WV1 1SB. Tel 01902 321000; www.wlv.ac.uk*

Worcester: *Worcester University, Henwick Grove, Worcester WR2 6AJ. Tel 01905 855000; www.worcester.ac.uk*

York: *The University of York, Heslington, York YO10 5DD. Tel 01904 433433; www.york.ac.uk*

York St John: *York St John University, Lord Mayor's Walk, York YO31 7EX. Tel 01904 624624; www.yorksj.ac.uk*

SECTION 2 UNIVERSITY COLLEGES AND COLLEGES AND INSTITUTES OF HIGHER EDUCATION

These institutions are in the UCAS scheme for their courses. (See also specialist and other colleges in Sections 3, 4, 5 and 6.)

Changes are taking place in this higher education sector, with some colleges merging with, or becoming affiliated to, universities. Changes are also taking place in the further education sector to give more degree course opportunities. All this means that you can study for a degree or diploma in a wide range of colleges, and it is important that you read prospectuses and check websites carefully and go to college Open Days to find out as much as you can about them and about their courses that interest you.

Birmingham University College Summer Row, Birmingham, West Midlands B3 1JB. Tel 0121 604 1000; www.ucb.ac.uk

Bishop Grosseteste University College Lincoln, Lincolnshire LN1 3DY. Tel 01522 527347; www.bishopg.ac.uk

Bradford College Great Horton Road, Bradford, West Yorkshire BD7 1AY. Tel 01274 433333; www.bradfordcollege.ac.uk

Colchester Institute Sheepen Road, Colchester, Essex CO3 3LL. Tel 01206 712777; www.colchester.ac.uk

University College for the Creative Arts, Rochester Campus Fort Pitt, Rochester, Kent ME1 1DZ. Tel 01634 888702; www.ucreative.ac.uk

Leeds Trinity University College Brownberrie Lane, Horsforth, Leeds LS18 5HD. Tel 0113 283 7100; www.leedstrinity.ac.uk

Marjon (UCP) St Mark and St John, Admissions Office, Derriford Road, Plymouth, Devon PL6 8BH. Tel 01752 636890; www.marjon.ac.uk

Newman University College Genners Lane, Bartley Green, Birmingham, West Midlands B32 3NT. Tel 0121 476 1181; www.newman.ac.uk

St Mary's University College Waldegrave Road, Twickenham TW1 4SX. Tel 020 8240 4000; www.smuc.ac.uk

Stranmillis University College: A College of the Queen's University of Belfast Stranmillis Road, Belfast, Northern Ireland BT9 5DY. Tel 028 9038 1271; www.stran.ac.uk

Suffolk New College Ipswich, Suffolk IP4 1LT. Tel 01473 382200; www.suffolk.ac.uk

UHI Millennium Institute (UHI) The UHI is based on a partnership of colleges and research institutes, each with its own distinctive character. Full-time undergraduate courses are provided by the following partner colleges. Institutions include Argyll College, Highland Theological College, Inverness College, Lews Castle College, Lochaber College, Moray College, Ness Foundation, North Atlantic Fisheries College, North Highland College, Orkney College, Perth College, Sabhal Mòr Ostaig, Scottish Association for Marine Science and Shetland College. Enquiries to the Registry. *(UHI Millennium Institute, Executive Office, 126, Ness Walk, Inverness IV3 5SQ. Tel 01463 279000; www.uhi.ac.uk)*

University of Wales Institute, Cardiff Llandaff Campus, Western Avenue, Cardiff CF5 2YB. Tel 029 2041 6070. www.uwic.ac.uk

SECTION 3 COLLEGES OF AGRICULTURE AND HORTICULTURE (see also Sections 2 and 6)

Some colleges are in the UCAS scheme (as indicated) for some or all of their courses (see UCAS *Directory* for details). Apply direct to colleges for courses outside UCAS.

Askham Bryan College Askham Bryan, York YO23 3FR. Tel 01904 772211; www.askham-bryan.ac.uk (UCAS)

Berkshire College of Agriculture (BCA) Hall Place, Burchett's Green, Maidenhead, Berkshire SL6 6QR. Tel 01628 824444; www.bca.ac.uk

Bishop Burton College York Road, Bishop Burton, Beverley, East Yorkshire HU17 8QG. Tel 01964 553000; www.bishopburton.ac.uk (UCAS)

Cambridgeshire College of Agriculture and Horticulture College of West Anglia, Landbeach Road, Milton, Cambridgeshire CB24 6DB. Tel 01223 860701.

Capel Manor College Bullsmore Lane, Enfield, Middlesex EN1 4RQ. Tel 08456 122122; www.capel.ac.uk (UCAS)

Cheshire College of Agriculture See **Reaseheath College**.

College of Agriculture Food and Rural Enterprise (CAFRE) Greenmount Campus, 22 Greenmount Road, Antrim, Northern Ireland BT41 4PU. Tel 028 9442 6666; www.cafre.ac.uk

Deeside College Northop, Mold, Flintshire, Wales CH7 6AA. Tel 01352 841000; www.deeside.ac.uk

East Durham Community College Houghall, Durham DH1 3SG. Tel 0191 375 4700; www.eastdurham.ac.uk

Harper Adams University College Edgmond, Newport, Shropshire TF10 8NB. Tel 01952 820280; www.harper-adams.ac.uk (UCAS)

Hartpury College Hartpury House, Hartpury, Gloucestershire GL19 3BE. Tel 01452 702345; www.hartpury.ac.uk

Lackham College See **Wiltshire College** in Section 6.

Myerscough College (an Associate College of the University of Central Lancashire) Myerscough Hall, St Michael's Road, Bilsborrow, Preston, Lancashire PR3 0RY. Tel 01995 642222; www.myerscough. ac.uk

Newton Rigg Cumbria Campus See **University of Central Lancashire** in Section 1.

Otley College Otley, Ipswich, Suffolk IP6 9NE. Tel 01473 785543; www.otleycollege.ac.uk

Pershore College Avonbank, Pershore, Worcestershire WR10 3JP. Tel 0300 456 0045; www.warwickshire. ac.uk (UCAS)

Reaseheath College Nantwich, Cheshire CW5 6DF. Tel 01270 625131; www.reaseheath.ac.uk

Royal Agricultural College Cirencester, Gloucestershire GL7 6JS. Tel 01285 652531; www.royagcol.ac.uk (UCAS)

Scottish Agricultural College (SAC) Ayr Campus, Auchincruive Estate, Ayr, Strathclyde, Scotland KA6 5HW. Tel 0800 269453; www.sac.ac.uk (UCAS)

Shuttleworth College Old Warden Park, Biggleswade, Bedfordshire SG18 9DX. Tel 01767 626222 www.shuttleworth.ac.uk

South Staffordshire College, Rodbaston Campus, Rodbaston, Penkridge, Stafford ST19 5PH. Tel 01785 712209; www.southstaffs.ac.uk

Sparsholt College, Hampshire, Westley Lane, Sparsholt, Winchester, Hampshire SO21 2NF. Tel 01962 776441; www.sparsholt.ac.uk (UCAS)

Writtle College Lordship Lane, Writtle, Chelmsford, Essex CM1 3RR. Tel 01245 424200; www.writtle.ac.uk (UCAS)

SECTION 4 COLLEGES OF ART

Many colleges of art are in UCAS for some or all of their courses (see the UCAS *Big Guide* for details). Some have now merged with universities – check with the UCAS *Big Guide* and prospectuses for details. Note that Art and Design courses are also offered by universities and higher and further education colleges. Apply direct for courses outside UCAS.

Architectural Association School of Architecture The School offers RIBA Parts I and II and the AA Diploma, and has an international reputation. It is situated in Georgian houses in the centre of London. There are approximately 260 fee-paying students. Architectural Association School, 36 Bedford Square, London WC1B 3ES. Tel 020 7887 4000; www.aaschool.ac.uk

Arts University College at Bournemouth Wallisdown Road, Poole, Dorset BH12 5HH. Tel 01202 533011; www.aucb.ac.uk (UCAS)

Camberwell College of Arts (University of the Arts) 45-65 Peckham Road, London SE5 8UF. Tel 020 7514 6302; www.camberwell.arts.ac.uk (UCAS)

Central Saint Martins College of Art and Design (University of the Arts) Southampton Row, London WC1B 4AP. Tel 020 7514 7022; www.csm.arts.ac.uk

Chelsea College of Art and Design (University of the Arts) 16 John Islip Street, London SW1P 4JU. Tel 020 7514 7751; www.chelsea.arts.ac.uk

City & Guilds of London Art School 124 Kennington Park Road, London SE11 4DJ. Tel 020 7735 2306; www.cityandguildsartschool.ac.uk

Cleveland College of Art and Design Green Lane, Linthorpe, Middlesbrough, Cleveland TS5 7RJ. Tel 01642 288888; www.ccad.ac.uk

Edinburgh College of Art (Heriot-Watt University) 74 Lauriston Place, Edinburgh, Lothian, Scotland EH3 9DF. Tel 0131 221 6000; www.eca.ac.uk

University College Falmouth (including Dartington College of Arts) Woodlane Campus, Falmouth, Cornwall TR11 4RH. Tel 01326 211077; www.falmouth.ac.uk

Glasgow School of Art 167 Renfrew Street, Glasgow, Strathclyde G3 6RQ. Tel 0141 353 4500. www.gsa.ac.uk

Heatherley's School of Fine Art 75 Lots Road, Chelsea, London SW10 0RN. Tel 020 7351 4190; www.heatherleys.org

Hereford College of Arts Folly Lane, Hereford HR1 1LT. Tel 01432 273359; www.hca.ac.uk

Kent Institute of Art & Design See University College for the **Creative Arts**.

Kirklees College (incorporating Batley School of Art and Design) Birkdale Road, Dewsbury, West Yorkshire, WF13 4HQ. Tel 01924 451649; www.kirkleescollege.ac.uk

Leeds College of Art and Design Jacob Kramer Building, Blenheim Walk, Leeds LS2 9AQ. Tel 0113 202 8000; www.leeds-art.ac.uk

London College of Communication (University of the Arts) Elephant and Castle, London SE1 6SB. Tel 020 7514 6500; www.lcc.arts.ac.uk

London College of Fashion (University of the Arts) 20 John Princes Street, London W1G 0BJ. Tel 020 7514 7400; www.fashion.arts.ac.uk

Coleg Morgannwg Ynys Terrace, Rhydyfelin, Pontypridd, Wales CF37 5RN. Tel 01443 662800; www.morgannwg.ac.uk

Norwich University College of the Arts Francis House, 3–7 Redwell Street, Norwich, Norfolk NR2 4SN. Tel 01603 610561; www.nuca.ac.uk

Oxfordshire School of Art and Design See **Oxford & Cherwell Valley College** in Section 6.

Plymouth College of Art and Design Tavistock Place, Plymouth, Devon PL4 8AT. Tel 01752 203434; www.plymouthart.ac.uk

Ravensbourne Walden Road, Chislehurst, Kent BR7 5SN. Tel 020 8289 4900; www.rave.ac.uk (UCAS)

Royal Academy Schools (Royal Academy of Arts) Burlington House, Piccadilly, London W1J 0BD. Tel 020 7300 8000; www.royalacademy.org.uk

Royal College of Art Kensington Gore, London SW7 2EU. Tel 020 7590 4444; www.rca.ac.uk (Royal Charter; postgraduate only).

Rycotewood College See **Oxford & Cherwell Valley College** in Section 6.

Sotheby's Institute of Art 30 Bedford Square, London WC1B 3EE. Tel 020 7462 3232; www.sothebys institute.com

Surrey Institute of Art & Design, University College See University College for the **Creative Arts**.

Wimbledon College of Art (University of the Arts) Merton Hall Road, London SW19 3QA. Tel 020 7514 9641; www.wimbledon.arts.ac.uk (UCAS)

Winchester School of Art See **Southampton University** in Section 1.

SECTION 5 COLLEGES OF DANCE, DRAMA, MUSIC AND SPEECH

Some colleges are in the UCAS scheme (as indicated) for some or all of their courses (see UCAS *The Big Guide* for details). Apply direct to college for courses outside UCAS.

Arts Educational London Schools Drama Department, Cone Ripman House, 14 Bath Road, London W4 1LY. Tel 020 8987 6666; www.artsed.co.uk

Birmingham Conservatoire Paradise Place, Fletchei Walk, Birmingham B3 3HG. Tel 0121 331 5901; www.conservatoire.bcu.ac.uk

Birmingham School of Acting G2, Millennium Point, Curzon Street, Birmingham B4 7XG. Tel 0121 331 7220; www.bssa.bcu.ac.uk

Bristol Old Vic Theatre School 1–2 Downside Road, Clifton, Bristol BS8 2XF. Tel 0117 973 3535; www.oldvic.ac.uk

Central School of Speech and Drama Embassy Theatre, 64 Eton Avenue, Swiss Cottage, London NW3 3HY. Tel 020 7722 8183; www.cssd.ac.uk (UCAS)

Drama Centre London (Central Saint Martins College of Art and Design) 1st Floor, 7 Saffron House, Back Hill, London EC1R 5LQ. Tel 020 7514 8778; www.csm.arts.ac.uk/drama

East 15 Acting School Hatfields, Rectory Lane, Loughton, Essex IG10 3RY. Tel 020 8508 5983; www. east15.ac.uk

GSA Conservatoire Guildford School of Acting Stag Hill Campus, Guildford GU2 7XH. Tel 01483 560701; www.conservatoire.org

Guildhall School of Music and Drama Silk Street, Barbican, London EC2Y 8DT. Tel 020 7628 2571; www.gsmd.ac.uk

Laban Contemporary Dance Creekside, London SE8 3DZ. Tel 020 8691 8600; www.laban.org

Leeds College of Music 3 Quarry Hill, Leeds, West Yorkshire LS2 7PD. Tel 0113 222 3400; www.lcm.ac.uk

Liverpool Institute of Performing Arts (LIPA) Mount Street, Liverpool L1 9HF. Tel 0151 330 3000; www.lipa.ac.uk (UCAS)

London Academy of Music and Dramatic Art (LAMDA) 155 Talgarth Road, London WI4 9DA. Tel 020 8834 0500; www.lamda.org.uk

London College of Music and Media See **University of West London** in Section 1.

Mountview Academy of Theatre Arts Ralph Richardson Memorial Studios, Clarendon Road, Wood Green, London N22 6XF. Tel 020 8881 2201; www.mountview.org.uk

Northern School of Contemporary Dance 98 Chapeltown Road, Leeds LS7 4BH. Tel 0113 219 3000; www.nscd.ac.uk

Rose Bruford College Lamorbey Park, Burnt Oak Lane, Sidcup, Kent DA15 9DF. Tel 020 8308 2600; www.bruford.ac.uk (UCAS)

Royal Academy of Dance 36 Battersea Square, London SW11 3RA. Tel 020 7326 8000; www.rad.org.uk (UCAS)

Royal Academy of Dramatic Art (RADA) 62-64 Gower Street, London WCIE 6ED. Tel 020 7636 7076; www.rada.org

Royal Academy of Music Marylebone Road, London NW1 5HT. Tel 020 7873 7373; www.ram.ac.uk

Royal Ballet School 46 Floral Street, Covent Garden, London WC2E 9DA. Tel 020 7836 8699; www.royal-ballet-school.org.uk

Royal College of Music Prince Consort Road, London SW7 2BS. Tel 020 7589 3643; www.rcm.ac.uk

Royal Northern College of Music 124 Oxford Road, Manchester M13 9RD. Tel 0161 907 5200; www.rncm.ac.uk

Royal Scottish Academy of Music and Drama 100 Renfrew Street, Glasgow, Strathclyde, Scotland G2 3DB. Tel 0141 332 4101; www.rsamd.ac.uk

Royal Welsh College of Music and Drama Castle Grounds, Cathays Park, Cardiff, Wales CF10 3ER. Tel 029 2034 2854; www.rwcmd.ac.uk (UCAS)

Trinity College of Music (Trinity Laban) King Charles Court, Old Royal Naval College, King William Walk, Greenwich, London SE10 9JF; Tel 020 8305 4444; www.tcm.ac.uk

Webber Douglas Academy of Dramatic Art See **Central School of Speech and Drama**.

SECTION 6 OTHER COLLEGES IN THE UCAS SCHEME OFFERING HIGHER EDUCATION COURSES

The following colleges appear under various subject headings in Chapter 4 and some are in the UCAS scheme.

Barking and Dagenham College Dagenham Road, Romford, Essex RM7 0XU. Tel 01708 770000; www.barkingcollege.ac.uk

Barnsley College Central Registry, PO Box 266, Church Street, Barnsley, South Yorkshire S70 2YW. Tel 01226 216216; www.barnsley.ac.uk

Basingstoke College of Technology Worting Road, Basingstoke, Hampshire RG21 8TN. Tel 01256 354141; www.bcot.ac.uk

Bedford College Cauldwell Street, Bedford MK42 9AH. Tel 01234 291000; www.bedford.ac.uk

Birmingham Metropolitan College, Matthew Boulton Campus, Jennens Road, Birmingham B4 7PS. Tel 0121 446 4545; www.bmetc.ac.uk

Blackburn College University Centre Fielden Street, Blackburn BB2 1LH. Tel 01254 55144; www.blackburn.ac.uk

Blackpool and The Fylde College Ashfield Road, Bispham, Blackpool, Lancashire FY2 0HB. Tel 01253 352352; www.blackpool.ac.uk

Bradford College University Centre Great Horton Road, Bradford, West Yorkshire BD7 1AY. Tel 01274 433333; www.bradfordcollege.ac.uk

Bridgwater College Bath Road, Bridgwater, Somerset TA6 4PZ. Tel 01278 441234; www.bridgwater.ac.uk

British College of Osteopathic Medicine (BCOM) Lief House, 120–122 Finchley Road, London NW3 5HR. Tel 020 7435 6464; www.bcom.ac.uk

British School of Osteopathy 275 Borough High Street, London SE1 1JE. Tel 020 7089 5300; www.bso.ac.uk

Brockenhurst College Lyndhurst Road, Brockenhurst, Hampshire SO42 7ZE. Tel 01590 625555; www.brock.ac.uk

Burton College Lichfield Street, Burton-upon-Trent, Staffordshire DE14 3RL. Tel 01283 494400; www.burton-college.ac.uk (UCAS)

Carmarthenshire College Graig Campus, Llanelli, Wales SA15 4DN. Tel 01554 748000; www.colegsirgar.ac.uk

Carshalton College Nightingale Road, Carshalton, Surrey SM5 2EJ. Tel 020 8544 4444; www.carshalton.ac.uk

Castle College Nottingham Maid Marian Way, Nottingham NG1 6AB Tel 0845 845 0500; www.castlecollege.ac.uk

Central Bedfordshire College Kingsway, Dunstable, Bedfordshire LU5 4HG. Tel 0845 355 2525; www.dunstable.ac.uk

Chesterfield College Infirmary Road, Chesterfield, Derbyshire S41 7NG. Tel 01246 500500; www.chesterfield.ac.uk

Chichester College Westgate Fields, Chichester, West Sussex PO19 1SB. Tel 01243 786321; www.chichester.ac.uk

City College, Birmingham Fordrough Campus, 300 Bordesley Green, Birmingham B9 5NA. Tel 0121 204 0000; www.citycol.ac.uk

City College, Coventry Sanswell Centre, 50 Sanswell Street, Coventry CV1 5DG. Tel 0800 616202; www.covcollege.ac.uk

City College Norwich Ipswich Road, Norwich, Norfolk NR2 2LJ. Tel 01603 773311; www.ccn.ac.uk

City and Islington College The Marlborough Building, 383 Holloway Road, London N7 0RN. Tel 020 7700 9200; www.candi.ac.uk

City of Bristol College Bedminster Centre, Marksbury Road, Bristol BS3 5JL. Tel 0117 312 5000; www.cityofbristol.ac.uk

City of Sunderland College Bede Centre, Durham Road, Sunderland SR3 4AH. Tel 0191 511 6260; www.citysun.ac.uk

Cliff College Calver, Hope Valley, Derbyshire S32 3XG. Tel 01246 584200; www.cliffcollege.ac.uk

Cornwall College Camborne Campus, Pool, Redruth, Cornwall TR15 3RD. Tel 01209 616161; www.cornwall.ac.uk

Craven College High Street, Skipton, North Yorkshire BD23 1JY. Tel 01756 791411; www.craven-college.ac.uk

Croydon College College Road, Croydon CR9 1DX. Tel 020 8760 5914; www.croydon.ac.uk

Dearne Valley College Manvers Park, Wath-upon-Dearne, Rotherham, South Yorkshire S63 7EW. Tel 01709 513333; www.dearne-coll.ac.uk

Doncaster College University Centre The Hub, Chappell Drive, Doncaster DN1 2RF. Tel 01302 553353; www.don.ac.uk

Dudley College The Broadway, Dudley, West Midlands DY1 4AS. Tel 01384 363000; www.dudleycol.ac.uk

Ealing, Hammersmith & West London College Hammersmith Campus, Gliddon Road, Hammersmith, London W14 9BL. Tel 020 8741 1688; www.wlc.ac.uk

East Surrey College Gatton Point, London Road, Redhill RH1 2JT. Tel 01737 788444; www.esc.ac.uk

European Business School London Regent's College, Inner Circle, Regent's Park, London NW1 4NS. Tel 020 7487 7505; www.ebslondon.ac.uk

European School of Osteopathy Boxley House, The Street, Boxley, Maidstone, Kent ME14 3DZ. Tel 01622 671558; www.eso.ac.uk

Exeter College Hele Road, Exeter, Devon EX4 4JS. Tel 0845 111 6000; www.exe-coll.ac.uk

Fareham College Bishopsfield Road, Fareham, Hampshire PO14 1NH. Tel 01329 815200; www.fareham.ac.uk

Farnborough College of Technology Boundary Road, Farnborough, Hampshire GU14 6SB. Tel 01252 407040; www.farn-ct.ac.uk

Gloucestershire College Llantony Road, Gloucester Gl2 5JQ. Tel 01452 532000; www.gloscol.ac.uk

Great Yarmouth College Suffolk Road, Southtown, Great Yarmouth, Norfolk NR31 0ED. Tel 01493 655261; www.gyc.ac.uk

Greenwich School of Management Meridian House, Royal Hill, Greenwich, London SE10 8RD. Tel 020 8516 7800; www.greenwich-college.ac.uk

Grimsby Institute of Further and Higher Education Nuns Corner, Laceby Road, Grimsby, North East Lincolnshire DN34 5BQ. Tel 0800 315002; www.grimsby.ac.uk

Guildford College Stoke Park, Guildford, Surrey GU1 1EZ. Tel 01483 448500; www.guildford.ac.uk

Gyosei International College See **University of Reading** in Section 1.

Havering College Ardleigh Green Campus, Ardleigh Green Road, Hornchurch, Essex RM11 2LL. Tel 01708 455011; www.havering-college.ac.uk

Henley College, Coventry Henley Road, Bell Green, Coventry, West Midlands CV2 1ED. Tel 024 7662 6300; www.henley-cov.ac.uk

Hereford College of Technology Folly Lane, Hereford HR1 1LS. Tel 08000 321986; www.hct.ac.uk

Hertford Regional College Ware Centre, Scott's Road, Ware, Hertfordshire SG12 9JF. Tel 01992 411400; www.hrc.ac.uk

Highbury College, Portsmouth Tudor Crescent, Portsmouth, Hampshire PO6 2SA. Tel 023 9238 3131; www.highbury.ac.uk

Holborn College Woolwich Road, London SE7 8LN. Tel 020 8317 6000; www.holborncollege.ac.uk

Hopwood Hall College Middleton Campus, Rochdale Road, Middleton, M24 6XH. Tel 0161 643 7560; www.hopwood.ac.uk

Huddersfield Technical College See **Kirklees College** in Section 4.

Hull College Queen's Gardens, Wilberforce Drive, Hull, East Yorkshire HU1 3DG. Tel 01482 329943; www.hull-college.ac.uk

Islamic College for Advanced Studies 133 High Road, Willesden, London NW10 2SW. Tel 020 8451 9993; www.islamic-college.ac.uk

Lakes College – West Cumbria Hallwood Road, Lillyhall Business Park, Workington, Cumbria CA14 4JN. Tel 01946 839300; www.lcwc.ac.uk

Lansdowne College 40–44 Bark Place, London W2 4AT. Tel 020 7616 4400; www.lansdownecollege.com

Leeds City College Park Lane Campus, Leeds LS3 1AA. Tel 0845 045 7275; www.leedscitycollege.ac.uk

Leeds: Thomas Danby College See **Leeds City College**

Leicester College Freemen's Park Campus, Aylestone Road, Leicester LE2 7LW. Tel 0116 224 2240; www.leicestercollege.ac.uk (UCAS)

Leo Baeck College – Centre for Jewish Education The Sternberg Centre, 80 East End Road, London N3 2SY. Tel 020 8349 5600; www.lbc.ac.uk

Lewisham College Lewisham Way, London SE4 1UT. Tel 020 8692 0353; www.lewisham.ac.uk

Lincoln College Monks Road, Lincoln LN2 5HQ. Tel 01522 876000; www.lincolncollege.ac.uk

Liverpool Community College Bankfield Centre, Bankfield Road, Liverpool L13 0BQ. Tel 0151 252 1515; www.liv-coll.ac.uk

Llandrillo College (Coleg Llandrillo Cymru) Llandudno Road, Rhos-on-Sea, North Wales LL28 4HZ. Tel 01492 546666; www.llandrillo.ac.uk

Loughborough College Radmoor Road, Loughborough, Leicestershire LE11 3BT. Tel 0845 166 2950; www.loucoll.ac.uk

Lowestoft College St Peter's Street, Lowestoft, Suffolk NR32 2NB. Tel 0800 854695; www.lowestoft.ac.uk

The Manchester College Ashton Old Road, Openshaw, Manchester M11 2WH. Tel 0800 068 8585; www.themanchestercollege.ac.uk

Manchester College of Arts and Technology See **The Manchester College**

Coleg Menai Ffriddoedd Road, Bangor LL57 2TP. Tel 01248 370125; www.menai.ac.uk

Mid-Cheshire College Hartford Campus, Chester Road, Northwich, Cheshire CW8 1LJ. Tel 01606 74444; www.midchesh.ac.uk

Nazarene Theological College Dene Road, Didsbury, Manchester M20 2GU. Tel 0161 445 3063; www.nazarene.ac.uk

Neath Port Talbot College Dwr-y-Felin Road, Neath SA10 7RF. Tel 01639 648000; www.nptc.ac.uk

Nescot Reigate Road, Ewell, Epsom, Surrey KT17 3DS. Tel 020 8394 3038; www.nescot.ac.uk

New College, Durham Framwellgate Moor Centre, Durham DH1 5ES. Tel 0191 375 4210; www.newcollegedurham.ac.uk

New College Nottingham The Adams Building, Stoney Street, Nottingham NG1 1NG. Tel 0115 910 0100; www.ncn.ac.uk

New College Stamford Drift Road, Stamford, Lincolnshire PE9 1XA. Tel 01780 484300; www.stamford.ac.uk

Newcastle College Rye Hill Campus, Scotswood Road, Newcastle upon Tyne NE4 7SA. Tel 0191 200 4000; www.ncl-coll.ac.uk

Newham College East Ham Campus, High Street South, London E6 6ER. Tel 020 8257 4000; www.newham.ac.uk

North East Worcestershire College Redditch Campus, Peakman Street, Redditch, Worcestershire B98 8DW. Tel 01527 570020; www.ne-worcs.ac.uk

North Tyneside College See **Tyne Metropolitan College**.

North Warwickshire and Hinckley College Hinckley Road, Nuneaton, Warwickshire CV11 6BH. Tel 024 7624 3000; www.nwhc.ac.uk

Northbrook College, Sussex Littlehampton Road, Durrington, Worthing, West Sussex BN12 6NU. Tel 0845 155 6060; www.northbrook.ac.uk

Northumberland College College Road, Ashington, Northumberland NE63 9RG. Tel 01670 841200; www.northumberland.ac.uk

Norton Radstock College South Hill Park, Radstock, Bath, Somerset BA3 3RW. Tel 01761 433161; www.nortcoll.ac.uk

Oldham College Rochdale Road, Oldham, Greater Manchester OL9 6AA. Tel 0161 624 5214; www.oldham.ac.uk

Oxford & Cherwell Valley College Banbury Campus, Broughton Road, Banbury, Oxfordshire OX16 9QA. Tel 01865 550550; www.ocvc.ac.uk

Oxford College of Further Education See **Oxford & Cherwell Valley College**.

Pembrokeshire College Haverfordwest, Pembrokeshire SA61 1SZ. Tel 01437 753000; www.pembrokeshire.ac.uk

The People's College, Nottingham See **Castle College Nottingham**

Peterborough Regional College Park Crescent, Peterborough, Cambridgeshire PE1 4DZ. Tel 0845 872 8722; www.peterborough.ac.uk

Regent's Business School London Inner Circle, Regent's Park, London NW1 4NS. Tel 020 7487 7505; www.rbslondon.ac.uk

Riverside College Kingsway Campus, Widnes, Cheshire WA8 7QQ. Tel 0151 257 2020; www.riversidecollege.ac.uk.

Rotherham College of Arts and Technology Town Centre Campus, Eastwood Lane, Rotherham, South Yorkshire S65 1EG. Tel 08080 722777; www.rotherham.ac.uk

Runshaw College Euxton Lane, Chorley, Lancashire PR7 6AD. Tel 01772 643005; www.runshaw.ac.uk

Ruskin College, Oxford Walton Street, Oxford OX1 2HE. Tel 01865 517832; www.ruskin.ac.uk

Rycotewood College See **Oxford & Cherwell Valley College**.

SAE Institute SAE House, 297 Kingsland Road, London E8 4DD. Tel 020 7923 9159; www.sae.edu

St Helens College Water Street, St Helens, Merseyside WA10 1PP. Tel 01744 733766; www.sthelens.ac.uk

St Loye's School of Health Studies See **University of Plymouth** in Section 1.

St Mary's University College 191 Falls Road, Belfast, Northern Ireland BT12 6FE. Tel 028 9032 7678; www.stmarys-belfast.ac.uk

Salisbury College See **Wiltshire College**

Sandwell College Central Enquiries, Oldbury Campus, Pound Road, Oldbury, West Midlands B68 8NA. Tel 0800 622006; www.sandwell.ac.uk

Sheffield College Central Admissions, Head Office, PO Box 345, Sheffield S2 2YY. Tel 0114 260 2600; www.sheffcol.ac.uk

Shrewsbury College of Arts and Technology London Road, Shrewsbury SY2 6PR. Tel 01743 342342; www.shrewsbury.ac.uk

Solihull College Blossomfield Campus, Blossomfield Road, Solihull, West Midlands B91 1SB. Tel 0121 678 7000; www.solihull.ac.uk

Somerset College of Arts and Technology Wellington Road, Taunton, Somerset TA1 5AX. Tel 01823 366366; www.somerset.ac.uk

South Birmingham College Hall Green Campus, Cole Bank Road, Hall Green, Birmingham, West Midlands B28 8ES. Tel 0121 694 5000; www.sbc.ac.uk

South Cheshire College Dane Bank Avenue, Crewe, Cheshire CW2 8AB. Tel 01270 654 654; www.s-cheshire.ac.uk

South Devon College Vantage Point, Long Road, Paignton TQ2 7EJ. Tel 01803 540540; www.southdevon.ac.uk

South Downs College College Road, Waterlooville, Hampshire PO7 8AA. Tel 023 9279 7979; www.southdowns.ac.uk

South East Derbyshire College Field Road, Ilkeston, Derbyshire DE7 5RS. Tel 0115 849 2000; www.sedc.ac.uk

South Essex College Luker Road, Southend-on-Sea, Essex SS1 1ND. Tel 01702 220400; www.southessex.ac.uk

South Kent College Folkestone Campus, Shorncliffe Road, Folkestone, Kent CT20 2TZ. Tel 0845 207 8220; www.southkent.ac.uk

South Leicestershire College Wigston Campus, Station Road, Wigston, Leicestershire LE18 2DW. Tel 0116 288 5051; www.slcollege.ac.uk

South Thames College Wandsworth Campus, Wandsworth High Street, London SW18 2PP. Tel 020 8918 7777; www.south-thames.ac.uk

Southport College Mornington Road, Southport, Merseyside PR9 0TT. Tel 01704 500606; www.southport-college.ac.uk

Staffordshire University Regional Federation Staffordshire University, College Road, Stoke on Trent ST4 2DE. Tel 01782 294000; www.surf.ac.uk

Stephenson College Thornborough Road, Coalville, Leicestershire LE67 3TN. Tel 01530 836136; www.stephensoncoll.ac.uk

Stockport College of Further & Higher Education Wellington Road South, Stockport, Greater Manchester SK1 3UQ. Tel 0161 958 3100; www.stockport.ac.uk

Stourbridge College Hagley Road, Stourbridge, West Midlands DY8 1QU. Tel 01384 344344; www.stourbridge.ac.uk

Stratford upon Avon College The Willows North, Alcester Road, Stratford upon Avon, Warwickshire CV37 9QR. Tel 01789 266245; www.stratford.ac.uk

Strode College Church Road, Street, Somerset BA16 0AB. Tel 01458 844400; www.strode-college.ac.uk

Sutton Coldfield College See **Birmingham Metropolitan College.**

Swansea College Tycoch Road, Swansea SA2 9EB. Tel 01792 284000; www.swancoll.ac.uk

Swindon College North Star Campus, North Star Avenue, Swindon SN2 1DY. Tel 01793 491 591; www.swindon-college.ac.uk

Tameside College Beaufort Road, Ashton-under-Lyne, Greater Manchester OL6 6NX. Tel 0161 908 6600; www.tameside.ac.uk

Totton College Calmore Road, Totton, Hampshire SO40 3ZX. Tel 023 8087 4874; www.totton.ac.uk

Trafford College Manchester Road, West Timperley, Altrincham, Cheshire WA14 5PQ. Tel 0161 886 7000; www.trafford.ac.uk

Truro College College Road, Truro, Cornwall TR1 3XX. Tel 01872 267 000; www.trurocollege.ac.uk

Tyne Metropolitan College Embleton Avenue, Wallsend, Tyne and Wear NE28 9NJ. Tel 0191 229 5000; www.tynemet.ac.uk

Uxbridge College Park Road, Uxbridge, Middlesex UB8 1NQ. Tel 01895 853333; www.uxbridge.ac.uk

Wakefield College Margaret Street, Wakefield, West Yorkshire WF1 2DH. Tel 01924 789111; www.wakefield.ac.uk

Walsall College Littleton Street West, Walsall WS2 8ES. Tel 01922 657000; www.walsallcollege.ac.uk

Warwickshire College, Royal Leamington Spa, Rugby and Moreton Morrell Warwick New Road, Leamington Spa, Warwickshire CV32 5JE. Tel 01926 318000; www.warwickshire.ac.uk

West Herts College Watford Hempstead Road, Watford, Hertfordshire WD17 3EZ. Tel 01923 812000; www.westherts.ac.uk

West Kent College Brook Street, Tonbridge, Kent TN9 2PW. Tel 01732 358101; www.wkc.ac.uk

West Nottinghamshire College Derby Road, Mansfield, Nottinghamshire NG18 5BH. Tel 01623 627191; www.wnc.ac.uk

West Suffolk College Out Risbygate, Bury St Edmunds, Suffolk IP33 3RL. Tel 01284 701301; www.westsuffolk.ac.uk

West Thames College London Road, Isleworth, Middlesex TW7 4HS. Tel 020 8326 2000; www.west-thames.ac.uk

Westminster Kingsway College St James's Park Centre, Castle Lane, London SW1E 6DR. Tel 0870 060 9800; www.westking.ac.uk

Weston College Knightstone Road, Weston-super-Mare, Somerset BS23 2AL. Tel 01934 411411; www.weston.ac.uk

Weymouth College Cranford Avenue, Weymouth, Dorset DT4 7LQ. Tel 01305 761100; www.weymouth.ac.uk

Wigan and Leigh College Parsons Walk, Wigan WN1 1RU. Tel 01942 761111; www.wigan-leigh.ac.uk

Wiltshire College Cocklebury Road, Chippenham, Wiltshire SN15 3QD. Tel 01249 464644; www.wiltshire.ac.uk

Wirral Metropolitan College Conway Park Campus, Europa Boulevard, Conway Park, Birkenhead CH41 4NT. Tel 0151 551 7777; www.wmc.ac.uk

Witan Hall See **University of Reading** in Section 1.

Worcester College of Technology Deansway, Worcester WR1 2JF. Tel 01905 725555; www.wortech.ac.uk

Yeovil College Holland Campus, Mudford Road, Yeovil, Somerset BA21 4DR. Tel 01935 423921; www.yeovil.ac.uk

York College Sim Balk Lane, York, North Yorkshire YO23 5RN. Tel 01904 770400; www.yorkcollege.ac.uk

Yorkshire Coast College Lady Edith's Drive, Scarborough, North Yorkshire YO12 5RN. Tel 01723 356192; www.yorkshirecoastcollege.ac.uk

Ystrad Mynach College Twyn Road, Ystrad Mynach, Wales CF82 7XR. Tel 01443 816888; www.ystrad-mynach.co.uk

APPENDIX 2
BOOKLIST AND USEFUL WEBSITES

STANDARD REFERENCE BOOKS

British Qualifications, 40th edition, Kogan Page, www.kogan-page.co.uk
British Vocational Qualifications, 12th edition, Kogan Page, www.kogan-page.co.uk
UCAS The Big Guide – University and College Entrance, The Official Guide for 2011 Entry, UCAS, www.ucas.com

OTHER BOOKS

HEAP 2011: University Degree Course Offers, Brian Heap, Trotman Publishing, www.trotman.co.uk
The Educational Grants Directory 2009/10, Directory of Social Change, www.dsc.org.uk
Experience Erasmus, The UK Guide to Socrates Erasmus Programmes, IFF, www.isco.org.uk
Destinations of Leavers from Higher Education, Higher Education Statistics Agency Services, www.hesa.ac.uk
Guide to UK Universities 2010, Klaus Boehm & Jenny Lees-Spalding
Guide to Uni Life, Lucy Tobin, Trotman Publishing, www.trotman.co.uk
Sixthformer's Guide to Visiting Universities and Colleges, IFF, www.isco.org.uk
Student Life, Natasha Roe, Lifetime Careers Publishing, www.lifetime-publishing.co.uk
University Scholarships, Awards and Bursaries, 8th edition, Brian Heap, Trotman Publishing, www.trotman.co.uk
Which Uni? Karla Fitzhugh, Trotman Publishing, www.trotman.co.uk

USEFUL WEBSITES

Don't forget that the internet can be an extremely useful resource. You can:

* search for job vacancies;
* send your CV to employment agencies and employers;
* find relevant careers information, including hints and tips on job hunting and CVs.

Try these websites:

www.jobsearch.co.uk	Vacancy site – you can submit your CV
www.reed.co.uk	A wide range of jobs sourced from Reed
www.peoplebank.com	Jobsearch, online CV writing
www.totaljobs.com	Search all types of jobs by location and type
www.Alec.co.uk	Interview techniques, CV writing, how to approach employers and how to use the internet effectively
www.fish4jobs.co.uk	Search for jobs by location and type
www.fulbright.co.uk	American universities
www.prospects.ac.uk	Information includes graduate employment, job search, graduate destinations
www.careerseurope.co.uk	Careers in Europe
www.allaboutcollege.com	European universities
www.aimhigher.ac.uk	Careers guidance and information about higher education courses, finance and university/college applications
www.yini.org.uk	Jobs for gap year students
www.nhscareers.nhs.uk	National Health Service
www.opendays.com	Information on Open Days
www.socialworkandcare.co.uk	New arrangements for social work/care training and social work/care careers
www.ucas.com	University application

COURSE INDEX

Choosing Your University And Degree Course... And Completing Your UCAS Form?

Why not contact Brian Heap, the author of *Degree Course Offers*, *Choosing Your Degree Course and University* and *University Scholarships and Awards*, for a personal interview or a telephone consultation for advice on such issues as:

Choosing A-level subjects (which are the best subjects and for which courses!)

Degrees and Diploma courses (making the right choice from a list of thousands!)

Completing your UCAS form (will the admissions tutor remember your personal statement?)

Choosing the right university or college (the best ones for you and your courses)

For details of services and consultation fees contact:
The Higher Education Advice and Planning Service

tel: 01386 859355 email: heaps@dsl.pipex.com

Essential exam tips
for every student

"Addresses
every exam–
related issue"
*Career Guidance
Today*

- Survive
  exams with
  confidence

- Tips on
  how to get
  organised

- Advice on
  managing
  stress levels

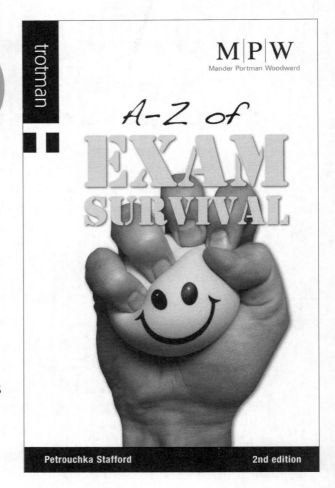

trotman

M|P|W
Mander Portman Woodward

A-Z of
EXAM
SURVIVAL

Petrouchka Stafford   2nd edition

978 1 84455 134 7   £9.99

Buy your copy today at **www.trotman.co.uk**   trotman

Get the inside track on the admissions process

For more university guides visit our website

The Daily Telegraph

INSIDER'S GUIDE TO APPLYING TO UNIVERSITY

KARLA FITZHUGH

978 1 84455 181 1   £12.99

Buy your copy today at **www.trotman.co.uk**

trotman **T**

Want to see the world but not be out of pocket?

Get the expert guide to working and travelling the globe

Work Your Way Around The World

"The globetrotter's bible"

Susan Griffith

SPECIAL OFFER
20% OFF
Only £10.39 RRP £12.99

"Guaranteed to give you wanderlust"
The Sunday Telegraph

Get your copy at www.trotman.co.uk and enter WYW20 at the checkout

The insider's guide to reaching the top

GETTING INTO THE UK'S BEST UNIVERSITIES & COURSES

The Daily Telegraph

BERYL DIXON

978 1 84455 179 8   £12.99

Buy your copy today at **www.trotman.co.uk**   trotman **T**

Create a personal statement to impress

HOW TO WRITE A WINNING UCAS PERSONAL STATEMENT

The Daily Telegraph

The UK's best-selling guide

SECOND EDITION   IAN STANNARD

978 1 84455 225 2   £12.99

Buy your copy today at **www.trotman.co.uk**   trotman **T**

A Guide to Uni Life
Save 10%!

ISBN: 978 1 84455 216 0
Was £9.99 **NOW** £8.99

Fresh from graduation, Lucy Tobin gives you the lowdown on everything you need to know to have a brilliant time at uni and get a great degree!

Order today at www.trotman.co.uk and enter SM3 at the checkout

The UK's leading education publisher

Save 10% on extra uni funding!

Discover over £1m in funding you never new about:

- University bursaries
- Commercial awards
- Sponsorship

ISBN: 978 1 84455 183 5
Was £22.99 NOW £20.69

Order today at www.trotman.co.uk
and enter SM1 at the checkout

The UK's leading education publisher